OXFORD MONOGRAPHS ON CLASSICAL ARCHAEOLOGY

Edited by

BERNARD ASHMOLE
MARTIN ROBERTSON
JOHN BOARDMAN

Madison (Wisconsin), Elvehjem Art Centre, EAC, 70.2
Timokrates Painter (near). *Scale* ½

ATHENIAN WHITE LEKYTHOI

Patterns and Painters

BY

DONNA CAROL KURTZ

OXFORD
AT THE CLARENDON PRESS
1975

Oxford University Press, Ely House, London W. 1

GLASGOW NEW YORK TORONTO MELBOURNE WELLINGTON
CAPE TOWN IBADAN NAIROBI DAR ES SALAAM LUSAKA ADDIS ABABA
DELHI BOMBAY CALCUTTA MADRAS KARACHI LAHORE DACCA
KUALA LUMPUR SINGAPORE HONG KONG TOKYO

ISBN 0 19 813214 X

*Printed in Great Britain
at the University Press, Oxford
by Vivian Ridler
Printer to the University*

To

MY PARENTS

PREFACE

Athenian White Lekythoi is a study of *lekythos* painters and workshops from *c.* 530 B.C. to *c.* 400 B.C., based on shape and pattern. It is neither a catalogue nor a stylistic analysis; Sir John Beazley's attributions are accepted without question. *Athenian White Lekythoi* is intended to supplement previous work on the vases by focusing attention on subjects hitherto neglected, especially on the continuity in production between *lekythoi* decorated in different techniques. I have, therefore, discussed and illustrated black- and red-figure vases, although they have not been my primary concern. The present monograph bears no relation to the doctoral thesis of the same title, submitted to the University of Oxford in the spring of 1968. The subject of the thesis was the iconography of white *lekythoi* and their use in Athenian rites of death and burial. The eschatological section of the thesis formed the basis of chapters six and seven in my part of *Greek Burial Customs* (Thames & Hudson, 1971). The iconographical section I hope to publish in detail elsewhere. In *Athenian White Lekythoi* iconography, like shape and pattern, is one of the criteria used to relate painters and workshops and an iconographical study of many of the vases illustrated has been included in the Notes on the Plates.

The monograph is divided into five unequal parts. Part One is the longest, and its subject—shoulder decoration—is the most difficult to justify. Part Two is the shortest and its subject—shape—is of recognized importance. The reasons for the disproportionate lengths are: (1) the shoulder is the richest source of pattern on white *lekythoi* with figure decoration and its patterns are executed in a manner as readily predictable as the figures on the body; (2) a detailed shape study is being prepared by Brian Cook of the British Museum. Part Three is devoted to side-palmette *lekythoi*. Part Four to black-bodied *lekythoi*—little-known vases whose importance deserves emphasis. Both clearly reveal the relation between figure and pattern, their interdependence, and their individual importance. Part Five—pattern *lekythoi*—is the logical conclusion to a study of pattern and in it abstract as well as floral motifs are described. It is intended primarily as an introduction to a large group of generally disregarded vases whose importance greatly exceeds their artistic value.

The illustrations, like the text, are designed to supplement previous publications. The line-drawings are by the author and some degree of inaccuracy is inevitable, and I hope, pardonable. I have adopted my own conventions, and these I have explained in the Notes on the Figures. The line-drawings illustrate details of pattern, the plates, with few exceptions, whole pots, photographed from an angle which includes patternwork without unduly distorting shape and figurework. White *lekythoi* are sometimes very beautiful and for this reason they are widely illustrated. But too often it is the exceptional piece which is featured, and only that part of it which pleases the author's fancy. My aim has been a representative selection of white *lekythoi*, the earliest and the latest, the masterpiece and the mass-produced hack-work—all in context, that is in relation to vases of other shapes and techniques, so far as this is practical and informative. The order of the plates follows the text, not chronology or style, which might have been easier for those who will 'read' the pictures and not the text. For 'picture readers' I have included a commentary on the plates with references to pages in the text where the vase illustrated is discussed.

References to museums follow Beazley's system, and references to attributed vases include museum, inventory number, and the relevant pages in *ABL*, *ABV*, *ARV*, and *Paralipomena*. Information on unpublished vases I have taken from my museum notes and from material available in the Beazley Archive. There is an Index of Collections, of Subjects, of Painters, Potters, and Workshops, and of Literary References.

Athenian White Lekythoi was written in Oxford, under the most favourable conditions, with opportunities for travel abroad virtually unlimited. There is, therefore, little excuse for errors of judgement and imperfect knowledge—little excuse but youth and lack of experience. I have concentrated on patterns and shapes not because I consider them more important than figures, but because they are easier to 'read'. In time I shall turn to figure-style and attribution.

D. C. K.

Somerville College, Oxford
Summer 1973

ACKNOWLEDGEMENTS

To the Editors of the Oxford Monographs on Classical Archaeology I owe more than a formal expression of thanks. Bernard Ashmole was largely responsible for my coming to Oxford; his wisdom and kindness have been an unfailing source of strength and inspiration. Martin Robertson supervised my doctoral thesis and first drew my attention to the importance of pattern. John Boardman taught me far more than how to extract a book from a thesis. All three have helped me organize the Beazley Archive to which I owe more than even they realize.

Athenian White Lekythoi was prepared in Oxford with the full resources of the Ashmolean Museum and Library, and it gives me great pleasure to thank the many people in the University who have helped me. I should like to thank the Craven Committee and the Committee for Advanced Studies, the Visitors of the Ashmolean Museum, the Department of Antiquities (especially Hector Catling, Ann Brown, and Michael Vickers), the Library (especially R. F. Ovenell, Clifford Currie, and Dorothy Deeming), the Principal and Fellows of Somerville College, the past Principal, Dame Janet Vaughan, and the late Isobel Henderson. Mrs. Henderson, Professor Ashmole, and Professor Hugh Lloyd-Jones made it possible for me to come to Oxford. Professor Lloyd-Jones has read the text and I have profited greatly from his sympathetic criticism. Lilian Jeffery, Colin Kraay, Roger Moorey, and Mr. and Mrs. Walter Oakeshott have assisted me on many occasions, as have Louise Berge, Beryl Bowen, Gerald Cadogan, Oliver Dickinson, Michael Lowe, Alexandra Marr, John Prag, Susan Sherwin-White, and Veronica Wilson.

The financial support of the United States of America and of Great Britain has enabled me to pursue my studies more widely than I had ever dared hope. The award of a Marshall Scholarship by the Association of Commonwealth Universities generously financed my doctoral research, and I should like to express my thanks to the Marshall Commission, especially to Lord Sherfield, Dr. J. F. Foster, and Miss Geraldine Cully. The Principal and Fellows of Somerville College enabled me to travel widely with the grant of a Katharine and Leonard Woolley Fellowship and their continued support, first in the form of a Mary Ewart Research Fellowship, then a College Research Fellowship, I gratefully acknowledge. In the United States I extend warm thanks to the Woodrow Wilson National Fellowship Foundation which financed my degree at Yale University, and to the Louise Taft Semple Fund of the University of Cincinnati. To the Classics Department of the University of Cincinnati I owe great thanks, especially to Cedric Boulter and John L. Caskey, to the Librarians, Janet Macdonald Moore and Jean Susorney, and to the Secretary, Betty Schneider. During that part of each year which I spend in Cincinnati they have made every facility of the Department available to me and have extended every kindness.

Many museums, institutes, and libraries, in Europe and in the United States, have supplied me with photographs and documentation, and I am happy to have this opportunity to thank them and their staff: (Austria) Kurt Gschwantler, (Belgium) Jean Ch. Balty, (Britain) Donald Bailey, Ann Birchall, Brian Cook, Richard Nicholls, John Ruffle, Brian Shefton, Brian Sparkes, (Canada) John Hayes, M. Catherine Twiss, (Denmark) Mette Moltesen, Steffen Trolle, (France) Lilly Kahil, A. Kauffmann, Roger Peyrefitte, Robert Richard, Angelica Waiblinger, (Germany) D. Ahrens, G. Beckel, Adolf Borbein, Christof Böhringer, U. Gehrig, H. Gropengiesser, Christiane Grunwald, Huberta Heres, Nicolas Himmelmann, Herbert Hoffmann, Erich Kukahn, Norbert Kunisch, Brina Otto, Elisabeth Rohde, Eberhard Reschke, Jurgen Thimme, (Greece) Karen Braun, Francis Croissant, George Dontas, Peter Fraser, Sharon Herbert, Bettina v. Freytag Löringhoff, Jean MacIntosh, Jean Michaud, Barbara Philippaki, Mary Philippides, Jane Rabnett, Henry Robinson, Effie Sakellarakis, Demetrios Skilardi, Eugene Vanderpool, K. Vierneisel, (Holland) J. H. Crouwel, C. H. E. Haspels, J. M. Hemelrijk, (Italy) C. Morigi Govi, Dolores Turesi, (Poland) B. Ruszczyc, (Spain) Ricardo Olmos, (Switzerland) Herbert Cahn, Christiane Dunant, Ines Jucker, Adrienne Lezzi-Hafter, Margot Schmidt, (U.S.S.R.) X. Gorbunova, (U.S.A.) Elaine Banks, Dietrich von Bothmer, Anne Pipin-Burnet, John Coleman, Emily Comer, Jiri Frel, Marvel Hart, John Hopkins, Sherman E. Lee, Thomas P. Lee, Kurt Luckner, Richard McFadden, Joan Mertens, Mary Moore, Robert Scranton, Deirdre Stamm, Loraine Turner, Lucy Ude, Gladys Weinberg, Lynn C. Yanok.

During the final preparation of the monograph the Archive secretary, Sarah Reason, was a great help, typing much of the text and correcting my mistakes. Marion Cox redrew the chronological chart on pp. 134 f. and the linear patterns in FIGURES 4 and 5; the drawing in PLATE 9. 3*a* is also hers. Pat Clarke gave advice on my own drawings and Bob Wilkins copied several photographs. John Boardman helped me design the plates.

I am grateful to the Delegates, the Secretary, the Printer, and their staffs, and especially to Dr. Graham Speake for the skill and patience with which he edited my typescript.

CONTENTS

ABBREVIATIONS   xv

GENERAL INTRODUCTION   xix

PART ONE
SHOULDER PATTERNS

Introduction   3

I. EARLY PAINTERS OF WHITE *LEKYTHOI*

  1. Lotus Chains   5

  2. Psiax and the Earliest White-ground   9

  3. The Leagros Group, the Edinburgh Painter and his Followers,
     the Theseus and Athena Painters   13

  4. Vertical Palmette Systems outside the Edinburgh Tradition   17
     Gela Painter   17
     Beldam Painter   18

  5. Horizontal Palmettes (Black)   20

  6. Horizontal Palmettes (Red-figure)   22

  7. Palmettes and Lotus Buds   26

  8. Douris   29

II. CLASSICAL PAINTERS OF WHITE *LEKYTHOI*   33

  9. Sabouroff Painter   34

  10. Bosanquet Painter   37

  11. Thanatos Painter   38

  12. Achilles Painter   41

  13. Phiale Painter   48

  14. Other Achillean White *Lekythoi*   50

  15. Bird Group   52

  16. Painter of Munich 2335   55

  17. Woman Painter   57

  18. Reed Workshop: Reed Painter and Group R   58

  19. Huge *Lekythoi*   68

  Conclusion   73

CONTENTS

PART TWO

SHAPES OF WHITE *LEKYTHOI*

Introduction   77

1. The Establishment of the Standard Cylinder   77

2. Type BL   79

3. Type DL   80

4. Type PL   81

5. Type ATL   82

6. Type CL   84

7. Type BEL   84

8. Chimneys   87

PART THREE

SIDE-PALMETTE *LEKYTHOI*

Introduction   91

1. The Principle of Decoration   91

2. Diosphos Workshop   96
   Diosphos Painter   97
   Diosphos Potter
      DLs with Lotus-bud Shoulder   99
      DLs with Palmettes on the Shoulder   101

3. PL   102

4. BL   104
   Black-figure   104
   Semi-outline   105
   Outline   107
   Athena-head *Lekythoi* and Coins   109

5. BELs and Chimneys   111

PART FOUR

BLACK-BODIED *LEKYTHOI*

Introduction   115

1. Black-figure Workshops   116
   Applied Colour, Incision, and Six's Technique   116
   Reservation   120
   Black-bodied *Lekythoi* of Secondary Shape   122

2. Red-figure Workshops   122

3. Syriskos Painter's *Lekythos* in Berlin   127

CONTENTS   xiii

PART FIVE

PATTERN *LEKYTHOI*

Introduction   131

1. Chronology   131

2. Proveniences   136
   Attica   136
   Eretria   137
   Corinth
      The North Cemetery   138
      The Lechaion Cemetery   139
   Sicily   139
   Southern Italy   141

3. Workshops   143
   Dolphin Group   144
   Phanyllis Group   144
   Cock Group   145
   Athens 581 Workshop and the Marathon Painter   147
   Contemporaries of the Marathon Painter
      i. Edinburgh and Gela Painters   148
      ii. Diosphos Workshop   149
   Haimon Workshop   150
      Haimon–Beldam Pattern *Lekythoi*   152
   Beldam Workshop   153

LIST OF FIGURES   157

FIGURES   163

LIST OF PLATES AND ICONOGRAPHICAL NOTES   197

INDEXES
   I. Collections   233
   II. Subjects   245
   III. Painters, Potters, and Workshops   252
   IV. Literary References   255

PLATES   at end

ABBREVIATIONS

AA	*Archäologischer Anzeiger*
ABL	C. H. E. Haspels, *Attic Black-figured Lekythoi* (1936)
ABV	J. D. Beazley, *Attic Black-figure Vase-painters* (1956)
AD	*Antike Denkmäler*
ADelt	*Archaiologikon Deltion*
AE	*Archaiologike Ephemeris*
Agora xi	E. B. Harrison, *Archaic and Archaistic Sculpture* (1965)
Agora xii	L. Talcott and B. A. Sparkes, *Black and Plain Pottery of the Sixth, Fifth and Fourth Centuries* B.C. (1970)
AJA	*American Journal of Archaeology*
AK	*Antike Kunst*
AK Beiheft i	L. Ghali-Kahil *et al.*, *Neue Ausgrabungen in Griechenland* (1963)
AK Beiheft vii	E. Walter-Karydi *et al.*, *Studien zur griechischen Vasenmalerei* (1970)
ALP	E. Buschor, *Attische Lekythen der Parthenonzeit* (from *Münchener Jahrbuch*, N.S. 2, 1925)
AM	*Mitteilungen des Deutschen Archäologischen Instituts: Athenische Abteilung*
Am	D. von Bothmer, *Amazons in Greek Art* (1957)
Anuari	A. Frickenhaus, 'Griechische Vasen aus Emporion', *Institut d'Estudis Catalans — Anuari* (1908)
ANY	D. von Bothmer, *Ancient Art from New York Private Collections* (1961)
ArchClass	*Archeologia classica*
ArchReps	*Archaeological Reports*
Arias, Hirmer, Shefton	P. E. Arias, M. Hirmer, and B. B. Shefton, *A History of Greek Vase Painting* (1963)
ARR	H. Hoffmann, *Attic Red-figured Rhyta* (1962)
*ARV*¹	J. D. Beazley, *Attic Red-figure Vase-painters* (1942)
ARV	J. D. Beazley, *Attic Red-figure Vase-painters* (1963)
Atti e Mem	*Atti e Memorie della Società Magna Grecia*
Auktion	Münzen und Medaillen AG., Basel
AWL	J. D. Beazley, *Attic White Lekythoi* (1938)
AZ	*Archäologische Zeitung*
BABesch	*Bulletin van de Vereeniging tot Bevordering der Kennis van de antieke Beschaving*
BCH	*Bulletin de correspondance hellénique*
Berl	J. D. Beazley, *Der Berliner Maler* (1930)
BerlMus	*Jahrbuch der Berliner Museen*
BMCat iii	C. H. Smith, *Catalogue of the Greek and Etruscan Vases in the British Museum*, iii (1896)
BMQ	*British Museum Quarterly*
Boll d'Arte	*Bollettino d'Arte*
BSA	*Annual of the British School at Athens*
BullMetr	*Bulletin of the Metropolitan Museum of Art*
CB	L. D. Caskey and J. D. Beazley, *Attic Vase Paintings in the Museum of Fine Arts, Boston* (1931–63)

ClRh	*Clara Rhodos*
Collignon	M. Collignon, *Les Statues funéraires dans l'art grec* (1911)
Collignon and Couve	M. Collignon and L. Couve, *Catalogue des vases peints du Musée National d'Athènes* (1902–4)
Conze	A. C. L. Conze, *Die attischen Grabreliefs* (1893–1922)
Corinth xiii	C. Blegen, H. Palmer, and R. Young, *The North Cemetery* (1964)
CQ	*Classical Quarterly*
CV	*Corpus Vasorum Antiquorum*
Délos xii	F. Courby, *Les Temples d'Apollon* (1931)
Délos xv	C. Dugas and C. Rhomaios, *Les Vases préhelléniques et géométriques* (1934)
Délos xvii	C. Dugas, *Les Vases orientalisants de style non mélien* (1935)
Délos xxi	C. Dugas and J. D. Beazley, *Les Vases attiques à figures rouges* (1952)
Dev	J. D. Beazley, *The Development of Attic Black-figure* (1951)
Diehl	E. Diehl, *Die Hydria* (1964)
Dumont and Chaplain	A. Dumont and J. Chaplain, *Les Céramiques de la Grèce propre* (1888)
Dunbabin	T. J. Dunbabin, *The Western Greeks* (1948)
EAA	*Enciclopedia dell'arte antica*
F	A. Fairbanks, *Athenian White Lekythoi*
i	Volume i (1907)
ii	Volume ii (1914)
FAS	H. Bloesch, *Formen attischer Schalen* (1940)
Felten	F. Felten, *Thanatos- und Kleophonmaler* (1971)
Follmann	B. Follmann, *Der Pan-Maler* (1968)
FR	A. Furtwängler and K. Reichhold *et al.*, *Griechische Vasenmalerei* (1904–32)
From the Coll	*From the Collection of the Ny Carlsberg Glypothek*
Furtwängler, *Beschreibung*	*Beschreibung der Vasensammlung im Antiquarium* (1885)
GazArch	*Gazette archéologique*
Gestalt und Geschichte	*Festschrift Karl Schefold, zu seinem 60. Geburtstag am 26. Jan. 1965* (1967)
Gomme iv	A. W. Gomme, A. Andrewes, and K. J. Dover, *A Historical Commentary on Thucydides*, iv (1970)
GP	C. M. Robertson, *Greek Painting* (1959)
GPP	R. M. Cook, *Greek Painted Pottery* (1972)
Graef	B. Graef and E. Langlotz, *Die antiken Vasen von der Akropolis zu Athen* (1909–?
GRBS	*Greek, Roman and Byzantine Studies*
Greifenhagen	A. Greifenhagen, *Griechische Eroten* (1957)
Guido	M. Guido, *Sicily, an Archaeological Guide* (1967)
*Hdbk Nich*²	A. D. Trendall, *Handbook of the Nicholson Museum*, edn. 2 (1948)
Hesp	*Hesperia*
Hoppin	J. C. Hoppin, *A Handbook of Attic Red-figured Vases* (1919)
Hoppin *Bf*	J. C. Hoppin, *A Handbook of Greek Black-figured Vases* (1924)
HSCP	*Harvard Studies in Classical Philology*
IG	*Inscriptiones Graecae*
Jacobsthal	P. Jacobsthal, *Ornamente griechischer Vasen* (1927)
Jb	*Jahrbuch des Deutschen Archäologischen Instituts*

Jh	*Jahreshefte des Österreichischen Archäologischen Institutes in Wien*
JHS	*Journal of Hellenic Studies*
Karouzou	S. Karouzou, *The Amasis Painter* (1956)
Kurtz and Boardman	D. C. Kurtz and J. Boardman, *Greek Burial Customs* (1971)
Langlotz	E. Langlotz, *Griechische Vasen in Würzburg* (1932)
Lippold	G. Lippold, *Die griechische Plastik* (1950)
Luschey	H. Luschey, *Die Phiale* (1939)
MadMitt	*Madrider Mitteilungen*
MdI	*Mitteilungen des Deutschen Archäologischen Instituts*
Mel	P. Jacobsthal, *Die melischen Reliefs* (1931)
Mingazzini	P. Mingazzini, *Vasi della collezione Castellani* (1930)
ML	*Monumenti antichi pubblicati per cura della Reale Accademia dei Lincei*
MMJ	*Metropolitan Museum Journal*
Möbius	H. Möbius, *Die Ornamente der griechischen Grabstelen* (1968)
MonPiot	*Monuments et Mémoires publiés par l'Académie des Inscriptions et Belles-Lettres*
Muse	*Annual of the Museum of Art and Archaeology*, University of Missouri, Columbia
MusJ	*The Museum Journal* (Philadelphia)
NC	*Numismatic Chronicle*
NSc	*Notizie degli Scavi di Antichità*
Olynthus xi	D. M. Robinson, *Olynthus XI—Necrolynthia* (1942)
Overseas	J. Boardman, *The Greeks Overseas* (1964)
PAE	*Praktika tes Archaiologikes Hetaireias*
Pan	K. Peters, *Studien zu den panathenäischen Preisamphoren* (1942)
Para	J. D. Beazley, *Paralipomena* (1971)
Payne	H. Payne, *Necrocorinthia* (1931)
Payne and Young	H. Payne and G. M. Young, *Archaic Marble Sculpture from the Acropolis* (1950)
PBSR	*Papers of the British School at Rome*
Perachora ii	T. J. Dunbabin *et al.*, *Perachora*, vol. ii (1962)
Pfuhl	E. Pfuhl, *Malerei und Zeichnung der Griechen* (1923)
Philippaki	B. Philippaki, *The Attic Stamnos* (1967)
PW	*Pauly–Wissowa, Real-Encyclopädie der klassischen Altertumswissenschaft*
RA	*Revue archéologique*
REA	*Revue des études anciennes*
Rhitsona	P. N. Ure, *Sixth and Fifth Century Pottery from Rhitsona* (1927)
Richter, *Korai*	G. Richter, *Korai: Archaic Greek Maidens* (1968)
Richter and Hall	G. Richter and L. Hall, *Red-figured Athenian Vases in the Metropolitan Museum of Art* (1936)
Riezler	W. Riezler, *Weissgrundige attische Lekythen* (1914)
RM	*Mitteilungen des Deutschen Archäologischen Instituts: Römische Abteilung*
Robinson and Harcum	D. Robinson, C. Harcum, and J. Iliffe, *A Catalogue of the Greek Vases in the Royal Ontario Museum of Archaeology, Toronto* (1930)

ABBREVIATIONS

Sammlung Funcke	N. Kunisch, *Antiken der Sammlung Julius C. und Margot Funcke* (1972)
Schmaltz	B. Schmaltz, *Untersuchungen zu den attischen Marmorlekythen* (1970)
Select	*Ashmolean Museum, Department of Antiquities. Select Exhibition of Sir John and Lady Beazley's Gifts to the Ashmolean Museum, 1912–1966* (1967)
SGK	R. Lullies, *Eine Sammlung griechischer Kleinkunst* (1955)
Sonderliste N	H. A. Cahn, *Attische rotfigurige Vasen* (1971)
Sonderliste G	H. A. Cahn, *Attische schwarzfigurige Vasen* (1964)
Starr	C. Starr, *Athenian Coinage, 480–449 B.C.* (1970)
TWL	S. Karouzou, *Ten White Lekythoi in the National Museum*, Athens, n.d.
VA	J. D. Beazley, *Attic Red-figured Vases in American Museums* (1918)
VPol	J. D. Beazley, *Greek Vases in Poland* (1928)
VPU	G. Pellegrini, *Catalogo dei vasi antichi dipinti delle collezioni Palagi ed Universitaria*, Bologna, (1900)
Watzinger	C. Watzinger, *Griechische Vasen in Tübingen* (1924)

GENERAL INTRODUCTION

> The Greek designers delighted in the facts of the human form, and became great
> in consequence; but the facts of lower nature were disregarded by them, and their
> inferior ornament became, therefore, dead and valueless.
>
> Ruskin, *The Stones of Venice*,
> vol. ii, ch. vi, paragraph 46.

PREVIOUS studies of Athenian white *lekythoi* have been concerned with style and iconography: Riezler's *Weissgrundige attische Lekythen* (1914), Fairbanks's two-volume *Athenian White Lekythoi* (1907, 1914), Buschor's *Attische Lekythen der Parthenonzeit* (1925), Miss Haspels's *Attic Black-figured Lekythoi* (1936), and Beazley's classic essay, *Attic White Lekythoi* (1938). Since 1938 there has been no detailed study of the vase despite greatly augmented painter lists in the second edition of *Attic Red-figure Vase-painters* (1963; the first edition (1925) included only white *lekythoi* by red-figure painters) and the discovery of classical graves and cemeteries in Athens and elsewhere. Now more is known about contemporary burial practices and, although our knowledge is still imperfect, the subject can profitably be studied again.

Classical *lekythoi*, white-ground with funerary iconography, were a fashion, limited in time and place (see pp. 135 ff.). They are not representative of Attic painted pottery, standing apart in iconography as well as technique. If white *lekythoi* figure prominently in studies of Greek vase-painting, it is because some are very beautiful and come closer than other Attic vases to the lost paintings on panel and wall. The scenes also have great appeal, partly because they are drawn not from the deeds of gods or heroes, but from the lives of men. Contemporary literature sometimes tells us what the Athenians did, white *lekythoi* show us.

From the second quarter of the fifth century to near its close the iconography of the white *lekythos* is almost exclusively funerary with scenes illustrative of Athenian rites of death and burial. How did the vase come to be so special? There are several reasons: (1) Oil was essential to the dead as well as to the living; oil pots are among the most common offerings in Athenian graves. (2) The white slip rendered the vase impractical for daily use, and at the same time afforded a neutral ground on which painters could express themselves freely. (3) Rites of death and burial were as important to Athenians as celebrations of birth or marriage; from the Geometric period onwards monuments of stone and of clay survive as memorials not only to the dead, but also to the honour with which the Athenians buried them.

The white *lekythos* is one element of Athenian funerary art, and its evolution is a result of restrictions imposed on grander monuments.[1] The Athenian's devotion to his dead is matched by his tendency towards extravagance in commemorating them. We

[1] Kurtz and Boardman, 90, 121 f.

have several accounts of sumptuary legislation passed in Athens, the fullest by Cicero in the *De Legibus* (ii. 26. 64). Cicero mentions Solon's legislation early in the sixth century, Demetrios of Phaleron's late in the fourth, and a third 'sometime after' Solon's. The date of the last is uncertain, but during most of the fifth century impressive private memorials of stone are conspicuously absent from excavated Athenian cemeteries and sumptuary legislation is a plausible explanation.

The tradition of funerary painting is well established in Attica from the Geometric period:[1] some of the scenes found on the great 'Dipylon' vases are reproduced without substantial alteration on white *lekythoi* of the classical period; between them stands the series of Protoattic and black-figure vases and plaques. Some of the latest in black-figure are by the Sappho and Theseus Painters (see pp. 80 f., 14 f.). Both artists were active in the years around 500 B.C. in workshops which came to specialize in white *lekythoi*— the Sappho Painter in the Diosphos Workshop, the Theseus Painter in the Athena Painter's Workshop. Both the technique and the iconography of the white *lekythos* develop from black-figure.

The essential elements of the black-figure technique are silhouette, incised detail, and added colour;[2] the ground may be dark or light. The earliest white *lekythoi* are fully black-figure and the history of the vase would be incomplete without a study of the black-figure artists who first decorated it. Even though the new red-figure technique was firmly established by the last decades of the sixth century B.C., black-figure was not abandoned. It was retained for the Panathenaic prize amphorae—traditional vases of great importance—and, for some time, for the subsidiary decoration on red-figure *loutrophoroi* —another traditional vase of ritual use—and on *lekythoi*. In the black-figure workshops which specialized in *lekythoi* the incised silhouette (black-figure) on white-ground first gives place to incised silhouette and outline (semi-outline) and then to outline. The early outlines are executed in undiluted glaze and added colours are the red, white, and purple of black-figure. Gradually, the glaze is diluted for freer lines and washes of a subtle polychromy; then, around the middle of the fifth century, matt paint is used as well as the dilute glaze, to be followed by matt paint on its own and pastel colours of fugitive pigments. The evolution is simple.

Before the iconography of the white *lekythos* became predominantly funerary, domestic and mythological scenes were standard. These early non-funerary white *lekythoi* were popular at home and abroad; their proveniences are as varied as those of the red-figured *lekythoi* with similar scenes, which were produced in several workshops throughout the fifth century (see pp. 136 f.). The funerary scenes on Athenian white *lekythoi* are either realistic portrayals of contemporary Athenian practices or traditional mythological renderings of the coming of death or, rarely, a conflation of the two.[3] The mythological scenes are not numerous and the principal figures are familiar to us from Greek art and literature: Charon, Hermes, Thanatos, and Hypnos. Charon plies his boat over the Acheron to collect the dead person, who faces death either alone (PLATE 47. 3), or in the

---

[1] Ibid. 61 ff., 77 ff., 102 ff., 148 f.

[2] J. D. Beazley, *The Development of Attic Black-figure* (1951), 1.

[3] See p. 50 n. 3, p. 63 n. 9, p. 83 n. 4.

company of a loved one (PLATE 42. 1), or of Hermes, in his role of *psychopompos*; the winged brothers—Thanatos and Hypnos, children of Night[1]—carry off the dead, the men (PLATE 32. 4), women, and children of Athens—as they had the legendary heroes of the past. This focus on the people of Athens is a characteristic feature of classical white *lekythoi*. The realistic portrayal of burial practices is a visual record of their rites and beliefs which contemporary literature rarely mentions and almost never explains. We see the dead on his bier, attended by his family, the men offering their respect and concealing their grief, the women lamenting more openly (PLATE 29. 1, 2); and we see the cemeteries, with monuments and mourners (PLATE 26). Grief is nobly, simply, and beautifully expressed; there is nothing unlovely or unpleasant. There are grander memorials to the dead, but few have the poignant human appeal of Athenian white *lekythoi*.

[1] Hesiod, *Theogony*, ed. M. L. West (1966), ll. 755 ff., and p. 368.

PART ONE

SHOULDER PATTERNS

INTRODUCTION

A SURVEY of painters and workshops based on patterns presupposes a regular co-ordination between pattern-hand and figure-hand. Such a co-ordination is an acknowledged hallmark of Attic vase-painting, and a fundamental part of Beazley's system of classification: 'A distinctive style of figurework is commonly accompanied by a distinctive set of patterns, executed in a distinctive way' (*Potter and Painter in Ancient Athens* (1944), 31); '. . . there is no reason to suppose that the patterns were not regularly executed by the same hand as the figures; the labour may sometimes have been divided, though I do not for a moment believe that it was often so; but even then the artist of the figures would naturally prescribe the patterns' ('*Citharoedus*', *JHS* xlii (1922), 88). We cannot be certain that pattern- and figure-hand are one and the same, but this is not so important. Even if the figure-man had a favourite pattern-man, the collaboration was so regular, the exceptions so few, that the two function virtually as one. Evidence drawn from Attic vase-painting generally, and from *lekythoi* particularly, indicates that one man nearly always executed both the patterns and the figures. Often the two elements are so harmoniously balanced that a division of labour seems unthinkable; not infrequently they are so intricately interwoven that collaboration would have been impractical, if not impossible.

The shoulder patterns on *lekythoi* of shoulder type do not seem to be a promising subject for a pattern-figure study, since structurally the shoulder field is distinct from the body; but black-figure *lekythoi* often have figures on the shoulder and their style is the same as that of the figures on the body. Red-figure *lekythoi* occasionally have shoulder figures (see pp. 126 f.), white *lekythoi* virtually never, but when they do, the style of the shoulder figures is that of the principal figures. Important for our purposes is the tendency for florals to be added to figure-compositions on the shoulder. Complementary to the phenomenon of figures on the shoulder is that of the florals on the body. The side-palmette *lekythoi* discussed in Part Two are the best, but not the only, example. The body florals are in the same style as the shoulder florals, and since some are structurally part of the figure scene collaboration once again seems highly unlikely.

In conclusion, I do not argue the pattern–figure connection; I accept it as fact. Beazley, Haspels, and Jacobsthal have studied the problem, concluding that figures and patterns, with very few exceptions, are the work of one man. My research supports this.

Part One is divided into 'early' and 'classical' painters of white *lekythoi*. The division is more than a chronological guide-line. 'Early' painters, for the most part, worked in more than one technique; 'classical' painters tended more and more to concentrate on *lekythoi* in the white-ground technique. Emphasis in the first half of the survey is, therefore, on the establishment of canons—of shape, technique, and pattern—and on the interrelations between workshops which are largely contemporary. In the second part of the survey emphasis is on continuity in production and community within workshops.

Because the canons have been established, accessory decoration is given somewhat less attention and iconography is given more.

Within the 'early' part there is a subdivision; a few pages are devoted to lotus buds which precede palmettes on the shoulders of *lekythoi*. Since our concern is primarily for later *lekythoi*, the lotus buds are treated summarily. My purpose is to illustrate how the lotus buds of mid- to late black-figure become the 'rays' of secondary *lekythoi* of the classical period.

Lastly, a word about the material on which I have based the survey of painters and workshops. A study of patterns on shoulders is beset by even more difficulties than a study of figures on bodies, for shoulders are often excluded from published photographs. For this reason I rely almost exclusively on my own museum notes. Here, too, there is a problem: like other students of Attic vase-painting, I was slow to realize the importance of pattern. My survey is not, therefore, based on the many museums in which I have once spent a short time, but on the few to which I have had the opportunity to return often—the British Museum; the National Museum, Athens; the Metropolitan Museum of Art, New York; the Museum of Fine Arts, Boston; and, most importantly, the Ashmolean Museum, Oxford.

I

EARLY PAINTERS OF WHITE *LEKYTHOI*

1. LOTUS CHAINS

FLORAL chains composed of lotus blossoms and lotus buds,[1] linked by simple arcs, first appear in Attica and Corinth towards the end of the first quarter of the sixth century B.C. The elements of composition and the manner of construction are Eastern (FIGURE 1*b*), imported via east Greece, and very unlike the Corinthian chain of interlaced palmettes and lotus blossoms which Attic vase-painters had taken over early in the black-figure style.[2]

In Attica the new type of floral was used by sculptors as well as vase-painters. The large marble statue in Berlin, known as the Berlin Goddess, dated around 580 B.C., wears a *polos* encircled with lotus blossoms and buds (FIGURE 1*a*).[3] The florals are lightly incised (as is the meander[4] pattern beneath them) and picked out in red paint. At the base of each calyx is a prominent circular protuberance.[5] The lack of linking tendrils is paralleled on a later but stylistically related *kore*, found recently in the Attic countryside at Merenta.[6] The Merenta *kore* is wreathed with lotus buds and blossoms, carved in high relief. Both she and the Berlin Goddess wear a *chiton* without a *peplos*. This is unusual. Until the middle of the century, when the fashion for Ionian dress takes Athens,[7] *korai* wear the *peplos* with a *chiton*. One of the first Attic *korai* in the new style of dress—*himation* worn diagonally over a *chiton*—is the so-called Lyons *kore*.[8] On her head is a *polos* with lightly incised florals, lotus blossoms alternating with palmettes and linked by simple arcs (FIGURE 1*g*).[9] During the second half of the century a lotus and palmette chain,

---

[1] Botanical terms cannot always be used with accuracy owing to the extreme stylization of the florals and the conventional archaeological terminology. Lotus 'blossom' is used here to describe all lotuses whose calyxes are not tightly closed; lotuses with closed calyxes are 'buds'.

[2] H. Payne, *Necrocorinthia* (1931), 154 ff. A general discussion of floral motifs in Egyptian, Near Eastern, and Greek art may be found in: A. Riegl, *Stilfragen, Grundlegungen zu einer Geschichte der Ornamentik* (1893), 48 ff., 86 ff.; M. Meurer, *Vergleichende Formenlehre des Ornamentes und der Pflanze* (1909), 42 ff., 379 ff. More recent studies with further bibliography are: R. M. Cook, *BSA* xxxiv (1933–4), 75 ff.; P. Jacobsthal, *Greek Pins* (1956), 145 f.; R. D. Barnett, *A Catalogue of the Nimrud Ivories* (1957), 57, 99 f.; pl. cxviii (T 24) and p. 225; pl. cxxi (V 6*a*) and pp. 227 f.; P. R. S. Moorey, *Catalogue of the Ancient Persian Bronzes in the Ashmolean Museum* (1971), 212 f.

[3] Berlin, Staatliche Museen, inv. 1800; C. Blümel, *Staatliche Museen, Berlin, Katalog der Skulpturen*, ii. 1 (1940), 6, A 1 (= Richter, *Korai*, no. 42). *Poloi* are discussed by the following: V. Müller, *Der Polos* (1915); H. Payne and G. M. Young, *Archaic Marble Sculpture from the Acropolis* (1950), 15 and n. 2.

[4] Compare the *polos*, decorated with a meander, worn by the best-preserved of the 'Dipylon ivories', Athens, National Museum, 776 (*AM* lv (1930), pl. v). For a discussion of the 'Dipylon ivories' and their relation to Near Eastern ivories, see T. J. Dunbabin, *The Greeks and their Eastern Neighbours* (1957), 38 f.

[5] Payne, 155 n. 1.

[6] *Athens Annals of Archaeology* v (1972), 298 ff., especially 313, fig. 15.

[7] Payne and Young, 16 ff.

[8] Ibid. 14 ff. (= Athens, Acropolis Museum, 269 = Richter, *Korai*, no. 89).

[9] H. Schrader, *Die archaische Marmorbildwerke der Akropolis* (1939), 67, fig. 32.

constructed with arc tendrils, appears on the dress[1] and/or headpiece[2] of a number of *korai*, among them Antenor's[3] and the *Peplos kore*.[4] If sculptors had not relied on paint without incision for so much of their patternwork, the numbers of florals of various types could doubtless be increased. On one of the latest of the *korai*, the early fifth-century *kore* of Euthydikos,[5] an interesting detail of painted decoration was preserved on one sleeve: a pair of racing chariots.[6]

The *korai* are relevant, for it is to dress patterns that Attic vase-painters initially applied the chain of florals linked by simple arcs.[7] Sophilos[8] and Kleitias[9] are the first to do this, and the dresses to which they apply florals are similar enough for a common model to have inspired them: richly ornamented robes with rows of florals alternating with rows of figures and other patterns, from neckline to hem. The figure scene most frequently represented is the chariot race, and the chariots painted on the sleeve of the Euthydikos *kore* are probably a later example of this type of elaborate pattern,[10] which was well established in the Near East.[11] I think it is possible that the lotus chain came into Greece from the East through textiles[12] and that Sophilos and Kleitias had seen, or at least knew of, these richly embroidered or woven robes. Perhaps there was in Athens such a garment, for the goddess Athena, made by immigrants or native artisans not unaware of Eastern textile traditions and luxury goods.[13] Our dress friezes could not, however, have been copied first-hand, for the iconographical details are sometimes confused and quite

[1] W. Lermann, *Altgriechische Plastik* (1907), pl. xviii (Athens, Acropolis Museum, 679 = Richter, *Korai*, no. 113); pl. xx (Athens, Acropolis Museum, 683 = Richter, *Korai*, no. 120).

[2] Ibid., pl. iii (Athens, Acropolis Museum, 671 = Richter, *Korai*, no. 111); pl. ix (Athens, Acropolis Museum, 696 = Richter, *Korai*, no. 126); pl. x (Athens, Acropolis Museum, 675 = Richter, *Korai*, no. 123); pl. xix (Athens, Acropolis Museum, 670 = Richter, *Korai*, no. 119); pl. xx (Athens, Acropolis Museum, 684 = Richter, *Korai*, no. 182).

[3] Athens, Acropolis Museum, 681 (= Richter, *Korai*, no. 110).

[4] Athens, Acropolis Museum, 679 (= Richter, *Korai*, no. 113).

[5] Athens, Acropolis Museum, 686 and 609 (= Richter, *Korai*, no. 180).

[6] Schrader, op. cit. 79, fig. 44.

[7] Payne, 155.

[8] When Payne described Sophilos' florals (*Necrocorinthia*, 155) he knew the fragmentary *dinos* from the Acropolis (Athens, Acropolis, 587. *ABV* 39, no. 15) but not the well-preserved *dinos* and stand recently acquired by the British Museum, on which the wedding of Peleus and Thetis is also represented (*ABV* 39, no. 16 *bis* and *Para* 19; *ArchReps*, 1971–2, 62, fig. 8; *BMQ* xxxvi (1972), 107 ff.).

[9] Florence, 4209; *ABV* 76, no. 1. Richly embroidered or woven dresses, like those worn by the goddesses, are worn by Amazons on some contemporary vases. The fragmentary vase by Kleitias from the Acropolis, his only attributed vase with Amazons (Athens, Acropolis, 597f–h. *ABV* 77, no. 4) preserves dresses with rows of figures alternating with rows of florals—like those worn by the goddesses. For other Amazons wearing richly embroidered dresses (rows of figures without florals) see D. von Bothmer, *Amazons in Greek Art* (1957), pl. 5 and pp. 17 f. (Boston, 98.916. *ABV* 98, no. 46); pl. 19. 1 and pp. 23 f. (Athens, Acropolis, 597; see above); pl. 25. 1 and p. 26 (Bonn, 37. *ABV* 99, no. 58); pl. 25. 2 and p. 29 (Munich, 1427. *ABV* 103, no. 16).

[10] Dress-patterns in Greek painting are discussed by A. Kloss, *MdI* v (1952), 80 ff., P. C. Cecchetti, *Studi Miscellanei* xix (1972).

[11] Dress-patterns on Assyrian reliefs are discussed by J. V. Canby, *Iraq* xxxiii (1971), 31 ff. I should like to thank Roger Moorey for drawing my attention to this article.

[12] The importance of textiles in the transmission of pattern is discussed by Canby, op. cit. 39. See also: H. Frankfort, *The Art and Architecture of the Ancient Orient* (1954), 232 f.; R. D. Barnett, *Catalogue of the Nimrud Ivories*, 57; *Studies Presented to Hetty Goldman* (1956), 34 (Barnett). E. Akurgal, *The Birth of Greek Art* (1966), 187, 214; G. Azarpay, *Urartian Art and Artifacts* (1968), 14, 21.

[13] T. J. Dunbabin, *The Greeks and their Eastern Neighbours* (1957); *Syria* xxxv (1958), 73 ff. (Amandry); J. Boardman, *The Greeks Overseas* (1973), ch. 3.

un-Eastern (for example, winged horses draw chariots),[1] just as the florals are selectively adapted and stylized. To these we now turn.

Sophilos relies on the old system of interlaced lotus blossoms and palmettes for conspicuous areas, rendering the new arc chain in miniature on the dresses of some of the goddesses attending the wedding of Peleus and Thetis.[2] Here he used the new manner of construction but the old elements—palmettes and lotuses, linked by simple arcs.

The wedding of Peleus and Thetis is also the subject of Kleitias' large volute-crater in Florence, the François Vase.[3] Kleitias, like Sophilos, displays the old Corinthian chain in conspicuous places and the new one on the dresses of some of the goddesses attending the wedding (FIGURE 1 e, f).[4] Like Sophilos he has combined the arcs with the palmettes and lotuses, but he has also introduced a second type of chain in which lotus blossoms, alternately upright and pendent, are joined by means of simple arcs (FIGURE 1d).[5] Chains of lotus blossoms, alternately upright and pendent, are not distinctively Eastern.[6] Their appearance on some of the so-called Melian vases is significant (FIGURE 1c).[7] In addition to the goddesses of the principal scene, two other figures on the François Vase wear these fancy dresses—a *potnia theron* (on the handle above the three Muses) and Theseus, leading the dance of youths and maidens, whom he has freed from the Minotaur.

The lotus blossoms painted by Sophilos and Kleitias are stylized, but the calyx with three distinct sepals and the corolla with several petals are carefully indicated. Nowhere on the vases of either are lotus blossoms linked to lotus buds. The first attributed Attic black-figure vase on which this scheme appears is Acropolis 606 (FIGURE 1h),[8] the name vase of a younger contemporary of Kleitias, working in a monumental style.[9] Above the figures on the Acropolis *dinos* the painter set a pendent chain of linked lotus buds and lotus blossoms, beneath them the Corinthian interlaced palmette and lotus. The florals are carefully executed, but the petals of the corolla have been omitted.

With the Amasis Painter, 'in whom the chief group of mid-sixth-century *lekythoi* centres',[10] we begin our study of the lotus chain as shoulder decoration on *lekythoi*. The Amasis Painter's early *lekythos* in the Louvre (PLATE 1. 1),[11] featuring a *potnia theron* not unlike Kleitias', is one of the first Attic *lekythoi* with a lotus chain on the shoulder.[12] Bud is linked to bud, blossom to blossom; the latter are clearly distinguished from the former by sepals carefully rendered. Later in his career, as illustrated by a *lekythos* found in the Kerameikos with a Dionysiac scene,[13] the Amasis Painter stylized the floral chain more severely. The sepals of the calyx become as thin as the stem arcs linking bud to bud, blossom to blossom. For want of a more appropriate term, I call these emaciated sepals

---

[1] I owe this information to Roger Moorey.

[2] Graef, pl. 26.

[3] See p. 6 n. 9, adding: FR pls. 1–3; *MdI* v. 84 (A 21 a and b).

[4] FR pl. 3 (Moira (second from the left), Hera, Urania, Hora (furthermost)).

[5] FR pl. 3 (Moira, Hera, Urania, Hora, and Theseus). Cf. also Graef, pl. 24 (Athens, Acropolis, 597 f. *ABV* 77, no. 4).

[6] But cf. Meurer, op. cit. 386 f. and pl. 5.

[7] A. Conze, *Melische Thongefässe* (1862), pl. 1. 5.

[8] Athens, Acropolis, 606. *ABV* 81, no. 1; Graef, pls. 30–2.

[9] *Dev* 38.

[10] *ABL* 10. The Amasis Painter: *ABV* 150 ff., 678 f., 714; *Para* 62 ff.

[11] Louvre, F 71. *ABV* 154, no. 49.

[12] *ABL* 11; S. Karouzou, *The Amasis Painter* (1956), 23.

[13] Athens, Kerameikos Museum, no number. *ABV* 155, no. 61; Karouzou, pl. 21. 3–4.

'sepal arcs', for they are little more than 'stem arcs' transposed (FIGURE 2*b*). The addition of 'sepal arcs' to buds as well as blossoms, and the lack of distinction between the florals, transform the chain of lotus blossoms linked to lotus buds into a lotus-bud chain, and this floral is one of the most common on Attic black- and red-figure vases.

The Amasean lotus-bud chain is reproduced for some time and without much variety on the shoulders of *lekythoi*.[1] Although the pendent chain is used by Attic painters during the second quarter of the sixth century on vases of different shapes,[2] the upright chain is regular on *lekythoi* until the time of the Pioneers and Leagrans, after the beginning of the last quarter of the sixth century (FIGURE 2*c*).[3] Through most, if not all, of the fifth century, the lotus-bud chain in various forms decorates the shoulders of shoulder-type *lekythoi* of secondary shape, palmettes being reserved for shoulder-type *lekythoi* of standard shape.[4] This distinction in shoulder decoration is characteristic of fifth-century *lekythoi*, black-figure, red-figure, and white-ground, and it is one of the criteria established by Beazley for the classification of standard and secondary shapes.[5] To illustrate the transformation of the lotus-bud chain I have selected a few *lekythoi* of representative painters.

The Cactus Painter, active in the years around 500 B.C., decorated two types of shoulder *lekythoi*. One is broader and more nearly cylindrical, the other is slimmer and more tapering.[6] On the shoulder of the former which is nearly standard shape, he painted palmettes (PLATE 4. 3),[7] and on the latter lotus buds (PLATE 4. 4).[8] The Cactus Painter's secondary shape is a personal version of the shape made popular by the Marathon Painter[9] and the Workshop of Athens 581,[10] with which he is closely associated (see pp. 147 ff.). Some of the Marathon Painter's largest and best *lekythoi* have shoulder palmettes,[11] but the great majority have pendent lotus buds. Beazley divided the Class of Athens 581 into two large groups on the basis of shoulder decoration: 581. i *lekythoi* have linked lotus buds on the shoulder;[12] 581. ii *lekythoi*, 'in general the smaller, slighter pieces', have rays—vestigial lotus buds, without stem or sepal arcs.[13]

Lekythoi of the Diosphos Workshop illustrate a similar transformation of the lotus-bud chain. The Sappho and Diosphos Painters, also active in the years around 500 B.C., decorate the shoulders of their *lekythoi* almost exclusively with pendent lotus chains.[14] On the Sappho Painter's *lekythoi* the stem arcs regularly skip two buds, on the Diosphos Painter's, one.[15] There is more variety in the Diosphos Painter's florals, just as there is more variety in his shapes. On the largest and finest *lekythoi*, lotuses are linked by stem arcs skipping one bud (FIGURE 2*d*).[16] On his smaller *lekythoi* he tends to omit the arcs or to paint the calyx white (cf. FIGURE 2*e*).[17] The shape of the independent buds is the same as that of the buds linked in chains. The latest of the Diosphos Painter's *lekythoi*[18]—very

[1] *ABL* 11.

[2] See above, p. 7 n. 8. Cf. also *ABL* 15, 44 and n. 1 (pendent lotus buds on the shoulder of *lekythoi* of the Dolphin Class); *Am* pl. 18 (lotus chain on the rim of a plate by Lydos, Bonn, 339 fr. *ABV* 111, no. 51).

[3] *ABL* 11.   [4] Ibid. 61.   [5] *ARV* 675.

[6] *ABL* 61 f.; *ABV* 472, 505; *Para* 212.

[7] Berlin, 3261. *ABL* 198, no. 3.

[8] Oxford, 512. *ABL* 198, no. 4.

[9] Ibid. 89 ff.; *ABV* 595.

[10] *ABV* 487 ff., 700 ff., 716; *Para* 222 ff.

[11] *ABL* 90.   [12] *ARV* 489.   [13] Ibid. 489.

[14] *ABL* 94 f.   [15] Ibid. 94 f.   [16] Ibid. 94.

[17] Ibid. 94, 107 and n. 2; *ANY* 50 f., no. 195.

[18] *ABL* 100.

slender vases, also decorated by the Haimon Painter, who follows the 581 Workshop in the mass production of small *lekythoi* (see pp. 150 ff.)[1]—have buds without arcs and the buds themselves are little more than rounded rays, barely distinguishable from the bars at the join of shoulder to neck. In the hands of the Haimon Painter degeneration continues. Better *lekythoi* of Diosphos type have round rays (FIGURE 2*f*),[2] lesser 'chimney' *lekythoi* (see p. 87), and the mass of Haemonian 581 *lekythoi* have bars (cf. FIGURE 2*g*).[3]

The Beldam Workshop, active later in the first half of the fifth century and continuing into the second half,[4] illustrates the same degeneration of bud into bar. The Beldam Painter preferred palmettes for the shoulder of his large *lekythoi* of shape BEL (PLATE 18. 1–2),[5] but even on these he sometimes paints the rays which are standard on smaller *lekythoi* (see p. 85).[6] At its worst, the vestigial bud/ray becomes a stroke or bar (FIGURE 2*h*). A series of concentric bars, hastily painted, is the characteristic shoulder decoration of *lekythoi* of the Tymbos Workshop (PLATES 22, 23), which is related to that of the Beldam Painter and active through much of the second half of the century.[7] Only a few of the most carefully fashioned *lekythoi* of shape ATL (cf. PLATE 21. 1–2), the Aischines and Tymbos Painters' favourite type (see p. 82),[8] have palmettes on the shoulder.[9] Among the other fifth-century *lekythoi* of secondary shape[10] the same distinction in shoulder decoration can be observed: a few of the finer pieces have palmettes on the shoulder, but the great majority have bars. The shoulder of *lekythoi* of secondary shape is regularly reserved, whether the vase is white-ground or red-figure.

2. PSIAX AND THE EARLIEST WHITE-GROUND

Palmettes begin to appear regularly on the shoulders of *lekythoi* during the period when the Leagros Group was dominating Attic black-figure, but white-ground is not common until the Edinburgh Painter, a younger member of the group, makes it fashionable on the new *lekythoi* of cylinder shape. Our earliest white *lekythos* is probably by Psiax.[11] Chronology is always a problem, but Psiax's affiliations are principally with the generation of painters which preceded the Leagros Group, and his *lekythos*, in shape, stands before the main series of cylinders.[12] The vase, in a private collection in Paris, is well preserved, and its white slip is without obvious technical imperfections.[13] The shoulder is white with three black palmettes linked by thin, gracefully curving tendrils, which terminate in open buds at the handle (FIGURE 7*a*). In black-figure, similar elegant palmettes appear on vases by the Antimenes Painter.[14] In red-figure Psiax reproduces them on the bottom of

---

[1] Ibid. 100, 131.
[2] Ibid. 131, pl. 41. 4.
[3] Ibid. 133, 137.
[4] Ibid. 170 ff.
[5] *ARV* 675, 750 ff.
[6] *ABL* 185.
[7] Ibid. 180 ff. The earliest *lekythoi* of the Tymbos Workshop may belong to the later second quarter of the century.
[8] *ARV* 675, 709.
[9] Cf. Basle Market (M.M.). *ARV* 715, no. 189 *bis*, and *Para* 409.
[10] *ARV* 675 f. (CL, PL).

[11] *ABV* 292 ff., 338, 609, 674, 675, 692; *ARV* 6 ff., 1617 f.; *Para* 127 f., 321.
[12] Cf. *ABL* 77, pl. 21 (Agrigento, 23. *ARV* 308, no. 5) and pl. 22. 4 (London, 1922.10–18.1. *ARV* 332, no. 1).
[13] Paris, Jameson. *ABV* 293, no. 11. I know the vase only from photographs.
[14] Cf. Munich, 1722. *ABV* 269, no. 33; Villa Giulia, 3556. *ABV* 269, no. 35; Swiss Private. *ABV* 269, no. 35 *bis*, and *Para* 119 f.

his *aryballos*, once in Bologna,[1] and in the tondo of some of his cups.[2] An early red-figure plate in Boston by Paseas has similar florals in the exergue.[3] We shall return to Paseas and the Antimenes Painter, for both are closely related to Psiax. Lastly, an early red-figure *lekythos* in Oxford may be compared (PLATE 5. 1).[4] The body tapers sharply and the figure decoration is very early or inept.[5] On the shoulder are three red-figure palmettes, linked by thin curving tendrils. If the Oxford vase is not our earliest red-figure *lekythos*, it is the first to have a red-figure shoulder.

A second white *lekythos* is near Psiax and probably from his hand (PLATE 1. 2).[6] Unfortunately, the vase is fragmentary (details of shape and shoulder decoration are unknown) but enough remains to establish that it was large and elaborately decorated. Beneath the figures there was a miniature frieze of horsemen and riders. Predella friezes are otherwise unknown on white *lekythoi*, but on Antimenean *hydriai* (PLATE 2. 1) they are common. Compare the *hydriai* of the Leagros Group (PLATE 57. 3) on which palmettes assume this position. A small number of black-figure *lekythoi* have palmettes similarly disposed (cf. PLATE 16. 4).[7]

If Psiax painted our earliest white *lekythoi*, from what source did he take his inspiration? To answer this question we must investigate Psiax' relation to his predecessors and to his contemporaries.

Psiax belongs to an era of experiment; Exekias had already exploited the black-figure technique to its fullest, leaving his successors to emulate or innovate. Psiax had a strong black-figure side, applying the technique in a traditional manner or more adventurously in new media—on a white[8] or coral-ground[9]—but he also worked in red-figure[10] and in Six's technique.[11] We know that he collaborated with Andokides,[12] for one of his Type-A amphorae[13] and one of special type[14] bear Andokides' signature as potter (special amphorae of the same type were decorated by the Antimenes Painter).[15] The Andokides Painter is the acknowledged inventor of red-figure, and it has been suggested that he also invented white-ground,[16] but Andokides the potter was a conservative, following closely in the line of Exekias, and the Andokides Painter one, and perhaps not the most important, of the early red-figure painters; his use of white-ground is hesitant and technically faulty.[17] Psiax' inspiration surely came from other quarters in the Kerameikos.

---

[1] Once Bologna, PU 322. *ARV* 7, no. 6.

[2] Swiss Private. *ARV* 7, no. 7; Munich, 2587. *ARV* 7, no. 8.

[3] Boston, 01.8025. *ARV* 163, no. 6.

[4] Oxford, 1949.751. *ARV* 9, no. 1.

[5] Compare the figure-style of the *kyathos* in Six's technique: London, B 693. *ABV* 609.

[6] Athens, Agora, P 5002. *ABV* 295, no. 2. See also *ARV* 8, for a third *lekythos* possibly by Psiax. Two of Psiax' hydriai have figure predelle (*ABV* 293, nos. 8 and 10); the third (*ABV* 293, no. 9; *Para* 127) has elaborate florals (PLATE 2. 2).

[7] Cf. *ABL* pl. 26. 3 (Gela Painter), and pp. 133, 137 (Haimon Painter), and see below, pp. 21 f.

[8] *ABV* 293, nos. 11–13; 294, nos. 16, 21, and 25.

[9] Ibid. 294, no. 22.

[10] *ARV* 6 ff.

[11] *ABV* 294, no. 25 (= *ARV* 8, no. 13).

[12] *ABV* 253 f., 715; *ARV* 1 ff., 1617; *Para* 113, 320 f.; *JHS* lxxi (1951), 29 ff. (Bloesch); *BullMetr*, February 1966, 201 ff. (Bothmer).

[13] Madrid, 11008. *ABV* 294, no. 24.

[14] Castle Ashby, Northampton. *ABV* 293, no. 7.

[15] Louvre, F 201. *ABV* 274, no. 120; Copenhagen, Thorwaldsen Museum, 38. *ABV* 274, no. 121.

[16] *BullMetr*, February 1966, 207.

[17] The mouth of an Type-A red-figure amphora in New York (63.11.6. *ARV* 3, no. 2 *bis*, and p. 1617; *Para* 320) has a white-ground mouth. See *BullMetr*, February 1966, 201 ff. A second Type-A amphora, in the Louvre (F 203. *ARV* 4, no. 13) is in a special technique, approximating red-figure: the figures are reserved on a white-ground.

Psiax' link with the preceding generation is through Amasis.[1] The potter Amasis was progressive and influential, and so was the Amasis Painter. On some of his black-figure vases the Amasis Painter explores the possibilities offered by outline and added colour, as if he were preparing the way for red-figure.[2] There is also a fragment of a very early red-figure cup which bears the letters AMA, which have been temptingly restored as Ama[sis].[3] Initially Beazley thought that the painter, too, was Amasis and that the fragmentary cup was 'a modest experiment in a wholly novel and unfamiliar technique',[4] but in *ABV* he decided: 'The style of drawing has no connection with the Amasis Painter.'[5] In a way more relevant to our study is Amasis' repertoire of shapes, which includes amphorae of various types, *oinochoai*, cups, *lekythoi*, plaques, a round *aryballos*,[6] and our earliest *alabastron*.[7] Psiax' vases, although less numerous, follow this shape sequence. Especially notable are the *lekythoi*, *aryballoi*, and *alabastra*. Plaques we might have expected by Psiax, and there are plaques close to him, but they have been attributed to Paseas, 'his nearest kin'.[8] Paseas' plaques are black-figure,[9] like the Amasis Painter's, or experiments in quasi-red-figure.[10] The use of white-ground on his plaques is not surprising, for a light or white-ground for plaques was known in Attica from late in the Geometric period.[11] This point brings out an important difference between red-figure and white-ground: although both develop in the period of experiment which followed the apogee of the black-figure style in the hands of Exekias, red-figure is invented and white-ground is rediscovered. Nor is white-ground exclusively a painter's technique, since a white slipped vase need not be decorated. The new fashion for white-ground is, I think, partly a rediscovery of the freedom of expression which outline on a neutral ground permits,[12] and partly (initially) a desire on the part of potters and painters to imitate vessels in other media, notably stone[13] (for example alabaster *alabastra*), but possibly also vases in metal. Some of these early white-ground vases are very fine, embellished with modelled handle attachments in the manner of metal vases, and I cannot help thinking that the artist applied the slip to set his vase somewhat apart from the others.[14]

Amasis stands before Psiax and probably influenced his choice of shapes, but this does not bring us any closer to Psiax' inspiration for white-ground, since we have no white-ground vases by Amasis. At this point the Antimenes Painter may be called in, for he is Psiax' brother,[15] and he is known to have decorated *hydriai* and neck-amphorae, with

---

[1] *ARV* 6.

[2] Karouzou 15 (outline), also, 8 (white women); *JHS* lxxviii (1958), 2 (Boardman).

[3] Florence, 1 B 6, frr. *ARV* 160.

[4] *JHS* li (1931), 275 (Beazley); Karouzou 38.

[5] *ABV* 158; *ARV* 160. Beazley compares a bilingual cup near the Goluchow Painter.

[6] New York, 62.11.11. *Para* 66.

[7] Athens, Agora, P 12628. *ABV* 155, no. 64; *Hesp* viii (1939), 247 ff.

[8] *ARV* 163.   [9] *ABV* 399 f.; *ARV* 164.

[10] Unpublished. I owe this reference to John Boardman.

[11] *BSA* xlix (1954), 196 ff., 200 (Boardman).

[12] This style of painting would have been kept alive in Attica during the black-figure style on plaques, which are generally thought to have been decorated by vase painters, not panel painters. See note 15.

[13] *AWL* 4.

[14] See below, p. 12 n. 15. Cf. also Petit Palais, 310. *ABV* 668, with the *kalos Karystios* which is inscribed on Psiax' *alabastron* in London (1900.6–11.1. *ABV* 294, no. 25) in Six's technique. PLATE I. 3.

[15] *ABV* 266 ff., 691; *Para* 117 ff.

white mouth, neck, or foot, left plain or enriched with figures or patterns.[1] Although the Antimenes Painter uses white-ground in a modest way, he is confident of himself in this technique;[2] he was prolific and his workshop was influential. Among the workshop's large number of black-figure *hydriai* with distinctive figure predelle (PLATE 2. 1) there are a few which are partly white-ground,[3] and which have been attributed to the Euphiletos Painter[4] whom we can date around 530 B.C. on the basis of his prize Panathenaic amphorae.[5] (The Antimenes Painter shares with the Euphiletos Painter the *kalos Euphiletos* otherwise unattested in Attic black-figure.)[6] Two of the Euphiletos Painter's finest vases, wholly black-figure,[7] are signed by the potter Pamphaios,[8] who collaborated with the early red-figure cup painters Oltos and Epiktetos. Pamphaios' partner is Nikosthenes,[9] whom he eventually succeeds. The chronology of Nikosthenes' career is not easily established. We know, however, that he collaborated with the black-figure painter Lydos[10] (from whom the Antimenes Painter seems to spring)[11] and with the red-figure painter Oltos.[12] We may, therefore, assume that he is an older contemporary of Andokides. We know him best for the numerous amphorae of Nikosthenic type (cf. PLATE 55. 2) (a shape which he seems to have borrowed from Etruscan bucchero, to attract the lucrative Etruscan market),[13] and it is on one of these signed amphorae that we have our earliest example of Six's technique (see pp. 116 ff.).[14] White-ground is also found in the Nikosthenic Workshop: two fine *oinochoai*, embellished with modelled heads at the handle, and signed by Nikosthenes.[15] From his successor Pamphaios we have one white-ground cup of special light make.[16] I should, therefore, like to suggest that, on the basis of present evidence, Psiax' inspiration for white-ground appears to have come from the Antimenes Painter and from members of the Nikosthenic circle. His use of Six's technique also betrays the Nikosthenic influence. Psiax' successors in the production of white *lekythoi* and *alabastra*, and in the perpetuation of Six's technique, are the Sappho and Diosphos Painters.

[1] *Hydriai*: Dresden, ZV 1779. *ABV* 268, no. 21; Dresden, ZV 1780. *ABV* 268, no. 22; London, B 316. *ABV* 268, no. 24 (*kalos Euphiletos*). Neck-amphorae: Villa Giulia, M. 487. *ABV* 270, no. 63; Boulogne, 18. *ABV* 272, no. 91.

[2] Compare the *hydriai* with black-figure mourners on the white neck: Dresden, ZV 1779 (E. Diehl, *Die Hydria* (1964), pl. 34 (T 203)), Dresden, ZV 1780, Diehl, pl. 34 (T 204)).

[3] *JHS* xlvii (1927), 82 and n. 46 (neck-amphorae), 86 and n. 54 (*hydriai*) (Beazley). For a recent discussion of these partly white-ground vases see: *RA* 1972, 131 ff. (Duplan).

[4] Munich, 1703. *ABV* 324, no. 26 (mouth); Copenhagen, 111. *ABV* 324, no. 29 (neck with floral pattern); Würzburg, 312. *ABV* 324, no. 35 (mouth); Louvre, F 290. *ABV* 324, no. 37 (mouth).

[5] *Dev* 89, 91 f.

[6] *ABV* 666 f. (except for the unattributed *olpe* in New York on p. 667).

[7] Cab. Méd. 254. *ABV* 324, no. 38; London, B 300. *ABV* 324, no. 39.

[8] *ABV* 216, 235 ff.; *ARV* 127 ff.; *Para* 109.

[9] *ABV* 216; *ARV* 122 f.; *Para* 108.

[10] Oxford, 1966.768. *ABV* 229, iv; *Para* 108.

[11] *Dev* 79.

[12] Florence, 2 B 11. *ARV* 54, no. 8. See also: *ARV* 55, nos. 10–11.

[13] R. M. Cook, *Greek Painted Pottery* (1972), 151 ff., 221 f.

[14] Louvre, F 114. *ABV* 226.

[15] Louvre, F 117. *ABV* 230, no. 1, and p. 690; Louvre, F 116. *ABV* 230, no. 2, and p. 690. Compare an *oinochoe* in Berlin (1922. *ABV* 444).

Other white-ground amphorae of Nikosthenic type which may be compared are: Boston, 01.17. *ABV* 319, no. 2; Class of Cab. Méd. 218. *ABV* 319, nos. 1–4, 10; Class of London B 620. *ABV* 425, 434; Class of London B 632. *ABV* 425.

And the following white-ground *oinochoai* may be associated with the Nikosthenic Workshop: New York, Kevorkian. *ABV* 435; the *oinochoai* of the Painter of Louvre F 118. *ABV* 440.

[16] New York, Mitchell. *ABV* 236, no. 7, and *Para* 102, 109.

3. THE LEAGROS GROUP, THE EDINBURGH PAINTER AND HIS FOLLOWERS, THE THESEUS AND ATHENA PAINTERS

'The Leagros Group represents a somewhat later stage of vase-painting than the work of the Andokides Painter or Psiax and his brother.'[1] It is the counterpart in black-figure of the red-figure Pioneer Group. The group consists of a large number of vases of different shapes, on which the name of Leagros is sometimes inscribed. The favourite shape is the *hydria*, and favourite subjects are the deeds of Herakles and the sack of Troy.[2] *Hydriai* were also very popular with the Antimenes Painter and members of his circle. These two great groups of late black-figure *hydriai* can be distinguished in decoration (notably the Leagran palmettes in place of the Antimenean figure predella), but also in shape: generally speaking Leagran *hydriai* are more slender; their horizontal handles tend to swing up and their vertical ridged handle to rise prominently above the lip (PLATE 57. 3).[3] But the *hydriai* of one group sometimes betray the influence of the other and although the bulk of Antimenean *hydriai* (PLATE 2. 1) precede the Leagran, there must have been a period of time when both were being painted in the Kerameikos (cf. PLATE 2. 2).[4]

The *lekythos* is one of the popular Leagran shapes and the Acheloos Painter[5] is one of its better-known exponents. He paints *lekythoi* of two principal types: near-cylinders and 'compromises' (a shape between the earlier shoulder-type *lekythos* and the new cylinder type (cf. PLATE 3. 2 and pp. 122 f.). On the shoulders of the near-cylinder *lekythoi* the Acheloos Painter disposes seven black palmettes, linked by tendrils, in groups of two, three, and two. At the neck he paints bars, unenclosed.[6] This is the typical Leagran scheme (cf. FIGURE 7*b*).

Initially the Edinburgh Painter[7] follows the Leagran model. On the shoulders of 'compromise' *lekythoi* (he is one of the last to decorate black-figure compromises)[8] he paints chains of linked lotus buds, as the Acheloos Painter had done before him.[9] On the shoulders of his red-ground cylinders he paints seven black palmettes in the Leagran scheme (FIGURE 7*c*).[10] The same Leagran palmettes appear on the reserved shoulders of the Gales (PLATE 6. 1)[11] and Roundabout Painter's (PLATE 5. 2)[12] early red-figure *lekythoi*, not on Oxford 1949.751 (PLATE 5. 1),[13] whose three shoulder palmettes are rendered in red-figure. The Edinburgh Painter soon moves away from the Leagrans, to concentrate more on white-slipped cylinders. On these *lekythoi* (PLATE 7. 2) he introduces a new shoulder pattern: five black palmettes linked by tendrils in groups of one, three, and one; the outer singletons turn towards the handle (FIGURE 8*a*).[14] These white-ground palmettes are drawn like those on the neck panel of his small neck-amphorae of special

[1] *Dev* 81.

[2] *ABV* 354 ff., 665, 695 f., 715, 716; *Para* 161 ff.; *Dev* 81 ff.

[3] *JHS* lxxi (1951), 35 ff. (Bloesch); *JHS* xlvii (1927), 86 (Beazley).

[4] Hartford, Connecticut. Wadsworth Atheneum. *ABV* 293, no. 9; *Para* 127; *JHS* xlvii. 80.

[5] *ABV* 382 ff., 696; *Para* 168 f.; *ABL* 47 f.

[6] *ABL* 48.

[7] *ABV* 476 ff., 670, 671, 700; *Para* 217 ff.; *ABL* 86 ff., 215 ff.

[8] *ABL* 48, 87.

[9] Ibid. 48, 87.

[10] Ibid. 87.

[11] Boston, 13.195. *ARV* 35, no. 1; Syracuse, 26967. *ARV* 36, no. 2.

[12] Athens, Agora, P 24061. *ARV* 131.

[13] Oxford, 1949.751. *ARV* 9, no. 1.

[14] *ABL* 87.

shape—doubleens (PLATE 7. 1);[1] the red-ground palmettes are like those on his ordinary neck-amphorae.[2]

The Edinburgh Painter stands at an important point in the development of the Attic *lekythos*. He firmly establishes the standard cylinder shape, the white slip, and the use of black paint for exposed female flesh.[3] His immediate successors in the production of *lekythoi*, the Theseus and Athena Painters, are the last to paint large black-figure *lekythoi* of standard shape.[4] From this point onwards important work is executed in red-figure; black-figure, apart from its special use on the Panathenaic prize amphorae and *loutrophoroi*, is relegated to small *lekythoi* of secondary shape.

Since the Edinburgh Painter stands at the beginning of the series of white-ground and red-figure cylinders of standard shape, it is greatly desirable to establish his chronological position and his relation to red-figure contemporaries. As a later member of the Leagros Group he must have begun his career in the last decade or so of the sixth century, continuing into the first decade of the fifth, if not later.[5] The Berlin Painter began his career just before 500 B.C.[6] and the doubleen (PLATE 7. 3) is one of his special shapes.[7] If the first doubleens were black-figure, as seems very likely, the Berlin Painter may have borrowed them from the Edinburgh Workshop.[8] The Berlin Painter also took up the cylinder for his *lekythoi* (PLATE 7. 4) and the earliest of these do not belong to the painter's very early years.[9] In black-figure the doubleen is taken up by a somewhat younger contemporary of the Edinburgh Painter, the Diosphos Painter,[10] whose large *lekythoi* of special shape (DL, see pp. 80 f.) are very nearly standard cylinders. The Diosphos Painter is related to the red-figure Dutuit Painter,[11] who specialized in small vases—Nolan amphorae (PLATE 55. 3), doubleens, and *lekythoi*. The Dutuit Painter can be related to the Berlin Painter's Circle through vases of the Floral Nolan Group (see pp. 125 f.; PLATE 66).[12]

The Edinburgh Painter's successors in the production of large black-figure cylinders are the Theseus and Athena Painters. The Theseus Painter[13] is the older of the two, probably not much younger than the Edinburgh Painter.[14] His *lekythoi* are certainly later (more or less contemporary with the Athena Painter's) but he does not specialize in *lekythoi* early in his career. He is one of the most important artists of the White Heron Group[15]—black-figure *skyphoi* with the eponymous birds rendered in added white—which flourished in the last decade or so of the sixth century.[16] The Theseus Painter also decorated *kyathoi*, some of them white-ground,[17] and these have been connected with the Nikosthenic Workshop in general, and with Psiax in particular.[18] The Theseus Painter's

---

[1] Doubleens: *ABV* 482; *Para* 220; *Berl* 11 n. 1; *VA* 38; *VPol* 6 f. and n. 4 on p. 6; *PBSR* xi (1929), 111.

[2] *ABL* 87.

[3] Ibid. 87.

[4] Ibid. 89, 164 f.

[5] Ibid. 87 f.

[6] *JHS* lxxi (1951), 23 ff. (C. M. Robertson).

[7] *ARV* 200, nos. 46–52; (?) 200, no. 53 to p. 201, no. 61. See also *Berl* 11 n. 1.

[8] *ABL* 89.   [9] *Berl* 20.

[10] *ABV* 482, 509 f.; *ARV* 300 ff.; *ABL* 94 ff., 225 ff.

[11] *ARV* 306 ff., 676, 1644; *Para* 357; *JHS* xxxiii (1913), 107 (Beazley).

[12] *ARV* 218 f.

[13] *ABV* 450, 518 ff., 703 f., 716; *Para* 255 ff.; *ABL* 141 ff., 249 ff.

[14] *AJA* lxxv (1971), 200 (Eisman).

[15] *JHS* liv (1934), 89 (Beazley). *ABV* 617 ff.; *Para* 306 ff.; *ABL* 142, 144, 253, 368.

[16] *JHS* lxxv (1955), 90 ff. (Ure).

[17] *ABV* 519, nos. 16–17; *Para* 259 f. ('related').

[18] *AJA* lxxv. 200.

free use of white-ground on vases of different shapes—among them *oinochoai*,[1] *kyathoi*, *lekythoi*, *alabastra*,[2] and a *hydria*[3] of *kalpis* type—brings him into line with both Nikosthenes and Psiax, as does his use of added white or yellow.

The Theseus Painter's earliest *lekythos* follows the Edinburgh Painter's model closely; in shape and shoulder decoration it looks like a product of the Edinburgh Workshop.[4] Most of his *lekythoi* are more slender than the Edinburgh Painter's, and also more slender than the Athena Painter's, but their reserved shoulders have five black palmettes arranged in the scheme favoured by the Athena Painter (FIGURE 8*b*), from whom he presumably borrowed it.[5] The Theseus Painter's *lekythoi* with Beldam florals are described in the section on the Beldam Painter (pp. 18 f.).

A *lekythos* by the Theseus Painter in Bonn[6] is very close to the Athena Painter in shape. The neck is black, the shoulder is reserved (with rounded rays beneath unenclosed bars); the shoulder–body join is marked by a black net pattern on reserved ground and the foot is flared. The iconography—a pyrrhicist—is paralleled on other *lekythoi* from the Athena–Bowdoin Workshop—notably on the red-figure *lekythos* in London with red-figure shoulder florals (PLATE 12. 2; see pp. 22 f.) and the shape is very nearly BL, the Bowdoin Painter's favourite type (see pp. 79 f.).

The Athena Painter[7] specialized in *lekythoi* and *oinochoai*; so far as we know these are the only shapes which he decorated. The proportion of white-slipped vases is high. His earliest *lekythoi* are red-ground, full cylinders in the Edinburgh manner with Edinburgh palmettes on the reserved shoulder.[8] *Lekythoi* of his mature period are white more often than not; for the shoulder, which is sometimes white, he introduces a new palmette system; the Edinburgh scheme enriched by spiral tendrils with thin closed buds at the first and fifth palmettes.[9] This system passes into red-figure through the Bowdoin Painter. During much of the fifth century a simplified version of the Bowdoin palmettes is 'common in the lower ranks of the standard lekythos' (cf. PLATE 20. 3, 4).[10] This often inelegant scheme is produced on red-figure and white-ground *lekythoi* by artists such as the Klügmann (FIGURE 8*c*)[11] and Dessypri[12] painters, contemporaneously with the elegant black palmettes on red-figure *lekythoi* by the Achilles Painter and his followers (see pp. 43 ff.; PLATE 34. 2–4).

The Athena Painter's relation to red-figure painters is acknowledged to be close and at the same time ill defined. His black-figure *lekythoi* are the first to have black neck and enclosed neck bars, and since these are characteristic features of red-figure *lekythoi* of standard shape, it is generally assumed that the Athena Painter borrowed them from painters of red-figure *lekythoi*—perhaps the Berlin Painter or the Brygos Painter.[13] Black necks are standard on standard *lekythoi*, just as reserved necks and reserved shoulders are

[1] *ABV* 519, no. 6.

[2] Ibid. 518, no. 5; *Para* 256 (Basle and Philadelphia markets).

[3] Madrid, 10930. *ABL* 146, 252, no. 73; *JHS* li (1931), 121.

[4] *ABL* 145, 163, 251, no. 55 (Cambridge, ex Borden Wood); *Para* 255.

[5] *ABL* 145.

[6] Bonn, 307. *ABL* 252, no. 66; p. 146 and pl. 44. 3.

[7] *ABV* 522 ff., 533, 704; *Para* 260 ff.; *ABL* 141 ff., 254 ff.

[8] *ABL* 147.

[9] Ibid. 147.

[10] *ARV* 692; *ARV*¹ 480.

[11] *ARV* 1198 ff., 1686; *Para* 462.

[12] *ARV* 1197, 1686, 1703; *Para* 461.

[13] *ABL* 148.

standard on *lekythoi* of secondary shape.[1] *Lekythoi* of shape BL (see pp. 79 f.),[2] the Bowdoin Painter's favourite, are cylinders with black necks which can be distinguished easily from standard cylinders only if the shoulder is reserved with black Bowdoin palmettes.

The Athena Painter's relation to the Bowdoin Painter[3] is complex. The Bowdoin Painter decorated red-figure and white *lekythoi* so like the Athena Painter's in shape, pattern, even style, that he has often been considered the black-figure Athena Painter working in the other techniques. Miss Haspels and Beazley studied the painters carefully, without conclusively deciding that they were one and the same. I keep them separate, not because I clearly see two distinct personalities, but because, like Haspels and Beazley, I cannot clearly see one. Also, chronology is difficult: at the latest the Athena Painter began his career around 490 B.C.;[4] the Bowdoin Painter is generally thought to have been active as late as the third quarter of the fifth century;[5] if the two are one, the span of the composite career is remarkable. For our purposes the Athena Painter's Workshop is responsible for black-figure *lekythoi*, the Bowdoin Workshop for red-figure and white-ground *lekythoi*, and the *lekythoi* in mixed techniques.

There are three groups of *lekythoi* which stand between the Athena and Bowdoin Painters; the first is the *lekythoi* in various techniques with red-figure shoulder palmettes (PLATES 12, 13), described on pp. 22 f.; the second is the white-ground Athena-head *lekythos* in Marburg (PLATE 63. 1), described on p. 108; the third is the pair of bilingual *lekythoi* in Brussels (PLATE 15).[6] Beazley attributed the two red-figure *lekythoi* in Brussels to the Bowdoin Painter, and their iconography (woman seated,[7] woman with wreath)[8] is characteristically Bowdoin. The shoulders are reserved in the Bowdoin manner, but the Bowdoin palmettes have been replaced by miniature scenes in silhouette. The shoulder figure is never as popular on red-figure *lekythoi* as it is on black-figure *lekythoi*, and on white *lekythoi* it is virtually unknown (see pp. 127 ff.). The iconography of the shoulder scenes (Gigantomachy and Theseus and the Bull) can be paralleled on vases by the Athena Painter.[9] Linked to these two bilinguals are two black-bodied *lekythoi*—one of them in Oxford (PLATE 67. 4)—full cylinders with black neck, whose reserved shoulders have miniature figures in silhouette—stag hunt,[10] hare hunt.[11] The black body links these *lekythoi* to the larger group of black-bodied *lekythoi*[12] from the Bowdoin Workshop (PLATE 67. 3; see pp. 121 ff.), whose reserved shoulders have Bowdoin palmettes, and the use of silhouette links them to the white-ground semi-outline of the Athena Bowdoin Workshop (pp. 105 f.),[13] on which black-figure, silhouette, and outline are combined.

Semi-outline, used somewhat differently, is a characteristic feature of some *lekythoi*

[1] *ABL* 148; *ARV* 675.

[2] *ARV* 675, 677 f., 692.

[3] Ibid. 677 ff., 1665 f., 1706; *Para* 405 ff.; *ABL* 157 ff.

[4] *ABL* 147, 150, 163.

[5] *ARV* 678.

[6] Brussels, A 3132. *ARV* 681, no. 91; Brussels, A 3131. *ARV* 682, no. 107; *ABL* 159 f. (Haspels adds a third *lekythos* decorated in this way.)

[7] Brussels, A 3132.

[8] Ibid., A 3131.

[9] Gigantomachy: *ABL* 255, nos. 13, 16, 30–2. Theseus and the Bull: *ABL* 257, no. 66.

[10] Oxford, 251. *ABL* 262, no. 1.

[11] Paris Market (Platt). *ABL* 262, no. 2.

[12] *ARV* 693 f., 1666; *Para* 407; *ABL* 262.

[13] *ARV* 689 f.; *ABL* 155, 262.

from the Diosphos Workshop (cf. PLATES 58, 59),[1] which also produced black-bodied *lekythoi*.[2] The hare hunt which is rendered in full on the body of a white-ground semi-outline *lekythos* from the Athena Bowdoin Workshop (PLATE 14. 2),[3] is popular in an abbreviated form on a group of *lekythoi* from the Diosphos Workshop.[4] Lastly, the Oxford *lekythos* has a mock inscription on the shoulder field.[5] Mock inscriptions are not usual on Athena or Bowdoin *lekythoi*, but they are on *lekythoi* from the Diosphos Workshop.[6]

From the Leagros Group and its later member, the Edinburgh Painter, we have followed the development of the standard cylinder to its demise in black-figure and to its position of prominence in red-figure and white-ground. The problem of the Athena and Bowdoin Painters is left unsolved (see pp. 104 ff.), but their importance has not been overlooked. In the next section we look briefly at black-figure *lekythoi* of other painters outside the Edinburgh tradition.

4. VERTICAL PALMETTE SYSTEMS OUTSIDE THE EDINBURGH TRADITION

During the period when the Edinburgh Painter and his followers were setting the future course for the standard cylinder, other painters in other workshops were decorating *lekythoi* of different shapes. Most of these painters are important only for a study of later black-figure and therefore need not concern us, but a few influenced the shape or decoration of later *lekythoi*, white-ground or red-figure. I have selected the Gela and Beldam Painters to represent other vertical palmette systems, because they specialize in *lekythoi* and are in some way related to the Edinburgh Workshop; also because their schemes of decoration vary significantly from those described previously. A separate section is devoted to horizontal shoulder palmettes.

GELA PAINTER

The Gela Painter[7] had a long career which we may follow from the Leagros period well into the fifth century B.C.[8] His career, therefore, runs parallel to that of the Edinburgh Painter and his followers. There is something peculiar about the Gela Painter.[9] He likes patterns, in quantity and variety. Some of these patterns are quite unusual and when they appear on vases by the Gela Painter's contemporaries, we may be reasonably certain that the painters are in some way related. The stylized ivy pattern is one: Psiax likes it (cf. PLATE 1. 3), so do the Sappho and Diosphos Painters.[10] The 'crossing meander' is another; the red-figure Pioneers like it,[11] but in black-figure it is rare, being occasionally

---

[1] *ABL* 110 ff.
[2] Ibid. 107, 108, 109. Cf. also ibid. 181, 270, beta, nos. 1–4.
[3] Athens, 1973. *ARV* 690, no. 9.
[4] *ABL* 118, 162.
[5] Ibid. 161.
[6] Ibid. 143, 150 (Athena Painter's Workshop). Cf. 96 ff. (Diosphos Workshop). For semi-outline

lekythoi from the Bowdoin Workshop with mock inscriptions see pp. 106 and 107 n. 8.
[7] *ABV* 473 ff., 699 f., 715; *Para* 214 ff.; *ABL* 78 ff.
[8] *ABL* 80.
[9] Ibid. 78 f.
[10] Ibid. 79, 101.
[11] Ibid. 79 ('labyrinthine meander'); *JHS* lxxi. 30.

used by the Antimenes Painter[1] and members of the Leagros Group.[2] There are several forms of the crossing meander (FIGURE 4*l–n*) and the Gela Painter's form (FIGURE 4*n*) is paralleled not in black-figure, but in red-figure, on vases by the Eucharides Painter.[3] Red-figure influence is probably also indicated by the distinctive buds which the Gela Painter likes to add to his shoulder palmettes.

The earliest *lekythoi* by the Gela Painter are Leagran red-ground cylinders with Leagran shoulder palmettes.[4] But soon he comes under the influence of the Edinburgh Painter, decorating Edinburgh white-ground cylinders with Edinburgh shoulder palmettes (PLATES 16. 4, 17. 3).[5] The Athena Painter seems to have influenced the Gela Painter's later white *lekythoi* (see pp. 21 f.).[6] The Gela Painter's shoulder florals may be distinguished from those of the Edinburgh Workshop by the presence of partially open buds. His five-palmette system has two prominent buds directed towards the handle (FIGURE 9*b*).[7] Even when these buds are missing, the Gela Painter's palmettes may be distinguished from those of the Edinburgh Painter by the direction of the outer tendrils: the tendrils of the first and fifth palmettes point towards the handle (as if to receive buds), not away from the handle as on *lekythoi* by the Edinburgh Painter.

The Gela Painter also has a three-palmette system (FIGURE 9*c*)[8] which at this time, in black-figure, is most unusual, although later in red-figure and white-ground it becomes common. The petals of the three palmettes are thin and widely spaced. Buds spring from tendrils which originate from the enclosing tendril of the central palmette, follow the base of the neck, and terminate in the handle area. In principle these tendrils with buds are prominent 'cross-overs', such as we find in diminutive form on red-figure and white *lekythoi* from the early classical period onwards.

Not all of the Gela Painter's *lekythoi* are standard cylinders; some are small, with a more tapering body (PLATE 17. 2)—*lekythoi* of the type sometimes decorated by the Marathon Painter.[9] There are three palmettes on the shoulder, hastily executed without buds.[10] The Marathon Painter occasionally decorated the shoulders of his better *lekythoi* with palmettes, arranged in a variety of ways,[11] but the lotus-bud chain, in a debased form, is more common, as it is on the numerous *lekythoi* of the Class of Athens 581.[12] The Gela and Marathon Painters share other patterns, for example the chequery on white-ground;[13] both like to decorate *lekythoi* exclusively with palmettes (see pp. 147 ff.).[14]

BELDAM PAINTER[15]

The Beldam Painter is younger than the Gela Painter, but like him influenced by the Edinburgh Painter's followers; he may have begun his career in the Edinburgh Workshop. The Beldam Painter's large cylinders are not standard type but special cylinders of

---

[1] *JHS* xlvii (1927), 86. In the manner of the Antimenes Painter: London, B 330. *ABV* 276, no. 1; Munich, 1693. *ABV* 280, no. 2.

[2] Leningrad, ex Basseggio. *ABV* 364, no. 59. Cf. also Copenhagen, 1636. *CV* iv. III H, pl. 120. 1.

[3] *BSA* xviii (1911–12), 231, fig. 6/6.

[4] *ABL* 80, 205 (I).   [5] Ibid. 80, 206 ff. (II).

[6] Ibid. 82 f.   [7] Ibid. 80.

[8] Ibid. 80 ff., 208 ff. (III).   [9] Ibid. 82.

[10] Ibid. 82.

[11] Ibid. 89 f.

[12] *ABV* 487 ff.; *Para* 222 ff.

[13] *ABL* 79 (Gela Painter), 89 (Marathon Painter). The pattern is used by early red-figure painters: *ARV* 9, 30.

[14] *ABL* 93 f. ('Marathon Painter'); 208, nos. 67–8, 200, no. 109, 212, no. 160 (Gela Painter).

[15] *ARV* 750 ff.; *ABL* 170 ff.

type BEL (PLATE 18; see pp. 84 f.) peculiar to himself and to his workshop.[1] It is, therefore, correct to call the Theseus and Athena Painters the last painters of large black-figure *lekythoi* of standard shape. Some of the Theseus Painter's latest *lekythoi* come nearer to those of the Beldam Painter than to those of the Athena Painter, for although they are standard cylinders, their neck is reserved (as on BELs, not black as on standard *lekythoi*); the bars at the join of neck to shoulder are not enclosed; and the shoulder palmettes are the Beldam Painter's.[2]

With few exceptions BELs are white-ground with palmettes on the shoulder. The earliest BELs, which are black-figure, display the Athena Painter's system of shoulder florals.[3] Occasionally, even these early florals may be distinguished from those of the Athena Painter by the addition of tiny arc tendrils to the large tendrils enclosing the palmettes (FIGURE 10a).[4] Later BELs are partly black-figure, partly outline (semi-outline),[5] or exclusively outline,[6] and both of these have five palmettes, basically in the Athena Painter scheme but modified. The palmettes of the semi-outline BELs have many thin petals;[7] the palmettes of the outline BELs have a few thin petals, widely spaced.[8] The reduction in the number of palmettes and their spatial disposition are probably explained by the original presence of alternate leaves in matt-red paint which has now disappeared. Alternately coloured petals soon become popular, and we know that the Beldam Painter liked this play of colour from his numerous small white-ground pattern *lekythoi* (PLATE 70. 6–8) on which traces of red paint have sometimes been preserved (see pp. 153 ff.).[9]

We have spoken only of white-ground BELs, but one red-figure BEL has been attributed to the Beldam Painter.[10] The shoulder is reserved with black palmettes, disposed rather like those on the shoulder of the black-figure BELs.[11] An important detail is the small tendril which springs from either side of the heart of the central palmette, 'crossing over' the large tendril which encloses it. In black-figure cross-overs are found only on the shoulder of a *lekythos* by the Athena Painter,[12] and in a somewhat different form on the body of several white *lekythoi* from the Athena Bowdoin Workshop (see p. 108).

Outside the Beldam Workshop the peculiar Beldam cylinder found little favour. BELs not by the Beldam Painter appear to have been painted by artists closely related to him, for example the Painter of London D65,[13] who takes over the Beldam patterns virtually without change (FIGURE 11a; PLATE 18. 3). Compare the BELs by the Carlsruhe Painter (PLATE 64. 1)[14] who seems to have been employed in the Beldam Workshop at one time, in other workshops at other times.[15] His BELs tend to have degenerate lotus buds (bars) instead of palmettes.[16] An artist not usually associated with the Beldam Workshop is the

---

[1] *ARV* 750.

[2] *ABL* 146 and pl. 44. 1; cf. pls. 45. 6 and 51. 1–3. Miss Haspels indicated that the Theseus Painter follows the Athena Painter's practice of enclosing neck-bars (p. 171), but this is not always the case.

[3] *ABL* 175.
[4] Ibid. 175 and pl. 51. 1.
[5] Ibid. 175.
[6] Ibid. 173.
[7] Ibid. pl. 51. 2.
[8] Ibid. pl. 51. 4.
[9] Ibid. 171 f. and n. 3. Cf. F i. 168 (Athens, 1982. *ABL* 267, no. 12), 175 (Athens, 1983. *ABL* 267, no. 13). See pp. 85 f. n. 15.

[10] Copenhagen, 1941. *ARV* 751, no. 3 (= *ABL* 266, no. 8).
[11] *ABL* 173 f.
[12] Havana, Lagunillas. *ABV* 523, no. 10.
[13] *ABV* 752; *ABL* 174, 270.
[14] *ARV* 730 ff., 1668; *Para* 411 f.; *ABL* 180 f.
[15] *ABL* 180 f.
[16] Cf. Cambridge, 4.17. *ARV* 734, no. 89; also Athens, 487. *ABL* 267, no. 11, and pl. 50. 1 (Beldam Painter).

Inscription Painter.[1] His earliest white *lekythos* (PLATE 19. 1)[2] is entered in *ARV* along with the rest (the painter is only known to have painted white *lekythoi*) as a standard cylinder, but the body of the vase curves in at the shoulder–body join, the neck is reserved (all his other *lekythoi* have black necks, as is usual on standard *lekythoi*), and the shoulder has five black palmettes beneath lines (FIGURE 11*b*); the others have the classical three palmettes beneath an egg band (FIGURE 11*c*). The Inscription Painter's *lekythoi* (PLATE 19) have false interiors[3] and their iconography is exclusively funerary.[4]

5. HORIZONTAL PALMETTES (BLACK)

From the introduction of the cylinder shape to the demise of the shoulder *lekythos*, the canonical scheme for shoulder palmettes is vertical; that is to say, the palmettes point towards or away from the neck ring instead of lying parallel to it. Although it was never very popular, there was a horizontal scheme which had almost as long a life, being found mostly in the decades around 500 B.C. Judging from preserved material the horizontal palmette was primarily a vase painter's motif. But horizontal palmettes in two different schemes were painted on the walls of the *pronaos* and *cella* of the Athenian Treasury at Delphi (FIGURE 3*a–b*), and probably on other buildings whose painted decoration has not survived. Dinsmoor studied the horizontal palmettes in connection with the date of the Athenian Treasury, distinguishing several different systems by which he classified Attic black-, red-figure, and white-ground vases.[5] (The controversy over the date of the Treasury need not concern us, since the date of the vases is not in question.)[6] Dinsmoor thought Psiax invented the new palmettes, painting them black on reserved ground on black-figure, bilingual, and red-figure vases.[7] But Psiax decorated neither his *lekythoi* nor his *hydriai* with horizontal palmettes. With one exception the *hydriai* have Antimenean figure predelle; the exception, a handsome *hydria* in the Wadsworth Atheneum, Hartford, Connecticut (PLATE 2. 2), has an elaborate system of palmettes and lotus buds, alternately upright and pendent, arranged vertically.[8] Early examples of the horizontal palmette on black-figure *lekythoi* are: a Leagran 'compromise' in Vienna, stylistically not far from the Acheloos Painter (PLATE 3. 1),[9] and a slightly later cylinder *lekythos* in Oxford not far from the Vienna compromise in style.[10] In the Leagros period horizontal palmettes were regularly painted beneath the picture panel on *hydriai* (cf. PLATE 57. 3). On *lekythoi* pattern bands in this position are common only on larger finer vases (cf. PLATE 17. 4). The upper pattern band, on the other hand, is common on all but the most hastily painted. Upper and lower pattern bands are usually the same width, often the same pattern; exceptional features of the horizontal palmette band, when it appears on

---

[1] *ARV* 748 f., 1668; *Para* 413.
[2] Madrid, 19497. *ARV* 748, no. 1.
[3] *ANY* 60 f., no. 239.
[4] Cf. Besançon, 957.4.2. *ARV* 749, no. 9. The iconography need not be funerary.
[5] W. B. Dinsmoor, 'The Athenian Treasury as Dated by its Ornament', *AJA* l (1946), 86 ff.; *JHS* xxxii (1912), 171 ff. (Beazley); *JHS* lxx (1950), 23 f.

(C. M. Robertson).
[6] *BCH* lxxvii (1953), 179 ff. (Coste-Messelière); *Agora* xi (1965), 9 ff. (E. Harrison).
[7] *AJA* l. 94.
[8] *ABV* 293, nos. 8 and 10.
[9] Vienna, 75. *ABV* 379, no. 270; *ABL* 49; *AJA* l. 104, 117, no. 88.
[10] Oxford, 249; *ABL* 49; *AJA* l. 117, no. 87.

the body of *lekythoi*, are its size and prominence. An unusually elaborate Leagran *lekythos* in Berlin may serve as example: the palmette band beneath the 'Herakles in Olympus' is more than twice the width of the upper band of linked dots; there are vertical palmettes on the shoulder.[1] Compare the two narrow pattern bands (key, ivy) beneath the figure on Psiax' Paris *lekythos*.

Chains of lotus buds may also appear on the body of *lekythoi*, above or below the figures.[2] The Rycroft Painter, who stands close to Psiax,[3] is known to have decorated only one *lekythos* and it has a band of lotus buds above the figures.[4] A 'compromise' *lekythos* in Vienna (PLATE 4. 2), near the Rycroft Painter but surpassing even him in attention to minute detail, has lotus buds beneath the picture, ivy above, and on the shoulder horizontal palmettes arranged in a highly personal system—small palmettes and buds alternating in a double row—reminiscent of the ivy-berry tendril composition.[5] The closest parallel for this shoulder decoration is the Cactus Painter's, and even his eccentric palmettes are more canonical than the Viennese.[6] The Cactus Painter also stands close to the Rycroft Painter, sharing his passion for detail and refinement,[7] but he seems to have been younger, painting cylinders of the Gales–Edinburgh type and experimenting freely with white slip.[8] Nearly all of his attributed vases are *lekythoi*;[9] those which are not full cylinders are the slimmer, more tapering 581 shape of the Marathon Painter and related artists,[10] and some of the Marathon Painter's better *lekythoi* have horizontal palmettes on the shoulder.[11] On the shoulder of *lekythoi* of 581 type (PLATE 4. 4) the Cactus Painter places lotus buds, on the full cylinders (PLATE 4. 3) horizontal palmettes, linked, with thin, closed bud and tiny cactus flowers in the spandrels.[12] Palmettes alternate in the same manner, but with the more common dots in the spandrels, on a group of black-figure *lekythoi*, squat cylinders, and 'compromises' by the Painter of Vatican G49, an artist who specializes in *oinochoai*, uses white-ground, and seems to have been closely connected with the workshop of the Athena Painter.[13] Another artist who decorated *oinochoai* in number, often white-ground, and who sometimes comes close to the Athena Painter, is the Gela Painter. His distinctive system of shoulder palmettes has already been described. The Gela Painter is not known to have decorated the shoulders of his *lekythoi* with horizontal palmettes, but horizontal palmettes do appear on the body of a few of his more unusual *lekythoi*: the slim white-ground cylinder in Syracuse with Erotes holding tendrils, flying over large cocks (PLATE 16. 4). Beneath the cocks there is a horizontal band of palmettes.[14] A fuller, earlier, white-ground cylinder in Göttingen

---

[1] Berlin, 1961. *ABV* 379, no. 273; *ABL* 49; *AJA* l. 117, no. 86.

[2] *ABL* 55; *ABV* 345; *Para* 157 (The Hague Class of the Michigan Painter).

[3] *ABV* 335 ff., 675, 692 (Petit Palais 311; for the Psiax/Rycroft Painter attribution, see also *ARV* 1618 and *Para* 128), 694; *Para* 148 ff.; *ABL* 60 f.

[4] Würzburg, 366. *ABV* 337, no. 31.

[5] Vienna, 753; *ABL* 61. Ivy-berry tendrils on pattern *lekythoi* are described on pp. 153 f.

[6] Cf. *ABL*, pl. 20. 3 (Vienna, 753) and pl. 20. 4 (Cactus Painter).

[7] *ABL* 61.

[8] Ibid. 61 f.

[9] Heidelberg, 158 (*olpe*). *ABL* 198, no. 7.

[10] *ABL* 61 f.

[11] Cf. Athens, 1011. *ABL* 221, no. 1, and pl. 30. 3.

[12] *ABL* 62 and pl. 20. 4.

[13] *ABV* 533 ff., 705; *Para* 267 f.; *ABL* 61 (New York, 26.60.76 = *ABV* 536, no. 41. See also *Para* 267); *AJA* l. 114, nos. 13–15. Beazley noted a connection with the Athena Painter's Workshop, *ABV* 534 ff., 537.

[14] Syracuse, 19854. *ABL* 212, no. 151.

(PLATE 17. 1) has a broad band of horizontal palmettes with thin closed buds in the spandrels at the join of shoulder to body. This *lekythos* is an example of the Gela Painter's obsession with pattern, which surpasses even that of his contemporary, the Marathon Painter: on the mouth there are vertical palmettes, on the neck chequery between linked dots, and on the shoulder, beneath tongues, palmettes with buds; and beneath the figures a narrow band of linked dots.[1]

The Haimon Painter,[2] like the Gela Painter, uses bands of horizontal palmettes both above and below the figures on some of his less typical *lekythoi*. He also painted some horizontal shoulder palmettes. Haemonian horizontal palmettes, unlike those we have described, often do not 'run'; their enclosing tendrils overlap without interconnecting; their hearts are regularly reserved, unless very hastily painted.[3] The Haimon Painter's usual shoulder decoration (degenerate lotus buds, inherited from the Diosphos Painter, together with the very slender Diosphan cylinder)[4] is given up for a small group of red-ground *lekythoi*, slimmed Edinburgh cylinders, exceptionally large for the Haimon Painter.[5] Most of these *lekythoi* have not only horizontal palmettes on the shoulder, but broad bands of horizontal palmettes on the body (PLATE 17. 4)—as if the painter were trying to decrease the height of the picture panel.[6] Similar bands may be found on a few of his white-ground 'chimneys' (PLATE 70. 4),[7] and one of his exceptionally large white-ground calyx-mouth *lekythoi* has horizontal palmettes on the shoulder.[8] Besides being accessory decoration on figure *lekythoi*, horizontal palmettes are the primary decoration of a number of the painter's pattern *lekythoi* (see pp. 153 ff.).

The Emporion Painter[9] who succeeds the Haimon Painter in the mass production of small cheap oil pots, and who is stylistically related to him and to the Beldam Painter, prefers hastily painted bars on the shoulders of his insignificant *lekythoi*. But he painted some side-palmette *lekythoi* (see p. 109) and, related to him, is a group of late black-figure *lekythoi*, nearly cylindrical with cup (calyx) mouth, linked as much by shoulder decoration (hastily painted horizontal palmettes) as by style and figurework.[10]

Some white-ground pattern *lekythoi* from the Beldam Workshop make use of horizontal palmettes, but the Beldam Painter is not known to have used them on his figure *lekythoi*.

6. HORIZONTAL PALMETTES (RED-FIGURE)

Horizontal palmettes executed in red-figure decorate the shoulder of a small number of *lekythoi*, which despite the variety in technique (black-figure (PLATE 13), red-figure (PLATE 12. 2), and black-bodied (PLATE 12. 3, 4)) are closely related.[11] They are standard

---

[1] Basle Market (M.M.). *Para* 215 (*Auktion* xxvi, no. 118). Cf. *ABL*, pl. 23. 1 (patterned neck).

[2] *ABV* 538 ff.; *Para* 269 ff.; *ABL* 131 ff.

[3] *ABL* 133.   [4] Ibid. 131.

[5] Ibid. 133, 241, nos. 1–4. Number 4 lacks the band.

[6] Ibid. 133.

[7] London, B 636. *ABL* 245, no. 79 (above); Louvre, CA 2218. *ABL* 245, no. 80 (below); Oxford, 1927.4457.

ABL 245, no. 81 (below).

[8] Leyden, xvii a. 20. *ABL* 241, no. 5, and p. 133 n. 2.

[9] *ABV* 584 ff., 708; *Para* 291 f.; *ABL* 165 ff.

[10] *ABV* 586. ii; *Para* 292; *ABL* 169, 266; *Hesp* xxxii (1963), pl. 36, A 8.

[11] *ABL* 162, 262; *ABV* 524; *ARV* 694, 1666; *Para* 262.

cylinders. Two of the black-figure *lekythoi* have reserved necks, as does one whose body has not been preserved.[1] The red-figure and black-bodied *lekythoi* have black necks, as we might expect, but so does a third black-figure *lekythos* of the group.[2] Technique did not, therefore, dictate the treatment of the neck. All of these *lekythoi* have bars at the join of the shoulder to neck, enclosed on one or both sides. At the join of shoulder to body most of the *lekythoi* have a net pattern; two of the black-bodied *lekythoi* have a simple running meander.[3] Some of the figured vases have a second pattern band beneath the figures.[4] The foot of the *lekythos* is either the minority flared form[5] or the more usual disc.[6] The similarities in shape and shoulder decoration point to a single workshop. The variety in technique and in treatment of the neck points to a workshop of the transitional period. Miss Haspels knew four of the *lekythoi*, initially recognized the group, and associated it with the workshop of the Athena Painter.[7] Beazley increased the number of examples to seven and confirmed the stylistic relation of the black-figure *lekythoi* to black-figure *lekythoi* by the Athena Painter, the red-figure *lekythoi* to red-figure *lekythoi* by the Bowdoin Painter.[8] I should like to make additions to the group, establish its position in relation to contemporary red-figure, and draw attention to the importance of black-bodied *lekythoi*, described in greater detail in Part Four.

A black-bodied *lekythos* in the Mormino Collection, Palermo, a standard cylinder with four red-figure palmettes arranged horizontally on the shoulder, should be added to the group and another in the Funcke Collection (PLATE 12. 3).[9] At the join of shoulder to neck, which is black, are enclosed bars; on the shoulder four linked horizontal palmettes, unribbed petals, and reserved dots in the field; at the join of shoulder to body, reserved lines. The black-bodied *lekythoi* of our group have enclosed bars at the neck–shoulder join and a simple running meander at the shoulder–body join. There are black-bodied *lekythoi* from several workshops in the years around 500 B.C. but most of these are secondary shape (see p. 122, PLATE 67). In the early fifth century the Bowdoin Workshop was the leading producer of black-bodied *lekythoi*[10] of standard shape, type BL (PLATE 67. 3). Some have Bowdoin palmettes on reserved shoulder[11] but others have black shoulders[12] in the manner of early red-figure *lekythoi* of standard shape.[13] At the join of shoulder to neck, which is black, there are enclosed bars;[14] at the join of shoulder to body there are simple running meanders, a net pattern, or more commonly, reserved bands. Apart from the Bowdoin Workshop, there was another producing black-bodied *lekythoi* of standard shape in the first quarter of the fifth century—a workshop greatly influenced by, if not closely associated with, the Berlin Painter.[15] From the Berlin Painter's own

---

[1] *ARV* 1666. [2] Ibid. [3] Ibid.
[4] Agrigento. *ABL* 262, no. 3. London, E 573. *ABL* 262, no. 1.
[5] CB iii. 27 f.; London, E 573. [6] *ABL* 75.
[7] Ibid. 162, 262. [8] *ABV* 524; *ARV* 694.
[9] Palermo, Mormino Collection. *CV* i. III L, pl. 3. 5 (no. 163) and p. 5 ('secondo quarto del V secolo a. C.'); Wuppertal, Funcke, no. 46. N. Kunisch, *Antiken der Sammlung Julius C. und Margot Funcke* (1972), 108 f. (Kat. no. 92).
[10] *ARV* 693 f., 1666; *Para* 407; *ABL* 262.

[11] *ARV* 693 f., nos. 1–30.
[12] Ibid. 694, nos. 31–7.
[13] Compare the Bowdoin Painter's *lekythoi* with black shoulders: Basle Market (M.M.). *ARV* 683, no. 122 *bis*, and p. 1665 (tongues at join of shoulder to neck); Bowdoin, 20. 1. *ARV* 684, no. 143 (bars at join of shoulder to neck).
[14] *ARV* 693. They are simple vertical black strokes—bars, not tongues.
[15] Ibid. 218 f.

hand we have a black-bodied *lekythos* with elaborate red-figure palmettes (type Iᴀ),[1] one with black shoulder bearing a lion without accessory decoration,[2] and another bearing a lioness amidst palmettes and blossoms.[3] The lion and lioness *lekythoi* are early (but not very early) in the Berlin Painter's career; the lioness *lekythos* has tongues at the shoulder–neck join,[4] the lion *lekythos*, a developed egg pattern.[5] The black *lekythoi* associated with the Berlin Painter are those of the Floral Nolan Group.[6] The vases of this group—Nolan amphorae (PLATE 66. 1, 2), *oinochoai*, and *lekythoi* (PLATE 66. 3, 4)—are essentially black, but a floral band is regularly placed on the body; the style of the florals is related to that of the Berlin and Dutuit Painters (see pp. 125 ff.).[7]

The black-figure *lekythoi* of our group are not exceptional iconographically: 'Achilles brought to Chiron' (Palermo) (PLATE 13. 2),[8] 'combat' (Agrigento),[9] 'satyrs and maenads' (Paris) (PLATE 13. 1).[10] Two of the three, as mentioned above, have black necks; all have a net pattern at the shoulder–body join—one of the Athena Painter's favourite patterns in this position.[11] The shoulder florals, although composed of four horizontal palmettes, differ in details. The Paris *lekythos* has pairs of opposed linked palmettes. The Agrigento *lekythos* has four linked palmettes with thin closed buds in the spandrels. The Palermo *lekythos* has four linked palmettes running left to right terminating in a convoluted spiral with a partly open bud; the petals of the palmettes are ribbed. The red-figure *lekythos* (PLATE 12. 2)[12] has a net pattern at the join of shoulder to body and beneath the single figure (pyrrhicist)[13] a very unusual meander and square pattern: meander and square alternate, but the two lines forming the broken meander enclose the cross square. On the shoulder three linked palmettes run horizontally, left to right; the fourth palmette is vertical, attached to the third palmette just like the blossom on the black-figure Agrigento *lekythos*. The petals of the palmette are not ribbed. The added spiral tendrils and reserved dots in the field are paralleled on the Agrigento *lekythos*. The pyrrhicist was a favourite subject of the Athena Painter[14] and Miss Haspels thought that the red-figure *lekythos* was painted by one of his imitators.[15] In *ARV* the vase is appended to the list of vases from the Bowdoin Workshop with the comment: 'Early. The figure work is not remote from the Bowdoin Painter.'[16]

---

[1] Basle, Cahn, 128. *ARV* 211, no. 202 *bis*, on p. 1635, and *Para* 343. For the relation of this *lekythos* to vases of the Floral Nolan Group see below, pp. 125 ff.

[2] Munich, 2475. *ARV* 211, no. 199.

[3] Adria, B 180. *ARV* 211, no. 200, and *Para* 343. The second fragment (B 404) associated with the vase in *CV* i. III I, pl. 5. 8–9, does not belong, as Mr. B. Cook has shown (*Para* 343). A comparison of the composition on the shoulder of the Adria *lekythos* with that of Douris' *lekythos* in Bologna (PU 321. *ARV* 446, no. 267. *VPU* 55, fig. 44) also makes it clear that the two fragments do not belong.

[4] These are proper tongues. Compare also the Adria fragment (last note). Munich 2475 has an egg pattern in this position, as do *lekythoi* of the Floral Nolan Group: F. Poulsen, *Aus einer alten Etruskerstadt*

(1927), pl. xi. 19 (= *ARV* 219, no. 14), and pl. xi. 20 (= *ARV* 219, no. 13).

[5] *Berl* pl. 12. 1.

[6] *ARV* 218 f., 1636; *Para* 346.

[7] *ARV* 218 f.

[8] Palermo, 2792. *ABL* 262, no. 2.

[9] Agrigento. *ABL* 262, no. 3.

[10] Paris, Peyrefitte. *ABV* 524; *Para* 262.

[11] *ABL* 148.

[12] London, E 573. *ABL* 262, no. 1.

[13] Compare the Theseus Painter's *lekythos* in Bonn (307. *ABL* 252, no. 66).

[14] *ABL* 162 and n. 1; *Para* 261; a recent discussion of pyrrhic dances may be found in *BCH* xcii (1968), 550 ff. (Poursat). [15] *ABL* 162.

[16] *ARV* 694.

The red-figure pyrrhicist *lekythos* resembles in shape, accessory decoration, and most important, shoulder decoration, a red-figure *lekythos* of Douris' early middle period in Boston (PLATE 12. 1).[1] The Douris *lekythos* is the only *lekythos* outside our group known to me with horizontal red-figure palmettes on the shoulder. The disposition of the shoulder palmettes is like that of the red-figure pyrrhicist but even more like that of the black-figure *lekythos* in Agrigento: four linked horizontal palmettes run left to right, terminating in a pendent partly opened bud. The bud is linked to the fourth palmette by a short tendril, in whose spandrel is a thin closed bud. The petals of the palmette are not ribbed. There are added spiral tendrils but no reserved dots in the field. At the join of shoulder to neck there are tongues;[2] at the join of shoulder to body a net pattern. Beneath the figure (an athlete) there is a partial pattern band (as on the pyrrhicist *lekythos*) composed of false meanders and cross squares; the units do not alternate in the Dourian manner nor are the pattern squares characteristically his.[3] Douris, like other early fifth-century painters of *lekythoi*, liked plain black shoulders[4] but occasionally painted elaborate florals. The best example of an elaborate red-figure shoulder is the lion amidst palmettes and buds (for the principle of composition compare the Berlin Painter's black-bodied *lekythos*) on his red-figure *lekythos* in Bologna,[5] bearing the *kalos* names *Diogenes*[6] and *Menon* (PLATE 8. 2). The Bologna shoulder seems to reflect the Berlin Painter just as the Boston shoulder seems to reflect the Bowdoin Painter.[7] Another probable indication of some relationship between Douris and the Bowdoin Workshop is the series of red-figure *lekythoi* of type BL, bearing the inscription *Doris*, attributed to the Cartellino Painter.[8] Stylistically these *lekythoi* are related to Douris. The shoulders are reserved with black Bowdoin palmettes. There are enclosed bars at the neck–shoulder join and a key or rough egg pattern at the shoulder–body join.

Other contemporary examples of horizontal red-figure palmettes have been collected by Dinsmoor.[9] The only ones which relate to our *lekythoi* appear on two head vases (*oinochoai*), signed by the potter Charinos.[10] On the head-dress of the women there are linked horizontal palmettes with added spiral tendrils and thin spandrel buds. Beazley compared the modelling of the female face with that of the Acropolis *kore* 674, who has been dated around 500 B.C. ('. . . contemporary with early Douris or early Panaitios Painter . . .').[11] Charinos was also interested in white-ground: two of his head vases (mugs) about a decade earlier than the *oinochoai* have white-ground *poloi* decorated with a black chequery,[12] a favourite pattern of the late black-figure and early red-figure painters.[13] We have a white-ground vase signed by Charinos, an *oinochoe* in London, decorated

[1] Boston, 95.41. *ARV* 447, no. 270; CB iii. 27, no. 134.

[2] CB iii. 27. [3] Ibid. 28.

[4] Vienna, University, 526a. *ARV* 447, no. 272; Boston, 13.194. *ARV* 447, no. 273.

[5] Bologna, PU 321. *ARV* 446, no. 267.

[6] *ARV* 1573 f., 1601. Diogenes is also praised on a round white-ground *aryballos* by the Syriskos Painter (Taranto, 3799. *ARV* 264, no. 57; C. Belli, *Il tesoro di Taras* (1970), 157).

[7] Beazley calls the London *lekythos* 'early' (*ARV*

694). If it is contemporary with 'early middle' Douris, the chronology of the Athena and Bowdoin Painters is further complicated.

[8] *ARV* 452.

[9] *AJA* l (1946), 86 ff.

[10] *ABV* 423, 697; *ARV* 1531 f. (Berlin, 2190, and Leningrad, 686); *JHS* xlix (1929), 43 ff. (C Group).

[11] *JHS* xlix. 44.

[12] Villa Giulia, fr. *ARV* 1531, no. 1; Tarquinia, 6845. *ARV* 1531, no. 2.

[13] *ARV* 9, 30.

with vine tendrils in black silhouette.[1] Black silhouette is also used for the frieze of miniature figures decorating the snood of one of his head vases (with white-ground chequery pattern on the *polos*).[2] The use of silhouette on white-ground and the treatment of the vine tendrils remind me of a white-ground silhouette and outline *lekythos* from the Athena Bowdoin Workshop in New York (Dionysos holding vine tendrils, attended by satyr and goat) (PLATE 14. 4).[3]

7. PALMETTES AND LOTUS BUDS

Apart from buds discreetly hidden in the handle area or added to subsidiary tendrils, lotus buds are not integral elements in the palmette compositions described thus far; the Gela Painter's shoulder florals are exceptional. Three palmettes, the central one embellished with two lotus buds, is the principal shoulder decoration of red-figure *lekythoi* from the first quarter of the fifth century. In white-ground the scheme had almost no following; the small number of examples, chronologically not far apart and to a certain degree stylistically related, probably reflect contemporary red-figure practice. White *lekythoi* with palmettes and lotus buds on the shoulder are either entirely white-ground or bilingual, that is to say, red-figure on the shoulder, white-ground on the body. None looks older than the earliest red-figure *lekythoi* with similar shoulder decoration. The first major painter who decorated red-figure *lekythoi* with palmettes and lotus buds in a regular manner is the Brygos Painter (PLATE 24. 1), and his *lekythoi* are not products of his very early years.[4] The first red-figure *lekythoi* displayed great variety in technique and style of shoulder decoration; those of standard shape, in the first decade of the fifth century, often have black undecorated shoulders without pattern bands below; the earlier *lekythoi* have tongues at the neck–shoulder join, later *lekythoi* an egg pattern.[5] The 'bare style' is, of course, favoured by the Berlin Painter, who likes to isolate figures in a field of glossy black paint.[6] Few of his *lekythoi* have shoulder florals.[7] One, from his early period, in Palermo, has five palmettes without lotus buds, arranged in a simple system, almost peculiar to himself and his circle of followers: the tendrils linking the second and fourth palmettes to the central palmette take their origin not from the latter's heart but from its terminal volutes.[8] This scheme is found on vases of the Floral Nolan Group,[9] on the shoulder of a neck-amphora (PLATE 66. 1),[10] and on two *lekythoi* (PLATE 66. 3, 4).[11]

Douris' early cups with few exceptions are 'bare style', essentially patternless,[12] and

---

[1] London, B 631. *ABV* 423, 697; *ARV* 1532; *JHS* xlix. 44 n. 30.

[2] Tarquinia, 6845; Arias, Hirmer, Shefton 335; *RM* v (1890), 315, figs. 1 and pl. xi.

[3] New York, 08.258.28. *ARV* 690, no. 7. Compare also a white *oinochoe* with handle-tendrils, decorated by the Painter of Vatican G 49 (Havana, Lagunillas. *ABV* 430, no. 26).

[4] *ARV* 383, no. 202, to p. 385, no. 223.

[5] CB iii. 27.

[6] *JHS* xxxi (1911), 290.

[7] *ARV* 211, nos. 191, 195, 199–200, 203.

[8] Palermo, V 670. *ARV* 211, no. 195.

[9] *ARV* 218.

[10] Birmingham, 1616.85. *ARV* 218, no. 10.

[11] Syracuse, no number. *ARV* 219, no. 13; Copenhagen, Ny Carlsberg, no number. *ARV* 219, no. 14.

[12] *ARV* 425.

we are not surprised to find that some of his red-figure *lekythoi* have black shoulders.[1] The palmettes and buds of his Bologna lion-shouldered *lekythos* (PLATE 8. 2*b*)[2] help to prepare us for the floral exuberance of the white-ground Atalanta *lekythos* in Cleveland (PLATES 10. 2, 11). The Kleophrades[3] and Eucharides[4] Painters rarely decorate *lekythoi*, but when they do they like to leave the shoulder black. The florals on some of the Eucharides Painter's vases of other shapes, especially neck-amphorae,[5] are close to those of the Floral Nolan Group (cf. PLATE 66. 2).

Red-figure shoulders were not acceptable to most painters of white *lekythoi*, probably because they look odd, the concentration of black on mouth, neck, and shoulder weighing heavily on the white slipped body. If the red-figure shoulder was borrowed from red-figure *lekythoi*, as seems likely, then we should expect painters of red-figure *lekythoi* who also painted white *lekythoi* to decorate the shoulders of their white *lekythoi* in red-figure, more often than those who worked exclusively in white-ground. With very few exceptions, for example the Brygos Painter's Aeneas and Anchises *lekythos* in Gela (PLATE 24. 1),[6] and the Pan Painter's Artemis in Leningrad (PLATE 24. 2),[7] this is not the case: painters tend to give the red-figure *lekythoi* either a red-figure or a reserved shoulder, with black palmettes, their white *lekythoi* a white-ground shoulder. White *lekythoi* with red-figure shoulders are known primarily from painters who specialized in white *lekythoi*. The vases are standard cylinders with three palmettes and two lotus buds on the shoulder, second white on the body, and often a *kalos* inscription. The total number is small and probably falls within the second quarter of the fifth century.

The Timokrates Painter[8] who painted exclusively white *lekythoi* liked white *lekythoi* with red-figure shoulders[9]—standard cylinders with second white (PLATE 25. 2, 3). The scenes are domestic and to some a *kalos* inscription has been added. Beazley related the painter to a better-known artist who occasionally worked in white-ground, but is not known to have painted a *lekythos* in this technique—the Pistoxenos Painter.[10] Among painters of white *lekythoi* the Timokrates Painter stands closest to the Vouni Painter[11] whose few attributed vases include three white *lekythoi*, two with white shoulders bearing outlined palmettes and lotus buds (FIGURE 12*a*; PLATE 26. 2),[12] the third with a red-figure version of the same.[13] The Painter of Athens 1826[14] also decorated a number of white *lekythoi* (apparently no vases of other shapes) in a variety of techniques.[15] Apart from a few with Bowdoin black palmettes on the white[16] or reserved ground,[17] his favourite shoulder decoration is palmettes and lotus buds, some in red-figure,[18] others

[1] Ibid. 446, no. 267 (palmettes and lion), and p. 447, no. 270 (horizontal palmettes).

[2] Bologna, PU 321. *ARV* 446, no. 267.

[3] Munich, 7517. *ARV* 189, no. 78.

[4] Oxford, 315. *ARV* 229, no. 47.

[5] London, E 279. *ARV* 226, no. 1; London, E 278. *ARV* 226, no. 2.

[6] Gela, no number. *ARV* 385, no. 223.

[7] Leningrad, 670. *ARV* 557, no. 121.

[8] *ARV* 743 f.

[9] The shoulders of two of the vases are missing: *ARV* 743, no. 8, and p. 744, no. 9.

[10] *ARV*¹ 578.

[11] Ibid. 580; *ARV* 744.

[12] *ARV* 744, nos. 1–2.

[13] Ibid. 744, no. 3.

[14] Ibid. 745 ff., 1668.

[15] Cab. Méd. 476. *ARV* 747, no. 29 (white squat *lekythos*).

[16] Athens, 1847. *ARV* 745, no. 2; London, D 26. *ARV* 746, no. 3.

[17] Athens, 1826. *ARV* 745, no. 1.

[18] *ARV* 746, no. 16, to p. 747, no. 28.

in white-ground (FIGURE 12*b*; PLATE 26. 1).[1] The red-figure shoulders scarcely differ from those of the Timokrates Painter.[2] The white-ground shoulders regularly have part of the pattern missing—alternate petals of the palmettes and the actual blossoms of the lotus buds; these were almost certainly added in red paint which has now disappeared. The painter uses quite a lot of red in the picture panel and second white not only for the flesh of women, but also for tombstones, which he painted with some care.[3] Beazley noted the influence of the Carlsruhe Painter in some of the *lekythoi* of the painter;[4] we think especially of the Carlsruhe Painter's BELs with funerary iconography,[5] stylistically related to other Beldam funerary scenes.[6] Beazley also associated some of the vases of the Painter of Athens 1826 with a large, not very well-defined, group of *lekythoi* (red-figure) 'recalling' the Ethiop Painter and the Painter of London E342.[7] No white *lekythoi* have been attributed to either. A white *lekythos* in Boston,[8] in the manner of the Painter of London E342, is important for its iconography as well as its shoulder decoration (FIGURE 12*c*): Hermes leads a child to Charon's waiting boat in the company of *eidola*— one of the earliest representations of the theme on white *lekythoi*;[9] it was a favourite of the Sabouroff Painter, to whom the Painter of London E342 is in some way related.[10] A very similar scene, from which, however, Charon's boat has been omitted, appears on a white *lekythos* in the Mormino Collection, Palermo,[11] Hermes' charge has second white for her exposed flesh, and a black silhouette *eidolon*, carrying a fillet (the Boston *eidola* also carry objects useful in the tendance of the dead), flies at Hermes' foot. The shoulder decoration (FIGURE 13*a*) of both vases is essentially the same: three palmettes and two lotus buds in black paint; the lotus buds are outlined; their actual blossoms, like the alternate petals of the palmettes, were added in red paint. A white *lekythos* in New York ('warrior and woman') has a comparable shoulder (FIGURE 13*b*; PLATE 27. 4).[12] Beazley placed the vase 'near' the Villa Giulia Painter, along with another, in London, with a red-figure palmette and lotus-bud shoulder.[13] (The New York vase does not have second white; the London vase does.) Although the Villa Giulia Painter was clearly interested in white-ground, applying it to calyx-craters,[14] *alabastra*,[15] and a cup,[16] only two white *lekythoi* have been attributed to him, both of secondary shape (near CL) with bars on reserved shoulders.[17]

The two white-shouldered white *lekythoi*[18] by the Vouni Painter, mentioned above in connection with the Timokrates Painter, are also comparable. The Vouni Painter's shoulders retain much of their original red paint (FIGURE 12*a*). All of his white *lekythoi*

---

[1] *ARV* 746, nos. 4–15.

[2] Cf. *AE*, 1950–1, 150, fig. 1 (Athens, 17279) and fig. 2 (Athens, 17933).

[3] *ARV* 746, no. 11; *AM* xv (1890), pl. 1.

[4] *ARV*¹ 466.

[5] *ARV* 735, nos. 99–102.

[6] Ibid. 753.

[7] *ARV*¹ 463. On this group of *lekythoi* see *ARV* 667 ff., 1664, and *Para* 404.

[8] Boston, 95.47. *ARV* 670, no. 17; F i. 191 f.

[9] *MadMitt* x (1969), 167 ff. (Brommer).

[10] *Para* 404, 424.

[11] 310. *CV* i. III Y, p. 6. and pl. 6. 2–4

[12] New York, 06.1021.134. *ARV* 626, no. 2.

[13] London, D 20. *ARV* 626, no. 3.

[14] Reggio, frr. *ARV* 619, no. 11 *bis*; Lausanne, 3700. *ARV* 619, no. 12.

[15] *ARV* 625, nos. 91–4.

[16] Athens, Acropolis, 443 *ARV* 625, no. 100. A second cup has been attributed to the Villa Giulia Painter by M. Vickers (*JHS* xciv (1974), 177 ff. and pl. xvii).

[17] Munich, ex Schoen. *ARV* 624, nos. 86–7, and *Para* 398.

[18] New York, 35.11.5. *ARV* 744, no. 1; Nicosia, Y 453. *ARV* 744, no. 2.

make use of second white; the *lekythos* in New York, with white shoulder, has an exceptionally liberal use of colour (PLATE 26. 2): the white tombstones bound with many fillets and wreaths, which dominate the scene, stand on a black base 'in front of' a low mound. On the black base, painted in white, with some details picked out in red, are a pair of *halteres*, an *aryballos*, and a wreath. The selection and disposition of objects on the tomb can be paralleled on a red-figure *askos* in Boston (PLATE 27. 1)[1] and on a red-figure *pelike* fragment in Oxford (PLATE 27. 2)[2] (both unattributed).

All of the white-ground palmette and lotus-bud shoulders described have tendrils in black paint, some of the petals and part of the buds in matt red. An unattributed white *lekythos* in New York[3] has a similar design executed in a different technique—solid black paint (in effect silhouette) on white-ground (FIGURE 13*c*; PLATE 27. 5). The vase is a standard cylinder and second white is used in the picture panel. An even more striking variation appears on an unattributed standard cylinder with second white in the British Museum (PLATE 27. 3).[4] On the white shoulder there are palmettes, with cross-overs, added spirals, and thin closed buds, and lotus buds rendered entirely in black outline; alternate red petals have an outline of black. The shoulder looks like an exact translation of reserved red-figure design.

8. DOURIS

The most exceptional palmette and lotus-bud composition is on a white *lekythos* by Douris.[5] Only one white *lekythos* by him was known—the imperfectly preserved 'Sacrifice of Iphigeneia' in Palermo (PLATE 10. 1)[6]—and since little of its shoulder remains, little attention was given the scheme of decoration.[7] Now we have a second, recently acquired by the Cleveland Museum of Art, perfectly preserved with a shoulder pattern of unparalleled complexity (PLATES 10. 2, 11).[8] Some details of the figurework are not what we have come to expect from Douris, initially making Beazley's firm attribution of the vase difficult to understand, but if we consider the place of both white *lekythoi* in Douris' total *œuvre*, we shall see that the Cleveland vase truly is 'just as the Palermo *lekythos*'.[9]

First the Palermo *lekythos* (PLATE 10. 1). It was found in the sanctuary of Demeter Malophoros, at Selinus.[10] Fragments of the picture panel are virtually all that remain. Two of the four principal figures (names inscribed) are preserved—Iphigeneia and Teucer—part of the altar at which the sacrifice will take place and the foot of the fourth figure.[11] The outlines are drawn in black paint with washes of dilute for some details.

[1] Boston, 13.169; *GRBS* viii (1967), 264 and n. 24. Beazley originally attributed the *askos* to the Tyszkiewicz Painter (*ARV*¹ 188, no. 59; *VA* 55), and later (*Etruscan Vase-painting* (1947), 195) compared a vase of the Praxias Group (Munich 3170) for the subject.

[2] Oxford, 1966.854; *Select*, pl. 43, no. 293.

[3] New York, 57.12.24.

[4] London, D 47.

[5] *ARV* 425 ff., 1652 ff., 1701, 1706; *Para* 374 ff., 521.

[6] Palermo, N.I. 1886. *ARV* 446, no. 226. There is also a fragmentary white cup by Douris (London, D 1. *ARV* 429, no. 20).

[7] *ML* xxxii (1928), 332.

[8] Cleveland, 66.114. *ARV* 446, no. 226 *bis*, and *Para* 376; *CV* i, pls. 32–5. 1, and pp. 21–3.

[9] *Para* 376.

[10] *ML* xxxii. 331 ff.

[11] Ibid. 334.

(Compare the Brygos Painter's red-figure shoulder and use of second white on the *lekythos* with Aeneas and Anchises (PLATE 24. 1)). Beazley placed the Palermo *lekythos* in Douris' early middle period.[1]

The Cleveland *lekythos* (PLATES 10. 2, 11) is a thick-set cylinder with deep mouth, short neck, broad base, and disc foot. It measures 32·5 cm.[2] The estimated height of the Palermo vase is 35 cm[3]—perhaps overestimated, in view of the heavy proportions of the Cleveland vase. The straight-sided cylinder with short neck and broad base is a product of the very late sixth and early fifth centuries.[4] Douris' *lekythos* in Boston (PLATE 12. 1), mentioned earlier in connection with the red-figure horizontal palmette scheme of the Athena–Bowdoin Painters, is a slimmer version of the shape, with similarly shaped mouth and short neck, but with the minority foot form.[5] The technique of the Cleveland vase is the same as the Palermo *lekythos*, with the exception of the partial misfiring: '. . . there is little downright black, either on the shoulder or the body, the black having mostly fired brown, thus accidentally enhancing the polychrome effect of the vase.'[6]

The subject of the Cleveland *lekythos* is Atalanta pursued by Erotes. Atalanta, like Iphigeneia, was a popular heroine, and the suggestion that both vases may initially have been conceived in a series illustrating the lives of famous women of myth and legend[7] is attractive, but the Brygos Painter used a well-known hero for the decoration of his white *lekythos* and both artists may be doing little more than applying grand themes to grand vases. Iphigeneia is not common in Attic vase-painting; Atalanta pursued by Erotes is unique. An impressive figure, Atalanta dominates the front of the vase, wearing a heavy *himation* over a highly patterned *chiton* (embattled-counter-embattled pattern, key, and lotus buds are represented) in the fashion of the best-dressed Acropolis *korai*. She lifts her *chiton*, freeing her leg for greater mobility. The central fold of the *chiton* looks odd but the detail can be paralleled on long dresses worn by other men[8] and women[9] on vases painted by Douris. From the right and left side of the vase fly Erotes (PLATE 11). The right-hand Eros holds a floral spray in his up-raised right hand, a large palmette and bud tendril in his left. The left-hand Eros—the principal Eros—carries a wreath in his left hand and a decidedly unlovely floral tendril in his right—the work of a modern restorer;[10] the handle and lashes of the original whip are clearly visible.[11] Behind the whip-bearing Eros is a handle-Eros, grasping in each hand the tendrils of a lotus-bud 'tree' (growing from the base-line). Eros and florals are little more than an elaborate handle ornament.

If our Atalanta is unique in Attic vase-painting, the pursuant Eros is not;[12] the theme was especially popular with Douris. We are most familiar with it from Douris' signed *aryballos* (PLATE 9. 2) found in a grave on Stadium Street in central Athens (see p. 132).[13] The principal Eros wields a whip, the boy flees in a pose very like Atalanta's, and in

[1] *ARV* 446, no. 266.
[2] *CV* Cleveland i, p. 21 (Boulter).
[3] *ML* xxxii. 331.
[4] Cf. *Auktion* xxxiv, no. 114; F i. 27, fig. 19.
[5] Boston, 95.41. *ARV* 447, no. 270; CB iii. 27.
[6] *CV* Cleveland i, p. 22.
[7] Ibid. 22.

[8] Meggen, Käppeli (ex Basle Market). *ARV* 430, no. 31, and *Para* 374.
[9] London, E 48. *ARV* 431, no. 47.
[10] *CV* Cleveland i, p. 21.
[11] Ibid., pl. 35. 1.
[12] A. Greifenhagen, *Griechische Eroten* (1957), 57 f.
[13] Athens, 15375. *ARV* 447, no. 274.

general the composition of the slightly later *aryballos* is very close to that of the Cleveland *lekythos*. Compare also a red-figure cup of the painter's early period in Berlin,[1] on whose exterior Eros pursues a boy with a sandal; between the two lies a whip (PLATE 9. 1). Returning for a moment to the handle Eros, we are reminded of the shoulder Eros on the white *lekythos* in Berlin by the Syriskos Painter (PLATE 8. 1*b*).[2] Both Erotes grasp the tendrils of the framing florals in a similar manner. The wings of the Syriskos Painter's Eros are attached to his shoulders, as are those of the two Erotes seen in profile on the Cleveland *lekythos*. Lastly, the shoulder florals of both vases are executed in a similar technique—glaze outlines and dilute washes. The Syriskos Painter's *lekythos* is described in greater detail on pp. 127 ff.

The shoulder decoration of the Cleveland *lekythos* (PLATE 11*c*) is as unusual as its iconography. (Even though we have very little of the Palermo shoulder, enough remains to establish kinship of style and technique.) We tend to think of Douris primarily as a cup painter, who in his early periods preferred a 'bare' style of decoration, with little or no patternwork.[3] But from the beginning of his career, Douris painted vases of different shapes whose accessory decoration is sometimes floral and sometimes exceedingly elaborate. These early to early-middle florals compare favourably with those on the Cleveland and Palermo shoulders, in general complexity of design and in particular elements of composition. On the shoulder of the Cleveland *lekythos* there are three palmettes and four large, partly open lotus buds, outlined in glaze and filled in with washes of varying strengths, and several small black buds, closed or partly open. On the body of the *lekythos* are palmettes and lotus buds combined in sprays, with stems crossing over, in the manner of the Athena–Bowdoin florals (cf. PLATE 60). The cross-overs with pendent lotus buds springing from the heart of the central shoulder palmette are also not unlike those on the shoulder of the Athena Painter's black-figure *lekythos* in Havana.[4] A significant feature of Douris' florals is the size and prominence of the lotus bud which is not infrequently as large as, if not larger than, the palmette with which it is combined. We find palmette and lotus buds alternating as equal elements in a horizontal chain on Douris' early-middle *psykter* in London (PLATE 9. 4)[5] and on the shoulder of his early-middle *lekythos* in Boston with horizontal palmettes completed by a pendent lotus bud, partly open (PLATE 12. 1).[6] The Bologna *lekythos* of the same period,[7] with the lion on the shoulder (PLATE 8. 2), combines palmettes and lotus buds but in a freer, more developed composition.[8] Shoulder lions framed by florals remind us of the Berlin Painter,[9] and some details of the Cleveland shoulder can be found in the work of this painter and in that of his followers, for example the direction of the side tendrils, taking their origin from the volutes of the central palmette, not from its heart,[10] the tri-lobed spandrel buds,[11] and the small circles in the field.[12] The closest parallel for the Cleveland florals may now be found

[1] Berlin, 3168. *ARV* 428, no. 13. Other vases with the same subject are listed in *ARV* 280, with no. 13.

[2] Berlin, 2252. *ARV* 263, no. 54.

[3] *ARV* 425.

[4] Havana, Lagunillas. *ABV* 523, no. 10.

[5] London, E 768. *ARV* 446, no. 262.

[6] Boston, 95.41. *ARV* 447, no. 270.

[7] *ARV¹* 293, no. 204.

[8] Bologna, PU 321. *ARV* 446, no. 267.

[9] *ARV* 211, nos. 199–200.

[10] Cf. Gela, 24. *ARV* 216, no. 18.

[11] Cf. Madrid, 11117. *ARV* 209, no. 167.

[12] Cf. Gela 24. *ARV* 216, no. 18.

in the work of Douris himself, on a newly found *aryballos* (PLATE 9. 3), bearing the painter's signature.[1] On the shoulder of the *aryballos* (PLATE 9. 3*a*), which is divided into two fields by the handles, there are two pairs of linked palmettes and lotus buds, aligned horizontally—very much as on the London *psykter*; each element is equal in size and is alternately placed, as if in a chain. The form of the lotus buds on the *aryballos*, with prominent central sepal(?) is very like that of the Cleveland *lekythos*. The single leaf which appears beside one handle of the *aryballos* may also be found on the Cleveland vase, on the left side of the shoulder and suspended from the cross-overs of the central palmette. The *aryballos* is a very early work by Douris,[2] earlier than our white *lekythoi*. The crossing meander with cross square at the shoulder join appears occasionally in the tondo of some early cups by Douris;[3] the elaborate palmette complexes beneath each handle, which act as frames for the single figures, recall the handle decoration of late black-figure amphorae which some early red-figure painters reproduced in the new technique.

In conclusion we see that the Cleveland white *lekythos* and its sister in Palermo, although exceptional in the manner of shoulder decoration, belong with those red-figure vases described above, painted by Douris in the early to early-middle periods of his career.

---

[1] Studies presented to G. Bakalakis, *Kernos* (1972) 197 ff. and pl. 54. 3 (Philippaki): Athens, T. E. 556. *ARV* 447, no. 273 *bis*, and *Para* 376.

[2] *Kernos* 200 f.; *Para* 376 ('earliest style').
[3] Cf. Berlin, 2283. *ARV* 429, no. 21.

II

CLASSICAL PAINTERS OF WHITE *LEKYTHOI*

THE remainder of Part One will be devoted to the white *lekythos* in its classical form—a standard cylinder, slip nearly pure white, outlines glaze or matt,[1] iconography almost exclusively funerary, and accessory pattern of an established type: three palmettes on the shoulder, an egg band at the join of neck to shoulder, and a meander band at the join of shoulder to body. With the standardization of shape, technique, and style of decoration there is also specialization: some artists chose to concentrate on white *lekythoi* to the exclusion of vases of other shapes decorated in other techniques. Because of this standardization and specialization it is necessary to treat the classical *lekythos* somewhat differently from its predecessors in mixed techniques and styles of decoration. A few painters have been chosen for detailed study, either because their work influenced the development of the vase or because their connections with other painters are clear enough to establish continuity in production and community within workshops.

Before turning to the painters, I should like to explain the terminology which I have used to describe their shoulder patterns. The standardization of the shoulder decoration affects the number of the palmettes more than it does the arrangement. The three palmettes are disposed in a variety of ways which look very similar. Without precise terms of reference it is impossible to distinguish one system from the other. For this reason I have classified the shoulder palmettes according to two details which vary significantly: the spirals of the central palmette and the point of origin of the lateral palmettes. If the tendrils enclosing the central palmette terminate in a single spiral, I call this type 'I' (FIGURE 6); if the tendrils terminate in a double spiral, I call this type 'II' (FIGURE 6). Within each type there are two sub-types: if the tendrils enclosing the lateral palmettes originate from the volute (a single or double spiral) of the central palmette's enclosing tendril, I call this sub-type 'A' (for mnemonic purposes A = apex, the area of the palmette tip); if they originate from the volutes forming the heart of the central palmette, I call this sub-type 'B' (B = base, the heart area of the palmette). Type-I and type-II florals appear on red-figure and white *lekythoi*, and very few palmette systems fall outside these categories; the Bosanquet Painter's are the most notable exceptions (see pp. 37 f.). Palmettes of type I may have a lotus bud, partly open, attached to the single volute; this is a common red-figure scheme. Most of the white-ground examples have been described (pp. 26 ff.) and those by the Sabouroff Painter and related artists are described below. Palmettes of type II have a double spiral in place of the bud. Significant sub-types are described in detail with reference to specific illustrations.

We begin with the Sabouroff and Achilles Painters, both of whom had long careers,

[1] See Notes on the Plates, p. 197.

beginning just before the full Classical period and continuing well into it.[1] On the one hand they have links with artists of the preceding generation, on the other they have a legacy in the future, their work being carried on by pupils into the last quarter of the fifth century.[2] They are also among the last painters of white *lekythoi* to decorate significant red-figure vases of other shapes. The Achilles Painter was a finer draughtsman, but the Sabouroff Painter was more progressive and more influential in technique and iconography: he was executing funerary scenes in matt outline quite early on, whereas the Achilles Painter retained glaze paint almost to the end of his career, often for domestic scenes favoured by red-figure artists for vases of different shapes. The lineage of the Achilles Painter has been traced by Beazley to the Berlin Painter in his later years. The lineage of the Sabouroff Painter remains to be charted.

9. SABOUROFF PAINTER

The Sabouroff Painter[3] worked extensively in red-figure on vases of different shapes, but his finest work is white-ground.[4] He is principally a painter of cups and *lekythoi*;[5] we have two cups with white-ground tondo from his hand. One is undecorated,[6] the other has a figure in glaze outline.[7] Cups constitute a great part of the painter's early work and the potter work of some has been associated with a follower of Brygos.[8] The other sizeable group of early vases consists of *lekythoi* and these early *lekythoi* are secondary shape; the rest of the painter's *lekythoi*, red-figure and white-ground, are standard cylinders, as are all the *lekythoi* attributed to the Achilles Painter. The two white secondary *lekythoi* are shape ATL[9] or near,[10] and their reserved shoulders have rays in the usual manner.[11] The published red-figure examples are PL[12] (see pp. 81 ff.) or near[13] with black palmettes on reserved shoulder in the scheme found on later PLs. One of the PLs[14] has a most unusual handle floral (PLATE 28. 1) which is paralleled on an equally unusual white *lekythos* 'near' the Two-row Painter (FIGURE 27a).[15] Details of iconography[16]

[1] *VPol* 32 (Sabouroff Painter); *AWL* 14 (Achilles Painter).

[2] Painter of Cambridge 28.2. *ARV* 855. See also below, p. 54, for the painter's relation to the Bird Group; Phiale Painter. *ARV* 1014 ff. See below, pp. 48 ff.

[3] *ARV*[1] 556 f.; *ARV* 837 ff., 1672, 1703, 1707; *Para* 423.

[4] *ARV* 837; *AWL* 16.

[5] *ARV* 837.

[6] Prague, private, fr. *ARV* 838, no. 21.

[7] Munich, 2685. *ARV* 837, no. 9.

[8] H. Bloesch, *Formen attischer Schalen* (1940), 87 f.

[9] Harvard, 60.336. *ARV* 846, no. 192.

[10] London Market (ex Northwick, Spencer-Churchill). *ARV* 846, no. 191, and *Para* 423.

[11] Beazley noted a certain resemblance in style between one of the painter's *lekythoi* of standard shape and a *lekythos* of shape ATL, related to the Tymbos Painter and his Group (*VPol* 34). Beazley compared

Goluchow, 86 (= Warsaw, 142302. *ARV* 850, no. 268) with Goluchow, 84 (= Warsaw, 142471. *ARV* 723, no. 1. *CV* Goluchow, pl. 43. 3). Goluchow 84 is shape ATL in the finer version used by the Painter of Munich 2774 (*ARV* 283) (see below, p. 82). Cf. *CV* Copenhagen iv, pl. 170. 1 (6328. *ARV* 283, no. 4) with *CV* Goluchow, pl. 43. 3; *Lekythoi* of shape ATL are described below on pp. 82 ff.

[12] San Francisco, Legion of Honor, 1621. *ARV* 844, no. 156.

[13] Laon, 37.960. *ARV* 844, no. 155; cf. Cracow, University, 1087. *ARV* 311, no. 11. *CV* Cracow, pl. 8. 11.

[14] Honolulu, 2892. *ARV* 844, no. 153.

[15] Greensboro, North Carolina, Jastrow. *ARV* 727, bottom.

[16] Seated Athena: Dunedin, E 30.202. *ARV* 311, no. 3 (PL or near. Painter of Palermo 4); Oxford, 1925.84. *ARV* 659, no. 50 (PL. Painter of the Yale *Lekythos*).

or figurework[1] on PLs by the Sabouroff Painter find parallels on PLs painted by other artists. With these early red-figure *lekythoi* Beazley compared a red-figure *lekythos*, in shape approximating PL, 'near' the Painter of Palermo 4;[2] another red-figure *lekythos* of standard shape, also 'near' the Painter of Palermo 4, is said to recall the manner of the Bowdoin Painter[3] who also decorated a *lekythos* of shape PL.[4]

The Sabouroff Painter's red-figured *lekythoi* of standard shape[5]—far fewer in number than the white-ground—for the most part have palmettes and lotus buds in the usual red-figure system (type I). A small number, however, have the shoulder reserved with 'elegant' black palmettes in the style of the Achilles Painter, from whom he borrowed them.[6] The close relation between the two artists is illustrated by the red-figure *loutrophoros* in Philadelphia on which both collaborated.[7]

The Sabouroff Painter's numerous white *lekythoi* of standard shape are homogeneous in their shoulder decoration—with the exception of a small group with lotus buds added to the palmettes (see below)—and they display a marked preference for an otherwise not very common scheme—Ia (FIGURE 17c). The Sabouroff Painter likes a very simple composition without cross-overs,[8] added spiral tendrils,[9] or dots in the field. His preference for lateral tendrils originating from the single (I) or sometimes double (II) spiral, is unusual, and this, together with his tendency to execute the florals, as well as the meander band below, in matt paint, make his decoration distinctive. Even the few painters who use Ia florals are not easily mistaken,[10] thanks to the wiry appearance of the Sabouroff florals with their thin tightly coiled tendrils.

The group of white *lekythoi* with palmettes and lotus buds on the shoulder (FIGURE 17 a, b)[11] differs from the painter's other white *lekythoi* of standard shape in the technique of the shoulder decoration as well as the design (PLATE 28. 2). They are not unrelated to white-ground palmette and lotus bud shoulders described earlier, of which the Charon *lekythos* in Boston, near the Painter of London E 342,[12] is representative (FIGURE 12c). The Painter of London E 342 is himself not unrelated to the Sabouroff Painter; both are among the first to paint Charon scenes on white *lekythoi*.[13] The florals of the Boston *lekythos* are outlined in black paint and some details are added in red. The Sabouroff

---

Nike flying: London Market. *ARV* 659, no. 47 (Painter of the Yale *Lekythos*); Vienna, 874. *ARV* 844, no. 154 (Sabouroff Painter).

[1] Floral sprays held in the hand are common enough, but the following examples deserve mention: Amsterdam, 3495. *ARV* 841, no. 76 (Sabouroff Painter); New York, 41.162.27. *ARV* 308, no. 21 (Dutuit Painter); Leningrad, from Olbia. *ARV* 676, no. 14 (unattributed *lekythos* of shape PL).

[2] Dunedin, E 30.202.

[3] London, E 642. *ARV* 311, no. 2.

[4] Athens, 1508. *ARV* 678, no. 23.

[5] *ARV* 843, no. 144, to p. 844, no. 152.

[6] New York, 26.60.78. *ARV* 844, no. 151; Laon, 37.957. *ARV* 844, no. 152 (I know the vase only from the photograph in *CV* Laon i, pl. 41. 5); cf. also Bowdoin, 1915.46. *ARV* 858, no. 7 (Trophy Painter).

[7] Philadelphia, 30.4.1. *ARV* 990, no. 45.

[8] New York, 21.88.17. *ARV* 846, no. 197.

[9] Berlin, 2455. *ARV* 846, no. 196.

[10] Athens, 2035. *ARV* 845, no. 174; Laon, 37.942. *ARV* 847, no. 208; Athens, 17324. *ARV* 847, no. 211.

[11] *ARV* 845, nos. 163–8. Compare also the unattributed white *lekythos*, Athens, 16422 (PLATE 28. 3). A recent addition to the group is a fragmentary *lekythos* by the Sabouroff Painter in the Getty Collection, on temporary loan to the Ashmolean Museum, Autumn 1973.

[12] Boston, 95.47. *ARV* 670, no. 17.

[13] *MadMitt* x (1969), 167 ff.; Painter of London E 342: *ARV*[1] 459 ff., *ARV* 667 ff., and *Para* 404. In *ARV* (p. 1664) Warsaw, 14769 was attributed to the Painter of London E 342; in *Para* (404 and 424) it has been transferred to the manner of the Sabouroff Painter.

florals are outlined in dilute glaze. The central petal of each palmette is angular and rendered in outline only, the others are rounded and filled in with dilute washes; the heart of the palmette is a double arc. The lotus buds, rendered in glaze, are long and thin with small calyxes and prominent petals. The use of glaze, instead of matt and of scheme B instead of A, set these white *lekythoi* apart from the others by the Sabouroff Painter. The use of glaze for the meander is also notable, as is the peculiar form which it assumes, on one of the *lekythoi*:[1] the initial stroke is horizontal, not vertical (cf. FIGURE 4*h*). This type of meander is exceedingly rare,[2] and its appearance on a red-figure *lekythos* by the Trophy Painter[3] deserves a mention. The painter is related through shape (*pelikai*) and pattern to the Achilles Painter,[4] and the reverse of one of his *pelikai* is painted not by himself but by an artist working in the Sabouroff manner.[5] Only one *lekythos* has been attributed to him.

The iconography of the palmette and lotus bud *lekythoi* also deserves mention. One, in the Vlasto Collection,[6] does not have a recognizably funerary scene; this detail alone sets it apart from the painter's other white *lekythoi* of standard shape. Exceptional, too, is the use of second white for the women's flesh; second white is otherwise unknown in the painter's work.[7] The reason why the Sabouroff Painter does not use second white, even in his early period,[8] probably lies in his training as a cup painter. The Achilles Painter, who seems not to have liked cups, retained the use of second white for some time.[9] Apart from the Vlasto *lekythos* (and two others which are too fragmentary for their iconography to be determined),[10] the palmette and lotus bud group is linked as closely by iconography as by shoulder design, and those which I have studied have a false interior,[11] as do some of the painter's other *lekythoi*.

The Sabouroff Painter's range of funerary iconography is remarkable: the visit to the tomb is the most common, but there are also scenes of the *prothesis* (PLATE 29. 2, 3)[12] and of Charon leading away the dead.[13] The visit to the tomb is the subject of the palmette and lotus-bud series (PLATE 28. 2). These differ from the painter's other tomb scenes in the attention given to the decoration of the monument which is decked with ribbons and laden with offerings—wreaths, fillets, and vases of different types, including *lekythoi*,

[1] Athens, 12747. *ARV* 845, no. 166.
[2] Meanders springing from vertical dividing lines are studied by Beazley (*JHS* xxxi (1911), 279, fig. 3/9) and by Martin Robertson (*JHS* lxx (1950), 30) in connection with the early work of the Berlin Painter. In the Sabouroff Painter's work variations on the vertical meander occur on the following vases: *ARV* 839, no. 47 (one unit in the cup tondo); *ARV* 841, no. 74 (one unit); *ARV* 844, no. 154; *ARV* 845, no. 166; *ARV* 845, no. 168.
I know of two examples in the work of the Trophy Painter: *ARV* 858, nos. 7–8, and variants in the work of the Painter of Munich 2335 (*ARV* 1161, no. 1; B side) and of the Thanatos Painter (*ARV* 1228, no. 11).
[3] Bowdoin, 1915.46. *ARV* 858, no. 7.
[4] *ARV* 900, nos. 47–52, and pp. 1676 f.
[5] Ibid. 857, no. 5.

[6] Athens, Vlasto. *ARV* 845, no. 163 ('woman and woman spinning top').
[7] F. Felten, *Thanatos- und Kleophonmaler* (1971), 33 and n. 9, 63; in the manner of the Sabouroff Painter: The Hague, Gemeente Museum, 1890. *ARV* 851.
[8] Compare the white cup by the painter in Munich: C. M. Robertson, *Greek Painting* (1959), 147.
[9] *AWL* 14.
[10] *ARV* 845, nos. 164–5.
[11] Athens, 12747. *ARV* 845, no. 166; Athens, 12739. *ARV* 845, no. 167.
[12] New York, 07.286.40. *ARV* 846, no. 190; New York, 21.88.17. *ARV* 846, no. 197; London, D 62. *ARV* 851, no. 273; Houston, 37.8. *ARV* 851, no. 273 *bis*, and *Para* 424; Mannheim, 195. *ARV* 851, no. 274.
[13] *ARV* 846, no. 193, to p. 847, no. 199.

plemochoai, and *oinochoai*. These objects appear on tombstones on other white *lekythoi* by the painter but not in such profusion:[1] a *lekythos* hangs from a tomb or stands at its base, a *plemochoe* and a *kantharos*.[2] This attention to the tomb is paralleled on a small number of *lekythoi* in the manner of the Sabouroff Painter (PLATE 29. 4)[3] and by the Bosanquet Painter (PLATE 30. 1, 2). The Bosanquet Painter, as mentioned earlier, decorates the shoulders of his *lekythoi* with unusual floral compositions but the Sabouroff palmette and lotus bud is not one of them. Related to the Bosanquet Painter is the Thanatos Painter. Sometimes, his tombs are well supplied with offerings and his shoulder palmettes arranged in the favourite Sabouroff scheme IA. The most striking parallel to the Sabouroff Painter's palmette and lotus bud shoulder is found on a small group of white *lekythoi* related to the Thanatos Painter (PLATE 31) (see p. 39).

10. BOSANQUET PAINTER

The Bosanquet[4] Painter, so far as we know, painted nothing but *lekythoi*. With one exception they are white-ground. The red-figure *lekythos*[5] has reserved shoulder with elegant black palmettes in the Achillean manner, but in the IA system favoured by the Sabouroff Painter. The white *lekythoi* tend to have figures in glaze outline, shoulder decoration in matt. The latter has not infrequently faded without a trace.[6] Those *lekythoi* whose shoulder decoration is still visible are most extraordinary (FIGURES 14, 15): the patterns are quite unlike anyone else's, even those of the Thanatos Painter (FIGURE 18) with whom some have identified him.[7] The three palmettes are enclosed by tendrils. The heart of the central palmette points towards the shoulder, the apex towards the neck. The lateral palmettes on at least one shoulder seem not to have been linked. On the others the lateral tendrils originate either from the apex of the central palmette or from its base. The central palmette has no volute, and these compositions are therefore neither type I nor type II. There are buds or traces of buds on all but one of the decorated shoulders and these, too, are unlike any we have described. The most elaborate and best-preserved example is Athens 1935, whose outline florals look like an adaptation of a red-figure shoulder design; compositionally the closest parallels for the Bosanquet Painter's shoulder decoration are red-figure.[8]

[1] Most of the tombs represented with offerings are early in the painter's career. One glaze outline *lekythos* (Basle Market (M.M.). *ARV* 846, no. 184 *bis*, and *Para* 424) has two *lekythoi* standing on the monument's base. A matt outline *lekythos* in the Vlasto Collection (*ARV* 847, no. 200) has a *plemochoe* on the base of the tomb and a *lekythos* suspended from its shaft. The matt outline New York, 51.11.4 (*ARV* 847, no. 203) has a *lekythos* suspended from the tombstone.

[2] A white *lekythos* in the Oundle School collection, which must be the entry 'once London, Revelstoke, 25' (*ARV* 850, no. 266), features a *kantharos* on the base of the tombstone. Compare the grave-reliefs,

Conze, no. 1685, pl. 357, and nos. 1686–8, pl. 358.

[3] Felten, 20 ff.

[4] *ARV*[1] 807 ff.; *ARV* 1226 f.; *Para* 466.

[5] Dresden, ZV 2777. *ARV* 1227, no. 11.

[6] Meggen, Käppeli. *ARV* 1227, no. 3; New York, 23.160.38. *ARV* 1227, no. 5.

[7] *ALP* 14; Felten, 12 ff.

[8] Athens, 1935. *ARV* 1227, no. 1; Athens, 1932. *ARV* 1227, no. 2; Berlin, 3291. *ARV* 1227, no. 9. Cf. Santa Barbara, Brundage. *ARV* 658, no. 27 (Painter of the Yale *Lekythos*); Wuppertal, Funcke. *ARV* 641, no. 87 *bis*, and *Para* 401 (Providence Painter).

With the exception of two fragmentary *lekythoi* whose iconography cannot be determined,[1] the Bosanquet Painter's scenes are funerary, and like the Sabouroff Painter's, rendered in detail. The tombs are bound with fillets and laden with offerings: *oinochoai* (whose thin convoluted handles suggest metal), cups, squat *lekythoi*, and *lekythoi* of cylinder shape (PLATES 30. 1–2).[2] The vases stand on the steps of the monument, sometimes holding wreaths in place,[3] and sometimes overturned[4]—a realistic detail which we might expect from such a careful artist. Another distinctive feature of the offerings is the variety in wreaths: some have thin black leaves, others have broader, outlined leaves. The latter are as characteristic of the Bosanquet Painter as the tubular fillets are of the Achilles Painter (cf. PLATES 35.1, 36.3).

The Bosanquet Painter is a fine artist: he has the technical excellence of the Achilles Painter and the iconographical interest of the Sabouroff Painter. The Thanatos Painter with whom he has been related also stands between these two artists and, in a way, stands in an even closer relation to them.

11. THANATOS PAINTER

The Bosanquet Painter belongs to the early part of the third quarter of the fifth century, the Thanatos Painter[5] to the later.[6] Both are mentioned before the older Achilles Painter, because of the lotus buds which sometimes appear on the shoulders of their *lekythoi*. Although the Bosanquet shoulders display lotus buds amidst palmettes, the composition is not at all like that of the Sabouroff Painter's or that of other white-ground shoulders with palmettes and lotus buds. The shoulders of the Thanatos Painter's *lekythoi* do not have lotus buds, and the palmettes are arranged in the usual manner (see below). But connected with him are two *lekythoi*[7] whose shoulders have palmettes and lotus buds arranged in a composition very like that of the Sabouroff Painter. Although both *lekythoi* were known to Beazley, neither was entered in *ARV*[1]. In *ARV* the one in New York

---

[1] Oxford, 1966.923. *ARV* 1227, no. 7, and *Para* 466; London, 1907–10.10, fr. *ARV* 1227, no. 10. See below, p. 39 n. 5.

[2] Meggen, Käppeli. *ARV* 1227, no. 3; New York, 23.160.39. *ARV* 1227, no. 4; New York, 23.160.38. *ARV* 1227, no. 5; New York Market. *ARV* 1227, no. 8.

Cf. Athens, 12747. *ARV* 845, no. 166, and Berlin, 3262. *ARV* 845, no. 128.

[3] Cf. Lausanne, private. *ARV* 849, no. 244.

[4] Vases overturned and broken at the grave are best explained as a realistic record of contemporary burial practice, not as an allusion to a specific rite (as S. Karouzou, *BCH* lxxii (1948), 388; O. M. Stackelberg, *Gräber der Hellenen* (1837), 37; Riezler, 108 and n. 47; *Corinth* xiii (1964), 82; *Olynthus* xi (1942), 182; *ClRh* iii (1929), 13).

Overturned vases appear on the following: Boston, 00.359. *ARV* 1229, no. 23 (Thanatos Painter) (PLATE 32. 1); New York, 23.160.38. *ARV* 1227, no. 5 (Bosan-

quet Painter); Athens, 12739.

Compare the painted Attic tombstone: *GP* 157.

Broken vases appear on the following: Athens, 1982. *ABL* 267, no. 12 (Beldam Painter) (PLATE 18. 2); Boston, 00.359. *ARV* 1229, no. 23 (Thanatos Painter); Amsterdam, Musée Scheurleer, 2703. *CV* i. III lc, pl. 2, no. 1; Louvre, CA 3758 (unattributed); Munich, 2170, F i, pl. 14. 2 (unattributed; the broken vase is a *hydria*; see Diehl, ch. 2); Berlin, 3209 (the broken vase is a *lekythos*, represented at the tomb on a red-figure *loutrophoros*. See *AK* xiv (1971), pl. 27. 2–3).

[5] *ARV*[1] 807 ff.; *ARV* 1228 ff.; *Para* 466 f.

[6] *AWL* 17, 18 f.

[7] Two other *lekythoi*, existing in fragments, do not have shoulders preserved: Oxford, 1966.924. *ARV*, 1231, no. 1, and *Para* 467 (near the painter); London, Russell, fr. *ARV* 1231, no. 3. An additional two *lekythoi* (Munich, 2791. *ARV* 1231, no. 1, and Athens, no number. *ARV* 1231, no. 2) I have not studied.

(PLATE 31. 2) is said to be 'also near him',[1] the other in Boston (PLATE 31. 1) is said to have 'a good deal in common with those of the Thanatos Painter, to whom Buschor attributed it as an early work'.[2] If the Boston vase is early in the painter's career, the New York florals are appreciably closer to the Sabouroff model (cf. PLATE 28. 2). The New York shoulder is almost indistinguishable from those by the Sabouroff Painter; the heart of the palmette is a double arc, the central petal is angular and rendered only in outline, the lotus buds have small calyxes and long thin petals. The Boston shoulder differs in small details: the heart of the palmette is triangular, petals are alternately outlined and filled in with glaze; the central petal of the lateral palmettes extends outside the enclosing tendril and the lotus buds, shorter and squarer, are partly outlined and partly filled in with glaze. The Boston *lekythos* has one of the Thanatos Painter's common meanders at the join of shoulder to body,[3] and in the figure scene two men at a low pedimented monument of unusual type, which is not without parallels in the Thanatos Painter's work (cf. PLATE 32. 1).[4] The New York *lekythos* features two women at a *stele*: one is seated in a pose which can be paralleled on a *lekythos* by the Bosanquet Painter (PLATE 30. 3),[5] on the Trophy Painter's red-figure *lekythos* mentioned earlier,[6] and on a white-ground *alabastron* by the Two-row Painter (PLATE 72. 1).[7]

Among the *lekythoi* firmly attributed to the Thanatos Painter there are several different shoulder schemes and none is anything like the Bosanquet Painter's, which is, I think, reason enough for keeping the two painters separate. Some of the shoulders are undecorated, the matt paint having faded;[8] others have florals in glaze,[9] glaze and matt,[10] or matt.[11] Alternate petals may be rendered in red.[12] The great part of the Thanatos Painter's *lekythoi* have glaze outlines.[13] The earliest of these is in the Baker Collection, New York. The vase clearly illustrates the Thanatos Painter's debt to the Achilles Painter: two women stand beside a simple shaft *stele* decorated only with two Achillean tubular fillets. The shoulder palmettes are executed in dilute golden glaze in one of the Achilles Painter's favourite schemes—IIA: the heart of the palmette is his distinctive shape; there are

[1] New York, 11.212.8. *ARV* 1231, no. 2.

[2] Boston, 01.8080. *ARV* 1231.

[3] Cf. Boston, 09.70. *ARV* 1230, no. 30 (glaze, F i. 253), and Boston, 94.127. *ARV* 1230, n. 40 (matt, F ii. 25) with broken meanders; *AA* 1955, 237 f. (unbroken meanders).

[4] Once Bonn, 66. *ARV* 1229, no. 15; Boston, 00.359. *ARV* 1229, no. 23.

[5] London, 1907.7–10.10, fr. *ARV* 1227, no. 10 (I take the vertical line behind the back of the seated woman to be the edge of the tombstone). Compare also an unattributed white *lekythos* in the British Museum (D 33; shoulder red-ground) with a seated woman (flesh in second white) at the tomb in a similar pose. The vase has been repainted; *BMCat* iii. 399. PLATE 20.4.

[6] Bowdoin, 1915.46. *ARV* 858, no. 7.

[7] Berlin, 2259. *ARV* 727, no. 20.

[8] New York, 15.165. *ARV* 1228, no. 6; Athens, 1797. *ARV* 1229, no. 14; Baltimore, Walters Art Gallery, 48.2012. *ARV* 1229, no. 20; Basle, 1958.170. *ARV* 1230, no. 32; Munich, 7678. *ARV* 1230, no. 36.

[9] New York, Baker. *ARV* 1228, no. 1; London, D. 57. *ARV* 1228, no. 5; Athens, 1822. *ARV* 1229, no. 22; Athens, 1942. *ARV* 1229, no. 27.

[10] Athens, 1960. *ARV* 1228, no. 4; New York, 12.299.10. *ARV* 1229, no. 26; Athens, 12792. *ARV* 1229, no. 28.

[11] Athens, 1933. *ARV* 1228, no. 8; Boston, 92.2609. *ARV* 1228, no. 10; Boston, 00.359. *ARV* 1229, no. 23; Boston, 09.70. *ARV* 1230, no. 30; London, D 60. *ARV* 1230, no. 37; Boston, 94.127. *ARV* 1230, no. 40 (matt outlines).

[12] Boston, 92.2609; Athens, 1761. *ARV* 1229, no. 17; Boston, 96.721. *ARV* 1229, no. 24; Boston, 09.70; Boston, 09.69. *ARV* 1230, no. 31.

[13] *ARV* 1228, no. 1, to p. 1230, no. 38 (glaze outline); 1230, no. 39, to p. 1231, no. 47 (matt outline).

cross-overs, spandrel buds, and added spiral tendrils (FIGURE 18*c*). This degree of elaboration is not common on *lekythoi* by the Thanatos Painter.[1] The meander at the shoulder–body join is Achillean,[2] as is the potter work, judging from the shape and position of the vent hole.[3] Another early *lekythos*[4] was found in a grave on Lenormant Street in central Athens, together with a squat white-ground *lekythos*, a black squat *lekythos*, and a black *lekanis*.[5] The figure scenes somewhat recall the Bosanquet Painter[6] and the shoulder palmettes, type IA, the Sabouroff Painter. Both IA (FIGURE 18*a*)[7] and IIA (FIGURE 18*b*)[8] palmettes are used by the Thanatos Painter, IIA being more common; type IB does not occur although it is the scheme of the two lotus bud *lekythoi*; IIB is not found either. Both are used by the Achilles Painter. The Thanatos Painter likes to execute his shoulder florals in matt and he prefers compositions uncluttered by too many tendrils and buds. The meander band is also simple: a neat series of stopt meanders without pattern squares.[9]

Iconographically the Thanatos Painter looks to both the Achilles Painter and the Sabouroff Painter. His most obvious borrowing from the former are the 'mistress and maid'[10] and 'warrior and woman at tomb'[11] scenes. The iconography of the glaze outline *lekythoi* is predominantly funerary,[12] the matt outline *lekythoi* are all funerary. In this the Thanatos Painter may be contrasted with the Achilles Painter, whose proportion of *lekythoi* with explicit funerary iconography is not very large. Another point of contrast is in the tomb scenes by the two painters: Achillean men and women stand by motionless; rarely do they engage in any apparent activity (cf. PLATES 35, 36). The Thanatos Painter's men[13] and women[14] not infrequently mourn openly (PLATE 32. 2). Such displays of grief may be found on earlier *lekythoi* by the Sabouroff Painter. The tomb monuments are most often tall shaft *stelai*, as are those of the Sabouroff and Achilles Painters, but some are lower and broader. One is crowned by a stool (PLATE 33. 1)[15] (as on two white *lekythoi*[16] by the Achilles Painter (PLATE 33. 2, 3)), another by a child[17] (as on a white *lekythos*[18] by the Sabouroff Painter). The child's tomb is featured on one[19] of three matt outline *lekythoi*

---

[1] 'Cross-overs': once Bonn, 66. *ARV* 1229, no. 15; Athens, 1822. *ARV* 1229, no. 22; London, D 60.

[2] *ANY*, pl. 88, no. 240; cf. *JHS* xxxiv (1914), 186.

[3] *ANY* 61 f.

[4] Athens, Agora, P 10369. *ARV* 1228, no. 2.

[5] *Hesp* xxxii (1963), 123 f. (F).

[6] Cf. *Hesp* xxxii, pl. 40 (F 1), and *JHS* xix (1899), 174, fig. 3 (Athens, 1932. *ARV* 1227, no. 2).

[7] IA palmettes: *ARV* 1228, no. 4; 1229, no. 25; 1230, nos. 30, 34, 44–6.

[8] IIA palmettes: *ARV* 1228, nos. 5, 7, 8, 10; 1229, nos. 15, 17, 22–4, 26–8; 1230, nos. 31, 37.

[9] Cf. *AA* 1955, 237 f.

[10] London, D 57. *ARV* 1228, no. 5; New York, 15.165; Basle Market (M.M.). *ARV* 1229, no. 19; Boston, 09.70; Munich, 7679. *ARV* 1230, no. 35.

[11] Boston, 92.2609; Athens, 1761. The *kalos* inscription on the Boston *lekythos* is unusual.

[12] See above, n. 10 for exceptions.

[13] London, D 67. *ARV* 1228, no. 7; Athens, 1993. *ARV* 1228, no. 8.

[14] Baltimore, Walters Art Gallery, 48.2012; Basle, 1958.170; Stockholm, G 2108. *ARV* 1230, no. 39; Berlin, 3964. *ARV* 1230, no. 42; New Orleans, private. *ARV* 1230, no. 46.

[15] New York, 12.229.10.

[16] Amiens, 3057.172.33; Vienna, 3746.

[17] New Orleans, private. *ARV* 1230, no. 44.

[18] Athens, 1815. *ARV* 845, no. 169; cf. also Boston, 10.220. *ARV* 845, no. 170 (seated woman on a tomb of similar shape); (?) Mannheim, 14. *ARV* 1372, no. 12; *CV* i, p. 45, fig. 14. Sculptural parallels: M. Collignon, *Les Statues funéraires dans l'art grec* (1911), 192 ff.

[19] *ARV* 1230, no. 44: For the child on the tomb, see note above; the snub-nosed girl may be compared with the girl on Berlin, 3291 (*ARV* 1227, no. 9).

ARV 1230, no. 45: the girl with the doll may be compared with girls with dolls on the following grave-reliefs: Conze, no. 880, pl. 170; no. 882, no. 171.

ARV 1230, no. 46: this vase does not look much like the Thanatos Painter; the figures are more slender and less substantial (cf. *ARV* 1230 f.).

of exceptional iconographical interest in a private collection in New Orleans.[1] At least one[2] of the *lekythoi* of this group has a false interior, as do the early Baker *lekythos*, and the *lekythos* from the Lenormant Street grave. False interiors are found in *lekythoi* by the Sabouroff and Achilles Painters, and by the Thanatos Painter's successor, the Painter of Munich 2335.

The matt outline *lekythoi* are iconographically interesting, but not without parallels. Three *lekythoi* by the painter are iconographically most unusual, virtually without parallel. Two feature a hare hunt at the tomb (PLATE 32. 3),[3] the third Persians.[4] For the former I compare a semi-outline *lekythos* from the Bowdoin Workshop (hare hunt in a rocky landscape without any funerary reference (PLATE 14. 2)),[5] for the latter two *lekythoi* by the Sabouroff Painter.[6] The Bowdoin *lekythos* is interesting but not strictly relevant; the Sabouroff *lekythoi* are, I think, very relevant. The Sabouroff Painter's Orientals stand at a tomb in the presence of a woman (on one of the vases the woman, too, seems to wear Persian dress).[7] The Thanatos Painter's Persians have no obvious funerary context, but the archer, dressed like an Oriental, at the tomb on another *lekythos* by this painter should perhaps be compared.[8] The significance of these scenes is not clear.

12. ACHILLES PAINTER

> It was the Achilles painter who determined what the white lekythos could be and was to be. Changes came when men of other times and temperaments succeeded him: but it bore his imprint to the end.[9]

The Achilles Painter[10] has come to be known as the classical painter *par excellence* of white *lekythoi*. His position of pre-eminence rests to a great extent on the exceptionally fine quality of his line—and in this he has no equal among painters of white *lekythoi*. He determined what the white *lekythos* became simply by revealing how very beautiful it could be. If he set a standard for others, it was more a standard of excellence, of sensitivity, and of serenity than of technique or of iconography.

The Achilles Painter had a long career[11] during which he decorated vases of different shapes in black-figure, red-figure, and white-ground. He began in the workshop of the

---

[1] *ARV* 1230, nos. 44–6. I know the vases only from photographs.

[2] *ARV* 1230, no. 44; cf. also Athens, Agora, P 10369. *ARV* 1228, no. 2 ('early'); *Hesp* xxxii, pl. 43 (F 1).

[3] London, D 60. *ARV* 1230, no. 37; Bonn, 1011. *ARV* 1230, no. 38. A third hare hunt at the tomb is said to have appeared on a white *lekythos* once in the Fröhner Collection (*Jb* xxii (1907), 105 ff.). Hare-hunts on other *lekythoi* are mentioned below on p. 121.

[4] Louvre, CA 2980. A second *lekythos* should probably be included: Athens, 1981. *ARV* 1229, no. 18 ('youth and archer at tomb'); *JHS* xix (1899), 184.

[5] Athens, 1973. *ARV* 690, no. 9.

[6] 'Persians' appear on the following *lekythoi*: Tübingen, E 67. *ARV* 850, no. 270 (Sabouroff Painter);

Paris Market (Geledakis). *ARV* 850, no. 271 (Sabouroff Painter); Cab. Méd. 496 *bis* ('oriental archer'). *ARV* 758, no. 94 (Tymbos Group); once Athens, Schliemann (Persian on a camel). *ARV* 1613 (unattributed).

For a recent discussion of Persians on Greek vases see: *BCH* lxxxvii (1963), 579 ff. (Bovon); *RA* 1972, 271 ff. (Kahil).

[7] C. Watzinger, *Griechische Vasen in Tübingen* (1924), 43 (E 67), and pl. 26.

[8] See above n. 4 (Athens, 1981).

[9] *AWL* 13.

[10] *ARV*[1] 634 ff.; *ARV* 986 ff., 1676 f.; *Para* 437 ff.

[11] *AWL* 14.

Berlin Painter, when the master was near the end of his career, and his pupils,[1] Hermonax and the Providence Painter,[2] were well along in theirs. One of his links with the Berlin Painter has been seen in his series of black-figure prize Panathenaics[3] which begins around 440 B.C.[4] The Achilles Painter follows the older artist's model for Athena without appreciable alteration of the type.[5] But Beazley retained some reservations about the Berlin Painter's authorship of the prize Panathenaics.[6] There is also a problem of chronology: even if the prize Panathenaics are by the Berlin Painter and date from the very end of his career there remains a gap which lost vases may or may not have bridged.[7]

The Achilles Painter's earliest vases are small neck-amphorae of Nolan type—a favourite shape of the Berlin Painter and of his school. One of the earliest[8] is so near the Berlin Painter that Beazley initially attributed it to the manner of the older artist, leaving open the possibility that it might be by the Achilles Painter in his very early period.[9] Some of the early Nolans bear *kalos* inscriptions—Kleinias,[10] Lichas,[11] and Meletos.[12] *Kalos* inscriptions are found on the Achilles Painter's Nolans, an early red-figure *lekythos* (Kleinias, son of Pedieus),[13] a high proportion of the painter's second white *lekythoi* (Lichas is one of those praised), and on a bell-crater in New York, also early.[14] The bell-crater was originally attributed to the Meletos Painter, named after the Nolan amphora on which the name occurs.[15] Later Beazley merged the Meletos and Achilles Painters, considering the former an early phase of the latter.[16]

Nolan amphorae were popular in the Berlin Painter's Workshop, but so were *lekythoi*. Those by the Berlin Painter have been mentioned earlier; all are red-figure, with black shoulders, red-figure florals, or figure compositions; in white-ground we have only a fragmentary plate by the master.[17] Hermonax[18] painted a number of red-figure *lekythoi*, with black shoulders,[19] red-figure florals,[20] or figure compositions;[21] he may have painted white *lekythoi* but we have only a fragmentary cup[22] in that technique. The Providence Painter[23] especially likes Nolan amphorae and *lekythoi*. His *lekythoi* are red-figure and white-ground, standard and secondary shape. The red-figure *lekythoi* display the same variety in shoulder decoration as Hermonax'.[24] The white-ground standard cylinders—

---

[1] *ARV* 986.   [2] *VA* 163.   [3] *ABV* 408.

[4] *AJA* xlvii (1943), 448 f. (Beazley).

[5] *ABV* 408.   [6] Ibid.   [7] *AJA* xlvii. 448 f.

[8] New York, 25.189.2. *ARV* 988, no. 6.

[9] *ARV*¹ 648.

[10] Kleinias: *ARV* 1589 f.; Berlin, 3759. *ARV* 988, no. 12; once London, Rogers. *ARV* 988, no. 13; London, E 300. *ARV* 988, no. 15.

[11] Lichas: *ARV* 1594 f.; Madrid, 11107. *ARV* 988, no. 14.

[12] Meletos: *ARV* 1599; Cab. Méd. 363. *ARV* 988, no. 11; *JHS* xxxiv (1914), 194 (Beazley).

[13] Syracuse, 21186. *ARV* 993, no. 80; *JHS* xxxiv. 195.

[14] New York, 07.286.81. *ARV* 991, no. 61, and p. 1677.

[15] *VA* 166; *JHS* xxxiv. 194 f., 205, 224, 226. Richter and Hall, 147, 151 ff.   [16] Richter and Hall, 152 n. 7.

[17] Athens, Acropolis, 427. *ARV* 214, no. 244, and p. 1635 (Acr. 428, fr.). A second example? (Acr. 428, fr. on p. 1635).

[18] *ARV* 483 ff., 1655, 1706; *Para* 379 f.

[19] New York, 26.60.77. *ARV* 490, no. 122; Palermo, V 673. *ARV* 490, no. 123.

[20] Aachen, Ludwig (ex Lucerne Market). *ARV* 490, no. 116 *bis*, and p. 1655; *Para* 379; Palermo, V 672. *ARV* 490, no. 119, and pp. 490 and 1655; Hartford, 30.184. *ARV* 490, no. 121.

[21] Cab. Méd. 489. *ARV* 490, no. 114; New York, 41.162.19. *ARV* 490, no. 115; Barcelona, 581. *ARV* 490, no. 116.

[22] Athens, fr., from Brauron. *ARV* 491, no. 132; *AK Beiheft* i, pl. 9 (Kahil).

[23] *ARV* 635 ff., 1663, 1702, 1708; *Para* 400 f.

[24] Black shoulders: *ARV* 640, no. 66 *bis*; 641, nos. 90, 92 *bis*, 93, 96, 97. Red-figure florals: *ARV* 640, no. 67; 641, nos. 70, 73 *bis*, 74–6, 80, 84, 87 *bis*. Figures: *ARV* 640, no. 77. There are also a very few reserved shoulders with black palmettes: *ARV* 641, no. 98 *bis*; 642, no. 99.

with unexceptional iconography, second white, and occasionally *kalos* inscriptions—have red-figure shoulders with type-I palmettes[1] or black Bowdoin palmettes on a white-ground.[2] The use of Bowdoin palmettes is not surprising, since the Providence Painter also decorated some *lekythoi* of the Bowdoin Painter's favourite shape—BL.[3] The red-figure and white *lekythoi* of the Providence Painter display neither of the Achilles Painter's characteristic schemes—elegant black palmettes on reserved shoulders of red-figure *lekythoi* and dilute glaze palmettes on the white-ground shoulders of white *lekythoi*.

The Achilles Painter's *lekythoi*, red-figure, and white-ground are standard cylinders. The shoulder decoration of the red-figure *lekythoi* is either red-figure (PLATE 34, 2) or black on reserved ground (PLATE 34. 4). The red-figure examples are few and early.[4] One in Cambridge[5] has palmettes and lotus buds (type IB) with reserved dots in the field; similar shoulders are found on *lekythoi* by the Berlin Painter and by members of his school. A second *lekythos*, in Syracuse (PLATE 34. 2), with a *kalos* inscription Kleinias, son of Pedieus,[6] has type-II palmettes with double spirals in place of the lotus buds. There are reserved dots and the v's in the field (see pp. 47 f.). A third red-figure *lekythos* in the Louvre,[7] later and larger, has a red-figure shoulder with figures (men and women) not florals. Shoulder figures were never very popular on red-figure *lekythoi* (see pp. 126 f.) but within the Berlin Painter's Workshop they enjoyed some favour; the Achilles Painter's pupil the Phiale Painter was decorating the shoulders of some of his red-figure *lekythoi* with figures down to the last quarter of the fifth century.

The great majority of the Achilles Painter's red-figure *lekythoi* have a reserved shoulder with black palmettes. These black palmettes differ from those of the Bowdoin Painter in number, form, and composition. Bowdoin palmettes are five in number; the petals are broad and do not vary much in length; the hearts are not clearly defined. The five palmettes are arranged in groups of one, three, and one, beneath the band of bars at the neck. Black dots and thin closed buds with spiral tendrils are often added. This system of shoulder decoration, either carefully rendered or hastily painted, beneath a neck-line instead of bars, remains common through much of the fifth century on second-rate standard cylinders,[8] and may even be found on *lekythoi* by the Achilles Painter himself.[9] The Achillean reserved shoulders have three palmettes, most often type IIB, beneath an egg band. Petals of the palmettes are thin; the central petal is appreciably longer than the others but no thicker. The heart is clearly indicated. To complement these elegant palmettes, there are thin gracefully curving tendrils, with thin closed spandrel buds and small black dots in the field. The Achilles Painter's black palmettes were taken up by other red-figure painters[10] and not only by those closely associated with him.[11] Most are carefully executed and reasonably close to the elegant Achillean model. There is no

---

[1] Oxford, 548. *ARV* 642, no. 112; Athens, 1828. *ARV* 642, no. 113; Syracuse, 21146. *ARV* 642, no. 115.

[2] Greifswald, 363. *ARV* 642, no. 114; Lyons, E 413. *ARV* 643, no. 116. The Greifswald *lekythos* has enclosed bars at the neck–shoulder join; the Lyons *lekythos* has a line.

[3] Athens, 1828; Greifswald, 363.

[4] *JHS* xxxix. 196.

[5] Cambridge, 37.29. *ARV* 993, no. 79.

[6] *ARV* 1007.

[7] Louvre, G 444. *ARV* 993, no. 91.

[8] *ARV* 692; *ARV*¹ 480.

[9] St. Louis, Washington University, 3275. *ARV* 997, no. 145, and p. 1677.

[10] *ARV* 1007.

[11] New York, 22.139.189. *ARV* 1147, no. 67 (Kleophon Painter).

precedent for the new style of black palmettes, and we must attribute their invention to the Achilles Painter.

The iconography of the red-figure *lekythoi* is essentially that of the Nolan amphorae (cf. PLATE 34. 2) but there are a few tomb scenes. These look like the earliest in red-figure (PLATE 34. 4),[1] but they are not early in the painter's career, nor are his white *lekythoi* with tomb scenes. We might wonder why the Achilles Painter was so slow to develop; it must have been quite clear by the middle of the century what the future course of the vase was going to be. Beazley noted that the Achilles Painter matured slowly: 'his art, both in red-figure and in outline, developed slowly, and none of his early lekythoi are among his best.'[2] But he was also a conservative artist well grounded in the red-figure style with little or no apparent contact with the late black-figure painters of *lekythoi* who are responsible for the introduction of funerary iconography on the white-ground vase.

White *lekythoi* by the Achilles Painter are far more numerous than red-figure.[3] Apart from a few late examples, all have glaze outlines. The earlier glaze outline *lekythoi* have second white, the later do not. The shoulders of all are white-ground. The second white *lekythoi*, although largely from Attica and Eretria, have been found as far afield as Gela in the west,[4] the Troad in the east,[5] and Naucratis in the south.[6] The iconography varies little: two women, often with a *kalos* inscription in the field—*Dromippos* and *Diphilos* are especially common.[7] The shoulder palmettes are most often type IIB—the scheme most common for the elegant black palmettes. The earliest of the white *lekythoi* (PLATE 35. 1)[8] has shoulder florals (FIGURE 19a) very like those on reserved shoulders of the painter's red-figure *lekythoi* (cf. PLATE 34. 4): the black paint is undiluted, the petals are numerous, and there are black dots in the field and thin spandrel buds. The palmettes are arranged according to the not very common IB system which is not otherwise found on the Achilles Painter's *lekythoi*. Another early second white *lekythos*[9] has the equally uncommon IA scheme which I have found on one of the painter's white *lekythoi* without second white.[10] The number of the petals of the palmettes has been reduced to five—the canonical Achillean number for palmettes rendered in diluted glaze. A third early second white *lekythos*[11] has IIB palmettes as do the majority of second white *lekythoi* by the painter.

These early second white *lekythoi* have not been properly studied. Beazley drew attention to the use of second white, suggesting that it may have been borrowed from panel and wall painting,[12] but not to the quality of the Achilles Painter's second white, or to his use of added white on black-figure vases. On some of the *lekythoi* the areas of second white are ill defined and undifferentiated by painted detail.[13] Some are finer,

---

[1] *JHS* xxxiv. 220. [2] *AWL* 14.

[3] *ARV* 993, no. 79, to p. 994, no. 104; 995, no. 118, to p. 1001, no. 212.

[4] Havana, Lagunillas. *ARV* 995, no. 124.

[5] Berlin, Völkerkundemuseum, 5252 and 5254. *ARV* 995, no. 127.

[6] London, 1937.10–26.1. *ARV* 996, no. 140.

[7] Dromippos, son of Dromokleides: *ARV* 1576; Diphilos, son of Melanopos: *ARV* 1574 f.

[8] Berlin, 2443. *ARV* 995, no. 118.

[9] Palermo, V 670. *ARV* 211, no. 188. Cf. also Syracuse, no number. *ARV* 219, no. 13 (*lekythos* of the Floral Nolan Group).

[10] Athens, 1923. *ARV* 995, no. 119.

[11] Athens, 1922. *ARV* 995, no. 120.

[12] *AWL* 14.

[13] Cf. C. Zervos, *L'Art en Grèce* (1934), fig. 269 (= Athens, 12789. *ARV* 750) and figs. 271–3 (= Achilles Painter, *ARV* 996, nos. 130, 141, and 132).

preserving painted details and considerable colour,[1] in the manner of the second white *lekythoi* of his contemporaries, the Timokrates Painter[2] and the Painter of Athens 1826.[3] Both painters decorated nothing but white *lekythoi* so far as we know. All of the Timokrates Painter's *lekythoi* (PLATE 25. 2, 3) have red-figure shoulders with type-I palmettes, scenes of mistress and maid or youth and woman, and *kalos* inscriptions; in general these *lekythoi* are rather like those by the Providence Painter.[4] The Painter of Athens 1826 varies his shoulder decoration: some are red-figure,[5] some are white with black Bowdoin palmettes,[6] and others have palmettes and lotus buds on white-ground (FIGURE 12*b*; PLATE 26. 1),[7] very like those of the Vouni Painter (FIGURE 12*a*; PLATE 26. 2).[8] His iconography is also sometimes funerary as is the Vouni Painter's, and there are details which recall the Inscription Painter (cf. PLATE 19) with whom he was equated by Buschor.[9] Apart from being contemporary with the Achilles Painter in his earlier period, these two painters share with him a preference for scenes of 'mistress and maid', rendered in second white, sometimes with a notable amount of polychromy.[10] There are also certain stylistic similarities. The Timokrates Painter stands close to the Pistoxenos Painter,[11] a painter of red-figure cups, whose master works are white-ground,[12] and the Pistoxenos Painter in turn stands close to the Penthesilea Painter,[13] another painter of red-figure cups who excelled in white-ground.[14] Beazley placed the Penthesilea Painter near Hermonax;[15] and Diepolder, in his monograph on the painter, saw the influence of both the Penthesilea and the Achilles Painters on the work of the Timokrates Painter.[16] The Painter of Athens 1826 comes from another tradition—probably that of the Beldam and Inscription Painters[17]—but he, too, is not unrelated to the Achilles Painter. The best example of Achillean influence is a standard cylinder in Athens (PLATE 39. 2) with IIB palmettes in dilute glaze in the Achillean manner with an Achillean meander band at the shoulder–body join.[18] The picture panel features a *stele* rendered in second white (as are those by the Painter of Athens 1826 and the Carlsruhe Painter),[19] and bound with red fillets; a man stands on one side, on the other a youth in a rosy beige *chiton*, who places his hands around the monument.

The Achilles Painter's glaze outline *lekythoi* without second white[20] differ from the earlier white *lekythoi* in several important respects: (1) although mistress and maid and youth and woman (or warrior and woman) are most common, tomb scenes appear;[21]

[1] *TWL* 12.

[2] *ARV* 743 f.; *Para* 413, 521.

[3] *ARV* 745 ff., 1668; *Para* 413.

[4] *ARV* 1582.

[5] Ibid. 746, no. 16, to p. 747, no. 28.

[6] Reserved: *ARV* 745, no. 1; white: *ARV* 745, no. 2, to p. 746, no. 3.

[7] *ARV* 746, nos. 4–15.

[8] Cf. Basle Market (M.M.). *ARV* 744.

[9] *ALP* 16 f.

[10] Cf. Bonn, 64. *ARV* 1582, no. 23.

[11] *ARV*[1] 578.

[12] *ARV* 859 ff., 1672 f., 1703; *Para* 425.

[13] *ARV* 879 ff., 1673, 1703, 1707; *Para* 428 f.

[14] New York, 07.286.36. *ARV* 890, no. 173 (*pyxis*);

New York, 28.167. *ARV* 890, no. 175 (bobbin); Athens, Kerameikos Museum. *ARV* 890, no. 176 (bobbin).

[15] *VA* 129.

[16] H. Diepolder, *Der Penthesilea-Maler* (1936), 23.

[17] *ARV* 745; *ARV*[1] 466.

[18] Athens, 13701. *ARV* 748, no. (3); cf. also Painter of Athens 12789, said to be 'related to the Inscription Painter' (*ARV*[1] 468).

[19] The Painter of Athens 1826: *ARV* 746, nos. 1 and 11; 747, no. 22 *bis*; Carlsruhe Painter: *ARV* 735, nos. 99–102.

[20] *ARV* 997, no. 146, to p. 1001, no. 206.

[21] Ibid. 998, nos. 160, 164–5, 168, 170; 999, nos. 171, 177, 185; 1000, nos. 187–8, 191–3, 200; 1001, nos. 205–6 and 212.

(2) *kalos* inscriptions are far less numerous and the names praised are different[1]—Hygiainon,[2] Axiopeithes,[3] and Alkimachos,[4] instead of Dromippos, Diphilos, and Lichas;[5] (3) the figures and patterns are rendered in glaze, diluted to a warm golden brown. By far the most common shoulder palmettes are type IIA (FIGURES 20*b*, *c*), although IIB (FIGURE 19*b*) also occurs[6] and IA at least once (FIGURE 20*a*).[7] The form of the florals scarcely differs from that of the second white *lekythoi*, but there tends to be a greater degree of elaboration—cross-overs, arc tendrils, and spandrel buds (occasionally lozenge shape (FIGURE 20*b*)).

The iconography of these *lekythoi* requires little attention; the non-funerary scenes are no different from those on the earlier second white *lekythoi* and the funerary scenes look as if they were painted by an artist who preferred his 'mistress and maid' but thought he must make some concession to the current fashion, placing a tomb between the two figures without altering their gesture or pose. Achillean men and women stand by the tomb in dignified inactivity (PLATES 34–6). The tomb is a tall slender *stele* with a simple finial, bound with ribbons and decked with the painter's characteristic tubular fillets (see pp. 50 f.).

The matt outline *lekythoi* are few in number and late.[8] Some are large, but size itself is not a sign of lateness.[9] Neither the shoulder decoration (FIGURE 19*c*) nor the iconography varies significantly from that of the glaze outline *lekythoi* without second white.

The distinctive features of the white *lekythoi* by the Achilles Painter are: standard cylinder shape, white-ground shoulder, and dilute glaze for patterns and figures. The vases are quite large (30–4 cm), well fashioned, and carefully painted. False interiors are not uncommon; and these may be recognized as Achillean by their bulbous shape (PLATE 35. 4).[10]

Our discussion of the Achilles Painter concludes with a fine white *lekythos* recently on the Basle Market, unknown to Beazley but attributed by others to the Achilles Painter (PLATE 37. 1).[11] This *lekythos* has a red-figure shoulder, which alone sets it apart from the Achilles Painter's *lekythoi*, and a single figure scene (the Achilles Painter prefers two figures) of unusual iconography: Akrisios seated at the tomb of Perseus. The vase is a good example of the importance of considering patternwork and iconography, as well as style, when trying to place a vase.

The *lekythos* is a tall cylinder of standard shape. At 42·5 cm[12] it is larger than many of the Achilles Painter's *lekythoi* but smaller than his largest, which is also one of his latest (45·4 cm).[13] The full cylinder with flat shoulder—fuller and flatter than usual for the

---

[1] With the exception of the 'early' Berlin 3970 (*ARV* 999, no. 146) on which Diphilos is praised.

[2] Hygiainon: *ARV* 1586 (used only by the Achilles Painter).

[3] Axiopeithes: *ARV* 1568.

[4] Alkimachos, son of Epichares: *ARV* 1561 f.

[5] Pistoxenos is also praised on one of the second white *lekythoi* and this is the only occurrence of the name: Havana, Lagunillas. *ARV* 995, no. 124, and p. 1607.

[6] Athens, 1818. *ARV* 998, no. 161; Athens, 12791.

ARV 999, no. 175; Oxford, 1947.24. *ARV* 1000, no. 192; New York, 07.286.42. *ARV* 1001, no. 209.

[7] New York, 06.1171. *ARV* 999, no. 179.

[8] *ARV* 1001, nos. 207–12.

[9] Cf. Boston, 13.201. *ARV* 997, no. 156 (38·3 cm; CB i. 46 f.); Athens, 1818. *ARV* 998, no. 161 (42·5 cm; Arias, Hirmer, Shefton, 364).

[10] *JHS* lxvi (1946), 11 and n. 3 (Beazley).

[11] *AK Beiheft* vii (1970), 47 ff. (I. Jucker).

[12] Ibid. 47.

[13] Boston, 08.368. *ARV* 1001, no. 210; CB i. 47 f.

Achilles Painter, even in his early period—is more at home in the decade before 450 than the decade immediately following.[1] The patternwork on the body consists of two bands of meanders alternating with pattern squares, one above (FIGURE 5*e*) and one below (FIGURE 5*f*) the figure scene. In both bands (and in the pattern band at the top of the monument) there is one meander unit per chequer square, meander alternately facing right and left so as to frame the squares. The squares of the lower band depend alternately from the upper and lower boundary line. When the Achilles Painter uses two pattern bands, as he does on occasion,[2] the lower band is regularly a running meander (less often stopt), the upper groups of meanders (two or more) alternately facing right and left, and pattern square alternately depending from the upper and lower boundary lines (FIGURE 5*d*).[3] I have not found the one meander/one square system on vases by the Achilles Painter, but it is used by the Berlin Painter and by other members of his school (FIGURE 5*b*).[4]

The great part of the figurework is executed in outlines of glaze, but some details have been added in matt, and Akrisios had a white beard.[5] The combination of glaze outlines and matt washes is not unusual, but it is unusual for some of the figurework to be outlined in glaze, some in matt.[6] The lion which crowned the monument was executed in outlines of matt and has now almost totally disappeared.[7] The iconography is without parallel on Attic vases. Vase-painters represented Akrisios but normally in the company of Danae, Perseus, or both (PLATE 37. 2).[8] The monument on which Akrisios sits is also without parallel but then there is tremendous variety in the types of monument represented on white *lekythoi*. The Achilles Painter's are simple shaft *stelai* on stepped bases, but a low broad monument on high stepped base appears on one of his late glaze outline *lekythoi*, crowned by a basket and a stool (PLATE 33. 3);[9] Danae's and Perseus' lion-crowned monument has parallels in sculpture[10] and on at least one white *lekythos*, later than ours, and decorated exclusively in matt (PLATE 36. 3).[11]

The red-figure shoulder, mentioned above, argues against an attribution to the Achilles Painter, but the scheme of palmettes, whose 'Ranken und Palmetten sind zum grössten Teil mit Relieflinien umfahren',[12] is at home in the Berlin Painter's Workshop. It is type IB with an unusual degree of elaboration; a similar arrangement appears on the shoulders of two vases of the Floral Nolan Group, a Nolan (PLATE 66. 1)[13] and a *lekythos*.[14] There are small reserved circles and v's around the central palmette and beside the handle. Similar circles and v's may be found not only on vases whose decoration is connected with the Floral Nolan Group (see p. 125) but also on the shoulder of *lekythoi*

---

[1] Cf. *AK Beiheft* vii. 47 n. 2.

[2] Double pattern bands are not as uncommon as Beazley thought in 1946 (*JHS* lxvi. 12).

[3] *JHS* xxxiv (1914), 186 (pattern delta) and 220 (two meanders per square).

[4] Ibid. xxxi (1911), 279, fig. 3 (4a, 8), 292, fig. 8 (4a), 293, fig. 9 (delta).

[5] *AK Beiheft* vii. 47.

[6] The Phiale Painter combines glaze outlines and matt on his two *lekythoi* from Oropos (*ARV* 1022, nos. 138–9).

[7] *AK Beiheft* vii. 47, 48.

[8] F. Brommer, *Vasenlisten zur griechischen Heldensage*[2] (1960), 205. Additional references are given in *Auktion* xl. 59 (no. 98).

[9] Amiens, 3057.172.33. *ARV* 1000, no. 200.

[10] Kurtz and Boardman, 135.

[11] Athens, 1938.

[12] *AK Beiheft* vii. 47 n. 3.

[13] Birmingham, 1616.85. *ARV* 218, no. 10.

[14] Syracuse. *ARV* 219, no. 13.

by the Berlin Painter's pupils, Hermonax[1] and the Providence Painter.[2] From the
Achilles Painter's own hand, the early red-figure *lekythos* from Syracuse (PLATE 34. 2)
offers the best comparison,[3] but the tendril arrangement is quite ordinary, as are the
double spirals and cross-overs; the formation of the palmettes is also different, but there
are reserved circles and v's in the field. A close parallel is supplied by a large fine red-
figure *lekythos* in Boston which Beazley placed 'close to his [Achilles Painter's] early
work' (PLATE 34. 1).[4] The shape of the palmettes is very similar and there are reserved v's
in the field. The size and the shape of the Boston *lekythos* are also comparable[5] although
the figure and patternwork on the body are not.[6]

In conclusion, the shape of the Akrisios *lekythos* suggests a date just before the middle
of the fifth century; the red-figure shoulder is without parallel on the Achilles Painter's
white *lekythoi* and its floral decoration and the pattern bands indicate some connection
with the late Berlin Painter and his followers. If the Akrisios *lekythos* is a work of the
Achilles Painter, it must be early; the painter's early work is not his best and it is precisely
the quality of the Akrisios *lekythos* that tempts us to think of him. Unless a closer parallel
can be found on a white *lekythos* by the Achilles Painter, it might be better to consider
the vase a master work of an older artist, working in the same tradition, who learned
much from the members of the Berlin Painter and his school.

13. PHIALE PAINTER

The Phiale Painter,[7] the Achilles Painter's pupil, worked in red-figure and white-ground
and like his master showed a marked preference for Nolans and *lekythoi*.[8] It is also
possible that he followed his master in the black-figure technique, taking over the painting
of the prize Panathenaic amphorae.[9] White-ground vases by the Phiale Painter are
exceedingly fine, but their place in his total *œuvre*, which is predominantly red-figure and
sometimes of high quality, should not be misjudged.

The Phiale Painter's *lekythoi* are standard cylinders of slender proportions (PLATE 38. 2);
some have false interiors.[10] The red-figure *lekythoi* have reserved shoulders with elegant
black Achillean palmettes. The elegant black palmettes follow the Achillean model
closely. Type-IIB palmettes are common.[11]—this was the Achilles Painter's favourite
for the black palmettes—but so are type-IIA[12]—an Achillean favourite for later white
lekythoi, not red-figure. The Phiale Painter adds thin spandrel buds and black dots,
rarely cross-overs—all in the Achillean manner. At least one of the red-figure *lekythoi*
has type-IA palmettes (FIGURE 21c)[13]—an uncommon scheme which the Achilles Painter

[1] Hartford, Connecticut, 30.184. *ARV* 490, no. 121.
[2] *Auktion* xl, pls. 40–1.
[3] See above, p. 43.
[4] Boston, 13.202. *ARV* 1002, no. 11.
[5] CB i. 43, no. 49 (41 cm).   [6] Cf. ibid. 45.
[7] *ARV* 1014 ff., 1678; *Para* 440 f.
[8] *ARV* 1014.
[9] K. Peters, *Studien zu den panathenäischen Preis-
amphoren* (1942), 89 f. Athens, Acropolis, 1185. *ABV*

696; Graef, pl. 69 (Peters attributes the vase to the
Phiale Painter; Beazley tentatively associates it with
the Achilles Painter.)
[10] Arias, Hirmer, Shefton, 364 f.
[11] *ARV* 1020, no. 100; 1021, nos. 104, 106, 107 *bis*,
108–9, 120.
[12] Ibid. 1021, nos. 110 *bis*, 112, 117 *bis*, 123, 123 *ter*,
123 *quater*, and *Para* 441.
[13] New York, 08.258.23. *ARV* 1021, no. 117.

also used only occasionally. The *lekythoi* with red-figure shoulders have figures and florals, not florals alone;[1] most have an enclosed palmette[2] with added tendrils and thin closed buds on either side of the figure composition. These *lekythoi* with red-figure shoulders do not have red-figure scenes on the body; they are black-bodied *lekythoi* (see p. 126). The iconography of the red-figure *lekythoi*, whose proveniences are predominantly Sicilian, is very like that of the painter's Nolan amphorae—scenes of pursuit, departure, arming, and two women. None of the red-figure *lekythoi* has a tomb scene.

White *lekythoi* by the Phiale Painter are few in number. Five have been attributed to him and all have Attic proveniences: two are said to have been found in Athens;[3] two were found in a grave at Oropos (see p. 137);[4] one was found not long ago in a sarcophagus burial at Anavyssos (see pp. 53 f.).[5] There is little difference in size or shape and the pattern-work, executed in dilute glaze, is Achillean. The meander band is regularly groups of stopt meanders alternating with saltire squares.[6] The palmettes are IIa (FIGURE 22c), the Achilles Painter's favourite for glaze outline without second white and matt outline *lekythoi*. There are thin spandrel buds, added spiral tendrils, and cross-overs; alternate petals are rendered in matt paint.[7] The outlines of the figures are rendered in glaze and matt and there is an important new use of matt—sketched in beside outlines of glaze, filling in the contours.[8]

Four of the white *lekythoi* have tomb scenes; the fifth has an Achillean mistress and maid. The iconography of three of the four tomb scenes is straightforward: two figures at the tomb, offering grief, music, or fillets to the dead. The tombs are tall shafts, bound with fillets, but the Achillean tubular fillets do not appear nor are the monuments exactly like those of the Achilles Painter. The most significant departure from the Achillean form is the round mound, crowned by a *loutrophoros*, bound with ribbons, on the *lekythos* from Anavyssos.[9] Significant, too, is the open display of grief on this vase. One of the Oropos *lekythoi* (PLATE 38. 2)[10] offers another point of contrast to the Achillean mood of noble detachment: a woman sitting beside a tomb rests her head on her hand, deeply absorbed in her own grief. This picture of introspection, like the new freer use of matt paint, anticipates the *lekythoi* of the late fifth century.

The iconography of the fourth *lekythos*,[11] also from Oropos, stands somewhat apart: Hermes has come to collect the dead person, not to the Styx in the company of Charon, but to the grave in the company of a woman who, like Alkestis, realizes that the time has come to put on the raiment of Death.[12] The mythological ministers of Death do not appear on white *lekythoi* by the Achilles Painter.[13] This vase, so often illustrated, is as untypical of *lekythoi* of the 430s as the Achilles Painter's Helicon *lekythos*[14] is of those of the 440s: in

---

[1] *ARV* 1022, nos. 133–7.

[2] The petals sometimes extend outside the enclosing tendril. Cf., for example, Lucerne Market. *ARV* 1022, no. 134.

[3] Berlin, 2449. *ARV* 1022, no. 140; Berlin, 2450. *ARV* 1022, no. 141.

[4] Munich, 2797. *ARV* 1022, no. 138; Munich, 2798. *ARV* 1022, no. 139.

[5] Athens, 19355. *ARV* 1022, no. 139 *bis*.

[6] Berlin, 2449 ('mistress and maid') has stopt

meanders without pattern squares.

[7] Athens, 19355. *AJA* lxv (1961), pl. 98. 3; Munich, 2797. Arias, Hirmer, Shefton, 365.

[8] *GP* 148.

[9] See above, n. 7.

[10] Munich, 2798.

[11] Munich, 2797.

[12] Euripides, *Alkestis*, 158 f.

[13] Hermes appears on Athens 1940 (*ARV* 1004, no. 41, 'manner').

[14] Munich (ex Lugano, Schoen, 81). *ARV* 997. no. 155.

the pursuit of beauty both painters have been led beyond the established iconography. The compositional device of placing two figures in a rocky landscape appealed to the Phiale Painter and his interest in the representation of landscape is notable.[1] The Achilles Painter's Muse sits primly, somewhat stiffly, on a Helicon whose rockiness is suggested rather than clearly indicated; the Phiale Painter's figures assume relaxed poses in a realistically rocky landscape. Figures seated amidst rocks remind us of Polygnotos, and the gesture of the Phiale Painter's woman seated on a rock, hand to chin in troubled thought, on the other Oropos *lekythos*, is also Polygnotan.[2] The Hermes *lekythos* is one of a small number of white *lekythoi* whose iconography conflates two types of scenes[3]— the realistic rendering of contemporary practice in death and burial and the mythological ministers of Death. The occasional conflation of the two scenes is understandable artistically if not iconographically. Hermes confronts a woman at the grave on another white *lekythos* whose patternwork is Achillean (PLATE 38. 1).[4] Beazley placed the vase in the manner of the Achilles Painter adding that it might be a work of the Phiale Painter, along with the second which is said to have been found in the Oropos grave with the Phiale Painter's two white *lekythoi*.[5] The tomb monument of the second Hermes *lekythos* is a mound like that of the Phiale Painter's Anavyssos *lekythos*. The shoulder decoration —IIA palmettes in dilute glaze with cross-overs, spandrel buds, and added spirals (FIGURE 22*a*)—is more Achillean than that of the second *lekythos*, in New York (FIGURE 22*b*), which introduces matt for the meander band at the shoulder join and for a few petals of the IIA palmettes. The same matt paint is used for the fillets around the tomb and for its finial.

14. OTHER ACHILLEAN WHITE *LEKYTHOI*

The Achilles Painter's model was followed in white-ground as it was in red-figure.[6] Among the Achillean white *lekythoi* which cannot be attributed to the master or to his pupil, there are few which display characteristic Achillean details absent from the Phiale Painter's white *lekythoi*: tubular fillets in the picture panel and dots or circles in the shoulder composition.

Fillets or *tainiai* are not specifically funerary; they have a general cult significance, setting off the object which they adorn from a common to a special use.[7] Their importance in Attic funerary rites is well known: fillets were painted on tombstones (PLATE 46. 3)[8] and rendered in relief,[9] as a lasting token of respect to the dead. On *lekythoi* they are carried by women or they hang suspended from the tombstone. Two different types of fillet are represented: flat strips of coloured material and tubular fillets with small

[1] A rocky landscape is indicated on the two white *lekythoi* in Munich; compare also the white crater in the Vatican (*ARV* 1017, no. 54; *GP* 123 ff.).

[2] *GP* 134, 149.

[3] Cf. Oxford, 1956.14. *ARV* 754, no. 13 (Tymbos Group); Athens 18813 (unattributed).

[4] Athens, 1940. *ARV* 1026, no. 1.

[5] New York, 22.53. *ARV* 1026, no. 2.

[6] *ARV* 1008 (vii).

[7] Kurtz and Boardman, 104 f., 123 f., 148, 167.

[8] Cf. Conze, no. 1324*a*, pl. 279; nos. 1325–7 and 1333, pl. 280.

[9] Athens, EM 6197. *AM* lxxxv (1970), pl. 45. 3.

dark dots at regular intervals on the light surface and dark terminal strings (PLATES 35.3, 36.1). The latter are substantial enough to lie like a wreath on the tomb's base, when secured in a circular position. The flat fillets are very common on white *lekythoi*, but the tubular fillets are a favourite of the Achilles Painter, and are not common on white *lekythoi* by other painters.[1] They appear on a small number of the Thanatos Painter's white *lekythoi*,[2] on a *lekythos* in Toronto near the Thanatos and Sabouroff Painters (PLATE 29. 4),[3] on an unattributed *lekythos* in Athens whose white-ground shoulder bears the Sabouroff Painter's distinctive palmettes and lotus buds (PLATE 28. 3),[4] on an unattributed Achillean *lekythos* in New York (PLATE 39. 1), easily remembered for the hare which surmounts the tombstone,[5] and on another Achillean *lekythos* in New York, attributed to the Painter of Athens 1943.[6] Only four vases (all white *lekythoi*) are known by this painter who is related to the Phiale Painter and to the Clio Painter, to whom the Phiale Painter himself is closely related.[7] His New York *lekythos* has IIA palmettes, rendered in dilute glaze with cross-overs, added spirals, and thin closed buds. The figures are also outlined in glaze.

The iconography of the other three *lekythoi* attributed to the Painter of Athens 1943 is not explicitly funerary, although the pose of the figures, their gestures, and offerings would not be inappropriate in this context.[8] Figures and patterns are rendered in dilute glaze. The shoulder palmettes are IIB and there are dots of glaze paint or circles outlined in glaze in the field.

Dots are not unusual in palmette compositions; in black-figure they are rendered in solid black, in red-figure they are reserved. On *lekythoi* with Bowdoin palmettes they are common. The Achilles Painter regularly adds them to the elegant black palmettes on reserved shoulders of red-figure *lekythoi* and to the shoulders of his early second white *lekythoi*, whose shoulder palmettes are sometimes very like the elegant florals of his red-figure *lekythoi*. Glaze dots are less common on his later white *lekythoi* but they are a

---

[1] *JHS* lxvi (1946), 11; CB i. 49. Fillets similar to those by the Achilles Painter appear on some *lekythoi* by the Timokrates Painter (Athens, 1929. *ARV* 743, no. 5) and by the Painter of Athens 1826 (Athens, 1845. *ARV* 746, no. 16) whose relation to the Achilles Painter is discussed above on pp. 44 f. Fillets like the Achilles Painter's, but less close to his model than those by the Timokrates Painter and the Painter of Athens 1826, appear on some *lekythoi* by the Quadrate Painter (Munich, 8499. *ARV* 1237, no. 6). See also the following note.

[2] New York, Baker. *ARV* 1228, no. 1; Athens, 1797. *ARV* 1229, no. 14; Athens, 1822. *ARV* 1229, no. 22. Cf. also the Bosanquet Painter's *lekythos* in New York (23.160.38. *ARV* 1227, no. 5. PLATE 30. 1) with similar fillets.

[3] Toronto, 929.22.7. *ARV* 855 (634).

[4] Athens, 16422.

[5] New York, 06.1075 (meander is matt, as are some petals of the palmettes). For the monument with an animal, cf. Conze, no. 66, pl. 28 (dog).

[6] New York, 34.155. *ARV* 1082, no. 4.

[7] The close relation between the Phiale and Clio Painters is illustrated by a white calyx-crater in the Vatican (*ARV* 1017, no. 54) which Beazley initially placed between the Eupolis and Clio Painters (*ARV*¹ 671). The Eupolis Painter in his earlier period is related to the Villa Giulia Painter and his group (*ARV* 634, 1072), producers of white calyx-craters. Beazley considered the possibility that the Eupolis Painter was the Clio Painter in his early years (*ARV*¹ 671), noting the resemblance between later vases by the Eupolis Painter and vases by the Phiale Painter (*ARV* 670), and that the Painter of Athens 1943 was the Clio Painter at an early period (*ARV*¹ 670). In *ARV* the painters are, for the most part, differentiated. The Clio Painter's *lekythoi* are given to the Painter of Athens 1943. The Phiale and Clio Painters are also related through their *pelikai*, which belong to the Class of the Achilles Painter's *Pelikai* (*ARV* 1676).

[8] Athens, 1943. *ARV* 1082, no. 1; Athens, 1945. *ARV* 1082, no. 2; Boston, 95.65. *ARV* 1082, no. 3.

notable feature of a *lekythos* in Oxford (PLATE 35. 3) and of a small group of *lekythoi*[1] which Beazley attributed to the Achilles Painter with the note: 'they are very close to the painter, but might be careful copies or imitations of him by an artist of the same character as the Bird Painter.'[2] All feature 'mistress and maid' except one[3] whose iconography is funerary: a youth and a woman stand at the tomb, a slender *stele* with palmette and volute *anthemion*, Achillean tubular fillet, and a prominently placed *plemochoe*.[4] The most notable iconographical detail is the *eidolon* which flies about the tomb. *Eidola* are popular with the Sabouroff Painter and with some later painters of white *lekythoi* but not with the Achilles Painter. I know of one other *eidolon* by the painter, on a white *lekythos* in London with a very similar scene (PLATE 36. 1),[5] but a late matt outline *lekythos*, in the manner of the painter, features an *eidolon* in the same context,[6] as does a *lekythos* by the Bird Painter (PLATE 39. 3),[7] with whom Beazley associated the group.

The Bird Painter's *lekythos* features a simple shaft *stele* on a two-step base. A youth leans against the tomb, placing his right hand on it in a meaningful gesture, not unlike that of a youth leading his horse to a *stele* on a red-figure *lekythos* in the manner of the Achilles Painter ('Late School', PLATE 34. 3).[8] On a white *lekythos* in the manner of the Bird Painter in Oxford (PLATE 39. 4)[9] an *eidolon* flies around the anthemion of a *stele* and one of the youths at the tomb performs a gesture of personal grief: he covers his face to conceal his emotion. This gesture is found on two unattributed *lekythoi*,[10] and on both of these the *stele* is a simple shaft on a step base, decorated only with the distinctively Achillean tubular fillets. A third unattributed *lekythos*[11] with Achillean patterns features a youth performing the same gestures at a tomb. There are no Achillean fillets, but there is an *eidolon*.

15. BIRD GROUP

This section and the following are devoted to two contemporaries, painting *lekythoi* in a not unrelated style, quite possibly in the same workshop[12]—the Painter of Munich 2335[13] and the Bird Painter.[14] The former painted red-figure vases in quantity, and their quality is often so low[15] that we wonder how one man could have painted both them and the fine white *lekythoi* attributed to him. The Bird Painter is known only for his white *lekythoi*, and these belong to a larger group, stylistically related and not always attributable to specific artists—the Bird Group.[16] The Bird Painter must have been slightly younger than the Painter of Munich 2335;[17] if we consider his work first, it is because here, and in the

[1] *ARV* 999, nos. 172–7; *JHS* lxvi. 12 (with references to other examples).

[2] *ARV* 999.

[3] Once Zürich, Ruesch. *ARV* 999, no. 177.

[4] *JHS* lxvi. 12; CB i. 49 f.

[5] London, D 54. *ARV* 1000, no. 193.

[6] Frankfurt, Univ. *ARV* 1003, no. 32.

[7] Marburg, 1016. *ARV* 1233, no. 19.

[8] Athens, 12133. *ARV* 1003, no. 20.

[9] Oxford, 544. *ARV* 1234, no. 21.

[10] Cambridge, 36.1937. Athens, Acropolis (unpublished).

[11] Cambridge *CV* ii, Ricketts and Shannon Collection, pl. 15, no. 3.

[12] *ARV* 1161.

[13] *ARV*[1] 779 ff., 964; *ARV* 1161 ff., 1685, 1703, 1707; *Para* 458 f.

[14] *ARV*[1] 811; *ARV* 1231 ff., 1687 f., *Para* 467.

[15] *ARV*[1] 779.

[16] *ARV* 1231.

[17] *AWL* 22; *ARV*[1] 811.

work of other members of the Bird Group, there are links with artists of the preceding generation—the Achilles and Sabouroff Painters. The Painter of Munich 2335 is not without such a heritage,[1] but it is his legacy in the future, in the work of the Woman Painter, that is, in a way, more notable.

The Bird Painter is the principal artist of the Bird Group; Beazley recognized others —among them the Carlsberg Painter[2] and the Painter of Athens 1934[3]—but he also pointed out that the personalities of these artists are often far from clear.[4] Bird *lekythoi* are, on the whole, modest in size and not very ambitious in their style of decoration; outlines tend to be matt, often fine and very pale; figures tend to be small, rather delicate, and child-like (PLATES 39. 3, 40. 2). Proveniences of the vases, when known, are Attic or Eretrian; iconography, without exception, is funerary, most often two figures at a tomb, one of which may be a child. There is little or no emotion in these scenes; they are Achillean in their quiet and calm.

The Bird Painter's shoulder palmettes are regularly matt, as is the meander, even when the figure outlines are glaze. At the neck–shoulder join there is either a band of eggs or a series of lines. With the exception of two important groups Bird palmettes are IIA without cross-overs or spandrel buds (FIGURE 23a). The heart of the palmette is an arc or a 'rounded triangle' and alternate petals are sometimes coloured.[5] The two exceptions to this simplified IIA scheme are the Achillean *lekythoi* with which we concluded the preceding section, and the *lekythoi* from a recently excavated sarcophagus burial at Anavyssos.

The Achillean *lekythoi* are attributed to the Achilles Painter himself. I take Beazley's suggestion that they 'might be careful copies or imitations of him by an artist of the same character as the Bird Painter' to mean: pattern- and figurework are Achillean, and the style is close, but something peculiarly Achillean is missing. There is his quiet and calm, and some of the figures are fine enough, but they are less impressive, more insubstantial —not unlike the Bird Painter's child-like people. The shoulder decoration, described in the preceding section for the dots or circles which appear on some, is executed in dilute glaze, in the Achillean manner. There are cross-overs, added tendrils, and thin closed buds—in the manner of the Achilles Painter's more elaborate shoulders.

The Anavyssos *lekythoi* have not yet been published. The following account is based entirely on the material on display in the National Museum, Athens, and on the attributions listed in *ARV* and *Paralipomena*. Two sarcophagi with white *lekythoi* have been found in recent years at Anavyssos, one in 1960,[6] the other a few years before.[7] The contents of the burials and their contexts are unknown to me. One of the sarcophagi had two *lekythoi* by the Bird Painter,[8] one by the Painter of Munich 2335,[9] and the Phiale Painter's *lekythos*[10] described earlier. The three painters were active around 430 and are not unrelated. The Phiale Painter is the Achilles Painter's acknowledged pupil, but the

[1] *AWL* 20 ('follower of the Thanatos Painter').
[2] *ARV* 1235 f.
[3] Ibid. 1236.
[4] Ibid. 1231.
[5] Harvard, 1925.30.54. *ARV* 1232, no. 2.
[6] *AJA* lxv (1961), 300.

[7] *ARV* 1687 f.; *AJA* lxv. 300.
[8] Athens, 19357. *ARV* 1232, no. 7; Athens, 19356. *ARV* 1232, no. 7 *bis*.
[9] Athens, 19354. *ARV* 1168, no. 131 *bis*.
[10] Athens, 19355. *ARV* 1022, no. 139 *bis*.

Painter of Munich 2335 also has Achillean associations,[1] and he stands close to the Thanatos Painter,[2] who is himself influenced by the Achilles Painter. The Bird Painter's relation to the Achilles Painter is established by the above-mentioned group of *lekythoi*, and his connection with the Painter of Munich 2335 is close: the white *lekythoi* of both look as if they were produced in the same workshop.

The second sarcophagus was exceptionally rich in *lekythoi*, white cylinders with figures[3] or patterns[4] and black squat *lekythoi*, red-figure[5] or undecorated.[6] Initially Beazley attributed all of these white *lekythoi* to the Bird Painter: 'they appear to me to be by the Bird Painter—unusually fine work of his later period, setting him in a new light',[7] but in *Paralipomena* the homogeneity of the group is questioned, and the large rather fine 19333 is set apart: '19333 may not be by the same hand as the rest; it somewhat recalls the Achilles Painter.'[8]

The influence of the Achilles Painter is understandable, in view of the Bird Painter's relation to him and to painters of his circle. 19333 is indeed like some vases by the Achilles Painter[9]—especially in the monumental quality of the figures, and the pose of the woman bearing the bundle of stuff, a motif found on two of the Achillean-Bird *lekythoi*[10]—but the acanthus leaves on the tomb[11] and the style of the palmettes on the shoulder[12] are what we should expect from later artists like the Woman (cf. PLATE 44. 1) and Quadrate Painters or the members of the Reed Group.[13] The shoulder of 19333 is more or less representative of the *lekythoi* from the second sarcophagus: type-IIA palmettes with arc-shaped hearts, dotted in red, and alternate petals in red (FIGURE 24b). The most characteristic feature of the shoulder decoration is the rendering of the spandrel buds: instead of the usual single stroke, representing a thin closed bud, there are two or more strokes, one of them in red. Polychrome, partly open, buds are very common on *lekythoi* of the Reed Group (FIGURE 24c) and the shoulder decoration of these *lekythoi* is, in fact, characteristically 'Reed', as is the meander band (FIGURE 5h). For the relation of these *lekythoi* to the Reed Workshop see pp. 58 f.; 19333 has an egg band at the neck-ring; some of the other *lekythoi* have a series of lines,[14] and one has a zigzag pattern.[15] The iconography of the Anavyssos *lekythoi* is exceptionally interesting—some of the scenes are without close parallel—and a detailed publication would be most welcome.

So much for the influence of the Achilles Painter on Bird *lekythoi*. The Sabouroff Painter's influence is best illustrated by the Painter of Cambridge 28.2,[16] whose four attributed *lekythoi* (with matt for figures and patterns, IIA palmettes with spiral tendrils

[1] Cf. *ARV* 1162, nos. 14–15; 1166, nos. 102–3; 1169 and 1676 f.

[2] *ARV*[1] 810.   [3] *ARV* 1687 f.

[4] Displayed with the *lekythoi* in the National Museum are the pattern *lekythoi*—Athens, 19345 and 19346—the squat red-figure *lekythos* of note 5 and the black-painted squat *lekythos* of note 6.

[5] Athens, 19348.   [6] Athens, 19350.

[7] *ARV* 1687.   [8] *Para* 467.

[9] Athens, 19333. *ARV* 1687, no. 1.

[10] Athens, 12791. *ARV* 999, no. 175; Berkeley, 8. 36. *ARV* 999, no. 176.

[11] Cf. Athens, 1955. *ARV* 1372, no. 4; Oxford, 574.

ARV 1373, no. 8 (manner).

[12] Polychrome, partly open buds are not common on earlier white *lekythoi*, but cf. Boston, 00.359. *ARV* 1229, no. 23.

[13] There are statuesque figures at acanthus-crowned tombs on some *lekythoi* by the Woman Painter, decorated in matt outlines, but the rendering of emotion is an important feature of these vases and this is absent from most of the Anavyssos *lekythoi*.

[14] Athens, 19341. *ARV* 1688, no. 8; Athens, 19338. *ARV* 1688, no. 11.

[15] Athens, 19336. *ARV* 1688, no. 6.

[16] *ARV* 855; *ARV*[1] 566.

tightly coiled in the Sabouroff Painter's manner) 'are very close to the Sabouroff Painter and might even be very late works from his own hand'.[1] They are very like the Sabouroff Painter's in shape, pattern, and simple two-figure composition (PLATE 40. 1), but Beazley preferred to keep them separate as a 'continuation of the Sabouroff Painter's white *lekythoi* in the period of the Bird Painter and in touch with him'.[2] The Sabouroff Painter, in his simplicity, can achieve a degree of grandeur[3] which is totally lacking in the unpretentious work of his follower. The Painter of Cambridge 28.2's people would be quite at home in the child-like world of the Bird Painter—but then so would some of the people of the Painter of Munich 2335[4]—and this is what I take Beazley to mean when he says both artists are 'akin' to the Bird Painter.[5]

The relationship between the Bird Painter and the Painter of Munich 2335 is most easily seen in the work of the Painter of Athens 1934.[6] Two *lekythoi* have been attributed to him[7] and two others have been compared.[8] All have matt outlines; the shoulder palmettes, when preserved, are matt, IIA, with spiral tendrils tightly coiled.[9] The scenes are funerary and the tombs are simple shafts. The figures, like the Bird Painter's, are 'little people' wearing opaque red cloaks, or nothing at all, the original matt colour having faded.[10] On both of the painter's attributed vases and on one of his probable vases (PLATE 41. 2)[11] one of the female figures performs a gesture of lament, twice on her knees (PLATE 40. 4).[12] The fourth vase features man and youth at the tomb in the usual Bird manner (PLATE 41. 1).[13] An expression of emotion—a display of grief—is not common on Bird *lekythoi* (cf. PLATE 39.3)[14] but is a prominent feature of several of the Anavyssos *lekythoi*.[15] The Painter of Munich 2335 is especially interested in the rendering of emotion, as is his follower, the Woman Painter. The New York *lekythos*, with woman mourning on her knees, has a false interior, and the position of the vent hole on the shoulder is like that of *lekythoi* with false interiors by the Painter of Munich 2335.

16. PAINTER OF MUNICH 2335

The Painter of Munich 2335[16] is a complicated artist; his white-ground vases (all *lekythoi*) are good, often very good indeed, but his red-figure vases, which exist in quantity, are

[1] *ARV* 855.   [2] Ibid.

[3] Compare the unattributed *lekythos* in Berlin (1941) illustrated by Riezler, pl. 41.

[4] Cf. Athens, *CV* i. III Jd, pl. 8. 1–2 (Painter of Cambridge 28.2); pl. 8. 3–4 (Painter of Athens 1934); pl. 8. 5–8 (Painter of Munich 2335).

[5] *ARV* 1232.   [6] Ibid. 1236; cf. *ARV*[1] 814.

[7] Athens, 1934. *ARV* 1236, no. 1; Athens, 12138 (b?). *ARV* 1236, no. 2.

[8] Berlin, 2454. *ARV* 1236; New York, 22.139.10. *ARV* 1236 (a).

[9] New York, 22.139.10.

[10] Cf. Athens, 2019. *ARV* 848, no. 216 (Sabouroff Painter); Athens, 12138. *ARV* 855, no. 1, and Lucerne, Roesli. *ARV* 855 n. 2 (Painter of Cambridge 28.2); Athens, 1769. *ARV* 1232, no. 9 (Bird Painter); Ny Carlsberg, 2780. *ARV* 1235, no. 4, and Athens, 1944. *ARV* 1235, no. 9 (Carlsberg Painter); Athens, 1933. *ARV* 1168, no. 135, and Athens, 1931. *ARV* 1168, no. 139 (Painter of Munich 2335); Athens, 1934. *ARV* 1236, no. 1, and Athens, 12138 (b?). *ARV* 1236, no. 2 (Painter of Athens 1934).

[11] New York, 22.139.10.

[12] Athens, 1934 and 12138 (b?).

[13] Berlin, 2454.

[14] Marburg, 1016. *ARV* 1233, no. 19; compare the Achillean red-figure *lekythos*, Athens 12133 (*ARV* 1003, no. 20).

[15] *ARV* 1687, no. 2 (man); 1688, no. 5 (woman) and no. 11 (woman kneeling).

[16] *ARV*[1] 779 ff., 964; *ARV* 1161 ff., 1685, 1703, 1707; *Para* 458 f.

sometimes very bad.[1] Beazley considered the white *lekythoi* (1) close to the late work of the Thanatos Painter,[2] and (2) 'akin' to the Bird Painter's, probably produced in the same workshop.[3] We have already drawn attention to the Bird Painter in this connection; the Thanatos Painter's connection is more direct:

His [the Thanatos Painter's] follower, however, worked chiefly in red-figure, if, as it seems, he is the same as the red-figure artist . . . the Painter of Munich 2335. His best works are his white *lekythoi*, which belong to the thirties and twenties of the fifth century. It is the same grave beauty as in the late vases of the Thanatos Painter, but tenderer and sweeter.[4]

No red-figure *lekythoi* are known by him. All of his white *lekythoi* have matt outlines and matt is used for the patternwork. Palmettes are IIA (FIGURE 23*b*) with petals sometimes rendered in a different colour from the tendrils,[5] and some of the petals in the more fugitive matt colours have entirely disappeared.[6] Several of the 2335 *lekythoi* have false interiors.[7] The proveniences are Attic or Euboean,[8] and the iconography, with one exception, is funerary. The exception is one of the many scenes from child life which now become acceptable in Greek art: mother, attended by maid, holds out a bird to a small boy-child.[9] A child is also the centre of attention on one of the painter's most appealing *lekythoi*: go-cart in hand, a little boy stands on a hillock to which Charon has drawn his bark; he beckons to his mother but she cannot help (PLATE 42. 1).[10] It is the poignancy of the scene, not its technical excellence, that is most remarkable; other painters of white *lekythoi* draw better, but few with such feeling. This interest in the rendering of emotion distinguishes 2335 *lekythoi* from those of the Bird Group. Compare the 2335 *lekythos* from one of the Anavyssos sarcophagi: a cemetery scene—man and woman at the grave.[11] The man is conventional enough, but the pose of the woman—bent over, head bowed, one hand laid upon the tomb, the other holding an *alabastron*, as offering to the dead—is new. It is a simple and very effective picture of intense grief, nobly expressed. Compare the pose of the woman seated in Charon's boat on another of the painter's *lekythoi*.[12] A few of his women mourn more openly, falling to the ground, hands to head in the traditional gesture of lament.[13] Open expressions of grief are not new—compare the Sabouroff Painter's *prothesis* scenes (PLATE 29. 1, 2)[14] and the Phiale Painter's Anavyssos *lekythos*[15]—but in the last quarter of the fifth century they become more numerous and more intense as more attention is given to the psychological content of art. The Woman Painter is not the only later painter of *lekythoi* to show an interest in this new art, but his work is often fine, and it is closely related to the Painter of Munich 2335, and to the Thanatos Painter; Beazley thought that there might have been an actual connection between the Thanatos Painter and the Woman Painter.[16]

[1] *ARV*[1] 779.   [2] *Ibid.* 810.   [3] *ARV* 1232.
[4] *AWL* 20.
[5] New York, 99.13.3. *ARV* 1169, no. 140.
[6] New York, 09.221.44. *ARV* 1168, no. 128.
[7] New York, 99.13.3 and 09.221.44; New York, 34.32.2. *ARV* 1168, no. 131.
[8] Copenhagen, 6590. *ARV* 1169, no. 142 (Chalkis).
[9] Athens, 1947. *ARV* 1168, no. 133.
[10] New York, 09.221.44.

[11] Athens, 19354. *ARV* 1168, no. 131 *bis*.
[12] Cracow, 1251. *ARV* 1168, no. 127.
[13] Athens, 1930. *ARV* 1168, no. 137; Oxford, 1966.925. *ARV* 1168, no. 138, and *Para* 459; *Select* pl. 53, no. 371.
[14] *ARV* 846, no. 190; 851, no. 273 *bis*.
[15] Athens, 19335. *ARV* 1022, no. 139 *bis*.
[16] *AWL* 23.

17. WOMAN PAINTER

The Woman Painter,[1] named from the beauty of his women, and their position of prominence in his art, painted nothing but white *lekythoi*. His patternwork requires little attention: IIA palmettes with rounded or angular hearts and alternate petals coloured (FIGURE 23*c*). At the neck-ring there is an egg band[2] or a line.[3] A characteristic feature of the Woman Painter's shoulder palmettes is simplicity—there are no cross-overs, no spandrel buds, no added spiral tendrils, and the tendrils have full round flowing curves. Compare the elaborate shoulder palmettes of his contemporary, the Quadrate Painter (FIGURE 24*a*).[4] The meander is regularly unbroken by pattern squares. Compare the Quadrate Painter's meanders, with the characteristic pattern square, from which the painter takes his name.[5] Matt paint is used for the pattern- and figurework, in a variety of colours—greens, blues, and reds are popular for the former, reds, pinks, mauves, and violet-blues for the latter. The iconography is funerary; the proveniences are Attic or Eretrian, with one possible exception—a vase which is said 'possibly' to have come from Melos.[6] The figure style has much in common with that of the Painter of Munich 2335.[7] A *lekythos* in the British Museum with warrior, woman, and child illustrates the relationship (PLATE 43. 1).[8] Beazley considered the vase an 'excellent work by the Painter of Munich 2335 in the spirit of the Woman Painter'.[9] The Painter of Munich 2335's figures are usually not so slight as the Bird Painter's, nor are they as massive as the Woman Painter's. Like the Bird Painter, the Painter of Munich 2335 prefers uncomplicated two-figure compositions. The Woman Painter's figures, on the other hand, are monumental—two, often three, or more, linked in a sequence of grand gestures.[10] The British Museum *lekythos* has the 'bigness' of the Woman Painter and the tenderness of the Painter of Munich 2335. Several of the Woman Painter's scenes are compositionally very like those of the Painter of Munich 2335: compare the pose of the woman seated at the tomb on Athens 1956 (PLATE 44. 1)[11] with that of the woman of the Anavyssos *lekythos*,[12] the woman offering a libation at the tomb on a *lekythos* in Carlsruhe (PLATE 43. 2)[13] with a 2335 *lekythos* in New York (PLATE 42. 2),[14] the women kneeling on several of the Woman Painter's *lekythoi*[15] with those of the 2335 *lekythos* in Oxford.[16] When Beazley wrote 'there is passion and grandeur in the best of the late *lekythoi*',[17] he had the Woman Painter's vases in mind.

[1] *ARV*[1] 818 ff.; *ARV* 1371 ff.; *Para* 485.

[2] London, D 70. *ARV* 1371, no. 1.

[3] Berlin, 3372. *ARV* 1371, no. 2.

[4] Cf. London, 1928.2–13.3. *ARV* 1240, no. 4.

[5] *ARV* 1236.

[6] Mannheim, 14. *ARV* 1372, no. 12 ('from Melos?'); *CV* i, p. 45; *AA* 1890, 153 ('aus Athen').

[7] *ARV* 1371.

[8] London, 1928.2–13.2. *ARV* 1169, no. (84). Cf. London, 1907.7–10.10. *ARV* 1227, no. 10 (Bosanquet Painter), and Los Angeles, A 5933.50.24. *ARV* 1242, no. 8 (Painter of the New York Hypnos, sometimes recalling the Bosanquet Painter).

[9] *ARV* 1169.

[10] Cf. *TWL* pls. 7–8.

[11] Athens, 1956. *ARV* 1372, no. 3.

[12] Athens, 19354. *ARV* 1168, no. 131 *bis*.

[13] Carlsruhe, 234. *ARV* 1372, no. 17.

[14] New York, 34.32.2. *ARV* 1168, no. 131. For the tomb, cf. New York Market. *ARV* 1227, no. 8 (Bosanquet Painter); Boston, 00.359. *ARV* 1229, no. 23 (Thanatos Painter), and Boston, 01.8080. *ARV* 1231 (Thanatos Painter, near).

[15] Athens, 1955. *ARV* 1372, no. 4; Louvre, CA 1329. *ARV* 1372, no. 20; Athens, 12534. *ARV* 1373, no. 21; Athens, 1795. *ARV* 1373, no. 22.

[16] Oxford, 1966.925. *ARV* 1168, no. 138, and *Para* 459.

[17] *AWL* 23.

18. REED WORKSHOP: REED PAINTER AND GROUP R

Lekythoi of the Reed Workshop include those by the Reed Painter himself, and those of Group R.[1] The workshop must have been one of the most influential in the last decades of the fifth century—at least a number of *lekythoi* attributed to different hands are connected with it—among them the Anavyssos *lekythoi*. The Reed shoulder palmettes and meander band of the Anavyssos *lekythoi* do not to my knowledge appear on *lekythoi* by the Bird Painter himself. His palmettes have been described; his meander, running or stopt, does not have pattern squares.[2] I know of one exception, a *lekythos* in a private collection in Basle,[3] with broken running meanders alternating with saltire squares; the pattern square is enclosed by the running meander. The same pattern occurs on *lekythoi* by the Carlsberg Painter,[4] the Woman Painter (and his manner),[5] at least one *lekythos* of Group R (PLATE 50. 1),[6] and two *lekythoi* of the Anavyssos Group (Athens 19333 (FIGURE 5g) and 19334). The Achilles Painter had alternated meanders and pattern squares, but in a different scheme: groups of stopt meanders alternately facing right and left and pattern squares depending alternately from the upper and lower horizontal lines bounding the pattern (FIGURE 5d).[7] The 19333 pattern is, in fact, much nearer the Reed (FIGURE 5h) form than the Achillean, differing principally in the formation of the pattern square, which is not enclosed by the broken running meander: next to the closing vertical of the meander unit comes a vertical line framing one side of the pattern square. All of the Anavyssos *lekythoi* (from the second grave), with the two stated exceptions and 19336 which has been reworked,[8] reproduce this distinctive Reed pattern. On the basis of patternwork, therefore, the Anavyssos *lekythoi* look as if they were produced in connection with the Reed Workshop. Nor is this unlikely, given the points of similarity between Bird and Reed *lekythoi* and the relationship between these painters and the Woman Painter. The Bird Painter specialized in small *lekythoi* with simple two-figure compositions; the Reed Painter decorated many small two-figure *lekythoi*. The Bird Painter's work is, on the whole, finer and more delicate than that of the Reed Painter's smaller *lekythoi*, but the two are sometimes not far apart in spirit, and somewhere near them stands the Anavyssos Group—more Bird than Reed in figurework, but unquestionably Reed in pattern, with a touch of something grander. Beazley looked to the Achillean following,[9] but the Woman Painter is nearer in time and he is not without Reed affiliations (see below). We think of the Woman Painter as a painter of large *lekythoi* with

[1] *ARV*[1] 823 ff., 965 ff.; *ARV* 1376 ff., 1692; *Para* 485 f.

[2] Basle, Hagemann. *ARV* 1232, no. 7 *qu.* Marburg, no number. *ARV* 1233, no. 19 (pattern squares); Harvard, 1925.30.54; *ARV* 1232, no. 2; Minneapolis, no number. *ARV* 1232, no. 8 (running meander); Bowdoin, 23.26. *ARV* 1232, no. 5; Athens, 19357. *ARV* 1232, no. 7; *ARV* 1232, no. 8 *bis*; Philadelphia, L 64.186. *ARV* 1232, no. 10 (stopt meander).

[3] Basle, Hagemann. *ARV* 1232, no. 4; *Auktion* xvi, pl. 37, no. 150.

[4] Greifswald, 365. *ARV* 1235, no. 1; Canberra, fr.

ARV 1235, no. 3; Munich (ex Lugano, Schoen, 81). *ARV* 1235, no. 10; Boston, Oddy. *ARV* 1235, no. 1.

[5] Lyons, no number. *ARV* 1373, no. 24; once Tarporley, Brooks. *ARV* 1374, no. 1, and Stockholm, no number. *ARV* 1374, no. 2 (Revelstoke Group, manner of the Woman Painter).

[6] Louvre, CA 537. *ARV* 1384, no. 18.

[7] *JHS* xxxiv. 186 (pattern delta); Beazley, *The Berlin Painter* (Melbourne, 1964), 7 ('ULFA').

[8] Athens, 19336. *Para* 467.

[9] *Para* 467.

statuesque figures, but a good number of his *lekythoi* are about the same size as the Reed Painter's[1] and their decoration is not much more impressive.[2]

Before turning to the patterns, the technique, and iconography of the Reed Workshop, a word about the distribution of its vases. All of the Group R *lekythoi* of known provenience are from Attica or Eretria. Several of the Reed *lekythoi*, on the other hand, have been found elsewhere, one at Gela,[3] one at Corinth,[4] two at Spina, in a single (unpublished) grave,[5] and others from south-eastern Yugoslavia.[6] Apart from these Reed *lekythoi*, the only white *lekythoi* of unquestionably funerary iconography which are known to have travelled in any significant numbers are from the Tymbos Workshop—a handful coming from the east (Rhodes),[7] the west (Italy),[8] and nearer home (Aegina,[9] Salamis,[10] and Corinth).[11] Both workshops specialized in the mass production of small, cheap funerary *lekythoi* for an undiscriminating public, which cared more about the nature of the offering than its aesthetic quality (proveniences are discussed on pp. 136 ff.).

The Reed Painter's *lekythoi* are mostly small and rather carelessly produced, but some are larger and finer, close enough to the *lekythoi* of Group R for a single workshop to have produced them (cf. PLATE 51. 1): shapes, patterns, and pigments are similar. Although some large Reed *lekythoi* are as good as some of the *lekythoi* of Group R, the quality, on the whole, is markedly lower, and the pigment, although similar, is applied differently. There are also iconographical differences. In short, as Beazley concluded, Group R *lekythoi* are not superior work by the Reed Painter, but are by another, related artist, active in the same workshop.[12]

Matt paint is used exclusively—regularly black for the patterns and red for the figures. Glaze, by now, is limited to the lines, framing the meander band, at the shoulder join; these lines are a characteristic feature of classical white *lekythoi*, regardless of the nature of their outlines, and were presumably applied in the initial stage of the vase's decoration. Both Reed and Group R *lekythoi* have a predominantly red colour scheme. Some have added black, and others have a greater degree of polychromy, with washes of violet, blue, green, and yellow, discreetly applied. Some of the Group R *lekythoi* are no more colourful than some of the Reed *lekythoi*, and there is no noticeable difference in polychromy among Reed *lekythoi* according to size.[13] Another technical feature should be mentioned

[1] Louvre, MNB 505. *ARV* 1372, no. 15 (29 cm; F ii. 45); Louvre, MNB 613. *ARV* 1372, no. 19 (33 cm; F ii. 140); Louvre, CA 1329. *ARV* 1372, no. 20 (33 cm; F ii. 44); Athens, 1795. *ARV* 1372, no. 22 (26 cm; F ii. 152). Cf. F ii. 136 ff. (Reed average is *c*. 30 cm).

[2] Cf. Louvre, CA 1329. *ARV* 1372, no. 20. See note above.   [3] London, D 63. *ARV* 1378, no. 34.

[4] Athens, 1811. *ARV* 1379, no. 54.

[5] Ferrara, T 136 C VP. *ARV* 1382, no. 123; Ferrara, T 136 C VP. *ARV* 1382, no. 124.

[6] *RA* 1973, 43 f.

[7] London, D 45. *ARV* 759, no. 7; London, D 44. *ARV* 762, no. 29.

[8] Munich, 2772. *ARV* 754, no. 5; Munich, 2771. *ARV* 757, no. 74; New York, 06.1021.127. *ARV* 757, no. 90 (? Cerveteri); Munich, 2770. *ARV* 759, no. 13.

[9] Cab. Méd. 501. *ARV* 759, no. 5.

[10] Athens, 1808. *ARV* 759, no. 14.

[11] Corinth, MP 91. *ARV* 759, no. 1.

[12] *ARV* 1376; *AWL* 24.

[13] Reed Painter (small): Athens, 1759. *ARV* 1376, no. 1 (F ii. 137); Athens, 1999. *ARV* 1376, no. 2 (F ii. 136); Athens, 2000. *ARV* 1376, no. 3 (F ii. 136); Athens, 2028. *ARV* 1376, no. 4 (F ii. 137); Athens, 1910. *ARV* 1379, no. 72 (F ii. 141); London, D 74. *ARV* 1380, no. 80 (F ii. 142); London, D 83. *ARV* 1380, no. 94 (F ii. 142). Reed Painter (large): Athens, 2011. *ARV* 1381, no. 112 (F ii. 184); Brussels, A 124. *ARV* 1381, no. 113 (F ii. 170). Group R: Louvre, CA 536. *ARV* 1383, no. 4 (F ii. 176); Athens, 1817. *ARV* 1383, no. 11 (F ii. 167); Athens, 1816. *ARV* 1383, no. 12 (F ii. 167); London, D 71. *ARV* 1384, no. 15 (F ii. 174).

—preliminary sketch.[1] Preliminary sketches have been detected both on the larger, grander *lekythoi* of Group R[2] and on Reed *lekythoi*, sometimes hastily painted.[3] The presence of a preliminary sketch on a hastily painted *lekythos* indicates that preliminary sketch is not of necessity a sign of careful workmanship. Conversely, its presence on some of the Group R *lekythoi* indicates that the vases were not painted 'spontaneously', as has been assumed from the impressionistic character of their lines.

Although both the Reed Painter and the artist or artists of Group R use matt paint for figurework, their method of expression is different: the Reed Painter's *lekythoi*, large and small, have broader even lines (cf. PLATES 47, 48. 1), those of Group R have thinner, broken lines, which give the effect of a sketch, spontaneously produced (cf. PLATES 49, 50). Where the Reed Painter paints a line, the Group R artist paints several. In doing this he achieves volume without the use of shading. The visual impression of weight is sometimes enforced by an almost oppressive atmosphere of brooding thought (PLATE 49. 1). On these *lekythoi* we have a glimpse of the troubled, introspective mood of the later war years, of which the light, pretty art of the Meidias Painter and his red-figure colleagues gives little indication. The ponderous large-limbed seated youths on the two best-known *lekythoi* of Group R command our attention by the expression on their faces.[4] Even though these two *lekythoi* are not truly representative their monumentality and mood are acknowledged hallmarks of Group R. The Reed Painter's people sometimes look spineless and spiritless, those of his colleagues look oppressed in body and soul.

According to Pliny,[5] volume through line, without the use of shadow, was the principal achievement of the great painter Parrhasios, who was active in Athens during the Peloponesian War. Although none of his work survives, it is not unreasonable to look for some reflection of it, however slight, on those Athenian vases whose white-slipped surfaces most nearly approximate to the neutral ground of panel and wall. Modern historians of art have been quick to associate the *lekythoi* of Group R with Parrhasios;[6] Rumpf's juxtaposition of a Group R *lekythos* and a Raphael sketch illustrated simply the grander quality of these vases.[7] Pliny also tells us, taking his information from Hellenistic sources,[8] that Parrhasios was especially interested in the representation of the face, the hair, and the mouth. This seems equally true of the artist (or artists) of Group R who tilts the face in three-quarter view, paints the hair nearly strand by strand, and purses the mouth in a thoughtful expression. Great care, too, is given to hands. In Group R the hands are as valid a vehicle of expression as the face: compare the sensitively drawn, prominently featured hands (PLATE 50. 3),[9] with the boneless expressionless hands of the Reed Painter's people.

[1] Beazley, *Potter and Painter in Ancient Athens* (1946), 38 f.; *ABL* 156; *JHS* lxxxv (1965), 16 ff. (Corbett).

[2] Cleveland, 28.859. *ARV* 1383, no. 10 (= Hirsch *lekythos* described in *AWL* 25); Louvre, CA 537. *ARV* 1384, no. 18 (F ii. 162); Louvre, CA 1264. *ARV* 1384, no. 19 (*MonPiot* xxii (1916), 37 f.).

[3] Athens, 1759. *ARV* 1376, no. 1 (F ii. 137); Athens, 2028. *ARV* 1376, no. 4 (F ii. 137); London, D 61. *ARV* 1377, no. 15 (F ii. 137).

[4] Athens, 1817. *ARV* 1383, no. 11 (*TWL* pl. 9); Athens, 1816. *ARV* 1383, no. 12 (*TWL* pl. 10).

[5] Pliny, *N.H.* 35. 67.

[6] *AJA* lv (1951), 1 ff. (Rumpf); *Antike und Abendland* v (1956), 71 ff. (Karouzou); *GP* 148 ff.

[7] *AJA* lv. 5.

[8] Pliny, *N.H.* 35. 60.

[9] Athens, 1817; Athens, 19280, fr. *ARV* 1384, no. 14; Athens, 17276. *ARV* 1384, no. 16.

Patternwork. Reed patternwork varies little and is easily recognized. The IIA shoulder palmettes (FIGURE 24c), beneath a line or two or, rarely, an egg band,[1] differ from those of the Anavyssos *lekythoi* only in the tendency towards broken lines: tendrils, executed in more than one stroke, often do not 'join';[2] heart-volutes, composed of two little arc-spirals, often do not 'join'. This tendency towards broken lines in the shoulder decoration of Group R *lekythoi* is complemented by a broken, impressionistic line in the picture panel. The meander, running (broken), alternating at two, three, or more unit intervals with saltire squares, scarcely differs from that on *lekythoi* by the Reed Painter.[3] The *lekythoi* of Group R admit somewhat more variety: the Reed meander is most common,[4] but there are also long thin running meanders,[5] squared stopt meanders,[6] a running meander enclosing a pattern square,[7] and once a 'false meander' (line terminating in the centre of the meander, instead of coming out again) alternates with a pattern square,[8] rather like the Quadrate Painter's favourite square.[9] On several *lekythoi* of Group R the patternwork has largely disappeared.[10]

Iconography. The elements of Reed and Group R iconography are more similar than disparate but there are notable differences: the Reed Painter prefers a simple two-figure composition, even for many of his large *lekythoi*;[11] Group R *lekythoi*, with few exceptions, have three[12] or four[13] figures. By far the commonest Reed scene is the visit to the tomb; the commonest tomb is a broad, rather low monument, crowned by a pediment or acanthus leaves.[14] Mounds[15] are more common than shaft *stelai*,[16] but neither is prominent in the painter's *œuvre*. A characteristic feature of these Reed tomb scenes is the illusion of several monuments behind the principal one (cf. PLATE 52. 2).[17] Visits to the tomb are the commonest scene on Group R *lekythoi*, but on these 'shadow monuments' do not appear (PLATE 49). (The 'shadow monuments' are presumably nothing more than a labour-saving version of the cemetery view, several monuments being kaleidoscoped.) The figures at the tomb on Reed *lekythoi* are reproduced with monotonous regularity: seated youth and standing woman, seated woman and standing youth, standing woman and leaning youth, etc. Seated figures on the smaller *lekythoi* more often than not sit beside the tomb; on the larger Reed *lekythoi* they tend to sit at the tomb, as do the people of Group R. Standing men hold spears or lean on a staff; women hold fillets or other offerings. A curious detail found on Reed *lekythoi*,[18] large and small, is the rolled fillet,

---

[1] Würzburg, 564. *ARV* 1383, no. 2.

[2] Athens, 1816. Cf. Athens, 1848. *ARV* 1379, no. 74.

[3] Leipsic, no number. *ARV* 1381, no. 109; cf. Würzburg, 564.

[4] Cf. Vienna, 143. *ARV* 1383, no. 1; New York, 07.286.45. *ARV* 1383, no. 3; London, D 71. *ARV* 1384, no. 15; New York, 41.162.11. *ARV* 1384, no. 2.

[5] Würzburg, 564.   [6] Louvre, CA 1264.

[7] Louvre, CA 537.

[8] Athens, 19280. *Athens Annals of Archaeology* ii (1969), cover (colour).   [9] *ARV* 1236.

[10] Cleveland, 28.859; Athens, 17276 (*CV* ii, p. 14).

[11] *ARV* 1382, no. 115 *qu*. and nos. 121–8 (*ARV* 1382, no. 136, has a third figure).

[12] *ARV* 1383, nos. 1–5, 8–12; 1384, nos. 15–17.

[13] Ibid. 1383, no. 7.

[14] *ADelt* viii (1923), 122, fig. 2.

[15] Athens, 1767. *ARV* 1378, no. 31; once Vienna. *ARV* 1378, no. 38.

[16] Athens, 1852. *ARV* 1379, no. 73.

[17] Bologna, PU 367. *ARV* 1377, no. 23; Heidelberg, L 41. *ARV* 1380, no. 78.

[18] Possible representations on *lekythoi* by other painters: Athens, 1761. *ARV* 1229, no. 17 (Riezler, 107, 'eine zusammengerollte Binde mit Fransen'); Athens 16422, unattributed (PLATE 28. 3). The shoulder is white with lotuses and palmettes in the manner of the Sabouroff and Thanatos Painters. See above, p. 35, FIGURE 16c. London, D 38 (*ARV* 757, no. 71) and

held by a woman, high behind the head (PLATE 46. 2). Much has been written about these fillets, largely because they have been taken to be 'tablets' and connected by some with 'Orphic' beliefs in an afterlife.[1] Orphism or Pythagoreanism is scarcely in question at this place and time. Fillets are important in Athenian funerary rites[2]—and in the art of the Reed Painter. In vase-painting[3] and in sculpture (PLATE 46. 3)[4] they are sometimes represented rolled, and the ribbons streaming from several Reed 'tablets'[5] establish their significance beyond reasonable doubt.

The Reed Painter is excessive in his representation of fillets. They hang in profusion, not only on tombstones, but on trees and reeds, even on the air (PLATES 47, 48). Fillets appear on Group R *lekythoi*, but they are not so prominent.[6] Fillets in profusion are a characteristic feature of two groups of *lekythoi* which on the basis of other details can be shown to be related to the Reed Workshop—the *lekythoi* of the Painters of Berlin 2464 and of London D 72. The Painter of Berlin 2464[7] is connected with the Reed Workshop by pattern and pigment.[8] His scenes of visits to the tomb are very like the Reed Painter's, and the monuments are similar, but the 'shadow' monuments do not appear. Some of his women wear their hair high in a chignon, like the Reed Painter's,[9] but others wear a *sphendone*,[10] like the Woman Painter's, and in their graceful line, too, they come quite close to the Woman Painter's model. The relation between the Woman Painter and the Reed Workshop is best illustrated by the Painter of London D 72 (PLATE 46. 1)[11]—unquestionably working in the Woman Painter's manner, but also under the influence of the Reed Workshop. Patternwork looks more Woman than Reed: beneath an egg band at the neck, the shoulder palmettes, with alternately coloured leaves, are enclosed by tendrils which flow in full, round curves.[12] The meander also assumes a form different from the Reed Painter's—neat and unbroken, not unlike the Woman Painter's. The tombs represented on the vases are characteristically Reed, without the 'shadows'; low, rather broad monuments with acanthus leaves are rare on *lekythoi* by the Woman Painter (cf. PLATE 44. 3).[13] Fillets hang around them and in the air, in the Reed manner. Like the *lekythoi* of the Painter of Berlin 2464, these are near the Reed Painter's, but better; in delicacy of line and feeling they come close to some of the less monumental *lekythoi* of Group R.[14]

Boston, 00.359 (*ARV* 1229, no. 23) should perhaps be added.

[1] *BSA* lv (1960), 155 and nn. 8–15 (Kardara).
[2] Kurtz and Boardman, 104 ff., 123 f., 148, 167.
[3] Exeter, University. *ARV* 1516, no. 80. *GPP*, pl. 50.
[4] *AM* lxxix (1964), *Beilage* 48. 1, and p. 94; *Jb* xxiv (1909), pl. 5.
[5] Copenhagen, 2789. *ARV* 1377, no. 12; Louvre, MNB 616. *ARV* 1378, no. 44; London, D 74. *ARV* 1380, no. 80.
[6] Meggen, Käppeli. *ARV* 1383, no. 6; Louvre, CA 1264. *ARV* 1384, no. 19.
[7] *ARV*¹ 822; *ARV* 1243 f.; Berlin, 2463. *ARV* 1244 (Reed-type tomb and hair-style).
[8] *ARV* 1243.
[9] Louvre, MNB 617. *ARV* 1244, no. 2 (cf. *ARV*¹ 822, 'No. 2 recalls the Woman Painter'). For the

basket of offerings, cf. Athens 1956 (*ARV* 1372, no. 3); Louvre, MNB 618. *ARV* 1244, no. 3; Athens, no number. *ARV* 1244, no. 4. For the pose of the seated woman cf. Athens, 1907 (*ARV* 1382, no. 119), Athens, 1755 (*ARV* 1385, no. 17); Athens, 1908 (*ARV* 1385, no. 19). For the necklace, cf. London, D 71 (*ARV* 1384, no. 15).
[10] Berlin, 2464. *ARV* 1244, no. 1; Athens, no number. *ARV* 1244, no. 4.
[11] *ARV*¹ 821; *ARV* 1375.
[12] London, D 72. *ARV* 1375, no. 1 (F ii, pl. 25. 1); Louvre, MNB 619. *ARV* 1375, no. 2 (Riezler 6, fig. 5, left).
[13] New York, 06.1169. *ARV* 1372, no. 6; Athens, 14517. *ARV* 1374, no. 18 (manner).
[14] With Athens, no number (*ARV* 1244, no. 4) cf. London, D 71 (Group R), Athens, 1907 (Reed Painter). With Athens, 17276 (*ARV* 1384, no. 16)

The Reed Painter takes his name from the reeds which are almost as much a signature of his hand as the profusion of fillets and the illusion of kaleidoscoped monuments. Reeds are landscape elements in Charon scenes (PLATE 47. 2, 3);[1] the Sabouroff Painter had used them earlier.[2] Among later painters of *lekythoi* Charon is not popular,[3] and the Reed Painter is one of the few to devote much attention to him. Charon appears on a number of small Reed *lekythoi*[4]—with monotonous regularity: he draws his boat over the water, which is sometimes indicated,[5] towards a centrally placed reed-tree, in whose 'branches' a fillet is regularly festooned. From the other side a woman approaches, bearing an offering or holding her cloak—looking very much as if she had been lifted from one of the painter's many tomb scenes. Half of Charon's boat is represented, as is usual on white *lekythoi* (cf. PLATE 23. 2);[6] the missing part is filled in with stylized reeds. The same boat comes over the same water, to the same centrally placed reed-tree on one of the Reed Painter's larger *lekythoi*,[7] but on this vase the Charon scene has been conflated with the visit to the tomb (PLATE 47. 1).[8] The one Charon *lekythos* of Group R has a similarly conflated iconography:[9] a woman bearing *alabastron* and basket (like other visitors to the grave) approaches a tomb, on which a large *lekythos* has been placed (PLATE 50. 1). From the other side a hastily transformed Charon (still looking rather like a visitor to the tomb—note the benign expression of the face) draws up his boat, the 'back' of which is filled in with stylized reeds. This is the only Group R *lekythos* on which reeds appear; it is also, in the opinion of Beazley, the closest of Group R *lekythoi* to the Reed Painter himself.[10] The figures are substantial; their hair is carefully rendered and their faces mirror some emotion; the lines are rather sketchy—all in the manner of Group R. The composition, however, is very close to one of the Reed Painter's *lekythoi* in London (PLATE 47. 3).[11]

Mythological ministers of Death appear on one other *lekythos* of Group R: Thanatos pursues a woman in the presence of Hermes; the figure of Hermes is largely effaced (PLATE 50. 2).[12] The Thanatos-Hypnos theme does not appear on Reed *lekythoi*.[13] It was used by the Triglyph Painter,[14] and was popular with the Quadrate Painter,[15] who at least once placed the brothers at a reed-tree.[16] (Among the large, late *lekythoi* by the Quadrate Painter Beazley noted the influence of Group R.)[17] The Group R *lekythos* is

cf. London, D 72 (*ARV* 1375, no. 1. Name-vase of the Painter of London D 72).

[1] Pausanias, 10.28.1 (*Nekyia* of Polygnotos).

[2] Athens, 1926. *ARV* 846, no. 193. Cf. Boston, 95.47. *ARV* 670, no. 17 (near the Painter of London E 342); Tübingen, E 60. *ARV* 744, no. 9 (Timokrates Painter).

[3] *MadMitt* x. 167 ff.

[4] *ARV* 1376, nos. 1–8; 1377, nos. 9–15.

[5] Athens, 1759. *ARV* 1376, no. 1 (F ii. 137).

[6] But cf. Carlsruhe, B2663. *ARV* 756, no. 63; Oxford, 547. *ARV* 756, no. 64.

[7] Hamburg, 1917.817. *ARV* 1381, no. 111.

[8] Cf. the conflated Charon scenes by the Triglyph Painter: Berlin, 2680. *ARV* 1385, no. 1; Berlin, 2681. *ARV* 1385, no. 2; Athens Market. *ARV*
1385, no. 3.

[9] Louvre, CA 537. *ARV* 1383, no. 18. For the woman with the offerings, cf. London, D 71.

[10] *ARV* 1384.

[11] London, D 61. *ARV* 1377, no. 15. Note the pose of Charon and the blurred outline of his cap protruding into the pattern band, also the pose of the woman, her ponderation, dress, and offering basket.

[12] Louvre, CA 1264. *ARV* 1384, no. 19.

[13] *MadMitt* x. 164 ff.

[14] Athens, 1796. *ARV* 1385, no. 7.

[15] Athens, 1928. *ARV* 1237, no. 3; Athens, 12783. *ARV* 1237, no. 11; Athens, 1939. *ARV* 1237, no. 12; Athens, no number. *ARV* 1237, no. 13.

[16] Athens, 12783.

[17] London, 1928.2–13.3. *ARV* 1240, no. 64. Other Reed-isms in the work of the Quadrate Painter include:

unusual in its iconography: Thanatos is represented without his brother, and instead of looking placid or sympathetic, he looks frighteningly menacing. We are reminded of the Thanatos of the *Alcestis*;[1] this Thanatos, in pose as well as countenance, would make a much better Charon. The object of his mission—a woman—seems to recoil in horror, but her countenance is serene, and her pose may be paralleled on Reed *lekythoi* with Charon scenes[2] and visits to the tomb.[3] A woman in the presence of Charon assumes nearly the same pose on one of the *lekythoi* from Anavyssos;[4] the scene is like the Reed Painter's and provides possible evidence for 'borrowing' in figure as well as patternwork.

Apart from visits to the tomb and mythological representations of the coming of Death, there are two other types of scene which, at this time, seem peculiar to the Reed Workshop, if not to the Reed Painter:[5] scenes of horsemen and scenes of battle (PLATE 48. 1, 2). Horsemen on smaller Reed *lekythoi* ride towards a reed-tree,[6] lead their horse from reeds to reed-tree,[7] ride it to the tomb,[8] or sit at the tomb,[9] leaving it tethered to a nearby reed-tree. On one of the larger Reed *lekythoi* man, woman, and horse gather at the tomb.[10] The Reed Painter especially liked horses—or at least he painted them with much more feeling than he did their masters. On red-figure *lekythoi* by the Achilles Painter (cf. PLATE 34. 3),[11] and on a small, but rather fine, red-figure *loutrophoros* by the Kleophon Painter (PLATE 45. 1),[12] horsemen come to the tomb. The appearance of horsemen on *loutrophoroi* is perhaps significant, for it is on these vases that scenes of combat become popular from the middle of the fifth century.[13] The earliest battle *loutrophoros* which we have is by Hermonax;[14] the Achilles Painter's *loutrophoros* in Philadelphia,[15] on which he collaborated with the Sabouroff Painter, is not much later. Funerary scenes on *loutrophoroi* are not new,[16] but scenes of combat are. It has been conjectured that these *loutrophoroi* were commissioned to commemorate the death of those fallen in battle.[17] Some are certainly fine enough and the recent discovery of a marble *loutrophoros* with battle-scenes in relief in the Diocharian Gate cemetery in Athens[18] tends to support this interpretation. Scenes of combat were inevitably popular during war years and suitable to grave monuments, public[19] and private.[20] The Reed Painter may have had such models

partly open buds on the shoulder of London, 1928.2–13.3, and the reed-tree on Athens, 12783.

[1] Euripides, *Alkestis*, 24 ff., 261, 843.
[2] Cf. Arlesheim, Schweizer. *ARV* 1376, no. 8.
[3] Bologna, PU 367. *ARV* 1377, no. 23.
[4] Athens, 19342. *ARV* 1688, no. 4.
[5] Berlin, 2677 (Riezler, pl. 95); New York, 53.107.
[6] Athens, 12275. *ARV* 1377, no. 16.
[7] Athens, 14521. *ARV* 1377, no. 18.
[8] Oxford, 263. *ARV* 1377, no. 17.
[9] London, D 63. *ARV* 1377, no. 34. *BMCat* iii. 406.
[10] Munich, 7620. *ARV* 1382, no. 129.
[11] Philadelphia, 30.51.2. *ARV* 993, no. 95; Athens, 1293. *ARV* 993, no. 96. Cf. also the Nolan amphorae, *ARV* 998, nos. 15–16, and an early red-figure *lekythos* near the painter featuring a fight (Athens, 12893. *ARV* 1002, no. 12). There is a horseman *lekythos* by the Berlin Painter (Athens, 1274.

ARV 211, no. 190).
[12] Athens, 1700. *ARV* 1146, no. 50.
[13] *MusJ* xxiii (1932), 5 ff.
[14] Ibid. 15 (Tübingen, E 90. *ARV* 488, no. 81). Cf. also the Berlin Painter's *loutrophoros* in Erlangen (526, frr. *ARV* 204, no. 108) with a fight between warriors and negroes.
[15] Ibid. 15 (Philadelphia, 30.4.1. *ARV* 990, no. 45).
[16] *MusJ* xxiii. 14 f.
[17] Ibid. 15.
[18] *Athens Annals of Archaeology* iii (1969), 331 ff.
[19] Pausanias 1.29.6; *MusJ* xxiii. 21 n. 20; Conze, 253 ff.; *AM* xxxv (1910), 191 ff., and pls. 11–12; H. von Roques de Maumont, *Antike Reiterstandbilder* (1958), 14 ff. Especially relevant are the following monuments: Nike Temple frieze, Lippold, 193, and pl. 69.3; Albani relief, Lippold, 195, and pl. 72.3.
[20] Monument of Dexileos: Conze, no. 1158, pl. 248; Lippold, 229, and pl. 80.1.

in mind when he reproduced fights (foot and horse at a fillet-festooned reed-tree) on a small number of his larger *lekythoi* (PLATE 48. 1).[1]

There are no horsemen and no warriors on Group R *lekythoi*, but one of two *lekythoi* from the Reed Painter's Workshop, '. . . inferior work, but hardly to be separated from Group R . . .', now in New York and previously in the Gallatin Collection, features a fight—foot and horse (PLATE 48. 2).[2] The action takes place at a fillet-festooned reed-tree; the combatants look like Group R people. The second Gallatin *lekythos* (PLATE 48. 3)[3] (youth seated at tomb, with youth and woman) presents similar difficulties of attribution. The seated youth, head lowered in thought, arm raised to hold a spear (which 'disappears' into the pediment of the tomb), appears on other *lekythoi* of Group R (PLATE 49. 2)[4] (once with spears 'disappearing' into the pediment),[5] but the man and woman, who join the youth, look enough like Reed people to have come from the Reed Painter's own hand.

Battle-scenes on *loutrophoroi* sometimes take place in the presence of a tomb;[6] battle-scenes of the Reed Workshop do not take place at the tomb. I know of one white *lekythos* with a combat at the tomb—a *lekythos* in Athens, attributed by Beazley to the manner of the Woman Painter (PLATE 44. 3).[7] The matt outlines are fine and now much faded; the patternwork has entirely disappeared. The encounter between two warriors on foot takes place in the presence of a low, broad, acanthus-crowned monument—a rather unusual monument for the Woman Painter. The combatants are fully armed. This vase has long been considered a visual record of the funeral games,[8] but at present we have no evidence for games being performed at the grave in classical Athens.[9]

An iconographical detail found on two *lekythoi* of Group R remains to be described: large *lekythoi* at the tomb. *Lekythoi* stand at the tomb on earlier vases, but they are small. The one certain representation of a large *lekythos* earlier than the Group R is an un-attributed and iconographically unparalleled white *lekythos* in Ithaca, New York, which shows a seated and a standing youth at a large *lekythos* (nearly three-quarter life-size) standing on a low stepped base (PLATE 53. 1).[10] The shape of the *lekythos*, its technique (glaze outline), and patternwork suggest a date near the middle of the fifth century, although the shape of the '*lekythos* monument' with trumpet mouth and distinctive handle looks later (see below). The *lekythoi* represented on Group R vases are smaller,[11] judging from the height of the human figures (*c.* 30 to 40 cm), and actually stand on the base of the tomb (PLATES 49. 4, 50. 1). Black paint added to the mouth, neck, and lower body suggests that a painted clay *lekythos* is intended. On *lekythoi* painted on *lekythoi*

[1] Louvre, S 1161. *ARV* 1382, no. 134; Hobart, 30a. *ARV* 1382, no. 135, and *Para* 486; Hobart, 30b. *ARV* 1382, no. 136, and *Para* 486.

[2] New York, 41.162.11. *ARV* 1384, no. 2.

[3] New York, 41.162.12. *ARV* 1384, no. 1.

[4] Louvre, CA 536. *ARV* 1383, no. 4.

[5] Cleveland, 28.859. *ARV* 1383, no. 10.

[6] *AK* xiv (1971), 74 ff.

[7] Athens, 14517. *ARV* 1374, no. 18; *AM* xxxv. 206 f. and 207 n. 1. The following may be added: Athens, 1834. *ARV* 1388, no. 2, 'fight, tomb', but neither Collignon and Couve (i. 583, CC 1842) nor

Fairbanks (ii. 192) mentions a tomb.

[8] *AM* xxxv. 100 ff.; L. Deubner, *Attische Feste* (1932), 230 f.

[9] Kurtz and Boardman, 121; *BCH* cxv (1971), 602 ff., 614 ff. (bibliography for the *epitaphios agon* is given by Amandry in note 73 on page 614); *ADelt* xxiv (1969), 1 ff. (Vanderpool).

[10] Ithaca, New York. F i. 209. B. Schmaltz, *Untersuchungen zu den attischen Marmorlekythen* (1970), 112 ff.

[11] London, D 71. *ARV* 1384, no. 15; Louvre, CA 537. *ARV* 1384, no. 18.

figure decoration is rare.[1] The two vases comprising the Revelstoke Group (in the manner of the Woman Painter) feature large *lekythoi* at the tomb,[2] with painted details, including figure decoration.[3] Both of the Revelstoke *lekythoi* are large, one is just under 50 cm,[4] the other is just over.[5] The shoulder palmettes are in the manner of the Woman Painter, but the meander band is the running Reed type, enclosing saltire squares, described above, in connection with the Anavyssos *lekythoi* and their relation to the Reed and Woman Painters. Iconographically the Revelstoke *lekythoi* have elements in common with the Woman Painter and the Reed Workshop. The women recall the Woman Painter as does the *eidolon*. The tombs are like those of the Painter of Berlin 2464, himself related in style to the Woman Painter, in pattern to the Reed Painter. The woman bearing an *alabastron* and an offering basket, who appears on both of the Revelstoke *lekythoi*, is similar to the offering-bearing woman on the one *lekythos* of Group R with the enclosed-saltire meander,[6] and the seated youth who appears on both of the *lekythoi* is a popular figure in the Reed Workshop.[7]

Representations of large *lekythoi* are otherwise known only from vases by the Triglyph Painter (PLATE 51. 3, 4), who is also in some way connected with the Reed Workshop. His *lekythoi* are large, some nearly 60 cm.[8] Their decoration consists of two figures simply composed, three at most. Tomb scenes predominate, although there are also scenes of *prothesis*,[9] Charon,[10] Thanatos and Hypnos.[11] The tombs are broad, and crowned with acanthus plants whose leaves are sometimes partly coloured.[12] A few tombs have palmette *anthemia*.[13] Pedimented monuments and shadow monuments do not appear.

---

[1] Compare the fragmentary *loutrophoros*, Athens, 17283.

[2] Once Tarporley, Brooks. *ARV* 1374, no. 1 (= *Cat. Sotheby*, 27 May 1929, 24 f., no. 136); Stockholm. *ARV* 1374, no. 2 (= *Cat. Sotheby*, 27 May 1929, 26 f., no. 137).

[3] The Revelstoke vases are not without modern restoration.

[4] *Cat. Sotheby*, 27 May 1929, 26.   [5] Ibid. 24.

[6] Cf. Louvre, CA 537. Riezler, pl. 89.

[7] Cf. Munich (ex Lugano, Schoen, 83). R. Lullies, *Eine Sammlung griechischer Kleinkunst* (1955), pl. 45; Cleveland, 28.859. *CV* i, pl. 36.

[8] Triglyph Painter: Athens, 1908. *ARV* 1385, no. 19 (60 cm; F ii. 180); Brussels, A 1022. *ARV* 1385, no. 15 (57·5 cm; F ii. 181); Athens, 1755. *ARV* 1385, no. 17 (57·5 cm; F ii. 177); Group R: London, D 71. *ARV* 1384, no. 15 (51 cm; F ii. 174); Athens, 1833. *ARV* 1384, no. 17 (52 cm; F ii. 169); Athens, 1817. *ARV* 1383, no. 11 (49 cm; F ii. 167); Louvre, CA 467. *ARV* 1384, no. 20 (49·5 cm; F ii. 172); Reed Painter: Athens, 1907. *ARV* 1382, no. 119 (55 cm; F ii. 180); Louvre, S 1161. *ARV* 1382, no. 134 (55 cm; F ii. 166); Brussels, A 124. *ARV* 1381, no. 52 (52 cm; F ii. 170). Smaller *lekythoi* by the Triglyph Painter: Athens, 1770. *ARV* 1386, no. 27 (18 cm (to the shoulder); F ii. 152); Athens, 1777. *ARV* 1387, no. 47 (25 cm; F ii. 197); Athens, Acropolis, the following five un-

numbered *lekythoi*: *ARV* 1385, no. 29 (29 cm; *AE* 1958, 77, and pl. 11); *ARV* 1385, no. 25 (20·5 cm; *AE* 1958, 80, and pl. 12); *ARV* 1387, no. 1 (25 cm; *AE* 1958, 100, and pl. 14 right); *ARV* 1387, no. 2 (25 cm; *AE* 1958, 100, and pl. 14 left); *ARV* 1387, no. 3 (22 cm; *AE* 1958, 100, and pl. 15 left). Stuttgart, KAS 140. *Para* 487, 'related to the Triglyph Painter'. *CV* i, p. 39 (24·9 cm). The *lekythos* has Bird-type palmettes and meander; the composition may be compared with Athens, 1944, by the Carlsberg Painter (*ARV* 1235, no. 19).

[9] Athens, 1756. *ARV* 1385, no. 4; Lyons, no number. *ARV* 1385, no. 5; Paris, Musée Rodin. *ARV* 1385, no. 6.

[10] Berlin, 2680. *ARV* 1385, no. 1; Berlin, 2681. *ARV* 1385, no. 2; Athens Market. *ARV* 1385, no. 3.

[11] Athens, 1796. *ARV* 1385, no. 7.

[12] Cf. Madrid, 11193. *ARV* 1375, no. 9; Market. *ARV* 1382, no. 122. Representative tomb types may be found on the following: Athens, 16461. *ARV* 1387, no. 43 (*BSA* lv, pl. 41*b*); Athens, 19273. *ARV* 1382, no. 127 (*BSA* lv, pl. 40*b*); Mannheim, 14. *ARV* 1372, no. 12 (*CV* i, p. 45).

[13] Berlin, 2680; Athens, 2038. *ARV* 1386, no. 31. The decoration of the shaft of the tomb may be compared with that on Würzburg, 564 (*ARV* 1383, no. 2), which is said to have been repainted (Langlotz, 114), and Toronto, 920.68.24 (*ARV* 1381, no. 199).

The Triglyph Painter's style and iconography are not far from the Reed Workshop: note especially the rubbery arms held awkwardly beside the head, the boneless fingers holding up a garment[1] (or nothing at all),[2] the pose of the figures seated at the tomb,[3] and the shrubbery growing about them.[4] Thanks to the Triglyph Painter's passion for eccentric details, his work is easily recognizable: tombs with triglyphs,[5] dresses with ivy-berry patterns,[6] biers and graves with ducks[7] and huge *lekythoi*.[8] Some of the *lekythoi* represented by the Triglyph Painter are very large. They differ from those represented on *lekythoi* of Group R and the Revelstoke Group in the formation of the mouth, which is decidedly trumpet shape. Some have painted details in black, and are, therefore, perhaps made of clay,[9] but others are without added details and are perhaps of stone.[10] The trumpet mouth can be found on several *lekythoi* decorated by the Triglyph Painter.[11] Neither the trumpet mouth nor the round moulding at the neck occurs on *lekythoi* from the Reed Workshop, with one exception—a large *lekythos* by the Reed Painter (man seated at tomb, with man and woman) in Chicago (PLATE 51. 1).[12] Both the pose of the seated man and the structure of the tomb can be paralleled on a *lekythos* by the Triglyph Painter.[13] Not so close, but unquestionably comparable, is the composition on a very large *lekythos* in Copenhagen (PLATE 52. 1), one of two members of the Class of Copenhagen 4986, connected not in style of drawing, but in shape: trumpet mouth, slender neck, strongly sloping shoulder (with moulded neck-ring), and somewhat ovoid body, tapering sharply towards a substantial disc foot.[14] The second *lekythos*, in New York, although essentially the same shape, is small (27·6 cm) (PLATE 52. 2).[15] The patterns are not characteristically Reed, but the style of figure decoration is: note especially the 'shadow monument' behind the principal acanthus-crowned tomb. Beazley thought that the New York vase had something in common with Berlin 2463,[16] itself close to the Painter of Berlin 2464 (see p. 62).[17]

A third large (48·3 cm) *lekythos* with Reed elements and a similar shape is unattributed, one of several offerings in an adult's tile-covered grave in the Kerameikos (PLATE 51. 2).[18] The scene is the visit to the tomb—a broad shaft with horizontal finial. On one side stands a woman (rather badly effaced), on the other sits a man, one hand on a shield, the

[1] Lidingo, Millesgården, 94. *ARV* 1385, no. 14. Cf. Paris Market. *ARV* 1382, no. 118; Basle, Geigy. *ARV* 1386, no. 32; once Athens, private. *ARV* 1385, no. 12.

[2] Athens, 1756.

[3] Athens, 1754. *ARV* 1385, no. 17; Sydney, 41.03. *ARV* 1386, no. 33; cf. also Athens, 1907. *ARV* 1382, no. 119.

[4] Brussels, A 1022; Munich (ex Lugano, Schoen, 82); Athens, 1756; Louvre, S 3893. *ARV* 1382, no. 115 *qu.*; Market. *ARV* 1382, no. 122; Athens, 16423 and 1832 (both unattributed).

[5] Carlsruhe (B2689). *ARV* 1386, no. 20; Louvre, MNB 440. *ARV* 1386, no. 21; *ARV* 1384.

[6] Zürich, University, 2568. *ARV* 1386, no. 38; Berlin, 2680 and 2681.

[7] Athens, 1756 (bier); Louvre, MNB 440 (grave); Warsaw 142406. *ARV* 1385, no. 8 (grave).

[8] Athens, 1756 (bier); Athens, 1908. *ARV* 1385, no. 19 (grave; see *AE* 1906, 16); Zürich, University, 2568 (grave).

[9] Athens, 1908; Zürich, University, 2568 (fillet around neck).

[10] Athens, 1756.

[11] Athens, 1755. *ARV* 1385, no. 17; Athens, Acropolis, no number. *ARV* 1385, no. 11 (*AE* 1958, pl. 6 left; cf. also *AE* 1958, pls. 6 right and 13).

[12] Chicago, Art Institute, 07.18. *ARV* 1381, no. 114.

[13] Lidingo, Millesgården, 94.

[14] Copenhagen, 4986. *ARV* 1389, no. 1; *CV* iv, pl. 173. 1 and p. 134 (55·4 cm).

[15] New York, 07.1. *ARV* 1389, no. 2; F ii. 196.

[16] This note is in the Beazley Archive.

[17] Berlin, 2463. *ARV* 1244.

[18] *AM* lxxxi (1966), 44 f. (90, hS 95).

other raised, holding spears. The pose of the seated man may be paralleled on the Reed Painter's large *lekythos* in Chicago (PLATE 51. 1) and on a *lekythos* by the Triglyph Painter.[1] Less close, but comparable, are the seated youths on Copenhagen 4986 (PLATE 52. 1) and on the Huge *Lekythoi* in Madrid (PLATE 54. 1) and Berlin (PLATE 54. 2). The patternwork of the Kerameikos vase is neither characteristically Reed, nor clearly anyone else's: the egg pattern at the neck-ring is carefully executed, as are the shoulder palmettes and the running meander without pattern squares. Great care, too, is given to a few details of figurework—the man's face, his hair, and his eyes. The heads of both figures are strictly profile, as are those on the Huge *Lekythoi*. There is a second 'shadow' monument and a sketchy indication of terrain.[2] Both details suggest a Reed affiliation. The type of tomb, although not very common on Reed *lekythoi*, does appear.[3]

The shape of the Kerameikos *lekythos* is very like Copenhagen 4986: trumpet mouth, moulded neck-ring, strongly sloping shoulder, high thin handle, and narrow base meeting a substantial (rilled) foot. The body is, however, more nearly cylindrical, nearer the shape of the Huge *Lekythoi*. The neck of the Kerameikos *lekythos* was white, apparently with some sort of red painted decoration,[4] a characteristic feature of the Huge *Lekythoi*, not found on other white *lekythoi*;[5] the mouth and foot, instead of being painted black in the usual manner, are red;[6] compare the treatment of the Huge *Lekythoi* (see below). Lastly, and most importantly, there is a limited use of shading—*skiagraphia*;[7] on white *lekythoi* shading only occurs on Huge *Lekythoi*.[8] The Kerameikos *lekythos*, therefore, in shape and technique stands between the Reed Workshop[9] and the Huge *Lekythoi*.

19. HUGE *LEKYTHOI*

The Huge *Lekythoi*,[10] five in number, share a common shape, technique, and style of decoration. They look like the work of one man in the last decade of the fifth century. Three of the five are approximately one metre high;[11] two are just under 70 cm,[12] not much larger than the Triglyph Painter's largest, or Copenhagen 4986. The shape of the best-preserved examples is a nearly straight-sided cylinder, with trumpet mouth, moulded neck-ring, and substantial foot (PLATE 54).[13] The proveniences of two are known: the two Huge *Lekythoi* in Berlin were found at Alopeke[14] (modern Ambelokepoi)[15] in 1872. The proveniences of the other three are unknown, but between the 1870s and very early

---

[1] Lidingo, Millesgården, 94.

[2] *AM* lxxxi. 44.

[3] *ADelt* viii (1923), 122, fig. 2 (zeta).

[4] *AM* lxxxi. 44.

[5] Cf. *MadMitt* x. 156 f.

[6] *AM* lxxxi. 44.

[7] Ibid.

[8] The Copenhagen *lekythos* may perhaps be compared: *CV* iv, pp. 134 f.

[9] *ARV* 1390. Beazley placed the Huge *Lekythoi* closest to Group R.

[10] *ARV* 1390; *MadMitt* x. 155 ff. (Brommer).

[11] *MadMitt* x. 155 n. 2 (Madrid, Paris, 'Erbach').

[12] Ibid. 155 n. 2 (Berlin).

[13] Ibid., colour plate 1; *MonPiot* xii (1905), 32, fig. 1 (without mouth).

[14] Furtwängler, *Beschreibung*, ii (1885), 768 f. Berlin, 2684. *ARV* 1390, no. 3; Berlin, 2685. *ARV* 1390, no. 4.

[15] W. Judeich, *Topographie von Athen* (1905), 158, 162; C. W. J. Eliot, *Coastal Demes of Attica* (1962), 148.

1890s one found its way to Madrid,[1] another to Paris,[2] and a third to Heidelberg[3] (now Basle).[4] It is not impossible that they came from Alopeke, which, despite its proximity to the heart of ancient Athens (less than two miles from the Acropolis), has yielded few attributed Attic vases. In *ARV* six vases are said to have been found at Alopeke, all but one white *lekythoi*; in addition to the two Huge *Lekythoi*, three by the Thanatos Painter,[5] acquired by the British Museum in 1876.[6] The sixth vase, a *lekanis* of Lycinic type (so named from the inscription on this example), was also found in the 1870s.[7] Furtwängler's 1885 Catalogue of the Berlin Collection has two more 1872 Alopeke *lekythoi*—one by the Triglyph Painter, 57 cm,[8] and one unattributed (75 cm).[9] Both Furtwängler and Fairbanks[10] connected the unattributed *lekythos* with the Huge Group, not only because of its size, but because of a technical feature of the figure decoration—*skiagraphia*—which according to Pliny was the great fame of the painter Apollodoros, and of his somewhat younger contemporary, Zeuxis of Heracleia (see below).[11] None of their paintings survives. We have Pliny's words (and those of a few other ancient writers) and little more—a few tantalizing glimpses, in various media, produced over several centuries, of what their art may have been—among them, the Huge *Lekythoi*. The development of *skiagraphia* in ancient Greece and Italy has been studied by Rumpf.[12] Here my purpose is not to place the Huge *Lekythoi* in relation to monumental painting, but in relation to other *lekythoi* of clay and of stone.

The shape of the Huge *Lekythoi* is, as we have noted, not very different from that of some late white *lekythoi* (cf. PLATE 51) and early stone *lekythoi* (PLATE 53. 2).[13] Unlike other white *lekythoi*, with the near exception of the Kerameikos vase (PLATE 51. 2), the white slip has been applied over the entire surface, not just to body—to mouth, neck, shoulder, and foot. The monumental size and the over-all application of white paint suggest that the potter is trying to attract a client who might be tempted to buy a stone model. Stone *lekythoi* were durable—therefore more suitable to the dead and marketable to the living. In the face of growing competition from sculptors, some potters and painters sought to revive a lagging trade by emulating, as best they could, contemporary *lekythoi* in stone. The rather attenuated trumpet mouth *lekythoi* by the Triglyph Painter are perhaps our earliest indications of this ill-fated movement, the Copenhagen *lekythos*

[1] Madrid, 11194. *ARV* 1390, no. 5; G. Leroux, *Vases grecs et italo-grecs du Musée Archéologique de Madrid* (1912), 168 ('acquis en Grèce par De la Rada'); F. Alvarez-Ossorio, *Vasos griegos etruscos e italo-griegos que se conservan en el Museo Arqueológico Nacional* (1910), p. vi (date of De la Rada's directorship).

[2] Louvre, CA 273. *ARV* 1390, no. 2; *MonPiot* xii. 35 ('acquis en 1889').

[3] Once Heidelberg, Stift Neuburg (*AA* 1893, 188 f.), now Basle, Cahn. *ARV* 1390, no. 1.

[4] According to Dr. Cahn the vase was never in Erbach.

[5] London, D 67. *ARV* 1228, no. 7; London, D 58. *ARV* 1228, no. 12; London, D 60. *ARV* 1230, no. 37.

[6] *BMCat* iii. 407 ('Athens'); cf. *ARV* 1228, no. 7

('Ambelokepoi'); *BMCat* iii. 405 ('Ambelokepos, near Athens, 1876').

[7] *ARV* 1556, once Athens, Carapanos; *BCH* ii (1878), 547; cf. *Agora* xii. 168 f.; *AE* 1958, 99, fig. 171, and pl. 22b.

[8] Berlin, 2682. *ARV* 1385, no. 13 ('Athens'); Furtwängler, *Beschreibung*, ii. 766 ('Alopeke bei Athen, 1872').

[9] Berlin, 2683; Furtwängler, op. cit. 767.

[10] F ii. 204 f.

[11] Pliny, *N.H.* 35. 60; *GP* 153.

[12] *Jb* xlix (1934), 6 ff. (Rumpf); *JHS* lxvii (1947), 10 ff. (Rumpf).

[13] Early stone *lekythoi* are described by Schmaltz, pp. 112 ff.

looks slightly later. During the last decades of the fifth century *lekythoi* were being produced in stone as well as clay and the stone vases did not come fully into line with other branches of Athenian funerary sculpture much before the end of the century.[1] Before this time there was considerable borrowing of decorative schemes: if the Huge *Lekythoi* show the potter and painter emulating the sculptor, the stone *lekythoi* with painted scenes of the visit to the tomb[2] show the sculptor following his prototype. Huge *Lekythoi*, like other late, large clay and stone *lekythoi*, were designed to be displayed, not to be filled.[3] Some of the Huge *Lekythoi* are without a bottom,[4] presumably so that they could be secured in place over a stake or on a stone base. Another curious feature of the Huge *Lekythoi* is the construction of the mouth: on the more complete examples, the mouth is separate from the body, held in position by a pin.[5] The separate mouth is probably a technical expedient, necessitated by the size and shape of the clay vase. Stone *lekythoi* do not have separate mouths, because they are structurally unnecessary.

The patternwork of the Huge *Lekythoi* comes nearer to the stone models than the figure-work.[6] Even the patternwork is sometimes traditional: the shoulder of the Louvre *lekythos* has palmettes, although their execution and arrangement are unusual.[7] The shoulder of the Basle Huge *Lekythos* has rays[8] like secondary clay *lekythoi*, but this is probably coincidental. The other three Huge *Lekythoi*—the two in Berlin and the one in Madrid—have wreaths of violet leaves.[9] Stone *lekythoi* with painted decoration rarely preserve much trace of it. There are, however, palmettes on the shoulder of a good number.[10] Leaves, or 'feathers',[11] are among the more common patterns cut in relief and since they appear in Attic funerary sculpture primarily on vases—*loutrophoroi*[12] and *alabastra*[13] as well as *lekythoi*—we are perhaps not wrong to see here a reflection of metal-work. Stone vases decorated entirely with this pattern certainly look like metal, as do the intricately convoluted handles.[14] Large metal vases were probably prized in the rites of death as they were in the service of the living, and if few have been found in excavated Athenian graves it is probably because the living felt their need was greater. Stone *lekythoi* with painted decoration regularly have framing pattern bands, meanders, and eggs.[15] A notable feature of all but one of the Huge *Lekythoi* is the apparent lack of

[1] Schmaltz, 115 f.

[2] Ibid. 68 f., 147 (B 12 = Athens, National Museum, 1049), 147 f. (B 13 = Athens, National Museum, 3585). Two additional examples are cited by Schmaltz on p. 68 n. 5. See also *AE* 1953–4 ii. 236 ff. (relief).

[3] Schmaltz, 76 ff. Some stone *lekythoi* have been found inside graves (Schmaltz, 68 (B 13)) in the usual manner of white clay *lekythoi*. See *AE* 1906. 16 f.

[4] *MadMitt* x. 156; *AE* 1906. 16 f.

[5] *MadMitt* x. 156 f.; *MonPiot* xii. 32, fig. 1.

[6] Schmaltz, 68 ff. 115 ff.

[7] *MonPiot* xii. 32. Cf. the palmettes on the shoulder of the large clay *lekythos* in Copenhagen (4986; PLATE 52. 1) and on the shoulder of a fragmentary *lekythos* in Berlin (*Jb* x (1895), 86 ff. and pl. 2; F ii. 212 f.). The tomb represented on the Berlin *lekythos* is crowned by an anthropomorphic *anthemion*. Cf. the multi-figure composition of the *anthemion*

from the central acroterion of the 'Temple of the Athenians' on Delos (*Délos* xii. 137 ff. and pls. 14 f.). and J. Marcadé, *BCH* lxxv (1951), 86 f. Martin Robertson drew my attention to the last reference.

[8] *MadMitt* x. 158.

[9] Ibid. 157 f.; cf. Furtwängler, *Beschreibung*, ii. 768 f. ('Rauten', 'Blattkranz').

[10] Schmaltz, 60 ff.

[11] Conze, no. 1695, pl. 360, and p. 361 (Schüppen-muster); no. 1699, pl. 363 (painted); nos. 1703–6 and 1708, pl. 365 (relief). The pattern on Attic vases is described by F. Johnson in *AJA* lviii (1954), 201 f.; on metal vases by P. Jacobsthal and A. Langsdorff, *Die Bronzeschnabelkannen* (1929), 99.

[12] Conze, no. 1354, pl. 284; no. 1409, pl. 290.

[13] Ibid., no. 1409, pl. 290.

[14] Cf. ibid., pls. 372–5.

[15] Schmaltz, 61.

pattern bands: the Basle *lekythos* has an egg and dart pattern at the shoulder join,[1] as do the large Copenhagen *lekythos* (PLATE 52. 1)[2] and some smaller red-figure *lekythoi* of various dates. The lack of framing pattern bands increases the already considerable picture field: on the largest of the vases the picture field itself is nearly 50 cm,[3] with little more than a ground line near the foot. If it were not for the strong traditional element in the iconography of these vases, we might be tempted to see in them the work of a man accustomed to freer painting on a grander scale.

Iconographically the Huge *Lekythoi* are canonical.[4] Four of the five feature people at the tomb, a low broad monument[5] with prominent acanthus leaves and *anthemia* with 'flame'[6] palmettes. This type of monument is most closely paralleled on *lekythoi* by the Triglyph Painter, on the Reed Painter's large *lekythos* in Chicago (PLATE 51. 1), and on Copenhagen 4986 (PLATE 52. 1). On the Madrid (PLATE 54. 1) and one of the Berlin *lekythoi* a youth sits at the tomb in a relaxed pose, looking, apart from the strictly profile face, like a brother to the Group R seated youths (PLATE 49. 1, 2). On the Louvre and Basle *lekythoi* two figures sit at the tomb—a more complicated composition made possible by the greater size of picture panel. The standing figures assume traditional poses: men lean on staves and women bear offerings. The fifth Huge *Lekythos*, in Berlin,[7] is equally traditional in its iconography—a *prothesis* (PLATE 54. 2), very little different from the Sabouroff Painter's of nearly half a century earlier (PLATE 29. 1, 2):[8] the bier, its trappings, the mourners, their gestures, even the *eidolon*. No significant detail of the iconography of the Huge *Lekythoi* departs from the established white-ground repertoire.

On the basis of sculptural[9] and numismatic[10] parallels, the Huge *Lekythoi* have been dated to the last decade of the fifth century. The man who painted them was, therefore, a contemporary of the man who painted the *lekythoi* of Group R, and both were contemporaries of Parrhasios and Zeuxis. That one vase-painter should have chosen to follow Parrhasios, another Zeuxis, seems altogether likely. The Group R man, like Parrhasios, valued line above all; his contours give the illusion of depth without the use of shadow. The attention which, he gives to face, hair, and mouth, on his finest pieces, is entirely in accord with Pliny's words about Parrhasios' art. The man who painted the Huge *Lekythoi*, on the other hand, like Zeuxis, and before him Apollodoros, was attracted to *skiagraphia*. One is technically no more advanced than the other and neither goes beyond the limits of other late fifth-century vase-painters working in red-figure.

Pliny tells us that Apollodoros 'was the first artist to give realistic presentation of

---

[1] *MadMitt* x. 157, fig. 1, and 158.

[2] Copenhagen, *CV* iv, pp. 134 f.

[3] F ii. 209 (Louvre, CA 273).

[4] Ibid. 214 f.

[5] The type of monument on the Basle *lekythos* is not clear, but neither acanthus leaves nor *anthemia* are visible. Cf. *MadMitt* x. 157, fig. 1.

[6] Cf. *MadMitt* x, colour plate 1, and W. Kraiker, *Das Kentaurenbild des Zeuxis* (1950), fig. 3. The shoulder palmettes may be compared with those on the stone *lekythos* (Schmaltz, B 13; *AE* 1913, 89, figs.

6–7) and the 'Boy with a Cat' *stele* (Conze, no. 1032, pl. 204; Möbius, 17, 106).

[7] Berlin, 2684.

[8] Cf. New York, 07.286.40. *ARV* 846, no. 190; London, D 62. *ARV* 851, no. 273; Mannheim, 195. *ARV* 851, no. 274 (Sabouroff Painter); Vienna, 3748. *ARV* 1372, no. 16 (Woman Painter); *AM* liii (1928), *Beilagen* 111 and 116; F ii. 214.

[9] *JHS* lxvii. 11 n. 13; *Jb* xlix. 16.

[10] *JHS* lxvii. 11 n. 12; *Jb* xlix. 15.

objects, and the first to confer glory as of right upon the paint brush',[1] and Plutarch calls him 'the first man to discover the art of mixing colours and chiaroscuro'.[2]

Shading in the form of light hatching appears on Attic vases for inanimate objects and landscape elements from the time of the Brygos Painter.[3] Apollodoros' contribution to Greek painting was not, therefore, the 'invention' of shading, rather its freer application, presumably to living creatures, including men, although we are not told this explicitly. *Skiagraphia*, as Rumpf has shown, was used selectively and restrictedly for a very considerable time after Apollodoros in Greek, Etruscan, and South Italian painting from around 400 B.C., but on the bodies of men, not women, probably because of the well-established sex differentiation through skin tones, fundamental to Greek as well as other earlier Mediterranean schools of painting. The flesh of women is outlined or lightly coloured; the flesh of men shaded and more deeply coloured.[4] The Huge *Lekythoi* are our earliest Attic vases on which this distinction in shading can be observed. Some of the Huge *Lekythoi* make more of it than others—for example, the two featuring youths seated at the tomb (PLATE 54. 1), their heavily shaded chest set off against a white mantle whose folds are hatched in. The *prothesis lekythos* (PLATE 54. 2) has a balance of shaded men (note the wrinkles on the face of the mourning man) and outlined women. The decoration of the Louvre *lekythos* with five women at the tomb consists largely of broad flat masses of colour, outlined and unshaded. The use of *skiagraphia* on the Huge *Lekythoi* is entirely in accord with late classical and Hellenistic monumental painting, as it has been preserved.[5]

The second technical feature of which the Huge *Lekythoi* have been considered representative is perspective—*skenographia*.[6] Perspective, as Vitruvius tells us, was the invention of Agatharchos of Samos,[7] a contemporary of Alkibiades[8] and Zeuxis,[9] and like shading had been applied hesitantly, and not very successfully, on Attic vases from the late Archaic period, most often to details of furniture or architecture.[10] The representation of objects in space on Attic vases is not very successful because the principles of perspective are not fully understood. It is a partial, linear perspective without a common vanishing point. The painter of the Huge *Lekythoi* is no more advanced in his *skenographia* than

---

[1] Pliny, *N.H.* 35. 60 (Loeb ix, p. 307 (Rackham)). Cf. J. J. Pollitt, *The Art of Greece* (1965), 112 and n. 143. *Iure* must be 'by right', not 'by a law' (as Pollitt, which would be *lege*).

[2] Plutarch, *De Glor. Athen.* 346 (Loeb, iv, p. 495 (Babbitt)).

[3] *Jb* xlix. 8 nn. 7–9.

[4] *JHS* lxvii. 11.

[5] The freer and wider application of *skiagraphia*, as seen on the Huge *Lekythoi*, is not common on other late fifth- or early fourth-century Attic red-figure vases. It is a marked feature of the Talos Painter's name vase in Ruvo (Jatta, 1501. *ARV* 1338, no. 1; H. Sichtermann, *Griechische Vasen in Unteritalien* (1966), 23 ff., and pl. 25) and on a related fragment with the same scene, from Spina (Ferrara, fr. *ARV* 1340) but it is limited to the white body of Talos (musculature shaded in), a giant whose body was made

of metal (Ap. Rhod., *Argon.* 4. 1638 ff.)—clearly a special case. Talos occupies the centre of the vase and the white focal point is very much in the style of later red-figure (cf. K. Schefold, *Kertscher Vasen* (1930), 8); compare the Talos Painter's *loutrophoros* in Amsterdam (Musée Scheurleer, 2474 frr. *ARV* 1339, no. 4) with a white tomb and a white horse, and a related fragment in Berlin (3209. *AK* xiv (1971), 74 ff.).

[6] Louvre, CA 273 (the tomb and the chest held by one of the women; *MonPiot* xii. 37, fig. 3, and pp. 36 ff.); Berlin, 2684 (the block beneath the bier).

[7] Vitruvius 7. 2.

[8] Plut., *Alc.* 16.

[9] Plut., *Per.* 13.

[10] Most recently, G. M. A. Richter, *Perspective in Greek and Roman Art* (1970), with bibliography.

other late fifth-century red-figure painters. The tomb monuments are as uncertain in their spatial disposition as is the block beneath the bier on the Berlin *prothesis lekythos* (PLATE 54. 2) or the chest held by one of the women on the Louvre *lekythos*.

CONCLUSION

Towards the end of the fifth century white *lekythoi* with figure decoration ceased to be favoured grave offerings (see pp. 133 ff.). The 'end' of white *lekythoi* cannot be dated closely owing to the lack of systematically excavated graves. Two recent excavations in Athens, one in the Kerameikos,[1] the other in Syntagma Square,[2] revealed late fifth- and early fourth-century graves but with few exceptions they were carelessly constructed and poorly furnished. Those with white *lekythoi* often had no other firmly datable offering.[3] None looks later than the last decade of the fifth century[4] and the fashion for the vase, despite the attempts by artists of Group R and of the Huge *Lekythoi* to revive it, seems to have passed a few years earlier.

A passage in the *Ecclesiazusae* of Aristophanes[5] has long been cited by students of Attic vase-painting as evidence for the demise of the white *lekythos*. In lines 994–6 of the play the old woman's lover is said to be 'the best of painters . . . the one who paints *lekythoi* for the dead'. The traditional interpretation of the lines, which is thought to produce the maximum comic effect, is: only one old man was carrying on the dying art form—a suitable lover for the moribund old woman.[6] This interpretation is not strictly in accord with the context of the rest of the play. The *Ecclesiazusae* dates from the late 390s;[7] the latest white *lekythoi* seem to be no later than 410/400 B.C. At several points in the play Aristophanes speaks of *lekythoi*,[8] some at the bier and at the grave;[9] his references are topical, to an object in common use. *Lekythos* is a generic term,[10] no more appropriate to the white slipped cylinders with painted decoration than to the squat oil pots, red-figured or black-painted, which were used by the living as well as the dead through much of the fourth century.[11] Aristophanes speaks of *lekythoi* without qualification and these *lekythoi* need be neither white nor cylindrical. *Lekythos* is an equally appropriate term for the stone vases whose shape was modelled after that of the clay cylinder. Stone *lekythoi* were fashionable in Aristophanes' day, and in one passage in the *Ecclesiazusae* he seems to refer to them. In lines 1098–1111 the young man, confronted by three amorous old women, entreats Zeus—should the necessity arise—to bury his

---

[1] *AM* lxxxi (1966), 4 ff. (B. Schlörb-Vierneisel), 112 ff. (U. Knigge).

[2] *AE* 1958, 1 ff. (S. Charitonides).

[3] Cf. *AM* lxxxi. 40 f. (81/ hS 173; all offerings are *lekythoi*) and 44 f. (90/ hS 95; *lekythoi* and a black cup-skyphos); *AE* 1958. 65 ff. (xliv/64).

[4] *AM* lxxxi. 44 (hS 95; one of the offerings is the large *lekythos*, near Group R).

[5] Aristophanes, *Ecclesiazusae*, ed. R. G. Ussher (1973), ll. 994–7.

[6] *GP* 149.

[7] Ussher, xxi ff.

[8] Ar., *Ecc.* 744, 996, 1101.

[9] Ibid. 538, 1032, 1111.

[10] *Lekythos*, as used by Aristophanes, is discussed by: J. H. Quincey, *CQ* xliii (1949), 32 ff., and, more recently, J. Henderson, *HSCP* lxxvi (1972), 133 ff.

[11] *AM* lxxxi, *Beilagen* 46–7 and p. 59 (graves); *Agora* xii. 150 ff., 153 ff. (squat *lekythoi*).

body at the mouth of the harbour[1] and to place above it, instead of a *lekythos*, one of the old women, blacked with pitch and leaded into position.[2]

Stone *lekythoi* are one aspect of the renaissance of Athenian funerary art which began around 430 B.C., when sculptors first turned to private commissions of a public unfettered by sumptuary restrictions (see p. 136.). During much of the fifth century, when ostentatious burial had been condemned, if not legally banned, the white *lekythos* enjoyed a special place in the funerary rites of Athenians. When the period of austerity came to an end, so did the pre-eminence of the vase. For a few decades *lekythoi* were produced in clay and stone—the former providing not only the inspiration, but also the model in shape, pattern, and figurework for the latter.[3] But the clay vase could not compete with the larger, more durable, stone monument. Soon the small oil pots, which had long been given to the dead, assumed the white *lekythos*' position as favoured offerings in the grave, and above ground the stone *lekythos* assumed its decorative role. The small oil pots were essential to the living and the dead, quite apart from eschatology. The demise of the white *lekythos*, therefore, marks a change in fashion, not a change in funerary practice: the small *lekythoi* of the late fifth and fourth centuries, and the fusiform *unguentaria* of the Hellenistic period which take their place, confirm the undiminished importance of oil in Athenian rites of death and burial.

[1] An allusion to the grave of Themistocles? Plut., *Them.*, 32, 5–6. A. W. Gomme, *A Historical Commentary on Thucydides*, i (1945), 445 f.

[2] Ussher, 226 f. Throughout the play there is an emphasis on the make-up of the old women; their faces are whitened with lead paint (ll. 878, 904, 929, 1072) and dabbed with rouge (Ussher, 195). The whiteness is as appropriate to most marble *lekythoi* as it is to clay *lekythoi* painted white (cf. *CQ* xliii. 39 f. and n. 6) and the inference that red on white alludes to white clay *lekythoi* with figures outlined in red paint (*CQ* xliii. 43 n. 39) is unnecessary. Stone vases were secured into bases with the help of molten lead (cf. A. Brückner, *Der Friedhof am Eridanos* (1909), 71, fig. 43; 91, figs. 56–8).

[3] Schmaltz, 76 ff.

PART TWO

SHAPES OF WHITE *LEKYTHOI*

INTRODUCTION

THE shapes of red-figure and white *lekythoi* have been classified by Beazley in *ARV*,[1] black-figure *lekythoi* by Miss Haspels in *ABL*. This section summarizes briefly the Beazley–Haspels classification without going beyond it, and is designed as a guide to *lekythoi* described in the monograph, especially to those in the following section devoted to side-palmettes. It considers only the principal shapes which were regularly decorated with figures in outline on white-ground. Some black-figure shapes are mentioned on pp. 143 f. A detailed study is being prepared by Brian Cook.

Lekythos is a generic term for oil bottle.[2] In classical Athens oil was essential for life and death, in the business, the home, the sanctuary, and the grave. Because of the many and varied uses for oil, receptacles of different shapes were designed for its storage and dispensation. Conventionally we restrict the term to a particular type of oil pot, although the ancient Greeks applied *lekythos* to vases of other shapes, for instance the *aryballos* (PLATE 9. 2, 3) and *alabastron* (PLATE 72).[3] Modern scholars recognize three types of *lekythos*:[4] Type One has a body which curves gently, without break from neck to base (PLATE 67. 1), Type Two has a shoulder sharply set off from the body (PLATE 67. 2–6), and Type Three is squat, generally without a sharply defined shoulder (PLATES 61. 2, 71. 3). Type One is essentially a black-figure shape; Type Three red-figure;[5] Type Two, although produced in black-figure, is the red-figure and white-ground shape *par excellence*. When we speak of *lekythoi* without qualification, we mean *lekythoi* of shoulder type. *Lekythoi* of Type Two are divided in *ARV* into two great classes—standard and secondary, secondary generally being smaller, less careful versions of standard.[6]

1. THE ESTABLISHMENT OF THE STANDARD CYLINDER

Some time in the second quarter of the sixth century *lekythoi* began to be fashioned with distinct shoulders[7] and this marks the beginning of Type Two *lekythoi* and the beginning of the end of Type One.[8] The first shoulder *lekythoi* retained the mouth and drip-ring characteristic of Type One, but by the middle of the century the Amasis Painter decorated a shoulder *lekythos* with a simple mouth and a token drip-ring which is little more than a thin raised line. The *Potnia Theron lekythos* in the Louvre (PLATE 1. 1),[9] which is early in his career, has linked lotus buds on the shoulder and a picture panel restricted to the front of the body. The former is a characteristic feature of secondary

[1] *ARV* 675.

[2] The etymology of *lekythos*, proposed by L. J. Elferink (*Lekythos* (1934), 21 ff.), is rejected by H. Frisk (*Griechisches etymologisches Wörterbuch* (1961), Lieferung 12, s.v. *lekythos*, p. 116).

[3] F i. 1–5; *BSA* xxix (1927–8), 187 ff. (Beazley); *ADelt* xi (1927–8), 91 ff. (S. Papaspyridi); *PW*, suppl. v (1931), 546–8 (H. Nachod); *EAA* iv (1961),

539 ff.; *Agora* xii. 150 ff.

[4] G. Richter and M. Milne, *Shapes and Names of Athenian Vases* (1935), 14–17.

[5] *Agora* xii. 153 and n. 16.

[6] *ARV* 675.

[7] *ABL* 7.

[8] Ibid. 6 and ch. 3.

[9] Louvre F 71. *ABV* 154, no. 49.

lekythoi throughout the fifth century,[1] the latter of almost all later Type Two *lekythoi*, black-figure, red-figure, or white-ground.[2]

The shoulder *lekythos* developed steadily through the third quarter of the sixth century,[3] and was decisively affected by the introduction of the new red-figure style towards its close.[4] The first cylinder *lekythoi* may have been decorated in red-figure—new shape and new technique appearing together—but our earliest examples are black-figure.[5] Unlike earlier shoulder *lekythoi*, whose body tapered sharply towards the base, the new *lekythos* of cylinder shape is nearly straight-sided; the base meets the foot in a full round curve. There is uncertainty of profile in the earliest examples,[6] but the shape stabilizes quickly. The cylinders painted by the members of the Leagros Group (PLATE 3. 1)[7] come close to the canon established by the Edinburgh Painter, and it is his shape which passes into red-figure through the Athena Painter and his Workshop. But the cylinder was not the only type of *lekythos* fashioned in the last quarter of the sixth century, nor were *lekythoi* decorated exclusively in black-figure.

Conservative members of the Kerameikos, less than certain that the cylinder would enjoy unqualified success, cautiously produced 'compromise' *lekythoi* which retained the sharply curving lower body of the earlier shape (PLATE 3. 2).[8] Compromises vary in shape, according to the degree of the painter's conservatism. Generally earlier 'compromises' are more tapering, later ones are more cylindrical. The experiment was short-lived. The Edinburgh Painter is one of the last to decorate this shape, and his 'compromise' *lekythoi*[9] tend to be more slender than those of the older Leagrans, for instance the Acheloos Painter.[10] The 'compromise' *lekythos* was a black-figure shape, and until recently the only red-figure example known was the cock and hen *lekythos* in Oxford (PLATE 65. 1).[11] Now there is another, and both are described in some detail on pages 122 ff.

Early red-figure *lekythoi*,[12] although few in number and roughly contemporary, are sufficiently varied to reveal the hands of different potters active in different workshops.[13]

---

[1] *ARV* 675.

[2] The *lekythos* of cylindrical shape has a long, flat surface which lends itself to extended compositions without distortion by the vase's profile or disruption by its handle (*RA* 1972, 108). But encircling compositions are not at all common because the cylindrical shape restricts the amount of surface area visible at one time. The frontal picture panel framed by pattern bands or florals or unframed is a characteristic feature of fifth-century *lekythoi* of Type Two, red-figure and white-ground (CB i. 11). In black-figure encircling compositions are not unusual (*ABL* 6, 14, 51, 99) and on some early red-figure *lekythoi* figures encircle the vase (as on the Roundabout Painter's *lekythos* from the Agora, P 24061. *ARV* 131, PLATE 5. 2; and the arming *lekythos* from Agrigento. *ARV* 308, no. 5. Plate 6. 2) or a large floral composition fills the handle zone (as on Gales's *lekythoi*. *ARV* 35 f. (PLATE 6. 1)).

Side-palmettes frame the picture and, although they do not extend over the back of the vase, they are in a way a link between the extended black-figure compositions and the restricted fields of red-figure and white *lekythoi* of cylindrical shape. It is worth noting that white pattern *lekythoi* are not decorated on the back, but *lekythoi* of the Floral Nolan Group are.

On white *lekythoi* with figure decoration in outline encircling compositions are rare. Douris' *lekythos* in Cleveland (see pp. 29 ff. and PLATES 10. 2, 11) is an example, but it is an exceptional piece, whose composition is closely paralleled on the painter's red-figure *aryballos* in Athens (15375. *ARV* 447, no. 274 PLATE 9. 2). The Sabouroff Painter's *lekythos* in Hamburg (1896.21. *ARV* 847, no. 206) is another example.

[3] *ABL* 33 ff.   [4] Ibid. 41 ff.   [5] Ibid.
[6] Ibid. 41 ff. and pl. 41. 1.   [7] Ibid. 43 ff.
[8] Ibid. 47 ff.   [9] Ibid. 87 and pl. 29. 2.
[10] Ibid. 48 ff.   [11] Oxford, 1932.733.
[12] Early red-figure *lekythoi*: *VA* 26; CB i. 11; *ABL* 69 ff.
[13] *ABL*. 69.

Some are the first red-figure examples of shapes which soon become established in the new style's repertoire of shapes, for instance the standard cylinders of Gales (PLATE 6. 1),[1] and the group of *lekythoi* in various techniques from the Athena Painter's Workshop (see pp. 23 f. and PLATES 12, 13). Others are isolated examples in red-figure of essentially black-figure shapes, for instance the Oinophile *lekythos* (PLATE 6. 3)[2] which in shape is related to the class of Athens 581 (see pp. 147 f.). Two others, the Agrigento arming[3] and Boston athletes[4] *lekythoi*, seem to stand before DL, the characteristic shape of the black-figure Sappho and Diosphos Painters, which was decorated in outline, or semi-outline, on white-ground, not red-figure (see pp. 80 f.). Even though the red-figure technique had pushed black-figure into the background by the end of the sixth century, the market for *lekythoi* decorated in black-figure was good for some time, but these fifth-century black-figure *lekythoi* are almost without exception small and unquestionably second-rate. The major work is now being done in red-figure.

The Edinburgh, Theseus, and Athena Painters are the last to decorate large-cylinder *lekythoi* in the black-figure technique (see pp. 14 ff.). The only other large black-figure cylinders are the exotic BELs of the Beldam Painter (PLATES 18, 70. 3, 5),[5] and these stand apart from the cylinders of standard shape, and are more important for technique and iconography than for the perpetuation of the black-figure technique (see pp. 84 f.).

2. TYPE BL

In the workshop of the Athena Painter, a personal version of the Edinburgh cylinder developed which, though occasionally decorated in black-figure, is essentially a red-figure and white-ground shape.[6] Without the characteristic Bowdoin palmettes on the shoulder (see pp. 15 f.) BLs are not easily distinguished from other *lekythoi* of standard shape (cf. PLATES 12, 13, 14, 15).[7] The neck is black. At the join of neck to shoulder there are enclosed bars,[8] not the more usual tongues of early red-figure *lekythoi* of standard shape.[9] The shoulder is reserved. Reserved shoulders are characteristic of secondary *lekythoi*, but also of two groups of standard *lekythoi*: (1) those by the Achilles Painter and his followers with three elegant black palmettes (see pp. 43 f.; PLATE 34. 2, 3) and (2) those of the Klügmann, Dessypri, and related painters, with five sub-Bowdoin black palmettes, inelegantly painted (see pp. 15 f.). The foot is reserved and often flared.[10] This is a minority form, which occasionally occurs on *lekythoi* of standard type (cf. PLATE 12. 1).

The Bowdoin Painter is not the only Painter of BLs nor are all his *lekythoi* this shape; we have PLs,[11] CLs,[12] and ATLs[13] by him. Some of the painters decorating BLs stand close to the Bowdoin Painter,[14] whose workshop must have been large and influential. Black-bodied Bowdoin *lekythoi* (PLATE 67. 3) are described in Part Four.

[1] Boston, 13.195. *ARV* 35, no. 1; Syracuse, 26967. *ARV* 36, no. 2.
[2] London, 1922.10–18.1. *ARV* 332, no. 1.
[3] Agrigento, 23. *ARV* 308, no. 5.
[4] Boston, 95.42. [5] *ABL* 78. [6] *ARV* 678.
[7] Ibid. 675. [8] Not 'tongues', as *ARV* 693.
[9] CB iii. 27.

[10] There is a considerable variety among *lekythoi* of shape BL, especially in the form of the foot. Cf. *Sonderliste N*, p. 25, nos. 21–4.
[11] *ARV* 678, no. 23; 686, no. 208.
[12] Ibid. 679, nos. 31–2; 680, no. 61; 681, no. 84.
[13] Ibid. 678, no. 22; 680, nos. 54–5.
[14] Ibid. 692 ff. and *ARV*[1] 480.

3. TYPE DL

DL, the Diosphos Painter's type, 'can hardly be classed as either standard or secondary'.[1] The finest examples are very straight-sided cylinders (PLATE 69. 1). The body meets the foot in a full round curve. The neck and shoulder are reserved. The mouth is a rather deep cup and the foot, in two degrees, is partly reserved, partly painted black.[2] DL is a black-figure shape, but it is also the most important of the shapes decorated with figures and palmettes on white-ground (PLATES 58, 59); these side-palmette *lekythoi* are a speciality, if not an invention, of the Diosphos Workshop (see pp. 96 ff.).

Miss Haspels considered the principal *lekythoi* decorated by the Diosphos Painter and his partner, the Sappho Painter, 'sister shapes of the early red-figure arming *lekythos* in Agrigento' (PLATE 6. 2).[3] The Agrigento *lekythos* is a tapering cylinder, with deep-cup mouth, prominent lip, reserved neck, and foot in two degrees.[4] The subject of the picture panel, which encircles the vase,[5] recalls the Kleophrades Painter,[6] and the patternwork of the red-figure shoulder[7] recalls the Berlin Painter and his circle.[8] The vase has been attributed to the Terpaulos Painter[9] who like the Dutuit Painter was associated not only with the black-figure Diosphos Workshop, but also with the red-figure workshop of the Berlin Painter. A red-figure *oinochoe* in St. Louis (PLATE 55. 4),[10] attributed to the painter, is, in principle of decoration, a side-palmette vase: the elaborate handle florals come to the front, to frame the single figure, a maenad. Vases were similarly decorated by the Dutuit Painter.[11]

The Sappho Painter's *lekythoi* come closer to the Agrigento shape than to the Diosphos Painter's. They tend to be fuller and squatter, with a shallower mouth.[12] Apart from these near-cylinders, the Sappho Painter also decorated smaller *lekythoi*, with long neck, flat shoulder, sharply tapering body, and simple disc foot. The shape,[13] which looks like the Sappho Painter's own invention, is called Little Lion, after the most usual decoration on the shoulder.[14] The Little Lion is almost exclusively a black-figure shape;[15] a semi-outline example, near the Diosphos Painter (PLATE 59. 4),[16] is mentioned with side-palmette *lekythoi*.

The Diosphos Painter's *lekythoi* tend to be slimmer than the Agrigento *lekythos* and those of the Sappho Painter.[17] This is the DL of *ARV*, not the fuller shape of the Sappho Painter. The finest (PLATE 58. 2) come close to the standard cylinder in profile, and these

---

[1] *ARV* 675.

[2] Ibid. 301, 676; *ABL* pl. 36. 4.

[3] *ABL* 94.   [4] Ibid. 70.

[5] See p. 78 n. 2.   [6] *ABL* 71.

[7] Jacobsthal, 153 ff.; *ABL* 70 ff.

[8] Red-figure horizontal palmettes enclosed by S-spirals are found on vases by the Berlin Painter and members of his circle (*JHS* xxxi (1911), 279, fig. 3/13; 292, fig. 8/13), and on vases of the Floral Nolan Group (*ARV* 218 f.), related to the Berlin Painter and his circle (see pp. 125 f.). In architecture the pattern was also used, cf. E. Buschor, *Die Tondächer von der Akropolis zu Athen* i (1929), pls. 6–10.

[9] Agrigento, 23. *ARV* 308, no. 5.

[10] St. Louis, Washington University, 3283. *ARV* 308, no. 4.

[11] Cf. Louvre, G 203. *ARV* 306, no. 1; London, E 511. *ARV* 307, no. 9.

[12] *ABL* 94 and pl. 32 (cf. pl. 36. 3, the Sappho Painter's slimmer type).

[13] Ibid. 98 and pl. 36. 1.

[14] *ARV* 301; *ABV* 512 ff., 703; *Para* 251 ff; *ABL* 98 ff.

[15] Little Lion *lekythoi* are also decorated in Six's technique or they are painted black without figure decoration (*ABL* 107). See pp. 120 f.

[16] Louvre, MNB 911. *ARV* 301, no. 1.

[17] *ABL* 100 and pl. 36. 4.

are the vases that the Diosphos Painter decorated with palmettes and figures,[1] or exclusively with palmettes,[2] on a white ground. Some of the Diosphos Painter's latest *lekythoi* are slimmer, with deep-cup mouth and a degenerate form of the lotus-bud chain on the shoulder.[3] This is the shape taken up by the Haimon Painter[4] and decorated either in black-figure or exclusively with patterns (see pp. 150 ff.).[5]

4. TYPE PL

PL—the Painter of Petit Palais 336's favourite type (PLATE 28. 1)—is related to DL, the Sappho Painter's version, not the Diosphos Painter's, and the Painter of Petit Palais 336 is 'akin' to both the Sappho and Diosphos Painters.[6] PL is not a black-figure shape. After DL it is the most important for side-palmette *lekythoi* and the popularity of this type of decoration is easily understood in view of the shape's connection with the Diosphos Workshop. Side-palmette *lekythoi* of shape PL (PLATE 61. 1) tend to make more use of outline, less of silhouette, and a number of the white-ground PLs are decorated exclusively in the outline technique (see pp. 102 f.). There are also red-figure PLs[7]—among them the Sabouroff Painter's in Honolulu with elaborate handle florals (PLATE 28. 1).[8] Most of the painters of red-figure PLs appear to be related in some way, as we might expect, since the vase, in its pure form, does not seem to have been produced over a very long period of time.[9]

PLs are generally small. The mouth is shallow and straight-sided. The neck is long and the shoulder is nearly flat. The body tapers sharply towards a simple disc foot.[10] This description is almost as appropriate to the Little Lions (cf. PLATE 59. 4). Little Lions are a speciality of the Sappho Painter and PL derives from the Sappho Painter's version of DL.

PL, as we have said, derives from the fuller form of DL, the Sappho Painter's version which stands closer to the Agrigento arming *lekythos* than the DL of the Diosphos Painter. The Agrigento *lekythos* (PLATE 6. 2) has a deep mouth, curved profile, prominent lip, and a foot in two degrees. Another early red-figure *lekythos*, the Oinophile *lekythos* in London (PLATE 6. 3),[11] has, in addition to the tapering body, the simple mouth and foot[12] which are characteristic features of PL. In style of drawing the Oinophile *lekythos* comes close to some Panaitian *kyathoi*,[13] in shape to the *lekythoi* of Class of Athens 581.[14] The shoulder decoration is in the manner of the Phanyllis Painter[15]—the chief proponent of the old-fashioned broad, sharply tapering *lekythos*, in the wake of the new cylinder,[16] which was connected with the Class of Athens 581, in decoration as well as shape (see pp. 147 f.).[17] Beazley noted the resemblance in shape between *lekythoi* of type PL and *lekythoi* of the Class of Athens 581.[18]

[1] Ibid. 110 f.
[2] Ibid. 110 f. (Athens, 12271. *ABL* 235, no. 66).
[3] *ABL* 100 and pl. 38. 3.
[4] Ibid. 131 and pl. 41.   [5] Ibid. 133.
[6] *ARV* 675, 1665, 1702; *Para* 405.   [7] *ARV* 676.
[8] Honolulu, 2892. *ARV* 844, no. 153.
[9] *ARV* 675 f. Most of the vases look as if they were

produced in the later 470s and 460s.
[10] Ibid. 676.   [11] London, 1922.10–18.1.
[12] *ABL* 74, 89.   [13] *ARV* 332, no. 1.
[14] Ibid. 333.   [15] *ABL* 63.   [16] Ibid. 63 f.
[17] Ibid. 42 f., 67 f., 93 and n. 3.
[18] *ARV* 676; *ABV* 466 ff., 471, 487, 498.

5. TYPE ATL

ATL is a favourite shape of the Aischines and Tymbos Painters (PLATE 21), and is related both to PL and to DL.[1] As the body of PL tapers less and as the mouth deepens, the shape becomes assimilated to the commoner type ATL.[2] The more cylindrical body, the deeper mouth, and the foot in two degrees[3] connect the shape with DL.[4] The cylinder tends to be slender, like the Diosphos Painter's later shape, taken up by the Haimon Painter.[5] The small calyx-mouth *lekythos* described by Miss Haspels in connection with the Beldam and Haimon Painters[6] is one of the versions of shape ATL, as it is recognized in *ARV*.[7] Miss Haspels connected the Tymbos Group with the Beldam Workshop not only in shape, but also in decoration.[8] The predominance of funerary scenes on *lekythoi* of the Tymbos Group is perhaps also a result of Beldam affiliation (see p. 83 n. 4). Significant in this regard is the Tymbos Painter's resemblance to the Inscription Painter,[9] another painter of funerary scenes, related to the Beldam Painter and his workshop (see p. 20).

ATL is a red-figure and a white-ground shape. Among ATLs there is considerable variety in shape and quality. Those which come closer to DL are finer, and not infrequently larger (PLATE 21. 1, 2).[10] A small group of these, red-figure and white-ground, has been connected with the Flying-Angel Painter (see p. 34 n. 11).[11] The neck and shoulder are reserved, as on all ATLs, but the shoulder is decorated with palmettes instead of the more usual degenerate buds or rays. The five black palmettes, beneath unenclosed bars, are arranged in a system like the Bowdoin Painter's. Earlier ATLs are roughly contemporary with the Bowdoin Painter's period of greatest influence, and one of the white-ground ATLs connected with the Flying-Angel Painter was buried with a red-figure Bowdoin *lekythos* of type BL in a grave at Gela.[12]

A large, fine, white-ground ATL, recently on the Basle Market, has been attributed to the Aischines Painter (PLATE 21. 2).[13] Although the Aischines and Tymbos Painters are members of the same workshop,[14] they have markedly different characters. The Aischines Painter's *lekythoi* are red-figure more often than white-ground and their iconography is not funerary.[15] In addition to *lekythoi* he painted vases of several different shapes, including cups.[16] His choice of shape and his iconography have more in common with the Carlsruhe Painter than the Tymbos Painter.

The Tymbos Group (PLATES 22, 23)[17] comprises a large number of small *lekythoi*,

[1] *ARV* 709; *BCH* xcv (1971), 610 ff. (P. Amandry, quoting B. F. Cook).

[2] *ARV* 675.

[3] *BCH* xcv. 612; cf. *ARV* 755, nos. 37 *bis* and 41; 757, no. 70.

[4] *ARV* 709.

[5] *ABL* 131.

[6] Ibid. 130 f., 178 ff.

[7] *ARV* 675, 709.

[8] *ABL* 180; cf. *ARV*[1] 503.

[9] Ibid. 503.

[10] Cf. Copenhagen, 6328. *ARV* 283, no. 4. *CV* iv,

p. 132 (27·4 cm); Gela, no number. *ARV* 283, no. 3. *NSc* 1956, 296 (26·3 cm).

[11] *ARV* 282 f., 709.

[12] *NSc*, 1956, 297, fig. 11 (= *ARV* 683, no. 126) and p. 12.

[13] *ARV* 715, no. 189 *bis*, and *Para* 409. *Auktion* xxxiv, no. 179 (p. 94, 27 cm).

[14] *ARV* 709, 721, 722 f. (Group of Athens 2025), 753; *ABL* 180.

[15] *ARV* 709 ff., 1667 ff., 1706; *Para* 408 ff.

[16] *ARV* 718, nos. 239–46.

[17] Ibid. 753 ff., 1668 f., 1702; *Para* 414 f.

produced over a considerable period of time, and decorated by the Tymbos Painter as well as by other related artists.[1] With very few exceptions the *lekythoi* are white-ground.[2] The earliest have glaze outlines; the later *lekythoi* have outlines in glaze mixed with matt, and the latest have matt outlines.[3] The iconography is predominantly funerary, and, despite the shockingly poor quality of the drawing, exceedingly interesting.[4] The poor quality of the draughtsmanship is matched by a generally low standard of potting: the work is coarse, the profile is slack, and the proportions are heavy and unattractive.[5] The usual shoulder decoration is hastily painted bars, which sometimes look like degenerate buds or rays;[6] palmettes are virtually unknown.[7]

[1] *ARV* 753.

[2] Ibid. 758, nos. 95–6 and nos. 1–2 ('near'); 762.

[3] Ibid. 753.

[4] The Tymbos Group (*ARV* 753 ff., 1668 f., 1702; *Para* 414 f.), just under 200 vases, almost all *lekythoi*, has been divided into three subgroups by Beazley (*ARV* 753): (i) vases by the Tymbos Painter; (ii) vases in his manner; (iii) late products of the workshop. The division is based partly on technique (glaze in (i), glaze and matt in (ii), and matt in (iii)) and partly on style. Roughly half of the vases, with few exceptions white *lekythoi*, are by the Tymbos Painter himself. Less than one-third of the *lekythoi* feature a single female (woman, Iris, Nike) in the manner of the Carlsruhe, Aischines, and Bowdoin Painters. The rest have tomb scenes. The monument most often represented is the round mound, or *tymbos*, from which the painter takes his name. A peculiar feature of *tymboi* by the Tymbos Painter is the 'interior view'—a figure is framed within the outline of the mound; it is not always clear whether the figure is meant to be in front of the mound or inside it (cf. *ARV* 753, and pp. 754, nos. 1–12, 756, no. 65). On at least one of the vases (London, D 35. *ARV* 756, no. 66. (PLATE 23. 1)) a figure seems like a corpse. (Cf. an unattributed *lekythos* in Tübingen (E 63. Watzinger, pl. 26); the head of the bier on the Tübingen *lekythos* may be compared with the ivory fitting with amber inlay found in a grave in the Kerameikos (*ADelt* xix (1964), B, pl. 39*a*).) Other tomb monuments represented on these *lekythoi* include *stelai* and broader tombstones which sometimes have figure decoration (cf. *ARV* 754, nos. 3, 7–9, 11, and p. 754, no. 14 (PLATE 22. 1)). There is also a sphinx monument (Athens, 1885. *ARV* 755, no. 40) which is not certainly funerary. (The fashion for sphinxes on graves had passed. See G. M. A. Richter, *The Archaic Gravestones of Attica* (1961), 6 f., but they are common subsidiary decoration on late fifth- and fourth-century gravestones. See B. F. Cook, *Antike Plastik* ix (1969), 67, and nn. 16–18.) Usually one figure stands beside the tombstone, most often a woman, who sometimes tears her hair (*ARV* 755, nos. 30–1; 756, no. 67) or falls to the ground in grief (*ARV* 755, no. 33). The youth charging with drawn sword on one of the *lekythoi* (New York, 06.1021.127. *ARV* 757, no. 90) is a conflation of two scenes: the youth running with spear or sword (*ARV* 757, nos. 86, 89) and the youth 'running' to the tomb (*ARV* 757, nos. 80–4). A similar example of conflation involves the seated woman (*ARV* 756, nos. 55–7), the seated woman 'in' a tomb (*ARV* 754, nos. 5–12), and the seated woman at the tomb (Oxford, 1956.14. *ARV* 754, no. 13. PLATE 22. 2). Two scenes on *lekythoi* by the Tymbos Painter fall outside these categories: the 'Oriental archer' (Cab. Méd. 496 *bis*. *ARV* 758, no. 94) and Charon (*ARV* 756, nos. 63–4). The Orientals are described on p. 41 n. 6. The Charon differs from others whom we have described in several respects: he is represented alone, in a complete boat, attended by sizeable *eidola* (PLATE 23. 2).

Vases in the manner of the Tymbos Painter (ii) are all white *lekythoi*, roughly fifty in number. The iconography is predominantly funerary and the compositions are very like those of the Tymbos Painter, although funerary monuments are represented more often, 'interior views' less often. Only one of the *lekythoi* requires special mention: the vase in Jena (*ARV* 760, no. 41) with 'Hermes at a *pithos*, charming souls'. The iconography has not been satisfactorily explained. The traditional interpretation (*JHS* xx (1900), 101 (J. Harrison)) that we have here a representation of the return of the souls at the end of the *Anthesteria* seems unlikely.

'Late products of the Workshop' (iii) number just under fifty, all white *lekythoi* whose iconography is almost exclusively funerary. The compositions continue virtually unchanged, but 'interior views' are no longer common and there is greater variety in the types of monuments. On one *lekythos* a woman stands between two *stelai* (Athens, 2026. *ARV* 761, no. 9), on another she sits on rocks, her head bowed in grief (Oxford, 1927.4463. *ARV* 761, no. 14). On one of the *lekythoi* a man rides a horse to the tomb (Winchester, 48. *ARV* 762, no. 32); see pp. 64 f.

[5] *ARV* 709.

[6] Ibid. 755, no. 37 *bis*; 756, no. 41; 757, no. 72.

[7] Ibid. 759, no. 9.

6. TYPE CL

CL[1] is the Carlsruhe Painter's favourite type of *lekythos* (PLATE 61. 4).[2] The upper body is cylindrical but the lower body tapers, sometimes sharply,[3] towards the foot—a simple disc[4] (reserved or concave), painted in imitation two degrees.[5] The neck and shoulder are reserved. The shoulder rises sharply and is decorated with hastily painted rays, beneath enclosed bars. The mouth tends to be shallow and rather straight-sided. Some CLs are large, well fashioned, and competently decorated; others are small, poorly fashioned, and carelessly decorated.

CL is a red-figure shape even more than white-ground—which is perhaps not surprising since the Carlsruhe Painter worked primarily in red-figure on a great variety of shapes, including a significant number of cups. Our earliest CL is red-figure,[6] a vase in a private collection,[7] whose style of figure-drawing is in the manner of Douris, especially of the Cartellino Painter, whose red-figure BLs bear the inscription *Doris* (see p. 25).[8] The Carlsruhe Painter decorates some BLs[9] and the Bowdoin Painter some CLs.[10] The Bowdoin Painter's CLs are red-figure, the Carlsruhe Painter's BLs are white-ground, with Bowdoin palmettes. Bowdoin palmettes also appear on the shoulder of one of his white *lekythoi* of standard shape.[11]

The iconography of the type CL *lekythos* is not funerary. A single figure, usually female, is most common.[12] A group of unattributed red-figure CLs[13] is decorated with an owl, sometimes with olive sprigs.[14] Similar owl *lekythoi* of other secondary shapes have been attributed to the Bowdoin Painter[15] and to the Icarus Painter.[16] Both painted CLs[17] and head-*lekythoi* (see pp. 109 f.). The Icarus Painter,[18] like the Carlsruhe Painter, was once associated with the Beldam Workshop.[19]

7. TYPE BEL

BEL[20] is the most easily recognized secondary shape (PLATE 18). The number of examples is small, and all of these are decorated by the Beldam Painter or by artists closely associated with him, within a short period of time. Miss Haspels dated the earliest BEL (the Beldam

[1] *ARV* 676 f., 1665; *Para* 405.

[2] *ARV* 730 ff., 1668; *Para* 411 f.

[3] Oxford, *CV* i, pl. 38. 2 (1914.9 = 733, no. 64).

[4] Tübingen, E 80. *ARV* 734, 84; Watzinger, pl. 25.

[5] Oxford, *CV* i, pl. 38. 1 (1916.15. *ARV* 733, no. 71).

[6] *AJA* lii (1948), 336.

[7] Coll. Seyrig. *ARV* 452.

[8] *AJA* lii. 336.

[9] *ARV* 732, no. 40 (red-figure); 734, nos. 93–5 (white).

[10] Ibid. 679, nos. 31–2; 680, no. 61; 681, no. 84.

[11] Corinth, MP 89. *ARV* 735, no. 97.

[12] The subjects are sometimes rather unusual: female pyrrhicist, with the painted inscription *Zephyria*

kale, on a red-figure *lekythos* of shape CL in Cape Town (18. *ARV* 677, no. 12); a satyr plunging into a *pithos* on a red-figure *lekythos* of shape CL in Carlsruhe (219. *ARV* 677, no. 13).

[13] Cf. Athens Market. *ARV* 734, no. 87 ('siren to right; on the right a sprig of olive').

[14] *ARV* 677, no. 14; 1665; *Para* 405.

[15] *ARV* 685, nos. 179–80.

[16] Ibid. 699, nos. 58–61.

[17] Ibid. 677.

[18] Ibid. 696 ff., 1666 f., 1702; *Para* 407.

[19] *ABL* 180.

[20] *ARV* 675, 750.

Painter's name vase in Athens) around 470 B.C.[1] BEL is a white-ground shape,[2] initially decorated in black-figure, later in outline. Despite the small number of examples, BELs are important to our study because of their technique, iconography, and false interiors.

The shape looks as if it were one potter's personal version of the standard cylinder.[3] BELs are large and well made, with a generous amount of white slip, not only for the body but also for the neck and shoulder. The neck is decorated[4] with an ivy-berry tendril,[5] the shoulder with palmettes,[6] whose arrangement varies according to the technique of the vases (see below). At the join of neck to shoulder there are bars, enclosed on the top only.[7] The mouth is deep and rounded; the neck is long and the shoulder rises sharply. But the most notable feature is the angle formed by the join of shoulder to body: instead of swelling out at this point, the body curves in.[8] The walls of the vase are nearly straight, apart from this angle, and meet the foot in a full round curve, as in *lekythoi* of standard shape. Characteristic too is the series of wet incised lines on the lower body.[9] The form of the foot varies: some are simple reserved discs,[10] others are flared and painted in imitation two degrees.[11]

The earliest BELs are fully black-figure and their shoulders bear five palmettes in the Athena Painter's favourite scheme (FIGURE 10a). Later BELs are semi-outline or outline and the shoulder palmettes are modified (FIGURE 10b, c): the number of petals is decreased and the space between them is increased. This system admits red for the alternate petals (now faded). The characteristic feature of BEL shoulders, regardless of the disposition of the palmettes, is the tiny arc tendrils which sprout from the larger tendrils linking palmettes. The Beldam palmettes and tiny arc tendrils are found in the latest work of the Theseus Painter,[12] and some of his cylinders come closer to the Beldam model than to any of those of his colleague, the Athena Painter.[13] It is possible that the Theseus Painter's tradition of funerary iconography within the Theseus–Athena Workshop also influenced the Beldam Painter.

The iconography of the black-figure BELs is not funerary.[14] Two semi-outline BELs feature tomb scenes (PLATE 18. 1)[15]—and one of the outline BELs (PLATE 18.

---

[1] *ABL* 171.

[2] There is one red-figure *lekythos* by the Beldam Painter (Copenhagen, 1941. *ARV* 751, no. 3) which at least in point of shape looks like an unsuccessful experiment (*ABL* 174).

[3] *ABL* 170 ff. Miss Haspels also draws attention to the distinctive clay of the Beldam Painter's cylinders; most of these of known provenience have been found in Eretria (*ABL* 266 ff.). See pp. 137 f.

[4] Decorated necks are not common on Attic *lekythoi*; the following examples are worth noting: Black-figure: Athens, 2246. *ABL* 203 and pl. 19. 4 (Chariot Painter); Palermo, 996. *ABL* 66 and pl. 19. 5 (unattributed); Athens, 12274. *ABL* 199, no. 14, and pl. 19. 1, and Athens, 574. *ABL* 200, no. 23, and pl. 19. 3 (Phanyllis Painter); Boston, 93.99. *ABL* 206, no. 5, and pl. 23. 1, and Athens, 399. *ABL* 222, no. 20, and pl. 31. 4 (Gela Painter). With the chequery on the neck of Athens 399, compare the painter's *lekythos* illustrated on

[PLATE] 17. 1. Red-figure: Zürich, Roš. *ARV* 656, no. 15 (Dresden Painter). PLATE 27. 6; Athens, 1626. *ARV* 663 f. (Mys).

[5] Phanyllis Painter: see above note; Painter of London, D 65, see p. 19 n. 13.

[6] Degenerate buds or bars are occasionally found on BELs by the Beldam Painter, e.g. Athens, 487. *ABL* 267, no. 11, and pl. 50. 1.

[7] The bars are not regularly enclosed on both sides (cf. ibid. 171).

[8] *ABL* 170 f.   [9] Ibid. 171.

[10] Ibid., pl. 50. 2, 4.   [11] Ibid., pl. 50. 1, 3.

[12] Ibid. 146.   [13] Cf. ibid., pl. 44. 2.

[14] Ibid. 172 f., 266 f.

[15] Athens, 12801. *ABL* 266, no. 2; Athens, 1948. *ABL* 266, no. 9. On both *lekythoi* the figures are fully black-figure and the tomb is rendered in outline. Solid black (silhouette) is used for some details (especially ribbons). The tomb on Athens 1948 is like that on the

2).[1] These *lekythoi* have all the essential elements of the tomb scene as it appears on later white *lekythoi*, including fillets, wreaths, and *lekythoi*—one broken at the grave. In addition to figure scenes, two of the white-ground BELs are decorated exclusively with patterns (PLATE 70. 5) (see pp. 153 ff.).[2]

Most of the BELs decorated by other painters also have tomb scenes. A group of them by the Carlsruhe Painter,[3] has tombs rendered in second white (one with a mock inscription[4]—in the manner of the Inscription Painter, who decorated at least one *lekythos* of BEL shape (PLATE 19. 1))[5], as do two by the Utrecht Painter,[6] whose style of drawing is also near the Carlsruhe Painter. Second white is used for the tomb on the two BELs by the Painter of London D 65 (PLATE 18. 3).[7] The use of second white for tombs on these *lekythoi*, but not for female flesh, is surely meaningful; the white probably indicates that the monument is not of wood but of marble, as were the finest of the contemporary gravestones. One of the unattributed BELs with a tomb scene[8] deserves special mention, for three tombs are represented sharing a common base[9] (as do the monuments on the Anavyssos *lekythos* by the Painter of Munich 2335 and the New York *lekythos* by the Vouni Painter (PLATE 26. 2)), and in the space between them are inscribed . . . *chos*, *Aristipos*, and *Diphilos*.[10]

False interiors are first known from Beldam *lekythoi*.[11] BELs are large and expensive to fill. The addition of a small interior chamber (cf. PLATE 35. 4) enabled the living to economize in an extravagant display of piety towards the dead. If later, very large, white *lekythoi* do not have false interiors, it is probably because the vase is no longer designed principally as a container for oil. Fashioning a vase with an interior compartment is difficult, but the idea caught on, and soon other potters began to make them. The shape of the interior receptacle (which can be determined by X-ray photography) and the

outline BEL (Athens 1982) of the following note. The horseman has been lifted from a valediction scene, of the type which occupies the subsidiary zones on some late black-figure and red-figure *loutrophoroi*. (The retention of the black-figure, or silhouette, technique for these friezes on some red-figure *loutrophoroi* is significant.) The horseman on the BEL cylinder, like those on *loutrophoroi*, performs the gesture of valediction (Aeschylus, *Choephoroi*, 9). Another important iconographic detail of this vase is the projection of the *stele* into the shoulder zone. Compare the similar treatment of *stelai* on white *lekythoi* by the Painter of Athens 1826 (London, 1928.2–13.1. *ARV* 746, no. 4. PLATE 26. 1; Athens, 1825. *ARV* 746, no. 11), whose relation to the Beldam Workshop is mentioned on pp. 27 f.; compare also the projecting *stele* on the un-attributed white *lekythos* in Boston (1970.428), PLATE 20. 2.

¹ Athens, 1982. *ABL* 267, no. 12.
² Athens, Kerameikos. *ABL* 266, no. 6; Munich Market. *ABL* 181, 266, no. 7; *ARV* 751. Smaller pattern *lekythoi* of secondary shape from the Beldam Workshop are mentioned on pp. 154 f.

³ *ARV* 735, nos. 99–102.
⁴ Paris Market. *ARV* 735, no. 100.
⁵ Madrid, 19497. *ARV* 748, no. 1.
⁶ *ARV* 753.
⁷ Ibid. 752. Cf. also Athens Market. *ARV* 751.
⁸ Chicago, University. *ARV* 752.
⁹ Compare the Vouni Painter's *lekythos* in New York (35.11.5. *ARV* 744, no. 1. PLATE 26. 2) and the Painter of Munich 2335's *lekythos* from Anavyssos (Athens, 19354. *ARV* 1168, no. 131 *bis*).
¹⁰ *ARV* 1575; *AJA* xii (1908), 428 ff. Compare the fragment of a large amphora or *loutrophoros* in the Allard Pierson Museum (*Hesp* xxxvi (1967), 324) which appears to be white-ground (cf. *Gestalt und Geschichte* (1967), 146 f. (L. Kahil)) with at least five tombstones. The monuments appear to share a common base, and on two the inscriptions 'in Byzantium' and 'in Eleutherai' can be detected—therefore, possibly a visual record of the Casualty Lists which the Athenians erected for their war dead (*Hesp* xxxvi. 324 f. (D. Bradeen)).
¹¹ A recent study of false interiors: *AA* 1972. 458 ff. (K. Waldstein). White *lekythoi* are mentioned on pp. 472 f. and in n. 101.

position of the all-important vent hole (which permitted the vase to be fired without breaking) vary according to different potters. A study of false interiors would take us a step forward in our knowledge of potter and painter relationships.

8. CHIMNEYS

The last secondary shape which we shall consider is one of the two types of smaller *lekythoi* produced by the Beldam Workshop. Both are named after the shape of the mouth; the calyx or cup-mouth *lekythoi* have been mentioned in connection with shape ATL. The chimney *lekythos* (PLATES 64. 2, 70. 4, 8), like the large BEL, is a curious shape with limited popularity.[1] Apart from the Beldam Painter himself, the Emporion and Haimon Painters are the only artists who specialized in them. The Emporion Painter's chimneys are like the Beldam Painter's: the shoulder is steep, the body is sharply tapered, and the concave foot is painted in imitation two degrees.[2] Haemonian chimneys, on the other hand, are nearly cylindrical, and the shoulders are quite flat.[3] The chimney is not a red-figure shape, nor is it popular in white-ground. It is included here because of the small number of white-ground examples decorated with side-palmettes (PLATE 64. 2; see pp. 111 f.) or exclusively with patterns (PLATE 70. 8; see pp. 151 f.).

[1] *ABL* 178 f.   [2] Ibid. 165 f.   [3] Ibid. 137.

PART THREE

SIDE-PALMETTE *LEKYTHOI*

PART THREE

SIDE-PALMETTE *LEKYTHOI*

INTRODUCTION

SIDE-PALMETTE *lekythoi* (cf. PLATES 58, 59)—the name is Beazley's[1]—like many of the vases chosen for study in the monograph, are relatively unknown, and, in a survey of Greek painting unimportant. For our purposes their importance is considerable: not only are virtually all side-palmette *lekythoi* white-ground, but the florals and figures on the body are often combined in such a way that the work of one hand, not two, seems assured. Side-palmette *lekythoi* are, therefore, one of the groups of *lekythoi* on which figures and patterns can be shown to be closely related, if not actually painted by one man. Another group consists of black-bodied *lekythoi* with figures and florals on the shoulder, described on pages 122 ff.

Side-palmette *lekythoi* are not numerous. Miss Haspels drew attention to *lekythoi* decorated in this way, especially to side-palmette *lekythoi* of the Diosphos Workshop,[2] and Beazley included them in *ARV*.[3] In this section side-palmette *lekythoi* are taken by shape, and reference should be made to the preceding pages in which the shapes of shoulder-type *lekythoi* are described.

With very few exceptions,[4] side-palmette *lekythoi* are white-ground. The palmettes are black, and black is sometimes retained for detail, but outline is more common for the figurework than black-figure[5] or silhouette. Added colour is restricted to touches of red or purple. These vases were first produced around 500 B.C., and most date to the first or early second quarter of the fifth century. Side palmettes are found on *lekythoi* of most secondary shapes, including the near-standard BL.

1. THE PRINCIPLE OF DECORATION

The principle of decoration—florals framing a central figure composition—is borrowed from contemporary vases of other shapes, whose handle florals are sometimes elaborate compositions extending towards the front or back of the vase, framing its figure scene (cf. PLATE 55). The florals painted beneath the handles on clay vases often look as if they were derived from metal vases, whose intricately worked handle attachments decoratively conceal the rivet holes joining handle to body.[6] Handle florals were painted on clay vases in the East before they became popular in Attica.[7] Fikellura amphorae are perhaps the best example; some of these made much of handle florals, which occasionally frame

---

[1] *ARV* 300 ff.

[2] *ABL* 110 ff.; cf. Fairbanks's 'scrolls and palmettes' (i. 29 ff., A: I) and 'vases with scrolls and large palmettes on each side of the main scene' (i. 59 ff., A: IIIa).

[3] *ARV* 300 ff., 1643 f.; *Para* 356 f.

[4] Berlin, 3261. *ABL* 198, no. 2, and Boston, 93.102. *ABL* 198, no. 3 (Cactus Painter).

[5] 'Semi-outline' is not as characteristic of side-palmette *lekythoi* as the classification in *ARV* (300 f.) suggests.

[6] Cf. Jacobsthal, 39, 144 and pl. 21 *a–c*. Metal vases with elaborate handle attachments are described by Jacobsthal (*Bronzeschnabelkannen* (1929)) and Miss Lamb (*Ancient Greek and Roman Bronzes* (1929); cf. white-ground *oinochoe*, *Sonderliste G*, no. 76).

[7] Jacobsthal, 23–45 ('Chalcidian' and Fikellura).

a central figure composition.[1] Jacobsthal studied the handle florals and distinguished two types on Attic vases: florals attached to the handle and florals floating freely beneath it.[2] The first is chronologically the earlier of the two, and in principle of decoration closer to the metal prototype.

Handle florals are found on a small number of *lekythoi*, black- and red-figure, but this type of ornament may have been more common on *lekythoi* than present evidence suggests. Some black-figure examples have been cited by Miss Haspels;[3] a few more are added here. Two black-figure shoulder *lekythoi* of special type in New York,[4] which Beazley thought recalled the Wraith Painter,[5] have palmettes, base to base, beneath the handle. On one[6] of the *lekythoi* the tendrils of the central palmette terminate in four lateral palmettes (FIGURE 25*b*); on the other[7] the tendrils of the central palmette terminate in spirals, with a partial palmette in the spandrel on either side of the central palmettes (FIGURE 25*a*). On neither vase are the central palmettes attached to the handles; they are static, as they are on a black-figure *lekythos* by the Gela Painter in Boston (FIGURE 25*c*).[8] The Gela Painter's florals are arranged like those on the first New York *lekythos*, but the central palmettes are apex to apex, not base to base.[9] The Boston vase has a scene from an oil shop (PLATE 17. 2), to which small florals have been decoratively added. On other *lekythoi* by the painter florals are held by Erotes (PLATE 16. 4)[10] and seated figures, deities,[11] or mortals;[12] palmette trees spring up from the ground line behind a fawn[13] or between large heads (PLATE 17. 3).[14]

The handle palmettes on a Leagran *lekythos* of compromise shape in the Funcke Collection (PLATE 3. 2)[15] are arranged differently; the composition is not static, and pairs of linked palmettes float freely beneath the handle. The arrangement of the palmettes, the treatment of their hearts, and the thin spandrel buds are not unlike those on an unattributed white-ground *oinochoe* in Dresden[16] and the white-ground column-crater in Carlsruhe (PLATE 55. 1)[17] by the Sappho Painter. The palmettes on the shoulder are the Leagran seven, linked in groups of two, three, and two. The Sappho Painter and his partner the Diosphos Painter are contemporary with the Leagros Group and not without some relation to it.[18]

The last examples of handle florals on black-figure *lekythoi* which I describe are by an artist closely related to the Sappho Painter, the Kephisophon Painter.[19] A small number

[1] *BSA* xxxiv (1933–4), 79 ff. (R. Cook).

[2] Jacobsthal, 23 ff., 46 ff.   [3] *ABL* 18 f.

[4] *ABV* 454. Painter of New York 07.

[5] Ibid.

[6] New York, 07.286.41. *ABV* 454, no. 1.

[7] New York, 07.286.43. *ABV* 454, no. 2. Cf. *Hesp* ix (1940), 218, fig. 41 (A-P 1665).

[8] Boston, 99.526. *ABL* 209, no. 81.

[9] The long tendrils with loops may be compared with some shoulder palmettes on *lekythoi* of the Leagros period (cf. *ABL*, pl. 20. 1; see also below, n. 15) and on some Leagran vases of different shapes, e.g. *stamnoi* (Brussels, R 251. *ABV* 388, no. 2; Maplewood, Noble, *ABV* 388, no. 2 *bis*, and p. 696) and on a *hydria* by the Antimenes Painter (Villa Giulia,

3556. *ABV* 269, no. 35; cf. Swiss Private. *ABV* 269, no. 35 *bis*, and *Para* 119).

[10] Syracuse, 19854. *ABL* 212, no. 151.

[11] Vienna, 84. *ABL* 212, no. 158.

[12] Compiègne, 1040. *ABL* 209, no. 86 (deities?, cf. *CV* p. 9).

[13] London Market. *ABL* 215, no. 152; *Sonderliste G*, no. 24.

[14] Vienna, 84.

[15] Wuppertal, Funcke, Inv. S. 496. *Sammlung Funcke*, 84 f., no. 76.

[16] Dresden, ZV 1608. Jacobsthal, pl. 49*b*.

[17] Carlsruhe, 167. *ABL* 228, no. 57.

[18] See p. 98 nn. 1 f.

[19] *ABV* 514, 669; *Para* 253.

of white *lekythoi* have been attributed to him, all Little Lions[1]—the Sappho Painter's special shape (see p. 81). At least two of them have handle florals. On a Little Lion in New York[2] linked circumscribed palmettes, neatly drawn, float in a free composition beneath the handle. The second Little Lion, now lost (PLATE 56. 2),[3] had exceptionally interesting handle florals (FIGURE 26a): four circumscribed palmettes, neatly drawn, bases directed towards a centre point on the handle axis. The two horizontally oriented palmettes are linked; the vertically oriented are not; in the spandrels formed by the four palmettes are four small black birds. Both *lekythoi* bear a *kalos* inscription in praise of Kephisophon.[4] Kephisophon is praised on another Attic vase—a red-figure Proto-Panaitian cup in the Cabinet des Médailles,[5] along with Dorotheos and Olympiodoros. Dorotheos and Olympiodoros are praised on other red-figure vases[6] and on other black-figure vases.[7] Among the latter is a *hydria* in the Vatican on which Olympiodoros is praised with Leagros,[8] and a black-bodied *oinochoe* in Munich (PLATE 57. 1)[9] whose shoulder bears palmettes with black birds, on which Dorotheos is praised with Memnon. Lastly, a white-ground Little Lion recently acquired by the Royal Ontario Museum, Toronto, and attributed by Beazley to the Kephisophon Painter (PLATE 56. 1),[10] bears five athletes and five names: Olympiodoros, Megakles, Spintharos, Dion, and P[y]this. The composition recalls the reliefs on three statue bases, two recovered from the Themistoklean Wall in Athens in 1922,[11] and a third from the Dipylon Gate in 1962.[12] In publishing the Dipylon base, which probably supported a *kouros*, Willemsen compared a group of white-ground *oinochoai*[13] by the Painter of London B 620 (PLATE 57. 2),[14] and these *oinochoai* were compared by Beazley[15] with the black-bodied *oinochoe* in Munich whose shoulder bears palmettes and black birds and the *kalos* inscriptions Dorotheos and Memnon.

Before turning to the handle ornament of red-figure *lekythoi* I should like to draw attention to other 'black-bird' vases.[16] Beazley dated the Munich *oinochoe* 'about 520 or not much later'.[17] The three statue bases have been dated around 510[18] and the lower date accords better with the ceramic evidence—a group of vases of different shapes with black palmettes and black birds on white ground, either beneath the handle or disposed on either side of the figure decoration. A white-ground amphora of Nikosthenic shape in Vienna (PLATE 55. 2; FIGURE 26b)[19] and a white-ground *oinochoe* in Dresden[20] have palmettes and birds beneath the handle. Miss Haspels compared the style and decoration of the

---

[1] *ABL* 117 f., 230 (top).

[2] New York, 08.258.30. *ABL* 230, no. 1.

[3] Once New York, Gallatin. Now lost. *ABL* 230, no. 3, and *ABV* 514, 669.

[4] *ABV* 669.

[5] Cab. Méd., 523. *ARV* 316, no. 4, and p. 1589.

[6] *ARV* 1575 f., 1604.

[7] *ABV* 666, 671.

[8] Vatican, 416. *ABV* 365, no. 65.

[9] Munich, 2447. *ABV* 425.

[10] Toronto, 963.59. *ARV* 1699 and *Para* 253.

[11] Athens, National Museum, nos. 3476 and 3477. *BSA* lvii (1962), 127 f. (L. Jeffery); *AM* lxxviii (1963), 133 ff. (Willemsen).

[12] Athens, Kerameikos, P 1002. *AM* lxxviii. 104, 129 ff. (no. 7).

[13] *AM* lxxviii. 132.

[14] *ABV* 434.   [15] Ibid. 425.

[16] *ABL* 118, no. 1; Jacobsthal, 76 f.; *CV* Fogg Museum and Gallatin Collection (1942), p. 91 (Pease). Miss Pease adds a black-figure *pyxis* in Athens (12149) about which I have no information. I add a black-figure *lekythos* (Agora, A-P 1665. See p. 92 n. 7), with birds amidst shoulder palmettes.

[17] *ABV* 425.

[18] *BSA* lvii. 127 f.; *AM* lxxviii. 129 ff.

[19] Vienna, 3607. *ABV* 319, no. 10.

[20] Dresden, ZV 1608.

Vienna amphora with the Diosphos Painter, its mock inscriptions with the Sappho Painter,[1] and the floating circumscribed palmettes are like those on the Sappho Painter's white-ground column-crater in Carlsruhe (PLATE 55. 1). The Dresden palmettes, which are embellished with lotus buds, are also like those on the Carlsruhe crater, and there are mock inscriptions in the field.[2] The Vienna birds fly on outstretched wings; they are few in number and enclosed by the palmettes. The Dresden birds are also few, but their silhouette is less crisp, and they fly outside the palmette composition.

Palmettes are disposed in a variety of ways on the other black-bird vases—*oinochoai* (PLATE 57. 1), a *hydria* (PLATE 57. 3), *onos* (PLATE 56. 3), *pyxis*, *lekythos*, and *alabastron*. The *alabastron*[3] is decorated in outline instead of black-figure and has a red-figure palmette on its base. Vertical bands of palmettes (with reserved hearts and thin closed buds) divide the picture panel. Above the figures is a horizontal band of smaller palmettes running left to right, with black birds flying right to left in the spandrels. Miss Haspels compared the palmettes and birds with those on the lost *lekythos* by the Kephisophon Painter (FIGURE 26*a*; PLATE 56. 2).[4] The *alabastron* belongs to the Paidikos Group[5] and two black *alabastra* of the same shape bear a *kalos* inscription in praise of Dorotheos.[6] The black-bird *lekythos*,[7] unlike those by the Kephisophon Painter, is decorated exclusively with patterns—two rows of horizontal palmettes.

The *onos* (PLATE 56. 3)[8] is related to the Golonos Group,[9] which resembles the Edinburgh Painter and includes *onoi* by the Sappho and Diosphos Painters. The modelled female head on the end of the *onos* is surrounded by circumscribed palmettes on whose tendrils black birds perch. On one other black-bird vase the birds perch instead of fly; this is a *hydria* recently acquired by the Louvre (PLATES 56. 4, 57. 3).[10]

In shape and style of decoration the Louvre *hydria* is more Leagran than Antimenean. The white mouth and neck are Antimenean. Decoration of the mouth is unusual,[11] but can be paralleled on some Leagran *hydriai*,[12] also on an exceptionally elaborate *hydria* in Minneapolis by the Antimenes Painter (PLATE 2. 1).[13] The Minneapolis vase has another unusual feature—palmettes on the reserved handles. On both the Louvre and Minneapolis *hydriai* there are tongues at the join of neck to shoulder, vertical bands of ivy leaves enclosing the picture panel, and rays on the foot. Also comparable is Psiax' black-figure *hydria* in Hartford (PLATE 2. 2), mentioned earlier for its Antimenean/Leagran affiliations (see p. 12).[14] Psiax' *hydria* has red-figure palmettes on the vertical handle. Palmettes are painted on the handle, mouth, neck, and lower body (predella) of the Louvre

---

[1] *ABL* 112; *ABV* 319.

[2] *AA* 1898, 133; Jacobsthal, 73 (vignette).

[3] Tübingen, E 48. *ARV* 100, no. 28.

[4] *ABL* 118, no. 1. The palmettes have reserved hearts like those of the Pasiades Painter (see p. 99) whose *alabastra* are the same shape (cf. PLATE 72. 2, 3), and also belong to the Paidikos Group (cf. *MonPiot* xxvi. 87, fig. 10). The red-figure palmette on the base of the Tübingen *alabastron* is also paralleled on the Pasiades *alabastra*.

[5] *ARV* 98 ff.

[6] Ibid. 1575, nos. 4–5.

[7] Compiègne, 881. *CV*, pl. 12, no. 23. See p. 93 n. 16.

[8] Athens, 2185. *ABV* 481, gamma.

[9] *ABV* 480.

[10] Louvre, CA 4176; *RA* 1972, 127 ff.

[11] *Minneapolis Institute of Arts Bulletin* li (1962), i. 8–9 (Beazley).

[12] Cab. Méd. 257. *ABV* 363, no. 47; London, B 320. *ABV* 364, no. 49 (both are red-ground).

[13] Minneapolis, 61.59. *ABV* 267, no. 8 *ter*, and *Para* 119.

[14] Hartford, Wadsworth Atheneum. *ABV* 293, no. 9, and *Para* 127.

hydria, black birds (some black-figure, not silhouette) on the mouth and neck. The predella palmettes are not unusual and those on the mouth and neck are not without parallel; long tendrils, heartless palmettes, and tri-lobed spandrel buds are found among Leagran[1] and Antimenean[2] florals. A distinctive feature of the florals on the neck of the Louvre *hydria* is the linked pairs of palmettes, one upright, the other pendent. The same arrangement is used on the back of the Leagran *lekythos* in the Funcke Collection (PLATE 3. 2) whose shoulder palmettes have long tendrils, like those on the Louvre *hydria*'s mouth (PLATE 56. 4). The Funcke *lekythos* has been associated with the Acheloos Painter.[3] The shape of the Louvre *hydria* and its scheme of decoration, including the attention to florals,[4] the figure style, and the iconography,[5] are near the Acheloos Painter.

The black-bird *oinochoai* are either black-figure or black-bodied. The black-figure vase is fragmentary,[6] and the palmettes are hastily painted: small birds fly between palmettes, above the figures, as on the Tübingen *alabastron*. The black-bodied *oinochoai*, on the other hand, are exceptionally fine, elaborately decorated, with modelled handle attachments, possibly produced in the Nikosthenic Workshop.[7] Pairs of linked, addorsed palmettes, carefully painted, decorate the white-ground shoulder. The *oinochoe* in Munich (PLATE 57. 1),[8] on which Dorotheos and Memnon are praised, has been mentioned; another, in the British Museum (PLATE 57. 2), has the addorsed palmettes and black birds, but no inscription.[9] A third, fragmentary *oinochoe*, in the Villa Giulia,[10] is decorated in the same style but there are no birds on the shoulder.

On red-figure *lekythoi* handle florals are equally uncommon.[11] The earliest are Gales' cylinders in Boston (PLATE 6. 1) and Syracuse.[12] Fancy palmette and lotus-bud compositions float freely beneath the handle. Jacobsthal likened the principle of composition to that of the red-figure *oinochoe* in St. Louis by the Terpaulos Painter (PLATE 55. 4), the style of the florals to those of the Dutuit (cf. PLATE 55. 3) and Eucharides Painters.[13] Two red-figure *lekythoi* by the Bowdoin Painter have handle florals of a very different type: a small palmette discreetly placed at the join of handle to body.[14] He may have painted *lekythoi* with larger, more complex handle florals, but none has survived. An artist related to the Bowdoin Painter,[15] the Dresden Painter,[16] decorated the handle area of at least one of his red-figure *lekythoi* with palmettes in an elaborate composition which nearly covers the back of the vase (PLATE 27. 6).[17] This *lekythos* is rich in floral decoration

---

[1] Cf. Cab. Méd. 255. *ABV* 361, no. 15 ('From the same workshop as the Leagran *hydriai*, but in a less masculine style'); Brussels, R 251 and Maplewood, Noble. See p. 92 n. 9.

[2] Minneapolis, 61.59; Villa Giulia, 3556. *ABV* 269, no. 35. Cf. Psiax' *hydria* in Berlin (1897. *ABV* 293, no. 8).

[3] *Sammlung Funcke*, 84.

[4] Cf. Amiens, no number. *ABV* 384, no. 25. There are vertical bands of ivy framing the picture on the body, palmettes below and on the mouth; a modelled female head is attached to the join of handle to mouth.

[5] Compare fragmentary volute-craters in Taranto (*ABV* 384, no. 21) and New York (*ABV* 384, no. 22) and the *hydria* in the Rothschild Collection, Pregny (*ABV* 386, no. 15, and *Para* 169).

[6] Parma, C 13a. *CV* i, pl. 9. 3 and p. 7.

[7] *ABV* 425.

[8] Munich, 2447. *ABV* 425 ('related to' the Class of London B 632).

[9] London, B 632. *ABV* 425, no. 1.

[10] Villa Giulia (M. 535), fr. *ABV* 425, no. 2.

[11] Some squat red-figure *lekythoi* have handle florals, cf. *ARV* 777 (Group of Oxford 1920).

[12] Boston, 13.195. *ARV* 35, no. 1; Syracuse, 26967. *ARV* 36, no. 2.

[13] Jacobsthal, 78.

[14] New York, 06.1021.90. *ARV* 682, no. 102; Paris Market. *ARV* 682, no. 107 *bis*.

[15] *ARV*[1] 448, 480.

[16] *ARV* 655 f., 1664; *Para* 403.

[17] Zürich, Roš. *ARV* 656, no. 15.

—on the neck, shoulder, and body. The Sabouroff Painter's *lekythos* in Honolulu (PLATE 28. 1 and pp. 34 f.)[1] is probably more or less contemporary with the Dresden Painter's. Florals on the back of the Honolulu *lekythos* are oriented on the handle axis, but they lie on the ground line and do not extend to the handle itself. The closest parallel for the floral composition is a white *lekythos* in a private collection in Greensboro, North Carolina[2]—the only white *lekythos* with a handle floral known to me (FIGURE 27*a*).

The Greensboro *lekythos* is fragmentary but most of the floral composition has been preserved: two palmettes, sharing a common base, are enclosed by tendrils which open at the apex of the palmette in a lyre formation. From the volutes of the lyre spring long spiralling tendrils which terminate in small partly open buds. Alternate petals and parts of the buds are rendered in outline instead of solid black. These areas were perhaps originally filled in with red paint. Lyre palmettes[3] become popular on red-figure vases around the end of the second quarter of the fifth century. This is one of the few figured *lekythoi* on which lyre palmettes appear, and the date is probably near 460 B.C. The Sabouroff Painter's *lekythos* in Honolulu features lyre palmettes and the more usual circumscribed palmettes. Note that the central petals of the Honolulu palmettes are angular, as they are on the Greensboro *lekythos*, and that the small, partly opened buds are similarly shaped. Beazley likened the palmettes of the Greensboro *lekythos* to those on a squat white-ground *lekythos* close to the Two-row Painter in Copenhagen (PLATE 61. 2).[4] The Copenhagen vase is actually a side-palmette squat *lekythos* (FIGURE 27*b*), for linked lyre palmettes hang suspended on either side of the single figure, rendered in outline.[5] The petals of the palmettes are alternately black and matt red.[6] Miss Haspels connected the Two-row Painter with the Beldam Workshop,[7] and lyre palmettes may be found on white-ground pattern *lekythoi* from that workshop (see pp. 153 f.; and cf. PLATE 70. 1).

2. DIOSPHOS WORKSHOP

White-ground side-palmette *lekythoi* of the type made popular by the Diosphos Painter, with figures partly or totally in outline, are our prime concern, but there are a few black-figure *lekythoi*, either earlier than the Diosphos Painter's or outside his immediate circle, which make use of florals of some sort in the picture panel. The Cactus Painter's[8] are perhaps the first. He likes vegetation, as his name implies, and he also likes snakes; *lekythoi* without florals may have snakes or branches, of the usual black-figure type, filling the background.[9] One of the painter's best *lekythoi*, in Berlin, featuring Herakles at the tree of the Hesperides (PLATE 4. 3), combines palmettes, snakes, and trees.[10] On this

[1] Honolulu, 2892. *ARV* 844, no. 153.
[2] Greensboro, North Carolina, Jastrow. *ARV* 727; *AM* lii (1927), *Beilage* 27. 1–3.
[3] Jacobsthal, 142 ff.
[4] Copenhagen, 3882. *ARV* 727.
[5] 'Lyre palmettes' may be found on the left side of the vase (lower palmette) and on the right (centre palmette).
[6] Copenhagen, *CV* iv, p. 136.
[7] *ABL* 182 f.; *ARV* 727, 728.
[8] *ABV* 472, 505; *Para* 212; *ABL* 61 f.
[9] *ABL* 61 f., 110.
[10] Berlin, 3261. *ABL* 198, no. 2.

vase the tree and the snakes are iconographically significant, and this is one of the few side-palmette *lekythoi* on which pattern and figure are so integrated. It is also one of the few red-ground side-palmette *lekythoi*. The palmettes are delicately drawn and easily distinguished from those of other painters by their cactus buds.[1] Characteristic, too, are the other added small spirals and the pairs of bars crossing the tendrils. On his *Herakles and the Lion lekythos* in Boston the tree is functional (it supports Herakles' quiver while he is engaged) but the palmettes are unrelated.[2] The Oxford *lekythos* with Ajax lifting the body of Achilles (PLATE 4. 4) comes closest to the canon established for side-palmette *lekythoi* by the Diosphos Painter.[3] The palmettes are integrated into the figure composition graphically if not iconographically: they extend towards the front of the vase behind the figures.

The Gela Painter's use of florals has been mentioned earlier in connection with handle decoration. Unlike the Cactus Painter, who clearly considered his florals important, the Gela Painter treats them as little more than minor filling ornament (cf. PLATES 16. 4, 17. 3). The thin tendrils with tiny blossoms are insignificant, and irrelevant to the decorative or iconographic scheme of the vase. On none of his vases are the florals disposed as side-palmettes.

The Diosphos Workshop[4] was the first to produce white-ground side-palmette *lekythoi* in quantity. The leading artists of the workshop are the Sappho and Diosphos Painters. They are closely related and often share shapes and patterns, but each has a distinct personality.[5] The Diosphos Painter likes florals[6] and outline technique,[7] which he combines in a highly successful way on side-palmette *lekythoi*. The Sappho Painter[8] was attracted by neither[9] and no side-palmette *lekythoi* by his hand are known. The Diosphos Painter specialized in *lekythoi* and small neck-amphorae.[10] The Sappho Painter decorated larger vases, as well as small,[11] among them the *kalpis hydria* in Six's technique with the inscription from which the painter takes his name,[12] and the white-ground column-crater in Carlsruhe with palmettes beneath the handle (PLATE 55. 1).[13] Another large vase, a black-figure amphora in Madrid,[14] is related to both the Sappho Painter[15] and the Leagros Group. A distinctive feature of some of the Sappho Painter's larger vases is the funerary iconography.[16]

DIOSPHOS PAINTER

The series of side-palmette *lekythoi* as recognized by Miss Haspels in *ABL* and by Beazley in *ARV* begins with the Diosphos Painter.[17] If he is not the first to frame figures

---

[1] *ABL* 62.
[2] Boston, 93.102. *ABL* 198, no. 3.
[3] Oxford, 512. *ABL* 198, no. 4.
[4] *ABV* 507 ff.; *ARV* 300 ff.; *Para* 246; *ABL* 94 ff.
[5] *ABL* 97, 114 f.   [6] Ibid. 110.   [7] Ibid. 111 f.
[8] *ABV* 507 f., 702; *ARV* 304; *Para* 246 ff.; *ABL* 94 ff.
[9] *ABL* 112.   [10] Ibid. 232 ff.   [11] Ibid. 225 ff.
[12] Warsaw, ex Czartoryski, 32. *ABL* 228, no. 56, and *Para* 246. Miss Haspels notes the significance of the size and technique of this vase (*ABL* 106).
[13] Carlsruhe, 167. *ABL* 228, no. 57. *ABV* 507. The

floral compositions on this vase are unusual in the work of the Sappho Painter as we know him, but there may have been other vases similarly decorated which have not survived.   [14] Madrid, 10916. *ABL* 508.
[15] *ABV* 508; Miss Haspels noted a resemblance between this painter and the red-figure painter, Hypsis (*ABL* 104 f.).
[16] *ABL* 115 f. and *Para* 247; Kurtz and Boardman, 148 ff.
[17] *ABV* 508 ff., 702 f., 716; *ARV* 303 f.; *Para* 248 ff.; *ABL* 94 ff.

with florals on white *lekythoi*, he seems to have firmly established this type of decoration, and his favourite shape, DL, is the principal side-palmette shape. The Diosphos Painter was active in the years around 500 B.C., probably beginning his career with the later Leagrans. He seems to have been connected with the Edinburgh Workshop in some way: he is one of the few black-figure artists to specialize in the Edinburgh Painter's special type of small neck-amphorae (doubleens, see p. 14 and cf. PLATE 7. 1)[1] and his larger, finer *lekythoi* are not far from the Edinburgh cylinder (cf. PLATE 7. 2).[2] His largest and finest *lekythoi* are white-ground with figures and florals in semi-outline; these side-palmette *lekythoi* form a small, but very important part of the painter's otherwise totally black-figure production.

The Diosphos Painter's side-palmette *lekythoi* are shape DL.[3] Black palmettes, in elaborate compositions, sometimes with lotus buds and touches of red for colour, frame figure decoration executed partly in black-figure and partly in outline (PLATES 58, 59).[4] A few of the *lekythoi* are decorated exclusively in black-figure[5] and the patternwork of these, and the others in semi-outline, is the same as that of the finer black-figure *lekythoi* of the Diosphos Workshop.[6] Semi-outline is a transitional technique,[7] standing between pure black-figure on white-ground and outline. The Diosphos Painter is not the only artist who employs semi-outline,[8] but he is one of the most successful. To him decorative effect is all important: there must be balance—between light and dark, between white-ground and black florals, between incised silhouette and outline, and between florals and figures. The florals are always black; the reserved hearts of the palmettes are red (FIGURE 28). In figurework black-figure and outline are used equally but unpredictably. On one *lekythos* (a warrior with a horse in Boston (PLATE 59. 1))[9] black-figure is used for the warrior (apart from his helmet, which is outlined) and outline for the horse (apart from his mane, which is black). On another (Herakles and the Lion, in the Louvre (PLATE 58. 2)),[10] Herakles is outlined (apart from hair, club, and cloak) and the Lion is black-figure. On a third (Perseus and Medusa, in New York (PLATE 59. 2))[11] Medusa is outlined (apart from her black-figure head, neatly tucked into Hermes' *kibisis*), Perseus and

---

[1] *ABL* 100, 238 ff.; *ABV* 482 ('small delicate variety'), 510.

[2] *ARV* 675; *ABL* 110f.

[3] With the exception of Louvre, MNB 911 (*ARV* 301, no. 1, and pp. 303 f.), which is a Little Lion and near the Diosphos Painter, decorated in his personal version of the semi-outline technique (*ABL* 100). PLATE 59. 4.

[4] *ABL* 235, nos. 67–71.

[5] Baltimore, Robinson Collection. *ABL* 235, no. 67. *CV* i, p. 53; Athens Market. *ABL* 235, no. 68.

[6] *ARV* 301.

[7] Semi-outline is used here, as it is in *ABL* (110), to describe white-ground vases decorated partly in black-figure (or silhouette with little or no incision) and partly in outline, not as it is in *ARV* (304) to describe white-ground vases on which human flesh is rendered in black-figure, other details in outline.

Miss Haspels has pointed out the similarities between Six's technique (see pp. 119 f.) and semi-outline, and that both techniques were favoured by the Diosphos Painter, not by his partner (*ABL* 111). A distinctive feature of the Diosphos Painter's semi-outline is the balance between light and dark, outline and incised silhouette.

[8] The most important group of white *lekythoi* decorated in semi-outline outside the Diosphos Workshop are the near-standard BLs of the Athena and Bowdoin painters. See pp. 105 ff.

[9] Boston, 99.528. *ARV* 301, no. 2 (= *ABL* 235, no. 69).

[10] Louvre, MNB 909. *ARV* 301, no. 4 (= *ABL* 235, no. 70).

[11] New York, 06.1070. *ARV* 301, no. 3 (= *ABL* 235, no. 71).

Pegasus are black-figure. On some there is added colour, red or purple, and on some a preliminary sketch.[1]

In principle of decoration, though not in technique, we may compare some of the painter's white *alabastra* on which zones of figures (black-figure) alternate with the zones of patterns (black with some red; see p. 149).[2] There are also white-ground *alabastra* decorated exclusively with palmettes[3] (and some of the painter's white DLs were decorated in this way (PLATE 69. 1)) in the manner of Pasiades' *alabastra* (see p. 149 and PLATE 72. 2, 3).[4] A distinctive feature of two of the *alabastra* fashioned by Pasiades and decorated with figures in outline on white ground is polychromy, achieved largely through washes of dilute glaze.[5] Such polychromy is not characteristic of side-palmette *lekythoi* but is found on a few. One of shape DL, fashioned by the Diosphos Potter, in the Louvre, is Diosphan in detail (PLATE 58. 1);[6] another, in Leningrad, is 'near the Sappho Painter'.[7]

DIOSPHOS POTTER

DLs with lotus-bud shoulder

This brings us to side-palmette *lekythoi* fashioned by the Diosphos Potter but decorated by different hands.[8] Most of the artists are unknown but clearly related to the Sappho and Diosphos Painters. The patternwork on the whole is homogeneous and characteristically Diosphan; exceptional is a small group of DLs with black palmettes on the shoulder instead of the Diosphan lotus buds (see below). Figure style sometimes comes close to the Sappho and Diosphos Painters' but the principle of decoration is not the Diosphos Painter's. The florals are neither so elaborate nor so evenly balanced against the figures, and the figures tend to be rendered in outline more often than black-figure. The work of two painters has been recognized among the DLs with lotus-bud shoulder —the Painter of Würzburg 517 and the Painter of Copenhagen 3830.

Most of the vases attributed to the Painter of Würzburg 517[9] are large, but 'he is not at home in large vases,' and 'his connexions are with the circle of the Diosphos and Sappho Painters'.[10] His *lekythoi* are white, shape DL, with lotus buds on the shoulders, and palmettes on the body, framing a single figure in outline.[11] There are two palmettes on each side, circumscribed but not linked; the base of the superior palmette rests on the top of the inferior (FIGURE 29a). There are added spirals and carefully drawn, partly opened buds, with one exception, pendent.[12] The disposition of the palmettes and of the buds is different from the Diosphos Painter's; the closest parallel is an unattributed

---

[1] Colour: F i. 63 (Louvre, MNB 909), 64 (New York, 06.1070). Preliminary sketch: F i. 63 (Louvre, MNB 909), 64 (New York, 06.1070).

[2] *ABL* 100, 237, nos. 114–15.

[3] Ibid. 237, nos. 116, 117, and 117 *bis*.

[4] *ABL* 104 (the shapes of *alabastra* are described on pages 101 ff.; those of Pasiades precede those from the Diosphos Workshop); *ARV* 98 ff.; *Para* 330 f.

[5] London, B 668. *ARV* 98, no. 1; Athens, 15002. *ARV* 98, no. 2.

[6] Louvre, MNC 650. *ARV* 301, no. 6, 304; *ABL* 112.

[7] Leningrad, 671. *ARV* 304; *ABL* 113.

[8] *ARV* 301 ff. Add: *ML* xlviii (1973), pl. 10. 4 (no. 11816), which is comparable with Syracuse, 43052. *ARV* 301, no. 8.

[9] *ARV* 305 f.

[10] Ibid. 305.

[11] Athens, 12769. *ARV* 305, no. 6; Thebes, R. 46.84. *ARV* 306, no. 7.

[12] Thebes, R. 46.84 (lower left palmette).

side-palmette *lekythos* of shape DL in New York (PLATE 59. 3; FIGURE 29*b*).[1] The figure-work of the Painter of Würzburg 517's *lekythoi* is essentially outline; black is restricted to minor details.

The Painter of Copenhagen 3830[2] specialized in *alabastra*. Three *lekythoi* have been attributed to him, two white-ground and one red-figure. The red-figure *lekythos* in Toronto[3] is shape BL, and the style of decoration as well as the shape are in imitation of the Bowdoin Painter.[4] Both white *lekythoi* are shape DL; one is in Warsaw;[5] the other in a Swiss private collection.[6] Beazley compared a third *lekythos*, not certainly shape DL, in Palermo.[7] All three feature a youth in outline, accompanied by a dog in silhouette, or leaning on a stick.[8] The palmettes on the Warsaw and Palermo *lekythoi* are very similar: two linked palmettes on each side with added spirals and without buds. The tendril encircling the upper palmettes swings around one side of the lower palmette, which is not otherwise enclosed, to form its base. Initially Beazley placed the Warsaw *lekythos* near the Painter of the Yale *Lekythos*, suggesting that it might even be by the painter's own hand.[9] In the Addenda to *ARV* a side-palmette *lekythos* is added to the vases attributed to the Painter of the Yale *Lekythos*—a nearly canonical DL (the mouth is near shape PL) found in a recently excavated cemetery at Sabucina in inland Sicily.[10] The vase, now in Caltanissetta, has an outline Nike, wearing black boots, 'running with caduceus and helmet'[11] towards a single large palmette on long stem with added spiral tendril (FIGURE 30*a*). A similar single-palmette tree springs up beside a woman on a white *lekythos* in Leningrad[12] and on a white *lekythos* of shape PL in New York a pair of long-stem palmettes, very like the Caltanissetta palmette, frame a wounded warrior (FIGURE 30*b*).[13] A *lekythos* of uncertain shape, once in the Barre Collection, now lost, has a pair of similar palmettes with added blossoms, buds, and spirals (FIGURE 30*c*) framing a Herakles, who leans on his club and holds a *kantharos* at a flaming altar.[14] Herakles has been excerpted from a scene in which Athena stands at his side with an *oinochoe* from which she fills his cup. The motif of Athena offering Herakles wine is most popular in the early part of the fifth century, and the classic example is by the Berlin Painter on the exceptionally fine amphora owned by the CIBA Corporation, now on display in the Antikenmuseum, Basle.[15] In publishing the CIBA amphora Beazley studied the motif and distinguished three versions, depending on Herakles' pose: seated, standing, or leaning.[16] The closest parallel for our leaning Herakles is on a Nolan amphora by the Dutuit Painter in the Louvre, with the full composition—Herakles leaning and Athena pouring (PLATE 55. 3).[17] The amphora is rich in patternwork: horizontal bands on the

---

[1] New York, 51.163. *ARV* 301, no. 7.

[2] *ARV* 723 f.; *Para* 410 f.

[3] Toronto, 366. *ARV* 724, no. 11.

[4] The Painter of Copenhagen 3830 is related to the Dresden Painter (*ARV*[1] 447) who is himself related to the Bowdoin Painter (*ARV*[1] 480). I take the predominance of black silhouette on vases by the Painter of Copenhagen 3830 to reflect Bowdoin practice. See p. 95.

[5] Warsaw, 142470. *ARV* 724, no. 9.

[6] Zürich, Schuh. *ARV* 724, no. 10.

[7] Palermo, no number. *ARV* 302, no. 16, and p. 724.

[8] See above n. 4.

[9] *VPol* 18.

[10] Caltanissetta, from Sabucina. *ARV* 660, no. 73 *bis*, and p. 1664.

[11] *ARV* 1664.

[12] Leningrad, PHC 97.

[13] New York, 41.162.95. *ARV* 303, no. 4.

[14] Once Barre. *ARV* 302, no. 1 (bottom).

[15] Basle, CIBA. *ARV* 196, no. 1 *bis*, and p. 1624.

[16] *AK* iv (1961), 56 ff.

[17] Louvre, G 203. *ARV* 306, no. 1.

lower body and palmettes and buds beneath the handles framing the figures. The Dutuit Painter, as we recall, is counted among the members of the Diosphos Painter's circle[1] and his vases offer perhaps the best contemporary examples in red-figure of the Diosphos Painter's florals and figures. If he had a black-figure side, we should expect a strong Diosphan influence. He liked florals and if he decorated a white *lekythos* exclusively with palmettes, we might expect it to look like the Diosphos Painter's.

DLs with palmettes on the shoulder

Five of the DLs fashioned by the Diosphos Potter have palmettes on the shoulder instead of the Diosphos Painter's linked, pendent lotus buds beneath enclosed bars.[2] The black palmettes, on reserved ground, are disposed in a manner most characteristic of the Athena Painter—a central group of three linked palmettes and a palmette on either side of the handle, with added spiral and thin closed bud. The bars at the neck–shoulder join, unlike the Athena Painter's, are not enclosed. The side palmettes on four of the five are very similar (FIGURE 31); those on the fifth (once on the Athens market)[3] look basically the same but their execution is less careful. The central petal of the palmettes tends to extend beyond the enclosing tendril; the heart is large and reserved. The figure decoration is almost exclusively outline, occasionally with washes of dilute glaze for colour. The most elaborate of the four finer *lekythoi* is in Warsaw.[4] The shoulder palmettes of this *lekythos* are quite large, with full petal and distinct hearts. The palmettes on the body, which frame a woman with mirror and basket, have an abbreviated six-lobed spandrel blossom in addition to spirals and thin closed bud (FIGURE 32a). The additional buds are as characteristic a feature of these *lekythoi* as the large reserved palmette heart.[5] Another feature is the inscription, *kalos* or *kale*. On the left side of the woman on the Warsaw vase *kale* is inscribed; on another of the *lekythoi*, in the Fogg Museum, Harvard University,[6] *kalos* is inscribed above the head of the 'hunter returning'. The booty of the hunter, a fox and hare on a pole, is coloured with washes of dilute glaze.[7] The palmettes framing the hunter are like those on a DL with palmette shoulder in the Mormino Collection, Palermo (woman with sceptre).[8] Beazley attributed both vases to the same

[1] *ARV* 306.

[2] *ARV* 302, nos. 19–21, and p. 1643 (no. 22); *Para* 357 (no. 19 *bis*).

[3] Athens Market. *ARV* 302, no. 20.

[4] Warsaw, 198554. *ARV* 302, no. 19, and *Para* 357.

[5] A comparable multi-lobed spandrel blossom is just visible behind the chair of a seated woman on a fragmentary white *lekythos* from the North Slope (Athens, Agora, North Slope AP 422). The vase is signed by Pasiades as painter, but the figure style, according to Beazley, is not by the same hand as the white *alabastra* fashioned by Pasiades (*ARV* 102). The polychromy of the *lekythos* is also a marked feature of the Pasiades figured *alabastra* (*ARV* 98). Too little remains of the florals for a comparison either with Pasiades' palmette *alabastra* (*ARV* 99, PLATE

72. 2, 3) or with other side-palmette *lekythoi*. Beazley did not include the Agora *lekythos* in his lists of side-palmette *lekythoi*. The shoulder of the *lekythos* is black (on which *Pasiades egraphsen* is incised) and the neck is decorated with a chequery pattern, in the manner of some *lekythoi* from the Diosphos Workshop (*ABL* 102 ff., 113, 118). There is a red-figure tongue pattern at the join of shoulder to neck, and this may be paralleled on a lost *lekythos* decorated in Six's technique, with a chequery on the neck, which has been attributed to the Sappho Painter (*ABL* 228, no. 50 *bis*).

[6] Harvard, 1925.30.51. *ARV* 302, no. 21.

[7] *CV* Robinson Collection i, p. 53.

[8] Palermo, Banco di Sicilia, 27. *ARV* 301, no. 22, and p. 1643 (= Mormino Collection, 179. *CV* i. III Y, pl. 4. 5).

hand; beside the woman *kale* is inscribed. The fourth DL, Thracian woman with the head of Orpheus, lacks an inscription, but the patternwork is similar.[1]

To this group of DLs with shoulder palmettes may be added a *lekythos*[2] found not long ago in a grave at Paestum,[3] whose offerings included four small *lekythoi*, two chimney *lekythoi* with figure decoration (one by the Haimon Painter),[4] one pattern *lekythos* of Beldam type, one black-bodied *lekythos* from the Beldam Workshop,[5] one large red-figure *lekythos*, a late work of the Brygos Painter,[6] and a bronze strigil. The side-palmette *lekythos* has five hastily painted black palmettes on the shoulder beneath un-enclosed bars. At the shoulder–body join there is a band of linked dots. Linked dots occur in this position on the DL with lotus-bud shoulder[7] which Beazley compared with the side-palmette *lekythoi* by the Painter of Copenhagen 3830; also on the fragmentary side-palmette *lekythos* from Brauron of uncertain shape[8] (nearer PL than DL), with rays on the shoulder. The palmettes of the Paestum *lekythos*, which frame a komast, are nearly effaced.

3. PL

After DL shape PL is the most common for side-palmette *lekythoi*.[9] The two shapes are related (see p. 81) and, although DL is generally considered a precursor of PL, they must have been produced concurrently for a time and the choice of shape must have been largely a matter of personal preference. Painters who decorated PLs seem not to have decorated DLs, and vice versa. The Painter of the Yale *Lekythos* comes closest to being an exception,[10] and if more than one *lekythos* of secondary shape were attributed to the Dutuit Painter we might have expected it to be shape DL. His red-figure *lekythos* of shape PL in New York (woman at thurible) has the lotus-bud shoulder characteristic of DL and of the Diosphos Workshop and nonsense inscriptions painted in the field.[11] The woman holds a gigantic flower which looks very much like some side-palmette florals. An almost identical gigantic flower is held by an Eros on an unattributed PL in Leningrad which 'Recalls the Dutuit Painter'.[12] The shoulder of the Leningrad vase has the decoration most characteristic of *lekythoi* of shape PL: five palmettes in groups of one, three, and one, beneath unenclosed bars. The scheme of decoration is essentially the same as that of the Harvard hunter *lekythos* of shape DL.[13] Palmettes on the shoulders of some DLs and lotus buds on the shoulders of some PLs provide another link between the shapes.

[1] Basle Market (M.M.). *ARV* 302, no. 19 *bis*, and *Para* 357.

[2] Paestum, no number. *ARV* 302 and 1643 f.

[3] *AJA* lviii (1954), 325 and pl. 68. 6; *Fasti Archaeologici* viii (1953), 128 and fig. 31.

[4] *ABV* 545, no. 210 *bis*, and p. 706.

[5] *ARV* 694, no. 36.

[6] Ibid. 384, no. 212.

[7] Palermo, no number. *ARV* 302, no. 16.

[8] Brauron, no number. *ARV* 302, no. 4, and p. 1643;

AK Beiheft i (1963), 14 and pl. 6. 3–4.

[9] *ARV* 303, no. 107, and p. 675.

[10] Caltanissetta, from Sabucina. *ARV* 660, no. 73 *bis*, and p. 1664.

[11] New York, 162.27. *ARV* 308, no. 21.

[12] Leningrad, from Olbia. *ARV* 676, no. 14. The floral may be compared with those by the Icarus Painter. See p. 103 nn. 14 ff.

[13] Harvard, 1925.30.51. *ARV* 302, no. 21

Most side-palmette *lekythoi* of shape PL are unattributed. Two in the Petit Palais—after which the shape is named—have been attributed to the Painter of Petit Palais 336, an artist 'Akin to the Sappho and Diosphos Painters',[1] and one has been attributed to the Vlasto Painter (PLATE 61. 1).[2] The side-palmettes of the Petit Palais *lekythoi* (FIGURE 33a) resemble those on DLs with palmette shoulders: two linked and circumscribed palmettes on each side, base to base, with added spiral tendrils. The central petal of each palmette extends outside the enclosing tendril, but the heart of the palmette is not reserved. The figure decoration is outline; black is restricted to the hair, beard, and boots of the komast on one of the *lekythoi*,[3] and the woman's hair on the other.[4]

The Vlasto Painter's[5] *lekythoi*, four red-figure and one white-ground, are shape PL. The white *lekythos* in Oxford (PLATE 61. 1) preserves florals distinctly on one side only: a pair of linked palmettes with added spirals. The central petal extends beyond enclosing tendrils, and there is a small partly opened pendent bud. Beazley compared another *lekythos* of shape PL once on the market (youth in black *chlamys*) on which similar palmettes and pendent bud appear,[6] and also another market PL (maenad in fawn skin).[7]

The Icarus Painter[8] is an artist of similar character to the Vlasto Painter, to whom a large number of small vases, mostly *lekythoi*, has been attributed. In shape his *lekythoi* are near PL.[9] Although none is decorated with side palmettes, there are florals on several, red-figure[10] and white *lekythoi*.[11] They are especially prominent on two white-ground vases of different shape—a white *chous* in Oxford (with a Nike flying with fillet in hand amidst black palmettes, PLATE 61. 3)[12] and a squat *lekythos* in Naples (with a female head framed by flowers).[13] The Icarus Painter liked head-*lekythoi* and he liked to frame heads with columns,[14] which in principle of decoration served much the same purpose as framing florals. The only large-scale work attributed to him is a red-figure *loutrophoros* with scenes of *prothesis* and valediction.[15] This is also his only attributed vase with funerary iconography. Miss Haspels connected the Icarus Painter with the Beldam Workshop on the basis of shape and pattern,[16] and I take the *loutrophoros* (which is unlikely to have been the painter's one picture of funerary practice) to reflect Beldam iconography. The Icarus Painter stands in the same relationship to the Beldam Workshop as the Carlsruhe Painter:[17] both were influenced by other workshops as well, notably that of the Bowdoin Painter (see pp. 108 n. 8, 110); both have an important red-figure side, painting vases of different shapes; and both prefer a single figure on their *lekythoi*, especially man, woman, Eros, or Nike. The Icarus Painter decorated at least one *lekythos* of shape CL (red-figure),[18]

[1] *ARV* 305.
[2] Oxford, 1922.18. *ARV* 696, no. 5.
[3] Petit Palais, 336. *ARV* 305, no. 1.
[4] Petit Palais, 335. *ARV* 305, no. 2.
[5] *ARV* 696.
[6] Market. *ARV* 303, no. 5, and pp. 1644, 1666.
[7] Market. *ARV* 303, no. 7.
[8] *ARV* 696 ff., 1666 f., 1702; *Para* 407.
[9] *ARV* 696.
[10] *ARV* 697, nos. 9–10 (man with flower); 698, nos. 32–4 (woman with flower and mirror), no. 42 (woman with flower), no. 46 *bis*, and p. 1667 (woman with flower and mirror).

[11] *ARV* 698, no. 61 *bis*, and p. 1667 (woman with flower and mirror).
[12] Oxford, 1927.4467. *ARV* 700, no. 84.
[13] Naples, from Cumae. *ARV* 700, no. 81.
[14] *ARV* 698, no. 53 (red-figure *lekythos*), 699, nos. 76–7 (white *lekythoi*), nos. 78 and 80 (red-figure squat *lekythoi*); Corinth, C 393. *ARV* 1667 'near' (red-figure squat *lekythos*).
[15] Louvain, fr. *ARV* 700, no. 85.
[16] *ABL* 180.
[17] Cf. *ABL* 180 f.
[18] Basle Market (M.M.). *ARV* 698, no. 50.

probably more,[1] and the Carlsruhe Painter decorated some *lekythoi* of shape PL (red-figure[2] and white-ground[3]). There is also one side-palmette *lekythos* of shape BEL (PLATE 64. 1)[4] attributed to the Carlsruhe Painter (see p. 86).

4. BL

There are florals in the picture panel of some white *lekythoi*[5] from the Bowdoin Workshop, but few are side-palmettes. Side-palmettes are also conspicuously absent from those Bowdoin *lekythoi* on which we should most expect them—the group decorated in semi-outline,[6] the technique characteristic of side-palmette *lekythoi* from the Diosphos Workshop. This section considers body florals on *lekythoi* by the Athena and Bowdoin Painters, according to the technique of the vase, black-figure, semi-outline, and outline. Since there are *lekythoi* by both painters and since some look as if they could have been painted by either, we are once again faced with the problem of the two painters' identity (see pp. 16, 121 ff.).

BLACK-FIGURE

A small number of *lekythoi* by the Athena Painter have florals on either side of the figure decoration which, with one exception (PLATE 60. 1),[7] is Athena—full figure (seated or standing) or bust (PLATE 62. 1). They are white-ground cylinders with the painter's five distinctive black palmettes on the shoulder. The florals framing Athena are side-palmettes in principle but their composition is unlike any we have described:[8] long, nearly straight tendrils, growing from the ground line, merging into small palmettes with added tendrils and thin closed buds. These side-palmettes look like trees, and the painter himself must have thought so, too, for he usually added small owls to the tendril branches.[9] Around the palmettes, whose hearts are sometimes coloured in purple or red, there are small black dots,[10] as there are on the shoulders of the painter's *lekythoi* and *oinochoai*.[11]

---

[1] *ARV* 701, 'with the Louvain *loutrophoros* compare . . .'. Oxford, 1934.294.

[2] *ARV* 731, no. 3; 733, no. 57.

[3] Ibid. 734, no. 91.

[4] Cambridge, GR 1.1895 (138). *ARV* 735, no. 98.

[5] A small number of Bowdoin red-figure *lekythoi* have florals in the picture panel: Paris Market (Segredakis). *ARV* 679, no. 42; Prague, National Museum, 775. *ARV* 683, no. 124; New Haven, Yale University, 144. *ARV* 685, no. 167.

[6] *ARV* 689 f.

[7] London, 1920.3–15.1. *ABL* 255, no. 27 (siren framed by columns); cf. London, B 651. *ABL* 256, no. 48 (siren framed by onlookers).

[8] They are closest to the long-stemmed palmettes on the following *lekythoi*: New York, 41.162.95 (*ARV*

303, no. 4), Leningrad, PHC 97, and Caltanissetta, from Sabucina (*ARV* 660, no. 73 *bis*, and p. 1664). See FIGURES 30 *a*, *b*.

[9] The Theseus Painter combined Athena, owls, and palmettes on some *skyphoi*; *ABL* 250, nos. 12–13. On the date of the Theseus Painter's *skyphoi*, see *AJA* lxxv (1971), 200, and lxxvi (1972), 232 (Eisman). A discussion of the owl of Athena may be found in: *BABesch* xliii (1968), 35 ff. Compare also the shield device of Athena on a red-figure *lekythos* from the south slope of the Acropolis, *BCH* xc (1966), 741, fig. 1.

[10] *ABL* 147 f., 157.

[11] Cf. *ABL*, pls. 45. 6 and 27 (*lekythos*) and pl. 25. 5 (*oinochoai*).

Athena appears on many of the painter's vases—hence his name—either alone or accompanied, not infrequently in combat;[1] sometimes a small owl perches on her spear.[2] On *lekythoi* with side-palmettes Athena is once in Panathenaic pose,[3] but more often she sits on a folding stool;[4] some of these vases were found on the Athenian Acropolis.[5] When Pausanias toured the Acropolis he saw a cult statue of the seated goddess by the sculptor Endoios,[6] and some scholars have thought the Athena Painter had such a statue in mind.[7] The source of the Athena Painter's inspiration is even more important for the *lekythoi* with palmette-trees framing a head or bust of the goddess. Two are firmly attributed to the Athena Painter,[8] and a third has been added as a 'late, decadent piece, probably by the painter's own hand',[9] but it has black-figure trees instead of side-palmettes (PLATE 63. 1). This *lekythos* is so like the Bowdoin Painter's of the same subject (PLATE 63. 2–4)[10] that we might be tempted to attribute the vase to his hand, were it not executed in black-figure, a technique which the Bowdoin Painter is assumed—perhaps incorrectly—not to have used. A fuller description of the Athena-head *lekythoi* by both painters may be found at the end of this section (pp. 109 ff.), together with a discussion of some contemporary Athenian coins with which the *lekythoi* have been compared.

SEMI-OUTLINE

Of all the vases attributed to the Athena and Bowdoin Painters the *lekythoi* in semi-outline are most easily attributed to either. Bowdoin semi-outline is more old-fashioned than the Diosphos Painter's; it is essentially black-figure.[11] The Diosphos Painter had rendered figures in outline or incised silhouette according to his fancy (cf. PLATES 58, 59); the painter of our *lekythoi* always renders figures in silhouette, sometimes barely incised.[12] Outline is secondary and is applied to accessory or minor details only. Since the decoration is predominantly black-figure, the Athena Painter is generally assumed to have executed it,[13] and parallels for some of the scenes may be found in his work.[14] But close parallels may be found in the work of the Bowdoin Painter as well,[15] and some details

[1] *ABL* 255, nos. 13, 16, 30–3; 258, no. 86.

[2] Ibid. 255, no. 33; 258, no. 86.

[3] Taranto, old no. 25. *ABL* 256, no. 37, and p. 157 n. 2.

[4] A not uncommon seat for deities: G. M. A. Richter, *Greek and Roman Furniture* (1966), 43 ff. and pls. 237–49; *Antike Plastik* vi (1967), 1 ff.

[5] *ABL* 256, nos. 38–9.

[6] Pausanias i. 26. 4. Payne and Young, 46 f.

[7] *ABL* 157 n. 5; C. Starr, *Athenian Coinage, 480–449* (1970), 19 n. 22.

[8] Dresden, ZV 1700. *ABL* 257, no. 75; Amsterdam, Allard Pierson Museum 3754 (ex Basle Market). *Para* 262.

[9] Marburg. *ABL* 258, no. 106 *ter*, and p. 157; *Para* 260; *Jb* lxxviii (1963), 305 (Athena is said to be holding an egg, but she probably holds a fruit, as she does on the *lekythos* by the Bowdoin Painter in the British Museum (D 22. *ARV* 687, no. 219); see *Mel* 97 n. 2).

[10] The Bowdoin Painter adds the right hand to his busts, the Athena Painter does not.

[11] *ABL* 153, 157; *ARV* 304, 689.

[12] Cf. Naples, Stg. 135. *ARV* 690, no. 8 (minimal incision) = *ABL* 258, no. 106 *bis*; Bonn, 538. *ARV* 690, no. 12 (no incision; *AA* 1935, 467, no. 35). With the Bonn *lekythos* compare the Diosphos Painter's Herakles and the Lion *lekythos* in semi-outline technique in the Louvre (MNB 909. *ARV* 301, no. 4. PLATE 58.2).

[13] Cf. *ARV¹* 478.

[14] Cf. Vienna, 86. *ABL* 257, no. 65 (black-figure) and Bonn 538 (see the preceding note); New York, 41.162. 146 (ex Gallatin. *ABL* 257, no. 72, and *ABV* 522 (black-figure)) and Athens, 1973. *ARV* 690, no. 10 (semi-outline).

[15] Cf. Palermo, V 686. *ARV* 683, no. 127 (red-figure), and Athens, 1809. *ARV* 689, no. 4 (semi-outline) (PLATE 60. 2); Lucerne Market. *ARV* 683, no. 127 *ter* (red-figure), and Bonn, 538 (PLATE 14. 5).

of these semi-outline *lekythoi* are more common on his *lekythoi*: a peculiar type of meander and a preference for silhouette animals and outline altars. The usual meander is a running rightward key,[1] but on several of the *lekythoi* pairs of linked stopt meanders alternate with patterned squares (FIGURE 5*j*).[2] This distinctive meander is one of the Bowdoin Painter's favourites on red-figure and white *lekythoi*. The Athena Painter's favourite pattern in this position is linked dots.[3] A simple running meander appears on a few of his *lekythoi*, whose figurework seems to be especially cursory black-figure;[4] the distinctive linked pairs of meanders alternating with patterned squares appear on a few.[5] The vases associated with both painters have different patterns in this position. The Athena-head *lekythoi* attributed to the Athena Painter have his favourite linked dots (PLATE 63. 1); those attributed to the Bowdoin Painter (PLATE 63. 2–3) have his favourite running key.[6] The bilingual *lekythoi* in Brussels—red-figure with shoulder figures in silhouette on reserved ground—have the pairs of linked meanders alternating with pattern squares (PLATE 15).[7]

Silhouette is not unknown in the Athena Painter's Workshop—the Theseus Painter used it on white-ground[8]—but it is a speciality of the Bowdoin Painter and not of his early period, as we might have expected.[9] He especially likes silhouette animals—fawns,[10] dogs,[11] bull-calves,[12] and birds,[13] but he also likes silhouette *himatia*[14] and vessels.[15] *Lekythoi* with details in silhouette not infrequently have florals and mock inscriptions,[16] the distinctive linked meander pattern, and outline altars.[17] Outline altars are almost as characteristic of the Bowdoin Painter as silhouette animals. An outline *lekythos* in

[1] There is considerable variety in the pattern band at the join of shoulder to body on Bowdoin *lekythoi*. Apart from running (right) key and the pairs of linked meanders alternating with pattern squares, and patternless black-shouldered *lekythoi* (see the following note), the following patterns may be found: Leftward-running key: Philadelphia Market. *ARV* 678, no. 1 *bis*, and p. 1665. Egg (simple): Basle Market (M.M.). *ARV* 679, no. 16 *bis*. Egg (developed): Beirut, 7393, fr. *ARV* 690, no. 7. Broken running meander: Naples, Stg. 135. *ARV* 690, no. 8. Stopt meander alternating with pattern square: Naples, 2438. *ARV* 689, no. 1 (the shoulder decoration is also unusual).

[2] London, E 582. *ARV* 679, no. 37; Brussels, Errera. *ARV* 679, no. 47; Athens, Agora, P 9470, fr. *ARV* 681, no. 88. Add the following *lekythoi* with black shoulders: Basle Market (M.M.). *ARV* 683, no. 122 *bis* (below figures); London Market. *ARV* 683, no. 126 *bis*, and *Para* 406; Bowdoin, 20.1. *ARV* 684, no. 143 (below figures); Athens, 1827. *ARV* 685, no. 181; Louvre, L 33. *ARV* 687, no. 222.

[3] *ABL* 148.

[4] Athens, 1067. *ABL* 258, no. 91; Havana, Lagunillas. *ABV* 523, no. 7; Berlin, 4982.9. *Para* 261; Neuchâtel, Seyrig. *Para* 262.

[5] Athens, 1133. *ABL* 256, no. 49; Athens, 1132. *ABL* 256, no. 50.

[6] The pattern on the Marburg *lekythos* is largely effaced.

[7] Brussels, A 3132. *ARV* 681, no. 91; Brussels, A 3131. *ARV* 682, no. 107.

[8] Philadelphia Market (white *alabastron*). *Para* 256.

[9] Oxford, 265. *ARV* 686, no. 187 ('late'); Greenwich, Bareiss, 104. *ARV* 686, no. 193 ('later'), and *Para* 406; Würzburg, H 4978. *ARV* 686, no. 204; Athens, 1792. *ARV* 686, no. 207; Mississippi (ex Robinson). *ARV* 687, no. 214 (late, judging from the shoulder decoration); Bronxville, Bastis. *ARV* 687, no. 215 ('late'). The unpublished *lekythoi* in Taranto (20308. *ARV* 686, no. 205; 20309. *ARV* 687, no. 212) probably also have silhouette animals. See also, F i. 40, 56.

[10] *ARV* 686, nos. 187, 204; 687, nos. 214–15.

[11] Ibid. 686, no. 207 (for the composition, compare Louvre, CA 599, mentioned in the following note).

[12] Louvre, CA 599. *ARV* 691, no. 27; probably also Taranto 20308 (see above n. 9).

[13] *ARV* 686, no. 204.

[14] Ibid. 686, nos. 187, 193, 204, 207; 687, no. 214.

[15] Ibid. 686, nos. 193 (*oinochoe*) and 202 (*hydria*). Compare the unattributed *lekythos* of Bowdoin type: Athens, private. F i. 45, and fig. 21.

[16] Compare the mock inscriptions on semi-outline *lekythoi* from the Bowdoin Workshop, below, p. 107 n. 8.

[17] *ABL* 157. Outline mounds may also serve as altars, cf. *ARV* 686, no. 193.

Würzburg[1] combines all these details (PLATE 16. 1). There is also an outline altar on a white *lekythos* which Miss Haspels associated with the Athena Painter,[2] as well as the Bowdoin Painter, and which Beazley included among his semi-outline *lekythoi* from the Bowdoin Workshop:[3] a black-figure Apollo, with the minimum of incision, attended by a silhouette fawn, approaches an outline altar. There is an inscription in the field and a peculiar leftward meander above the scene.[4] There is a very similar Apollo on a *lekythos*, recently on the Basle Market, which should be added to the list of semi-outline *lekythoi* from the Bowdoin Workshop (PLATE 14. 3):[5] Apollo is rendered in silhouette; his *himation* in outline; a silhouette fawn accompanies him and a mock inscription fills the background.

None of the semi-outline *lekythoi* has side-palmettes but vegetation of the old black-figure type, trees (PLATE 14. 1, 2)[6] and vine tendrils (PLATE 14. 4),[7] is prominent on some, and on others nonsense inscriptions, scattered in the background, serve much the same purpose (PLATE 14. 5).[8] One of the semi-outline *lekythoi*,[9] and possibly others, of which we have only fragments,[10] is nearly a side-palmette *lekythos*: a black-figure Eros on outline wings flies amidst palmettes (FIGURE 34b; PLATE 60. 2).[11] The composition of the florals is very like the Athena Painter's but there are no small black dots around the palmettes; the floral composition may also be compared with the Bowdoin Painter's Athena-head *lekythoi*. The Eros *lekythos* has the linked meanders alternating with pattern squares above the figure scene.

OUTLINE

A few Bowdoin white *lekythoi* have florals in the picture panel, in a circular or linear composition. The circular compositions are small and insignificant or large and prominent, and sometimes disposed in the manner of side-palmettes. On the Würzburg *lekythos* (PLATE 16. 1), a small circular floral is held by a woman wearing a silhouette *himation*: a forked tendril terminating in volutes and blossoms with a palmette and spandrel buds. Despite its small size, this floral has all the essential elements of circular Bowdoin compositions. Notice especially the crossing-over tendril of the pendent blossom and the black dot inside it.[12] Notice also the nonsense inscription decoratively

[1] Würzburg, H 4978. *ARV* 686, no. 204.

[2] *ABL* 157 and 258 (Naples, Stg. 235).

[3] Naples, Stg. 135. *ARV* 690, no. 8.

[4] See above, p. 106 n. 1, adding: Küsnacht, Hirschmann (ex Philadelphia Market). *ARV* 691, no. 26 *bis*, and p. 1666; *Para* 521.

[5] London, Embiricos.

[6] Cf. Athens, 1973. *ARV* 690, no. 9. Compare the tree on Louvre, CA 599. *ARV* 691, no. 27.

[7] New York, 08.258.28. *ARV* 690, no. 7. Compare a white *oinochoe* decorated only with a black tendril, signed by the potter Charinos, London, B 631 (*ABV* 423).

[8] Naples, Stg. 135. *ARV* 690, no. 8; Cab. Méd. 299. *ARV* 690, no. 11; Bonn, 538. *ARV* 690, no. 12; the three *lekythoi* with the same scene—black-figure man in outline dress, leaning on stick, with outline lyre and

black-figure cock—have vertical inscriptions (Naples, 2438. *ARV* 689, no. 1; Nicosia, Pierides. *ARV* 689, no. 2; Berlin, 2250. *ARV* 689, no. 3); compare the similarly placed inscription on Louvre, CA 599. *ARV* 691, no. 27.

[9] Athens, 1809. *ARV* 689, no. 4.

[10] Eros appears on an unpublished *lekythos* (Swiss private. *ARV* 689, no. 5) and on the fragment from Byblos (Beirut, 7393, fr. *ARV* 690, no. 6).

[11] Compare the Nike flying amidst palmettes on the white *chous* by the Icarus Painter in Oxford 1927.4467 (*ARV* 700, no. 84. PLATE 61. 3).

[12] Tendrils crossing-over each other and dotted circles are known from at least one vase by the Athena Painter, where they appear on the shoulder: a black-figure white *lekythos* in conde de Lagunillas's collection in Havana (*ABV* 523, no. 10).

scattered in the field. There is a larger circular floral on a *lekythos* in Athens, to the left of an outline altar to which a Nike flies (PLATE 60. 4).[1] The figure flying with *phialai* reminds us of the Eros flying with *phialai* and lyre on the semi-outline *lekythos* in Athens (PLATE 60. 2), and the patternwork of both vases is the same. The floral beside the altar is composed of a circular tendril which crosses over itself and terminates in blossoms; inside the circle formed by the tendril is a dotted circle. Nike flying to an altar is the subject of another Bowdoin *lekythos* with body florals (PLATE 60. 3).[2] Nike wears a black-figure *himation* (the folds are incised), and beneath her outlined wings there are letters of a nonsense inscription; to the left of the outline altar a tendril, springing from the groundline, bends, terminating in volutes—like the floral held by the woman on the Würzburg *lekythos* (PLATE 16. 1). From one of the volutes springs a tendril with a blossom. On the other side of the altar is a side-palmette composition of familiar type: a pair of linked circumscribed palmettes. Notice the spandrel blossom and the small bars crossing the tendrils;[3] notice also the pattern bands framing the scene—pairs of linked meanders alternating with patterned squares.

Two white *lekythoi* in the manner of the Bowdoin Painter are proper side-palmette *lekythoi*, with pairs of black palmettes framing a figure in outline (FIGURE 34*a*).[4] The palmettes are circular but not linked: the superior palmette, which is aligned vertically, rests on the inferior palmette, which is aligned horizontally. The palmettes do not look like the Bowdoin Painter's, nor is the meander pattern one of his favourites,[5] but the composition is familiar, as is the outline technique, with thick lines of black paint. Floral decoration on these *lekythoi* is not limited to side-palmettes: scattered in the field are smaller florals—circular tendrils crossing each other and terminating in blossoms with a central black dot.

Linear florals appear only on Bowdoin *lekythoi* decorated with a head or bust (PLATE 63. 2, 3 and see pp. 109 ff.). The florals, like the Athena Painter's, are long, nearly straight tendrils, terminating in palmettes, but the Athena Painter's small black dots and owls are missing (cf. PLATE 62. 3).[6] The Marburg Athena head *lekythos* (PLATE 63. 1) which Miss Haspels attributed to the Athena Painter as a late piece, has black-figure trees in place of palmettes[7] and, instead of small owls on the branches of the trees, large owls stand beside them; single large owls are the decoration of a group of red-figure *lekythoi* by the Bowdoin Painter.[8] Two of his white *lekythoi* are decorated with the bust of a woman, wearing a *sakkos* and playing a lyre; on one[9] a palmette tree fills the

---

[1] Athens, 1827. *ARV* 685, no. 181. The floral on Berlin 2249 (*ARV* 685, no. 186) is compared by Fairbanks (i. 40 f.).

[2] Richmond, Va., 56.27.4. *ARV* 685, no. 182.

[3] The small cross-bars appear on a black-figure *lekythos* with palmette-trees by the Athena Painter (Athens, 1138. *ABL* 257, no. 73), on the Bowdoin semi-outline Eros *lekythos* (Athens, 1809. *ARV* 689, no. 4). They do not appear on the Athena Painter's head *lekythoi*.

[4] Munich, 7657. *ARV* 303, no. 10 *bis*, and p. 1644 (= *ARV* 691, no. 26, and p. 1666); Küsnacht, Hirsch-mann. *ARV* 303, no. 10 *ter*, and p. 1644 (= *ARV* 691, no. 26 *bis*, and p. 1666).

[5] Above the figures is a running (left) meander. See above, p. 106 n. 1, for Bowdoin patterns.   [6] *ABL* 157.

[7] Cf. Berlin, 1933. *ABL* 260, no. 128, and pl. 45. 3.

[8] *ARV* 685, nos. 179–80. There are also owl *lekythoi* by the Icarus Painter (*ARV* 699, nos. 58–61 *ter*) and a number of unattributed *lekythoi* of shape CL are decorated in this way (*ARV* 677, nos. 14 and 15, and p. 1665, nos. 16–17, and *Para* 405).

[9] Eleusis, from Eleusis. *ARV* 687, no. 223 (palmette behind and to the right).

background, on the other columns.[1] The head motif was well established in Attica before *lekythos* painters took it up at the end of the sixth century[2] and there are head *lekythoi* before the Athena Painter's,[3] but he and the Bowdoin Painter seem to be responsible for the popularity of the motif on *lekythoi* of cylindrical shape. Outside the Bowdoin Workshop the fashion had a limited appeal. In black-figure the Painter of the Half-palmettes reproduces the Athena Painter's scheme most faithfully (PLATE 62. 1). He is a second-rate artist closely associated with the Haimon Painter,[4] and the Haimon Painter used the head motif at least twice on red-ground chimney *lekythoi*.[5] No *lekythoi* have been attributed to the Painter of the Half-palmettes, apart from a group of Haemonian *lekythoi* which Beazley thought might be by him.[6] He specialized in *kalpides*, *oinochoai*, and *olpai*, which he sometimes decorated with sanctuary scenes.[7] The basic elements of the sanctuary scene are columns, owls, and females, either full figure or bust. Since the bust of Athena appears on some, her bird on others, we are perhaps not wrong in thinking that the sanctuary is hers. In the manner of the Athena Painter's goddess, she wears a high-crested helmet, and there are florals, the distinctive half-palmettes from which the painter takes his name. The addition of an owl to the half-palmette suggests that the artist is following the same model as the Athena Painter.[8] Miss Haspels had noticed that the style of the Painter of the Half-palmettes sometimes comes close to the Gela Painter, who also painted a head *lekythos* (PLATE 17. 3), even closer to the Emporion Painter.[9] Since the Emporion Painter specialized in chimney *lekythoi* of the same type as the Haimon Painter (a single workshop for both seems likely),[10] a stylistic connection between the two painters is fully understandable. With the passing of the black-figure style the head motif becomes rare on *lekythoi* of cylindrical shape, but on squat *lekythoi*, one of the shapes born with the new red-figure style,[11] this form of decoration holds its own well into the fourth century in Attica and in the west.

ATHENA-HEAD *LEKYTHOI* AND COINS

The Athena-head *lekythoi* by the Bowdoin Painter have a place of importance in Attic vase-painting far beyond their artistic merit, because the principal elements of the composition—the head of the goddess and her owl—are the insignia of some contemporary coins (PLATE 62. 2) from which it has been assumed the painter drew his inspiration.[12] Numismatists have relied upon the *lekythoi* to establish the chronology of early

---

[1] Louvre, L 33. *ARV* 687, no. 222.

[2] *ABL* 10, 16, 26, 67, 82 and n. 3. E. Buschor, *Feldmäuse* (1937); H. Metzger, *Les Représentations dans la céramique attique du IVe siècle* (1951), 81 ff., 85.

[3] Cf. Athens, 1699. *ABL* 67 and pl. 19. 2 (Phanyllis shape); Vienna, 84. *ABL* 212, no. 158 (Gela Painter).

[4] *ABL* 136, 248 f.; *ABV* 429, 573, 708; *Para* 287 f.

[5] Tübingen, D 72. *ABL* 245, no. 77; Utrecht, University. *ABL* 245, no. 78.

[6] *ABV* 573.

[7] *ABL* 248, nos. 3, 5–7, 15; *ABV* 573, no. 3; *Para*

288 (Gotha, 42 and 43).

[8] London, B 359. *ABL* 248, no. 5; Rhodes, 12962. *ABV* 573, no. 3. For the position of the half-palmettes, at the base of altars, cf. Mingazzini, pl. 98. 7; Basle Market *olpe*, *Para*, 288.

[9] *ABL* 136.

[10] Ibid.

[11] *VA* 177.

[12] Owls and palmettes by the Theseus Painter (see p. 104 n. 9) may indicate that a vase painter's version of this motif existed independent of coins.

fifth-century Athenian coinage, especially the date of the reopening of the Athenian mint after the Persian invasion. The most recent study of the coins dates the reopening of the mint in the 470s, 'before 470 at the very latest'.[1] I shall not comment on the evidence from coins, but I should like to clarify the nature of the ceramic evidence.

Athena-head *lekythoi* by the Athena and Bowdoin Painters are few in number and, although in general similar, different in minor details of major importance to numismatists. The goddess of the Athena Painter's *lekythoi* (PLATE 62. 3)[2] wears the old-fashioned high-crested helmet, as does the goddess of the Bowdoin Painter's *lekythoi* (three white (PLATE 63. 2, 3),[3] one red-figure (PLATE 63. 4)).[4] The Athena Painter's helmet is undecorated; the Bowdoin Painter's has olive leaves on the frontlet and a spiral tendril with palmette at the base of the bowl. On coins Athena does not wear the high-crested helmet,[5] presumably because it is not suited to the circular field.[6] On the 'early owls', the coins which replace the *Wappenmünzen* towards the end of the sixth century B.C.,[7] Athena's helmet is usually undecorated. But at some time in the first half of the fifth century it is embellished with olive leaves on the frontlet and curving tendril and palmette on the bowl; on the coin's reverse a small crescent is added to the field at this time.[8] These innovations mark the end of the early 'owls' and mark the beginning of the standard series.[9] Understandably numismatists would like to be able to date them and, since the same innovations can be detected on Bowdoin *lekythoi*, these vases have been cited as chronological evidence. But the chronology of the Athena and Bowdoin Painters is far from clear, and the presence of the innovations is not altogether reliable. The crescent is not easily explained,[10] and the curving tendril might be little more than fancy decoration,[11] but the olive leaves are traditionally symbolic of victory,[12] and Athena had won a decisive victory over the Persians in 479. At this time the addition of olive leaves to her helmet would be appropriate and politically significant. But even if the leaves were added to commemorate the event, and this is not certain,[13] their appearance on vases cannot be linked to the new 'owls' without caution since there are wreathed Athenas on Attic vases before 479, and since the number of leaves on the vases varies considerably.[14] On coins, with the exception of the earliest issues, with four upright olive leaves, Athena's helmet has three leaves.[15] The Bowdoin Painter's Athena has five leaves on her helmet as does the Icarus Painter's.[16] The curving tendril with palmette at the base of the bowl, to my knowledge, is first prominent on Attic vases by the Bowdoin Painter. On coins the

---

[1] Starr, 19. The numismatic evidence cited is the series of Arcadian hemidrachms featuring the head of Athena to which three olive leaves have been added.

[2] See pp. 104 f.

[3] London, D 22. *ARV* 687, no. 219; Athens, Vlasto, fr. *ARV* 687, no. 220; Oxford, 1965.129 (ex Spencer-Churchill). *ARV* 687, no. 221, and *Para* 406.

[4] Bonn, 84. *ARV* 685, no. 165.

[5] An exception: C. T. Seltman, *Athens—Its History and Coinage before the Persian Invasion* (1924), 72, fig. 45.

[6] C. Kraay, 'The Archaic Owls of Athens: Classification and Chronology', *Numismatic Chronicle* xvi (1956), 43 ff.

[7] Ibid. 59.

[8] Starr, 8 f.; *NC* xvi. 58.

[9] Cf. Starr, 77.

[10] Starr, 11 ff.; *NC* xvi. 56.

[11] Starr, 11.

[12] Ibid., 11 f.; *NC* xvi. 56.

[13] Starr, 11 f.

[14] *ABL* 157 n. 5; *Mel* 97 n. 2.

[15] Starr, 8.

[16] Palermo, no number. *ARV* 698, no. 53 ('female head in *sakkos*'). On later red-figure vases the five leaves also appear: compare the Group of the Athena-head *Pyxides* (*ARV* 1224) and Palermo, Mormino Collection, *CV* i, pl. 85.

position of the palmette changes gradually and so regularly that numismatists have been able to classify them on the basis of this detail.[1] But on vases the position of the palmettes is variable and not strictly comparable to the coins.[2]

The date of the *lekythoi* is not easily determined, owing to the ambiguous relation of the red-figure Bowdoin Painter to the black-figure Athena Painter. It is generally agreed that the Bowdoin Painter had a long career;[3] Beazley thought that he probably 'went on working as late as the third quarter of the fifth century'.[4] If he did, and if he is the black-figure Athena Painter working in red-figure, the length of the composite career is remarkable. If we put aside the problem of the Bowdoin Painter's relation to the Athena Painter and the relation between his *lekythoi* decorated with the head of Athena and contemporary coins, we are left with four vases, whose motif is not without parallel in Attic vase-painting and whose shape and accessory decoration are very similar but not homogeneous. The *lekythos* in Oxford (PLATE 63. 3) looks like the latest of the four, and it need not be earlier than 470 or even as early as that.[5]

BELS AND CHIMNEYS

Apart from side-palmette *lekythoi* of undetermined shape,[6] two other types of *lekythoi* are known to have been decorated in this way—BELs and chimneys. Since the number of examples of each is small and since the two shapes are related, they are treated together. The Carlsruhe Painter decorated several *lekythoi* of shape BEL.[7] One, in Cambridge,[8] is a side-palmette *lekythos* (PLATE 64. 1): on either side of a woman standing with a basket

[1] Starr, 8 f.

[2] On London, D 22, and Oxford, 1965.129, the palmettes lie parallel to the frontlet; on the Vlasto fragment the palmette hangs down beside the frontlet. On numismatic evidence the Vlasto helmet is the latest of the three (cf. Starr, 8 f.) but ceramic evidence suggests that the Oxford *lekythos* is later. The Bowdoin Painter renders the florals with some care, but we cannot expect him to achieve the precision of a die-cast (cf. Starr, 77 and n. 2).

[3] *ARV* 677 f.

[4] Ibid. 678.

[5] *Mel* 97 n. 2.

[6] The side-palmette *lekythoi* of undetermined shape (*ARV* 303, nos. 10–13, and pp. 1644 and 1666 (10 *bis*, *ter*, and 11 *bis*); *Para* 357) are nearly standard, but the neck and shoulder are reserved in the manner of secondary *lekythoi*. One of these undetermined shapes (*ARV* 303, no. 11) is classified among the BELs (*ARV* 303, no. 11 = 735, no. 98) and described here with that shape (see below n. 8). The characteristic sharp-angle join of this vase is more apparent in the *CV* plate (Cambridge, *CV* i, pl. 30. 1) than it is in our PLATE 64. 1.

The *lekythos* in Athens (2023. *ARV* 303, no. 10) 'Recalls the Providence Painter and, a little, the school of Douris' (*ARV* 303). The side-palmettes are not

unlike those on the Carlsruhe Painter's side-palmette *lekythos* of shape BEL (*ARV* 303, no. 11. Below, n. 8), but the hearts of the palmettes are not reserved.

The Dresden *lekythos* (ZV 2963. *ARV* 303, no. 12) is restored and the surface of the vase is damaged, but the composition of the side-palmettes is comparable to that of Athens 2023. (I should like to thank Dr. B. E. Bowen for notes and photographs of the vase which I have not personally examined.)

The fourth *lekythos* in Cambridge (GR 3.1917 (PLATE 64. 3), *ARV* 303, no. 13) is unusual. Beazley describes it: 'Full size. Late straggler' (*ARV* 303) and attributes it, together with three other white *lekythoi* of secondary shape, to the Painter of Cambridge 3.17 (*ARV* 1241 f.). The shoulder decoration is nearer the Beldam Painter's than to anyone else's (cf. *ABL*, pl. 51. 1–4); note the little arc-tendrils. The side palmettes (the *CV* plate (*CV* i, pl. 30. 3b) displays the florals more fully than our PLATE 64. 3, which emphasizes the shoulder decoration) have no close parallel. The three other *lekythoi* attributed to the painter have rays on the shoulders and peculiar meanders without pattern squares. The Cambridge *lekythos* also stands apart from these in the use of second white (*CV* i, p. 32).

[7] *ARV* 752.

[8] Cambridge, GR 1.1895 (138). *ARV* 735, no. 98.

before a chair there are pairs of circumscribed linked palmettes with dotted, reserved hearts and added spiral tendrils. Similar palmettes with added spirals and reserved dotted hearts frame Apollo on a *lekythos* recently on the Basle market (FIGURE 32*b*; PLATE 64. 2).[1] The body of the *lekythos* curves in sharply at the shoulder join, in the manner of BELs, but the mouth is a chimney. Beazley described the Basle *lekythos* as a chimney of Haemonian type,[2] but Haemonian chimneys, like those of the Emporion Painter, have a rounded base, very flat shoulder, and foot in two degrees; the chimneys of the Beldam Painter have tapering body, curving in sharply below the shoulder, sloping shoulder, and an imitation foot in two degrees.[3] Apart from having a foot in two degrees the Basle *lekythos* resembles Beldam chimneys more than Haemonian. The patternwork of the Basle *lekythos* is also quite like the Carlsruhe Painter's side-palmette *lekythos* of shape BEL.[4]

There is possibly another side-palmette *lekythos* of shape BEL[5]—a *lekythos*, with Persian archer[6] between pairs of linked palmettes, which is said to have been found in a grave at Tanagra[7] late in the nineteenth century.[8] The palmettes have small arc-tendrils (FIGURE 33*b*), like those on the shoulders of *lekythoi* by the Beldam Painter[9] and on some pattern *lekythoi* (see pp. 153 ff; PLATE 70. 1).[10]

Chimney *lekythoi* were the speciality of the Haimon and Emporion Painters and of the Beldam and Pholos Painters. None of the Beldam type, with the possible exception of the Basle *lekythos*, has side-palmettes, nor does any of the Haemonian by the Haimon Painter, but in time we may find side-palmette *lekythoi* by him, for he stood in close relation to the Diosphos Painter[11] and he liked palmettes.[12] There are side-palmette chimney *lekythoi* by the Emporion Painter, black-figure on white ground.[13] The workmanship is hasty and careless but the palmette compositions are canonical—a pair, circumscribed on each side of the figure scene. The Emporion Painter also decorated *alabastra* with patterns,[14] sometimes with patterns and figures in horizontal registers,[15] in the manner of the Diosphos Painter,[16] and the Diosphos Painter may have influenced the Emporion Painter in his choice of decoration.

---

[1] Basle Market (M.M.). *Auktion* xxxiv, no. 177; *Para* 357 ('a late member').

[2] *Para* 357.

[3] Cf. *ABL*, pl. 38. 3–5 and pp. 137, 165 (Emporion Painter), and *ABL*, pl. 53 and p. 178 (Beldam Painter).

[4] Iconographically, vases by the Carlsruhe Painter may also be compared, especially the covered white cup in Boston (00.356) which Beazley associated with the painter (*ARV* 741); compare also a white cup from Delphi (*AE* 1970, 27 ff.).

[5] Tanagra. *ARV* 303, no. 10 *ter*, and p. 1644.

[6] *BCH* lxxxvii (1963), 585, no. 12, and 588, fig. 12.

[7] *AM* xxiii (1898), 404 ff.

[8] Ibid. 404.

[9] Cf. *ABL*, pl. 51. 1.

[10] *ABL* 175; Jacobsthal, pl. 34a (= *ABL* 266, no. 7).

[11] *ABL* 130.

[12] Ibid. 133.

[13] Ibid. 167, 265, nos. 42–6; cf. *AM* lxxxi (1966), *Beilage* 25. 1–2; *Hesp* xxxvii (1968), 359.

[14] *ABL* 263, nos. 18–20; 264, nos. 21–6.

[15] Ibid. 263, nos. 1, 11; 264.

[16] Ibid. 165, 167.

PART FOUR

BLACK-BODIED *LEKYTHOI*

INTRODUCTION

BLACK-BODIED *lekythoi* (PLATE 67) were produced in the same workshops as the black-, red-figure, and white *lekythoi*, and their subsidiary decoration is fully comparable. A study of the figured *lekythoi* would be incomplete without some consideration of them. In this section black-bodied *lekythoi* are divided broadly into black- and red-figure workshops, and special attention is given to their shoulder decoration.

Before turning to the black-figure workshops the term black-bodied must be explained. Black-bodied vases are not entirely black. Black-glaze (or black-painted) ware has recently been studied in detail by Talcott and Sparkes;[1] these all-black vases may be decorated in a variety of ways including simple reservation, added colour, ribbing, relief-work, and patternwork, stamped or incised.[2] Black-bodied vases are not ribbed, worked in relief, incised, or stamped, but they are reserved and coloured. For purposes of clarity, most black vases with minimal reserved or painted decoration, for example a narrow band on the black body, are classed as black-glazed ware; black vases with more prominent painted or reserved decoration (regularly adapted to figures and florals) are black-bodied.[3] The black-bodied vases were certainly produced in figured workshops,[4] and it is reasonable to assume that black-glaze vases were too,[5] although the shape distribution among the latter sometimes varies significantly from figured and black-bodied.[6] For example, the cylinder *lekythos* (Type II)—the most important black-, red-figure, and white-ground shape—is rare in black glaze.[7] Conversely, the range of black-glaze shapes is wider than that of black-bodied.[8] In the second half of the sixth century and early in the fifth century other shapes are occasionally black-bodied, for example *oinochoai*,[9] volute-craters,[10] *dinoi*,[11] *stamnoi*,[12] *hydriai*,[13] and some types of amphorae[14] and neck-*pelikai*;[15] but the richer patternwork of the mature red-figure style soon undermined this decorative scheme.

[1] L. Talcott and B. Sparkes, *Black and Plain Pottery*, *Agora* xii (1970). On p. 1 n. 2, the term 'black glaze' is explained; cf. *GPP* 211 ('black painted').

[2] *Agora* xii. 17 ff.   [3] Cf. ibid. 153.

[4] Shapes, patterns, and figures support this, as I attempt to demonstrate.

[5] *Agora* xii. 14.   [6] Ibid. 3, 9 f.

[7] Ibid. 152 f.

[8] Ibid. 9 ff.

[9] Black-bodied *oinochoai* are described with black-bird vases, pp. 93 ff. Cf. also Class of Agora P 1256, *ABV* 427 (entirely black *oinochoai*, with red lines).

[10] Louvre, F 198. *ABV* 280, no. 55 (Antimenes Painter); Acropolis, 655. *ABV* 289, no. 26 (Antimenes Painter, manner); London, B 364. *ABV* 229 vi. (Nikosthenes, 'Fairly good and early'); Taranto, fr. *ABV* 384, no. 21, and New York, 41.162.64, a–c, and e, frr. *ABV* 384, no. 22 (Leagros Group); *ABV* 195 (Golvol Group). Unattributed: Copenhagen, 3835 (*CV* iii, pl. 124. 2), and Agora, P 1251 (*Hesp* vii (1938), 387,

no. 36, and pp. 400 f.). The black-figure tradition of black-bodied volute-craters is mentioned by Beazley (*JHS* xxxi (1911), 282).

[11] Villa Giulia, 50599. *ABV* 146, no. 20 (Exekias); Madrid, 10902. *ABV* 275, no. 133 (Antimenes Painter), and *ABV* 279, nos. 50–1 (Manner). Unattributed: Copenhagen, 4219. *CV* iii, pl. 124. 3.

[12] Basle Market (M.M.), *Auktion* xvi, no. 120, and p. 33.

[13] Black-bodied *hydria*, Würzburg, 322. Langlotz, pl. 247.

[14] Black-bodied neck-amphorae of the Uprooter Class have palmettes on their reserved necks (*ABV* 589, nos. 4–6). A neck-amphora related to the Class (Bologna, 44. *ABV* 589) has black bands on the body. A black-bodied neck-amphora of the Leagros Group (*ABV* 375, no. 218) has figures on the shoulder.

[15] Black-bodied neck-*pelikai*: *Agora* xii. 50 ('The closest parallels to the black neck-*pelikai* are those with black body but with black-figured palmettes on

1. BLACK-FIGURE WORKSHOPS

The earliest black *lekythoi* are type I (Deianeiras) and they are black-glaze (PLATE 67. 1): the dark surface is broken by bands of added colour, most often red or purple.[1] The simple scheme was attractive and widely used on vases of different shapes. The earliest *lekythoi* decorated in this way have been dated to the beginning of the sixth century.[2] The earliest black-bodied *lekythoi* are considerably later; they are shoulder *lekythoi* (Type II), and their subsidiary decoration is painted either in a light colour on the black body or in a dark colour on the reserved shoulder.

APPLIED COLOUR, INCISION, AND SIX'S TECHNIQUE

Dark vases with decoration in added, lighter colours had been favoured at various times and in various places in the Greek world.[3] In Corinth from around the middle of the seventh century B.C. these elements were employed in the 'black-polychrome' style, which was popular at home and imitated abroad.[4] In the East, especially on the islands of Rhodes[5] and Chios,[6] some Orientalizing fabrics were decorated in this way and in Etruria some vases of the Etrusco-Corinthian style.[7] In Attica colour had been applied to black-painted vases early in the sixth century,[8] but incised detail is not a regular feature until later.[9] It is important to distinguish applied colour[10] from applied colour with incision. The latter is generally known as Six's technique, after the Dutch scholar who first studied it.[11] Within Six's technique two variations are conventionally recognized; each uses incision differently.[12] The first has decoration entirely in added colour; incision is restricted to interior details of minor importance (PLATE 4. 1). The second has decoration partly incised and partly in added colour, to which incision may be added (PLATE 6. 4). The first looks like an amplification of the early red (or purple) on black scheme,[13]

the neck.') and n. 7 on p. 50. Cf. *ClRh* iv. 216, fig. 231 (horizontal palmettes on the reserved neck).

Black-figured neck-*pelikai* (*JHS* lxxi (1951), 46 f. (Bothmer)) are largely unattributed, but one (London, Winslow Collection) has been attributed to the Theseus Painter (*ABV* 519, no. 10). The decoration of the necks of the black-figure neck-*pelikai* is either three linked palmettes, alternately upright and pendent (*JHS* lxxi. 46, nos. 4–6), as on the necks of doubleens by the Edinburgh and Diosphos Painters and small Panathenaic amphorae associated with the Painter of Oxford 218b (*ABV* 339; *Para* 150 f.) or upright palmettes-on-Os (*JHS* lxxi. 46, no. 2).

Red-figure neck-*pelikai* are known by the Berlin Painter (Ferrara, T. 367. *ARV* 205, no. 114; Ferrara, T. 41 VP. *ARV* 205, no. 114 *bis*). These vases are black-bodied; the neck bears a red-figure lion on one side, a lioness on the other, in the manner of the painter's black-bodied *lekythos* in Munich (2475. *ARV* 211, no. 199). The vases are early in the Berlin Painter's career.

[1] *Agora* xii. 151 f.; *ABL* 4 f.
[2] *Agora* xii. 151; *ABL* 5.

[3] H. Luschey, *Die Phiale* (1939), 152; Pfuhl, 350 ff.; Carlsruhe *CV* i, p. 37; *Muse* iii (1969), 24 f. (Haspels).
[4] Payne, 18 f. ('black-polychrome' style); cf. *GPP* 139 (influence of Corinth).
[5] *GPP* 139 f.
[6] J. Boardman, *Excavations in Chios, 1952–1955— Greek Emporio* (1967), 169; *Report of the Department of Antiquities, Cyprus* (1968), 14 (Boardman).
[7] W. Llewellyn Brown, *The Etruscan Lion* (1960), 58 f.
[8] *Agora* xii. 18 f., 151 (*lekythoi*); Boardman, op. cit. 14 f. (*phialai*).
[9] Luschey, 151 f.
[10] Cf. *GPP* 372; *Muse* iii. 24; Boardman, op. cit. 14; *AA* 1970. 475 ff. and p. 481 (Six = incision).
[11] *GazArch* xiii (1888), 193 ff., 281 ff.
[12] *Muse* iii. 24; *JHS* lxxxv (1965), 24 (Corbett).
[13] The simple Six's technique is often considered 'easy red-figure' (cf. *Muse* iii. 25; *GPP* 372), but the red lines painted on earlier black vases indicate that this type of decoration was appreciated in its own right: figures in added colour, with or without incised details, need not have been directly inspired by developments

possibly inspired by one of the above-mentioned centres which specialized in dark fabrics decorated in added colour. The second is a modification of the first, inspired by the movement which spawned several other experimental techniques before culminating in developed red-figure.[1]

The earliest Attic vase whose figure decoration is executed in simple Six's technique[2] is a black-bodied amphora of Etruscan (Villanovan)[3] shape, fashioned by Nikosthenes,[4] a potter who specialized in the so-called Nikosthenic amphorae, with an eye to the lucrative Etruscan market.[5] (Nikosthenes was an acknowledged innovator in the Athenian Kerameikos and the amphora of Nikosthenic shape is not the only evidence we have which suggests he was influential in the development of Six's technique in Athens.)[6] Decoration is limited to the conical neck and ribbon handles of the amphora; on the former a nude woman and a dog, in added white with incised details and a touch of red; on the latter tripods in added white. A few other Nikosthenic amphorae are very nearly black-bodied,[7] and black-bodied vases of other shapes are known from the workshop, for example a volute-crater[8] and a neck-amphora of special shape,[9] but their subsidiary decoration is black-figure.

We have three black-bodied vases signed by the potter Andokides, but none in Six's technique. They are neck-amphorae of special shape (unlike the Nikosthenic) with black-figure decoration on the neck. Two have been attributed to the Antimenes Painter,[10] the third to his 'brother' Psiax.[11] The Antimenes Painter is not known to have worked in Six's technque but Psiax worked in several techniques, including Six's. An *alabastron* in the British Museum (PLATE 1. 3)[12] illustrates his varied interests: the body is white slipped and covered with neat registers of pattern except the centre which is black with figure decoration in added colour lightly incised.[13] The *alabastron* was probably painted

in red-figure. See p. 120 n. 4 (red lines), and page 117 n. 6.(*phialai* decorated in added colour on dark ground, with and without incision).

[1] *Muse* iii. 24 f.; *GPP* 372.

[2] Six's technique had been used by earlier black-figure painters for shield blazons; see below, n. 6.

[3] *GPP* 221.

[4] Louvre, F 114. *ABV* 226.

[5] *GPP* 151 ff., 221 (Etruscan bucchero).

[6] A few black-painted *phialai* signed by Nikosthenes have a tongue pattern in added red around the *omphalos* (*ABV* 234, xii). The mesomphalic *phiale* is a shape derived from metalwork. It was introduced to Greece from the East in the Geometric period (*Perachora* ii. 80 and n. 8) and soon copied in clay. The earliest Attic clay *phialai* have been dated to the middle of the seventh century (ibid., n. 6). In the later sixth century black-painted *phialai* with decoration in added colour, with or without incision (Boardman, *Report of the Department of Antiquities, Cyprus* (1968), 14), were especially popular in Athens, judging from the finds on the Athenian Acropolis (Langlotz, pls. 85 ff.). It has been conjectured that the fashion came from Ionia (Luschey, 149 ff.), where 'black-polychrome' *phialai*

are well attested, especially on the island of Chios, from the earlier sixth century (Boardman, op. cit. 15). The Nikosthenic *phialai* are not incised (apart from the potter's signature), and the decoration in added colour is very simple. There is, however, closely related to them, a fragmentary *phiale*, found at Eleusis, signed by Sosimos and decorated in a Six-like technique (*ABV* 350). A fragmentary cup from the Acropolis, which also seems to bear Sosimos' signature, is decorated in proper Six's technique (Acropolis ii, 1078, fr. *ABV* 350. Langlotz, pl. 84).

[7] Cf. Hanover, 1961.23. *ABV* 222, no. 58 *bis*, and *Para* 106.

[8] London, B 364. *ABV* 229, vi. Compare the similar disposition of the patterns (especially the upright palmettes-on-Os) on the two unattributed volute-craters mentioned on p. 115 n. 10.

[9] Tarquinia, RC 1076. *ABV* 223, no. 59.

[10] Louvre, F 201. *ABV* 274, no. 120; Copenhagen, Thorwaldsen Museum, 38. *ABV* 274, no. 121.

[11] Castle Ashby, Northampton. *ABV* 293, no. 7.

[12] London, 1900.6–11.1. *ABV* 294, no. 25.

[13] Karystios and Smikrion occur as *kalos* inscriptions on this vase. Karystios (*ABV* 668) is known from one other vase, an exceptionally fine white-ground *oinochoe*

around 510 B.C., for its shape is connected with Pasiades' (PLATE 72. 2, 3) and the *alabastra* of the Paidikos Group.[1] It is slimmer than the Amasis Painter's black-figure *alabastron*—our earliest clay *alabastron* with black-figure decoration[2]—but fuller than those of the Sappho and Diosphos Painters, with which it is, none the less, related in figure- and patternwork.[3] The Sappho and Diosphos Painters are the major exponents of Six's technique in the years around 500 B.C., but before turning to them we shall look briefly at other late sixth- and early fifth-century black-bodied *lekythoi* in Six's technique.[4]

The Nikosthenic Workshop was productive, influential, and probably largely responsible for the dissemination of Six's technique in the decades around 500 B.C. One of the earliest *lekythoi* in this technique is Phanyllis shape (PLATE 4. 1)—a broad-shoulder *lekythos*—a type by now decidedly old-fashioned—which was revived by the Phanyllis Painter and the members of his workshop (see pp. 144 f.). The reserved neck of the *lekythos* is decorated with rays,[5] the reserved shoulder with upright palmettes-on-Os, one of the favourite patterns of the Nikosthenic Workshop.[6] The black body bears three figures in added white (details incised) dancing above a painted red line.[7] The artist is the Chariot Painter.[8] The Chariot Painter's Phanyllis *lekythoi* are somewhat slimmer than the Phanyllis Painter's and, apart from their generally larger size and steeper shoulder, their profile is not unlike the Little Lions of the Diosphos Workshop.[9] Between the Phanyllis and Little Lion *lekythoi* stands the Cock Group (see pp. 145 f.)[10]—near the Phanyllis in shape, near the Little Lion in size. The Cock *lekythoi* are sometimes decorated in imitation of Phanyllis *lekythoi* and are somewhat later in date.[11] They derive their name from

in the Petit Palais (310), whose patternwork (tongues, embattlement, and double ivy band (*ABL* 101)) is very similar to that on the *alabastron*. Smikrion (*ABV* 674) is known from one other vase, a fragmentary band-cup (Acropolis, 1742. Graef, pl. 86), about which Beazley wrote: 'The exceptional technique makes one think of Psiax, but so little remains' (*ABV* 674).

[1] *ABL* 101 ff.; *ARV* 98 ff.

[2] Athens, Agora, P 12628. *ABV* 155, no. 64; *Hesp* viii (1939), 248 ff.

[3] *ABL* 101.

[4] Attic vases of other shapes are, of course, decorated in Six's technique.

Stamnoi: Philippaki, 25 ff. One of the *stamnoi* is thought to be the work of the same potter as a black-figure *stamnos* of the Antimenean Circle (Naples, Stg. 175. *ABV* 289, no. 25), and two, decorated exclusively with florals, make one think of palmette vases, such as those by the Gela, Diosphos, and Haimon Painters.

Neck-amphorae: *JHS* lxxviii (1958), 21 and pl. 10 *b*, *c*. Two small neck-amphorae of similar shape and style of decoration are related to the above-mentioned *stamnoi* (*ABV* 672). They are Six vases, except for the neck, which is reserved (*ML* xxx (1925), 652 and

decorated with black palmettes, very like those on the Diosphos Painter's doubleens (cf. *ABL* 238, nos. 130–1, and 239, no. 138), except those on the 'B' side of the Florence amphora (*ML* xxx. 654, fig. 34) which are very like the palmettes on the Diosphos Painter's palmette *lekythos* in Athens (2213. *ABL*, pl. 36. 5).

Choes: *AA* 1970. 475 ff. A sizeable group of *choes* with decoration in added colour has been collected by Green (*AA* 1970. 475 ff.), mentioned earlier by van Hoorn (*Choes and Anthesteria* (1951), 54). Most do not make use of incision (*AA* 1970. 481).

[5] Rays: *ABL* 63 and n. 2, 64, 65, 87 (581 Class), 89 (Oinophile *lekythos*).

[6] Upright palmettes-on-Os: *ABL* 63, 64 and n. 1, 65, 66. The pattern is applied to architectural decoration, FIGURE 3*c*.

[7] See p. 120 n. 4.

[8] *ABL* 65 f.; *ABV* 699; *Para* 205 f.

[9] *ABL* 65. An exceptionally slight version of the shape, near LL (see p. 81), is represented by a *lekythos* in Carlsruhe (B 985, *CV* i, pl. 31. 2) whose black body bears two dancers in added white, with red lines painted above and below (*CV* i, p. 37, and fig. 9).

[10] *ABL* 67 f.; *ABV* 466 ff., 699; *Para* 208 ff.

[11] *ABL* 68.

the cocks which regularly decorate the shoulders. Six's technique is not unknown among Cock *lekythoi* but at present it is not well represented.[1] Some Cock *lekythoi* were produced in the 581 Workshop which is connected with the Phanyllis Workshop in both shape and pattern.[2] Black-bodied *lekythoi* are not known to have been a speciality of the 581 Workshop,[3] but pattern *lekythoi* were and these we shall consider in Part Five. The Marathon Painter, the leading artist of the 581 Workshop, was a contemporary of the Sappho and Diosphos Painters,[4] and interrelation might be expected: some 581 *lekythoi* 'are close to the Little Lion Class in shape, and might indeed be counted as belonging to it'.[5] The patternwork of both is sometimes similar.

Six's technique in the hands of the Sappho and Diosphos Painters generally looks different: significant parts of the composition are incised without added colour. This 'outline—Six' is a modification of the simple Six's technique,[6] as mentioned above. (There are black-bodied vases by the Sappho Painter in the simpler technique.)[7] It is a transitional technique just like semi-outline, standing between black-figure (incised painted areas) and red-figure (outlined areas). Semi-outline vases from the Diosphos Workshop dispose outlined and solid areas of colour on a light ground; the Six vases dispose outline (incised) and solid (applied colour) on a dark ground (cf. PLATES 58, 59 and 6. 4).[8] The Sappho Painter seems to have been more old-fashioned than his colleague and generally less interested in the outline styles.[9] The Diosphos Painter's use of Six's technique is similar to his use of semi-outline; just as he liked to balance light (outline) and dark (silhouette) on white ground, he likes to balance dark (incised) and light (added colour) on black. In both techniques his chief concern is decorative effect. One of his exceptionally elaborate Six *lekythoi* (PLATE 6. 4)[10] features a warrior (body incised) striding over his fallen adversary (body in added flesh tones), displaying a shield with a blazon in Six's technique, as it had been used by earlier black-figure painters.[11] On some other Six *lekythoi* the decorative scheme suits the theme: a black (incised) satyr pursues a white (added colour) maenad, one figure overlapping the other for maximum decorative effect.[12]

Most of the Six *lekythoi*, of both the Sappho and Diosphos Painters, are the workshop's normal shape, DL, and some *lekythoi* of this shape are black-bodied without accessory decoration (PLATE 67. 2).[13] We know that the Sappho Painter decorated at least one

[1] Boston, 10.556. *ABV* 471, no. 122.

[2] *ABL* 93, n. 3; *ABV* 467.

[3] A black-bodied *lekythos* in Oxford (1938.732) (PLATE 67. 5), related in shape to Phanyllis and 581, preserves traces of decoration in added colour: on the shoulder an abbreviated Phanyllis palmette (red and white); the body decoration is effaced.

[4] *ABL* 89.

[5] *Para* 253.

[6] *Muse* iii. 25; *JHS* lxxxv (1965), 24.

[7] The following may serve as examples: *Onos* (Athens, 2184. *ABL* 228, no. 53). On the end of the *onos*, with a modelled female head, two Erotes in added white, details incised, fly with tendrils. The

attached female head is white slipped and details were picked out in colour. *Lekythos* (Athens, 2262. *ABL* 228, no. 47). The figures (Theseus and the Minotaur) are rendered entirely in added colour.

[8] *ABL* 111.

[9] Ibid. 112.

[10] *Muse* iii. 24 f., figs. 1–2 (attributed by Haspels).

[11] Luschey, 151 f.

[12] Athens, 2137. *ABL* 228, no. 45. Cf. Carlsruhe B 34 (*CV* i, pl. 31. 1).

[13] Corinth, T 3161–P1980. *ABL* 228, no. 50. Taranto (old museum, no. 5). *ABL* 236, no. 82; Rhodes, 13491. *ABL* 236, no. 83; Agrigento. *ABL* 236, no. 87; Oxford, 1928.41. *ABL* 236, no. 88.

larger vase in the Six's technique, the *kalpis hydria* in Warsaw,[1] but the other favourite Six shape in the Diosphos Workshop is the Little Lion,[2] which was also sometimes black-bodied without accessory decoration.[3]

RESERVATION

Many black-bodied *lekythoi* from the Diosphos Workshop, shape DL and LL, were not enhanced by figure decoration in Six's technique: their bodies were left black, brightened only by the old system of fine bands of added red or purple paint, at the shoulder–body join, the lower body, and not infrequently at the mouth and foot.[4] The necks and shoulders of these plain black-bodied *lekythoi*, like those of the black-bodied *lekythoi* in Six's technique, are reserved, normally also part of the foot plate.[5] The larger *lekythoi* of the workshop's normal shape (DL) usually have reserved shoulders with linked lotus buds in the painters' favourite schemes (PLATE 67. 2),[6] but some have a white slipped shoulder and a white slipped pattern band at the join of shoulder to body. The smaller black-bodied *lekythoi* of Little Lion type (plain and Six's technique) are similarly reserved. Their shoulders frequently have lotus buds instead of the eponymous lions.[7] A distinctive feature of some of these Little Lions (plain and Six's technique) is the addition of white paint to the shoulder florals: in place of stem-arcs linking bud to bud, two white lines are added to alternate buds. The white lines splay out towards the shoulder edge, giving the effect of white petals.[8] This is not Six's technique because there is no incision,[9] nor is it a decorative invention of the Diosphos Workshop: white petals are found earlier on *lekythoi* of the Dolphin Group (see p. 144; cf. PLATE 68. 3).

The reserved shoulders of one of the Diosphos Painter's black-bodied *lekythoi* in Six's technique has five black palmettes disposed in the Athena Painter's favourite scheme, in place of the workshop's usual lotus buds.[10] The Athena Painter's shoulder decoration is the most characteristic feature of black-bodied *lekythoi* of shape BL (PLATE 67. 3) which are generally assumed to have come from the red-figure Bowdoin Workshop. Before describing them, mention should be made of some earlier black-bodied *lekythoi* of standard shape from black-figure workshops.

No black-bodied *lekythoi* have been attributed to the Edinburgh Painter, but he may have decorated *lekythoi* of this type.[11] A black-bodied *lekythos* in the Petit Palais betrays

---

[1] Warsaw, ex Czartoryski, 32. *ABL* 228, no. 56, and *Para* 246. *ABL* 106 (Haspels compares a *stamnos* fragment in Heidelberg, E 51).

[2] *ABL* 107, no. 3; *Para* 252.

[3] *Agora* xii. 153; *ABV* 515 f., 703; *Para* 253 f.

[4] Cf. Palermo, Mormino Collection, *CV* i. III L, pls. 1–3, and pp. 3–5. Miss Haspels was inclined to credit the Sappho Painter with the introduction of black-bodied Little Lions, because the red lines which appear on these vases also appear on those which the painter decorated in Six's technique. She suggested that the presence of red lines on the body of black *lekythoi* indicated that the vase was originally intended to be decorated in Six's technique (*JHS* lviii (1938), 257 f.). Mrs. Ure has pointed out the earlier use of red

lines on black-bodied *lekythoi* and has emphasized that they need not indicate that decoration in Six's technique was originally intended (*JHS* lvii (1937), 265; lviii (1938), 258).

[5] Cf. Palermo, Mormino Collection, *CV* i. III L, pls. 1–3.

[6] The Sappho Painter's stem-arcs regularly skip two buds, the Diosphos Painter's one (*ABL* 94).

[7] *Agora* xii. 153; *ABL* 107.

[8] *ABL* 107.

[9] Cf. ibid.

[10] Carlsruhe, 231. *ABL* 235, no. 78.

[11] The painter's association with the Berlin and Diosphos Painters leads me to think this. A white-ground black-figure *lekythos* by the Edinburgh Painter

his influence.[1] It is a tall, slim, straight-sided cylinder with reserved neck, shoulder, and foot plate. The shoulder bears seven black palmettes—the old Leagran scheme which the Edinburgh Painter used on his earlier *lekythoi*[2]—with single small ivy-leaves in the field.[3] The shape and enclosed bars at the neck–shoulder join suggest a later date than the seven-palmette scheme. The Gela Painter decorated pattern (see pp. 148 f.)[4] and black-bodied *lekythoi*. The latter are slim standard cylinders, presumably work of his later years. The shoulder of one has the Edinburgh Painter's later five-palmette scheme;[5] the shoulder of the other has the painter's own distinctive three palmettes with two lotus buds.[6] The Gela Painter follows the Edinburgh Painter's practice of leaving the neck reserved.

The introduction of the black neck to *lekythoi* of standard shape is credited to the Athena Painter; contemporary developments in red-figure are thought to have influenced him.[7] The Athena Painter's relation to red-figure has been mentioned on several occasions. Here our concern is the group of standard cylinders decorated in different techniques whose shoulders bear red-figure palmettes disposed horizontally. Some are black-figure (PLATE 13), some are black-bodied (PLATE 12. 3, 4), and one is red-figure (PLATE 12. 2). Two of the three black-figure *lekythoi* have reserved necks. The black-bodied and red-figure *lekythoi* have black necks.[8] The shoulder decoration scarcely varies: four horizontal red-figure palmettes beneath enclosed bars (black vertical strokes on reserved ground, not red-figure tongues). The shoulder–body join is decorated with a dot pattern or a meander. These *lekythoi* are standard cylinders. The black-bodied *lekythoi* associated with the red-figure Bowdoin Workshop (PLATE 67. 3)[9] are near standard, with black neck. Between them stand two black-bodied *lekythoi*—standard cylinders with black necks whose reserved shoulders bear figures instead of florals. One was once on the Paris Market;[10] the other is in Oxford (PLATE 67. 4).[11] The shoulders of both are black-figure and their scenes are very similar. The Paris shoulder had two men and two hounds chasing a hare with *lagobola*[12]—a scene found on black-figure (PLATE 14. 1) and semi-outline (PLATE 14. 2) *lekythoi* from the Athena Bowdoin Workshop;[13] beneath, a net pattern. The Oxford shoulder features a stag hunt with lines painted at the shoulder–body

---

in Switzerland (*ABV* 476, no. 5, PLATE 7. 2), is unexceptional in shape and style of figures, and in shoulder ornament, but exceptional in the pattern at the join of shoulder to body: stopt meanders alternate with saltire squares in a scheme similar to that favoured by the Berlin Painter. Especially interesting is the meander which takes its origin from the vertical dividing line (left of centre). In *JHS* lxx (1950), 30, Martin Robertson cited three examples of such meanders—all from the Berlin Painter's very early period, adding, 'nor do I know of other examples of this peculiarity in Attic vase-painting'. The Swiss *lekythos* features 'Ariadne mounting chariot, with Dionysos and two satyrs'. The satyr on the right is attended by a goat. The satyrs and goat on the B-side of the Gorgos cup, also associated with the early Berlin Painter (Athens, Agora, P 24113. *ARV* 213, no. 242. *AJA* lxii (1958), pl. 7) come to mind.

[1] Petit Palais, 436. *CV* i, pl. 3. 3.
[2] *ABL* 87.
[3] These small ivy-leaves are not to be confused with the larger ivy-leaves which frame central palmettes on some *lekythoi* of the Phanyllis, Fat Runner, and Cock groups. See p. 146.
[4] Castelvetrano, 126. *ABL* 212, no. 160.
[5] Taranto (old museum, no. 3). *ABL* 212, no. 157.
[6] Agrigento. *ABL* 212, no. 161.
[7] *ABL* 148.
[8] *ARV* 1666.
[9] Ibid. 693 f.; *Para* 407.
[10] Paris Market (Platt). *ABL* 262, no. 2.
[11] Oxford, 251. *ABL* 262, no. 1.
[12] *ABL* 161 f.
[13] New York, 41.162.146 (ex Gallatin). *ABL* 257, no. 72, and *ABV* 522; Athens, 1973. *ARV* 690, no. 9.

join. In the field the letters of an inscription are scattered. Space-filling inscriptions are a characteristic feature of semi-outline *lekythoi* from the Bowdoin Workshop. Two other *lekythoi* from the workshop may be compared, for even though they are red-figure, their reserved shoulders are decorated with figures instead of florals—the bilingual *lekythoi* in Brussels attributed to the Bowdoin Painter (PLATE 15).[1] The figures on the Brussels shoulders are rendered in silhouette—as are some of the figures on semi-outline *lekythoi*, and the compositions recall the Athena Painter[2] and the semi-outline *lekythoi* associated with him and the Bowdoin Painter.[3] There are letters scattered in the field, in the manner of semi-outline *lekythoi*. At the shoulder–body join there is the peculiar meander pattern—pairs of linked meanders alternating with patterned squares.

The black-bodied *lekythoi* of the Bowdoin Workshop are shape BL and most have the Athena Painter's five palmettes on their shoulder,[4] but some have black shoulders.[5] At the join of the black neck to the reserved body there are enclosed black bars;[6] at the join of shoulder to body painted lines or pattern band—dots or a meander. The black-bodied Bowdoin *lekythoi* have been found over much of the Mediterranean.[7] They were in wide use over a considerable period of time, but most were probably produced during the second quarter of the fifth century B.C.[8]

BLACK-BODIED *LEKYTHOI* OF SECONDARY SHAPE

There are black-bodied *lekythoi* of virtually all the secondary shapes decorated in red-figure or white-ground. The subsidiary decoration is generally abbreviated florals or rays on reserved ground, and for this reason I keep them separate from black-bodied *lekythoi* with subsidiary decoration in red-figure. Decoration is restricted to the reserved shoulder: PLs normally have five black palmettes,[9] BELs,[10] CLs,[11] and ATLs[12] have rays. They are small and inexpensive vases, widely exported and freely imitated. They serve much the same purposes as the small pattern *lekythoi*.

2. RED-FIGURE WORKSHOPS

The earliest black-bodied *lekythoi* with subsidiary decoration in red-figure are earlier than the black-bodied *lekythoi* with red-figure shoulders associated with the Athena

---

[1] Brussels, A 3132. *ARV* 681, no. 91; Brussels, A 3131. *ARV* 682, no. 107.

[2] The striding Athena of A 3132 (probably in a Gigantomachy (*ABL* 160)) may be compared with the following: *ABL* 255, nos. 30–2, and 258, no. 100. The Herakles and the Bull of A 3131 may be compared with Vienna, 86. *ABL* 257, no. 65, and with the Theseus and the Bull on Cab. Méd. 300. *ABL* 257, no. 66.

[3] The wounded, falling combatant on A 3132 may be compared with the wounded warrior on Cab. Méd. 299. *ARV* 690, no. 11. The Herakles and the Bull on A 3131 may be compared with Bonn, 538. *ARV* 690, no. 12.

[4] *ARV* 693, no. 1, to p. 694, no. 30.

[5] Ibid. 694, nos. 31–7.

[6] Beazley calls the bars 'tongues' (*ARV* 693) but they are vertical black strokes on reserved ground, enclosed by lines.

[7] *ARV* 693 f. The great majority comes from the west, especially Sicily; there is also a significant number from the east, especially the islands of Rhodes and Cyprus. The distribution of these and of pattern *lekythoi* is discussed on pp. 136 ff.

[8] Cf. *ARV* 678.

[9] Palermo, Mormino Collection, *CV* i. III L, pl. 3. 1 (535) and pl. 3. 2 (529).

[10] *ML* xxiii (1914), 914, fig. 154.

[11] Palermo, Mormino Collection, *CV* i. III L, pl. 3. 4 (183).

[12] Ibid., pl. 3, centre row.

Painter. They are not standard cylinders, but old-fashioned 'compromises' (PLATE 3. 2)
—a shape which compromised between the old type of shoulder *lekythos* and the new
cylinder.[1] In black-figure the shape is short-lived; the Edinburgh Painter is one of the
last to use it;[2] and in red-figure only two examples are known, both black-bodied,[3] one
in Oxford (PLATE 65. 1),[4] the other recently on the Basle Market.[5] The two vases are so
nearly identical in shape, size, and style of decoration that one hand seems assured.
Beazley never attributed the Oxford *lekythos* and he did not know the Basle *lekythos*.
The Oxford 'compromise' whose shoulder bears cock and hen between palmettes offers
less scope for attribution than the Basle 'compromise', whose shoulder bears four figures
framed by palmettes. On the basis of shape the *lekythoi* cannot be much later than
500 B.C.

The Oxford *lekythos* has a black neck,[6] tongues at the join of neck to shoulder, and a
leftward key at the join of shoulder to body. A large cock and small hen (inscribed *kalos*
and *kale*) are framed by a pair of linked, circumscribed palmettes with ribbed petals.
The closest parallel Beazley could find for the fowl is a cock by the Harrow Painter on
a column-crater in Naples.[7] The closest parallel Haspels could find for the florals are
palmettes by the Eucharides and Tyszkiewicz Painters.[8] The composition is paralleled
on a *lekythos* shoulder fragment from the Acropolis, stylistically not comparable,[9] and
cocks are, of course, common on the shoulders of *lekythoi* of the Cock Group. Cocks
alternate with smaller fowl on the Gela Painter's white *lekythos* in Syracuse (PLATE 16. 4),[10]
and cocks fight on the back of one of the Sappho Painter's *lekythoi* in Six's technique.[11]
In red-figure cock and hen, framed by florals, are the principal decoration of a janiform
head vase in the Louvre (PLATE 64. 5, 65. 2).[12] The composition is closely comparable with
the Oxford *lekythos* but the style is not. The head vase belongs to the Epilykos Class[13]
and dates around 520 to 510 B.C.;[14] the love name Epilykos[15] is used by Skythes, too,[16] who
also worked in black-figure on coral ground,[17] possibly in black-figure on white ground.[18]

The Basle 'compromise' has a black neck, tongues at the join of neck to shoulder, and
a most unusual pattern at the join of shoulder to body—a crossing ('labyrinthine')
meander.[19] In black-figure the crossing meander is rare; the Gela Painter liked it,[20] and the
Antimenes Painter used it occasionally.[21] In red-figure the crossing meander is used more

[1] *ABL* 47 f., 50 ff.   [2] Ibid. 48.

[3] The fact that the only red-figure *lekythoi* known
of 'compromise' shape are black-bodied seems to
support the black-figure tradition of this form of
decoration. The red-figure painters who are best
known for black-bodied *lekythoi* are themselves close
to black-figure—the Bowdoin and Berlin Painters.

[4] Oxford, 1932.733. *ARV* 1644 (to p. 308); *ABL* 75.

[5] I should like to thank Herbert Cahn for allowing me to study the vase, which is to be published by
M. I. Davies.

[6] The black neck is an example of red-figure practice earlier than the Athena Painter's adoption of black
necks on cylinder *lekythoi*, black-figure and white-
ground.

[7] Naples, 3155. *ARV* 275, no. 60.

[8] *ABL* 75.   [9] *ARV* 1644.

[10] Syracuse, 19854.

[11] 'Formerly in the van Branteghem Collection.'
ABL 228, no. 50 *bis*; *GazArch* 1888, 200, figs. 6–7.

[12] Louvre, CA 987.

[13] *ARV* 1530, no. 2; *JHS* xlix (1929), 41 ff. (Beazley).

[14] *JHS* xlix. 43.   [15] *ARV* 1578.   [16] Ibid. 82.

[17] *ABV* 352, 399; *ARV* 84, no. 20, and p. 85, no. 21.

[18] *ABV* 352; *ARV* 82.

[19] *JHS* lxx (1950), 30 (C. M. Robertson).

[20] *ABL* 79 and n. 13.

[21] *JHS* xlvii (1927), 86. On an unattributed *onos* in
Copenhagen (1636. *CV* iii, pl. 120. 1) the crossing-
meander and leftward key appear. The modelled
female head on the end of the *onos* may be compared
with those on *onoi* of the Golonos Group (*ABV* 480),
and by both the Sappho and Diosphos Painters (*ABV*
481).

extensively and in a wider variety of forms—by the Pioneers, by the Berlin Painter, and by some of his contemporaries and followers; in later red-figure it is rare.[1] The Berlin Painter himself seems to have been attracted to the crossing meander only in his early years,[2] when he executed it in a form different from that regularly used by the Gela and Eucharides Painters (a stopt key alternating with a stopt step) (FIGURE 4*n*) and by the Pioneers (a more flowing pattern, both step and key run) (FIGURE 4*l*), the running key is crossed by a stopt step (FIGURE 4*m*). I know this pattern only from the Eucharides Painter's name vase, a *stamnos* in Copenhagen.[3] The Eucharides Painter was specially attracted to the crossing meander which he executed in at least three different forms. The Basle 'compromise' has stopt key crossed by a stopt step—the form found in black-figure on vases by the Gela Painter and in red-figure on vases by the Eucharides Painter.

The four-figure composition on the Basle shoulder reproduces the death of Aigisthos. Red-figure *lekythoi* with shoulder figures do not have more than two figures;[4] the extended composition on our vase is possibly a reflection of black-figure practice.[5] The closest parallel which I have been able to find for the scene, which is in fact a parody of the death of Aigisthos, comes from a small group of *kalpis hydriai* by a little-known artist associated with the early Eucharides and Harrow Painters.[6] There is also something about the composition of the figures, not of course about the style, which makes one think of the Berlin Painter in his early years.[7]

The Berlin Painter liked the effect of the glossy black surface. Many of his vases have a minimum of patternwork and a single figure on each side;[8] some are black-bodied.[9] Two black-bodied *lekythoi* by this painter, one in Munich[10] and one in Adria,[11] have figured shoulders. They are standard cylinders with an egg pattern at the neck–shoulder join and a meander pattern at the shoulder–body join.[12] On the Munich shoulder there

---

[1] *JHS* lxx. 30.

[2] The pattern may be found beneath the figures on the *hydria* in Aberdeen (695. *ARV* 209, no. 164), on the corselet of Orestes on the *pelike* in Vienna (3725. *ARV* 204, no. 109), and (according to Martin Robertson, *JHS* lxx. 23 n. 3, and p. 30 n. 33. I have not seen the vase) on the B side of the neck of a volute-crater in the Villa Giulia (fr. *ARV* 206, no. 131).

[3] Copenhagen, 124. *ARV* 229, no. 35. The pattern is incorrectly copied in the table of patterns in *BSA* xviii (1911–12), 231, fig. 6, no. 7 (no. 14).

[4] *JHS* xxxiv (1914), 197 and n. 15 (Beazley).

[5] There are shoulder figures, not infrequently extended to multi-figure narrative compositions on black-figure *lekythoi* of shoulder type. Cf. *ABL*, pls. 2 (1, 2), 5 (2); Karouzou, pl. 43 and p. 44.

[6] Painter of Florence 3984. *ARV*[1] 174; *ARV* 271.

[7] The Basle shoulder has two two-figure compositions, each self-contained and independent. They look like condensed versions of the figures on the Berlin Painter's early *pelike* in Vienna (see above, n. 2). Compare the Clytemnestra–Telamedes (an unusual name; the painter's error?) group with the B side of the Berlin Painter's *pelike*, noting especially the turn

of Clytemnestra's head and the way in which she wields the instrument of death. Compare the Orestes–Agamemnon group with the B side of another early *pelike* by the Berlin Painter (Florence, 3985. *ARV* 204, no. 110), on which Theseus is seen killing the Minotaur. Theseus and Orestes, Aigisthos, and the Minotaur are composed in significantly similar ways. Both of these *pelikai* have, on their B sides, reserved pattern bands above the figures—a minor point, but one worth notice, because the Berlin Painter, unlike many of his contemporaries who maintained the old-fashioned scheme of black patternwork on reserved ground, seems to have broken more sharply with this black-figure practice. Only a few of his vases, and these are mostly *lekythoi* and doubleens, have reserved pattern bands.

[8] *JHS* xlii (1922), 71 (Beazley).

[9] Cf. *ARV* 206, nos. 127–32 (excepting no. 131 *bis*).

[10] Munich, 2475. *ARV* 211, no. 199; *JHS* xxxiv. 198 n. 16.

[11] Adria, B 180. *ARV* 211, no. 200, and *Para* 343.

[12] The Adria fragment does not have the neck preserved. See *Para* 343 for the redistribution of fragments.

is a lion, on the Adria shoulder a lioness amidst florals. Both *lekythoi* are early in the painter's career. The lion shoulder is familiar in black-figure from *lekythoi* of the Little Lion Class, and in red-figure a similar composition occurs on the shoulder of Douris' red-figure *lekythos* in Bologna (PLATE 8. 2).[1]

Connected with the Berlin Painter is a group of essentially black-bodied vases—*lekythoi*, *oinochoai*, and Nolan amphorae—with floral shoulders and subsidiary pattern bands—the Group of the Floral Nolans (PLATE 66).[2] The *lekythoi* (PLATE 66. 3, 4) are standard cylinders with black neck, an egg pattern[3] at the join of neck to shoulder, a meander pattern at the join of shoulder to body, a subsidiary band of florals on the body, and sometimes a second meander band towards the base.[4] There are four *lekythoi* in the group, but the number of examples could be increased.[5] The shoulder decoration is not exceptional. Two have five palmettes (Type I) with lotus buds added to the volutes of the central palmette,[6] and two have five palmettes (Type Ia) without lotus buds.[7] Type-I palmettes are common in red-figure but the classical system has three palmettes, not five.[8] The Dutuit Painter's shoulders regularly have Type-I palmettes,[9] and the Dutuit Painter is closely connected with the Floral Nolan Group (see below). Type-Ia palmettes are uncommon on red-figure shoulders just as they are on white-ground shoulders but the Berlin Painter and his followers occasionally use them.[10] Type-Ia palmettes are also applied to the shoulder of a Nolan amphora of the group in Birmingham (PLATE 66. 1)[11] and the shoulder of another Nolan in New York[12] is decorated with a double chain of lotuses and palmettes—a pattern which encircles the body of a *lekythos* of the group in Gela.[13] The body florals on the *lekythoi* are restricted to a narrow centrally placed band.

---

[1] Bologna, PU 321. *ARV* 446, no. 267. Diogenes, praised on the vase, is also praised on the white-ground round *aryballos* by the Syriskos Painter.

[2] *ARV* 218 f., 1636; *Para* 346.

[3] Compare the tongues on the Adria fr. (B 404. *CV* i, pl. 5. 8) and on the fragment in Cahn's Collection (128. *ARV* 211, no. 202 *bis*, and *Para* 343).

[4] Cf. Gela, from Gela. *ARV* 218, no. 11.

[5] *ARV* 218, no. 11, to p. 219, no. 14. These *lekythoi* might be added: Adolphseck, Landgraf Philip of Hesse, 50. *CV* i, pl. 37. 2 and pl. 39. 3, and our PLATE 66. 4. The standard cylinder, 36·2 cm, is thought to have come from Gela. At the join of neck to shoulder there is an egg pattern; on the shoulder five palmettes, in the Ia scheme, with tri-lobed spandrel buds. Apart from the spandrel buds (for which, cf. Madrid 11117. *ARV* 209, no. 167. 'On the shoulder, Eros, between florals') the palmettes are very like those on the shoulder fragment in Cahn's Collection (128: see above, n. 3), which Beazley compared (*Para* 343 and *ARV* 1635) with other Ia shoulder palmettes by the Berlin Painter. At the shoulder–body join there is a key pattern; on the body a band of slanting palmettes, enclosed by S-spirals.

New York, 24.97.26. The standard cylinder, 40·05 cm, has an egg pattern at the join of neck to shoulder

(D. 13·9 cm), and Type-I palmettes on the shoulder. There are three palmettes, with lotus buds attached to the volutes of the central palmettes. The first and third palmette are enhanced with added spiral tendrils. At the join of shoulder to body there is a meander pattern (stopt meanders not very carefully executed), and a second, on the lower body. In the centre of the body a rather wide band: a double chain of lotus and palmette. The same pattern may be found on a Nolan amphora of the group in New York (06.1153. *ARV* 218, no. 5).

[6] *ARV* 218, nos. 11–12.

[7] Ibid. 219, nos. 13–14.

[8] The three-palmette system may, however, be 'extended' by the addition of spiral tendrils or buds, as on the *lekythos* in New York (above, n. 5).

[9] Cf. New York, 13.227.16. *ARV* 307, no. 17. Gela, 21. *ARV* 307, no. 18 *bis*, and *Para* 357 (the vase was first attributed to the School of the Berlin Painter, *ARV* 215, no. 14).

[10] Cf. Palermo, V 670. *ARV* 211, no. 195; Copenhagen, Ny Carlsberg, 2701. *ARV* 211, no. 196. See also above, n. 5.

[11] Birmingham, 1616.85. *ARV* 218, no. 10.

[12] New York, 06.1153. *ARV* 218, no. 5.

[13] Gela. *ARV* 218, no. 11.

On the basis of linear[1] and floral patternwork Beazley placed the group near the Berlin Painter, finding closest parallels during the painter's middle period.[2] The style of florals is close to the Dutuit Painter, who is known to have been under the influence of the Diosphos Painter as well as the Berlin Painter.[3] His elaborate handle florals have already been likened to the Diosphos Painter's side-palmettes and the possibility of floral vases by his hand has been suggested. There are also some black-bodied vases by the Dutuit Painter: a doubleen (a shape favoured by the Berlin and Diosphos Painters) in the Louvre bears only a single figure on either side of the neck,[4] and several *oinochoai* (shape 5B, not the Floral Nolan shape)[5] are black-bodied with a single figure on the neck. Another black-bodied *oinochoe* of the same shape with two figures on the neck, which Beazley initially placed with the Dutuit Painter's *oinochoai*,[6] he later associated with the Syriskos Painter.[7] The Eucharides Painter, whose hand also appears among patterns on Floral Nolan vases,[8] is probably the artist of the patternwork on the doubleen in PLATE 66. 2.[9]

The Berlin Painter's school seems to have been selective about black-bodied *lekythoi* and about shoulder figures. Hermonax,[10] the Providence,[11] Achilles,[12] and Phiale[13] Painters all tried their hands at shoulder figures, but neither the Providence nor the Achilles Painter seems to have been very interested in them. Black-bodied *lekythoi* are known only from the Phiale Painter and his black-bodied *lekythoi* have shoulder figures. One black-bodied *lekythos* with figured shoulder has been attributed to the Manner of the Achilles Painter.[14]

Outside the Berlin Painter's School black-bodied *lekythoi* are rare and so are shoulder figures.[15] We have spoken of Douris' red-figure *lekythos* in Bologna (PLATE 8. 2), which

---

[1] *ARV* 219. Beazley noted that the linear patterns admit more variety than the floral.   [2] *ARV* 219.

[3] The relationship between these painters has been mentioned on pp. 14, 80, 115 f. n. 15. Here I should like to draw attention to another shape which is shared by the Berlin and Diosphos Painters—a small neck-amphora of special shape, fat, with triple handles. Black-figure amphorae of this shape have been attributed to the Diosphos Painter (*ABV* 510, no. 26) and to an artist who 'recalls' him, the Philon Painter (*ABV* 516 f., 703; *Para* 254 f.). The black-figure amphorae have reserved necks with palmettes disposed in a variety of ways. The Berlin Painter's amphora, in Oxford (1924.3. *ARV* 201, no. 62, 'early'), has a black neck. In the Oxford *CV* (i, p. 15) Beazley described the vase: '. . . unique shape . . . about 490', but another vase of the same shape, recently on the Basle Market (*Sonderliste N*, no. 1) has been attributed to the Berlin Painter.

[4] Louvre, G 137. *ARV* 307, no. 6.

[5] *ARV* 307, nos. 12, 14, 15.

[6] Ibid. 1644.   [7] *Para* 357.

[8] Beazley noted the resemblance between some Eucharidean florals and those on a neck-amphora by the Berlin Painter (*ARV* 199, no. 30 *bis*, and p. 1634).

[9] The doubleen in Brooklyn looks like a work of the Eucharides Painter, judging from the style of the florals; especially close is the painter's small red-figure doubleen in Brussels (A 71. *ARV* 226, no. 5. Jacobsthal, pl. 74*a*). His interest in black-bodied vases is established by the amphora recently acquired by Hamburg (*ARV* 227, no. 8 *ter*, and *Para* 347). There are no doubleens in the Floral Nolan Group in *ARV* (pp. 218 f.).

[10] Cab. Méd. 489. *ARV* 490, no. 114; New York, 41.162.19. *ARV* 490, no. 115; Barcelona, 581. *ARV* 490, no. 116.

[11] New York, 41.162.18. *ARV* 640, no. 77.

[12] Louvre, G 444. *ARV* 993, no. 91; *JHS* xxxiv. 190.

[13] Lucerne Market. *ARV* 1022, nos. 133–4; London, 1910.4–30.1. *ARV* 1022, no. 135; Syracuse, 24596, fr. *ARV* 1022, no. 136; Syracuse. *ARV* 1022, no. 137.

[14] Athens, 16283. *ARV* 1003, no. 14.

[15] Red-figure *lekythoi* with shoulder figures outside the Berlin Painter's circle of influence: Greifenhagen, 71 (with references).

I noted the following examples: Maplewood, Noble. *ARV* 423, no. 130 (Painter of the Paris Gigantomachy. The painter liked elaborate florals; cf. Boston, 24.450. *ARV* 423, no. 123). Athens, 1626. *ARV* 663 (Mys; a most unusual *lekythos*); Leningrad. *ARV* 1326, no. 72 (Meidias Painter).

From the Berlin Painter's Workshop, or closely associated with it, are two *lekythoi*, one attributed to

was probably painted late in the first quarter of the fifth century.[1] There is a fine black-bodied *lekythos*, not much later, from the hand of the Pan Painter.[2] The vase is large and very handsome; it has a Sicilian provenience, as do many of the black-bodied *lekythoi* (see pp. 136 f.). Two Erotes, holding tendrils, fly across the black shoulder. Eros was a popular subject at this time.[3] The Pan Painter's *lekythos* may serve as introduction to a vase which has no place in this section; it is not black-bodied, but I include it because the shoulder is figured.

3. SYRISKOS PAINTER'S *LEKYTHOS* IN BERLIN

One *lekythos* has been attributed to the Syriskos Painter[4]—the only white *lekythos* known to me whose shoulder bears figure decoration (PLATE 8. 1).[5] The Syriskos Painter was the Copenhagen Painter's 'brother', 'An academic artist, akin to the later phase of Douris',[6] and a younger contemporary of the Berlin Painter,[7] who worked for the potters Syriskos and Pistoxenos,[8] probably also for the potter of some of the Brygos Painter's head vases.[9] (The Brygos Painter and Douris are among the first to take up the fashion for plastic vases which seems to have come to the Athenian Kerameikos in the years immediately following the close of the Persian wars;[10] the Syriskos Painter also decorated some head vases and his are not much later.)[11] There are several white-ground vases by the Syriskos Painter: our *lekythos*, a round *aryballos*,[12] *alabastra*,[13] and a head vase,[14] whose style of decoration links the painter with the group of the Negro *Alabastra*.[15]

The white *lekythos* is modest in size[16] and unusual in shape: although very cylindrical, it is unlike any other *lekythos* of standard shape we have described. It looks like an unsuccessful experiment. The body is thick, the neck is long, and there is no pattern band at the join of neck to shoulder. The iconography is not exceptional: a woman, seated on a chair with a bird on her knee, and a man leaning on a stick. Outlines are glaze and a sober polychromy is achieved through dilute washes of glaze.[17] A *kalos* inscription is decoratively scattered in the field; the *kalos* Olympichos is otherwise unknown.[18] There are two pattern bands and both are unusual: above the figures an embattled pattern with chequered squares in the gaps and, below, an embattled-counter-embattled pattern.

the manner of the Berlin Painter, late (*Auktion* xxxiv no. 161; *Para* 346), the other, earlier, connected by pattern (*Auktion* xxvi, no. 134, and p. 71).

[1] *ARV*[1] 293, no. 204.
[2] Adolphseck, Landgraf Philip of Hesse, 51. *ARV* 557, no. 119.
[3] J. D. Beazley, *The Lewes House Collection of Ancient Gems* (1920), 27 f.; Greifenhagen, *Griechische Eroten* (1957).
[4] *ARV* 259 ff., 1640 f., 1705; *Para* 351.
[5] Berlin (East), 2252. *ARV* 263, no. 54.
[6] *ARV* 256.
[7] *Para* 352.
[8] *ARV* 259.

[9] *ARR* 12; *AK* iv (1961), 24.
[10] *AK* iv. 21 ff.
[11] *JHS* xlix. 51.
[12] Taranto, 4553. *ARV* 264, no. 57. The pattern-work on the vase may be found on *alabastra* of the Negro Group, and the *kalos* Diogenes on Douris' red-figure *lekythos* with lion shoulder, in Bologna.
[13] *ARV* 264, nos. 58–65.
[14] Boston, 98.928. *ARV* 265, no. 78. The palmettes on either side of the woman on side A are essentially side-palmettes.
[15] *ARV* 267.
[16] Furtwängler, *Beschreibung* ii. 557 (18 cm).
[17] Cf. *Die Antike* i (1925), pl. 30 (colour).
[18] *ARV* 1603.

Despite the many unusual features of this *lekythos*, its authenticity is secure: it was found in a grave near Haghia Triada in the Athenian Kerameikos in 1879.[1]

On the shoulder (PLATE 8. 1*b*), our chief concern, Eros flies grasping in each hand a tendril with palmettes and added blossom. The composition is quite like the Pan Painter's, but much more like Douris', on the Atalanta *lekythos* in Cleveland (PLATES 10. 2, 11). The Eros beneath the handle on the Cleveland *lekythos* flies with two palmette tendrils in his hands in a pose almost exactly like the Syriskos Painter's Eros. Notice that these Erotes have their wings attached to their shoulders, not to their backs, as the Pan Painter's, and remember that the Cleveland *lekythos* makes extensive use of dilute washes of glaze to achieve subtle polychromy. The elements of both pattern bands on the Berlin *lekythos* may be found on the Cleveland vase,[2] and the execution of the florals on the shoulders is in many respects quite similar (see p. 31).

The picture on the body of the *lekythos* finds a close parallel in the work of the Bowdoin Painter, on a *lekythos* in New York mentioned earlier for its handle palmette.[3] Douris liked to represent Eros and so did the Bowdoin Painter.[4] I have suggested that Douris had some relation with the Bowdoin Workshop (see p. 30), and the Syriskos Painter's *lekythos* perhaps lends support to this. Close attention to the florals on the Cleveland *lekythos* reveals a prominence of cross-overs—tendrils crossing over each other and terminating in blossoms. Similar cross-overs are a characteristic feature of florals on white-ground semi-outline *lekythoi* from the Bowdoin Workshop (PLATE 60). Cross-overs do not appear on the Syriskos Painter's *lekythos* (whose thick black lines and solid blossoms are more like those of the Pistoxenos Painter)[5] but they do appear on his red-figure *astragalos* in the Villa Giulia, signed by the potter Syriskos.[6]

[1] *AE* 1880, 134.

[2] The embattled-counter-embattled pattern may be found on the dress of Atalanta; the chequer squares in the pattern band above the figure scene.

[3] New York, 06.1021.90. *ARV* 682, no. 102.

[4] Greifenhagen, 72 f.

[5] Compare especially the palmettes on the white tondo of the cup in London (D 2. *ARV* 862, no. 22)

and on the exterior of the white cup from the Acropolis (439. *ARV* 860, no. 2). The latter is exceptional not only for being white-slipped on the exterior as well as the tondo, but also for the predominance of black, figures, and florals.

[6] Villa Giulia, 866. *ARV* 264, no. 67. The elements of the composition—lion, Eros, and Nike amidst florals—remind one of the Berlin Painter.

PART FIVE

PATTERN *LEKYTHOI*

INTRODUCTION

WE have looked at figures and florals on shoulder and body and, indirectly, at linear motifs comprising framing pattern bands. We conclude with pattern *lekythoi* (PLATES 68–71)[1] which, like the black-bodied of the preceding section, are contemporary with figure *lekythoi* and produced in the same workshops. A *lekythos* with figure decoration, unless very poor work, was more expensive than one painted black or hastily covered with patterns, and its market was more restricted, since the iconography was not always intelligible abroad. The white *lekythos* with funerary iconography had the most restricted market; the specialized iconography rendered it intelligible only to those familiar with Athenian rites of death and burial, and since the white *lekythos* came to serve the dead, it is not often found in domestic deposits. Pattern and black-bodied *lekythoi*, on the other hand, served the needs of the living and the dead, at home and abroad; numbers and distribution—chronological and geographical—give them a place of importance in Attic vase-painting beyond their artistic merit, and for these reasons I have prefaced the section with a discussion of their chronology and provenience.

1. CHRONOLOGY

The chronology of Attic vase-painting has been studied by many and is now reasonably secure.[2] Recently, non-Attic, pre-, and post-classical fabrics have received more attention than Attic black- and red-figure, and this is because students of Attic vase-painting have come to rely upon Beazley's chronology—a schematic arrangement of painters, potters, and workshops, based on the assumption that Attic vase-painting, like other branches of Greek art, developed in a straightforward predictable manner—as indeed it seems to have.[3] Although Beazley himself was fully aware of the relationships between painters and although he sometimes dated vases closely, chronological aids are almost totally absent from *ABV*, *ARV*, and *Paralipomena*. Consequently, when we try to date Attic black-, red-figure, and white-ground vases we tend to compare one vase with another in Beazley's list for which he has given a date. Beazley's chronology can be used effectively only if one's eyes are sensitive to subtle differences in style and if one is well aware of the external evidence for dating the vases on which he based his system. It is this external evidence which I should like to summarize.

Athenian chronology during our period is determined by absolute and relative dates. The latter are provided by a series of deposits in which Attic vases, and *lekythoi* of various types, have been found. Their dates depend not only on the vases, but also on stratigraphy and the other contents, which sometimes include *ostraka*, coins, or other readily datable material. The absolute dates are well known: the battle of Marathon (490 B.C.),

---

[1] 'Pattern *lekythos*' is used here to describe *lekythoi* of Type Two, whose decoration is composed of patterns instead of figures; the term is sometimes applied to *lekythoi* of Type Three, but these are red-figure or black-bodied more often than not, and I do not include them.

[2] *GPP* 259 ff. Follmann, 20 ff.

[3] Cf. *JHS* lxxxv (1965), 99 (C. M. Robertson).

the sack of the Athenian Acropolis by the Persians (480 B.C.), the refoundation of Camarina in Sicily (461 B.C.), the purification of Delos (426/5), the battle of Delion (424 B.C.),[1] and the burial of the Lacedaimonians in the Kerameikos (403 B.C.).

Charts I and II (on pp. 134 f.) present the evidence bearing on the date of Attic *lekythoi* from the late sixth century to around 400 B.C. Chart I is designed primarily to illustrate the topographical distribution, Chart II the typological; both are based on the same material. Chart I may be applied to Attic vase-painting more generally, since nearly all the deposits listed contained black- or red-figure vases of other shapes; but the limitations of the selection must be kept in mind: (1) most of the deposits have been chosen because *lekythoi* are prominent; (2) the time-span of each is that of the excavators and defines the deposits, not necessarily the contents. (When the span of the deposit exceeds that of a specific type of *lekythos* I have indicated this in the charts by a broken line.)

The Athenian evidence is full and reasonably well documented. Funerary deposits greatly outnumber domestic, but the latter are represented by the wells in the Agora which have been so carefully excavated and published that they provide a firm foundation for our chronological table.[2] Funerary deposits are very numerous because many late archaic and classical Athenian graves are known,[3] but few have received detailed publication. I have therefore selected two cemeteries to represent our period, both well published and carefully dated—the Kerameikos (south side of the Sacred Way)[4] and Lenormant Street (between the Agora and Kolonos Hippios).[5] I also include a grave from the excavations along Stadium Street—the so-called Douris grave, whose offerings included a large number of *lekythoi* in addition to the *aryballos* by Douris (PLATE 9. 2).[6] A selection of non-Attic deposits is included for comparison; all are funerary except the 'foundation deposit' beneath the Heraion on the island of Delos[7] and the purification deposit on the island of Rheneia;[8] neither of these is especially important for us.[9] Rhitsona and the North Cemetery at Corinth have been chosen to represent burials outside Athens[10]

[1] Some of the dead from the battle were buried in the *polyandrion* at Thespiae (Thucydides iv. 101). See *PAE* 1911. 153 ff.; *AM* lxv (1940), 8 ff., and pls. 4–6. Among the offerings buried with the dead were three Boeotian red-figure *lekythoi* (*ARV* 1010, ix). One of the three (*ARV* 1010, no. 1) is a copy of a red-figure *lekythos* by the Achilles Painter (Boston, 01.8077. *ARV* 993, no. 84); the other two are less directly inspired by him, but betray his influence. The shoulder palmettes are black on reserved ground, nearer the elegant Achillean type than the inelegant Bowdoin, but there are added spiral tendrils and spandrel buds on either side of the central group of three palmettes, many thin petals, and reserved, dotted hearts. At least one of the shoulders (*AM* lxv, pl. 5. 2) has small arc-tendrils added to the central palmette.

[2] *Agora* xii. 45 n. 126, and Index of Deposits, part ii, 383 ff.

[3] Kurtz and Boardman, chs. v and vi.

[4] *AM* lxxxi (1966), 21 ff., 116 ff.

[5] *Hesp* xxxii (1963), 113 ff.

[6] *ADelt* xi (1927–8) B, 91 ff. I exclude the more recently published graves from this area (*AE* 1958. 1 ff.) because many of the excavator's dates require adjustment. They span a large part of the fifth century and their grave-goods, though not distinguished, include *lekythoi* of different types.

[7] *Délos* x (1928). The terminal dates are adjusted by Payne (*JHS* xlviii (1928), 274 f.).

[8] *Délos* xxi (1952).

[9] The Heraion series ends c. 480 B.C. (*JHS* xlviii. 274 f.) and has the usual selection of black-figure *lekythoi*; the Rheneia deposit had a small number of white *lekythoi*, standard cylinders, with figure decoration largely or totally effaced. The shape suggests a date in the later 430s. None of the *lekythoi* has been attributed. Two preserve figures (nos. 126 and 127), and one of them a tomb (no. 127).

[10] *Lekythoi* from Sicilian graves might have been included in the chart, but no one site has a sequence of published burials with offerings strictly relevant to our study. Gela is the best site for our purposes and it is treated in some detail on pp. 139 ff.

because they are well published and Attic *lekythoi* were found in significant numbers. The evidence presented in the charts may be summarized:

1. In Athens *lekythoi* of all types are represented throughout the period.

2. Outside Athens the pattern of distribution becomes noticeably less even towards the middle of the century—that is, when the white *lekythos* with funerary iconography comes into its own.

The geographical distribution of the white *lekythos* towards the middle of the fifth century reflects the change in the iconography of the vase; by this time the white *lekythos* had become decidedly funerary. Attic funerary art has a long tradition;[1] in vase-painting it is well represented from the Geometric period,[2] and in black-figure it is found on vases and plaques from the very beginning of the style.[3] The earliest white *lekythoi* with unquestionably funerary iconography are the Beldam Painter's and are probably not much earlier than 470.[4] This is somewhat surprising since older black-figure artists who specialized in *lekythoi*, some of them white-ground, decorated black-figure vases of other shapes with detailed scenes of burial rites—for example the Sappho and Theseus Painters. The Sappho Painter's funerary vases are in the black-figure tradition—red-ground plaques[5] and *loutrophoroi*[6] with scenes of *prothesis*, valediction, and interment. They are exceptional only in the wealth of detail.[7] The date is probably not later than around 500 B.C. and possibly somewhat earlier. The Theseus Painter's funerary vases are the traditional red-ground *loutrophoroi*,[8] with scenes of *prothesis* and mourning, and a group of *skyphoi*.[9] (Funerary *skyphoi* are otherwise unknown but there are black-figure *kantharoi*[10] and cups of other types[11] with similar decoration.) More important for us is an *alabastron* by the painter with a *prothesis* scene in black-figure on white ground (with a miniature fawn hunt in silhouette above).[12] This, to my knowledge, is the earliest white-ground vase with unquestionably funerary iconography. Judging from the shape, the date of the *alabastron* is the later 470s,[13] certainly later than the *skyphoi* or *loutrophoroi*, and it is presumably one of the Theseus Painter's latest works. Some late *lekythoi* by the painter are connected with the Beldam Painter in shape and in shoulder decoration,[14] and the funerary iconography is another link between the two artists. The Beldam Painter's funerary *lekythoi* are white-ground BELs; the earliest are black-figure, the latest outline. They have false interiors,[15] and the combination of funerary iconography and false interiors is evidence of the acknowledged funerary role of the white *lekythos* at this time.

The period during which the white *lekythos* with funerary iconography was the most

[1] Kurtz and Boardman, 27 f.

[2] Ibid. 58 ff.

[3] *BSA* l (1955), 51 ff. (Boardman).

[4] *ABL* 171.

[5] Louvre, MNB 905. *ABL* 229, no. 58; Kurtz and Boardman, pl. 33.

[6] Athens, 450. *ABL* 229, no. 59; Kurtz and Boardman, pl. 36; London, 1928.7–16.1. *ABL* 229, no. 60.

[7] Compare the bail-amphora in Lausanne recently added to the painter's attributed works (*Para* 247), Kurtz and Boardman, 148 f., and pls. 37 f.

[8] Oxford, 1930.20. *ABL* 252, no. 74; Athens

Market. *ABL* 252, no. 75; *Para* 257.

[9] Basle, Cahn. *Para* 257 f.

[10] Cf. *ABV* 346, nos. 7–8; Kurtz and Boardman, pls. 34–5.

[11] Cf. Athens, Kerameikos. *ABV* 113, no. 81 (special cup, near Proto-A, by Lydos).

[12] Havana, Lagunillas. *ABV* 518, no. 5.

[13] Cf. *ABL* 101 ff. (shapes of *alabastra*) and Oxford *CV* i, pl. 41, nos. 5–6 (= Haspels's Type III), nos. 1–4 (= Haspels's) Type I nos. 7–8 (= Haspels's Type II)

[14] *ABL* 146, 178 f.

[15] Ibid. 175 nn. 4–10.

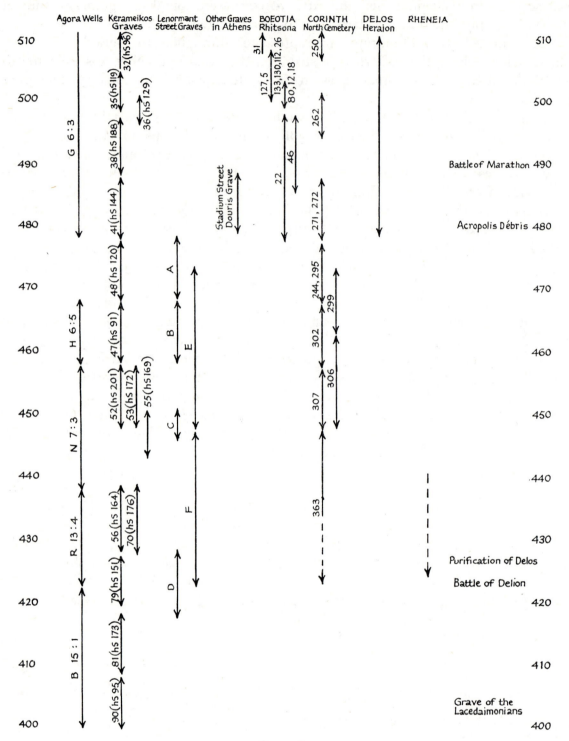

CHART I.

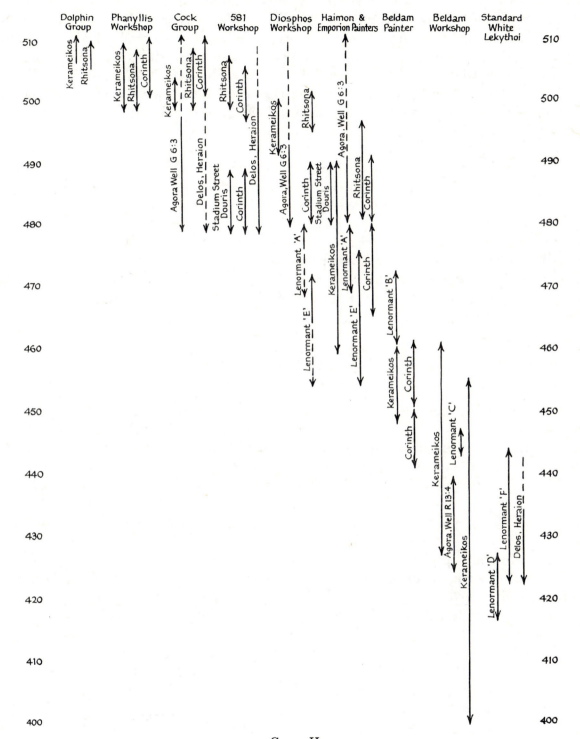

CHART II.

favoured offering to the dead is from the 460s to around 410 B.C. (allowing a margin
on either side for the not very numerous earlier and later examples). The application of
funerary iconography to the vase is not surprising in view of the established tradition of
funerary vase-painting in Attica and the prominence of oil in rites of death and burial,
but the lack of white *lekythoi* with funerary iconography before this time is somewhat
surprising. I think the fashion for the vase is due to restrictions on more extravagant
forms of Athenian funerary art which seem to have been in effect from around 500 B.C.
to some time in the third quarter of the fifth century (see p. 74).[1] There also seems to
be literary evidence for sumptuary legislation at this time,[2] and there is a noticeable lack
of impressive private grave monuments with fine sculptural decoration from Athenian
cemeteries during most of the fifth century.[3] The Athenian tendency towards extravagance in funerary art, well illustrated by the fourth-century family plots in the Eridanos
Cemetery,[4] with handsome decorated tombstones, large marble vases, and figures carved
in the round, must have been greatly frustrated by these restrictions. A clay vase with
explicit funerary iconography was better than nothing, but a poor substitute for a grander
monument in stone. When sculptors were again free to cut private memorials,[5] the white
lekythos began its decline. The sculptors' new offering to the sepulchral market—large
stone *lekythoi*—hastened its end.

2. PROVENIENCES

ATTICA

The market for clay vases with specialized iconography is unlikely to extend beyond the
area in which it is understood, unless the contents are especially valuable; and the market
for a vase whose iconography is devoted to Athenian funerary rites and eschatological
beliefs (and whose contents are not especially valuable) will not extend beyond Athens
and Athenian areas of influence. Only a fraction of the attributed Attic white *lekythoi*
have a known provenience, and these are recorded in the Index of Proveniences in *ABV*,[6]
ARV,[7] and *Paralipomena*.[8] There is no convenient index of proveniences for unattributed
figure *lekythoi* or for the many white *lekythoi* decorated exclusively with patterns, but
their distribution is probably very similar to that of the attributed vases: white *lekythoi*
with funerary iconography are found in Attica and Eretria, on the nearby island of
Euboea; white *lekythoi* without funerary iconography (figured and patterned) are found
in many parts of the Greek world where they were not infrequently copied locally.

Before turning to specific non-Attic sites which I have selected to illustrate the geographical distribution of white *lekythoi*, the Attic sites need brief mention. Unfortunately,
none of them has been systematically excavated or properly published. If I speak of
'Athenian white *lekythoi*' it is not because I think all of the vases were made in Athens,
but because I think that most of them were and that those which were not were inspired

---

[1] Kurtz and Boardman, 90, 121 f., 143, 166.

[2] Ibid. 90, 121 f.

[3] Modest gravestones were not affected by the restrictions on grander funerary monuments; cf. ibid. 123 f.

[4] A. Brückner, *Der Friedhof am Eridanos* (1909).

[5] Kurtz and Boardman, 121 f., 130 ff.

[6] *ABV* 707 ff.

[7] *ARV* 1707 ff.

[8] *Para* 527 ff.

by the Athenian model. Also the published white *lekythoi* from Attic sites are unmistakably Athenian, some by the leading painters. The provincial sites which have yielded white *lekythoi* with figure decoration are, for the most part, either near Athens (Pikrodaphni, Ambelokepoi) or on main lines of communication between Athens and the sea (Trachones, Anavyssos) or between Athens and the Mesogaia (Koropi, Markopoulo). An interesting apparent exception is Oropos, where a grave was found with two white *lekythoi* by the Phiale Painter (PLATE 38. 2) and a third of related style.[1] Oropos is quite far from Athens, due north, but near Eretria which lies across the Euripus. The vases are fine and the grave can scarcely have been unique. Oropos lies on the inland route to Eretria.[2]

ERETRIA

Outside Attica the largest number of attributed Attic white *lekythoi* is from Eretria, but unfortunately they were found during the nineteenth-century excavations of the site for which there is no record; even in the 1890s Bosanquet lamented the lack of information on the Eretrian graves.[3] Eretria is the only site whose large-scale importation of Attic *lekythoi* does not cease when the iconography of the white *lekythos* becomes decidedly funerary.

Why were white *lekythoi* popular in Eretria? Eretria is not too far from Attica; only the narrow Euripus separates them, but physical proximity seems not to have been the only reason. Eretrians imported funerary and non-funerary *lekythoi*, which suggests that at least some of the people understood the iconography. They also imported Attic *choes*, and these vases are almost as peculiar to Athens and to Athenian rites and beliefs as white *lekythoi*.[4] The reason normally given for the close relations between Athens and Eretria is the establishment of an Athenian colony on the site some time around the middle of the fifth century B.C., for which there is literary evidence.[5] But Attic *lekythoi* were imported before this: the Beldam Painter's white *lekythoi* with funerary iconography were found at Eretria, and the earliest of them is probably not later than 470 B.C.[6]

The high proportion of attributed Attic white *lekythoi* with an Eretrian provenience has suggested to some scholars local production.[7] *Lekythoi* were made locally,[8] but apparently not the finer figured vases with which we are most familiar. Among the painters best represented at Eretria is the Achilles Painter, whose Athenian-ness can scarcely be questioned. Among the Eretrian *lekythoi* included in *ARV*, there is a small group which Beazley thought might have been made locally: three *lekythoi* by the Torch Painter (PLATE 45. 2–4)[9] and one of similar fabric by another hand.[10] The most distinctive

---

[1] Oropos is also well situated for connections with Boeotia.

[2] Munich, 2797. *ARV* 1022, no. 138; Munich, 2798. *ARV* 1022, no. 139; New York, 22.53. *ARV* 1026, no. 2.

[3] The most recent and fullest bibliography for the Attic vases of Eretria is: *Historia* xix (1970), 515 ff. (J. R. Green and R. K. Sinclair). Eretrian pottery has been studied by Boardman (*BSA* xlvii (1952), 46 ff., and lii (1957), 1 ff.) and more recently by Bothmer

(*MMJ* ii (1969), 27 ff.) and Ure (*BSA* lxiii (1973), 25 ff.).

[4] *Historia* xix. 523 ff. (*choes*).   [5] Ibid. 516 ff.

[6] *ABL* 171; *Historia* xix. 523 n. 40.

[7] Cf. *BSA* xlvii. 47.

[8] *BSA* xlvii. 47; lii. 19. See also p. 144 ff. on the *lekythoi* of the Dolphin Group.

[9] Athens, 1970. *ARV* 1246, no. 1; Athens, 1979. *ARV* 1246, no. 2; Athens, 1985. *ARV* 1246, no. 3.

[10] Athens, 11730. *ARV* 1246.

feature of these *lekythoi* is a coarse fabric. The shape and pattern could be Athenian, although some details are a little peculiar, for example the style of the shoulder palmettes.[1] The figure style is executed with care, and the attention to anatomical detail is not what we have come to expect from Athenian white *lekythoi*.[2] The outlines are matt red, very fine and sure, and this contrasts with the rest of the vase's decoration. The painter takes his name from an athlete on one of the *lekythoi* (PLATE 45. 3)[3] who is seen at a tomb, with discus and 'torch' in hand; the 'torch' looks more like a technical slip which the painter has tried to correct,[4] and certainly should not be used as evidence for the torch race at the grave.[5] The torch used in races, which are not known to have been funerary in classical Athens,[6] is very short with a shield to protect the hand.[7]

CORINTH

The North Cemetery[8]

The graves of the North Cemetery at Corinth span a considerable period of time and are especially numerous during the sixth and fifth centuries B.C.[9] Corinthian *lekythoi* in imitation of Attic black Deianiras first appear around the middle of the sixth century;[10] *lekythoi* of Type II do not appear until its end.[11] During the fifth century Athenian *lekythoi* were popular grave offerings. They were imported in quantity until the outbreak of the Peloponnesian War; after that time they were copied locally.[12] The chronology of the fifth-century graves relies heavily on Attic *lekythoi*;[13] the excavators found it difficult to date the last Corinthian imitations, but their assumption that the white *lekythos* disappeared in Athens and in Corinth at about the same time[14] seems reasonable.

The Attic white *lekythos* which the Corinthians imported in the greatest numbers was decorated with patterns (PLATE 70. 8), not figures,[15] and it is the pattern *lekythos* which they had copied most often. The attributed Attic white *lekythoi* with figure decoration are not numerous.[16] The few with funerary iconography are either products of the two large workshops whose geographical distribution is wide and whose funerary *lekythoi* do occasionally travel outside Athenian areas of influence—the Tymbos[17] and Reed[18] Workshops—or of a small, virtually unknown workshop—the Group of Athens 1810

---

[1] The shoulder palmettes preserve some features of late black-figure florals, for example the many, thin, feathery petals. Compare the Beldam Painter's shoulder palmettes, *ABL*, pl. 51.

[2] Collignon and Couve, 548 (nos. 1970, CC 1702), 549 (no. 1979, CC 1703), 561 (no. 1985, CC 1747).

[3] Athens, 1979.

[4] Cf. Athens, 1762. Riezler, pl. 66.

[5] L. Deubner, *Attische Feste* (1932), 230 f.; *AM* xxxv (1910), 200 ff. (Brückner).

[6] The evidence for torch races in Athens in funerary rites is late, *I.G.*² 1011. 9.

[7] Cf. S. Aurigemma, *La necropoli di Spina in Valle Trebba*, i (1960), pls. 1–7, 16, and pp. 38, 39 n. 1. Aeschylus, *Agamemnon*, ed. E. Fraenkel (1962), ii 166 ff.

[8] *Corinth* xiii. *The North Cemetery*.

[9] Ibid. 65.

[10] Ibid. 115; *Agora* xii. 151.

[11] *Corinth* xiii. 180.

[12] Ibid. 121.

[13] Ibid. 120 f.

[14] Ibid. 121 f.

[15] Cf. *Corinth* xiii. 81, 'The white-ground figured 'lekythos', during the second half of the fifth century, was the chief grave offering in Corinth as elsewhere in Greece.' The finds published in the volume do not support this; white *lekythoi* are indeed common in the graves, but their decoration is most often patternwork, not figures.

[16] Cf. Corinth, MP 89. *ARV* 735, no. 97; MP 90. *ARV* 752; *ARV* 1198, no. 13.

[17] MP 91. *ARV* 759, no. 2.

[18] Athens, 1811. *ARV* 1379, no. 54.

(five matt outline vases not certainly by the same hand, which Buschor connected with the Woman Painter in his late period)[1] and the Painter of the Corinth *Lekythos*, to whom three white *lekythoi* have been attributed (two found on the road to Vouliagmeni, the third at Corinth).[2] These vases are late[3] and must have been imported after the outbreak of the Peloponnesian War.[4] The Corinthian white *lekythoi* preserve little of their figure decoration.[5] The iconography, as preserved, is very simple: a single figure. The shape, fabric, and polychromy of these vases help to distinguish them from contemporary white *lekythoi* made in Athens.

THE LECHAION CEMETERY[6]

In 1954 a smaller cemetery was found not far from Corinth, east of the Lechaion Gulf, near the Bronze Age site of Korakou.[7] Among the graves, which date from the early seventh century to the second half of the fourth century B.C.,[8] there were seven from the first half of the fifth century and two from the second.[9] The distribution of Attic *lekythoi* corresponds to that in the North Cemetery; pattern *lekythoi* are especially popular[10] and black-bodied *lekythoi* are well represented;[11] the figured *lekythoi* are Haemonian,[12] and there is a side-palmette *lekythos* by the Emporion Painter;[13] there are no later white *lekythoi* with funerary iconography. In the Lechaion Cemetery, as in the North Cemetery, imported Attic vases are not found in the graves of the later third and fourth quarters of the century; in their place are local imitations, whose decoration, so far as it is preserved, is floral.[14]

SICILY

The distribution of Attic figured vases in Sicily[15] is wide but uneven, and geography probably determined this less than contemporary political events. Gela has been the most productive of all the Sicilian sites and the number of Attic vases, black-[16] and red-figure,[17] is impressive. The city lay on the south coast, well situated for communications inland[18]

[1] Athens, 1810. *ARV* 1375, no. 3.

[2] MP 93. *ARV* 1245, no. 3.

[3] The egg pattern at the join of shoulder to body, although found on red-figure *lekythoi* of different dates, is a late feature on white *lekythoi*.

[4] *Corinth* xiii. 121 n. 105 (other Attic vases imported after the outbreak of the Peloponnesian War).

[5] Ibid. 143 (Corinthian white *lekythoi* with figure decoration are cited).

[6] *Hesp* xxxvii (1968), 345 ff.

[7] Ibid. 345.

[8] Ibid. 346.

[9] Ibid. 347.

[10] The date proposed for the *lekythoi* in grave C 3 (354 f.) seems too early.

[11] Ibid. 356, 357, 363.

[12] Ibid. 357, 359.

[13] Ibid. 359.

[14] Ibid. 364 (grave C 11).

[15] Thucydides describes the settlement of Sicily (vi. 1–5), and his text has recently been given a full commentary by A. W. Gomme, A. Andrewes, and K. J. Dover (*A Historical Commentary on Thucydides*, iv (1973), 197 ff.). The archaeological and literary evidence is discussed by: T. J. Dunbabin, *The Western Greeks* (1948), ch. I; J. Boardman, *The Greeks Overseas* (1973), ch. V; M. Guido, *Sicily, an Archaeological Guide* (1967). Excavations in Sicily are reviewed periodically in the *Anzeiger* of the *Jahrbuch des Deutschen Archäologischen Instituts*, most recently, *AA* 1964, 657 ff.

[16] *ABV* 719; *Para* 528.

[17] *ARV* 1712; *Para* 528.

[18] A map of the environs of Gela may be found in *NSc* 1960. 212, fig. 1. Among the inland sites recently excavated which have produced attributed Attic vases is Sabucina (*ArchClass* xv (1963), 86 ff.; *Kokalos* viii (1962), 69 ff.) where the side-palmette *lekythos* by the Painter of the Yale *Lekythos* was found. See p. 102 n. 10.

and by sea. Unlike most Sicilian cities, her fifth-century history is not marked by a series of cataclysmic upheavals:[1] Gela was politically stable and materially prosperous throughout most of the fifth century.[2] In addition she seems to have enjoyed a position of cultural pre-eminence in the west; Aischylos passed the last years of his life in Gela,[3] and other Athenians were probably also attracted by the flourishing western city.[4] Lastly, Gela seems to have maintained reasonably amicable relations with Athens, even during the latter part of the century, when Syracuse's[5] animosities erupted in the open hostilities which occasioned the ill-fated Sicilian expedition of 415 B.C.[6]

Lekythoi are among the most numerous Attic vases found in Geloan graves; the great part of the figured *lekythoi* is red-figure,[7] and many of these are fine works by the leading painters, such as the Berlin Painter[8] and members of his school,[9] Douris,[10] the Brygos[11] and Pan[12] Painters. The latter two, like Douris, rarely painted white *lekythoi* but there is one by each painter from Gela.[13] (Douris' white *lekythos* with the sacrifice of Iphigeneia (PLATE 10. 1) was also found in Sicily, at Selinus.)[14] Most of the attributed white *lekythoi* look as if they were painted before 450 B.C.[15] Later white *lekythoi* with outlines in matt

---

[1] Cf. Camarina (Guido, 153 f.; *Overseas*, 196) and Megara Hyblaea (G. Vallet and F. Villard, *Megara Hyblaea*, ii (1964), 114 ff.). Here published *lekythoi* could antedate the destruction of the city in 483 B.C. by Gelon (Thucydides vi. 4. 1–2) but some (e.g. pls. 103, nos. 9–12, and 114, no. 3) could be later. Cf. Follmann, 23 and n. 108.

[2] Cf. Agrigento (*Overseas*, 198 f.; Guido, 107 ff.) which enjoyed periods of uninterrupted prosperity. Among the imported Attic *lekythoi* found at Agrigento is the red-figure 'compromise' in Oxford (PLATE 65. 1).

[3] *Vita Aeschyli*, 10–11; *JHS* lxxxvii (1967), 74 ff. (C. J. Herington). I should like to thank Peter Brown for the last reference.

[4] This is one of the possible explanations for the larger number of white *lekythoi* with matt outlines and funerary iconography.

[5] Dunbabin, 13 ff.; *Overseas*, 186 ff.; Guido, 159 ff.; *ABV* 721; *ARV* 1717; *Para* 529.

[6] Thucydides vi: Gomme iv. 197 ff.

[7] The number of attributed black-figure *lekythoi* is smaller, but the leading painters are represented. So many vases by the Gela Painter have been found on the site that Miss Haspels named him after it; she suggested that he may even have had Sicilian connections (*ABL* 78).

[8] *ARV* 211, nos. 188, 193–4, 198, 207 *bis*; p. 212, nos. 210–11. Manner of the painter: *ARV* 215, no. 14; 216, nos. 17–18, 20.

[9] *ARV* 490, nos. 119–20, 123 (Hermonax); *ARV* 640, nos. 67, 72; 641, nos. 80, 82–7, 91; 642, nos. 108–9 and no. 115 (white) (Providence Painter); *ARV* 993, nos. 80, 85, 87, 93 (red-figure); 995, no. 124; 997, no. 156; 998, no. 166; 1000, no. 195 (white). (Achilles Painter). Considering the number of *lekythoi* by him this is not a high proportion. Compare the

Phiale Painter: *ARV* 1020, nos. 101–3; 1021, nos. 108, 110–11, 118–19, 122; 1022, nos. 128, 130, 136–7 (red-figure). The Floral Nolan Group, associated with the Berlin Painter School, is also represented among the finds at Gela: *ARV* 218, nos. 9, 11–12.

[10] *ARV* 447, nos. 269–73.

[11] Ibid. 384, nos. 208, 211, 214–16, 219.

[12] Ibid. 556, nos. 102, 104, 106, 109; 557, nos. 113–14, 117–19.

[13] Gela (ex Navarra-Jacona). *ARV* 385, no. 223; Syracuse, 19900. *ARV* 557, no. 122. The second white *lekythos* by the painter, in Leningrad (*ARV* 557, no. 121), may also have come from Sicily. These *lekythoi* stand close to the red-figure decoration in technique, and in the preservation of the red-figure shoulder decoration. See pp. 26 ff.

[14] Palermo, from Selinus: *ARV* 446, no. 266; *ML* xxxii (1927), 331 f.; Selinus: Guido, 85 ff.; *Overseas*, 197 f.; *ABV* 720; *ARV* 1716; *Para* 529. At Selinus white *lekythoi* have been found both in the sanctuaries and in the cemeteries.

[15] *ARV* 743, nos. 2–3 (Timokrates Painter); 746, nos. 4, 19, 20 (Painter of Athens 1826). The Painter of Athens 1826, who does not use *kalos* inscriptions on his *lekythoi*, is also well represented at other sites in Sicily. Two of his *lekythoi* were found at Camarina (*ARV* 746, nos. 7–8) and one at Selinus (*ARV* 746, no. 10). Of the painters represented at Gela the Bowdoin Painter should be mentioned, since a good number of his *lekythoi* have been found there, but his vases had a wide distribution, and the fact that they have been found in some quantity at Gela is not particularly significant. More important are the two white *lekythoi* by the Painter of Munich 2774 (*ARV* 283, nos. 3–4) with a Geloan provenience. Only four vases have been attributed to him, all white *lekythoi*;

paint are not numerous, nor are white *lekythoi* with funerary iconography, but they do seem to have been less rare at Gela than elsewhere on the island.[1] There is a tomb scene on one *lekythos* by the Painter of Athens 1826 (PLATE 26. 1),[2] another on a *lekythos* from the Tymbos Workshop.[3] There are outline *lekythoi* with tomb scenes by the Sabouroff[4] and Reed Painters.[5]

The distribution of pattern[6] and black-bodied[7] *lekythoi* in Sicily is more even. Most sites have yielded a variety of each and some of these vases were probably produced locally.[8]

SOUTHERN ITALY

Attic white *lekythoi* have been found in fifth-century graves of the Greek cities in the south,[9] notably, Locri,[10] Metaponto,[11] and Taranto.[12] The number of examples from the north is small;[13] Etruria imported quantities of black- and red-figure vases from Athens, but not white *lekythoi*.[14] The types of *lekythoi* found in south Italian graves are the types found in greater numbers in Sicilian graves: black- and red-figure *lekythoi*, white *lekythoi* with glaze outlines and non-funerary iconography, black-bodied and pattern *lekythoi*.

the proveniences of the other two (*ARV* 283, nos 1–2) are unknown. In shape these *lekythoi* are notable: a refined version of ATL, used by the Flying Angel Painter (*ARV* 282 f., 709; see pp. 82 ff. on shape ATL). Two *lekythoi*, red-figure, have been attributed to the Flying Angel Painter (*ARV* 282, nos. 40–1), who showed a preference for larger vases, especially column-craters. Both of the *lekythoi* were found at Gela. Beazley suggested that the Painter of Munich 2774 was in fact the Flying Angel Painter working in white-ground (*ARV* 282).

[1] I know of no attributed white *lekythos* with explicit funerary iconography from a Sicilian grave outside Gela.

[2] London, 1928.2–13.1. *ARV* 764, no. 4. Compare another white *lekythos* by the painter with similar iconography, found at Eretria: Athens, 1825. *ARV* 764, no. 11.

[3] Syracuse, from Gela. *ARV* 760, no. 33.

[4] Christchurch (New Zealand), Canterbury University Collection, 16. *ARV* 849, no. 239. Compare the *lekythos* by the painter, of unknown provenience, in Rome: Villa Giulia, 15729. *ARV* 849, no. 246.

[5] London, D 63. *ARV* 1378, no. 34.

[6] Cf. *NSc* 1960, 142, fig. 8*b*; *ABL* 183; 208, no. 67.

[7] Cf. *ARV* 693, no. 11; 694, nos. 16, 26, 33–4.

[8] *Boll d'Arte*, 1954. 78 nn. 19 (Megara Hyblaea), 20 (Syracuse), 21 (Gela).

[9] Excavations in and around Paestum are offering more evidence for the importation of Attic *lekythoi*. At present the number of attributed white *lekythoi* is small, but this picture may change with future excava-

tions. A grave at Pila near Paestum, which contained a side-palmette *lekythos*, a red-figure *lekythos* by the Brygos Painter, black-figure, black-bodied, and pattern *lekythoi*, has been mentioned (p. 102 n. 3). A black-bodied *lekythos* from the Bowdoin Workshop was found in the 'Tomb of the Diver' at Paestum, recently published by M. Napoli (*La tomba del tuffatore* (1970)).

[10] *ABV* 719; *ARV* 1713; *Para* 528.

[11] *ARV* 1714; *NSc* 1966. 227 f.

[12] *ABV* 721; *ARV* 1717 f.; *Para* 529; *Atti e Mem* vii (1967), 59 ff.

[13] The two matt outline *lekythoi* with funerary iconography, by the Reed Painter, which were found in the Valle Pega cemetery at Spina, are unpublished (*ARV* 1382, nos. 123–4). There was a significant Greek element in the population at Spina and it is not impossible that the grave in which the *lekythoi* were found belonged to an Athenian, although I should not consider the presence of the vases sufficient evidence for such an assumption. References to other 'stray' white *lekythoi* and possible travelling Athenians are mentioned in *Overseas*, 235 f., and *RA* 1973. 39 ff. (Demir Kapija, Yugoslavia). A white *lekythos* with funerary iconography from the Tymbos Workshop is said to have been found at Cerveteri (New York, 06.1021.127. *ARV* 757, no. 90).

[14] Black-bodied and pattern *lekythoi* and squat *lekythoi* have been found in several of the published graves: S. Aurigemma, *La necropoli di Spina in Valle Trebba*, i (1960), pls. 139 (T. 311), 183 (T. 183); i. 2 (1965), pls. 4 (T. 436), 101 (T. 133), 160 (T. 165); S. Aurigemma, *Il R. Museo di Spina* (1936), 105 (T. 671, with forty-four squat *lekythoi*).

As in Sicily, importation of white *lekythoi*[1] falls off sharply around the middle of the fifth century.[2]

In the nineteenth century French scholars spoke of 'Locrian' vases—*lekythoi* with yellow-white slip, non-funerary iconography, and wide geographical distribution.[3] They never maintained that all of these vases were made in that city; the term was adopted for convenience.[4] Early in the twentieth century Fairbanks gave reasons for abandoning the term,[5] but he left open the possibility of south Italian production for a small number of white *lekythoi* whose shape, technique, pattern, or figure style was peculiar.[6] Some of these vases may have been produced locally, but the greater part is now recognized to be Athenian.[7] The problem of the production of white *lekythoi* in southern Italy has recently been considered by Felten,[8] who suggests that Beazley's Lupoli Painter[9] was a local artist. The painter takes his name from Lupoli, near Taranto, where two[10] of his three[11] attributed white *lekythoi* were found. The three vases are standard cylinders, with white slip, glaze outlines, and second white. The subject of two is a woman with a *plemochoe*, the third is 'Oedipus and the Sphinx (or rather, youth at tomb surmounted by the image of sphinx)'.[12] Felten draws special attention to the physiognomy of the figures,[13] for which he offers south Italian parallels, but this in itself is not convincing evidence for the south Italian production of the vases.[14] To judge from its shape and shoulder decoration, the vase is a product of the 450s. The shoulder palmettes are type IA, with small volutes and long tendrils—like those on some white *lekythoi* by the Sabouroff Painter.[15] The monument is the most important feature of the vase. Whether or not a tomb is intended, the details are sufficiently Attic to establish the place of manufacture of the vase. The stept base with low broad monument is easily paralleled: for example, on the Sabouroff Painter's *lekythoi* in Athens[16] and the Akrisios *lekythos* in Berne (PLATE 37. 1). The moulding on the Lupoli monument may also be compared with that on the Akrisios *lekythos*; the coloured platform, on which the sphinx sits, with monuments by the Vouni Painter (PLATE 26. 2)[17] and the Painter of Athens 1826 (PLATE 26. 1).[18] Both of these painters decorated standard cylinders with second-white and distinctive shoulder palmettes, and Beazley placed the Lupoli Painter between them. Lastly, the sphinx. In Athenian funerary art the sphinx is known from the sixth century B.C.[19] On a white *lekythos* from the Tymbos Workshop there is a sphinx on a low stept base;[20] in view of the marked funerary iconography of the workshop and the variety of monuments

---

[1] Some of the painters whose work is found in Sicily, for example the Bowdoin, Icarus, Seireniske, and Aischines Painters, are represented in southern Italy; others, for example the Timokrates Painter and the Painter of Athens 1826, are not.

[2] Cf. Felten, 55 ff.

[3] Ibid. 55 n. 15.

[4] Dumont and Chaplain, 64.

[5] F i. 6 f.

[6] Ibid. 72, 78, 196, 328.

[7] Cf. Naples, 2763. *ARV* 302, no. 13 (F i. 72), and Tarquinia. *ARV* 1242, no. 4 (F i. 78).

[8] Felten, 57 f.

[9] *ARV* 745.

[10] Taranto, 4567. *ARV* 745, no. 2; Basle Market. *ARV* 745, no. 3.

[11] Felten adds a fourth *lekythos*: Lecce, 566.

[12] Taranto, 4566. *ARV* 745, no. 1.

[13] Felten, 58.

[14] *Gnomon* xlv (1973), 218 ff. (Kurtz).

[15] Cf. Athens, 17324. *ARV* 847, no. 211.

[16] Athens, 1815. *ARV* 845, no. 169.

[17] New York, 35.11.5. *ARV* 744, no. 1.

[18] London, 1928.2–13.1. *ARV* 746, no. 4.

[19] M. Collignon, *Les Statues funéraires dans l'art grec* (1911), 214 ff.; B. Ridgway, *The Severe Style in Greek Sculpture* (1970), 36.

[20] Athens, 1885. *ARV* 755, no. 40.

represented, I think that there can be little doubt that this monument is sepulchral.[1] But the Lupoli Painter's sphinx assumes a different pose on a higher base. She is not unlike the marble sphinx from Aigina, often associated with the sculptor Onatas,[2] which was found beneath the Temple of Apollo and which is almost certainly not funerary.[3]

3. WORKSHOPS

Pattern *lekythoi* are cheap, mass-produced oil-pots which served the needs of the living and the dead in many parts of the Greek world for more than a century. The earliest are among the earliest shoulder *lekythoi* (Type II), and the latest are among the last. The widespread, undiminished popularity of the vase is explained by its low price and universal acceptability: there are no problems of iconography, and the patternwork, sometimes enhanced with added colour, is not unattractive. Despite the number of pattern *lekythoi*, they are not easily studied: excavators do not always include them in detailed field reports (because they do not realize the importance of the vases), and curators often place them in museum stores (because not all pattern *lekythoi* are attractive). I cannot, therefore, offer a comprehensive, or even a representative, study, but I can try to trace the development of the pattern *lekythos* in an uninterrupted sequence over more than one hundred years, and recognize workshops which specialized in its production. The material on which I base this study is my museum notes, the *Corpus Vasorum Antiquorum*,[4] and a selection of excavation reports.[5]

[1] But compare the sphinx monument on a red-figure *lekythos* by the Bowdoin Painter (Yale University, 144. *ARV* 685, no. 167). For vases illustrating Oedipus and the Sphinx, see: F. Brommer, *Vasenlisten*[2] (1960), 340 ff. *Jahrbuch der Staatlichen Kunstsammlungen in Baden-Württemberg*, ix (1972), 18 ff. (U. Hausmann).

[2] Ridgway, op. cit. 64. See also p. 83 n. 4.

[3] Ibid. 36; Lippold, 101.

[4] The following fascicules of the *Corpus Vasorum Antiquorum* have a selection of pattern *lekythoi*; those marked with asterisks are especially useful:

Brussels ii. III Ja, pl. 1.
Copenhagen iii, pl. 112; viii, pl. 333.
Braunschweig i, pls. 10–11.
Vienna ii (Matsch Collection), pl. 6.
*Carlsruhe i, pl. 32.
Mannheim i, pl. 19.
Altenburg i, pl. 42.
Stuttgart i, pls. 24–5.
Frankfurt ii, pl. 50.
Heidelberg iv, pl. 177.
Como i. III H, pl. 7.

Ferrara ii. III H pls. 42–4.
**Palermo (Mormino Collection) i. III H, pl. 20; III Y, pls. 11–12.
*Norway i, pl. 36.
Warsaw i, pls. 33, 44–5.
*Bucarest (National Museum) i, pl. 30.
**Bucarest (Private Collections) ii, pls. 21–2.

[5] The selection of excavations is arbitrary; I have found the following reports and summaries useful:

Athens, Kerameikos: *AM* lxxxi (1966), 4 ff., 112 ff. Syntagma Square: *AE* 1958, 1 ff.
Attica: Thorikos; H. Mussche *et al.*, *Thorikos*, i (1968), 62; ii (1967), 40, 98; iv (1969), 111.
Corinth: the North Cemetery, *Corinth* xiii.
Argos: *ADelt* xv (1933–5), 16 ff.
Spain: Ampurias: M. Almagro, *Las Necrópolis de Ampurias*, i (1953), 179, 185, 188, 195, 243, and pls. 7–8, 11.
Near East: C. Clairmont, 'Greek Pottery from the Near East', *Berytus* xi (1955), 85 ff.
Black Sea: I. Venedikov *et al.*, *Apoloniya* (1963), 373 ff. (French summary) and 80 ff. (types of *lekythoi*).

DOLPHIN GROUP

The earliest shoulder *lekythoi* with patterns instead of figures belong to the Dolphin Group.[1] Small *lekythoi* comprise the greater part of the Group,[2] but there are also vases of other shapes, notably small *hydriai*, which are occasionally decorated with patterns instead of figures.[3] Beazley included the Group in *ABV*, but subsequent studies of the vases have established that some were made in Euboea.[4] For our purposes the place of manufacture is less important than the principle of decoration. A relatively small number of the *lekythoi* and *hydriai* have floral chains on the body, either summary lotus buds and blossoms—with white arc-petals (PLATE 68. 4),[5] like the florals which sometimes take the place of the more characteristic dolphins on the shoulders of Dolphin *lekythoi* (see p. 8 n. 2)[6]—or more detailed renderings of palmettes and lotus buds.[7] There are also Dolphin *lekythoi* decorated with abstract patterns—a series of black bands (cf. PLATE 68. 2)[8]—or black-bodied, with figure decoration restricted to the shoulder. Vases connected with the Dolphin Group are sometimes also decorated with patterns.[9] Linked pendent lotus buds encircle the body of two small ring-collar *oinochoai*[10] found in a single grave at Ialysos, on the island of Rhodes.[11] Another floral ring-collar *oinochoe* belongs to the Dolphin Group,[12] which on the basis of shape Beazley related to Amasis' *oinochoe* of Shape I in London.[13] Other Amasean connections seem to be indicated by the ring around the shoulder of one of the Dolphin *lekythoi*,[14] a characteristic feature of Amasean *lekythoi* of the type.[15] Miss Haspels noted a Lydan element in some of the Dolphin *lekythoi*,[16] and among the *lekythoi* 'descended' from the Lydan Painter of Louvre F6[17]—the Group of Vatican G52[18]—there is one palmette *lekythos*,[19] found at Camiros, on the island of Rhodes.[20] The Group is related to the Fat Runner and Cock Groups, to which we shall return.[21] The Amasean and Lydan affiliations date the Dolphin Group to the late second and third quarters of the sixth century B.C.

PHANYLLIS GROUP

The Phanyllis Group[22] is the name given to a large number of small *lekythoi* from the workshop in which the Phanyllis Painter was the dominant artist. The Phanyllis Painter

[1] *ABV* 457 f., 698; *Para* 199 ff.; *ABL* 14 ff.

[2] *ABV* 457 f.; *MMJ* ii. 38.

[3] *ABV* 458; *MMJ* ii. 32 f.

[4] Cf. *MMJ* ii. 38 ('all' the Dolphin vases are claimed to be Euboean); *BSA* lxviii (1973), 276 f. (Boardman).

[5] Cf. Oxford, 1937.301. *ABV* 457, no. 17, and Oxford, 1938.726. *ABV* 457, no. 18.

[6] *ABL* 15.

[7] Cf. Brussels, A 2127. *ABL* 193, no. 9. *CV* ii, pl. 21. 3; New York, Lykiardopoulos. *MMJ* ii. 35, fig. 35.

[8] Oxford, 1872. 1248A. *ABV* 457, no. 22. Beazley placed a similarly decorated *lekythos* in the Class of Athens 581 (Agora, P 24531); a *lekythos* in Norway (*CV* i, pl. 26. 5) may also be compared. Amphorae of the Light-make Class are also decorated with bands (*ABV* 600, no. 3; Norway, *CV* i, pl. 11; Mingazzini, pl. 78, nos. 2, 4).

[9] Thebes, R. 49.250. *Para* 201, no. 3; Athens, Agora, P 15431. *ABV* 458, no. 1, 'near' the Dolphin Group.

[10] Rhodes, 10495 and 10496. *ABV* 418, nos. 1–2, and *Para* 178. Cf. also the black-bodied ring-collar *oinochoai*, *ABV* 419, iii.

[11] *ClRh* iii. 166, fig. 158.

[12] Prague, National Museum, 1688. *Para* 179, no. 9.

[13] *Para* 179 (London, B 524. *ABV* 154, no. 47). The curious little *oinochoai* of the Dubois Class (*ABV* 423 f., 697, *Para* 182), decorated with florals on the body, may also be mentioned, although there is no apparent connection with the Dolphin Group.

[14] Zürich, Private. *ABV* 457, no. 2, and *Para* 199.

[15] *Para* 199.   [16] *ABL* 15 f.

[17] *ABV* 123 ff., 685, 714; *Para* 50 ff.

[18] *ABV* 460 ff., 698 f., 715; *Para* 202 f.

[19] Rhodes, 12475. *ABV* 461, no. 37.

[20] *ClRh* iv. 249, right.

[21] Cf. *ABV* 459; *ABL* 16 ff.

[22] *ABV* 463 ff., 699; *Para* 205 ff.

himself decorated large cylinders[1] as well as *lekythoi* of Phanyllis shape (cf. PLATE 67. 4)
—broad, old-fashioned, shoulder *lekythoi*,[2] not unrelated to the *lekythoi* of the Dolphin
Group.[3] Between the two stand the *lekythoi* of the Fat Runner Group,[4] which Miss
Haspels considered '. . . a late off-shoot of the Dolphin Class'.[5] Some of the Fat Runners
are related to the smaller Phanyllis *lekythoi* through the style of shoulder decoration;
none of the Fat Runners is known to have been decorated with patterns instead of
figures. The most characteristic feature of the *lekythoi* of Phanyllis shape is the shoulder
decoration—an abbreviated version of the upright palmettes-on-Os[6] popular with the
artists of the Nikosthenic Workshop,[7] in which the volutes of the hearts of the palmettes
are omitted: palmettes alternate with lotus buds (which look like exclamation marks) on
a chain of Os. Heartless palmettes also appear on the shoulders of cylinder *lekythoi* by the
Phanyllis Painter in a different arrangement: enclosed by a heart-shaped tendril without
lotus buds (FIGURE 9a).[8] Phanyllis *lekythoi* are figured, and most of the scenes are reproduced
with monotonous regularity.[9] There is, however, at least one published pattern *lekythos*
of Phanyllis shape[10] and there were almost certainly others. The body of the *lekythos* is
covered with rows of dots, giving the effect of a chequery pattern. On the shoulder
are heartless palmettes, enclosed by heart-shaped tendrils; on the neck, rays.[11] Rows of
dots in a more regular chequery decorate the body of a small Cock *lekythos* from Rhitsona[12]
and another small *lekythos* from the Heraion deposit on the island of Delos of about the
same date.[13]

COCK GROUP

With the *lekythoi* of the Cock Group[14] we come to the decades around 500 B.C.[15] and
from this time onwards the number of pattern *lekythoi* increases noticeably. The Cock
Group is the name given to a large number of small *lekythoi* of not very high quality,
whose most characteristic shoulder decoration is a cock framed by single ivy-leaves.[16]
Cock *lekythoi* are related to both Phanyllis and 581 *lekythoi*: some are decorated in
imitation of Phanyllis *lekythoi*,[17] and others come close to the 581 shape and were probably
produced in that workshop.[18] Cock *lekythoi* are also related to the Fat Runner Group.
Most Fat Runners have abbreviated lotus buds on the shoulder ('pointed leaves')[19] but
a few have an upright palmette framed by single ivy-leaves,[20] a scheme which is found on

---

[1] *ABL* 63 f.   [2] Ibid.
[3] Principally through the Fat Runner Group. Cf.
Para 208.
[4] *ABV* 459 f., 698; *Para* 201 f.; *ABL* 16 ff.
[5] *ABL* 16.   [6] Ibid. 64.
[7] An early form of the pattern (pendent) appears on
the shoulder of an *oinochoe* found in the Athenian
Agora (P 1233), of the Burgon Group (*ABV* 90, no. 5).
Compare also the *simae* of the Hekatompedon,
FIGURE 3c. Some of the amphorae from the Nikosthenic
Workshop are decorated largely or entirely with
florals (as are some amphorae of the Fikellura style:
ClRh iv. 152, fig. 149; 245, fig. 265): Louvre, *CV* v,
pl. 36, nos. 4, 8 (F 113): Hoppin, *BF* 249 (*ABV* 219,
no. 27), 251 (*ABV* 219, no. 28), 252 (*ABV* 220, no.

32), 269 (*ABV* 220, no. 29), 273 (*ABV* 221, no. 43).
The upright palmettes-on-Os continue through much
of the fifth century on the necks of Panathenaic prize
amphorae, also on Floral Band Cups.
[8] Cf. *ABL*, pl. 20. 6.
[9] *ABV* 463 ff.; *ABL* 63 ff.
[10] Carlsruhe, B 2319. *ABL* 203, no. 3. *CV* i, pl. 32. 7.
[11] Neck-rays on 581 *lekythoi*: *ABL* 63 and n. 2.
[12] Thebes, R. 112.66. *ABV* 471, no. 1.
[13] Delos, 566. *Délos* x, pl. 42.
[14] *ABV* 461 ff., 699; *Para* 208 ff; *ABL* 67 f.
[15] *ABL* 68.   [16] Ibid. 67.   [17] Ibid. 68.
[18] Ibid. 99 and n. 3; *ABV* 466; Cf. *Para* 233, 238.
[19] *ABV* 459.
[20] Ibid. 459; *ABL* 18, 67.

small Phanyllis *lekythoi*[1] and on *lekythoi* related to the Cock Group.[2] The pattern *lekythoi* of the Cock Group comprise a small part of the vases, but the variety in decoration is wide and these vases were probably more common than present evidence indicates. The chequery *lekythos* from Rhitsona has been mentioned. Its shoulder has the characteristic cock between ivy-leaves, as does a *lekythos* of the Group found in a well in the Athenian Agora,[3] whose body is decorated with upright palmettes enclosed by heart-shaped tendrils. The palmettes differ from those on the chequery Phanyllis *lekythos*—and on the shoulder of the Phanyllis Painter's cylinders—only in the addition of the volutes to the hearts. A different palmette arrangement is found on the *lekythos* from Ferrara[4] whose shoulder bears a cock between ivy-leaves; it has three conventional palmettes, alternately upright and pendent, linked by tendrils, with dots in the field—similar triads of palmettes occupy the neck-panel on small amphorae of the decades around 500 B.C.[5]

A small red-figured *lekythos* in Oxford (PLATE 68. 6) may be mentioned here, because its body is decorated with florals and its shoulder with a version of the upright palmette between ivy-leaves.[6] No other red-figure pattern *lekythos* is known from the early fifth century B.C., but this may well be due to the luck of excavations. The *lekythos* is small and in shape not far from the Cock-581 type. Beazley called it a rarity[7] and found the nearest parallel in a small *lekythos* from the Agora, which is slimmer and tighter in profile, but otherwise comparable (PLATE 68. 7).[8] The decoration of the Oxford vase is cursory black-figure—upright palmettes-on-Os on the body, and a pendent lotus bud between upright palmettes on the shoulder. The Oxford florals are more a red-figure adaptation of a black-figure motif than a design conceived in the red-figure technique. Black paint is applied to the front of the vase only; the back, beneath the handle, and the shoulder are reserved. Reddish-brown lines encircle the body, including the reserved handle area, at the shoulder and beneath the floral—upright palmettes-on-Os. Unlike the most characteristic Phanyllis upright palmettes-on-Os, these have an arc, painted in white above each palmette. The arcs appear above palmettes on 581 *lekythoi*,[9] and on the Agora *lekythos* with which Beazley compared our vase. Other notable features of the Oxford florals are the red hearts of the palmettes and the dotted arc enclosing them. The dotted arc is a feature of 581[10] and Haemonian palmettes.[11] The shoulder florals are a combination of diverse elements: in the centre an upright palmette framed by ivy-leaves (as on some of the Fat Runners, smaller Phanyllis, and Euboean Dolphins). But on either side of this triad there are additional florals: on the left an upright palmette and a single ivy-leaf, on the right a pendent bud.

---

[1] *ABL* 67; *Para* 208.

[2] Cf. Delos 566. *Délos* x, pl. 42.

[3] Athens, Agora, P 16767. *ABV* 471, no. 116. Another *lekythos* from the Agora (P 24546), which Beazley placed near the Little Lion Class (*Para* 252), is decorated with three palmettes on the body and a figure on either side of the palmettes (PLATE 68. 8); the vase is essentially a palmette *lekythos*, and is one of those Little Lions which illustrates the relation of the Class to *lekythoi* of the Cock Group and to *lekythoi* of the Class of Athens 81.

[4] Ferrara, T. 349.

[5] Cf. Rhodes, from Ialysos. *ABV* 482, no. 9. *ClRh* viii. 144, fig. 130 (Edinburgh Painter).

[6] Oxford, 1934.329.

[7] *ARV* 1644 (to p. 308).

[8] Athens, Agora, P 20750.

[9] Cf. *ABL*, pl. 22. 5.

[10] Cf. *ABL*, pl. 22. 5; this detail may also be found on Dolphin *lekythoi* (*MMJ* ii. 35, fig. 35), and on some Floral Band Cups (*BCH* xcii (1968), 406, fig. 52).

[11] *Corinth* xiii, pl. 42 (T. 294, nos. 4, 5).

ATHENS 581 WORKSHOP AND THE MARATHON PAINTER

The Oxford *lekythos* displays features of palmette *lekythoi* from the 581 Workshop (PLATE 68. 4),[1] the leading producer of less distinguished[2] pattern *lekythoi* in the early years of the fifth century. The most prominent personality in the 581 Workshop is the Marathon Painter,[3] named after the *lekythoi* found in the tumulus at Marathon. Since it is generally agreed that the tumulus was erected in honour of those who fell at the Battle of Marathon in 490 B.C.,[4] we have in these vases a useful chronological guideline. Furthermore, relative chronology, based on the style of the figures and patterns, also places the Marathon Painter in this period. The 581 Workshop can be connected with the later Phanyllis Workshop in both shape and pattern,[5] and the upright palmettes-on-Os common to both,[6] appear on the shoulder of the red-figure Oinophile *lekythos* in London (PLATE 6. 3),[7] whose shape points to the 581 Workshop[8] and whose style of figure decoration comes close to Onesimos,[9] one of the most influential cup painters of the early fifth century.[10]

The 581 Workshop must have been large and pattern *lekythoi* were only one of its products. The *lekythoi* of the Marathon deposit are black-figure, with the exception of four pattern *lekythoi*.[11] These are smaller and somewhat slimmer than the others. Their florals, although basically very similar, differ in details: three have single chains of upright palmettes-on-Os,[12] one a double chain (PLATE 68. 4);[13] one has many thin petals, indicated by thin hair-like incision marks,[14] and the others have fewer fuller petals.[15] There is considerable use of added white paint.[16] Beazley distinguished subgroups within the palmette *lekythoi* according to the style of florals: those with many fine, 'feathery' petals are Type A (alpha),[17] those with fewer, fuller petals are Type B (beta).[18] He also divided all 581 *lekythoi*, figured and patterned, into two large subgroups according to the shoulder decoration: 581-i *lekythoi* have linked lotus buds;[19] 581-ii *lekythoi* have rays.[20] Outside this division are some of the finer *lekythoi* by the Marathon Painter whose shoulders bear palmettes in a variety of schemes.[21] Since the florals of the Marathon *lekythoi* are both single and double chains, composed of feathery and full petals, it is inadvisable to use these details as chronological indicators, but the feathery petals are peculiar,[22] and, if not actually earlier, they are not copied by later artists who favoured the fuller petals. The fuller petals are also characteristic of palmettes on the Floral Band Cups[23]—a large number of not very high-quality cups, sometimes found in graves with our *lekythoi*,[24] and probably like them enjoying long life over a wide area.[25]

[1] *ABV* 487 ff., 700 ff., 705, 716; *Para* 222 ff.

[2] Finer pattern *lekythoi* of other shapes are discussed in the following pages on different workshops.

[3] *ABL* 89 ff.; *ABV* 487.

[4] *JHS* lxxxviii (1968), 13 ff. (N. Hammond), reprinted in *Studies in Greek History* (1973), 170 ff.

[5] *ABL* 74, 89.   [6] Ibid. 64, 93 f.

[7] London, 1922.10–18.1; *ARV* 332, no. 1.

[8] *ARV* 333; *ABL* 74, 89.

[9] *ARV* 332.   [10] *CB* ii. 23 ff.

[11] Athens, *CV* i, pl. 10, nos. 2, 3, 4, 13.

[12] Ibid., pl. 10, nos. 2, 3, 13.

[13] Ibid., pl. 10, no. 4.   [14] Ibid., pl. 10, no. 4.

[15] Ibid., pl. 10, nos. 2, 3, 15.

[16] Added white and white ground appealed to the Marathon Painter, *ABL* 89.

[17] *Para* 242.   [18] Ibid.   [19] *ABV* 489.

[20] Ibid.   [21] Cf. *ABL* 89 f.

[22] *ABL* 93 f. The 'feathery' palmettes are also found on a *lekythos* of Cock type from the Kerameikos excavations (*AM* lxxxi, *Beilage* 21. 6 and p. 25).

[23] *ABV* 197; *REA* xlviii (1946), 169 ff.; *Corinth* xiii. 158 f.; *BCH* xcii (1968), 405 f.

[24] *Corinth* xiii, pl. 40 (T. 281). *AM* lxxxi, *Beilage* 23. 4.

[25] *Corinth* xiii. 158 f.

The Marathon *lekythoi* were cheap vases 'bought wholesale for the funeral'.[1] The offerings in the Stadium Street Douris grave[2] have the same 'wholesale lot' appearance, with the notable exception of the *aryballos* signed by Douris (PLATE 9. 2), which must have been a treasured possession of the dead or of his family for some years before the burial.[3] This grave has been dated to the later 480s,[4] largely on the basis of the numerous *lekythoi* which nearly all look as if they were from one workshop, that of the Haimon Painter—successor to the 581 Workshop in the mass production of cheap vases for the grave.[5] Before taking up pattern *lekythoi* of the Haimon Workshop, let us look briefly at some of the Marathon Painter's contemporaries who also painted pattern vases.

CONTEMPORARIES OF THE MARATHON PAINTER

(i) *Edinburgh and Gela Painters*

The most important painter of large black-figure cylinder *lekythoi* around 500 B.C. is the Edinburgh Painter.[6] No pattern vases have been attributed to him, but there is a pattern *lekythos* of cylinder shape which betrays his influence.[7] It is large, with reserved neck and shoulder and white slipped body. There are bars at the neck,[8] not enclosed below, and five black palmettes in groups of one, three, and one on the shoulder. The cylinder is slimmer than the Edinburgh Painter's usual type[9] and near the later cylinders by the Gela Painter.[10] On the body there are two registers with palmettes and lotus buds, alternately upright and pendent, divided by a meander band; and at the join of shoulder to body there is a meander band. The formation of the palmettes is not unlike the Gela Painter's,[11] but the lotus buds are unusual and more difficult to parallel.[12]

The Gela Painter was also active in the years around 500 B.C. and pattern vases of two shapes have been attributed to him—*lekythoi*[13] and *oinochoai*.[14] The *lekythoi* are white ground, the *oinochoai* red. There are also black-bodied *lekythoi* by the painter.[15] The patterns on the *lekythoi* are either abstract (chequery)[16] or floral (palmettes).[17] The vases

[1] *ABL* 93. [2] *ADelt* xi (1927–8), 91, fig. 1.

[3] Athens, 15375. *ARV* 447, no. 274; *BSA* xxix (1927–8), 206 ('about 490', Beazley).

[4] *ABL* 133.

[5] Ibid. 132; *Para* 228, 232, 283. Miss Haspels noted that all the vases looked as if they were produced in the same workshop (132), but wondered about the three small *lekythoi* with upright palmettes (132 n. 1), which she thought resembled the Beldam Painter's (186). I take the vases to be Haemonian, produced in the same tradition (that of the 581 Workshop) as those by the Beldam Painter and his associates.

[6] *ABL* 86.

[7] Palermo, Mormino Collection. *CV* i. III Y, pl. 11, no. 10 (299).

[8] The reserved neck and unenclosed neck-bars may be contrasted with the Athena Painter's regular practice. Compare also the black-bodied *lekythos* in the Petit Palais (*CV* i, pl. 3, no. 3) which looks as if it were roughly contemporary.

[9] Cf. *ABL*, pl. 29.

[10] Cf. Vienna, 84 (PLATE 17. 3) and Syracuse, 19854 (PLATE 16. 4).

[11] Cf. *ABL*, pl. 27.

[12] Eccentric floral ornament is not unknown at this time. Compare, for example, the right-hand pattern band on the unattributed *hydria* published in *ML* xxii, pl. 60. 3, and on the unattributed *hydria* (Jahn 112), published by T. Lau *et al.*, *Die griechischen Vasen* (1877), pl. 13. 2.

[13] Syracuse, 45048. *ABL* 208, no. 67; Agrigento, Giudice Collection, 893. *ABL* 208, no. 68; Taranto, old museum no. 28. *ABL* 210, no. 109; Castelvetrano, 126. *ABL* 212, no. 160.

[14] Palermo, 1272. *ABL* 214, no. 184. Compare the elaborate palmette composition beneath the handle of a white-ground *oinochoe* (*Sonderliste G*, no. 76).

[15] Taranto, old museum no. 3. *ABL* 212, no. 157; Agrigento, Giudice Collection. *ABL* 212, no. 161.

[16] Cf. *ABL* 210, no. 109.

[17] Cf. *ABL* 208, no. 68.

are straight cylinders,[1] some very slender,[2] with the Gela Painter's distinctive palmette and lotus buds on the shoulder (see pp. 17 f.) The painter's interest in florals is clear not only from his special shoulder decoration, but also from the rows of palmettes which he introduces beneath the figures (PLATE 16. 4), and the palmette-trees and tendrils which spring up between them (PLATE 17. 3).

(ii) *Diosphos Workshop*

The Sappho and Diosphos Painters, also, were contemporaries of the Marathon Painter. The Sappho Painter decorated at least one vase, the white-ground column-crater in Carlsruhe (PLATE 55. 1),[3] with a handsome floral composition, but no pattern vases are known from his hand. The Diosphos Painter, on the other hand, seems to have been especially taken by florals, and a number of vases have been attributed to him which either combine figures and patterns or dispense with figures altogether. The pattern *lekythoi* are white-ground either cylinders of his normal shape (DL or near)[4] or smaller vases.[5] The shoulders of the *lekythoi* have the painter's usual linked lotus buds; the palmettes on the body are aligned vertically[6] or horizontally[7] (cf. PLATE 68. 5). The hearts of the palmettes are reserved and filled in with red paint; the tendrils which enclose the palmettes are not drawn with the surest hand, but the florals are attractive: they appear to float freely over the surface of the vase. There are often small arc-tendrils added to the larger enclosing tendrils and small spandrel buds. The palmettes on these pattern *lekythoi* may be compared with those on the painter's side-palmette *lekythoi*; the florals are similarly composed, and sometimes enhanced with open buds or blossoms (PLATES 58, 59). Palmettes and open buds are the sole decoration of a number of white *alabastra* by the Diosphos Painter.[8] White palmette *alabastra* by Pasiades are also known (PLATES 72. 2, 3).[9] In shape Pasiades' are earlier than the Diosphos Painter's.[10] In principle of decoration they are similar but significantly different. Pasiadean palmettes have reserved hearts, but they are not filled in with added colour;[11] the enclosing tendrils are executed with a sure hand and the florals themselves are more regularized; each looks like the last and all produce a static composition, not a mobile one like the Diosphos Painter's. Other white *alabastra* by the Diosphos Painter combine figures and florals in registers,[12] and in these there is considerable variety in the types of florals: there are running, linked horizontal palmettes,[13] independent upright palmettes,[14] and chains of palmettes, alternately upright and pendent.[15]

Loosely connected with the Diosphos Workshop in shape is a group of pattern *lekythoi*,

---

[1] *ABL* 208, nos. 67–8; 210, no. 109.

[2] Ibid. 212, no. 160.

[3] Carlsruhe, 167. *ABL* 228, no. 57.

[4] Athens, 2213. *ABL* 233, no. 36; Syracuse, 43051. *ABL* 233, no. 37; Athens, 12271. *ABL* 234, no. 66.

[5] Athens, Empedokles. *ABL* 234, no. 51.

[6] Athens, 2213. *ABL* 233, no. 36.

[7] Syracuse, 43.051. *ABL* 233, no. 37.

[8] Cagliari. *ABL* 237, no. 116; Gerona. *ABL* 237, no. 117; Gerona. *ABL* 237, no. 117 *bis*.

[9] *ARV* 99, nos. 3–6.

[10] The shapes are compared by Miss Haspels, *ABL* 101 ff.

[11] Compare the palmettes on a *lekythos* in the Mormino Collection (154), *CV* i. III Y, pl. 11, no. 2.

[12] Naples, RC 209. *ABL* 237, no. 114; Barcelona, Montanauer Collection. *ABL* 237, no. 115.

[13] *ABL* 237, no. 115.

[14] Ibid. 237, no. 115.

[15] Ibid. 237, no. 114.

Little Lions,[1] and squatter fuller models, near PL,[2] white-ground and red-ground. They are decorated with florals more often than abstract patterns, and the florals are usually palmettes, arranged horizontally, in a single or double row (PLATE 69. 4). The hearts of the palmettes are sometimes reserved, sometimes not; small arc-tendrils are common, as are abbreviated spandrel buds or groups of tiny dots. The shoulder decoration on the finer pieces is linked lotus buds, on the less careful pieces, rays; pattern *lekythoi* of shape PL, like figured *lekythoi* of the shape, not infrequently have black palmettes on reserved ground.

HAIMON WORKSHOP

A very large number of late, small, black-figure *lekythoi* have been attributed to the Haimon Painter[3] or to his manner. Some of them have florals in the picture panel, others are decorated exclusively with patterns[4] and the patterns are most often palmettes, arranged in a variety of ways. The Haimon Painter's pattern *lekythoi* probably span the later years of the first quarter of the fifth century and the earlier years of the second quarter. They follow those of the 581 and Diosphos Workshops, and are also related to the pattern *lekythoi* of the Beldam Workshop. First, the 581 Workshop. Among the Marathon *lekythoi* there are Haemonian elements,[5] and one is a chimney *lekythos* of the type often decorated by the Haimon Painter.[6] In style of figures and choice of pattern the Haimon Painter looks back to the Marathon Painter,[7] and some of his palmette *lekythoi* are very like the 581,[8] except in shape. The Haimon Painter took over the slim *lekythoi* of Shape DL which the Diosphos Painter was decorating in his later years;[9] some of his patterns are derived from the Diosphos Workshop,[10] and his figure style sometimes comes close to that of the Diosphos Painter.[11] Other connections with the workshop are the Little Lions decorated by the Haimon Painter[12] and the shape and style of decoration of his white *alabastra*,[13] on which registers of patterns alternate with miniature figure friezes[14] or rows of palmettes are arranged horizontally.[15] The Haimon Painter's relation to the Beldam Workshop is discussed below.

---

[1] Little Lions: Cambridge, G 134. *CV* i, pl. 22, no. 34; Schloss Fasanerie. *CV* i, pl. 12, no. 2; Stuttgart, KAS 93. *CV* i, pl. 24, no. 7; Como, *CV* i. III H, pl. 7, no. 5; Toronto, 923.13.40 (335). Robinson and Harcum, pl. 51, no. C. 670.

[2] PLs: Cambridge, 111. *CV* i, pl. 22, no. 25; Izmir, from Smyrna. *BSA* liii–liv (1958–9), pl. 39, no. 113; Palermo, Mormino Collection, *CV* i. III Y, pl. 11, no. 3; Bucarest. *CV* i, pl. 22, no. 1; Heidelberg, L 11. *CV* iv, pl. 177, no. 1. A *lekythos* nearer PL than any other recognized shape, in the Mormino Collection (*CV* i. III Y, pl. 11, no. 1, no. 591) has a doubled ivy tendril on the body and may be compared with Cambridge, G 137 (*CV* i, pl. 22, no. 32).

[3] *ABV* 538 ff., 705 ff., 716; *Para* 269 ff.; *ABL* 132 ff.

[4] *Para* 283; *ABL* 132 f.

[5] *ABL* 93.

[6] Athens, *CV* i, pl. 10, no. 12 (Athens, 1033); *ABL* 166.

[7] *ABL* 131.

[8] *ADelt* xi. 91, fig. 1, top row, nos. 1, 3, and 4, from the right.

[9] *ABL* 131.

[10] Ibid. 131. Two cup-*skyphoi* in Hamburg (*ABV* 567, nos. 630–1), which Miss Haspels attributed to the Haimon Painter (*ABL* 245, nos. 86 and 85), have carefully executed handle florals whose composition recalls the Diosphos Painter.

[11] *ABL* 134.

[12] Delos, 567. *ABL*, 244, no. 71; Taranto. *ABL* 244, no. 72.

[13] *ABL* 134.

[14] Gerona. *ABL* 245, no. 82. Athens, 12768. *ABL* 245, no. 83.

[15] Bologna, 100. *ABV* 555, no. 426.

Since the Haimon Painter adds florals to the figures on some of his *lekythoi*,[1] certain types of palmettes can be recognized as Haemonian, just as others are recognizably Diosphan or Pasiadean. On a small number of large red-ground cylinders (PLATE 17. 4),[2] whose shoulders are decorated with horizontal palmettes, instead of the painter's more usual rays or abbreviated lotus buds, palmettes and horizontal bands have been added to the picture panel, above or below the figures.[3] A similar use of palmettes is found on the Gela Painter's cylinder *lekythos* in Syracuse (PLATE 16. 4). Haemonian palmettes, like those of the Diosphos Painter, have reserved hearts, but they are not filled in with the touch of added colour, nor are they as carefully or as regularly rendered as those of Pasiades. The less carefully executed palmettes and most of the smaller palmettes have the heart filled in with black paint from the palmettes' petals.[4] The larger, more carefully executed palmettes with reserved hearts have an arc above, which is dotted in white.[5] Arc-tendrils are added to the hearts of both types, but buds or blossoms are less common. In addition to these large cylinders with horizontal palmettes, there are a few smaller *lekythoi*, chimneys, on which palmettes of a different type appear in the picture panel.[6] One of them, in Oxford (PLATE 70. 4),[7] may serve as example: beneath the figure scene —Herakles and Kyknos—there are pairs of addorsed palmettes, with hearts filled in.[8]

Haemonian pattern *lekythoi* are rarely large or very carefully decorated.[9] The patterns are floral more often than abstract and palmettes more often than florals of other types. Some of the vases are red-ground,[10] some are white-ground. The red-ground *lekythoi* are small, tapering shoulder *lekythoi*, slimmer versions of the 581 type, with upright palmettes-on-Os in the 581 style[11] or straight-sided cylinders, descendants of the Diosphos Painter's DL, with rows of palmettes disposed horizontally.[12] In the Stadium Street grave there were small red-ground *lekythoi* with upright palmettes-on-Os and larger light-ground[13] *lekythoi* with horizontal palmettes.[14] The disposition of the horizontal palmettes, the addition of partly open buds, and the subsidiary chequery pattern at the shoulder–body join, reflect the Diosphos Workshop,[15] and the shape is near DL; Diosphan patterns are also found on Haemonian chimneys.[16] A slender white *lekythos* in the

[1] *ABL* 133. Haemonian florals are, of course, not limited to *lekythoi* from the workshop; complementary to the *lekythoi*, and of the same generally low quality, are cups of different types produced in quantity by the Haimon Workshop, *ABV* 583, nos. 27–8; *Para* 290; their handle florals are comparable to those on the *lekythoi*.   [2] *ABL* 241, nos. 1–4.

[3] The subsidiary pattern band occurs on all but *ABL* 241, no. 4.   [4] *ABL* 133.

[5] Cf. *Corinth* xiii, pl. 42 (T. 294, nos. 4–5).

[6] *ABL* 245, nos. 79–81.   [7] Oxford, 1927.4457.

[8] Cf. Bucarest, *CV* i, pl. 30, no. 2 (shapes near DL with Beldam patterns).

[9] The *lekythoi* illustrated in *ADelt* xi. 91, fig. 1, bottom row, nos. 1–3, are exceptions.

[10] *Para* 245; *ADelt* xi. 91, fig. 1, nos. 1, 3, 4 top row, from the right.

[11] The most noticeable difference between 581 and Haemonian *lekythoi* is the shape of the *lekythos*.

Haemonian *lekythoi* are more slender. The change in proportions occurred some time in the early 480s, judging from the shapes represented in the Heraion deposit (*Délos* x, pl. 43, no. 565 (broad) and pl. 42, no. 570 (slender)) and in the Stadium Street Douris grave (*ABL* 132, 164, 186). Haemonian and Beldam *lekythoi* are not easily distinguished if the sharp shoulder angle characteristic of Beldam *lekythoi* is not pronounced, and if the 'wet-incised' lines (*ABL* 171, 185) are missing.

[12] Cf. Gerona. *Anuari* 217, fig. 32; *ABL* 133.

[13] *ADelt* xi. 92.

[14] Ibid. 91, fig. 1, top row, nos. 1, 3, 4, from the right (small), bottom row, nos. 1–3 (large).

[15] Cf. *ADelt* xi. 91, fig. 1, bottom row, no. 2, with *ABL* 235, no. 67 (Robinson Collection, *CV* i, pl. 38, no. 7).

[16] Cf. Amsterdam, Musée Scheurleer, 3323. *CV* i. III Jb, pl. 1, no. 4.

Conservatori,[1] comparable in size and shape, has rows of horizontal palmettes beneath a chequery, and differs from the larger Stadium Street palmette *lekythoi* only in the more elaborate shoulder decoration—horizontal palmettes like those on the shoulder of the Haimon Painter's large red-ground cylinders.

Haimon–Beldam pattern lekythoi

The pattern *lekythoi* which seem to be associated with the Haimon Workshop are generally straight-sided cylinders, with cup or chimney mouth, minimal abstract patterns, and a single or double row of horizontal palmettes. It is not always clear whether pattern *lekythoi* of the second quarter of the fifth century are Haemonian or whether they are from the Beldam or some other workshop. To judge from the number of pattern *lekythoi* of undetermined shape and not easily paralleled patternwork, there must have been other workshops producing pattern *lekythoi* at this time.[2] On the basis of this summary and highly selective study of the vases, I tentatively offer the following criteria for distinguishing Beldam from Haemonian pattern *lekythoi*:

1. Shape—most Beldam *lekythoi* have the sharp angle at the join of shoulder to body, characteristic of shape BEL.

2. Ground colour—Beldam pattern *lekythoi* are usually light-ground.

3. Patternwork (abstract)—prominent, especially meanders, lattice and lozengy.

4. Patternwork (florals)—palmettes, regularly upright, either old-fashioned or 'lyres', ivy-berry—very common; laurel—late.

5. Disposition of pattern—horizontal registers.

6. Added colour—red paint.

The Haimon and Beldam painters are closely related. Between them stand painters who seem to have been connected with both, and some of the pattern *lekythoi* which cannot easily be assigned to either may have been decorated by some of them.[3] There are tall, very straight-sided cylinders with deep-cup mouths—Haemonian in the Diosphan tradition—decorated exclusively with rectilinear patterns—more characteristic of the Beldam Workshop;[4] and there are fuller cylinders—nearer shape DL, with Beldam ivy-berry tendrils, a Beldam lozengy, and Haemonian palmettes.[5]

The Haimon and Beldam pattern *lekythoi* which are the most like each other are the

---

[1] Rome, Conservatori, 73. Capitoline Museums, *CV* i, pl. 28, no. 2, and p. 23.

[2] Cf. Bucarest, *CV* i, pl. 22, nos. 2, 4; Frankfurt, *CV* ii, pl. 50, nos. 4, 5; Mingazzini, pl. 86, no. 9.

[3] Pholos Painter: *ABV* 571 ff.; *Para* 287. 'There are probably a few *lekythoi* by the Pholos Painter among those described above as in the manner of the Haimon' (*ABV* 572).
Painter of the Half-palmettes: *ABV* 573, 708; *Para* 287 f.; *ABV* 573, 'There are probably *lekythoi* by the Painter of the Half-palmettes among those classed as Haemonian.'
Brno Painter: *Para* 288 f., 'companion of the Haimon Painter'; p. 289, *lekythoi* of the Beldam Workshop.

Emporion Painter: *ABV* 584 f., 708 f.; *Para* 291.
Two-row Painter: *ARV* 726 ff.; *Para* 411. Miss Haspels (*ABL* 181 ff.) noted the resemblance in patternwork to the Beldam Workshop, especially in Athens 1725 (*ARV* 726, no. 9, and p. 728). The combination of figures and patterns in registers on this vase also recalls the Diosphos Painter's *alabastra* and those of the Haimon Painter. The reticular pattern on the base recalls the Emporion Painter.
Icarus Painter: *ARV* 696 ff., 1666 f., 1702; *Para* 407 f. *ABL* 180.

[4] Cf. Cambridge, G 118. *CV* i, pl. 22, no. 23 (cf. Athens, Agora, P 3881).

[5] Cf. Bucarest, *CV* i, pl. 30, no. 1.

ones which are the least characteristic of each painter—the *lekythoi* decorated with upright palmettes-on-Os in the old 581 scheme (cf. PLATE 69. 2, 5).[1] The Beldam *lekythoi* reproduce the upright palmettes-on-Os with little or no variation. They differ from Haemonian *lekythoi* of the type more in the shape of the vase itself than in its decoration. How long were these old-fashioned pattern *lekythoi* produced? Probably well into the second half of the fifth century,[2] but not as late as the ivy-berry[3] and laurel[4] *lekythoi*.

BELDAM WORKSHOP

Since Miss Haspels recognized the importance of the Beldam Workshop[5] there has been a tendency to attribute to it all pattern *lekythoi* from the 460s onwards. The workshop was influential and probably large, but it can scarcely be responsible for the number of pattern *lekythoi* of different shapes and styles of decoration which are known from the second half of the fifth century. The pattern *lekythoi* of this period require more detailed treatment than is possible here, to distinguish what is Beldam from what is not. I shall limit myself to the Beldam Painter, his immediate workshop, and painters who are known to have been influenced by him, and to pattern *lekythoi* which are not decorated with the upright palmettes-on-Os.

The Beldam Painter's career probably covers most of the second quarter of the fifth century B.C. He does not seem to have been active earlier;[6] his heritage seems to lie within the Workshop of the Athena and Theseus Painters, and certain details of shape, pattern, and iconography point to the Theseus Painter himself (see p. 19). Two of the Beldam Painter's large white-ground BELs are decorated exclusively with patterns and these may be taken as representative of the painter. One of the vases was found in a grave in the Athenian Kerameikos and is now in the Kerameikos Museum (PLATE 70. 5);[7] the whereabouts of the second, once on the Munich Market,[8] is unknown. The Munich *lekythos* has undecorated neck, rays on the shoulder, and a combination of patterns on the body which may be paralleled on *lekythoi* of other shapes from the workshop:[9] a central palmette composition framed above by a key and lattice, below by a reserved zigzag and double ivy chain. The central floral composition is two addorsed lyre palmettes, whose tendrils terminate in lateral palmettes. Lyre palmettes (see p. 96) are popular on Beldam pattern *lekythoi* (cf. PLATE 69. 3, 6). The earlier lyres are fully formed, the later lyres are 'sunken', that is the base of the palmette is submerged beneath the ground line. Beldam *lekythoi* with lyre palmettes are generally larger and finer than the majority of the workshop's pattern *lekythoi*; some have clusters of small dots disposed decoratively in the field,[10] and a very few incorporate figures into the floral composition

[1] *ABL* 185 f. Cf. Carlsruhe, *CV* i, pl. 32. 3 (*ABL* 269, no. 73); Cambridge, *CV* i, pl. 22, no. 25.

[2] Cf. *AE* 1958, 75 f. (T. 27, no. 67, with the fragment of a matt outline white *lekythos* (p. 75, fig. 129) and Beldam pattern *lekythoi* (p. 76, fig. 131).

[3] Cf. *AE* 1958, pl. 17.

[4] *Corinth* xiii. 254 f. (T. 367), and p. 143; *AM* lxxxi. 37 (70/176).

[5] *ABL* 170 ff., especially 181 ff.

[6] Ibid. 171. The sub-Deianeira *lekythos* in Amiens (*ABV* 709, add as no. 7 to p. 587) I have not seen.

[7] Athens, Kerameikos. *ABL* 266, no. 6, and pls. 50. 4 and 51. 3.

[8] Munich Market. *ABL* 266, no. 7. Jacobsthal, pl. 34a.

[9] Cf. Bucarest, *CV* i, pl. 30, nos. 1, 3, 4; Bucarest *CV* ii, pls. 21, nos. 7–8.

[10] Beldam *lekythoi*: London, B 659; Madrid, 11171; *BCH* lxxxvi (1962), 650, fig. 12; Berkeley, 8.35. *ABL*

(PLATE 70. 1).[1] The second BEL (PLATE 70. 5) is equally characteristic of Beldam pattern-work. On the neck there is an ivy-berry tendril, as on some of the painter's figured BELs.[2] (The ivy-berry neck had appeared earlier on Phanyllis *lekythoi*,[3] and it is also found later on a few pattern *lekythoi* (PLATE 70. 3.).)[4] On the shoulder there are palmettes of the type which the Beldam Painter uses on his black-figure BELs.[5] On the body the area to be decorated with patterns is marked off by vertical lines.[6] At the shoulder–body join there is a meander and pattern square, below a large lozengy (dotted); beneath the lozengy are the following narrow bands: reserved zigzag, lattice, and ivy-berry tendril. Many of pattern *lekythoi* from the Beldam Workshop employ one or more of the motifs found on these two *lekythoi*; on some the florals predominate,[7] on others rectilinear patterns.[8] Of all the motifs, the ivy-berry tendril (cf. PLATE 70. 6–8)[9] seems to have been the most common in the second half of the century. It is simpler and easier to execute than the palmette compositions and, framed by lattice work and embellished with a touch of red paint,[10] it is not unattractive. These ivy-berry *lekythoi* were being buried with the dead in the last quarter of the fifth century B.C.[11] Some especially late specimens were found in the graves around Syntagma Square.[12] Not all of these vases can be related to the Beldam Workshop with any degree of certainty. Among the artists associated with the Beldam Painter and his workshop, Miss Haspels recognized the Carlsruhe, Icarus, and Two-row Painters.[13] No pattern *lekythoi* have been attributed to the Carlsruhe Painter, but there are pattern *lekythoi* of shape CL.[14] The Icarus Painter's liking for palmettes has been mentioned earlier and, although no pattern *lekythoi* have been attributed to him, he probably decorated vases of this type.[15] The shape of his small figure *lekythoi* is distinctive;[16] there are pattern *lekythoi* of this shape—one has red-figure palmettes.[17] The Icarus Painter is known to have painted black palmettes on white-

---

247, no. 1 (Pholos Group). Non-Beldam *lekythoi*: Toronto, 923.13.40 (335) (Little Lion); Madrid, 19497. Inscription Painter (PLATE 19. 1, FIGURE 11*b*).

[1] London, B 659 (mentioned, *ABL* 182); Philadelphia Market. *Hesperia Art* xlix, no. 7*b* (not Beldam shape; cf. no. 7*a*); Beirut (I do not have the number). On the London vase the figure decoration is human (warrior), on the market vase animal (duck), and on the Beirut vase (deer). The combination of patterns and silhouette figures is found on cups decorated by the Marlay and Lid Painters (*ARV* 1279, nos. 51, 51 *bis*, and p. 1280, no. 67 (Marlay Painter), and *ARV* 1282, nos. 10–12, and p. 1283, no. 13 (Lid Painter)) who Miss Haspels thought betrayed the influence of the Beldam Workshop (*ABL* 183 f.).

[2] *ABL* 171.   [3] Cf. *ABL*, pl. 19, nos. 1, 3.

[4] Cassel, T. 437. *CV* i, pl. 47. 3. Basle Market (M.M.). Compare also the unattributed black-figure *lekythos*, Athens, *CV* i, pl. 7, no. 6.

[5] *ABL*, pl. 51. 1 and pp. 175 f. The palmettes in pl. 51. 1 may be compared with the central group on the pattern BEL once on the Munich Market, above, p. 153 n. 8.

[6] Cf. Palermo, Mormino Collection, *CV* i. III Y, pl. 11, no. 10, and pl. 12, no. 9; Bucarest, *CV* i, pl. 30. 2; Norway, *CV* i, pl. 26. 1. 4.

[7] Cf. Copenhagen, Chr viii 392. *CV* iii, pl. 112. 16. *NSc* 1960, 142, fig. 8*b*.

[8] Louvre, F 523 and 524; Bucarest, *CV* i, pl. 30, no. 11.

[9] *ABL* 181 f.; *Hesp* xxii. 71; *Corinth* xiii. 164 f. The pattern is found in red-figure from the time of the Berlin Painter (*JHS* xxxi. 279, fig. 3, no. 14).

[10] *ABL* 182.

[11] *Corinth* xiii. 121 f., 142 f., and pl. 65 (T. 404).

[12] *AE*, 1958, pl. 17.

[13] *ABL* 181 ff.

[14] Philadelphia Market. *Hesperia Art* xxxii, pl. 37, B 4; *Hesp* xxxii (1963), pl. 37, B 4.

[15] Cf. Athens, Vlasto. *ARV* 699, no. 65. The patterns are mentioned by Miss Haspels and related to the Beldam Workshop (*ABL* 180 and pl. 54. 5).

[16] *ARV* 696.

[17] *Anuari*, 217, fig. 31, no. 72. For the shape compare Cracow, *CV* i, pl. 8, no. 12 (*ARV* 700, no. 8). A red-figure palmette *lekythos* in Cracow (*CV* i, pl. 10. 10) has palmettes not unlike the Icarus Painter's, but the

ground vases[1] and red-figure palmettes on red-figure vases.[2] The Two-row Painter specialized in *alabastra*,[3] and just as there are *alabastra* earlier in the fifth century decorated with patterns, there are later pattern *alabastra*, with abstract and floral ornament, in the manner of pattern *lekythoi*.[4] Some of these have characteristic Beldam patterns and were probably painted by members of that workshop, such as the Two-row Painter (cf. PLATE 71. 4).[5]

shape is near ATL, and there is applied white in a central band to which a meander in black paint was added; similar pattern bands at the shoulder and beneath the figures are not uncommon on red-figure *lekythoi* of shape ATL.

A late red-figure palmette *lekythos*, with sunken lyres, found at Camarina in Sicily (*ML* xiv. 785, fig. 6) indicates that the vases were probably produced in red-figure during most of the fifth century.

[1] Cf. Oxford, 1927.4467. *ARV* 700, no. 84.
[2] Cf. Cologny, Bodmer. *ARV* 699, no. 80 (palmettes on the shoulder of the vase).
[3] *ARV* 726 ff.
[4] *ABL* 182.
[5] *ARV* 728.

LIST OF FIGURES

EXPLANATION

The figures are drawn by the author and should not be taken for a strictly accurate reproduction of the original. When the source of the drawing is not my museum notes, I have cited the published photograph or drawing from which I have taken it and to which reference should be made.

Figures 1 and 2 (Lotus Chains) and Figure 3 (Architectural Decoration) are taken from publications, for the reader's convenience.

Figures 4 and 5 (Meanders) are a compilation of linear patterns taken from Beazley's publications, especially:

BSA xviii (1911–12), 231, fig. 6; xix (1912–13), 242, fig. 10.

JHS xxx (1910), 54 f.; xxxi (1911), 279, fig. 3; 292, fig. 8; 293, fig. 9; xxxiv (1914), 186, 218; xlii (1922), 86 ff.

CB iii.

Figure 6 (Types of Shoulder Palmettes) is explained on pages 33 f.

Figures 7 to 24 (Shoulder Patterns)

The shoulder field, regardless of its diameter, is represented by a circle of uniform size; the handle is omitted and the neck is represented by a central, smaller circle. Differences in technique, which cannot be indicated in the drawing, are noted in the entry for each vase.

Figures 25 to 27*a* (Handle Decoration)

The handle is not indicated; it forms the central axis of the floral composition on all of the vases.

Figures 27*b* to 34 (Side-Palmettes)

The central figure composition framed by the palmettes is represented by a blank space. Reference to plates 58–9 will make this clear.

Figure 1. Lotus Chains

a. *Polos* of the Berlin Goddess. Incised on marble and picked out in paint. K. Blümel, *Katalog der Sammlung antiker Skulpturen, Staatliche Museen zu Berlin*, ii. 1 (1940), pls. 5–6.

b. Incised ivory panel, lower border. From Küyünjik, Nineveh. Late eighth century. R. D. Barnett. *A Catalogue of the Nimrud Ivories* (1957), pl. 128 (T 24).

c. 'Melian' amphora, Athens. National Museum, 474. A. Conze, *Melische Thongefässe* (1862), pl. 1. 5.

d. François Vase, Florence, Archaeological Museum, 4209. *ABV* 26, no. 1; FR, pl. 3. 5.

e. François Vase. FR, pl. 3. 3.

f. François Vase. FR, pl. 3. 3.

g. *Polos* of the Lyons *kore*. Incised on marble and picked out in paint. Lyons Museum. H. Schrader, *Die archaische Marmorbildwerke der Akropolis* (1939), 67, fig. 32.

h. Black-figure *dinos*, Athens, Acropolis, 606. *ABV* 81, no. 1. Graef, pls. 30–2.

Figure 2. Lotus Chains

a. Black-figure column-crater, Delos, 593. *ABV* 122, no. 22 (Lydan). *Délos* x, pl. 45.

b. Black-figure neck-amphora, Paris. Cab. Méd., 222. *ABV* 152, no. 25 (Amasis Painter); Karouzou, pl. 31.

c. Black-figure *lekythos* (shoulder), Palermo, GE 1896.1. *ABV* 379, no. 276 (Leagros Group); *ABL*, pl. 14.2.

d. *Lekythos* (shoulder), Six's Technique, Paris, Louvre, MNB 912. *ABL* 235, no. 76 (Diosphos Painter); *ABL*, pl. 37. 3.

e. *Lekythos* (shoulder), Six's Technique, Athens, National Museum, 2262. *ABL* 228, no. 47 (Sappho Painter). *ABL*, pl. 36. 3.

f. Black-figure *lekythos* (shoulder), Athens, National Museum, 472. *ABL* 241, no. 14 (Haimon Painter). *ABL*, pl. 41. 2.

g. Black-figure *lekythos* (shoulder), Athens, National Museum, 609. *ABL* 265, no. 42 (Emporion Painter). *ABL*, pl. 48. 5.

h. Black-figure *lekythos* (shoulder), Athens, National Museum, 610. *ABL* 268, no. 45 (Beldam Painter). *ABL*, pl. 53. 6.

Figure 3. Architectural Decoration (*BSA* lvii (1960), 218 ff. (Plommer); *Hesp* xxxix (1970), 236 f. (L. Shoe-Meritt)).

a. Athenian Treasury, Delphi (*cella*). Painted on marble. J. Audiat, *Fouilles de Delphes*, ii (1933), pl. 23.

b. Athenian Treasury, Delphi (*cella*, cross-wall). Painted on marble. Audiat, op. cit., pl. 23.

c. Hekatompedon, Athenian Acropolis (*sima*). Incised and painted on marble. Acropolis Museum, 3976 and M 71; *AD* i, pl. 50*a*.

d. Knidian Lesche, Delphi (*sima*). Painted on marble. J. Pouilloux, *Fouilles de Delphes*, ii (1960), pl. 71. 1 and p. 132. (Compare the pattern painted on the dress of some of the marble *korai* from the Athenian Acropolis: W. Lermann, *Altgriechische Plastik* (1907), pl. 9 (Acropolis 696), 10 (Acropolis 675), 19 (Acropolis 670).)

e. Stoa Poikile, Athenian Agora (pier capital). Painted on limestone. Agora Museum, A 1559. *Hesp* xxxix (1970), pl. 64 *a, c* and pp. 236 ff.

Figure 4. Meanders and Pattern Squares (*JHS* xlii. 37 f.)

Figure 5. Meanders

a. *JHS* xxxi. 279, fig. 3/2, *The Berlin Painter* (Melbourne, 1964), 7 (ULFA).

b. *JHS* xxxi. 279, fig. 3/4*a*.

c. *JHS* xxxi. 293, eta.

d. *JHS* xxxiv. 186, delta.

e. Berne, Jucker. Akrisios *lekythos*. Plate 37. 1.

f. Berne, Jucker. Akrisios *lekythos*. Plate 37. 1.

g. Athens, National Museum, 19333. *ARV* 1687, no. 1.

h. Reed Workshop. Page 58.

i. Paris, Louvre, CA 537. *ARV* 1384, no. 18. Group R.

j. Bowdoin Workshop. Page 106.

k. *JHS* xxx. 54; xlvii. 86, lxx. 30; *BSA* xviii. 232.
The pattern appears in architectural decoration (E. Buschor, *Die Tondächer der Akropolis*, i (1929), pl. 12) and on the dress of some of the marble *korai* (*Korai* 40, no. 43; 71, no. 111; 75, no. 117; 78, no. 122). It is also found (earlier) in the East, in the Fikellura (*BSA* xxxiv. 73 and pl. 15*b*) and Clazomenian styles (*CV*, British Museum, viii, pl. 614. 4).

l. The pattern also appears in architectural decoration (Buschor, op. cit., pl. 5) and on the *korai* (*Korai* 40, no. 43; 71, no. 111; 78, no. 122).

m. Cf. *Korai* 75, no. 117.

n. CB iii. 44.

Figure 6. Types of Shoulder Palmettes. Pages 33 f.

Figures 7 to 24. Shoulder Patterns. Pages 33 f.

7*a.* Paris, Jameson Collection. Psiax. *ABV* 293, no. 11 (black on white ground). *AJA* xlv (1941), 591, figs. 10–11. Page 9.

b. Delos, Heraion, 547. Leagros Group. *ABV* 379, no. 274 (black on red ground). *ABL*, pl. 20. 1. Pages 9, 13.

c. London, British Museum, 99.2–18.67. Edinburgh Painter. *ABL* 216, no. 1 (black on red ground). *ABL*, pl. 27. 5. Page 13.

8*a.* Athens, National Museum, 1124. Edinburgh Painter. *ABL* 216, no. 16 (black on white ground). *ABL*, pl. 27. 6. Page 13.

b. New York, Metropolitan Museum of Art, 41.162.146. Athena Painter. *ABL* 257, no. 72 (black on white ground). Page 15.

c. New York, Metropolitan Museum of Art, 10.210.11. Klügmann Painter. *ABV* 1200. no. 38 (black on reserved ground). Page 15.

9*a.* Athens, National Museum, 12274. Phanyllis Painter. *ABL* 199, no. 14 (black on red ground). *ABL*, pl. 20. 6. Page 145.

b. Syracuse, Museo Nazionale, 2287. Gela Painter. *ABL* 206, no. 10 (black on white ground). *ABL*, pl. 27. 1. Page 18.

c. Syracuse, Museo Nazionale, 2358. Gela Painter. *ABL* 228, no. 63 (black on red ground). *ABL*, pl. 27. 3. Page 18.

10*a.* Athens, National Museum, 1129. Beldam Painter. *ABL* 266, no. 1 (black on white ground). Pages 19, 85.

b. Athens, National Museum, 12801. Beldam Painter. *ABL* 266, no. 2 (black on white ground). Page 85. Plate 18. 1.

c. Athens, National Museum, 1982. Beldam Painter. *ABL* 267, no. 12 (black on white ground). Page 85. Plate 18. 2.

11*a.* London, British Museum, D 65. Group of London D 65. *ARV* 652, no. 2 (black on white ground). Page 19. Plate 18. 3.

b. Madrid, Museo Arqueológico Nacional, 19497. Inscription Painter. *ARV* 748, no. 1 (black on white ground). Pages 20, 153 f. n. 10. Plate 19. 1.

c. New York, Metropolitan Museum of Art, 41.162.102. Inscription Painter. *ARV* 749, no. 8 (black on white ground). Page 20.

12*a.* New York, Metropolitan Museum of Art, 35.11.5. Vouni Painter. *ARV* 744, no. 1 (black on white ground; alternate petals of the palmettes and central lobes of the lotus blossoms are matt red). Pages 27, 28, 45. Plate 26. 2.

b. London, British Museum, 1928.2–13.1. Painter of Athens 1826. *ARV* 746, no. 4 (black on white ground; central petals of the palmettes and central lobes of the lotus blossoms are matt red; the centre palmette is partly covered by the *stele* in the picture panel). Pages 28, 45. Plate 26. 1.

c. Boston, Museum of Fine Arts, 95.47. Painter of London E 342, near. *ARV* 670, no. 17 (black on white ground; the added matt red paint has largely disappeared). Pages 28, 35.

13*a.* Palermo, Mormino Collection, 310. Unattributed. *CV* Mormino Collection i. III Y, pl. 6, no. 2 (black on white ground; alternate petals on the palmettes are matt red; the matt red which was originally applied to the lotus blossoms has largely disappeared). Page 28.

b. New York, Metropolitan Museum of Art, 06.1021.134. Villa Giulia Painter, near. *ARV* 626, no. 2 (black on white ground; the missing petals of the palmettes and the lotus blossoms were originally added in matt red). Page 28. Plate 27. 4.

c. New York, Metropolitan Museum of Art, 57.12.24. Unattributed (black on white ground). Page 29. Plate 27. 5.

14*a.* Athens, National Museum, 1935. Bosanquet Painter. *ARV* 1227, no. 1 (glaze on white ground). Page 37.

b. Athens, National Museum, 1932. Bosanquet Painter. *ARV* 1227. 2 (glaze on white ground). Page 37.

15*a.* New York, Metropolitan Museum of Art, 23.160.39. Bosanquet Painter. *ARV* 1227, no. 4 (glaze on white ground). Page 37. Plate 30. 2.

b. Berlin (East), Staatliche Museen, 3291. Bosanquet Painter. *ARV* 1227. no. 9 (glaze on white ground). Page 37.

16*a.* Boston, Museum of Fine Arts, 01.8080. Thanatos Painter, near. *ARV* 1231 (glaze on white ground). Page 39. Plate 31. 1.

b. New York, Metropolitan Museum of Art, 11.212.8. Thanatos Painter, near. *ARV* 1231 (glaze on white ground). Page 39. Plate 31. 2.

c. Athens, National Museum, 16422. Unattributed (glaze on white ground). Page 61 n. 18. Plate 28. 3.

17*a.* Athens, National Museum, 12739. Sabouroff Painter. *ARV* 845, no. 167 (glaze on white ground). Pages 35 f.

b. Athens, National Museum, 12747. Sabouroff Painter. *ARV* 845, no. 166 (glaze on white ground). Pages 35 f.

c. New York, Metropolitan Museum of Art, 21.88.17. Sabouroff Painter. *ARV* 846, no. 197 (glaze on white ground). Page 35.

18*a.* Athens, National Museum, 1960. Thanatos Painter. *ARV* 1228, no. 4 (glaze tendrils and hearts of palmettes; matt black petals; white ground). Page 40.

b. New York, Metropolitan Museum of Art, 12.229.10. Thanatos Painter. *ARV* 1229, no. 26 (glaze tendrils and hearts of the palmettes; matt petals; white ground). Page 40. Plate 33. 1.

c. New York, Baker Collection. Thanatos Painter. *ARV* 1228, no. 1 (glaze on white ground). *ANY*, pl. 88. Page 40.

19*a.* Berlin (West), Staatliche Museen, 2443. Achilles Painter. *ARV* 995, no. 118 (glaze on white ground). Pages 44, 46. Plate 35. 1.

b. Athens, National Museum, 1818. Achilles Painter. *ARV* 998. no. 161 (glaze on white ground). Page 46.

c. New York, Metropolitan Museum of Art, 07.286.42. Achilles Painter. *ARV* 1001, no. 209 (glaze on white ground). Page 46.

20*a.* New York, Metropolitan Museum of Art, 06.1171. Achilles Painter. *ARV* 999, no. 179 (glaze on white ground). Page 46.

b. New York, Metropolitan Museum of Art, 08.258.18. Achilles Painter. *ARV* 999, no. 180 (glaze on white ground). Page 46.

c. Boston, Museum of Fine Arts, 13.187. Achilles Painter. *ARV* 998, no. 157 (glaze on white ground). Page 46.

21*a.* Oxford, Ashmolean Museum, 1938.909. Achilles Painter. *ARV* 993, no. 93 (red-figure *lekythos*; black palmettes on reserved shoulder). Pages 43 f.

b. Boston, Museum of Fine Arts, 93.103. Painter of Boston 93.104. *ARV* 1007, no. 2 (red-figure *lekythos*; black palmettes on reserved shoulder). Pages 43 f.

c. New York, Metropolitan Museum of Art, 08.258.23. Phiale Painter. *ARV* 1021, no. 117 (red-figure *lekythos*; black palmettes on reserved shoulder). Page 48.

22*a.* Athens, National Museum, 1940. Phiale Painter? *ARV* 1004, no. 41 and p. 1026, no. 1. (glaze on white ground). Page 50. Plate 38. 1.

b. New York, Metropolitan Museum of Art, 22.53. Phiale Painter? *ARV* 1026, no. 2 (glaze on white ground, except the two petals of each palmette which are rendered in matt black). Page 50.

c. Athens, National Museum, 19355. Phiale Painter. *ARV* 1022, no. 139 *bis* (glaze on white ground, except the alternate petals of the palmettes which are rendered in matt red). Page 49.

23*a.* London, British Museum, D 66. Bird Painter. *ARV* 1233, no. 23 (matt black on white ground). Page 53.

b. New York, Metropolitan Museum of Art, 09.221.44. Painter of Munich 2335. *ARV* 1168, no. 128 (matt brown on white ground). Page 56. Plate 42. 1.

c. London, British Museum, D 70. Woman Painter. *ARV* 1371, no. 1 (matt black on white ground, except the alternate petals of the palmettes which are rendered in matt red). Page 57.

24*a.* New York, Metropolitan Museum of Art, 75.2.5. Quadrate Painter. *ARV* 1238, no. 28 (matt black on white ground). Page 57.

b. Athens National Museum, 19333. Bird Painter? *ARV* 1687, no. 1; *Para* 467, (glaze on white ground, except the alternate petals of the palmettes and some of the buds, which are rendered in matt). Pages 54, 58.

c. Athens, National Museum, 1816. Group R. *ARV* 1383, no. 12 (matt black on white ground, except the alternate petals of the palmettes, which are rendered in matt red). Pages 54, 61. Plate 49. 1.

Figures 25 to 27*a*: Handle Decoration

25*a.* New York, Metropolitan Museum of Art, 07.286.43. Painter of New York 07. *ABV* 454 (black on red ground). Page 92.

b. New York, Metropolitan Museum of Art, 07.286.41. Painter of New York 07. *ABV* 454 (black on red ground). Page 92.

c. Boston, Museum of Fine Arts, 99.526. Gela Painter. *ABL* 209, no. 81 (black on red ground). Page 92. Plate 17. 2.

26*a.* Once New York, Gallatin. Kephisophon Painter. *ABL* 230, no. 3; *ABV* 514 and p. 669, no. 2 (black on white ground). Pages 93, 94. Plate 56. 2.

b. Vienna, Kunsthistorisches Museum, 3607. Diosphos Workshop? *ABV* 319, no. 10 (black on white ground). Page 93. Plate 55. 2.

27*a.* Greensboro, North Carolina, Jastrow Collection. Two-row Painter, near? *ARV* 727 (black on white ground; alternate petals of the palmettes and part of the lotus blossoms matt red). *AM* lii (1927), *Beilagen* 27 and 28.1. Pages 34, 96.

Figures 27*b* to 34. Side-Palmettes

27*b.* Copenhagen, National Museum, 3882. Two-row Painter, close. *ARV* 727 (black on white ground, except the alternate petals of the palmettes and the lotus blossoms). Page 96. Plate 61. 2.

28*a.* Once Baltimore, Maryland, Robinson Collection. Diosphos Painter. *ABL* 235, no. 67 (black on white ground; the hearts of the palmettes are red). *CV* Robinson Collection i, pl. 38, no. 7. Page 98.

b. New York, Metropolitan Museum of Art, 06.1070. Diosphos Painter. *ABV* 301, no. 3 (black on white ground; the hearts of the palmettes are red). Page 98. Plate 59. 2.

29*a.* Thebes, Museum, R. 46.84. Painter of Würzburg 517. *ARV* 306, no. 7 (black on white ground). *JHS* xxix (1909), pl. 24. Page 99.

b. New York, Metropolitan Museum of Art, 51.163. Diosphos Workshop. *ARV* 301, no. 7 (black on white ground). Page 100. Plate 59.3.

30*a.* Caltanissetta, from Sabucina. Painter of the Yale *Lekythos*. *ARV* 660, no. 73 *bis.*, and p. 1664; *Para* 403 (black on white ground). Pages 100, 104 n. 8.

b. New York, Metropolitan Museum of Art, 41.162.95. *ARV* 303, no. 4 (black on white ground). Page 104 n. 8.

c. Once Barre Collection. Diosphos Workshop? *ARV* 302, no. 1 (black on white ground). *Collection de M. Albert Barre* (Paris, 1878), 45, no. 353. Page 100.

31*a.* Palermo, Museo Nazionale. Diosphos Workshop. *ARV* 302, no. 16 (black on white ground). *AM* lii (1927), *Beilage* 28. 1. Page 101.

    b. Cambridge, Massachusetts, Fogg Museum, 1925.30.51. Diosphos Workshop. *ARV* 302, no. 21 (black on white ground). *CV* Hoppin Collection i, pl. 19. 5. Page 101.

32*a.* Warsaw, National Museum, 198554. Diosphos Workshop. *ARV* 302, no. 19 (black on white ground). Page 101.

    b. Basle Market (M.M.). *ARV* 303; *Para* 357 (black on white ground). Page 112. Plate 64. 2.

33*a.* Paris, Petit Palais, 335. Painter of Petit Palais 336. *ARV* 305, no. 2 (black on white ground). *CV* Petit Palais i, pl. 33, nos. 1–2. Page 103.

    b. Athens Market, from Tanagra. *ARV* 303, no. 11 *bis*, and p. 1644 (black on white ground). *AM* xxiii (1888), pl. 5. Page 112.

34*a.* Küsnacht, Hirschmann. Bowdoin Workshop. *ARV* 691, no. 26 *bis*, and p. 1666; *Para* 521 (black on white ground). *Hesperia Art* xv. 7, no. 93. Page 108.

    b. Athens, National Museum, 1809. Bowdoin Workshop. *ARV* 689, no. 14 (black on white ground; the hearts of the palmettes are purple). Page 107. Plate 60. 2.

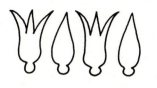

a. Polos of the Berlin Goddess

b. Ivory Panel from Küyünjik, Nineveh

c. 'Melian' amphora

d. François Vase

e. François Vase

f. François Vase

g. Polos of the Lyons *kore*

h. Black-figure *dinos*, Acropolis 606

FIGURE 1. LOTUS CHAINS

a. Black-figure column-crater, Delos, 593.
Lydan

b. Black-figure neck-amphora, Paris, Cab. Méd., 222.
Amasis Painter

c. Black-figure *lekythos* (shoulder), Palermo, GE 1896.1.
Leagros Group

d. Lekythos (shoulder), Six's technique, Louvre, MNB 912.
Diosphos Painter

e. Lekythos (shoulder), Six's technique, Athens, National Museum, 2262.
Sappho Painter

f. Black-figure lekythos (shoulder), Athens, National Museum, 472.
Haimon Painter

g. Black-figure *lekythos* (shoulder), Athens, National Museum, 609.
Emporion Painter

h. Black-figure *lekythos* (shoulder), Athens, National Museum, 610.
Beldam Painter

FIGURE 2. LOTUS CHAINS

a. Athenian Treasury, Delphi (*cella*)

b. Athenian Treasury, Delphi (*cella,* cross-wall)

c. Hekatompedon, Athenian Acropolis (*sima*)

d. Knidian Lesche, Delphi (*sima*)

e. Stoa Poikile, Athenian Agora (pier capital)

FIGURE 3. ARCHITECTURAL DECORATION

a. Key (simple meander), running right

b. Key (simple meander), running left

c. Key, stopt

d. Meander, running

e. Meander (broken), running

f. Meander, stopt

g. Meander (broken), stopt

h. Meander taking its origin from the vertical edge

i. Pairs of opposed meanders (broken and stopt)

j. False meander

k. Pairs of linked meanders (broken)

l. Crossing ('labyrinthine') meanders (running)

m. Crossing ('labyrinthine') meander (running key crossed by stopt step)

n. Crossing ('labyrinthine') meander (stopt key crossed by stopt step)

 o. Saltire square

 p. Saltire square with a dot between each pair of arms

 q. Saltire square, blackened

 r. Saltire square, with dots on the arms

 s. Saltire square, Achillean

 t. Cross square

 u. Cross square, with a dot in each corner

 v. Cross square, blackened

 w. Cross square, blackened, Dourian

 x. Dourian cross square, modified, with black corners voided

y. Chequer square, blackened

z. Chequer square

aa. Blackened square

bb. Voided square

FIGURE 4. MEANDERS AND PATTERN-SQUARES

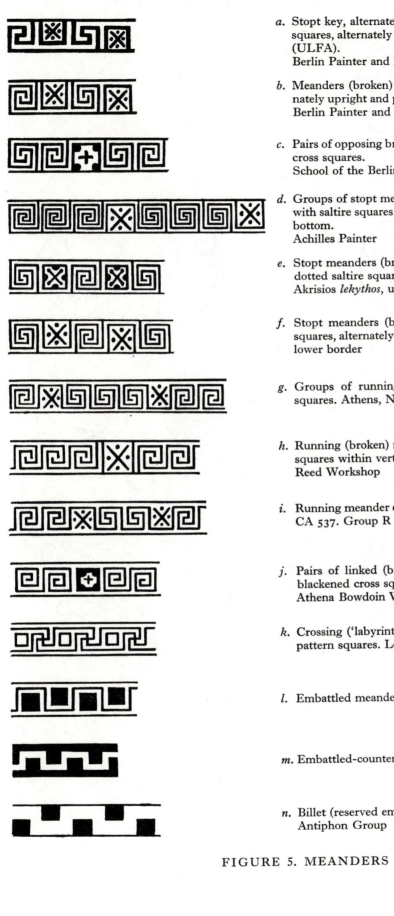

a. Stopt key, alternately facing right and left, and saltire squares, alternately attached to the upper and lower border (ULFA).
Berlin Painter and his school

b. Meanders (broken) alternating with saltire squares, alternately upright and pendent.
Berlin Painter and his school

c. Pairs of opposing broken meanders alternating with dotted cross squares.
School of the Berlin Painter

d. Groups of stopt meanders facing alternately right and left with saltire squares depending alternately from the top and bottom.
Achilles Painter

e. Stopt meanders (broken), alternating with blackened dotted saltire squares, alternately upright and pendent.
Akrisios *lekythos*, upper border

f. Stopt meanders (broken) alternating with dotted saltire squares, alternately upright and pendent. Akrisios *lekythos*, lower border

g. Groups of running (broken) meanders enclosing saltire squares. Athens, National Museum, 19333

h. Running (broken) meanders alternating with saltire squares within vertical hedges.
Reed Workshop

i. Running meander enclosing saltire squares. Paris, Louvre, CA 537. Group R

j. Pairs of linked (broken) meanders alternating with blackened cross squares.
Athena Bowdoin Workshop

k. Crossing ('labyrinthine') meander, running and enclosing pattern squares. Leagrans and Pioneers

l. Embattled meander with blackened squares in the gaps

m. Embattled-counter-embattled meander

n. Billet (reserved embattled-counter-embattled)
Antiphon Group

FIGURE 5. MEANDERS

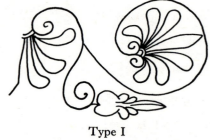

Type I

Type I B

Type II B

Type I A

Type II A

Type I AA

Type II AA

FIGURE 6. TYPES OF SHOULDER PALMETTES

a. Paris, Jameson Collection.
Psiax

b. Delos, Heraion, 547.
Leagros Group

c. London, British Museum, 99.2–18.67.
Edinburgh Painter

FIGURE 7. SHOULDER PATTERNS

a. Athens, National Museum, 1124.
   Edinburgh Painter

b. New York, Metropolitan Museum of Art,
   41.162.146.
   Athena Painter

c. New York, Metropolitan Museum of Art,
   10.210.11.
   Klügmann Painter

FIGURE 8. SHOULDER PATTERNS

a. Athens, National Museum, 12274.
Phanyllis Painter

b. Syracuse, Museo Nazionale, 2287.
Gela Painter

c. Syracuse, Museo Nazionale, 2358.
Gela Painter

FIGURE 9. SHOULDER PATTERNS

a. Athens, National Museum, 1129.
Beldam Painter

b. Athens, National Museum, 12801.
Beldam Painter

c. Athens, National Museum, 1982.
Beldam Painter

FIGURE 10. SHOULDER PATTERNS

a. London, British Museum, D 65.
   Group of London D 65

b. Madrid, Museo Arqueológico Nacional, 19497.
   Inscription Painter

c. New York, Metropolitan Museum of Art,
   41.162.102.
   Inscription Painter

FIGURE 11. SHOULDER PATTERNS

a. New York, Metropolitan Museum of Art,
35.11.5.
Vouni Painter

b. London, British Museum, 1928.2–13.1.
Painter of Athens 1826

c. Boston, Museum of Fine Arts, 95.47.
Painter of London E 342, near

FIGURE 12. SHOULDER PATTERNS

a. Palermo, Mormino Collection, 310.
Unattributed

b. New York, Metropolitan Museum of Art,
06.1021.134.
Villa Giulia Painter, near

c. New York, Metropolitan Museum of Art,
57.12.24.
Unattributed

FIGURE 13. SHOULDER PATTERNS

a. Athens, National Museum, 1935.
Bosanquet Painter

b. Athens, National Museum, 1932.
Bosanquet Painter

FIGURE 14. SHOULDER PATTERNS

a. New York, Metropolitan Museum of Art,
23.160.39.
Bosanquet Painter

b. Berlin (East), Staatliche Museen, 3291.
Bosanquet Painter

FIGURE 15. SHOULDER PATTERNS

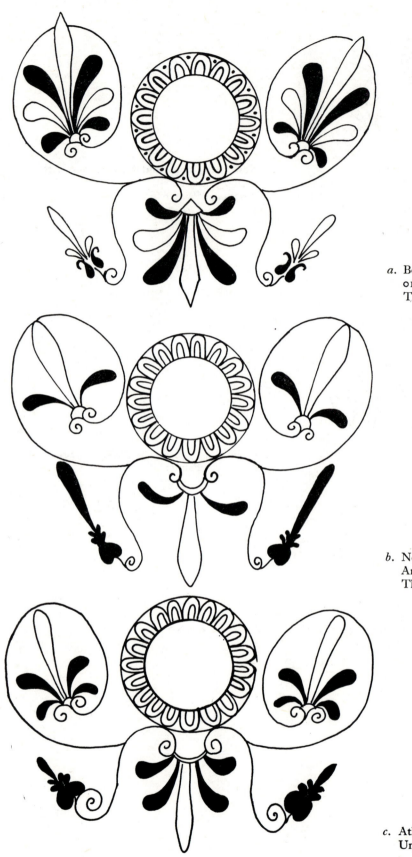

a. Boston, Museum of Fine Arts,
01.8080.
Thanatos Painter, near

b. New York, Metropolitan Museum of
Art, 11.212.8.
Thanatos Painter, near

c. Athens, National Museum, 16422.
Unattributed

FIGURE 16. SHOULDER PATTERNS

a. Athens, National Museum, 12739.
   Sabouroff Painter

b. Athens, National Museum, 12747.
   Sabouroff Painter

c. New York, Metropolitan Museum of
   Art, 21.88.17.
   Sabouroff Painter

FIGURE 17. SHOULDER PATTERNS

a. Athens, National Museum, 1960.
Thanatos Painter

b. New York, Metropolitan Museum of
Art, 12.229.10.
Thanatos Painter

c. New York, Baker Collection.
Thanatos Painter

FIGURE 18. SHOULDER PATTERNS

a. Berlin (West), Staatliche Museen, 2443.
Achilles Painter

b. Athens, National Museum, 1818.
Achilles Painter

c. New York, Metropolitan Museum of Art, 07.286.42.
Achilles Painter

FIGURE 19. SHOULDER PATTERNS

a. New York, Metropolitan Museum of
Art, 06.1171.
Achilles Painter

b. New York, Metropolitan Museum of
Art, 08.258.18.
Achilles Painter

c. Boston, Museum of Fine Arts,
13.187.
Achilles Painter

FIGURE 20. SHOULDER PATTERNS

a. Oxford, Ashmolean Museum,
1938.909.
Achilles Painter

b. Boston, Museum of Fine Arts,
93.103.
Achillean, Painter of Boston 93.104

c. New York, Metropolitan Museum of
Art, 08.258.23.
Phiale Painter

FIGURE 21. SHOULDER PATTERNS

a. Athens, National Museum, 1940.
Achillean, Phiale Painter?

b. New York, Metropolitan Museum of
Art, 22.53.
Achillean, Phiale Painter?

c. Athens, National Museum, 19355.
Phiale Painter

FIGURE 22. SHOULDER PATTERNS

a. London, British Museum, D 66.
Bird Painter

b. New York, Metropolitan Museum of
Art, 09.221.44.
Painter of Munich 2335

c. London, British Museum, D 70.
Woman Painter

FIGURE 23. SHOULDER PATTERNS

a. New York, Metropolitan Museum of
Art, 75.2.5.
Quadrate Painter

b. Athens, National Museum, 19333.
Bird Painter?

c. Athens, National Museum, 1816.
Group R

FIGURE 24. SHOULDER PATTERNS

a. New York, Metropolitan Museum of
Art, 07.286.43.
Painter of New York 07

b. New York, Metropolitan Museum of
Art, 07.286.41.
Painter of New York 07

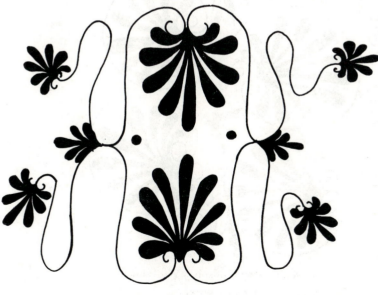

c. Boston, Museum of Fine Arts,
99.526.
Gela Painter

FIGURE 25. HANDLE DECORATION

a. Once New York, Gallatin Collection. Kephisophon Painter

b. Vienna, Kunsthistorisches Museum, 3607. Diosphos Workshop?

FIGURE 26. HANDLE DECORATION

a. Greensboro, North Carolina, Jastrow Collection. Two-row Painter, near?

b. Copenhagen, National Museum, 3882. Two-row Painter, close

FIGURE 27. HANDLE DECORATION AND SIDE-PALMETTES

a. Once Baltimore, Robinson Collection. Diosphos Painter

b. New York, Metropolitan Museum of Art, 06.1070. Diosphos Painter

FIGURE 28. SIDE-PALMETTES

a. Thebes, Museum, R. 46.84. Painter of Würzburg 517

b. New York, Metropolitan Museum of Art, 51.163. Diosphos Workshop

FIGURE 29. SIDE-PALMETTES

a. Caltanissetta, from Sabucina. Painter
of the Yale *Lekythos*

b. New York, Metropolitan Museum of Art, 41.162.95.
Diosphos Workshop?

c. Once Barre Collection. Diosphos Worskhop?

FIGURE 30. SIDE-PALMETTES

a. Palermo, Museo Nazionale. Diosphos Workshop

b. Cambridge, Massachusetts, Fogg Museum, 1925.30.51. Diosphos Workshop

FIGURE 31. SIDE-PALMETTES

a. Warsaw, National Museum, 198554. Diosphos Workshop

b. Basle Market (M.M.)

FIGURE 32. SIDE-PALMETTES

a. Paris, Petit Palais, 335. Painter of Petit Palais 336

b. Athens, Market

FIGURE 33. SIDE-PALMETTES

a. Küsnacht, Hirschmann. Bowdoin Workshop

b. Athens, National Museum, 1809. Bowdoin Workshop

FIGURE 34. SIDE-PALMETTES

LIST OF PLATES AND ICONOGRAPHICAL NOTES

THE information given for each object may include: museum inventory number, attribution, date, basic dimensions, and provenience. I also give text and figure references. The attributions are Beazley's (*Attic Black-figure Vase-painters*, *Attic Red-figure Vase-painters*, and *Paralipomena*) or Haspels's (*Attic Black-figured Lekythoi*) unless specified. Most of the dates are in terms of quarter-centuries, not because I wish to be elusive, but because it is very difficult to date more precisely, with any degree of accuracy (see pp. 131 ff. on Chronology). Closer dates are based largely on Beazley's remarks in *Vases in American Museums*, *Attic Vase Paintings in the Museum of Fine Arts, Boston*, and the Oxford *Corpus Vasorum Antiquorum*; errors are my own.

Little or nothing is said about the technique of white *lekythoi*, beyond noting 'glaze outline', 'matt outline', or 'second white', according to Beazley's lists. Much of the colour which originally enhanced these vases has faded, and we cannot be certain that what remains has not sometimes been altered by time or the elements; a technical history of white *lekythoi* remains to be written. For the present, the following studies may be useful:

White slip	Addendum by Mavis Bimson in R. A. Higgins, *Catalogue of the Terracottas in the Department of Greek and Roman Antiquities, British Museum* (1954), p. viii; Beazley, *Attic White Lekythoi*, 3.
Second white	Beazley, *AWL* 14. C. M. Robertson, *Greek Painting*, 127 ff.
Glaze and matt paint	J. V. Noble, *The Techniques of Painted Attic Pottery* (1966), 61 f.; Beazley, *AWL* 4 ff.; *ARV* 753, 846, 1022 and 1227, 1242 (the two are not always distinguishable). Robertson, *GP* 148 f. Arias, Hirmer, and Shefton, 359 ff., 363 ff.
Added colours	R. A. Higgins, *Catalogue*, 3 ff. Beazley, *AWL* 6 f. Noble, *Techniques*, 61 f.
Preliminary sketch	*JHS* lxxxv (1965), 18. (P. E. Corbett).

ICONOGRAPHICAL NOTES ON PLATES 18–54

The vases in Plates 1–72 have been selected because they illustrate, broadly and representatively, the origins and development of white *lekythoi*; since this development is dependent on vases of other shapes in other techniques, black- and red-figure, vases of different shapes are also illustrated. The basic information for each object is given in the List of Plates; the Iconographical Notes are supplementary. Almost all of the vases in Plates 18–54 are white *lekythoi*, and most have funerary iconography, reflecting the special use of the vase. Those whose iconography is not drawn from contemporary Athenian rites of death and burial are not described in detail.

The order of the Plates follows the text more than strict chronology or style but Plates 18–54, with very few exceptions, may be taken as a pictorial history of the Athenian white *lekythos*. Unattributed and little-known *lekythoi* are illustrated, as well as those by well-known painters, for the minor works help us to appreciate the major and, often, they show us how closely the two are related.

LIST OF PLATES

Plate

1. 1 Paris, Musée du Louvre, F 71. Black-figure *lekythos* by the Amasis Painter (*ABV* 154, no. 49). Third quarter of the sixth century.
Photograph: Museum, and Chuzeville, Paris.   Pages 7, 77

1. 2 Athens, Agora Museum, P 5002. Fragments of a white *lekythos* (black-figure) by Psiax (*ABV* 295, no. 2). Last quarter of the sixth century. Dimensions of the largest fragment: 8 cm by 7·8 cm.
Photograph: Agora Excavations, American School of Classical Studies, Athens.   Page 10

1. 3 London, British Museum, 1900.6–11.1. *Alabastron* in Six's technique by Psiax (*ARV* 8, no. 13). Last quarter of the sixth century. From Eretria.
Photograph: Museum.   Pages 11 n. 14, 17, 117 f. and n. 13

2. 1 Minneapolis (Minnesota), Institute of Arts, 61.59 (John R. van Derlip Fund, 1962). Black-figure *hydria* by the Antimenes Painter (*ABV* 267, no. 8 *ter*, and *Para* 119). Last quarter of the sixth century. Height: 51·11 cm.
Photograph: Museum.   Pages 10, 12, 13, 94

2. 2 Hartford (Connecticut), Wadsworth Atheneum, 1961.8. Black-figure *hydria* by Psiax (*ABV* 293, no. 9). Last quarter of the sixth century. Height: 46·99 cm.
Photograph: Museum.   Pages 10 n. 6, 13, 20, 94

3. 1 Vienna, Kunsthistorisches Museum, 75. Black-figure *lekythos* of the Leagros Group (*ABV* 379, no. 270. 'Recalls the Acheloos Painter and the Antiope Group'). Last quarter of the sixth century. Height: 30 cm. Shoulder diameter: 11·5 cm.
Photograph: Photo Meyer, Vienna.   Pages 20, 78

3. 2 Bochum, Ruhr University, Funcke Collection, S 496. Black-figure *lekythos* ('compromise' shape) of the Leagros Group, possibly by the Acheloos Painter (Kunisch, *Sammlung Funcke*, 84 f., no. 76). Last quarter of the sixth century. Height: 27·7 cm. Shoulder diameter: 11·4 cm.
Photograph: Museum.   Pages 13, 78, 92, 95, 123

4. 1 Athens, National Museum, 2246. *Lekythos* in Six's technique by the Chariot Painter (*ABL* 203, no. 1). Last quarter of the sixth century. Height: 21·8 cm.
Photograph: from *ABL*, pl. 19. 4.   Pages 116, 118

4. 2 Vienna, Kunsthistorisches Museum, 753. Black-figure *lekythos* ('compromise' shape) near the Rycroft Painter (*ABL* 55, 61). Last quarter of the sixth century. Height: 28·2 cm. Shoulder diameter: 13·8 cm.
Photograph: Photo Meyer, Vienna.   Page 21

4. 3 Berlin (West), Staatliche Museen, 3261. Black-figure *lekythos* by the Cactus Painter (*ABL* 198, no. 2). Last quarter of the sixth century. Height: 27 cm.
Photograph: Museum.   Pages 8, 21, 96

4. 4 Oxford, Ashmolean Museum, V.512 (1895.75). Black-figure *lekythos* (white-ground) by the Cactus Painter (*ABL* 198, no. 4). Last quarter of the sixth century. Height: 23·3 cm. Shoulder diameter: 8·55 cm.
Photograph: Museum.   Pages 8, 21, 97

5. 1 Oxford, Ashmolean Museum, 1949.751. Red-figure *lekythos* by the Painter of Oxford 1949 (*ARV* 9, no. 1). Last quarter of the sixth century. Height (as preserved): 17·2 cm. Shoulder diameter: 7·65 cm. Photograph: Museum.   Pages 10, 13

5. 2 Athens, Agora Museum, P 24061. Fragmentary red-figure *lekythos* by the Roundabout Painter (*ARV* 131). Late sixth to early fifth century. Height (as preserved): 13·8 cm. Shoulder diameter: 8·1 cm. Photograph: Agora Excavations, American School of Classical Studies, Athens.   Pages 13, 78 n. 2

6. 1 Boston, Museum of Fine Arts, 13.195. Red-figure *lekythos* by Gales (*ARV* 35, no. 1). Last quarter of the sixth century. From Gela. Height: 31 cm. Shoulder diameter: 11·5 cm. Photograph: Museum.   Pages 13, 78 n. 2, 79, 95

6. 2 Agrigento, Museo Civico, 23. Red-figure *lekythos* probably by the Terpaulos Painter (*ARV* 308, no. 5). Early fifth century, from Agrigento. Height: 22 cm. Photograph: from *ABL* pl. 21*c*.   Pages 80, 81

6. 3 London, British Museum, 1922.10–18.1. Red-figure *lekythos* by the Oinophile Painter (*ARV* 332, no. 1). Early fifth century. From Sicily. Height: 20·4 cm. Photograph: Museum.   Pages 79, 81, 147

6. 4 Columbia (Missouri), University Museum of Art and Archaeology, 58.12. *Lekythos* in Six's technique (shape DL) by the Diosphos Painter (Haspels, *Muse* iii (1969), 24 ff.). Late sixth to early fifth centuries. Height: 19·6 cm. Photograph: Museum.   Pages 116, 119

7. 1 London, British Museum, B 188. Black-figure neck-amphora (doubleen) by the Edinburgh Painter (*ABL* 219, no. 64). Late sixth to early fifth centuries. Height: 27·9 cm. Photograph: Museum.   Pages 14, 98

7. 2 Swiss Private Collection. Black-figure *lekythos* by the Edinburgh Painter (*Para* 217). Early fifth century. Height: 30 cm. Shoulder diameter: 12 cm.   Pages 13, 98, 120 f. n. 11

7. 3 Greenwich (Connecticut), Bareiss Collection, 15. Red-figure neck-amphora (doubleen) by the Berlin Painter (*ARV* 200, no. 51, and page 1700; *Para* 342). Early fifth century. Height: 30·5 cm. Photograph: Widmer, Basel.   Page 14

7. 4 Basle, Cahn Collection. Red-figure *lekythos* by the Berlin Painter (*ARV* 211, no. 201 *bis*, and *Para* 345). Early fifth century. Height: 20 cm. Photograph: Widmer, Basel.   Page 14

8. 1 Berlin (East), Staatliche Museen, 2252. White *lekythos* (glaze outline) by the Syriskos Painter (*ARV* 263, no. 54, and p. 1641). Early fifth century. From Athens. Height: 18 cm. Photograph: Museum.   Pages 31, 127 f.

8. 2 Bologna, Museo Civico Archeologico, PU 321. Red-figure *lekythos* by Douris (*ARV* 446, no. 267). Early fifth century. Height: 31·8 cm. Shoulder diameter: 11·5 cm. Photograph: Fotofast, Bologna.   Pages 25, 27, 31, 125 n. 1, 126, 127 n. 12

9. 1 Berlin (East), Staatliche Museen, 3168 (detail). Red-figure *kylix* (exterior, side A) by Douris (*ARV* 428, no. 13). Early fifth century. Photograph: Museum.   Page 31

9. 2 Athens, National Museum, 15375. Red-figure *aryballos* (round) by Douris (*ARV* 447, no. 274). First quarter of the fifth century. From Athens. Height. 10 cm. Photograph: Museum.   Pages 30 f., 77, 78 n. 2, 132, 148

9. 3 Athens, National Museum, T.E. 556. Red-figure *aryballos* (round) by Douris (*ARV* 447, no. 273 *bis*, and *Para* 376). Around 500. From Athens.

Photograph: from *Kernos* (1972), pl. 54, no. 1.

Drawing: from *Kernos*, pl. 54, no. 3 (Marion Cox).   Pages 32, 77

9. 4 London, British Museum, E 768 (detail). Red-figure *psykter* (floral pattern at the join of bowl to foot) by Douris (*ARV* 446, no. 262). First quarter of the fifth century. From Cerveteri. Height: 28·58 cm.

Photograph: Museum.   Page 31

10. 1 Palermo, Museo Nazionale, N.I. 1886. White *lekythos* (glaze outline) by Douris (*ARV* 446, no. 266). First quarter of the fifth century. From Selinus. Height: 32·9 cm. Shoulder diameter: 11·7 cm. (The mouth, neck, part of the shoulder, and foot are restored.)

Photograph: Museum.   Pages 29 f., 140

10. 2; Cleveland, Museum of Art, 66.114 (Leonard C. Hanna Jr. Bequest). White *lekythos* (glaze outline)
11   by Douris (*ARV* 446, no. 266 *bis*, and *Para* 376). First quarter of the fifth century. Height: 31·7 cm. Shoulder diameter: 13 cm.

Photograph: Museum.   Pages 27, 29 ff., 78 n. 2, 128

12. 1 Boston, Museum of Fine Arts, 95.41. Red-figure *lekythos* (standard shape) by Douris (*ARV* 447, no. 270). First quarter of the fifth century. From Athens. Height: 30·2 cm. Shoulder diameter: 10 cm.

Photograph: Museum.   Pages 16, 25, 30, 31, 79

12. 2 London, British Museum, E 573. Red-figure *lekythos* (standard shape) from the Bowdoin Workshop (*ARV* 694; *ABL* 262, no. 1). First quarter of the fifth century. Height: 29·23 cm.

Photograph: Museum.   Pages 15, 22, 24, 79, 121

12. 3 Bochum, Ruhr University, Funcke Collection, S 502. Black-bodied *lekythos* (standard shape; red-figure shoulder) from the Bowdoin Workshop (Kunisch, *Sammlung Funcke*, 108, no. 92). First quarter of the fifth century. Height: 29 cm. Shoulder diameter: 10 cm.

Photograph: Museum.   Pages 16, 23, 79, 121

12. 4 London, British Museum, 63.7–28.45.1 (detail). Black-bodied *lekythos* (standard shape; red-figure shoulder) from the Bowdoin Workshop (*ABL* 262, no. 4; *ABV* 524). First quarter of the fifth century. Height: 32 cm. Shoulder diameter: 11 cm.

Photograph: Museum.   Pages 16, 22, 79, 121

13. 1 Paris, Peyrefitte Collection. Black-figure *lekythos* (standard shape; red-figure shoulder) from the Bowdoin Workshop (*ABV* 524; *Para* 262). First quarter of the fifth century.   Pages 22, 24, 79, 121

13. 2 Palermo, Museo Nazionale, 2792. Black-figure *lekythos* (standard shape; red-figure shoulder) from the Bowdoin Workshop (*ABL* 262, no. 2; *ABV* 524). First quarter of the fifth century. Height: 31 cm. Shoulder diameter: 10·5 cm.

Photograph: Museum.   Pages 16, 22, 24, 79, 121

14. 1 New York, Metropolitan Museum of Art, 41.162.146 (Rogers Fund, 1941). Black-figure *lekythos* (white ground, near shape BL) by the Athena Painter. First quarter of the fifth century. (*ABV* 522; *ABL* 257, no. 72). Height: 23·4 cm. Shoulder diameter: 8·8 cm.

Photograph: Museum.   Pages 107, 121

14. 2 Athens, National Museum, 1973. Semi-outline *lekythos* (shape BL) from the Bowdoin Workshop (*ARV* 690, no. 9). First quarter of the fifth century. From Eretria. Height: 29 cm.

Photograph: Museum, and Ioannidou and Bartsioti, Athens.   Pages 17, 41, 121

14. 3 London, Embiricos Collection. Semi-outline *lekythos* (shape BL) from the Bowdoin Workshop (*Auktion* xl, no. 82). First quarter of the fifth century. Height: 28 cm.
Photograph: Widmer, Balse.   Page 107

14. 4 New York, Metropolitan Museum of Art, 08.258.28 (Rogers Fund, 1908). Semi-outline *lekythos* (shape BL) from the Bowdoin Workshop (*ARV* 690, no. 7). Height: 23·7 cm. Shoulder diameter: 8·3 cm.
Photograph: Museum.   Pages 26, 107

14. 5 Bonn, Akademisches Kunstmuseum, 538. Semi-outline *lekythos* (shape BL) from the Bowdoin Workshop (*ARV* 690, no. 12). First quarter of the fifth century. Height: 20·2 cm. Shoulder diameter: 7 cm.
Photograph: Museum, and Professor E. Kukahn.   Pages 105 n. 15, 107

14. 6 Lucerne Market (A.A.). Red-figure *lekythos* (shape BL) from the Bowdoin Workshop (*ARV* 683, no. 127 *ter*). First to second quarters of the fifth century. Height: 18 cm.

15. 1 Brussels, Musées Royaux d'Art et d'Histoire, A 3131. Red-figure *lekythos* (shape BL; silhouette shoulder) by the Bowdoin Painter (*ARV* 682, no. 107). First quarter of the fifth century. Height: 19 cm. Shoulder diameter: 6·3 cm.
Photograph: Museum.   Pages 16, 106, 122

15. 2 Brussels, Musées Royaux d'Art et d'Histoire, A 3132. Red-figure *lekythos* (shape BL; silhouette shoulder) by the Bowdoin Painter (*ARV* 681, no. 91). First quarter of the fifth century. Height: 20 cm. Shoulder diameter: 6·8 cm.
Photograph: Museum.   Pages 16, 106, 122

16. 1 Würzburg, Martin von Wagner-Museum, H 4978. White *lekythos* (shape BL; glaze outlines) by the Bowdoin Painter (*ARV* 686, no. 204). First to second quarters of the fifth century. Height: 18·5 cm. Shoulder diameter: 6·3 cm.
Photograph: Museum.   Pages 106 f., 107 f.

16. 2 Athens, National Museum, 1792. White *lekythos* (glaze outline and silhouette; shape BL) by the Bowdoin Painter (*ARV* 686, no. 207). First to second quarters of the fifth century. From Pikrodaphne. Height: 26 cm. Shoulder diameter: 8·1 cm.
Photograph: Museum.

16. 3 Erlangen, Kunstsammlung der Universität, I. 275. White *lekythos* (glaze outline; shape BL) by the Bowdoin Painter (*ARV* 685, no. 183). Second quarter of the fifth century. Height: 26·5 cm. Shoulder diameter: 8·9 cm.
Photograph: Museum.

16. 4 Syracuse, Museo Nazionale, 19854. Black-figure *lekythos* (white ground; standard shape, early) by the Gela Painter (*ABL* 212, no. 151). First quarter of the fifth century. Height: 32 cm.
Photograph: Museum.   Pages 10, 18, 21, 92, 97, 123, 148 n. 10, 149, 151

17. 1 Göttingen, Archäologisches Institut der Universität, ZV 1964/139. Black-figure *lekythos* (white ground; cylinder shape) by the Gela Painter (*Para* 215). First quarter of the fifth century. Height: 30·6 cm. Shoulder diameter: 11·8 cm.
Photograph: Widmer, Balse.   Pages 21 f., 85 n. 4

17. 2 Boston, Museum of Fine Arts, 99.526. Black-figure *lekythos* (standard shape, early) by the Gela Painter (*ABL* 209, no. 81). First quarter of the fifth century. From Gela. Height: 24·6 cm. Shoulder diameter: 9·4 cm.
Photograph: Museum.   Pages 18, 92 FIGURE 25c

17. 3 Vienna, Kunsthistorisches Museum, 84. Black-figure *lekythos* (white-ground; standard shape) by the Gela Painter (*ABL* 212, no. 158). First quarter of the fifth century. Height: 30·3 cm. Shoulder diameter: 9·5 cm.

Photograph: Photo Meyer, Vienna.   Pages 18, 92, 97, 109, 148 n. 10, 149

17. 4 New York, Metropolitan Museum of Art, 41.162.13. Black-figure *lekythos* (standard shape) by the Haimon Painter (*ABL* 241, no. 1; *ABV* 538). First quarter of the fifth century. Height: 34·6 cm. Shoulder diameter: 11·1 cm.

Photograph: Museum.   Pages 20, 22, 151

18. 1 Athens, National Museum, 12801. Semi-outline *lekythos* (shape BEL) by the Beldam Painter (*ABL* 266, no. 2). First to second quarters of the fifth century. From Eretria. Height: 20·3 cm.

Photograph: Museum, and Ioannidou and Bartsioti, Athens.   Pages 9, 19, 79, 84 ff.   FIGURE 10*b*

One of the earliest white *lekythoi* with the 'visit to the tomb'—the most common funerary scene on Athenian vases of this type during the fifth century B.C. The Beldam Painter, who worked in a variety of techniques, has combined black-figure (the women) and outline (the tomb) in a transitional technique known as semi-outline (see p. 98 n. 7).

The woman on the left brings a basket of offerings and a circlet of flowers to a broad monument draped with ribbons. The tomb rests on a platform on which there is a series of small black circles at regular intervals (see notes on PLATE 19. 3); it is crowned by a pediment with a palmette *anthemion* framed by two small black owls. The woman on the right of the tomb (not shown) seems to carry similar offerings. She is largely effaced.

18. 2 Athens, National Museum, 1982. White *lekythos* (glaze outline; shape BEL) by the Beldam Painter (*ABL* 267, no. 12). Second quarter of the fifth century (early). From Eretria. Height: 35 cm.

Photograph: Museum, and Ioannidou and Bartsioti, Athens.   Pages 9, 19, 38 n. 4, 79, 84, 86. FIGURE 10*c*

A technically more advanced work by the Beldam Painter (black-figure has been replaced by outline) with all of the essential elements of the 'visit to the tomb', as it is known from classical white *lekythoi*.

The woman on the left holds a basket of offerings in one hand (the mouth, neck, and handle of a black *lekythos* are clearly visible), an *alabastron* in the other. Her companion (not shown) holds a wreath and a *plemochoe*. Next to the tomb—a *stele* bound with ribbons and crowned with a palmette *anthemion*— stands a stool supporting a basket of offerings, like that held by the woman on the left. Above the basket hangs a lyre. A broken *lekythos* lies at the base of the *stele* (mouth, neck, shoulder, and handle are visible to the left of the monument's base). The broken *lekythos* is a realistic detail added by a painter who was deeply concerned about the funerary use of *lekythoi* (see p. 38 n. 4).

18. 3 London, British Museum, D 65. White *lekythos* (glaze outline; shape BEL) from the Group of London D 65 (*ARV* 752, no. 2). Second quarter of the fifth century. Height: 38·7 cm.

Photograph: Museum.   Pages 19, 86   FIGURE 11*a*

The Group of London D 65 betrays the influence of the Beldam Painter in shape (BEL), accessory decoration (ivy-berry tendril on the neck, palmettes on the shoulder; the ivy-berry pattern at join of shoulder to body is unusual), and iconography. Technically the vase is less competent work than Athens 1982, but iconographically it is no less interesting.

The woman on the left holds an *alabastron* and a wreath; the woman on the right (not shown) holds a ribbon over a basket placed beside the tomb, as on Athens 1892. On the steps of the *stele* stands a large white *lekythos* (care has been taken to follow the profile of shape BEL) and a small *plemochoe*.

19. 1 Madrid, Museo Arqueológico Nacional, 19497. White *lekythos* (glaze outline; secondary shape, near BEL) by the Inscription Painter (*ARV* 748, no. 1). Second quarter of the fifth century. Height: 35 cm. Shoulder diameter: 11 cm.

Photograph: Museum.   Pages 20, 45, 86, 153 f. n. 10   FIGURE 11*b*

An early vase by the Inscription Painter, who began his career in the Beldam Workshop. The shape is closer to BEL than to the painter's other white *lekythoi* and the shoulder palmettes are more like the Beldam Painter's than anyone else's; notice the groups of small black dots between the palmettes and cf. PLATE 70. 1. See also p. 153 n. 10.

The tomb—a shaft-like *stele* on a high, three-step base —bears a mock inscription of the type which has given the painter his name. For the *kantharos* placed above the *stele* see p. 37 n. 2. On either side of the tomb hang a bag and a *sakkos*. The woman on the right holds out a ribbon which she will tie around the *stele*; the woman on the left holds an object which may be a rolled ribbon. See note on PLATE 46.

19. 2 Athens, National Museum, 1790. White *lekythos* (glaze outline; standard shape) by the Inscription Painter (*ARV* 749, no. 5). Second quarter of the fifth century. From Athens. Height: 34·5 cm.
Photograph: Museum, and Ioannidou and Bartsioti, Athens.   Pages 20, 45

The woman holds a basket of offerings at a *stele* with a palmette *anthemion*. Many of the ribbons and wreaths which adorned the *stele* have faded. The youth extends his right hand in a gesture of salutation (cf. Euripides, *Helen*, 1165).

19. 3 Athens, National Museum, 1958. White *lekythos* (glaze outline; standard shape) by the Inscription Painter (*ARV* 748, no. 2). Second quarter of the fifth century. From Eretria. Height: 36·5 cm.
Photograph: Museum, and Ioannidou and Bartsioti, Athens.   Pages 20, 45

The woman on the left, overcome with grief, dries her tears and sadly presents her offering. The woman on the right brings a basket of offerings. The tomb is a *stele* with ovolo finial and palmette *anthemion* and *acroteria*, resting on a three-step base. On the shaft there is a five-line mock inscription and a draped ribbon. In the field, on either side, hang *lekythoi*.

The four circles on the lower step of the base are like those on Athens 12801 (PLATE 18. 1). The detail also occurs on another early, unattributed, white *lekythos* (Fairbanks i. 96, fig. 31) and on several later *lekythoi*. Various explanations have been offered for the circles, which are certainly not meaningless decoration (cf. Fairbanks i. 96, 207). One of the most careful painters of white *lekythoi*, the Bosanquet Painter, added them to the base of a tomb on his most carefully painted *lekythos* (Athens, 1935. *ARV* 1227, no. 1. Riezler, pl. 23), as did his almost equally precise 'follower', the Thanatos Painter (Athens, 1960. *ARV* 1228, no. 4. Riezler pl. 29). A plausible explanation for the circles is that they are the artist's conception of the circular indentations found on the horizontal face of the base of some tombstones, which held offerings and smaller, accessory monuments (stone vases) in place.

20. 1 Paris, Musée du Louvre, CA 1640. White *lekythos* (glaze outline; standard shape). Unattributed. Second quarter of the fifth century. Height: 39 cm. Shoulder diameter: 12 cm.
Photograph: Museum, and Chuzeville, Paris.

The woman presents a basket of offerings (ribbons, wreaths, and two large black *lekythoi*), the youth a ribbon, at a *stele* on a four-step base. See the following note.

20. 2 Boston, Museum of Fine Arts, 1970.428. White *lekythos* (glaze outline and second white; standard shape). Unattributed. Second quarter of the fifth century. Height: 37 cm. Shoulder diameter: 11·5 cm.
Photograph: Widmer, Basel.   Pages 85 f. n. 15

The woman holds an offering basket like that on the preceding vase (partly shown) at a tomb rendered in second white—a *stele* on a high base. The shaft of the monument, on which two palmette *anthemia* have been painted, projects into the shoulder field. (The *stele* on the preceding vase projects through the upper pattern band.) This detail is found on a small number of *lekythoi* and is especially popular with the Painter of Athens 1826, who is related to the Inscription Painter in his early period. (See notes on PLATES 26. 1, 39. 2.) If the Paris and Boston *lekythoi* are not by the same hand, they are contemporary and closely related in shape, pattern, technique, and style.

20.3   Athens, National Museum, 1975. White *lekythos* (glaze outline; shape BL). Unattributed. From Eretria. Height: 31 cm.

Photograph: Museum, and Ioannidou and Bartsioti, Athens.   Page 15

A woman holds an offering basket to the right of a *loutrophoros* (only traces of the distinctive long neck and handles remain).

The *loutrophoros* was a special vase which Athenians used in rites of marriage and death (Kurtz and Boardman, 151 ff.) Like *lekythoi*, *loutrophoroi* were produced in stone and metal as well as clay, and they were frequently set up in cemeteries. The clay funerary *loutrophoros* very often has a funerary iconography (cf. PLATE 45), and one of the most common subsidiary scenes on black- and red-figure *loutrophoroi* is the procession of horsemen, filing past with their right hands extended in a gesture of valediction (cf. Arias, Hirmer, Shefton, pl. 126 and p. 331).

20.4   London, British Museum, D 33. White *lekythos* (glaze outline and second white; standard shape). Second quarter of the fifth century. Unattributed. From Eretria. Height: 30·1 cm.

Photograph: Museum.   Pages 15, 39

A damaged and repainted *lekythos* illustrated for the pose of the woman, sitting with her back to the tomb (cf. Athens, 1959. *ARV* 748, no. 3. Inscription Painter. Riezler, pl. 16). Modern inscriptions tell us that she is Elektra and that the youth standing before her is Orestes. That is an interesting 'addition', for the children of Agamemnon assume similar poses at his grave—on vases and on the 'Melian' plaques (see Jacobsthal, *Die melischen Reliefs*, 11 ff., 192 ff.)

21.1   London, British Museum, 1914.5–12.1. White *lekythos* (glaze outline; shape ATL, refined) by the Painter of Munich 2774 (*ARV* 283, no. 1). Second quarter of the fifth century. Height: 26·5 cm. Shoulder diameter: 9 cm.

Photograph: Museum.   Pages 9, 82

A representative example of the refined version of shape ATL, possibly the Flying Angel Painter, working in white ground. See p. 140 f. n. 15.

21.2   Basel Market (M.M.). White *lekythos* (glaze outline; shape ATL, refined) by the Aischines Painter (*ARV* 715, no. 189 *bis*, and *Para* 409). Second quarter of the fifth century. Height: 27 cm.

Photograph: Widmer, Basel.   Pages 9, 82

An exceptionally careful version of shape ATL by the Aischines Painter. The Aischines and Tymbos Painters were the principal painters of *lekythoi* of this shape.

21.3   Athens, National Museum, 2025. White *lekythos* (glaze outline; shape ATL) from the Group of Athens 2025 (*ARV* 722, no. 1). Second quarter of the fifth century. Height 23 cm.

Photograph: Museum, and Ioannidou and Bartsioti, Athens.   Page 82

See note on the following.

21.4   Athens, National Museum, 1875. White *lekythos* (glaze outline; shape ATL) from the Group of Athens 2025 (*ARV* 722, no. 2). Second quarter of the fifth century.

Photograph: Museum, and Ioannidou and Bartsioti, Athens.   Page 82

Representative examples of the more common shape ATL, at its best. Note the rays on the shoulders of these two *lekythoi* and the palmettes on the two preceding. Both *lekythoi* belong to the Group of Athens 2025 which stands between the Aischines and Tymbos Painters. The iconography of the Group is largely non-funerary.

The woman on Athens 1875 is going to place a ribbon on the *tymbos* (mound) or *stele* (with triangular pediment). The semicircular objects beneath the mound do not look like the circles on Athens 12801 (PLATE 18. 1) and Athens 1958 (PLATE 19. 3), nor are they part of the *stele*'s base. The few descriptions which we have of *tymboi* sometimes mention encircling bases of stones or tiles which helped the earth mound retain its shape (cf. Pausanias, 2.29.2; 6.21.3; 8.4.9; 8.11.14; 8.16.3).

Notice the empty pattern band beneath the figure scene.

22. 1 Paris, Musée du Louvre, MNB 3059. White *lekythos* (glaze outline; shape ATL) by the Tymbos Painter (*ARV* 754, no. 14). Second quarter of the fifth century. Height: 22·2 cm. Shoulder diameter: 7·5 cm. Photograph: Museum, and Chuzeville, Paris. Page 83 n. 4

Tombstones on white *lekythoi* rarely have figure decoration, and this is what we should have expected, for during most of the fifth century fine monuments with figures cut in relief seem to have been officially discouraged, if not legally banned.

A woman with a wreath approaches a grave-relief.

22. 2 Oxford, Ashmolean Museum, 1956.14. White *lekythos* (glaze outline; shape ATL) by the Tymbos Painter (*ARV* 754, no. 13). Second quarter of the fifth century. Height: 18·9 cm. Shoulder diameter: 6·25 cm.

Photograph: Museum. Page 83 n. 4

One of the clearest examples of the conflation of two scenes on a white *lekythos* (see p. xx and n. 3). On the front of the vase the woman, seated, holding a sash, could be in the women's quarters, but the tomb (a *stele*) on the side of the vase, suggests that she is somehow connected with it. The painter has not connected his compositions structurally or iconographically.

23. 1 London, British Museum, D 35. White *lekythos* (glaze outline; shape ATL) by the Tymbos Painter (*ARV* 756, no. 66). Second quarter of the fifth century. From Athens. Height: 19·6 cm.

Photograph: Museum. Page 83 n. 4

A distinctive feature of *lekythoi* from the Tymbos Workshop, especially those by the Tymbos Painter, is the 'figure . . . on this side of the tomb (citra), giving the effect of a stele decorated with a relief' (*ARV* 754; in Beazley's lists these vases are marked by a 'C'). But the tombs are *tymboi*, not *stelai*, and the figures are not unquestionably relief decoration, as Paris MNB 3059. London D 35 differs from other 'C' *lekythoi* in the representation of a figure, prone like a corpse in a *prothesis* (cf. PLATE 29. 1–2). An unattributed *lekythos* in Tübingen (E 63. Watzinger, pl. 26), which looks as if it were produced in the Tymbos Workshop, features a shrouded figure on a bier within a similar mound 'frame'. If the Tymbos Painter is giving us his conception of the dead, lying in his grave, he is following contemporary artistic convention (compare the white-ground cup by the Sotades Painter in London with Polyidos and Glaukos in the tomb (D 5. *ARV* 763, no. 2. Robertson, *Greek Painting*, 133 f.)), not contemporary burial practice (Kurtz and Boardman, 79 f., 105 f.).

23. 2 Oxford, Ashmolean Museum, 547 (G 258). White *lekythos* (glaze outline; shape ATL) by the Tymbos Painter (*ARV* 756, no. 64). Second quarter of the fifth century. Height: 20·8 cm. Shoulder diameter: 7·6 cm.

Photograph: Museum. Pages 63, 83 n. 4

The iconography of Charon scenes on white *lekythoi* admits little variety (cf. PLATES 42. 1, 47, 50. 1). This vase and another by the Painter in Carlsruhe (B 2663. *ARV* 756, no. 63) stand apart in several details: Charon is alone, his boat is complete, and the *eidola* are substantial, recognizably human figures, not diminutive stick-men. There are reeds at the stern of the boat, as there were in Polygnotos' painting of the *Nekyia* (Underworld) at Delphi (Pausanias 10.28.1).

23. 3 Paris, Musée du Louvre, CA 3758. White *lekythos* (glaze outline; secondary shape). Unattributed. Second quarter of the fifth century. Height: 20·8 cm. Shoulder diameter: 7 cm.

Photograph: Museum, and Chuzeville, Paris. Pages 82 f.

An unusual view of a monument decked with sprays and laden with offerings: a lyre, two *alabastra*, and two *lekythoi*, lying on their sides. Notice the series of small black circles on the base of the monument, and see note on PLATE 19. 3.

24.   White *lekythoi* with red-figure shoulders by red-figure painters.

24. 1   Gela, Museo Civico. White *lekythos* (glaze outline; standard shape; red-figure shoulder) by the Brygos Painter (*ARV* 385, no. 223). First quarter of the fifth century. From Gela. Height: 38 cm.
Photograph: Heidelberg, Archaeological Institute, Photographic Archive.   Pages 26, 27, 30

24. 2   Leningrad, Museum of the Hermitage, 670. White *lekythos* (glaze outline and second white; standard shape, red-figure shoulder) by the Pan Painter (*ARV* 557, no. 121). First quarter of the fifth century. Height: 38 cm. Shoulder diameter: 7·8 cm.
Photograph: Museum.   Page 27

24. 3   Syracuse, Museo Nazionale, 19900. White *lekythos* (glaze outline; standard shape; red-figure shoulder) by the Pan Painter (*ARV* 557, 122). First to second quarters of the fifth century. Height: 35 cm.
Photograph: Museum.

25.   White *lekythoi* with red-figure shoulders by painters who specialized in this type of vase.

25. 1   Paris, Musée du Louvre, CA 1142. White *lekythos* (glaze outline; standard shape; red-figure shoulder). Unattributed. From Eretria. Second quarter of the fifth century. Height: 24·5 cm. Shoulder diameter: 8·5 cm.
Photograph: Museum, and Chuzeville, Paris.

An unattributed *lekythos* with damaged surface, closely related to the following by the Timokrates Painter.

25. 2   Athens, National Museum, 1929. White *lekythos* (glaze outline and second white; standard shape; red-figure shoulder) by the Timokrates Painter (*ARV* 743, no. 5). Second quarter of the fifth century. From Eretria. Height: 32 cm.
Photograph: Museum.   Pages 27, 45

The basket which the women are filling is like that placed next to the tomb on Athens 1982 (PLATE 18. 2), and since the offerings (ribbons, wreaths, a *lekythos*, and an *alabastron*) are essential to Athenian rites of death and burial, there can be little doubt that the women are preparing a basket for the grave. See the following.

25. 3   Madison (Wisconsin), Elvehjem Art Center, University of Wisconsin, EAC 70.2 (Edna G. Dyar Fund and Fairchild Foundation Fund). White *lekythos* (glaze outline and second white; standard shape; red-figure shoulder) near the Timokrates Painter (*Auktion* xl, no. 111). Second quarter of the fifth century. Height: 40·3 cm. Shoulder diameter: 13·1 cm.
Photograph: Widmer, Basel.   Pages 27, 45

The women have prepared their basket and are now proceeding to the cemetery.

These three vases have second white for the flesh of the women, tubular fillets (see pp. 50 f.) in addition to flat ribbons (not certainly, Paris CA 1142) and a *kalos* inscription. The inscription on the Madison vase is Glaukon, a popular *kalos* of the Providence Painter, who also painted some white *lekythoi* with red-figure shoulders and second white (see p. 42 f.).

25. 4   Athens, National Museum, 2032. White *lekythos* (glaze outline; standard shape; red-figure shoulder) probably by the Painter of Athens 1826 (*ARV* 747, no. 1). Second quarter of the fifth century. Height: 25 cm.
Photograph: Museum, and Ioannidou and Bartsioti, Athens.   Pages 27, 45

Most of the white *lekythoi* by the Painter of Athens 1826 have no funerary scenes. The significance of the inverted bird between the two women on this *lekythos* is not clear.

26. 1 London, British Museum, 1928.2–13.1. White *lekythos* (glaze outline and second white; standard shape) by the Painter of Athens 1826 (*ARV* 746, no. 4). Second quarter of the fifth century. From Gela. Height: 34 cm. Shoulder diameter: 10·4 cm.

Photograph: Museum.   Pages xxi, 28, 45, 85 f. n. 15, 141 f.   FIGURE 12*b*

The figures are as undistinguished as those on the preceding vase, and unquestionably related (note the prominence of outline and the absence of details in colour); the painter's chief interest is the tomb—a *stele* on a high base of unusual structure, 'in front of' a *tymbos* on a platform. Both are rendered in second white (which is not used for the flesh of the woman holding the ribbon).

The white *tymbos* is a realistic detail: layers of plaster were applied to the surface of earth mounds to retain their shape and offer protection from the elements (Kurtz and Boardman, 79 ff., 105 f.). The ribbons which originally hung around the monuments have faded (the terminal strings of one can be seen to the right of the *stele*'s base) as has the painted decoration of the *anthemion*. The projection of the *stele* into the shoulder field, and the adjustment of the palmettes and lotus buds to accommodate it are notable features of another *lekythos* by the painter (Athens, 1825. *ARV* 746, no. 11. Riezler, pl. 11). See also the notes on PLATE 20. 2. This vase, early in the painter's career, was found at Gela. Several of his vases have a Sicilian provenience, but none of them has funerary iconography. See p. 141.

26. 2 New York, Metropolitan Museum of Art, 35.11.5 (Alexander M. Bing Gift Fund, 1935). White *lekythos* (glaze outline and second white; standard shape) by the Vouni Painter (*ARV* 744, no. 1). Second quarter of the fifth century. Height: 42·2 cm. Shoulder diameter: 12·9 cm.

Photograph: Museum.   Pages xxi, 27, 29, 45, 86 and n. 9, 142   FIGURE 12*a*

Like the preceding vase this one features *stelai* projecting into a shoulder decorated with palmettes and lotus buds. Technically it is superior and iconographically more interesting, thanks to the wealth of detail which the Vouni Painter has added. The mound and *stelai* are covered with wreaths and ribbons; the woman and youth bring more. Two *stelai* are represented, not one (cf. Athens, 2026. *ARV* 761, no. 9. Tymbos Workshop; Athens, 19354, *ARV* 1168, no. 131 *bis*. Painter of Munich 2335); standing on a dark, apparently communal, base (for 'family plots' see, Kurtz and Boardman, 106 ff.) on which offerings, in added colour, hang suspended: a wreath, a pair of *halteres*, and an *aryballos*.

27. 1 Boston, Museum of Fine Arts, 13.169. Red-figure *askos*. Unattributed. Second quarter of the fifth century.

Beazley described the unusual scene on this red-figure *askos*: 'a bearded hero with spear and shield rising out of a large mound: attached to the mound, and leaning against it, a diskos, a pair of halteres, two fillets, and three akontia . . .' (*VA* 55). The disposition of the offerings is like that on the Vouni Painter's *lekythos*.   Page 29

27. 2 Oxford, Ashmolean Museum, 1966.854. Fragment of a red-figure *pelike*. Unattributed. Second quarter of the fifth century. Dimensions: 11·4 cm × 7·5 cm.

Photograph: Museum.   Page 29

A fragment of a red-figure *pelike* with a similar disposition of objects on a mound, to which someone has come to pay homage.

27. 3 London, British Museum, D 47 (detail). White *lekythos* (glaze outline; standard shape). Unattributed. Second quarter of the fifth century. From Gela. Height: 45·4 cm.

Photograph: Museum.   Page 29

The shoulder decoration looks like an adaptation of the red-figure florals on a white ground.

27. 4–6 These vases have been chosen for variety in shoulder decoration, not iconography.

27. 4 New York, Metropolitan Museum of Art, 06.1021.134. White *lekythos* (glaze outline; standard shape) near the Villa Giulia Painter (*ARV* 626, no. 2). Second quarter of the fifth century. Height: 37·5 cm. Shoulder diameter: 11·7 cm.

Photograph: Museum.   Page 28   FIGURE 13*b*

27. 5 New York, Metropolitan Museum of Art, 57.12.24 (Gift of Ernest Brummer, 1957). White *lekythos* (glaze outline standard shape). Unattributed. Second quarter of the fifth century. Height: 29·2 cm. Shoulder diameter: 10·3 cm.

Photograph: Museum.   Page 29   FIGURE 13*c*

27. 6 Zürich, Roš Collection, Red-figure *lekythos* (standard shape) by the Dresden Painter (*ARV* 656, no. 15). Second quarter of the fifth century. Height: 28 cm.

Photograph: Widmer, Basel.   Pages 85 n. 4, 95

The florals on the neck and beneath the handles are exceptional. See p. 95.

28. 1 Honolulu, Academy of Arts, 2892 (gift of Mrs. Charles M. Cooke, 1930) by the Sabouroff Painter (*ARV* 844, no. 153). Second quarter of the fifth century. Height: 15·9 cm. shoulder diameter: 5·7 cm.

Photograph: Museum.   Pages 34, 81, 96

The Sabouroff Painter rarely used the 'mistress and maid' theme (the wreath held by the seated woman has faded). He painted many more white *lekythoi* than red-figure, and all of these are standard shape. This secondary *lekythos* of shape PL is early in his career. The handle florals are remarkable. See p. 96.

28. 2 Berlin (West), Staatliche Museen, inv. 3262. White *lekythos* (glaze outline; standard shape) by the Sabouroff Painter (*ARV* 845, no. 168, and p. 1672). Second quarter of the fifth century. Height: 29 cm. Shoulder diameter: 9·7 cm.

Photograph: Museum.   Pages 35, 36, 39

A small number of the Sabouroff Painter's white *lekythoi* stand apart in shoulder decoration (palmettes and lotus buds. See p. 35), and in attention to the offerings placed at the tomb (neat rows of carefully drawn vases). The low monument supports a lyre and a chest; three *lekythoi*, an *oinochoe*, and a *plemochoe* stand on the top step. The youth is presenting a wreath (not visible in the photograph). The woman's pose and dress find parallels in the work of the Bosanquet Painter (cf. PLATE 30).

28. 3 Athens, National Museum, 16422. White *lekythos* (glaze outline; standard shape). Unattributed. Second quarter of the fifth century. Height: 30·2 cm. Shoulder diameter: 9·7 cm.

Photograph: Museum.   Pages 35 n. 10, 51, 61 n. 18   FIGURE 16*c*

This *lekythos*, and another, also attributed, in Madrid, have shoulder florals like those of Berlin 3262. The tomb is a *stele* with an ovolo moulding. A ribbon hangs around the shaft and another, tubular fillet, around its base. The profile face of the woman who is presenting a ribbon, is not far from the Bosanquet Painter's woman on New York 23.160.38 (PLATE 30. 1).

29. 1–2 *Prothesis* scenes by the Sabouroff Painter in glaze (New York, 07.286.40) and matt (London, D 62) outlines. The *prothesis*, the formal lying in state, took place on the day after death in the home of the deceased. During the *prothesis* the women of the family performed the traditional lament in honour of the dead (Kurtz and Boardman, 143 ff.) In Athenian vase-painting the subject is known from the Geometric period (ibid. 58 ff., 148 f.). On white *lekythoi* the scene scarcely varies. Cf. Plates 44. 2, 51. 4, 54. 2.

29. 1 New York, Metropolitan Museum of Art, 07.286.40 (Rogers Fund, 1907). White *lekythos* (glaze outline; standard shape) by the Sabouroff Painter (*ARV* 846, no. 190). Second quarter of the fifth century. Height: 31·7 cm. Shoulder diameter: 9·5 cm.

Photograph: Museum.   Pages xxi, 56, 71

A heavily mantled man stands at the head of the bier—the position of greatest importance. At the foot (not shown) a woman mourns. In the centre of the bier a young girl tears her hair, which has been cut short, as a sign of mourning. Despite intense grief, her lovely face is in no way disfigured. The dead is covered with blankets and adorned with ribbons. The pillows beneath his head provide the elevation necessary to keep the jaws from gaping in an unsightly manner.

29. 2   London, British Museum, D 62. White *lekythos* (matt outline; standard shape) by the Sabouroff Painter (*ARV* 851, no. 273). Third quarter of the fifth century (early). From Eretria. Height. 33·02 cm.

Photograph: Museum.   Pages xxi, 36, 56, 71

The woman behind the bier is older; she tends the dead while making an authoritative gesture towards a youth who shows every sign of losing his manly reserve: women mourned openly, men did not. The young woman at the foot of the bier (not shown) extends her right hand to the dead (cf. Aischylos, *Choephoroi*, 9.)

29. 3   Athens, National Museum, 2021. White *lekythos* (matt outline; standard shape) by the Painter of Athens 2020 (*ARV* 854, no. 1). Third quarter of the fifth century (early). Height: 26·5 cm.

Photograph: Museum, and Ioannidou and Bartsioti, Athens.   Page 36

Beazley placed this vase in the manner of the Sabouroff Painter. Compositionally it is very like his numerous tomb scenes. The woman (partly shown) extends her left hand to her head in grief, her right to the tomb (her fingers are visible on the shaft) in respect (cf. Athens, 12133. PLATE 34. 3). The old man (his hair and beard are grey) covers his face to conceal the tears (cf. London, D 67. PLATE 32. 2; Oxford, 544. PLATE 39. 4). The *stele* is decorated with ribbons and with a sword, hanging in its scabbard. The family brings a warrior's armour to his grave so that everyone will know that he fell courageously.

29. 4   Toronto, Royal Ontario Museum, 929.22.7 (old number, 634). White *lekythos* (glaze outline; standard shape) in the manner of the Sabouroff Painter (*ARV* 855). Second to third quarter of the fifth century. Height: 32·4 cm. Shoulder diameter: 6·8 cm.

Photograph: Museum.   Pages 37, 51

Beazley also placed this vase in the manner of the Sabouroff Painter, but the shape (a full, rather broad cylinder), the matt shoulder (whose decoration has disappeared), the glaze meander pattern (the Sabouroff Painter preferred matt, except for the small group of white *lekythoi* with palmettes and lotus buds on the shoulder), and details of the figurework suggest the Bosanquet Painter's influence.

The simple *stele* and the row of vases at its base, holding garlands in place, are as close to the Bosanquet Painter's *lekythoi* in New York (PLATE 30. 1–2) as they are to the Sabouroff Painter's *lekythos* in Berlin (PLATE 28. 2); they are especially close to the Bosanquet Painter's fine *lekythos* in Athens (1935. *ARV* 1227, no. 1. Riezler, pl. 23). The woman on the left of the *stele* (partly shown) is not unlike the woman on New York 23.160.39 (PLATE 30. 1) or on the Thanatos Painter's early *lekythos* in the Baker Collection (*ARV* 1288, no. 1. *ANY*, pl. 88, no. 240). The woman with the basket of offerings has something of the beauty of the Bosanquet Painter's woman, on a fragmentary *lekythos* in London (PLATE 30. 3). Her pose is statuesque: the heavy *peplos* and the barely perceptible ponderation make us think of Pheidias' Lemnian Athena (as represented by the copy in Dresden, Lippold, pl. 51. 3) with which Beazley compared the finest of the Bosanquet Painter's women (*AWL* 17).

30. 1   New York, Metropolitan Museum of Art, 23.160.38 (Rogers Fund, 1923). White *lekythos* (glaze outline; standard shape) by the Bosanquet Painter (*ARV* 1227, no. 5). Third quarter of the fifth century (early). Height: 38·7 cm. Shoulder diameter: 12·7 cm.

Photograph: Museum.   Pages 37, 38

See note on the following.

30. 2   New York, Metropolitan Museum of Art, 23.160.39 (Rogers Fund, 1923). White *lekythos* (glaze outline;

standard shape) by the Bosanquet Painter (*ARV* 1227, no. 4). Third quarter of the fifth century (early). Height: 36·1 cm. Shoulder diameter: 11·3 cm.

Photograph: Museum.   Pages 37, 38   FIGURE 15*a*

The Bosanquet Painter's white *lekythoi* are grand; the compositions are clear and simple, and the figures follow the classical canons of Pheidias and Polykleitos. The rows of vases holding garlands and wreaths in place are highly characteristic of the painter. On New York 13.160.38 we see three cylindrical *lekythoi* (one of them overturned), and a squat *lekythos* on the top step, an overturned, partly hidden *lekythos* on the centre step, and a *kylix* and *lekythos* on the lowest step. The overturned vases, like the draped garlands, are realistic details which the Bosanquet Painter would have seen in Athenian cemeteries.

30. 3 London, British Museum, 1907.7–10.10. Fragment of a white *lekythos* (glaze outline; standard shape) by the Bosanquet Painter (*ARV* 1227, no. 10). Third quarter of the fifth century (early). Height: 13·2 cm. (max.). Width: 15·2 cm. (est.).

Photograph: Museum.   Page 39

This *lekythos*, of which a body fragment is preserved, must have been one of the Bosanquet Painter's loveliest, to judge from the aristocratic, fine-boned woman sitting in a gracefully relaxed pose (?at a tomb. Cf. London, D 33. PLATE 20. 4). She looks to a baby held by a maid (only her hands are shown). The baby wears a protective string of amulets and extends his tiny hand (cf. Berlin 2443. PLATE 35. 1). The man on the right is not shown.

31.   Two white *lekythoi* near the Thanatos Painter which differ from his attributed vases in the unusual decoration of the shoulder: palmettes and lotus buds.

31. 1 Boston, Museum of Fine Arts, 01.8080. White *lekythos* (glaze outline; standard shape) near the Thanatos Painter (*ARV* 1231). Third quarter of the fifth century (early). From Athens. Height: 31·5 cm. Shoulder diameter: 10 cm.

Photograph: Museum.   Pages 37, 39   FIGURE 16*a*

Although individual elements of the monument can be paralleled, the composite structure is probably fantastical. The diminutive Polykleitan athletes (cf. the youths on Athens, 1822. *ARV* 1229, no. 22. Fairbanks i, pl. xv; Boston, 00.359. *ARV* 1229, no. 23. PLATE 32.1) acting as *acroteria* are unlikely, at this time, to represent funerary sculpture in the round. They, like the relief in the pediment, tell us that the dead excelled in athletics. A *diskos* hangs to the left of the tomb, a lyre to the right. For the broad monument with palmette *anthemion*, cf. Boston, 00.359. The pose of the bearded man is unusual. He is perhaps paying his respect to the dead, possibly in the act of *proskynesis* (cf. Sophokles, *Elektra* 1374 f.).

31. 2 New York, Metropolitan Museum of Art, 11.212.8 (Rogers Fund, 1911). White *lekythos* (glaze outline; standard shape) near the Thanatos Painter (*ARV* 1231, no. 2). Third quarter of the fifth century (early). Height: 30·3 cm. Shoulder diameter: 9·8 cm.

Photograph: Museum.   Pages 37, 38 f.   FIGURE 16*b*

The *stele* is unadorned, except for the ovolo moulding in the centre of the shaft. Terminal strings are all that remain from the ribbons which were once tied around it. The profile of the seated woman recalls the Bosanquet Painter's woman on New York 23.160.39 (PLATE 30. 2) and the Thanatos Painter's on London D 67 (not shown in PLATE 32. 2). Her pose may be compared with that of the woman on the Bosanquet Painter's fragmentary *lekythos* in London (PLATE 30. 3).

32. 1 Boston, Museum of Fine Arts, 00.359. White *lekythos* (glaze outline; standard shape) by the Thanatos Painter (*ARV* 1229, no. 23). Third quarter of the fifth century (early). Height: 40 cm. Shoulder diameter 13·5 cm.

Photograph: Museum.   Page 39

The girl, who is carrying a *plemochoe* and an object largely faded to a broad monument with a palmette *anthemion*, is not nude; her clothes have faded. The tomb is very like that on the *lekythos* in Boston near the painter (PLATE 31. 1), but in place of sculptural decoration there is a secondary *stele* (not shown) whose relation to the primary monument is not clear. A black wreath and an overturned *lekythos* (not shown) have been placed on the base of the tomb.

The youth on the left (not shown) is a full-size version of the diminutive Polykleitan athletes surmounting the tomb on Boston 01.8080.

32. 2   London, British Museum, D 67. White *lekythos* (glaze outline; standard shape) by the Thanatos Painter (*ARV* 1228, no. 7). Third quarter of the fifth century (early). From Ampelokepoi/Athens. Height: 26·7 cm.

Photograph: Museum.   Pages 38 n. 4, 40

An old man (his head is bald) leans on his staff for support as he places his hand on his forehead in a sorrowful gesture (cf. PLATES 29. 3, 39. 4). Notice how the contours of his body are outlined beneath the cloak, which has greatly faded, and compare the 'nude' girl on Boston 00.359 (PLATE 32. 1). The woman on the left (not shown) approaches with a basket of offerings.

32. 3   London, British Museum, D 60. White *lekythos* (glaze outline; standard shape) by the Thanatos Painter (*ARV* 1230, no. 37). Third quarter of the fifth century. From Ampelokepoi. Height: 31·7 cm.

Photograph: Museum.   Page 41

The youths of Athens did not hunt hares in the cemetery, and this unusual *lekythos* is one of a small number in which two scenes have been conflated (see p. xx n. 3 and cf. PLATES 22. 2, 44. 3, 47. 1, 50. 1). The Thanatos Painter has given us his personal version of a funerary scene suitable to a dead youth who delighted in the hunt. The elements of the composition including the rocky terrain are familiar from black-figure (cf. PLATES 14. 2, 67. 4). The hound's front feet are shown, but not the youth with *lagobolon*, on the right.

There is another *lekythos* by the Thanatos Painter in Bonn (1011. *ARV* 1230, no. 38. *Jb* xxii (1907), pl. 3) with the same unusual subject.

32. 4   London, British Museum, D 58. White *lekythos* (glaze outline; standard shape) by the Thanatos Painter. (*ARV* 1228, no. 12). Third quarter of the fifth century. From Ampelokepoi. Height: 48·8 cm.

Photograph: Museum.   Page xxi

There are two Charon *lekythoi* by the Thanatos Painter (Munich 2777. *ARV* 1228, no. 11. Riezler, pl. 26 and Berlin, 3160. *ARV* 1229, no. 29. Riezler, pl. 27) and one with Thanatos and Hypnos (from which the painter takes his name).

Just as the youth did not hunt hares in Athenian cemeteries, the winged children of Night did not there enact a heroic *ekphora*. The *stele* with its helmet indicates that the dead is a warrior. He is in full panoply, and although the angle of his face is not very successfully managed, the closed eyes and tight-set lips leave us in no doubt of his mortality.

According to Hesiod (*Theogony* 763 ff.) one of the brothers was kind, the other pitiless; according to Pausanias (whose description of the brothers, as they appeared on the chest of Kypselos at Olympia, is the fullest which we have) one was fair, the other was dark (5.18.1). The youthful, clean-shaven figure, whose flesh is coloured, must be Hypnos (Sleep); the older, bearded figure, stern of countenance, must be Thanatos (Death).

The subject was treated in a similar manner by the Sabouroff Painter on a matt outline *lekythos*, also in London (D 59. *ARV* 851, no. 272. *GP* 150 f. (colour)).

33.   Three white *lekythoi* with the same subject. The first is by the Thanatos Painter, the second and third are by the Achilles Painter. The Thanatos Painter's relation to the Achilles Painter is mentioned on p. 39 f.

The similarities are obvious, but notice the significant differences:

(1) shoulder palmettes: the Thanatos Painter's are composed differently and executed partly in matt paint (see FIGURE 18);

(2) meander band: the Thanatos Painter prefers single stopt meanders to groups of meanders alternating with pattern squares;

(3) style: the Thanatos Painter's figures are fuller and fleshier; his tombs are unadorned shafts, without the characteristically Achillean tubular fillets (see p. 80) and centrally placed *plemochoe*.

33. 1 New York, Metropolitan Museum of Art, 12.229.10 (Rogers Fund, 1912). White *lekythos* (glaze outline; standard shape) by the Thanatos Painter (*ARV* 1229, no. 26). Third quarter of the fifth century. Height: 43·8 cm. Shoulder diameter: 13·06 cm.

Photograph: Museum.   Page 40   FIGURE 18*b*

33. 2 Vienna, Kunsthistorisches Museum, 3746. White *lekythos* (glaze outline; standard shape) by the Achilles Painter (*ARV* 998, no. 164). Third quarter of the fifth century. Height: 30·8 cm. Shoulder diameter: 9·3 cm.

Photograph: Photo Meyer, Vienna.   Page 40

33. 3 Amiens, Musée de Picardie, 3057.172.33. White *lekythos* (glaze outline; standard shape) by the Achilles Painter (*ARV* 1000, no. 200). Third quarter of the fifth century. Height: 37 cm. Shoulder diameter: 11·5 cm.

Photograph: Museum.   Pages 40, 47

Beazley described the Thanatos Painter's *lekythos*: ' . . . On top of the tomb there is a seat. That is not copied from actual life, for neither real seats nor carved ones were put on tombs. It is short for a statue of a seated woman.', and the Achilles Painter's *lekythos* in Vienna:

. . . On a vase by the Achilles Painter the symbol is still clearer, for beside the seat the artist has placed one of those wool baskets that are constantly seen in pictures of women spinning or winding skeins. Sculptured groups are sometimes represented on lekythoi; but they look dwarfed between the full sized human figures: to avoid this the painter has had recourse to a symbol. *AWL* 19 f.

We cannot know that stools were not placed on Athenian graves, and in view of the wide variety of objects found in this position on white *lekythoi*, it seems entirely possible that they were. The symbolic interpretation is unnecessary.

Notice the circular break on the shoulder of the Amiens *lekythos*. This marks the join of the false interior oil compartment to the body of the vase (cf. PLATE 35. 4). See p. 86.

34. 1 Boston, Museum of Fine Arts, 13.202. Red-figure *lekythos* (standard shape) in the early manner of the Achilles Painter (*ARV* 1002, no. 11). Second quarter of the fifth century. Height: 40·8 cm. Shoulder diameter: 14·5 cm.

Photograph: Museum.   Pages 46, 48

An early work in the manner of the Achilles Painter, with a *kalos* inscription in praise of Alkimachos son of Epichares, which also occurs on white *lekythoi* by the Timokrates and Vouni Painters (*ARV* 1561 f.).

34. 2 Syracuse, Museo Nazionale, 21186. Red-figure *lekythos* (standard shape) by the Achilles Painter (*ARV* 993, no. 80). Second to third quarter of the fifth century. Height: 41 cm.

Photograph: Museum.   Pages 15, 43, 44, 46, 48, 79

34. 3 Athens, National Museum, 12133. Red-figure *lekythos* (standard shape) in the manner of the Achilles Painter (*ARV* 1003, no. 20). Third quarter of the fifth century (later). From Eretria. Height 38 cm.

Photograph: Museum, and Ioannidou and Bartsioti, Athens.   Pages 15, 46, 52, 64, 79

The youth has come to the tomb—a simple *stele*—with his horse (cf. Athens 1700. PLATE 45. 1) to pay his respect to the dead. He extends his right hand to the tomb, in a gesture not unlike the woman on the *lekythos* in Athens in the manner of the Sabouroff Painter (PLATE 29. 3) (cf. Euripides, *Helen*, 1165).

This vase is a late school piece; notice especially the pattern bands, hastily painted and not character-istically Achillean.

34. 4 Brussels, Musées Royaux d'Art et d'Histoire, A 1379. Red-figure *lekythos* (standard shape) by the Achilles Painter (*ARV* 994, no. 97). Third quarter of the fifth century. Height: 38·3 cm. Shoulder diameter: 10·5 cm.

Photograph: Museum, and ACL, Brussels. Pages 15, 43, 44, 46, 86

An even slimmer, more elongated *lekythos*, by the Achilles Painter with three elegant black palmettes on the reserved shoulder. See p. 43.

There are not many tomb scenes on red-figure *lekythoi*, and the earliest are probably by the Achilles Painter and members of his circle (*JHS* xxxiv (1914), 199 and n. 18). They are not early in the painter's career.

The youth on the left side of the *stele* holds his spears, the woman on the right a ribbon. (She is a 'mantle figure' on one of his Nolan amphorae: Dresden 315. *ARV* 990, no. 38. *JHS* xxxiv. 185, fig. 5*p*.) On the Achilles Painter's use of stock figures in tomb scenes, see p. 44.

The false interior oil compartment (see p. 86) of this vase is illustrated in PLATE 35. 4.

35. 1 Berlin (West), Staatliche Museen, 2443. White *lekythos* (glaze outline and second white; standard shape) by the Achilles Painter (*ARV* 995, no. 118). Second quarter of the fifth century (late). From Pikrodaphne. Height: 36·8 cm. Shoulder diameter: 11·3 cm.

Photograph: Museum. Pages 38, 40, 44, 46, 51 FIGURE 19*a*

One of the earliest white *lekythoi* by the Achilles Painter. The shoulder has the elegant black palmettes of his red-figure *lekythoi*; the women's flesh is rendered in second white. The *kalos* inscription, in praise of Dromippos son of Dromokleides, is used by the painter only on his early white *lekythoi* (*ARV* 1576).

35. 2 London, British Museum, D 48. White *lekythos* (glaze outline; standard shape) by the Achilles Painter (*ARV* 997, no. 148). Third quarter of the fifth century. From Athens. Height: 36·2 cm.

Photograph: Museum. Pages 38, 40, 46, 51

The Achilles Painter is best known for the many scenes of 'mistress and maid', and this glaze outline *lekythos* without second white is highly characteristic. The *kalos*, in praise of Hygiainon, is a favourite of the painter in his maturity, being added to a number of 'mistress and maid' white *lekythoi* (*ARV* 1586). The maid extends her hands to receive a '*himation* rolled up' (as *ARV* 997, no. 156). Although women sometimes hold similar bundles of cloth at the tomb (cf. Athens 1799. *ARV* 1372, no. 10. Riezler, pl. 68) there is no reason to attribute a funerary significance to this scene.

35. 3 Oxford, Ashmolean Museum 1947.24. White *lekythos* (glaze outline; standard shape) by the Achilles Painter (*ARV* 1000, no. 192). Third quarter of the fifth century. Height: 43·8 cm. Shoulder diameter: 12·8 cm.

Photograph: Museum. Pages 38, 40, 46, 51, 52

A woman carrying a *plemochoe* in her left hand, a ribbon in her right, stands to the right of a *stele*, bound with ribbons and crowned by a triangular pediment with *acroteria*. Two tubular fillets lie around the base of the monument. The nude youth to the left does not stand on the ground line, but on an uneven line less than 1 cm above it. When Beazley published the vase, which was once in his possession, he spoke of a 'rocky platform' and concluded that 'the boy is probably the dead' (*JHS* lxvi (1946), 11). A boy stands on a similar 'platform' on another white *lekythos* by the painter in the Victoria and Albert Museum (*ARV* 1000, no. 191), and on a third, almost certainly by his hand, in Leningrad (ex Botkin. *ARV* 1677). The 'platform' has suggested a statue to some (cf. E. Götte, *Frauengemachbilder in der Vasenmalerei des fünften Jahrhunderts* (1957), 81), but the figures look less statuesque than many of those on roughly contemporary *lekythoi* by the Bosanquet and Thanatos Painters, and one (on the Lenin-grad *lekythos*) is copied from the youth with the bag of astragals on London D 54 (PLATE 36. 1). A more likely representation of funerary sculpture (to judge from the form of the base, its position, and coloration) is the horseman on a large, fragmentary, red-figure *loutrophoros* in Athens and Berlin (3209) recently published in *AK* xiv (1971), 74 ff., and pls. 25 ff. This equestrian monument (cf. H. von Roques de Maumont, *Antike Reiterstandbilder* (1958), 16) should be distinguished from visitors who come to the tomb with their horses, as on the red-figure *lekythos*, Athens 12133 (PLATE 34. 3) and *loutrophoros*, Athens 1700 (PLATE 45. 1).

35.4 See PLATE 34.4.

36. 1 London, British Museum, D 54. White *lekythos* (glaze outline; standard shape) by the Achilles Painter (*ARV* 1000, no. 183). Third quarter of the fifth century. From Eretria. Height: 33 cm.

Photograph: Museum.　　　　　　　　　　　　　　　　　　　　Pages 38, 40, 46, 51, 52

Tomb scenes occur on a relatively small number of the Achilles Painter's white *lekythoi* (about 20 per cent). The composition is simple: a figure on either side of a *stele*, bound with ribbons and tubular fillets (see p. 50), often with a large *plemochoe* prominently placed in the centre of its base.

The youths on this vase are joined by an *eidolon*, flying in the air to the left of the *stele*. There is an *eidolon* in a similar scene on one other *lekythos* by the painter (once Zürich, Ruesch. *ARV* 999, no. 177) —a vase which Beazley thought might be a careful copy of the Achilles Painter by the Bird Painter, or an artist of similar character (see p. 52); similar scenes are known by the Bird Painter (Marburg, University 1016. PLATE 39. 3) and an artist working in his manner (Oxford, 544. PLATE 39. 4). The presence of the *eidolon* does not always mean that the person about whom it flies is dead; several *eidola* fly about the living mourners attending the bier of a single dead person (cf. Vienna 3748. PLATE 44. 2).

36. 2 Oxford, Ashmolean Museum, 545 (1896.41). White *lekythos* (glaze outline; standard shape) by the Achilles Painter (*ARV* 998, no. 165). Third quarter of the fifth century. Height: 35·8 cm. Shoulder diameter: 11·3 cm.

Photograph: Museum.　　　　　　　　　　　　　　　　　　　　　　Pages 38, 40, 46, 51

A woman brings an *alabastron* and a *plemochoe* to a *stele* on a high, multi-step base—a rather unusual form for the Achilles Painter; the characteristic tubular fillets are lacking. The boy on the right, with his hand lowered, either holding something which has faded (a ribbon) or gesticulating, may be compared with the nude youth in PLATE 35. 3, and with the youth on the *lekythos* in the Victoria and Albert Museum, mentioned in that note.

36. 3 Athens, National Museum, 1938. White *lekythos* (matt outline; standard shape). Unattributed. From Eretria. Height: 40 cm.

Photograph: Museum, and Ioannidou and Bartsioti, Athens.　　　　　　Pages 38, 40, 46, 47

An unattributed *lekythos* illustrated here not because it is distinctively Achillean, but because its iconography is unusual and not without bearing on the fine 'Achillean' *lekythos* in PLATE 37. 1. A woman holds a basket of offerings at a tomb surmounted by a lion. Lions, cut in relief or sculpted in the round, were favoured monuments in Athenian cemeteries. As free-standing sculpture they surmounted tombs or marked the limits of family plots (Kurtz and Boardman, 135 ff.)

The luxuriant acanthus growth (at the bottom of the tomb on this vase) is common on white *lekythoi* from the time of the Woman Painter onwards (cf. Athens 1956. PLATE 44. 1) to whom the artist of this *lekythos* is not unrelated. (For the relation between the Woman Painter and later members of the Achilles Painter's circle see p. 57.) Athenians placed acanthus plants, living or cut in stone (for a more lasting memorial), around and on top of their tombs.

37. 1 Berne, Jucker Collection. White *lekythos* (glaze and matt outlines; standard shape; red-figure shoulder). Achilles Painter (Jucker). Second quarter of the fifth century (late). Height: 42·5 cm.

See note on the following.　　　　　　　　　　　　　　　　　　　Pages 46 ff., 142

37. 2 Toledo (Ohio), Museum of Art, 69.369. Red-figure *lekythos* (standard shape) by the Providence Painter

(*Auktion* xl, no. 98). Second quarter of the fifth century (later). Height: 40·5 cm. Shoulder diameter: 13·95 cm.

Photograph: Widmer, Basel.   Page 47

The story of Akrisios, king of Argos, his daughter Danae, and her son Perseus (fathered by Zeus), is told by Apollodorus (2.2–4) and by Pausanias (2.16.2; 2.25.7). The red-figure *lekythos*, by an artist of the Berlin Painter's following, probably the Providence Painter, shows us a familiar part of the story: Akrisios supervising the preparation of the chest in which Danae and Perseus are to be put adrift. The story behind the white *lekythos*, also by an artist working in the Berlin Painter's following, but probably not the Achilles Painter (see p. 48), is not included in the accounts of Apollodoros and Pausanias. Akrisios sits on the steps of a tomb, which he has presumably had built for Perseus and Danae. Perseus' name is clearly visible on the second step; what is not visible is the lion (in matt outlines) which surmounts the tomb. Cf. Athens 1938. PLATE 36. 3.

38. 1 Athens, National Museum, 1940. White *lekythos* (matt outline; standard shape) in the manner of the Achilles Painter (*ARV* 1004, no. 41). Third quarter of the fifth century. From Eretria. Height: 37·6 cm. Shoulder diameter: 11 cm.

Photograph: Museum.   Pages xx, 50   FIGURE 22a

Beazley placed the vase in the manner of the Achilles Painter, suggesting that it might be by the painter himself (*ARV* 1004). Shape, patterns, and figures are Achillean, but the iconography is without parallel in the painter's work.

Hermes *psychopompos* is not very common on white *lekythoi*, and when he does appear, it is in the company of Charon (as, Athens 1926. *ARV* 846, no. 193. Riezler, pl. 44) or of Thanatos and Hypnos (as Athens, 12783. *ARV* 1237, no. 11. *TWL* 24).

Hermes confronts a woman at the grave on another attributed white *lekythos*, by the Achilles Painter's pupil, the Phiale Painter (Munich 2797. *ARV* 1022, no. 138. Arias, Hirmer, Shefton, pls. xli–xlii). The addition of the tomb serves the same iconographical purpose here that it does on the Thanatos–Hypnos *lekythos* by the Thanatos Painter (another Achillean artist) on London D 58 (PLATE 32. 4).

38. 2 Munich, Museum antiker Kleinkunst, 2798. White *lekythos* (matt outline; standard shape) by the Phiale Painter (*ARV* 1022, no 139). Third quarter of the fifth century. From Oropos. Height: 37 cm.
Photograph: Museum.   Pages 48, 49, 137

This *lekythos*, by the Phiale Painter, and the Hermes *lekythos* mentioned in the preceding note, were found in a single grave at Oropos in northern Attica (see p. 137). Both stand apart from the mass of contemporary white *lekythoi* in technique (matt paint applied with the lightness and freedom of a charcoal sketch; Munich 2797 combines glaze and matt paint for maximum colouristic effect) and iconography.

The ribbon-bearing woman is a stock figure (cf. Berlin 2450. *ARV* 1023, no. 141. Riezler, pl. 48; Athens 1943. PLATE 38. 3), but the woman seated in a rocky landscape, who rests her head on her hand, is new: she reminds us of figures whom Polygnotos painted in his *Nekyia* (Underworld) at Delphi (cf. Robertson, *Greek Painting*, 149). She is deeply absorbed in her own thoughts. To Achillean calm the Phiale Painter has added emotion (cf. Athens 19355. *ARV* 1022, no. 139 *bis*. *AJA* lxi (1957), pl. 98. 3).

38. 3 Athens, National Museum, 1943. White *lekythos* (glaze outline; standard shape) by the Painter of Athens 1943 (*ARV* 1082, no. 1). Third quarter of the fifth century. From Eretria. Height: 37·7 cm. Shoulder diameter: 11 cm.
Photograph: Museum.

A tighter, mannered version of the Achillean 'mistress and maid' theme by a contemporary of the Phiale Painter.

38. 4 Athens, National Museum, 1995. White *lekythos* (matt outline; standard shape). Unattributed. Third quarter of the fifth century. From Eretria. Height: 29 cm.

Photograph: Museum, and Ioannidou and Bartsioti, Athens.

Shape and pattern are Achillean; the figure style is not. The woman with short hair is clearly a mourner; her companion (now largely effaced) holds a basket for the tomb. The pose and drapery of the mourning woman find sculptural parallels in the 430s.

39. 1 New York, Metropolitan Museum of Art, 06.1075. White *lekythos* (glaze outline; standard shape). Unattributed. Third quarter of the fifth century (early). Height: 38·3 cm. Shoulder diameter: 11 cm. Photograph: Museum.   Page 51

The shoulder palmettes are Achillean, as are the tubular fillets at the base of the tomb, but the matt meander band (now greatly faded) is not, nor is the style of the figures: tall women with expressionless faces and wooden gestures. Only the hare surmounting the *stele* suggests an artist with some imagination. Given the variety of animals in Athenian funerary art, there is no reason to think such a monument did not exist.

39. 2 Athens, National Museum, 13701. White *lekythos* (glaze outline and second white; standard shape). Achillean patternwork (*ARV* 748). Second to third quarters of the fifth century.
Photograph: Museum, and Ioannidou and Bartsioti, Athens.   Page 45
Patternwork is characteristically Achillean, but the figure style and the use of second white for the tomb are not. The boy places his hands around the *stele* in a reverent gesture (cf. Athens, 12133. PLATE 34. 3; Marburg, University, 1016. PLATE 39. 3). The man has the elongated proportions of the women on New York 06.1075 (PLATE 39. 1); also of the woman on the later Athens 1943 (PLATE 38. 3), and of the man on Boston 1970.428 (PLATE 20. 2) who stands at a tomb rendered in second white. Beazley thought that Athens 13701 bore some resemblance to a white *lekythos* by the Painter of Athens 1826 (Athens 1825. *ARV* 746, no. 11. Riezler, pl. 11), and the relation between this painter and the Painter of Boston 1970. 428 is mentioned in the note on that vase.

39. 3 Marburg, University, 1016. White *lekythos* (matt outlines; standard shape) by the Bird Painter (*ARV* 1233, no. 19). Third to last quarters of the fifth century. Height: 26·8 cm. Shoulder diameter: 9 cm. Photograph: Museum.   Pages 52, 53, 55

The patternwork of this matt-outline *lekythos* by the Bird Painter, rendered in glaze, is very near the Achillean model, and the figures may be compared with those on London D 54 (PLATE 36. 1). Note the *eidola* flying about the *stelai* on both vases.

The youth who places his hand on the *stele* is probably sadly performing a gesture of respect for the dead (cf. Athens, 12133. PLATE 34. 3; Athens, 2021. PLATE 29. 3).

39. 4 Oxford, Ashmolean Museum, 544 (G. 254). White *lekythos* (matt outline; standard shape) in the manner of the Bird Painter (*ARV* 1234, no. 21). Third quarter of the fifth century (late). From Athens. Height: 28·6 cm. Shoulder diameter: 8 cm.
Photograph: Museum.   Page 52

Stylistically in the manner of the Bird Painter and iconographically comparable with the *lekythos* in Marburg (PLATE 39. 3). A boy steps up to a *stele* (not shown), apparently to tie a ribbon around it. To the right of the tomb flies an *eidolon*, performing a gesture of grief. The man, heavily mantled and leaning on his staff to the left of the *stele*, covers his face with his hand to conceal his sorrow. Cf. Athens 2021 (PLATE 29. 3).

40.   This plate and the following are designed to illustrate the development of the Bird Workshop.

40. 1 Cambridge, Fitzwilliam Museum, GR 2.1928. White *lekythos* (matt outline; standard shape) by the Painter of Cambridge 28.2 (*ARV* 855, no. 4). Third quarter of the fifth century (later). Height: 29 cm. Shoulder diameter: 9·4 cm.
Photograph: Museum.   Page 55
The name vase of the Painter of Cambridge 28·2, whose work is a 'continuation of the Sabouroff Painter's

white lekythoi, in the period of the Bird Painter and in touch with him'. (*ARV* 855). Shape and pattern are related to both painters (cf. the *lekythoi* by the Sabouroff Painter in PLATES 28, 29, and London D 66, PLATE 40. 2, by the Bird Painter). The dress of the woman standing with the chest can be paralleled in the work of the Sabouroff Painter (cf. Tübingen, E 67. *ARV* 850, no. 270. Watzinger, pl. 26), her slight proportions in the work of the Bird Painter. The seated woman is largely effaced.

40. 2 London, British Museum, D 66. White *lekythos* (matt outline; standard shape) by the Bird Painter (*ARV* 1233, no. 23). Third to last quarters of the fifth century. Height: 20·9 cm.

Photograph: Museum. Page 53 FIGURE 23*a*

A typical example of the more modest work by the Bird Painter: small figures, simply drawn, with a minimum of detail, and a contrast between outlined and matt painted areas. Matt paint is used exclusively; compare the 'Achillean' *lekythos* by the painter in Marburg (PLATE 39. 3).

The youth who is approaching the *stele* may have held a ribbon, for the ribbons which once encircled the tomb have faded, leaving only a few terminal strings on the shaft and base.

The single figure composition is unusual, but fully compatible with the Bird Painter's simple style. Notice that the *stele* is off centre.

40. 3 Athens, National Museum, 1941. White *lekythos* (matt outline; standard shape). Unattributed. Third to last quarter of the fifth century. From Eretria. Height: 32 cm.

Photograph: Museum, and Ionannidou and Bartsioti, Athens.

An unattributed *lekythos* of the wider circle of the Bird Painter, to judge from the shape, pattern, technique, and simple figure style.

The man to the left of the *stele* (not shown) may have held a ribbon, now faded, like the one which the woman is tying. (Notice the pair of black terminal strings beneath her hands.) The ribbons, which once filled the offering basket, on the steps of the tomb have also faded.

40. 4 Athens, National Museum, 1934. White *lekythos* (matt outline; standard shape) by the Painter of Athens 1934 (*ARV* 1236, no. 1). Third quarter of the fifth century (late). From Eretria. Height: 25 cm.

Photograph: Museum and Ioannidou and Bartsioti, Athens. Page 55

The name-vase of the Painter of Athens 1934, who is 'related to the Bird Painter, but nearer than he to the Painter of Munich 2335' (*ARV* 1236), as a comparison of Athens 1934 with London D 66 (PLATE 40. 2) and Athens 1933 (PLATE 41. 3) makes clear. To the left of a *stele*, once bound with many ribbons (notice the faded horizontal bands on the shaft and the pairs of vertical lines of the terminal strings), a woman stands, arranging the ribbons in her basket (her hand and part of the basket are shown). The mourning woman on the right has fallen to her knees, beating her breast with her right hand. The profile face recalls the later work of the Thanatos Painter (cf. Boston 09.70. *ARV* 1230, no. 30. Fairbanks ii, pl. v, right; Boston 94.127. *ARV* 1230, no. 40. Fairbanks ii, pl. 32. 3) who influenced both the Bird Painter and the Painter of Munich 2335 (*ARV* 1232).

41. 1 Berlin (East), Staatliche Museen, 2454. White *lekythos* (matt outline; standard shape) near the Painter of Athens 1934 (*ARV* 1236). Third to last quarter of the fifth century. From Athens. Height: 23·5 cm.

Photograph: Museum. Page 55

The figure style is nearer to that of the Bird Painter and the Painter of Munich 2335 than the pattern-work; both are executed with a tight, wiry style.

The youth on the left of the *stele* seems to be talking expressively with the woman on the right, who holds a basket and a floral spray. Her dress has almost entirely faded.

41. 2 New York, Metropolitan Museum of Art, 22.139.10 (Rogers Fund, 1922). White *lekythos* (matt outline; standard shape) in the Circle of the Bird Painter (*ARV* 1236). Third to last quarter of the fifth century. Height: 30·25 cm. Shoulder diameter: 9·3 cm.

Photograph: Museum.   Page 55

The importance of this vase lies less in the pose of the woman who has fallen to her knees in grief (cf. Athens 1934, PLATE 40. 4) at a beribboned *stele*, than in the style of the drawing. There are elements which recall the Sabouroff Painter, as well as the Bird Painter, the Painter of Munich 2335, and Athens 1934.

41. 3 Athens, National Museum, 1933. White *lekythos* (matt outline; standard shape) by the Painter of Munich 2335 (*ARV* 1168, no. 135). Third to last quarter of the fifth century. From Eretria. Height: 32 cm. Photograph: Museum, and Ioannidou and Bartsioti, Athens.

One of the simpler compositions by the Painter of Munich 2335 (cf. also New York 99.13.3. *ARV* 1169, no. 140. Fairbanks ii, pl. vi. 2) in which his close relation to the Bird Painter is clearest.

The woman, whose dress has faded, is presenting a ribbon, which has faded (notice the terminal strings above her feet) at a *stele*, most of whose ribbons have also faded. The youth on the right is somewhat effaced.

42. 1 New York, Metropolitan Museum of Art, 09.221.44 (Rogers Fund, 1909). White *lekythos* (matt outline; standard shape) by the Painter of Munich 2335 (*ARV* 1168, no. 128). Third to last quarter of the fifth century. Height: 31·8 cm. Shoulder diameter: 10·2 cm.

Photograph: Museum.   Pages xxi, 56 f.   FIGURE 23*b*

The art of the Painter of Munich 2335's white *lekythoi* is as delicate as its spirit is tender. His version of the familiar Charon theme has a special appeal, for the object of Charon's mission is a truly human child, standing on a hillock, with his favourite toy (a go-cart) in hand. He beckons to his mother, but she cannot help him; even Charon himself seems to be touched by the pathos of the child's untimely death.

42. 2 New York, Metropolitan Museum of Art, 34. 32. 2 (Gift of the Estate of Julius Sachs, 1934). White *lekythos* (matt outline; standard shape) by the Painter of Munich 2335 (*ARV* 1168, no. 131). Third to last quarter of the fifth century. Height: 39·15 cm. Shoulder diameter: 12·1 cm.

Photograph: Museum.   Page 57

Offerings of food and drink, although rarely shown on white *lekythoi*, are as much a part of Athenian funerary rites as the wreaths, ribbons, and vases (Kurtz and Boardman, 144 ff.) The importance of the proper performance of the libation is stressed in contemporary literature, and is most familiar to us from the *Choephoroi* of Aischylos. On this *lekythos* by the Painter of Munich 2335 we see a girl holding a *hydria* (by its two horizontal handles) at a *tymbos* and low broad monument with palmette *anthemion*. The features of the girl's sadly downcast face and the structure of the tomb recall the Thanatos Painter's *lekythos* in Boston (PLATE 32.1).

43. 1 London, British Museum, 1928.2–13.2. White *lekythos* (matt outline; standard shape) by the Painter of Munich 2335, in the spirit of the Woman Painter (*ARV* 1169). Third to last quarter of the fifth century. Height: 31·5 cm. Shoulder diameter: 11·8 cm.

Photograph: Museum.   Page 57

The Painter of Munich 2335 looks back to the Thanatos Painter and forward to the Woman Painter, whose spirit Beazley saw in this 'excellent work by the Painter of Munich 2335' (*ARV* 1169). The lines are faded and do not photograph well, but the woman, seated in a graceful pose with a child on her knee, can still command our attention, not only by her physical beauty, but by her meaningful gaze, received and exchanged by the helmeted warrior, who extends a hand in consolation.

The pedimented *stele*, hastily executed and not very carefully drawn, was clearly not the painter's chief interest.

43. 2 Carlsruhe, Badisches Landesmuseum, 234 (B 1528). Fragment of a white *lekythos* (matt outline; standard shape) by the Woman Painter (*ARV* 1372, no. 17). Third to last quarter of the fifth century. Height: 25 cm.

Photograph: Museum.   Page 57

The Woman Painter's figures are fuller, some are almost monumental. They wear heavy dresses, often elaborately patterned. Their gestures are grand; their spirit is grave. Compare the earlier libation scene by the Painter of Munich 2335 (PLATE 42. 2) with this fragmentary *lekythos* by the Woman Painter. The woman who steps up to the tomb (compare the pose of the warrior on Athens 14517 (PLATE 44. 3)) to make the libation, holds the *hydria* by the vertical (pouring) handle, not by its two horizontal (carrying) handles. Her companion (not shown) holds out a phiale. The tomb is a *stele* with palmette and volute *anthemion*, bound with ribbons. In the field a festooned ribbon hangs.

44. 1 Athens, National Museum, 1956. White *lekythos* (matt outline; standard shape) by the Woman Painter (*ARV* 1372, no. 3). Third to last quarter of the fifth century. From Eretria. Height: 39 cm.

Photograph: Museum. Pages 54, 57

One of the Woman Painter's most highly characteristic scenes: beautiful women at the tomb. Two of the three hold offerings; the seated woman an *alabastron*, the woman standing behind her a basket. The third woman (partly shown, on the left) performs a gesture of lament.

There is something in the pose of the seated woman that recalls the Painter of Munich 2335's *choephoros* (PLATE 42. 2). The tomb is a slender shaft (possibly columnar) with a luxuriant acanthus growth.

44. 2 Vienna, Kunsthistorisches Museum, 3748. White *lekythos* (matt outline; standard shape) by the Woman Painter (*ARV* 1372, no. 16). Third to last quarter of the fifth century. Height: 52·5 cm. Shoulder diameter: 13·5 cm.

Photograph: Photo Meyer, Vienna. Page 71 n. 8

Stately women, mourning in a grand manner, attend the bier of an elegantly dressed woman, who wears her necklace and her ear-rings to the grave: (cf. Euripides, *Alkestis* 161).

A woman with a basket of offerings in her left hand stands at the head of the bier, fanning the corpse— probably to discourage the insects, as much as to circulate the air. The woman at the foot (not shown) extends her right hand to the dead (cf. Aischylos, *Choephoroi* 9), her left to her head, to tear her hair. In the centre of the bier a woman tears her short hair in grief. Three *eidola* hover in the air, repeating the gestures of the living mourners.

44. 3 Athens, National Museum, 14517. White *lekythos* (matt outline; standard shape) in the manner of the Woman Painter (*ARV* 1374, no. 18). Last quarter of the fifth century (early).

Photograph: Museum, and Ioannidou and Bartsioti, Athens. Pages 62, 65

A fight at the tomb is known from no other attributed Attic white *lekythos* (a second *lekythos* is described in *ARV* 'Fight. Tomb' (Athens 1834. *ARV* 1388, no. 2)), but there is no record of a tomb on the vase (cf. Fairbanks, ii. 193, no. 1; Collignon and Couve, 583 (CC 1842)).

This unique vase-painting has been considered a representation of the funeral games (cf. *AM* xxxv (1910), 200 ff.) which according to Plato (*Menex.* 249 b) included athletic contests, equestrian events, and musical performances; according to Lysias (ii. 80) contests of strength, wisdom, and wealth; according to Demosthenes (60. 13), athletic and horse events. But we do not know that mock battles were staged at the grave in classical Athens (Kurtz and Boardman, 121), and since battle-scenes are not uncommon on contemporary vases, red-figure and white *lekythoi*, this unique scene may be little more than a conflation of themes for artistic emphasis. Just as the Thanatos Painter depicted a hare hunt at the grave, for one who delighted in the chase, the artist of this *lekythos*, working in the manner of the Woman Painter, may have depicted a battle at the tomb for one who fell fighting.

45. 1 (*a, b, c*) Athens, National Museum, 1700. Fragments of a red-figure *loutrophoros* by the Kleophon Painter (*ARV* 1146, no. 50). Third quarter of the fifth century. Height (as preserved): 32 cm.

Photograph: Museum, and Ioannidou and Bartsioti, Athens. Page 64

No white *lekythoi* have been attributed to the Kleophon Painter, and only one red-figure *lekythos*, whose iconography is not funerary (New York 22.139.89. *ARV* 1147, no. 67), but some of his red-figure *loutrophoroi* have unquestionably funerary iconography (*ARV* 1146, nos. 49 and 52 *bis. Para* 457) and others (*ARV* 1146, nos. 51–2, and p. 1147, nos. 55–7) scenes of battle which probably commemorate the dead. Battle *loutrophoroi* are mentioned on p. 64. On this small fragmentary *loutrophoros* men gather at the cemetery: a youth with a shield, a warrior, and an old man and a youth leading a horse. There are three tombs, *stelai*, bound with ribbons.

The old man leans on his staff, with his hand to his head in grief (cf. Athens 2021. PLATE 29. 3).

The warrior leans on his spear, in a sombre pose reminiscent of the 'Mourning Athena' (Athens, Acropolis Museum, 645. Lippold, pl. 35. 1).

45. 2 Athens, National Museum, 1985. White *lekythos* (matt outline; standard shape) by the Torch Painter (*ARV* 1246, no. 3). Third to last quarter of the fifth century. From Eretria. Height: 28 cm. See note on PLATE 45. 4.
Photograph: Museum, and Ioannidou and Bartsioti, Athens.   Pages 137 f.

45. 3 Athens, National Museum, 1979. White *lekythos* (matt outline; standard shape) by the Torch Painter (*ARV* 1246, no. 2). Third to last quarter of the fifth century. From Eretria. Height: 28 cm. See note on PLATE 45. 4.
Photograph: Museum, and Ioannidou and Bartsioti, Athens.   Pages 137 f.

45. 4 Athens, National Museum, 1970. White *lekythos* (matt outline; standard shape) by the Torch Painter (*ARV* 1246, no. 1). Third to last quarter of the fifth century. From Eretria. Height: 28 cm.
Photograph: Museum, and Ioannidou and Bartsioti, Athens.   Pages 137 f.

Three *lekythoi* from Eretria, attributed by Beazley to the Torch Painter, named after the object held by the youth on 1979. Fabric, shape, pattern, and technique differ slightly from those of most Athenian white *lekythoi*, and Beazley suggested that the three were possibly local imitations of Athenian *lekythoi* (*ARV* 1246).

All three feature a single figure at the tomb; two of the three figures are clearly tying a ribbon around the tombstone (1985 and 1970). The third (1979) carries a *diskos* in his left hand (not shown), and a 'torch' in his right.

Iconographically 1979 is unique, and like Athens 14517 (PLATE 44. 3) it has been associated with the funeral games, largely because of the 'torch' (cf. Deubner, *Attische Feste* (1936), 230 f.). But the evidence for funerary torch races in Athens is late (second-century ephebic inscription, *IG*² 1011. 9), and the torch which runners carry on other Athenian vases bears no resemblance to this object.

46. 1 London, British Museum, D 72. White *lekythos* (matt outline; standard shape) by the Painter of London D 72 (*ARV* 1375, no. 1). Last quarter of the fifth century (early). From Athens. Height: 40·6 cm.
Photograph: Museum.   Page 62

The name vase of the Painter of London D 72, who stands between the Woman Painter and the Reed Workshop. His women are elegant, if somewhat languid in pose and gesture; his tombs are broad monuments with dark pediments and *acroteria*. Ribbons tend to fill the background. The vase has suffered from time and modern restoration; its iconography is not exceptional.

46. 2 Paris, Musée du Louvre, MNB 616. White *lekythos* (matt outline; standard shape) by the Reed Painter (*ARV* 1378, no. 44). Last quarter of the fifth century. From Piraeus. Height: 33·7 cm. Shoulder diameter: 9·6 cm.
Photograph: Museum, and Chuzeville, Paris.   Page 62

The Reed Painter's tomb scenes are all very much alike: the tomb is a broad monument with dark pediment and *acroteria*; behind it there is often a second smaller monument (not shown on this *lekythos*. Cf. Athens, Kerameikos. PLATE 51. 2); ribbons hang festooned in the air; the figures (usually two; one seated and one standing) hold offerings or nothing at all.

This vase has been selected to represent the painter's tomb scenes because it is also an exceptionally good example of an iconographical detail peculiar to him: the rolled ribbon which the seated woman holds behind her head. See p. 62. Rolled ribbons are represented in vase-paintings (cf. Exeter, red-figure *pelike*, *GPP*, pl. 50. The rolled ribbon lies on the steps of the tomb) and in sculpture. See below.

46. 3 Athens, Kerameikos Museum, P 1169. Marble grave-relief of Eupheros (detail) from a grave on the Sacred Way, in the Kerameikos. Dimensions of the complete relief: 1·47×0·75 m.

Photograph: Deutsches Archäologisches Institut, Athens. Pages 50, 62

The upper portion of the marble grave-relief of Eupheros, found during recent excavations in the Kerameikos (*AM* lxxix (1964), 101 f.). On the shaft (not shown) Eupheros is represented, full figure, in low relief. The pedimental decoration is painted: a panther and a lion, framed by snakes, confront each other in the pediment; above, several rolls of ribbons are rendered in perspective; the black terminal strings are clearly shown.

46. 4 Private Collection. Cornelian scaraboid gem (14×11 mm). Mid fifth century. The pigeon carries a rolled ribbon by its terminal strings (cf. Beazley, *The Lewes House Collection of Ancient Gems* (1920), pl. 5, no. 81, which is a near replica). Boardman, *Intaglios and Rings* (1975), no. 40.

47. 1 Hamburg, Museum für Kunst und Gewerbe, 1917.817. White *lekythos* (matt outline; standard shape) by the Reed Painter (*ARV* 1381, no. 111). Last quarter of the fifth century. Height: 42 cm. Shoulder diameter: 11·3 cm.

Photograph: Museum. Pages 60, 62, 63

The great majority of the Reed Painter's *lekythoi* have tomb scenes; of the rest Charon scenes are most numerous. On this vase the painter has conflated the two. Between them he has placed the reeds, from which he takes his name. (To the right of the reeds the stern of Charon's boat is visible.)

47. 2 Basle Market (M.M.). White *lekythos* (matt outline; standard shape) by the Reed Painter (*ARV* 1377, no. 15 *bis*, and p. 1692, and *Para* 285). Last quarter of the fifth century. Height: 23·9 cm.

Photograph: Widmer, Basel. Pages 60, 62, 63

A typical Charon scene by the Reed Painter. Charon and a youth meet at a reed-tree in which a ribbon hangs festooned. The quality of the draughtsmanship is low; mass production has taken its toll.

47. 3 London, British Museum, D 61. White *lekythos* (matt outline standard shape) by the Reed Painter (*ARV* 1377, no. 15). Last quarter of the fifth century. From Athens. Height: 29·3 cm.

Photograph: Museum. Pages 60, 62, 63

Essentially the same composition, painted somewhat more carefully and mentioned below in connection with Paris CA 537 (PLATE 50. 1).

48. 1 Paris, Musée du Louvre, S 1161. White *lekythos* (matt outline; standard shape) by the Reed Painter (*ARV* 1382, no. 134). Last quarter of the fifth century.

Photograph: Museum, and Chuzeville, Paris. Pages 60, 62, 64, 65

Horses figure prominently on some of the Reed Painter's *lekythoi*. Horsemen appear at the tomb or they engage in a fight at a reed-tree. These fight scenes, like those on contemporary *loutrophoroi*, probably commemorate the deeds of men who fell in battle.

This *lekythos* is attributed to the painter himself. The following two *lekythoi*, one of which features a fight with horse (PLATE 48. 2), belong to the Reed Workshop, but seem to stand closer to Group R (*ARV* 1384).

48. 2 New York, Metropolitan Museum of Art, 41.162.11 (Rogers Fund, 1941). White *lekythos* (matt outline; standard shape) from the Reed Workshop (*ARV* 1384, no. 2). Last quarter of the fifth century. Height: 52·8 cm. Shoulder diameter: 14·7 cm.

Photograph: Museum. *Pages 62, 64, 65*

A fight (foot and horse; the horse's forefeet are shown) at a reed-tree. See above note.

48. 3 New York, Metropolitan Museum of Art, 41.162.12 (Rogers Fund, 1941). White *lekythos* (matt outline; standard shape) from the Reed Workshop (*ARV* 1384, no. 1). Height: 54 cm. Shoulder diameter: 13·7 cm.

Photograph: Museum. *Pages 62, 65*

The brooding youth seated at the tomb, in the company of a second youth and a woman, is familiar from Group R (cf. PLATE 49). The Reed Painter's figures sometimes sit at the tomb (cf. Hamburg 1917. 817. PLATE 47. 1) but their faces are not rendered in three-quarter view—an angle favoured by the artist(s) of Group R, and their eyes are not rendered with such care; note the lashes, lids, and pupils of the seated youth. His awkwardly posed right arm, with the spear disappearing into the pediment, is paralleled on a *lekythos* of Group R in Cleveland (*ARV* 1383, no. 10).

49. 1 Athens, National Museum, 1816. White *lekythos* (matt outline; standard shape) from Group R (*ARV* 1383, no. 12). Last quarter of the fifth century. From Eretria. Height: 47·8 cm. Shoulder diameter: 13 cm.

Photograph: Museum. *Pages 60, 61, 71* FIGURE 24*c*

One of the best-known and most widely illustrated white *lekythoi*. Technically no better than the other three *lekythoi* illustrated on this plate, its appeal is greater because of the powerful expression on the seated youth's face, reflecting a troubled soul and a heavy heart.

See note on London D 71 (PLATE 49. 4).

49. 2 Paris, Musée du Louvre, CA 536. White *lekythos* (matt outline; standard shape) from Group R (*ARV* 1383, no. 4). Last quarter of the fifth century. From Eretria.

Photograph: Museum, and Chuzeville, Paris. *Pages 60, 61, 65, 71*

The pose of the youth seated at the tomb is more relaxed than that of his clothed 'brother' of Athens 1816 (PLATE 49. 1); there are no weapons to allude to battle, but otherwise the compositions are very similar. See note on London D 71 (PLATE 49. 4).

49. 3 Athens, National Museum, 17276. White *lekythos* (matt outline; standard shape) from Group R (*ARV* 1384, no. 16). Last quarter of the fifth century. Height: 40·6 cm. Shoulder diameter: 10·9 cm.

Photograph: Museum. *Pages 60, 61*

The seated women of Group R are less well known than the youths, but no less important technically or iconographically. The woman seated at the tomb, her arms gently crossed in her lap, looks out at us as if she were posing for her portrait. Her face is one of the loveliest in Group R. The woman to the right, offering a basket, is hastily rendered in profile, but the figure on the right, seen from the back, is very gracefully handled. Note the sensitively drawn hands.

The composition compares favourably with the pencil-like sketches of the Herculaneum Marble, which is generally thought to be a Roman copy of Greek painting of the classical period (cf. A. Maiuri, *Roman Painting* (1953), 104 f.).

49. 4 London, British Museum, D 71. White *lekythos* (matt outline; standard shape) from Group R (*ARV* 1384, no. 15). Last quarter of the fifth century. Height: 50·8 cm. Shoulder diameter: 13 cm.

Photograph: Museum. *Pages 60, 61, 65*

A woman sits at a broad monument, draped with ribbons and laden with offerings: a white *lekythos* on the step beside her; two *alabastra* and a black *loutrophoros* on the finial above her head. There appears to be a secondary monument—a shaft with triangular pediment—surmounting the primary one. Beside the shaft there is a strigil, suspended in the field.

The woman standing to the right with a basket of ribbons is partly shown, as are the feet of a second figure, seated on a mound to the left of the tomb.

The figure seated at the tomb on Group R *lekythoi* is regularly taken for the dead, even though he can in no way be distinguished from the other 'visitors' to the tomb. The iconography of some of the *lekythoi*, for example, London D 71, makes this interpretation unlikely, if not impossible. If the woman seated at the tomb is the dead, why does a strigil hang at the tomb—an object traditionally associated with men? And if she is 'dead' because she is seated, why is not the second seated person also dead? Consider Athens 1816 (PLATE 49. 1): the seated youth is assumed to be a dead warrior, whose armour is being brought to the grave by his family, but on some *lekythoi* (not of Group R) a woman sits at the tomb to which others bring armour (cf. Geneva Market. *ARV* 1241, no. 7; Athens 1907. *ARV* 1382, no. 119); the armour cannot be hers.

The motif of the seated mourner is well established in fifth-century literature and art. Niobe sat on the tomb of her children, slaughtered by Apollo and Artemis and mourned her fate (Aischylos, *Niobe*, fr. 277, 6 (Loeb, ed. by H. Lloyd-Jones)), and Elektra sat on the tomb of her father, Agamemnon, as Orestes stood by (Jacobsthal, *Mel* 192 ff.).

50. 1 Paris, Musée du Louvre, CA 537. White *lekythos* (matt outline; standard shape) from Group R (*ARV* 1384, no 18). Last quarter of the fifth century. From Eretria.

Photograph: Museum, and Chuzeville, Paris.   Pages 58, 60, 63, 65

Beazley described the vase: slighter, and specially close to the Reed Painter (*ARV* 1384).

The only Group R *lekythos* on which Charon appears, and the reeds (stylized verticals behind Charon)—hallmarks of the Reed Painter. The woman's three-quarter face, her offering basket, the *alabastron*, and the white *lekythos* on the step of the tomb are all in the manner of Group R. The composition recalls the Reed Painter's *lekythos* in London (PLATE 47. 3), and the conflation of tomb and Charon scenes can be paralleled on his large *lekythos* in Hamburg (PLATE 47. 1).

50. 2 Paris, Musée du Louvre, CA 1264 (detail). White *lekythos* (matt outline; standard shape) from Group R (*ARV* 1384, no. 19).

Photograph: Museum, and Chuzeville, Paris.   Pages 60, 63

A detail from the only Group R *lekythos* on which a mythological minister of Death appears. Not pictured is the object of the figure's mission—a woman at a tomb, recoiling in fear (her feet are partly shown) and Hermes *psychopompos*, sitting on a rock to the side.

The figure is winged and he has no boat; therefore, he cannot be Charon. His countenance is menacing, and this in itself is unusual on white *lekythoi*. He must be Thanatos (see note on PLATE 32. 4)—a unique representation of him without his milder brother, Hypnos.

We are reminded of the Thanatos/Hades of Euripides' *Alkestis* (cf. ll. 24 ff.; 74, 261, 843), and in the original publication of the vase the figure was equated with the Euripidean *daimon*. But there is something of Charon in the pose and dress (cf. Paris CA 537. PLATE 50. 1), and the painter himself seems to have been uncertain for he redrew the left foot.

50. 3 Athens, National Museum, 19280. Fragments of a white *lekythos* (matt outline; standard shape) from Group R (*ARV* 1384, no. 14). Dimensions (as preserved): 12 × 10 cm.

Photograph: Museum.   Pages 60 n. 9, 61 n. 8, 223

The artist(s) of Group R devoted much care to the representation of the human face, especially to the eyes, the mouth, and the hair, as did the great painter Parrhasios, who was active in Athens at this time (Pliny, *N.H.* 35. 60), and who probably influenced vase painters as well as other painters of panel and wall (see p. 60). The artist(s) of Group R also gives his attention to the hands of his figures; they are large and prominently placed, with fingers sensitively drawn.

51. 1 Chicago, The Art Institute, 07.18. White *lekythos* (matt outline; standard shape) by the Reed Painter (*ARV* 1381, no. 114). Last quarter of the fifth century. Height: 48·26 cm.

Photograph: Museum. Pages 59, 67, 68, 69, 71

A large *lekythos* by the Reed Painter, illustrated here because of its unusual shape, which is more like some of the very latest white *lekythoi* (cf. PLATES 51. 3–4; 52) than his other large vases (cf. Hamburg 1917.817. PLATE 47. 1). The pose of the man seated at the tomb (roughly drawn and crowned by an acanthus) is very like that of the youth on the peculiarly shaped late *lekythos* in Copenhagen (PLATE 52. 1), and comparable with that of the man on the Kerameikos *lekythos* (PLATE 51. 2).

To the left of the tomb stands a youth with a helmet and a sword (not shown); to the right, a woman, who seems to have held a ribbon in her hand, extended above a shield. The elements of the composition are those of Athens 1816 (PLATE 49. 1), and the same problems of interpretation arise.

51. 2 Athens, Kerameikos Museum, 3146. White *lekythos* (matt outline; standard shape). Unattributed. From the Kerameikos. Height: 48·3 cm. Shoulder diameter: 12·5 cm.

Photograph: Deutsches Archäologisches Institut, Athens. Pages 67 f., 69

A recent find from the excavations of a classical cemetery along the Sacred Way in the Athenian Kerameikos, of exceptional importance because of its technique and iconography.

The late shape—with curved mouth and white-slipped neck—is not far from the Huge *Lekythoi* (PLATE 54); details of drawing (especially of the seated man's face, hair, beard, and eyes) recall Group R; the pose of the seated man with a shield at his feet recalls the Reed Painter's large, late *lekythos* in Chicago (PLATE 51. 1); another detail (scarcely visible in the photograph), the second 'shadow' monument behind the principal one (see p. 61), is characteristically Reed. Notable is the use of shading (*skiagraphia*, see p. 71) on the man's chest and on the shield, which is not known from any *lekythoi* except those of the Huge Group.

51. 3 Zürich, University, 2518. White *lekythos* (matt outline; standard shape) by the Triglyph Painter (*ARV* 1386, no. 38). Last quarter of the fifth century. Height: 40·5 cm. Shoulder diameter: 10·6 cm.

Photograph: Museum. Pages 66, 69

The Triglyph Painter, named after the triglyphs on some of his tombs (not clear on the Zürich vase), was active in the last quarter of the fifth century. His *lekythoi* tend to have deeply curved mouths, long necks, and mediocre, but interesting scenes. His eccentric style is easily recognized by the following details: triglyphs on tomb, large *lekythoi*, ducks and dresses with dots (stylized florals). The youth seated beside an acanthus-crowned tomb wears a dotted cloak. The mound on which he sits is draped with ribbons, as is the neck of the large *lekythos* standing beside the tomb.

51. 4 Athens, National Museum, 1756. White *lekythos* (matt outline; standard shape) by the Triglyph Painter (*ARV* 1385, no. 4). Last quarter of the fifth century. From Athens. Height: 46·1 cm. Shoulder diameter: 11·2 cm.

Photograph: Museum. Pages 66, 69

The centre of a bier is shown and a woman mourning behind it; her 'rubbery' arms and hands convey little feeling; compare the *prothesis* scene by the Woman Painter (PLATE 44. 2). Beneath the bier there is a duck; at either end a large *lekythos* at the head of the bier is partly shown.

52. 1 Copenhagen, National Museum, 4986. White *lekythos* (matt outline; late shape) from the Class of Copenhagen 4986 (*ARV* 1389, no. 1). Last quarter of the fifth century. From Athens. Height: 55·4 cm. Shoulder diameter: 14·4 cm.

Photograph: Museum. Pages 67, 68, 71

The Class of Copenhagen 4986 is composed of two *lekythoi*, similar in shape, but different in size and style (see p. 67). The pose of the youth seated at the tomb has already been compared with the Reed Painter's large *lekythos* in Chicago (PLATE 51. 1) and the Kerameikos *lekythos*, which shows the influence of the Reed Workshop (PLATE 51. 2). The zigzag pattern on the tomb and the prominent dark areas (for example, the 'acroteria'—stylized acanthus leaves?) are comparable with the New York *lekythos*, associated with the Reed Painter and Group R (PLATE 48. 3). Notice the egg-and-dart pattern at the join of shoulder to body. This pattern is found on one of the Huge *Lekythoi*, and is common on stone *lekythoi* (see p. 71).

52. 2 New York, Metropolitan Museum of Art, 07.1 (gift of P. H. Reynolds, 1907). White *lekythos* (matt outline; late shape) from the Class of Copenhagen 4986 (*ARV* 1389, no. 2). Last quarter of the fifth century. Height: 27·8 cm. Shoulder diameter: 7·7 cm.

Photograph: Museum. Pages 61, 67

This very ugly little *lekythos* also seems to show the influence of the Reed Workshop, especially in the second 'shadow' monument, clearly visible behind the principal acanthus-crowned tomb. Both the youth and the women hold ribbons, but these have faded as have most of the ribbons tied around the tomb.

53. 1 Ithaca (New York), Museum. White *lekythos* (glaze outline; standard shape). Unattributed. Height: 30 cm.

Photograph: Museum. Page 65

A modest vase which has acquired an importance far beyond its artistic merits, because it is the only white *lekythos* on which a large *lekythos*-monument is unquestionably represented. See p. 65. In the centre of the vase a large *lekythos* stands on a platform base. The youth seated on the right is shown, not his companion standing on the left.

53. 2 Copenhagen, Ny Carlsberg Glyptotek, Kat. 221. Marble *Lekythos*. Fourth century. Height: 1·05 m. Shoulder diameter: 0·265 m.

Photograph: Museum. Page 69

On *lekythoi* of Group R and by the Triglyph Painter large *lekythoi* are seen at the tomb and at the bier. We cannot be certain whether these vases are made of clay or of stone, for both were being used by Athenians in the later fifth century.

Stone *lekythoi* vary greatly in size, shape, and decoration. Some of the earliest borrow themes from vase-painters, but most repeat subjects common in contemporary grave-reliefs. See pp. 73 ff.

The central group of two figures on the Copenhagen *lekythos* clasp hands in a gesture of *dexiosis*; they are framed by a shield bearer and a grieving man.

The hand-clasp, or *dexiosis*, is a gesture capable of many meanings, including agreement or greeting, and is prominent in decree- and grave-reliefs. On white *lekythoi* it is virtually unknown (cf. G. Neumann, *Gesten und Gebärden* (1965), 290). The prominence of the gesture on stone monuments and its absence from white *lekythoi* suggest that the two art forms are iconographically distinct.

54. 1 Madrid, Museo Arqueológico Nacional, 11.194. White *lekythos* (matt outline; late shape) from the Group of the Huge *Lekythoi* (*ARV* 1390, no. 5). Last quarter of the fifth century. Height: 95 cm. Shoulder diameter: 28 cm.

Photograph: Museum. Pages 68, 71, 72

Vase painters vied with sculptors for the lucrative Athenian sepulchral art market, but their offering—the Huge *Lekythoi*—could not compete with the more permanent stone memorials. This last phase in the development of the white *lekythos* is described on pp. 73 ff. The Huge *Lekythoi* differ from other white *lekythoi* in technique (the over-all application of white slip, the detachable mouth and *skiagraphia*, or shading), not in iconography.

The youth seated at the acanthus-crown tomb differs from seated youths on other late white *lekythoi* only in the treatment of his exposed flesh, which is shaded in light hatching. A second youth, leaning on a staff, is shown to the left.

54. 2 Berlin (East), Staatliche Museen, F. 2684. White *lekythos* (matt outline; late shape) from the Group of

the Huge *Lekythoi* (*ARV* 1380, no. 3). Last quarter of the fifth century. From Ampelokepoi. Height: 68 cm.

Photograph: Museum.   Pages 68, 71, 72, 73

The artist(s) of the Huge *Lekythoi* applied *skiagraphia* selectively, as was the custom of the time, to the flesh of men, not of women (see p. 72), and on this *lekythos* there is a balance between shaded and outlined areas.

The dead youth lies on a bier, covered with patterned blankets. The head of the bier is elevated by a small block, seen in partial perspective. The block, like the pillows, elevated the head of the dead and prevented his jaws from gaping; *lekythos* painters tended to omit the chin strap (cf. Arias, Hirmer, and Shefton, pl. 128). Beneath the bier stands a *lekythos*, containing the oil with which the dead was anointed.

The woman in the centre of the bier is about to embrace the head of the dead (cf. Homer, *Iliad* 24. 710–12) in a gesture conveying deep affection (cf. Oxford 1923.69. *CV* i, pl. 49. 1–3. Red-figure *loutrophoros*).

The old man at the head of the bier also touches the head of the dead, while striking his own in grief; his hair and beard are grey; the contours of his exposed chest are carefully modelled with light hatching. At the foot of the bier (not shown) a second woman mourns. In the air an *eidolon* flies, repeating the gesture of the living mourners.

55. 1 Carlsruhe, Badisches Landesmuseum, 167. Black-figure column-crater (white-ground; handle view) by the Sappho Painter (*ABL* 228, no. 57). Around 500 B.C. From Locri. Height: 32 cm. Maximum diameter: 34 cm.
Photograph: Museum.   Pages 91, 92, 94, 97, 149

55. 2 Vienna, Kunsthistorisches Museum, 3607. Black-figure neck-amphora (white-ground; side B) from the Diosphos Workshop (*ABV* 319, no. 10). Around 500 B.C. Height: 25·5 cm. Maximum diameter: 12·5 cm.
Photograph: Photo Meyer, Vienna.   Pages 12, 91, 93   FIGURE 26*b*

55. 3 Paris, Musée du Louvre, G 203. Red-figure neck-amphora of Nolan type (handle view) by the Dutuit Painter (*ARV* 306, no. 1). First quarter of the fifth century (early). Height: 32·5 cm.
Photograph: Museum, and Chuzeville, Paris.   Pages 14, 91, 95, 100

55. 4 St. Louis (Missouri), Washington University, 3283. Red-figure *oinochoe* (shape 1) probably by the Terpaulos Painter (*ARV* 308, no. 4). First quarter of the fifth century (early). Height: 24·13 cm.
Photograph: Museum.   Pages 80, 95

56. 1 Toronto, Royal Ontario Museum, 963. 59. White *lekythos* (black-figure; Little Lion shape) by the Kephisophon Painter (*ARV* 1644, and *Para* 253). Around 500 B.C. Height (as preserved): 9 cm. Shoulder diameter: 4·7 cm.
Photograph: Museum.   Page 93

56. 2 Once New York, Gallatin Collection. Now lost. White *lekythos* (black-figure; Little Lion shape) by the Kephisophon Painter (*ABL* 230, no. 3; *ABV* 669, no. 2). Around 500 B.C.   Pages 93 f.   FIGURE 26*a*

56. 3 Athens, National Museum, 2185. Fragment (end) of a black-figure *onos* (white-ground) akin to the Golonos Group (*ABV* 481). Around 500 B.C. Diameter: 12 cm.
Photograph: Museum.   Page 94

56. 4 See PLATE 57. 3.

57. 1 Munich, Museum antiker Kleinkunst, 2447. Black-bodied *oinochoe* (shape 2; white-ground shoulder, with patterns in black, and *kalos* inscriptions in praise of Nikolaos, Dorotheos, and Memnon). Related to

the Class of London B 632 (*ABV* 425). Last quarter of the sixth century. From Vulci. Height: 7·7 cm. Diameter: 7 cm.

Photograph: Museum. Pages 93, 94, 95

57. 2 London, British Museum, B 632. Black-bodied *oinochoe* (shape 1; white-ground shoulder) from the Class of London B 632 (*ARV* 425, no. 1). Around 500 B.C. Height: 24·13 cm.

Photograph: Museum. Pages 93, 95

57. 3 Paris, Musée du Louvre, CA 4176. Black-figure *hydria* (partly white-ground). Unattributed (*RA* 1972, 127 ff.). Last quarter of the sixth century. Height: 48·2 cm.

Photograph: Museum, and Chuzeville, Paris. Pages 10, 13, 20, 94

58. 1 Paris, Musée du Louvre, MNC 650 (detail). Side-palmette *lekythos* (glaze outline; shape DL) from the Diosphos Workshop (*ARV* 301, no. 6). First quarter of the fifth century (early). Height: 20·3 cm.

Photograph: Museum, and Chuzeville, Paris. Pages 17, 80, 91, 98, 99, 105, 149

58. 2 Paris, Musée du Louvre, MNB 909. Side-palmette *lekythos* (semi-outline; shape DL) by the Diosphos Painter (*ARV* 301, no. 4). First quarter of the fifth century (early). Height: 25·7 cm.

Photograph: Museum, and Chuzeville, Paris. Pages 17, 80, 91, 98, 105 n. 12, 149

59. 1 Boston, Museum of Fine Arts, 99.528. Side-palmette *lekythos* (semi-outline; shape DL) by the Diosphos Painter (*ARV* 301, no. 2). First quarter of the fifth century (early). From Palermo. Height: 26·1 cm. Shoulder diameter: 9·2 cm.

Photograph: Museum. Pages 17, 80, 91, 98, 105, 149

59. 2 New York, Metropolitan Museum of Art, 06.1070 (Rogers Fund, 1906). Side-palmette *lekythos* (semi-outline; shape DL) by the Diosphos Painter (*ARV* 301, no. 3). First quarter of the fifth century. Height: 25·45 cm. Shoulder diameter: 8·5 cm.

Photograph: Museum. Pages 17, 80, 91, 98 f., 105, 149 FIGURE 28*b*

59. 3 New York, Metropolitan Museum of Art, 51.163 (gift of Dietrich von Bothmer, 1951). Side-palmette *lekythos* (glaze outline; shape DL) from the Diosphos Workshop (*ARV* 301, no. 7). First quarter of the fifth century. Height: 21·85 cm. Shoulder diameter: 7·5 cm.

Photograph: Museum. Pages 60, 80, 91, 98, 100, 105, 149 FIGURE 29*b*

59. 4 Paris, Musée du Louvre, MNB 911. Side-palmette *lekythos* (semi-outline; Little Lion shape) near the Diosphos Painter (*ARV* 301, no. 1). First quarter of the fifth century (early). From Athens.

Photograph: Museum, and Chuzeville, Paris. Pages 17, 80, 81, 98 n. 3, 105, 149

60. 1 London, British Museum, 1920.3–15.1. Black-figure *lekythos* (near standard shape) by the Athena Painter (*ABL* 255, no. 27). Around 500 B.C. Height: 21·5 cm.

Photograph: Museum. Pages 31, 104, 128

60. 2 Athens, National Museum, 1809. Side-palmette *lekythos* (semi-outline; shape BL) from the Bowdoin Workshop (*ARV* 689, no. 4). First quarter of the fifth century (earlier). From Aigina. Height: 30·9 cm. Shoulder diameter: 10 cm.

Photograph: Museum. Pages 31, 105 n. 15, 107, 108, 128 FIGURE 34*b*

60. 3 Richmond (Virginia), Museum of Fine Arts, 56.27.4. White *lekythos* (glaze outline and silhouette; shape BL) by the Bowdoin Painter (*ARV* 685, no. 182). First to second quarter of the fifth century. Height: 19·05 cm. Shoulder diameter: 6·98 cm.

Photograph: Widmer, Basel. Pages 31, 108, 128

60. 4 Athens, National Museum, 1827. White *lekythos* (glaze outline; shape BL) by the Bowdoin Painter (*ARV*

685, no. 181). First to second quarter of the fifth century. From Eretria. Height: 26·5 cm. Shoulder diameter: 8·5 cm.

Photograph: Museum.   Pages 31, 108, 128

61. 1 Oxford, Ashmolean Museum, 1922.18. Side-palmette *lekythos* (glaze outline; shape PL) by the Vlasto Painter (*ARV* 696, no. 5). Second quarter of the fifth century. Height: 16·3 cm. Shoulder diameter: 7·0 cm.

Photograph: Museum.   Pages 81, 108

61. 2 Copenhagen, National Museum, 3882. White squat *lekythos* (glaze outline) close to the Two-row Painter (*ARV* 727). Second quarter of the fifth century (later). Height: 18·5 cm. Maximum diameter: 5·8 cm.

Photograph: Museum.   Pages 77, 96   FIGURE 27*b*

61. 3 Oxford, Ashmolean Museum, 1927.4467. White *oinochoe* (glaze outline; shape 3, *chous*) by the Icarus Painter (*ARV* 700, no. 84). Second quarter of the fifth century (later). Height: 9·6 cm.

Photograph: Museum.   Pages 103, 107 n. 11

61. 4 Oxford, Ashmolean Museum, 1927.4460. Red-figure *lekythos* (shape CL). Second quarter of the fifth century. Height: 10·8 cm. Shoulder diameter: 4·1 cm.

Photograph: Museum.   Page 84

62. 1 London, British Museum, B 359. Black-figure *hydria* (small, *kalpis* type) by the Painter of the Half-palmettes (*ABL* 248, no. 5). First quarter of the fifth century (later). Height: 15·24 cm.

Photograph: Museum.   Pages 104, 106, 109

62. 2 Athenian tetradrachm. Around 470 B.C. (Starr, Class II. B, no. 37). Photograph from a cast of the coin in the Heberden Coin Room, Ashmolean Museum.   Pages 109 ff.

62. 3 Amsterdam, Allard Pierson Museum, 3754. White *lekythos* (black-figure; shape BL) by the Athena Painter (*Para* 262). First quarter of the fifth century. Height: 21·6 cm. Shoulder diameter: 8 cm.

Photograph: Widmer, Basel.   Pages 108, 110

63. 1 Marburg, University. White *lekythos* (black-figure; shape BL) from the Bowdoin Workshop (*ABL* 258, no. 106 *ter*). First quarter of the fifth century. From Eretria. Height: 28·8 cm. Shoulder diameter: 10 cm.

Photograph: Museum.   Pages 16, 105, 108

63. 2 London, British Museum, D 22. White *lekythos* (glaze outline; shape BL) by the Bowdoin Painter (*ARV* 687, no. 219). First quarter of the fifth century. From Eretria. Height: 25·4 cm.

Photograph: Museum.   Pages 105, 106, 108, 110

63. 3 Oxford, Ashmolean Museum, 1965.129. White *lekythos* (glaze outline; shape BL) by the Bowdoin Painter (*ARV* 687, no. 221, and *Para* 406). Second quarter of the fifth century. Height: 27·5 cm. Shoulder diameter: 8·75 cm.

Photograph: Museum.   Pages 105, 106, 108, 110, 111

63. 4 Bonn, Akademisches Kunstmuseum, 84. Red-figure *lekythos* (shape BL) by the Bowdoin Painter (*ARV* 685, no. 165). Second quarter of the fifth century. Height: 23·5 cm. Shoulder diameter: 8 cm.

Photograph: Museum, and E. Kukahn.   Pages 105, 110

64. 1 Cambridge, Fitzwilliam Museum, GR 1.1895 (G. 138). Side-palmette *lekythos* (glaze outline and second white; shape BEL) by the Carlsruhe Painter (*ARV* 735, no. 98). Second quarter of the fifth century. Height: 21·1 cm. Shoulder diameter: 7·1 cm.

Photograph: Museum.   Pages 19, 104, 111 n. 6, 112

64. 2 Basle Market (M.M.). Side-palmette *lekythos* (glaze outline; chimney type). Unattributed (*Para* 357). Height: 24·1 cm.

Photograph: Widmer, Basel. Pages 87, 112 FIGURE 32*b*

64. 3 Cambridge, Fitzwilliam Museum, GR 3.1917 (3.17). Side-palmette *lekythos* (glaze outline and second white; secondary shape) by the Painter of Cambridge 3.17 (*ARV* 1241, no. 1). Second to third quarter of the fifth century. Height: 21·1 cm. Shoulder diameter: 7·3 cm.

Photograph: Museum. Page 111 n. 6

64. 4 Boston, Museum of Fine Arts, 99.928. Head-*kantharos* (white-ground; side A) by the Syriskos Painter (*ARV* 265, no. 78). First to second quarter of the fifth century. From Tanagra. Height: 17·2 cm. Maximum diameter: 10·8 cm.

Photograph: Museum. Pages 127 n. 14, 229

64. 5 See PLATE 65. 2.

65. 1 Oxford, Ashmolean Museum, 1932.733. Black-bodied *lekythos* ('compromise shape' with red-figure shoulder). Unattributed (*ARV* 1644). Around 500 B.C. Height: 32·0 cm. Shoulder diameter: 14·85 cm.

Photograph: Museum. Page: 78, 123 f., 140 n. 2

65. 2 Paris, Musée du Louvre, CA 987. Red-figure janiform head-vase from Class B (Epilykos Class; *ARV* 1530, no. 2). First quarter of the fifth century.

Photograph: Museum, and Chuzeville, Paris. Page 123

66. 1 Birmingham, City Museum and Art Gallery, 1616.85. Black-bodied amphora (of Nolan type with red-figure florals) from the Floral Nolan Group (*ARV* 218, no. 10). First quarter of the fifth century. From Nola. Height: 33 cm. Maximum diameter: 20·2 cm.

Photograph: Museum. Pages 14, 24, 26, 47, 125

66. 2 Brooklyn (New York), The Brooklyn Museum, 29.1. Black-bodied neck-amphora (doubleen, with red-figure florals) from the Floral Nolan Group (Kurtz). First quarter of the fifth century. Height: 32·3 cm. Maximum diameter: 17·5 cm. From Nola.

Photograph: Museum. Pages 14, 24, 27, 125, 126 and n. 9

66. 3 Copenhagen, Ny Carlsberg Glyptotek, V. 26. Black-bodied *lekythos* (standard shape with red-figure florals) from the Floral Nolan Group (*ARV* 219, no. 14). First quarter of the fifth century. From Orvieto. Height: 34 cm. Shoulder diameter: 10·5 cm.

Photograph: Museum. Pages 14, 24, 26, 125 f.

66. 4 Adolphseck, Landgraf Philip of Hesse, 50. Black-bodied *lekythos* (standard shape with red-figure florals) from the Floral Nolan Group (*CV* i. 24). First quarter of the fifth century. Height: 36·2 cm.

Photograph: Foto Claus, Fulda. Pages 14, 24, 26, 125 and n. 5

67. 1 Oxford, Ashmolean Museum, 1936.113. Black-bodied *lekythos* (Deianeira type, with bands of added colour on the body). Later sixth century. Height: 17·7 cm.

Photograph: Museum. Pages 23, 77, 115, 116

67. 2 Oxford, Ashmolean Museum, 1928.41. Black-bodied *lekythos* (shape DL) from the Diosphos Workshop (*ABL* 236, no. 88). Early fifth century. Height: 21·1 cm. Shoulder diameter: 6·5 cm.

Photograph: Museum. Pages 23, 77, 115, 119, 120

67. 3 Oxford, Ashmolean Museum, Queen's College loan, 1935.2. Black-bodied *lekythos* (shape BL). Bowdoin Workshop. First to second quarter of the fifth century. Height: 25·6 cm. Shoulder diameter: 9·2 cm.

Photograph: Museum. Pages 16, 23, 79, 115, 120, 121

67. 4 Oxford, Ashmolean Museum, 251 (1889.1013). Black-bodied *lekythos* (shape BL with black-figure shoulder) from the Bowdoin Workshop (*ABL* 262, no. 1). From Sicily. First quarter of the fifth century. Height: 32.9 cm. Shoulder diameter: 11·7 cm.

Photograph: Museum.   Pages 16, 23, 77, 115, 121, 145

67. 5 Oxford, Ashmolean Museum, 1938.732. Black-bodied *lekythos*. Late sixth to early fifth century. Height: 16·9 cm. Shoulder diameter: 8·1 cm.

Photograph: Museum.   Pages 23, 77, 115, 119 n. 3

67. 6 Oxford, Ashmolean Museum, 1935.229. Black-bodied *lekythos* (shape DL). Not from the Diosphos Workshop (*ABL* 107, n. 1). First quarter of the fifth century. Height: 18·8 cm. Shoulder diameter: 6·6 cm.

Photograph: Museum.   Pages 23, 77, 115

68. 1 Athens, Agora Museum, P 24532. Pattern *lekythos* (black bands; secondary shape). First half of the fifth century. Height (as preserved): 11·5 cm. Shoulder diameter: 6 cm.

Photograph: Agora Excavations, American School of Classical Studies, Athens.   Pages 131 ff.

68. 2 Oxford, Ashmolean Museum, 1872.1248A. Pattern *lekythos* (black bands), not certainly Attic. Early fifth century. Height: 12·4 cm.

Photograph: Museum.   Pages 131 ff., 144

68. 3 Oxford, Ashmolean Museum, 1836.68. Pattern *lekythos* (upright lotus buds, linked), not certainly Attic. Early fifth century. From Agrigento. Height: 9 cm. Shoulder diameter: 4·2 cm.

Photograph: Museum.   Pages 131 ff., 120

68. 4 Oxford, Ashmolean Museum, 1938.736. Pattern *lekythos* (pendant lotus buds), probably Euboean (cf. *BSA* lxxviii (1973), 276). Later sixth century. Height: 11·3 cm.

Photograph: Museum.   Pages 131 ff., 144, 147

68. 5 Athens, National Museum, 12714. Palmette *lekythos* (581 shape) from the Class of Athens 581 (*ABL* 225, no. 1; *ABV* 497, no. 195.) First quarter of the fifth century (early). From Marathon. Height: 18 cm.

Photograph: from *ABL*, pl. 22, no. 5.   Pages 80, 99, 131 ff., 149

68. 6 Oxford, Ashmolean Museum, 1934.329. Floral *lekythos* (secondary shape; *ARV* 1644, to p. 308). First quarter of the fifth century. Height: 10·1 cm. Shoulder diameter: 4·95 cm.

Photograph: Museum.   Pages 131 ff., 146

68. 7 Athens, Agora Museum, P 20750. Black-figure floral *lekythos* (secondary shape; *ARV* 1644, to p. 308). First quarter of the fifth century. Height (as preserved): 9·6 cm. Shoulder diameter: 5·5 cm.

Photograph: Agora Excavations, American School of Classical Studies, Athens.   Pages 131 ff., 146

68. 8 Athens, Agora Museum, P 24546. Black-figure *lekythos* with florals (Little Lion shape; *Para* 252). First quarter of the fifth century. Height (as preserved): 6·5 cm. Shoulder diameter: 4 cm.

Photograph: Agora Excavations, American School of Classical Studies, Athens.   Pages 131 ff., 146 n. 3

69. 1 Athens, National Museum, 12271. Palmette *lekythos* (white-ground; shape DL) by the Diosphos Painter (*ABL* 235, no. 66). First quarter of the fifth century (early). From Boeotia. Height: 25·4 cm. Shoulder diameter: 8·5 cm.

Photograph: Museum.   Pages 131 ff.

69. 2 Oxford, Ashmolean Museum, 1927.4456. Palmette *lekythos* (secondary shape). First half of the fifth century. Height: 16·7 cm. Shoulder diameter: 5·9 cm.

Photograph: Museum.   Pages 131 ff., 153

69. 3 Eden Collection, Corsham (Wiltshire). Palmette *lekythos* (secondary shape). First half of the fifth century. Height: 19·6 cm.
Photograph: Michael Vickers.   Pages 131 ff., 153

69. 4 Toronto, Royal Ontario Museum, 923.13.40 (335). Palmette *lekythos* (white-ground; Little Lion shape). First quarter of the fifth century. Height: 10·1 cm. Shoulder diameter: 4·2 cm.
Photograph: Museum.   Pages 131 ff., 150

69. 5 Oxford, Ashmolean Museum, 1940.148. Palmette *lekythos* (secondary shape). First half of the fifth century. Height: 14·2 cm. Shoulder diameter: 4·4 cm.
Photograph: Museum.   Pages 131 ff., 153

69. 6 Oxford, Ashmolean Museum, 1927.4458. Palmette *lekythos* (secondary shape). First half of the fifth century. Height: 24·2 cm. Shoulder diameter: 8·1 cm.
Photograph: Museum.   Pages 131 ff., 153

70. 1 London, British Museum, B 659. Pattern *lekythos* with a single figure (white-ground; secondary shape) from the Beldam Workshop (*ABL* 182). First half of the fifth century. Height: 22·86 cm.
Photograph: Museum.   Pages 79, 86, 112, 131 ff., 154

70. 2 London, British Museum, 36 2-D 341. Pattern *lekythos* (white-ground; secondary shape) from the Beldam Workshop (Kurtz). Height: 23·1 cm.
Photograph: Museum.   Pages 131 ff.

70. 3 Basle Market (M.M.). Pattern *lekythos* (white-ground; secondary shape).
Photograph: Widmer, Basel.   Pages 131 ff., 154

70. 4 Oxford, Ashmolean Museum, 1927.4457. Black-figure *lekythos* (chimney type) by the Haimon Painter (*ABL* 245, no. 81). Second quarter of the fifth century. Height: 19·8 cm. Shoulder diameter: 5·8 cm.
Photograph: Museum.   Pages 22, 87, 131 ff., 151

70. 5 Athens, Kerameikos Museum. Pattern *lekythos* (white-ground; shape BEL) by the Beldam Painter (*ABL* 266, no. 6). First to second quarter of the fifth century. Height: 32 cm.
Photograph: from *ABL*, pl. 50, no. 4.   Pages 79, 86, 131 ff., 153 f.

70. 6 Oxford, Ashmolean Museum, 1940.149. Pattern *lekythos* (white-ground; secondary shape) from the Beldam Workshop. Second to third quarter of the fifth century. Height: 19·9 cm. Shoulder diameter: 6·8 cm.
Photograph: Museum.   Pages 19, 131 ff., 154

70. 7 Oxford, Ashmolean Museum, 1879.210. Pattern *lekythos* (white-ground, secondary shape) from the Beldam Workshop. Height: 13·6 cm. Shoulder diameter: 4·6 cm.
Photograph: Museum.   Pages 19, 131 ff., 154

70. 8 Corinth, Museum, T 566–118. Pattern *lekythos* (white-ground; chimney type) from the Beldam Workshop (*ABL* 268, no. 52). Middle quarters of the fifth century. Height: 20·8 cm. Shoulder diameter: 6·4 cm.
Photograph: Museum, and American School of Classical Studies, Athens.   Pages 19, 87, 131 ff., 138, 154

71. 1 Athens, Kerameikos Museum. Pattern and black-bodied *lekythoi* from a grave on the Sacred Way, in the Kerameikos.
(A) Height: 21·3 cm. Shoulder diameter: 7·4 cm.
(B) Height: 18·75 cm. Shoulder diameter: 6·0 cm.
(C) Height: 15·5 cm. Shoulder diameter: 5·0 cm.

(D) Height: 11·4 cm. Shoulder diameter: 3·85 cm.
(E) Height: 11·05 cm. Shoulder diameter: 3·9 cm.
Photograph: Deutsches Archäologisches Institut, Athens.   Pages 131 ff.

71. 2 Oxford, Ashmolean Museum, 1879.209. Pattern *lekythos* (secondary shape). Second to third quarter of the fifth century. Height 19·4 cm. Shoulder diameter: 6·6 cm.
Photograph: Museum.   Pages 131 ff.

71. 3 London, British Museum, 64.10–7.1722. Pattern *lekythos* (white-ground) from the Beldam Workshop (*ABL* 183). First half of the fifth century. Height: 10·8 cm. Diameter: 7 cm. (max.).
Photograph: Museum.   Pages 77, 131 ff.

71. 4 Oxford, Ashmolean Museum, 1930.617. Pattern *alabastron* (Columbus type) from the Beldam Workshop (*ABL* 182). Second quarter of the fifth century. Height: 9·6 cm.
Photograph: Museum.   Pages 131 ff., 155

72. 1 Berlin (West), Staatliche Museen, F. 2259. White *alabastron* (glaze outline) by the Two-row Painter (*ARV* 727, no. 20). Second quarter of the fifth century. Height: 29·1 cm.
Photograph: Museum.   Pages 39, 77

72. 2 New York, Metropolitan Museum of Art, 06.1021.92. Palmette *alabastron* (white-ground) from the Paidikos Group (*ARV* 99, no. 6). First quarter of the fifth century. Height: 15·2 cm.
Photograph: Museum.   Pages 77, 94 n. 4, 99, 101 n. 5, 118, 149

72. 3 New York, Metropolitan Museum of Art, 21.80 (gift of Welles Bosworth, 1921). Palmette *alabastron* (white-ground) from the Paidikos Group (*ARV* 99, no. 5). First quarter of the fifth century. Height: 12·7 cm.
Photograph: Museum.   Pages 77, 94 n. 4, 99, 101 n. 5, 118, 149

72. 4 New York, Metropolitan Museum of Art, 91.1.442 (bequest of Edward C. Moore, 1891) *alabastron* (white-ground). First quarter of the fifth century. Height: 13·7 cm.
Photograph: Museum.   Page 77

72. 5 Oxford, Ashmolean Museum, 1934.67. Pattern *alabastron*. Second to third quarter of the fifth century. From Sicily. Height: 12·9 cm.
Photograph: Museum.   Page 77

72. 6 London, British Museum, 64.10–7.1809. Pattern *alabastron* (red-figure) probably from the Haimon Workshop. First half of the fifth century. Height: 19·5 cm. Diameter: 6·5 cm.
Photograph: Museum.   Page 77

72. 7 London, British Museum, 1836.2–24.33 (Durand 1106). Pattern *alabastron* (white-ground) from the Beldam Workshop (*ABL* 182). First half of the fifth century. Height: 19·6 cm. Diameter: 6·6 cm.
Photograph: Museum.   Page 77

72. 8 Oxford, Ashmolean Museum, 1936.616. Black *alabastron* with pattern bands. First half of the fifth century. Height: 25 cm.
Photograph: Museum.   Page 77

INDEX OF COLLECTIONS

AACHEN, Ludwig
— (Hermonax, red-figure *lekythos*)   42 n. 20
ABERDEEN, University
695   124 n. 2
ADOLPHSECK, Landgraf Philip of Hesse
50   14, 24, 125 and n. 5, 229. Plate 66.4
51   127 n. 2
ADRIA, Museo Civico
B 180   24 nn. 3, 4, 124 nn. 11, 12
B 404   125 n. 3
AGRIGENTO, Giudice Collection (in Museo Civico)
893   148 n. 13
— (Gela Painter, black-bodied *lekythos*)   148 n. 15
AGRIGENTO, Museo Civico
23   9 n. 12, 78 n. 2, 79 n. 3, 80 and n. 9, 81,
                                   199. Plate 6.2
— (Bowdoin black-bodied *lekythos*)   23 n. 4,
                                          24 n. 9, 25
— (black-bodied *lekythos*)   119 n. 13
— (Edinburgh Painter, *lekythos*)   121 n. 6
AMIENS, Musée de Picardie
3057.172.33   40, 47, 212. Plate 33.3
— (Acheloos Painter, *hydria*)   95 n. 4
— (Beldam Painter, *lekythos*)   153 n. 6
AMSTERDAM, Allard Pierson Museum
2474   72 n. 5
2703   38. n. 4
3323   151 n. 16
3495   35 n. 1
3754   105 n. 8, 108, 110, 228. Plate 62.3
— (white ground *loutrophoros*?)   86 n. 10
ARLESHEIM, Dr. Samuel Schweizer
— (Reed Painter, *lekythos*)   64 n. 2
ATHENS, Acropolis Museum
— (Achillean white *lekythos*)   52 n. 10
— (Triglyph Painter, white *lekythos*)   66 n. 8
— (Triglyph Painter, white *lekythos*)   66 n. 8
— (Triglyph Painter, white *lekythos*)   67 n. 11
— (Related to Triglyph Painter, white *lekythos*)
                                             66 n. 8
— (Related to Triglyph Painter, white *lekythos*)
                                             66 n. 8
— (Related to Triglyph Painter, white *lekythos*)
                                             66 n. 8
ATHENS, Agora Museum
P 1233   145 n. 7
P 1251   115 n. 10
P 3881   152 n. 4
P 5002   10 n. 6, 198. Plate 1.2
P 9470   106 n. 2
P 10369   40 n. 4, 41 n. 2
P 12628   11 n. 7, 118 n. 2
P 15431   144 n. 9

P 16767   146 n. 3
P 20750   131, 146, 230. Plate 68.7
P 24061   13 n. 12, 78 n. 2, 199. Plate 5.2
P 24113   120 nn. 11f.
P 24531   114 n. 8
P 24532   131, 230. Plate 68.1
P 24546   131, 146 n. 3, 230. Plate 68.8
ATHENS, Agora Museum, North Slope
AP 422   101 n. 5
Once ATHENS, Carapanos
— (*lekanis*, Lykinic type)   69 n. 7
ATHENS, Empedokles
— (Diosphos Painter, pattern *lekythos*)   149 n. 5
ATHENS, Kerameikos Museum
3146   67, 68, 69, 220, 224. Plate 51.2
— (Amasis Painter, *lekythos*)   7 n. 13
— (Penthesilea Painter, bobbin)   45 n. 14
— (Beldam Painter, pattern-*lekythos*)   79, 86 n. 2,
                     131, 153 n. 7, 154, 231. Plate 70.5
— (black-bodied *lekythos*)   131, 231.
                                             Plate 71.1
— (Theseus Painter, cup)   133 n. 11
ATHENS, Market
— (Triglyph Painter, white *lekythos*)   63 n. 8,
                                             66 n. 10
— (Carlsruhe Painter, *lekythos*)   84 n. 13
— (Beldam Painter, *lekythos*)   86 n. 7
— (Diosphos Painter, black-figure *lekythos*) 98 n. 5
— (Side-palmette *lekythos*)   101 n. 3
— (Theseus Painter, *loutrophoros*)   133 n. 8
— (Side-palmette *lekythos*)   161. Figure 33b
ATHENS, National Museum, Acropolis Collection
427   42 n. 17
439   128 n. 5
443   28 n. 16
587   6 n. 8
597 f–h   6 n. 9, 7 n. 5
606   7, 157. Figure 1h
645   220
655   115 n. 10
1078   117 n. 6
1185   48 n. 9
ATHENS, National Museum
399   85 n. 4
450   133 n. 6
472   157. Figure 2f
474   157. Figure 1c
487   19 n. 16, 85 n. 6
574   85 n. 4
609   157. Figure 2g
610   157. Figure 2h
1011   21 n. 11
1033   150 n. 6

ATHENS, National Museum (*cont.*):

1067	106 n. 4
1124	158. Figure 8a
1129	158. Figure 10a
1132	106 n. 5
1133	106 n. 5
1138	108 n. 3
1274	64 n. 11
1293	64 n. 11
1508	35 n. 4
1626	85 n. 4, 126 n. 15
1699	109 n. 3
1700	64 n. 12, 212, 214, 219. Plate 45.1
1725	152 n. 3
1742	117 nn. 13 f.
1754	67 n. 3
1755	62 n. 9, 66 n. 8, 67 n. 11
1756	66 and n. 9, 67 nn. 2, 4, 7, 8, 10, 69, 208, 224. Plate 51.4
1759	59 n. 13, 60 n. 3, 63 n. 5
1761	39 n. 12, 40 n. 11, 61 n. 18
1762	138 n. 4
1767	61 n. 15
1769	55 n. 10
1770	66 n. 8
1777	66 n. 8
1790	20, 45, 203. Plate 19.2
1792	106 n. 9, 201. Plate 16.2
1795	57 n. 15, 59 n. 1
1796	63 n. 14, 66 n. 11
1797	39 n. 8, 51 n. 2
1799	213
1808	59 n. 10
1809	31, 105 n. 15, 107 and n. 9, 108 and n. 3, 128, 161, 227. Figure 34b. Plate 60.2
1810	139 n. 1
1811	59 n. 4, 138 n. 18
1815	40 n. 18, 142 n. 16
1816	59 n. 13, 60 and n. 4, 61 and n. 2, 71, 160, 222, 223, 224. Figure 24c. Plate 49.1
1817	59 n. 13, 60 nn. 4, 9, 66 n. 8
1818	46 nn. 6, 9, 159. Figure 19b
1822	39 n. 9, 40 n. 1, 51 n. 2, 210
1825	85 n. 19 f., 141 n. 2, 207, 216. Plate 26.1
1826	27 n. 17
1827	31, 106 n. 2, 108 n. 1, 128, 227. Plate 60.4
1828	43 nn. 1, 3
1832	67 n. 4
1833	66 n. 8
1834	65 n. 7, 219
1845	51 n. 1
1847	27 n. 16
1848	61 n. 2
1852	61 n. 16
1875	82, 204. Plate 21.4
1885	83 n. 4, 142 n. 20
1907	62 nn. 9, 14, 66 n. 8, 67 n. 3, 223
1908	62 n. 9, 66 n. 8, 67 nn. 8, 9
1910	59 n. 13
1922	44 n. 11
1923	44 n. 10
1926	63 n. 2, 215. Plate 38.1
1928	63 n. 15
1929	27, 51 n. 1, 206. Plate 25.2
1930	56 n. 13
1931	55 n. 10
1932	37 n. 8, 40 n. 6, 159. Figure 14b
1933	39 n. 11, 55 n. 10, 217, 218. Plate 41.3
1934	55 nn. 7, 10, 12, 217, 218. Plate 40.4
1935	37 n. 8, 159, 203, 209. Figure 14a
1938	38, 40, 47 n. 11, 50 f., 214, 215. Plate 36.3
1939	63 n. 15
1940	xx, 50 n. 4, 159, 215. Figure 22a, Plate 38.1
1941	217. Plate 40.3
1942	39 n. 9
1943	51 n. 11, 215, 216. Plate 38.3
1944	55 n. 10, 66 n. 8
1945	51 n. 11
1947	56 n. 9
1948	85 nn. 19 f.
1955	54 n. 11, 57 n. 15
1956	54, 57 n. 11, 62 n. 9, 214, 219. Plate 44.1
1958	20, 45, 202, 203, 204. Plate 19.3
1959	204
1960	39 n. 10, 159, 203. Figure 18a
1970	137 n. 9, 220. Plate 45.4
1973	17 n. 3, 41 n. 5, 105 n. 14, 107 n. 6, 121 and n. 13, 200. Plate 14.2
1975	15, 204. Plate 20.3
1979	137 n. 9, 138 n. 3, 220. Plate 45.3
1981	41 nn. 4, 8
1982	9, 19 and n. 9, 38 n. 4, 79, 84, 85 n. 19, 86 n. 1, 158, 202, 206. Figure 10c, Plate 18.2
1983	19 n. 9
1985	137 n. 9, 220. Plate 45.2
1993	40 n. 13
1995	215. Plate 38.4
1999	59 n. 13
2000	59 n. 13
2011	59 n. 13
2019	55 n. 10
2021	209, 211, 212, 216, 217, 220. Plate 29.3
2023	111 n. 6
2025	82, 204. Plate 21.3
2026	83 n. 4, 207
2028	59 n. 13, 60 n. 3
2032	206. Plate 25.4
2035	35 n. 10
2038	66 n. 13
2137	119 n. 12
2184	119 n. 7
2185	94 and n. 8, 226. Plate 56.3
2213	118 n. 4, 149 nn. 4, 6
2246	85 n. 4, 116, 118, 198. Plate 4.1
2262	119 n. 7, 157. Figure 2e
11730	137 n. 10
12133	15, 46, 55 n. 14, 64, 79, 209, 212, 214, 216. Plate 34.3
12138	55 nn. 7, 10, 12
12149	93 n. 16

12271   81 n. 2, 119, 131, 149 n. 4, 230. Plate 69.1
12274   85 n. 4, 158. Figure 9a
12275   64 n. 6
12534   57 n. 15
12714   80, 99, 131, 230. Plate 68.5
12739   36 n. 11, 38 n. 4, 159. Figure 17a
12747   36 nn. 1, 11, 38 n. 2, 159. Figure 17b
12768   150 n. 14
12769   99 n. 11
12783   63 nn. 15, 16, 17 f., 215
12789   44 n. 13
12791   46 n. 6, 54 n. 10
12792   39 n. 10
12801   9, 19, 79, 84, 85 n. 19, 158, 202, 203, 204.
        Figure 10b, Plate 18.1
12893   64 n. 11
13701   45 n. 18, 216. Plate 39.2
14517   62 n. 13, 65 n. 7, 211, 219, 220. Plate 44.3
14521   64 n. 7
15002   99 n. 5
15375   30 n. 13, 77, 78 n. 2, 132, 148 n. 3, 199.
        Plate 9.2
16283   126 n. 14
16422   35 n. 11, 51 n. 4, 61 n. 18, 159, 208, 217.
        Figure 16c, Plate 28.3
16423   67 n. 4
16461   66 n. 12
17276   60 and n. 9, 61 and n. 10, 62 n. 14, 222.
        Plate 49.3
17279   28 n. 2
17283   66 n. 1
17324   35 n. 10, 142 n. 15
17933   28 n. 2
18813   50 n. 3
19273   66 n. 12
19280   60 n. 9, 61 n. 8, 223. Plate 50.3
19333   54 and n. 9, 58, 157, 160. Figures 4g, 24b
19334   58
19335   56 n. 15
19336   54 n. 15, 58 n. 8
19338   54 n. 14
19341   54 n. 14
19342   64 n. 4
19345   54 n. 4
19346   54 n. 4
19348   54 n. 5
19350   54 n. 6
19354   53 n. 9, 56 n. 11, 57 n. 12, 86 n. 9, 207
19355   49 nn. 5, 7, 50, 53 n. 10, 160, 215.
        Figure 22c
19356   53 n. 8
19357   53 n. 8, 58 n. 2
T.E. 556   32 n. 1, 77, 200. Plate 9.3
(connected with Thanatos Painter, *lekythos*) 38 n. 7
(Hermonax, cup)   42 n. 22
(Painter of Berlin 2464, white *lekythos*)
        62 nn. 9, 10, 14
(Quadrate Painter, white *lekythos*)   63 n. 15
Once ATHENS, Private
(Triglyph Painter, *lekythos*)   67 n. 1

(Bowdoin-type *lekythos*)   106 n. 15
Once ATHENS, Schliemann
— (*lekythos*)   41 n. 6
ATHENS, Vlasto Collection
— (Sabouroff Painter, *lekythos*)   36 n. 6
— (Sabouroff Painter, *lekythos*)   37 n. 1
— (Bowdoin Painter, *lekythos*)   110 n. 3, 111 n. 2
— (Pattern *lekythos*, Beldam Workshop)   154 n. 15

Once BALTIMORE, Maryland, Robinson Collection
— (Diosphos Painter, Side-palmette *lekythos*)
        98 n. 5, 161. Figure 28a
BALTIMORE, Walters Art Gallery
48.2021   39 n. 8, 40 n. 14
BARCELONA, Montanauer Collection
— (Diosphos Painter, white *alabastron*)   149 n. 12
BARCELONA, Museo Arqueológico
581   42 n. 21, 126 n. 10
Once Barre Collection
— (Diosphos Workshop, Side-palmette *lekythos*)
        100 n. 14, 162. Figure 30c
BASLE, Antikenmuseum
1958.170   39 n. 8, 40 n. 14
BASLE, Cahn Collection
128   24 n. 1, 125 nn. 3, 5
— (Berlin Painter, red-figure *lekythos*)   14, 199.
        Plate 7.4
— (Huge *Lekythos*, once Heidelberg)
        68 n. 11, 69 n. 3, 70, 71 and n. 5
— (Theseus Painter, *skyphos*)   133 n. 9
BASLE, CIBA AG
— (Berlin Painter, amphora)   100 n. 15
BASLE, J. R. Geigy AG
— (Triglyph Painter, *lekythos*)   67 n. 1
BASLE, Hagemann Collection
— (Bird Painter, *lekythos*)   58 n. 2
BASLE, Market, M.M.
— (Aischines Painter, *lekythos*)
        9 n. 9, 82, 204. Plate 21.2
— (Theseus Painter, *alabastron*)   15 n. 2
— (Gela Painter, *lekythos*)   22 n. 1
— (Bowdoin Painter, *lekythos*)   23 n. 13, 106 n. 2
— (Sabouroff Painter, *lekythos*)   37 n. 1
— (Thanatos Painter, *lekythos*)   40 n. 10
— (like Vouni Painter, *lekythos*)   45 n. 8
— (Reed Painter, *lekythos*)   60, 62, 63, 205, 221.
        Plate 47.2
— (Side-palmette, chimney *lekythos*)
        87, 112 n. 1, 161, 229. Figure 32b, Plate 64.2
— (*lekythos*, shape DL)   102 n. 1
— (Icarus Painter, *lekythos*)   103 n. 18
— (Bowdoin Painter, *lekythos*)   106 n. 1
— (Painter of Half-palmettes, *olpe*)   109 n. 8
— (black-bodied *stamnos*)   115 n. 12
— (black-bodied *lekythos*, 'compromise')   123
— (Berlin Painter, amphora)   126 n. 3
— (white-ground pattern *lekythos*)
        131, 154, 231. Plate 70.3
— (Lupoli Painter, white *lekythos*)   142 n. 10

BEIRUT, Museum
7393   106 n. 1, 107 n. 10
— (Beldam Workshop, *lekythos*)   154 n. 1
BERKELEY (California), University of California
8.35   153 n. 10
8.36   54 n. 10
BERLIN, Staatliche Museen
1897   95 n. 2
1922   12 n. 15
1933   108 n. 7
1941   55 n. 3
1961   21 n. 1
2190   25 n. 10
2249   108 n. 1
2250   107 n. 8
2252   31 n. 2, 127 n. 5, 128, 199. Plate 8.1
2259   39 n. 7, 77, 232. Plate 72.1
2283   32 n. 3
2443   38, 40, 44 n. 8, 46, 50 f., 159, 210, 213. Figure 19a, Plate 35.1
2449   49 n. 3, 6
2450   49 nn. 3 f., 215
2454   55 nn. 8, 13, 217. Plate 41.1
2455   35 n. 9
2463   62 n. 7, 67 n. 17
2464   62 n. 10
2677   64 n. 5
2680   63 n. 8, 66 nn. 10, 13, 67 n. 6
2681   63 n. 8, 66 n. 10, 67 n. 6
2682   69 n. 8
2683   69 n. 9
2684   68 and nn. 12, 14, 70, 71 and n. 7, 72 and n. 6, 73, 208, 224, 225. Plate 54.2
2685   68 nn. 12, 14, 70
inv. 3160   211
inv. 3168   31 n. 1, 199. Plate 9.1
inv. 3209   38 n. 4, 72 n. 5, 214
inv. 3261   8 n. 7, 21, 91 n. 4, 96 n. 11, 198. Plate 4.3
inv. 3262   35, 36, 38 n. 2, 39, 208, 209, 217. Plate 28.2
inv. 3291   37 n. 8, 40 n. 19, 159. Figure 15b
inv. 3372   57 n. 3
inv. 3759   42 n. 10
inv. 3964   40 n. 14
inv. 3970   46 n. 1
inv. 4982.9   106 n. 4
— (*Lekythos*, fragment)   70 n. 7
BERLIN, Völkerkundemuseum
5252   44 n. 5
5254   44 n. 5
BERNE, Jucker Collection
— (Achilles Painter, white *lekythos*)
46 n. 11, 47, 48, 142, 157, 214. Figure 4e, f, Plate 37.1
BIRMINGHAM, City Museum and Art Gallery
1616.85   14, 24, 26 n. 10, 47 n. 13, 125 and n. 11, 229. Plate 66.1
BOCHUM, Ruhr University, Funke Collection
S 496   13, 78, 95, 123, 198. Plate 3.2
S 502   16, 22, 23, 27, 79, 121, 200. Plate 12.3

BOLOGNA, Museo Civico
44   115 n. 14
100   150 n. 15
PU 321   24 n. 3, 25, n. 5, 27 n. 2, 31 n. 8, 125 n. 1, 126, 127 n. 12, 199. Plate 8.2
PU 322   10 n. 1
PU 367   61 n. 17, 64 n. 3
BONN, University, Akademisches Kunstmuseum
37   6 n. 9
64   45 n. 10
66   39 n. 4, 40 n. 1
84   105, 110 n. 4, 228. Plate 63.4
307   15 n. 6, 24 n. 13
339   8 n. 2
538   79, 105 nn. 12, 14, 15, 107 n. 8, 122 n. 3, 201. Plate 14.5
1011   41 n. 3, 211
BOSTON (Massachusetts), Museum of Fine Arts
92.2609   39 nn. 11, 12, 40 n. 11
93.99   85 n. 4
93.102   91 n. 4, 97 n. 2
93.103   159. Figure 21b
94.127   39 nn. 3, 11, 217. Plate 40.4
95.41   16, 25 n. 1, 27, 30 n. 5, 31 n. 6, 79, 200. Plate 12.1
95.42   79 n. 4
95.47   28 n. 8, 35 n. 12, 63 n. 2, 158. Figure 12c
95.65   51 n. 11
96.721   39 n. 12
98.916   6 n. 9
98.928   127 n. 14, 229. Plate 64.4
99.526   18, 92 n. 8, 160, 201. Figure 25c, Plate 17.2
99.528   17, 80, 91, 98 and n. 9, 105, 149, 227. Plate 59.1
00.356   112 n. 4
00.359   38 n. 4, 39 nn. 4, 11, 54 n. 12, 57 n. 14, 61 nn. 18 f., 210, 211, 218. Plate 32.1
01.17   12 n. 15
01.8025   10 n. 3
01.8077   132 n. 1
01.8080   37, 39 n. 2, 57 n. 14, 159, 210, 211. Figure 16a, Plate 31.1
08.368   46 n. 13
09.69   39 n. 12
09.70   39 nn. 3, 11, 12, 40 n. 10, 217
10.220   40 n.18
10.556   119 n. 1
13.169   29 n. 1, 207. Plate 27.1
13.187   159. Figure 20c
13.194   25 n. 4
13.195   13 n. 11, 78 n. 2, 79 n. 1, 95 n. 12, 199. Plate 6.1
13.201   46 n. 9
13.202   46, 48 n. 4, 212. Plate 34.1
24.450   126 n. 15
1970.428   85 nn. 19 f., 203, 216. Plate 20.2
BOSTON, Oddy Collection
— (Carlsberg Painter, *lekythos*)   58 n. 4
BOULOGNE, Musée Communal
18   12 n. 1

BRAURON, Museum
— (Side-palmette *lekythos*) 102 n. 8
BRONXVILLE, Bastis Collection
— (Bowdoin Painter, *lekythos*) 106 n. 9
BRUNSWICK (Maine), Bowdoin College
20.1 23 n. 13, 106 n. 2
23.26 58 n. 2
1915.46 35 n. 6, 36 n. 3, 39 n.6
BRUSSELS, Errera
— (Bowdoin Painter, *lekythos*) 106 n. 2
BRUSSELS, Musées Royaux
A 71 126 n. 9
A 124 59 n. 13, 66 n. 8
A 1022 66 n. 8, 67 n. 4
A 1379 15, 43, 44, 46, 213. Plate 34.4
A 2127 144 n. 7
A 3131 16 nn. 6, 8, 106 n. 7, 122 nn. 1, 2, 3, 201.
Plate 15.1
A 3132 16 nn. 6, 7, 79, 106 n. 7, 122 nn. 1, 2, 3,
201. Plate 15.2
R 251 92 n. 9, 95 n. 1
Once Brussels, van Branteghem Collection
— (Sappho Painter, *lekythos*) 123 n. 11

CAGLIARI, Museo
— (Diosphos Painter, white *alabastron*) 149 n. 8
CALTANISSETTA, Museum
— (Painter of the Yale *Lekythos*. Side-palmette
lekythos) 100 n. 10, 102 n. 10, 104 n. 8, 160.
Figure 30a
CAMBRIDGE, Fitzwilliam Museum
111 150 n. 2
4.17 19 n. 16
36.1937 52 n. 10
37.29 43 n. 5
G 118 152 n. 4
G 134 150 n. 1
G 137 150 n. 2
GR 1.1895 19, 104 n. 4, 111 nn. 6, 8, 112, 228.
Plate 64.1
GR 2.1928 55, 216. Plate 40.1
GR 3.1917 111 n. 6, 229. Plate 64.3
— (Theseus Painter, *lekythos*) 15 n. 4
CAMBRIDGE (Massachusetts), Harvard University, Fogg
Museum
60.336 34 n. 9
1925.30.51 101 n. 6, 102 n. 13, 161. Figure 31b
1925.30.54 53 n. 5, 58 n.2
CANBERRA, Australian National University
— (Carlsberg Painter, *lekythos*) 58 n. 4
CAPE TOWN, South African Museum
18 84 n. 12
CARLSRUHE, Badisches Landesmuseum
167 91, 92 n. 17, 94, 97 n. 13, 149 n. 3, 226.
Plate 55.1
219 84 n. 12
231 120 n. 10
234 57 n. 13, 218. Plate 43.2
B 34 119 n. 12
B 985 118 n. 9

B 2319 145 n. 10
B 2663 63 n. 6, 205
(B 2689) 67 n. 5
CASSEL, Hessisches Landesmuseum
T 437 154 n. 4
CASTELVETRANO, Museo
126 121 n. 4, 148 n. 13
CASTLE ASHBY, the Marquess of Northampton
— (Psiax, neck-amphora) 10 n. 13, 117 n. 11
CHICAGO, Art Institute
07.18 59, 67 n. 12, 68, 69, 71, 223, 224. Plate 51.1
— (Beldam Workshop, *lekythos*) 86 n. 8
CHRISTCHURCH (New Zealand), University of Canter-
bury
16 141 n. 4
CLEVELAND (Ohio), Museum of Art
28.859 60 n. 2, 61 n. 10, 65 n. 5, 66 n. 7
66.114 27, 29 n. 8, 30, 31, 32, 78 n. 2, 128, 200.
Plates 10.2, 11
1873.28 222
COLOGNY, Dr. Martin Bodmer
— (Icarus Painter, squat *lekythos*) 155 n. 2
COLUMBIA (Missouri), University of Missouri
58.12 116, 119, 199. Plate 6.4
COMPIÈGNE, Musée Vivenel
881 94 n. 7
1040 92 n. 12
COPENHAGEN, Nationalmuseum
82 160. Figure 27b
111 12 n. 4
124 124 n. 3
1636 18 n. 2, 123 n. 21
1941 19 n. 10, 85 n. 2
2789 62 n. 5
3835 115 n. 10
3882 77, 96 n. 4, 228. Plate 61.2
4219 115 n. 11
4986 67 n. 14, 68 and n. 8, 69, 71 and n. 2, 224.
Plate 52.1
6328 82 n. 10
6590 56 n. 8
Chr. viii, 392 154 n. 7
COPENHAGEN, Ny Carlsberg Glyptotek
2701 125 n. 10
2780 55 n. 10
V. 26 14, 24, 26 n. 11, 125, 229. Plate 66.3
COPENHAGEN, Thorvaldsen Museum
38 10 n. 14, 117 n. 10
CORINTH, Museum
C 393 103 n. 14
MP 89 84 n. 11, 138 n. 16
MP 90 138 n. 16
MP 91 59 n. 11, 138 n. 17
T 566–118 19, 87, 131, 138, 154, 231. Plate 70.8
T 3161–P 1980 119 n. 13
CORSHAM (Wiltshire), Eden Collection
— (Palmette *lekythos*) 119, 131, 153, 231. Plate 69.3
CRACOW, University
1087 34 n. 13
1251 56 n. 12

DELOS, Museum
547   158. Figure 7b
566   145 n. 13, 146 n. 2
567   150 n. 12
593   157. Figure 2a
DRESDEN, Albertinum
315   213
ZV 1608   92 n. 16, 93 n. 20
ZV 1700   105 n. 8
ZV 1779   12 n. 1, 2
ZV 1780   12 n. 1, 2
ZV 2777   37 n. 5
ZV 2963   111 n. 6
DUNEDIN, Otago Museum
E 30.202   34 n. 16, 35 n. 2

EDEN Collection, see Corsham (Wiltshire)
ELEUSIS, Museum
— (Bowdoin Painter, *lekythos*)   108 n. 9
— (Sosimos, *phiale*)   117 n. 6
ERLANGEN, University
526   64 n. 14
I 275   201. Plate 16.4
EXETER, University
— (Reed Painter, *lekythos*)   62 n. 3
— (red-figure *pelike*)   221

FERRARA, Museo Nazionale di Spina
T.41   115 nn. 15 f.
T.136 C VP   59 n. 5
T.136 C VP   59 n. 5
T.349   146 n. 4
T.367   115 nn. 15 f.
— (Talos Painter, calyx-crater, fr.)   72 n. 5
FLORENCE, Museo Archeologico Etrusco
1 B 6   11 n. 3
2 B 11   12 n. 12
3985   124 n. 7
4209   6 n. 9, 7, 157. Figure 1 d, e, f
— (black-figure doubleen)   118 n. 4
FRANKFURT, University
— (Manner of the Bird Painter, *lekythos*)   52 n. 6
Once FRÖHNER Collection
— (white *lekythos*)   41 n. 3

GELA, Museo Civico
21   125 n. 9
24   31 nn. 10, 12
— (Brygos Painter, *lekythos*) 26, 27 n. 140 n. 13, 6, 30, 206. Plate 24.1
— (Painter of Munich 2774, *lekythos*)   82 n. 10
— (Group of the Floral Nolans, *lekythos*)   125 nn. 4, 13
GENEVA, Market
— (Painter of New York 23. 166.41, *lekythos*)   223
GERONA, Museo Arqueológico Provincial
— (Diosphos Painter, white *alabastron*)   149 n. 8
— (Diosphos Painter, white *alabastron*)   149 n. 8
— (Haimon Painter, white *alabastron*)   150 n. 14

Once GOLUCHOW, Prince Czartoryski
84   34 n. 11
86   34 n. 11
GOTHA, Museum
42   109 n. 7
43   109 n. 7
GÖTTINGEN, University
ZV 1964/139   85 n. 4, 201. Plate 17.1
GREENSBORO (North Carolina), Jastrow Collection
(*lekythos* near the Two-row Painter)   34 n. 15, 96 n. 2, 160. Figure 27a
GREENWICH (Connecticut), Bareiss Collection
15   14, 199. Plate 7.3
104   106 n. 9
GREIFSWALD, University
363   43 nn. 2, 3
365   58 n. 4

THE HAGUE, Gemeente Museum
1890   36 n. 7
HAMBURG, Museum für Kunst und Gewerbe
1896.21   78 n. 2
1917.817   60, 62, 63 and n. 7, 205, 211, 221, 222, 223, 224. Plate 47.1
— (Eucharides Painter, black-bodied amphora)   126 n. 9
— (Haimon Painter, cup-*skyphoi*)   150 n. 10
HANOVER, Kestner Museum
1961.23   117 n. 7
HARTFORD (Connecticut), Wadsworth Atheneum
30. 184   42 n. 20, 48 n. 1
1961.8   10 n. 6, 13 n. 4, 20, 94 n. 14, 198. Plate 2.2
HAVANA, Conde de Lagunillas Collection
(Athena Painter, *lekythos*)   19 n. 12, 31 n. 4, 107 n. 12
(Painter of Vatican G 49, *oinochoe*)   26 n. 3
(Achilles Painter, *lekythos*)   44 n. 4, 46 n. 5
(Athena Painter, *lekythos*)   106 n. 4
(Theseus Painter, *alabastron*)   133 n. 12
HEIDELBERG, University
158   21 n. 9
E 51   120 n. 1
L 11   150 n. 2
L 41   61 n. 17
HOBART, University of Tasmania
30a   65 n. 1
30b   65 n. 1
HONOLULU, Academy of Arts
2892   34 n. 14, 81 and n. 8, 96 n. 1, 208, 217. Plate 28.1
HOUSTON (Texas), Museum of Fine Arts
37.8   36 n. 12

ITHACA (New York), Museum
— (white *lekythos*)   65 n. 10, 225. Plate 53.1
IZMIR, Museum
(Pattern *lekythos*)   150 n. 2

JENA, University
(Manner of the Tymbos Painter, *lekythos*)   83 n. 4

KÜSNACHT, Hirschmann
(Manner of the Bowdoin Painter, *lekythos*)
107 n. 4, 108 n. 4, 161. Figure 34a

LAON, Musée
37.942   35 n. 10
37.957   35 n. 6
37.960   34 n. 13
LAUSANNE, Musée
3700   28 n. 14
LAUSANNE, Private
(Sappho Painter, bail-amphora)   133 n. 7
(Sabouroff Painter, *lekythos*)   38 n. 3
LECCE, Museo Provinciale
566   142 n. 11
LEIPSIC, University
(Reed Painter, *lekythos*)   61 n. 3
LENINGRAD, Museum of the Hermitage
670   27 n. 7, 45, 140 n. 13, 206. Plate 24.2
671   99 n. 7
686   25 n. 10
PHC 97   100 n. 12, 104 n. 8
(Leagros Group, *hydria*)   18 n. 2
(*lekythos* from Olbia)   35 n. 1, 102 n. 12
(Meidias Painter, *lekythos*)   126 n. 15
(white *lekythos*)   213
LEYDEN, Rijksmuseum van Oudheden
xvii a. 20   22 n. 8
LIDINGÖ, Millesgården
94   67 nn. 1, 13, 68 n. 1
LONDON, British Museum
B 188   14, 98, 199. Plate 7.1
B 300   12 n. 7
B 316   12 n. 1
B 320   94 n. 12
B 330   18 n. 1
B 359   104, 106, 109 and n. 8, 228. Plate 62.1
B 364   115 n. 10, 117 n. 8
B 524   144 n. 13
B 631   26 n. 1, 107 n. 7
B 632   93, 95 n. 9, 227. Plate 57.2
B 636   22 n. 7
B 651   104 n. 7
B 659   79, 96, 112, 131, 153 n. 10, 154 n. 1, 203,
                231. Plate 70.1
B 668   99 n. 5
B 693   10 n. 5
D 1   29 n. 6
D 2   128 n. 5
D 5   205
D 20   28 n. 13
D 22   105 and n. 9, 106, 108, 110 n. 3, 111 n. 2,
                228. Plate 63.2
D 26   27 n. 16
D 33   15, 39 n. 5, 204, 210. Plate 20.4
D 35   9, 82, 83 n. 4, 205. Plate 23.1
D 38   61 n. 18
D 44   59 n. 7
D 45   38, 46, 59 n. 7
D 47   29 n. 4, 207. Plate 27.3

D 48   40, 46, 50 f., 213. Plate 35.2
D 54   38, 40, 50 f., 52 n. 5, 213, 214, 216. Plate 36.1
D 57   39 n. 9, 40 n. 10
D 58   xxi, 69 n. 5, 211, 215
D 59   211. Plate 32.4
D 60   39 n. 11, 40 n. 1, 41 n. 3, 69 n. 5, 211.
                Plate 32.3
D 61   60 and n. 3, 62, 63 and n. 11, 205, 221,
                223. Plate 47.3
D 62   xxi, 36 n. 12, 40 n. 1, 41 n. 3, 69 n. 5, 208,
                209, 217. Plate 29.2
D 63   59 n. 3, 64 n. 9, 141 n. 5
D 65   19, 79, 84, 86, 157, 202. Figure 11a,
                Plate 18.3
D 66   53, 160, 217. Figure 23a, Plate 40.2
D 67   38 n. 4, 40 n. 13, 69 n. 5, 209, 210, 211.
                Plate 32.2
D 70   57 n. 2, 160. Figure 23c
D 71   59 n. 13, 60, 61 and n. 4, 62 nn. 9, 14, 63
                n. 9, 65 and n. 11, 66 n. 8, 222. Plate 49.4
D 72   62 and nn. 12, 14 f., 220. Plate 46.1
D 74   59 n. 13, 62 n. 5
D 83   59 n. 13
E 48   30 n. 9
E 278   27 n. 5
E 279   27 n. 5
E 300   42 n. 10
E 511   80 n. 11
E 528   106 n. 2
E 573   15, 16, 22, 23 n. 4, 24 n. 12, 25, 27, 79,
                200. Plate 12.2
E 642   35 n. 3
E 768   31 n. 5, 32, 200. Plate 9.4
63.7–28.45.1   16, 22, 27, 79, 121, 200. Plate 12.4
64.10–7.1722   77, 131, 232. Plate 71.3
64.10–7.1809   77, 232. Plate 72.6
99.2–18.67   158. Figure 7c
1836.2–24.33   77, 232. Plate 72.7
1900.6–11.1   11 n. 4, 117 n. 12, 198. Plate 1.3
1907.7–10.10   38 n. 1, 39 n. 5, 57 n. 8,
                209, 210. Plate 30.3
1910.4–30.1   126 n. 13
1914.5–12.1   9, 82, 204. Plate 21.1
1920.3–15.1   31, 104 n. 7, 128, 227. Plate 60.1
1922.10–18.1   9 n. 12, 79 n. 2, 81 n. 11, 119,
                147 n. 7, 199. Plate 6.3
1928.2–13.1   xxi, 28, 85 nn. 19 f., 141 n. 2, 142
                n. 18, 158, 207. Figure 12b, Plate 26.1
1928.2–13.2   57 n. 8, 218. Plate 43.1
1928.2–13.3   57 n. 4, 63 n. 17
1928.7–16.1   133 n. 6
1929.2–13.3   63 nn. 17 f.
1937.10–26.1   44.6
1971.11–1.1   6 n. 8
36 2-D 341   131, 231. Plate 70.2
LONDON, Embiricos Collection
— (Bowdoin Workshop, *lekythos*)   79, 107, 201.
                Plate 14.3
LONDON, Market
— (Sabouroff Painter, *lekythos*)   34 n. 10

LONDON, Market (*cont.*):
— (Painter of the Yale *Lekythos, lekythos*)   34 n. 16
— (Gela Painter, *lekythos*)   92 n. 13
— (Bowdoin Painter, *lekythos*)   106 n. 2
Once LONDON, Rogers Collection
— (Nolan-amphora)   42 n. 10
LONDON, Russell Collection
   (connected with Thanatos Painter, *lekythos*)
       38 n. 7
LONDON, Victoria and Albert Museum
   C 2491.1910   213, 214
LONDON, Winslow Collection
— (Theseus Painter, neck-*pelike*)   115 nn. 15 f.
LOS ANGELES, County Museum
   A 5933.50.24   57 n. 8
LOUVAIN, University
— (Icarus Painter, *loutrophoros*)   103 n. 15
LUCERNE, Market
— (Phiale Painter, *lekythos*)   49 n. 2, 126 n. 13
— (Bowdoin Workshop, *lekythos*)   79, 201.
       Plate 14.6
— (Bowdoin Painter, *lekythos*)   105 n. 15
LUCERNE, Roesli
— (Painter of Cambridge 28.2, *lekythos*)   55 n. 10
LUGANO, Schoen Collection (now MUNICH, Museum
   antiker kleinkunst)
LYONS, Musée
   E 413   43 n. 2
— (Woman Painter, *lekythos*)   58 n. 5
— (Triglyph Painter, *lekythos*)   66 n. 9

MADRID, Museo Arqueológico Nacional
   10902   115 n. 11
   10916   97 n. 14
   10930   15 n. 3
   11107   42 n. 11
   11117   31 n. 11, 125 n. 5, 153 n. 10
   11193   66 n. 12
   11194   68 and n. 11, 69 n. 1, 70, 71, 72,
       224, 225. Plate 54.1
   19497   20 n. 2, 45, 86 n. 5, 153 nn. 10 f., 158,
       202. Figure 11b, Plate 19.1
MALIBU (California), Getty Museum
— (Sabouroff Painter, *lekythos*)   35 n. 11
MANNHEIM, Reiss-Museum
   14   40 n. 18, 57 n. 6, 66 n. 12
   195   36 n. 12, 71 n. 8
MAPLEWOOD (New Jersey), Noble Collection
— (Leagran *stamnos*)   92 n. 9
— (Leagran *hydria*)   95 n. 1
— (Painter of the Paris Gigantomachy, *lekythos*)
       126 n. 15
MARBURG, University
   1016   52 n. 7, 53, 55 n. 14, 58 n. 2, 214, 216,
       217. Plate 39.3
— (Bowdoin Workshop, white *lekythos*)
       16, 105 n. 9, 106 n. 6, 108, 228. Plate 63.1
MEGGEN, Käppeli
— (Douris, cup)   30 n. 8

— (Bosanquet Painter, *lekythos*)   37 n. 6, 38 n. 2
— (Group R, *lekythos*)   62 n. 6
MINNEAPOLIS (Minnesota), Institute of Arts
   61.59   10, 12, 13, 94 n. 13, 95 n. 2, 198.
       Plate 2.1
— (Bird Painter, *lekythos*)   58 n. 2
MISSISSIPPI, University
— (Bowdoin Painter, *lekythos*)   106 n. 9
MUNICH, Bareiss Collection, see Greenwich
   (Connecticut)
MUNICH, Market
— (Beldam Painter, *lekythos*)   86 n. 2, 153 n. 8
Once MUNICH Market
   (Pattern *lekythos*)   154 n. 5
MUNICH, Museum antiker Kleinkunst
   1427   6 n. 9
   1693   18 n. 1
   1703   12 n. 4
   1722   9 n. 14
   1798   137 n. 2
   2170   38 n. 4
   2447   93 n. 9, 94, 95 n. 8, 226. Plate 57.1
   2475   24 nn. 2, 4, 25, 115 nn. 15 f., 124 n. 10
   2587   10 n. 2
   2685   34 n. 7
   2770   59 n. 8
   2771   59 n. 8
   2772   59 n. 8
   2777   211
   2791   38 n. 7
   2797   49 nn. 4, 7, 11, 50 and n. 1, 137 n. 2, 215
   2798   48, 49 nn. 4, 10, 50 and n. 1, 137 n. 2, 215.
       Plate 38.2
   inv. 3170   29 n. 1
   inv. 7517   27 n. 3
   inv. 7620   64 n. 10
   inv. 7657   108 n. 4
   inv. 7678   39 n. 8
   inv. 7679   40 n. 10
   inv. 8499   51 n. 1
— (Villa Giulia Painter, *lekythoi*)   28 n. 17
— (Sabouroff Painter, white cup)   36 n. 8
— (Helicon *lekythos*)   49, 58 n. 4
— (Reed Workshop, *lekythos*)   66 n. 7
— (Triglyph Painter, *lekythos*)   67 n. 4

NAPLES, Museo Nazionale
   2438   106 n. 1, 107 n. 8
   2763   142 n. 7
   3155   123 n. 7
   RC 209   149 n. 12
   Stg. 135   105 n. 12, 106 n. 1, 107 nn. 3, 8
   Stg. 175   118 n. 4
   Stg. 235   107 n. 2
— (Icarus Painter, *lekythos*)   103 n. 13
NEW HAVEN (Conn.), Yale University
   144   104 n. 5, 143 n. 1
NEW ORLEANS (Louisiana), Private Collection
— (Thanatos Painter, *lekythoi*)   40 nn. 14, 17; 41

New York, Baker Collection
— (Thanatos Painter, *lekythos*)   39 nn. 9, 14, 41,
                         51 n. 2, 159, 209. Figure 18c
New York, Brooklyn, The Brooklyn Museum
29.1   14, 24, 27, 125, 126 and n. 9, 229.
                                    Plate 66.2
Once New York, Gallatin Collection
—   93 n. 3, 94, 160, 226. Figure 26a, Plate 56.2
New York, Market
—   38 n. 2, 57 n. 14
New York, Metropolitan Museum of Art
06.1021.47   12 n. 6
06.1021.90   95 n. 14, 128 n. 3
06.1021.92   77, 94 n. 4, 99, 101 n. 5, 118, 149,
                             232. Plate 72.2
06.1021.127   59 n. 8, 83 n. 4, 141 n. 13
06.1021.134   28 n. 12, 158, 208. Figure 13b,
                                    Plate 27.4
06.1070   17, 80, 91, 98 and n. 11, 99 n. 1, 105,
             149, 160, 224. Figure 28b, Plate 59.2
06.1071   99 n. 1
06.1075   51 and n. 5, 216. Plate 39.1
06.1153   125 nn. 5, 8, 12
06.1169   62 n. 13
06.1171   46 n. 7, 159. Figure 20a
07.1   61, 67 n. 15, 224, 225. Plate 52.2
07.286.36   45 n. 14
07.286.40   xxi, 36 n. 12, 56, 71 n. 8, 205, 208,
                             217. Plate 29.1
07.286.41   92 n. 6, 160. Figure 25b
07.286.42   46 n. 6, 159. Figure 19c
07.286.43   92 n. 7, 160. Figure 25a
07.286.45   61 n. 4
07.286.81   42 n. 14
08.258.18   159. Figure 20b
08.258.23   48 n. 13, 159. Figure 21c
08.258.28   26 n. 3, 79, 107 n. 7, 201. Plate 14.4
08.258.30   93 n. 2
09.221.44   xxi, 56 nn. 6, 7, 10, 160, 218. Figure
                             23b, Plate 42.1
10.210.11   158. Figure 8c
11.212.8   37, 39 n. 1, 159, 210. Figure 16b,
                                    Plate 31.2
12.299.10   39 n. 10, 40, 159, 212. Figure 18b,
                                    Plate 33.1
13.227.16   125 n. 9
15.165   39 n. 8, 40 n. 10
21.80   77, 94 n. 4, 99, 101 n. 5, 118, 149, 232.
                                    Plate 72.3
21.88.17   35 n. 8, 36 n. 12, 159. Figure 17c
22.53   50 n. 5, 137 n. 2, 159. Figure 22b
22.139.10   55 nn. 8, 9, 11, 217. Plate 41.2
22.139.189   43 n. 11, 219
23.160.38   37 and n. 6, 38 nn. 2, 4; 51 n. 2, 208,
                             209. Plate 30.1
23.160.39   37, 38 n. 2, 160, 209 f. Figure 15a,
                                    Plate 30.2
24.97.26   125 n. 5
25.189.2   42 n. 8
26.60.76   21 n. 13

26.60.77   42 n. 19
26.60.78   35 n. 6
28.167   45 n. 14
34.32.2   56 n. 7, 57 n. 14, 219. Plate 42.2
34.155   51 n. 6
35.11.5   27, 28 n. 18, 29, 45, 86 and n. 9, 142
             n. 17, 158, 207. Figure 12a, Plate 26.2
41.162.11   61 n. 4, 62, 64, 65 n. 2, 221. Plate 48.2
41.162.12   62, 65 n. 3, 222, 225. Plate 48.3
41.162.13   20, 22, 151, 202. Plate 17.4
41.162.18   126 n. 11
41.162.19   42 n. 21, 126 n. 10
41.162.27   35 n. 1, 102 n. 11
41.162.64   95 n. 5, 115 n. 10
41.162.95   100 n. 13, 104 n. 8, 160. Figure 30b
41.162.102   158. Figure 11c
41.162.146   79, 105 n. 14, 107, 121 and n. 13, 158,
                 200. Figure 8b, Plate 14.1
51.11.4   37 n. 1
51.163   17, 80, 91, 98, 100 n. 1, 105, 149, 160,
                 227. Figure 29b, Plate 59.3
53.107   64 n. 5
57.12.24   29 n. 3, 158, 208. Figure 13c, Plate 27.5
62.11.11   11 n. 6
63.11.6   10 n. 16
75.2.5   160. Figure 24a
91.1.442   77, 232. Plate 72.4
99.13.3   56, nn. 5, 7, 218
New York, Mitchell Collection
— (Pamphaios, cup)   12 n. 16
Nicosia, Cyprus Museum
Y 453   28 n. 18
Nicosia, Pierides Collection
— (Semi-outline *lekythos*)   107 n. 8

Oundle, School Collection
— (*lekythos*)   37 n. 2
Oxford, Ashmolean Museum
249   20 n. 10
251   16 n. 10, 17, 23, 77, 115, 121 n. 11, 145,
                 211, 230. Plate 67.4
263   64 n. 8
265   106 n. 9
315   27 n. 4
437   9, 63, 82, 83 n. 4, 205. Plate 23.2
512   8 n. 8, 21, 97 n. 3, 198. Plate 4.4
544   52 n. 9, 209, 211, 214, 216. Plate 39.4
545   38, 40, 50 f., 214. Plate 36.2
547   63 n. 6
548   43 n. 1
574   54 n. 11
1836.68   120, 131, 230. Plate 68.3
1872.1248A   131, 144 n. 8, 230. Plate 68.2
1879.209   131, 232. Plate 71.2
1879.210   19, 131, 154, 231. Plate 70.7
1914.9   84 n. 3
1916.15   84 n. 5
1922.18   81, 103 n. 2, 228. Plate 61.1
1923.69   226
1924.3   126 n. 3

OXFORD, Ashmolean Museum (*cont.*):

1925.84	34 n. 16
1927.4456	119, 131, 153, 230. Plate 69.2
1927.4457	22 n. 7, 87, 131, 151, 231. Plate 70.4
1927.4458	119, 131, 153, 231. Plate 69.6
1927.4460	84, 228. Plate 61.4
1927.4463	83 n. 4
1927.4467	103 n. 12, 107 n. 11, 155 n. 1, 228. Plate 61.3
1928.41	23, 77, 115, 119 n. 13, 120, 229. Plate 67.2
1930.20	133 n. 8
1930.617	131, 155, 232. Plate 71.4
1932.733	78 n. 11, 123 n. 4, 140 n. 2, 229. Plate 65.1
1934.67	77, 232. Plate 72.5
1934.294	104 n. 1
1934.329	131, 146 n. 6, 230. Plate 68.6
1935.2	16, 23, 77, 79, 115, 120, 121, 229. Plate 67.3
1935.229	23, 77, 115, 230. Plate 67.6
1936.113	23, 77, 115, 116, 229. Plate 67.1
1936.616	77, 232. Plate 72.8
1937.301	144 n. 5
1938.726	144 n. 5
1938.732	23, 77, 115, 119 n. 3, 230. Plate 67.5
1938.736	131, 144, 147, 230. Plate 68.4
1938.909	159. Figure 21a
1940.148	119, 131, 231. Plate 69.5
1940.149	19, 131, 154, 231. Plate 70.6
1947.24	38, 40, 46 and n. 6, 50 f., 52, 213, 214. Plate 35.3
1949.751	10 n. 4, 13 n. 13, 199. Plate 5.1
1956.14	9, 50 n. 3, 82, 83 n. 4, 205, 211. Plate 22.2
1965.129	105, 106, 108, 110 n. 3, 111 and n. 2, 228. Plate 63.3
1966.768	12 n. 10
1966.854	29 n. 2, 107. Plate 27.2
1966.923	38 n. 1
1966.924	38 n. 7
1966.925	56 n. 13, 57 n. 16

PAESTUM, Museum

— (Side-palmette *lekythos*)	102 n. 2

PALERMO, Banco di Sicilia (Mormino Collection)

27	101 n. 8
310	28 n. 11, 158. Figure 13a

PALERMO, Museo Nazionale

V 670	26 n. 8, 44 n. 9, 125 n. 10
V 672	42 n. 20
V 673	42 n. 19
V 686	105 n. 15
996	85 n. 4
1272	148 n. 14
2792	16, 22, 24 n. 8, 79, 121, 200. Plate 13.2
GE 1896.1	157. Figure 2c
N.I.1886	29 and n. 6, 30, 31, 32, 140 n. 14, 200. Plate 10.1

— (Diosphos Workshop, Side-palmette *lekythos*)	100 n. 7, 102 n. 7, 161. Figure 31a
— (Icarus Painter, *lekythos*)	110 n. 16

PARIS, Bibliothèque Nationale, Cabinet des Médailles

222	157. Figure 2b
254	12 n. 7
255	95 n. 1
257	94 n. 12
299	107 n. 8, 122 n. 3
300	122 n. 2
363	42 n. 12
476	27 n. 15
489	42 n. 21, 126 n. 10
496 *bis*	41 n. 6, 83 n. 4
501	59 n. 9
523	93 n. 5

PARIS, Jameson

— (Psiax, *lekythos*)	9 n. 13, 21, 158. Figure 7a

PARIS, Market

— (Black-bodied *lekythos*)	16 n. 11, 121 n. 10
— (Sabouroff Painter, *lekythos*)	41 n. 6
— (Triglyph Painter, *lekythos*)	67 n. 1
— (Carlsruhe Painter, *lekythos*)	86 n. 4
— (Bowdoin Painter, *lekythos*)	95 n. 14

PARIS, Musée du Louvre

F 71	7, 77 n. 9, 198. Plate 1.1
F 114	12 n. 14, 117 n. 4
F 116	12 n. 15
F 117	12 n. 15
F 198	115 n. 10
F 201	10 n. 14, 117 n. 10
F 203	10 n. 16
F 290	12 n. 4
F 523	154 n. 8
F 524	154 n. 8
G 137	126 n. 4
G 203	14, 80 n. 11, 91, 95, 100 n. 17, 226. Plate 55.3
G 444	43 n. 7, 126 n. 12
CA 273	68 n. 11, 69 n. 2, 70, 71 and n. 3, 72 and n. 6, 73
CA 467	66 n. 8
CA 536	59 n. 13, 60, 61, 65 n. 4, 71, 222. Plate 49.2
CA 537	58 n. 6, 60 and n. 2, 61 n. 7, 62, 63 n. 9, 65 and n. 11, 66 n. 6, 157, 205, 211, 221, 223. Plate 50.1
CA 599	106 nn. 11, 12, 107 nn. 6, 8
CA 987	123 n. 12, 229. Plate 65.2
CA 1142	206. Plate 25.1
CA 1264	60 and n. 2, 61 n. 6, 62 n. 6, 63 n. 12, 223. Plate 50.2
CA 1329	57 n. 15, 59 nn. 1, 2
CA 1640	203. Plate 20.1
CA 2218	22 n. 7
CA 2980	41 n. 4
CA 3758	9, 38 n. 4, 82, 205. Plate 23.3
CA 4176	10, 13, 20, 94 n. 10, 95, 227. Plate 57.3
L 33	106 n. 2, 109 n. 1

MNB 440   67 nn. 5, 7
MNB 505   59 n. 1
MNB 613   59 n. 1
MNB 616   61, 62 n. 5, 220. Plate 46.2
MNB 617   62 n. 9
MNB 618   62 n. 9
MNB 619   62 n. 12
MNB 905   133 n. 5
MNB 909   17, 80, 91, 98 and n. 10, 99 n. 1, 105 and n. 12, 119, 149, 227. Plate 58.2
MNB 911   17, 80 and n. 16, 81, 91, 98 and n. 3, 105, 149, 227. Plate 59.4
MNB 912   157. Figure 2d
MNC 650   17, 80, 91, 98, 99 n. 6, 105, 119, 149, 227. Plate 58.1
S 1161   60, 62, 64, 65 n. 1, 66 n. 8, 221. Plate 48.1
S 3893   67 n. 4
PARIS, Musée Rodin
— (Triglyph Painter, *lekythos*)   66 n. 9
PARIS, Petit Palais
310   11 n. 14, 117 nn. 13 f.
311   21 n. 3
335   103 n. 4, 161. Figure 33a
336   103 n. 3
436   121 n. 1
— (Black-bodied *lekythos*)   148 n. 8
PARIS, Peyrefitte Collection
— (Bowdoin Workshop, *lekythos*)   16, 22, 24 n. 10, 79, 121, 200. Plate 13.1
Once PARIS, Seyrig
— (Manner of Douris, *lekythos*)   84 n. 7
— (Athena Painter, *lekythos*)   106 n. 4
PARMA, Museo Nazionale di Antichità
C 13a   95 n. 6
PHILADELPHIA, Market
— (Theseus Painter, *alabastron*)   15 n. 2, 106 n. 8
— (Bowdoin Painter, *lekythos*)   106 n. 1
— (Beldam Workshop, *lekythos*)   154 n. 1
— (Pattern *lekythos*)   154 n. 14
PHILADELPHIA (Pennsylvania), University Museum
30.4.1   35 n. 7, 64 n. 15
30.51.2   64 n. 11
L 64.186   58 n. 2
PRAGUE, Private
— (Sabouroff Painter, cup)   34 n. 6
PRAGUE, National Museum
775   104 n. 5
1688   144 n. 12
PREGNY, Rothschild Collection
— (Manner of the Acheloos Painter, *hydria*)   95 n. 5
REGGIO CALABRIA, Museo Nazionale
— (Villa Giulia Painter, calyx-crater)   28 n. 14
RHODES, Museum
10495   144 n. 10
10496   144 n. 10
12475   144 n. 19
12962   109 n. 8
13491   119 n. 13
— (amphora)   146 n. 5

RICHMOND (Virginia), Virginia Museum of Art
56.27.4   31, 108 n. 2, 128, 227. Plate 60.3
ROME, Museo Nazionale di Villa Giulia
866   128 n. 6
3556   9 n. 14, 92 n. 9, 95 n. 2
15729   141 n. 4
50599   115 n. 11
M 487   12 n. 1
M 535   95 n. 10
— (Charinos, head-vase)   25 n. 12
— (Berlin Painter, volute-crater)   124 n. 2
ROME, Museo del Palazzo dei Conservatori
73   152 n. 1
ROME, Museo Vaticano
416   93 n. 8
— (Phiale Painter, calyx-crater)   50 n. 1, 51 n. 10
RUVO, Museo Jatta
1501   72 n. 5
ST. LOUIS (Missouri), Washington University
3275   43 n. 9
3283   80 n. 10, 91, 95, 226. Plate 55.4
SAN FRANCISCO (California), Palace of the Legion of Honor
1621   34 n. 12
SANTA BARBARA (California), Avory Brundage Collection
— (Painter of the Yale *Lekythos, lekythos*)   37 n. 8
STOCKHOLM, National Museum
G 2108   40 n. 14
— (Woman Painter, *lekythos*)   58 n. 5, 66 n. 2
STUTTGART, Museum
93   150 n. 1
KAS 140   66 n. 8
SWISS Private Collections
(Antimenes Painter, *lekythos*)   9 n. 14, 92 n. 9
(Psiax, cup)   10 n. 2
(Edinburgh Painter, *lekythos*)   13, 98, 199, 120 nn. 11 f. Plate 7.2
(Semi-outline, *lekythos*)   107 n. 10
SYDNEY, University, Nicholson Museum
41.03   67 n. 3
SYRACUSE, Museo Nazionale
2287   158. Figure 9b
2358   158. Figure 9c
19854   10, 18, 21 n. 14, 92 n. 10, 97, 123 n. 10, 148 n. 10, 149, 151, 201. Plate 16.4
19900   45, 140 n. 3, 206. Plate 24.3
21146   43 n. 1
21186   15, 42 n. 13, 43, 44, 46, 48, 79, 212. Plate 34.2
22789   140 n. 15
22952   140 n. 15
26967   13 n. 11, 79 n. 1
43051   149 nn. 4, 7
43052   99 n. 8
45048   148 n. 13
(Floral Nolan Group, *lekythos*)   26 n. 11, 44 n. 9, 47 n. 14
(Phiale Painter, *lekythos*)   126 n. 13

SYRACUSE, Museo Nazionale (*cont.*):
(Workshop and manner of the Tymbos
Painter)   141 n. 3

TANAGRA, Museum
(Side-palmette *lekythos*)   112 n. 5
TARANTO, Museo Nazionale
3 (old no.)   121 n. 5, 148 n. 15
5 (old no.)   119 n. 13
25 (old no.)   105 n. 3
28 (old no.)   148 n. 13
3799   25 n. 6
4553   127 n. 12
4566   142 n. 12
4567   142 n. 10
20308   106 nn. 9, 12
(Acheloos Painter, volute-crater)   95 n. 5, 115 n. 10
(Haimon Painter, *lekythos*)   150 n. 12
Once TARPORLEY, Brooks Collection
(Woman Painter, *lekythos*)   58 n. 5, 66 n. 2
TARQUINIA, Museo Nazionale Tarquiniense
6845   25 n. 12, 26 n. 2
RC 1076   117 n. 9
(white *lekythos*)   142 n. 7
THEBES, Museum
R.46.84   99 nn. 11, 12, 160. Figure 29a
R.49.250   144 n. 9
R.112.66   145 n. 12
TOLEDO (Ohio), Museum of Art
69.369   47, 214. Plate 37.2
TORONTO, Royal Ontario Museum
366   100 n. 3
920.68.24   66 n. 13
923.13.40   119, 131, 150 and n. 1, 153 nn. 10 f., 231. Plate 69.4
929.22.7   37, 51 n. 3, 209, 217. Plate 29.4
963.59   93 n. 10, 226. Plate 56.1
TÜBINGEN, University
D 72   109 n. 5
E 48   94 nn. 3, 4
E 60   63 n. 2
E 63   83 n. 4, 205
E 67   41 n. 6, 217
E 80   84 n. 4
E 90   64 n. 14

UTRECHT, University
(Haimon Painter, *lekythos*)   109 n. 5

VIENNA, Kunsthistorisches Museum
75   20 n. 9, 78, 198. Plate 3.1
84   18, 92 nn. 11, 14, 97, 109 and n. 3, 148 n. 10, 202. Plate 17.3
86   105 n. 14, 122 n. 2
143   61 n. 4
753   21 nn. 5, 6, 198. Plate 4.2
874   35
3607 (234)   12, 91, 93 n. 19, 160, 226. Figure 26b, Plate 55.2
3725   124 nn. 2, 7
3746   40, 212. Plate 33.2
3748   208, 214, 219, 224. Plate 44.2
Once VIENNA
(Reed Painter, *lekythos*)   61 n. 15
VIENNA University
526a   25 n. 4
3748   71 n. 8

WARSAW, National Museum
32   97 n. 12, 120 n. 1
14769   35 n. 13
142302   34 n. 11
142406   67 n. 7
142470   100 n. 5
142471   34 n. 11
198554   101 n. 4, 161. Figure 32a
WINCHESTER, Winchester College,
48   83 n. 4
WISCONSIN, Madison, Elvehjem Art Center
EAC 70.2   27, 206. Plate 25.3
WÜRZBURG University, Martin von Wagner-Museum
312   12 n. 4
322   115 n. 13
366   21 n. 4
564   61 nn. 1, 3, 5, 66 n. 13
H 4978   106 n. 9, 107 and n. 1, 108, 201. Plate 16.1

WUPPERTAL, Funcke, see BOCHUM

ZÜRICH, Private
(Dolphin *lekythos*)   144 n. 14
ZÜRICH, Rŏs
(Dresden Painter, *lekythos*)   85 n. 4, 95 n. 17, 208. Plate 27.6
Once ZÜRICH, Ruesch
(close to the Bird Painter)   52 n. 3
(Achilles Painter, *lekythos*)   214
ZÜRICH, Schuh
(Painter of Copenhagen 3830)   100 n. 6
ZÜRICH, University
2568   66, 67 nn. 6, 8, 9, 69, 224. Plate 51.3

INDEX OF SUBJECTS

Principal references are italicized.

acanthus, 54, 61, 62, 65, 66, 67, 71, 214, *passim*

Acheron, xx

Achilles, 97

Acropolis, *see* Athens

Agamemnon, 124 n. 7, 204, 223

Agatharchos of Samos, 72

Agora, *see* Athens

Agrigento, 140 n. 2

Aigina, 59
    marble sphinx, 143
    Temple of Apollo, 143

Aigisthos, death of, 124

Aischylos, 140

Ajax, 97

akontia at tomb, 207

Akrisios, 46 f., 142, *215*

alabastra, 11, 15, 28, 56, 63, 66, 77, 94, 99 and n. 4,
    100, 101 n. 5, 106 n. 8, 112, 117 f., 127, 133, 149, 150,
    155, 202

Albani relief, 64 n. 19

Alkestis, 49

Alkibiades, 72

Alopeke, *see* Ambelokepoi

altar, 100, 106, 107, 108

Ambelokepoi, 68 f., 137

Anavyssos, 49, *53* f., 56, 58, 64, 66, 86, 137

animals, representation of, 106, 107, 154 n. 1, 216

Anthesteria, 83 n. 4, 118 n. 4

Apollo, 107, 112, 223

Apollodoros, 69, 71, 72

arc tendrils, 85, 111 n. 10, 112, 132 n. 1, 150, 151

Arcadia, coins, 110 n. 1

architectural patterns, 80 n. 8, 118 n. 8. Figure 3

Argos, 143 n. 5

Ariadne, 120 f. n. 11

Aristippos, 86

armour, 223

Artemis, 223

aryballoi, 10, 11, 30 ff., 77, 78 n. 2, 125 n. 1, 127, 132, 148

askos, 207

astragals, 213

Atalanta, *30*, 128

Athena, 104 and n. 9, 105, 122 n. 2
    Lemnia, 209
    'Mourning', 220
    pouring libation, 100
    seated, 34 f. n. 16, 105

Athena-head *lekythoi*, 16, 107, 108

Athens:
    Acropolis, 69, 117 n. 6, 128 n. 5, 132
        'Hekatompedon', Figure 3c

Agora, 132, 146. *See also* wells
    Stoa Poikile, Figure 3e
    Diocharian Gate, 64
    Kerameikos, 7, 10, 67, 73, 127, 128, 132, 143 n. 5,
        147 n. 22
        Dipylon Gate, xx, 5, 93
        Eridanos Cemetery, 136
        Sacred Way, 132
    Lenormant Street, 40, 132
    Stadium Street, 30 f., 40, 132, 148, 151
    Syntagma Square, 73, 132 n. 6, 143 n. 5, 154

Athens 581, see *lekythoi*, shapes of

athlete at tomb, 138, 210

ATL, see *lekythoi*, shapes of

baby at tomb, 210. *See also* child on tomb

bail-amphora, 133

'bars', shoulder decoration, 22, 28
    at join of neck to shoulder on *lekythoi*, 19 and n. 2,
        23 and nn. 13 f., 25, 43, 79, 82, 83, 85 and nn. 6 f.,
        101, 122 n. 6, 148

basket:
    of offerings, 62 n. 9, 63, 66, 202, *passim*
    of wool, 212
    on tomb, 47, 202

'battle *loutrophoroi*', see *loutrophoroi*

battle scenes, *64*, 65, 221. *See also* tomb, fight at

BEL, see *lekythoi*, shapes of

'Berlin Goddess', 5

bier, 67, 71, 72 n. 6, 73, 83, n. 4, 209, 214, 219, **224**,
    226. See also *prothesis*

bilingual *lekythoi*, 16, 106, 122

birds:
    black, *see* black birds
    upside-down, 207

BL, see *lekythoi*, shapes of

black bands, 115 n. 14, 144

black birds, 93

black-bodied *lekythoi*, 16, 23, 49, 79, 80 n. 15, 91, 102,
    115 ff., 124, 125, 126, 131, 139, 141 n. 9, 148 and n. 8

black circles painted on base of tomb, 202, *203*, 204,
    206

black female flesh, 14

'black-polychrome' style, 116, 117 n. 6

Black Sea, 143 n. 5

black shoulders of *lekythoi*, 23 n. 13, 25, 26, 27, 42 n. 24,
    106 nn. 1 ff., 122

bobbin, 45 n. 14

Boeotia, 137 n. 1
    lekythoi, 132 n. 1

botanical terminology, 5 n. 1

Bowdoin palmettes, *see* palmettes
'Boy and Cat' *stele*, 71 n. 6
Brauron, 102
broken vases, representation of, *see* vases
bundle of stuff, 54, 213
burial practices, xx, xxi, 38 n. 4, 50, 62, 70, 131, 133, 136, 205
busts, 92, 103, 104, 105 and n. 10, 108, *109* ff. *See also* Athena-head *lekythoi*
Byblos, 107 n. 10
Byzantium, 86 n. 10

cactus flowers, 21, 97
Caltanissetta, 100, 102 n. 10, 104 n. 8
calyx-craters (white ground), 28, 50 n. 1, 51 n. 8
Camarina, 132, 140 n. 1, 154 f. n. 17
Camiros, 144
Casualty Lists, 86 n. 10
cemeteries:
    excavation of, xix, 73
    representation of, xxi, 56, 61, 86
Cerveteri, 59 and n. 8, 141 n. 9
'Chalcidian' vases, 91 n. 7
Charon, xx, 28, 35, 36, 49, 56, 63, 64, 66, 83 n. 4, 205, 215, 218, 221 f., 223
    boat of, *63* and n. 6, 83 n. 4, 205
chequery pattern, 18 and n. 13, 22, 25, 85 n. 4, 101 n. 5, 146, 148, 152
chest:
    at tomb, 208
    of Kypselos, *see* Kypselos
chiaroscuro, 72
child on tomb, 40 and n. 19, 56, 57, 218
chimney *lekythoi*, see *lekythoi*, shapes of
chin strap, 226
Chios, 116, 117 n. 6
chous, 103, 107 n. 11, 118 n. 4, 137
chronology, 14, 16, *131* ff.
CL, see *lekythoi*, shapes of
clay, 85 n. 3
Clytemnestra, 124 n. 7
cock, between ivy-leaves, 21, 107 n. 8, 118 f., 123 ff., 146
coins, 71, 105, *109* ff., 131
colour, applied to black ground, 116
column-crater (white ground), 92, 140 f. n. 15, 149
conflation of scenes, xx and n. 3, 50, 63 and n. 8, 83 and n. 4, 205, 211, 219, 221, 223
coral red, 10
Corinth, 5, 59, 103 n. 14, 116, *138* f., 147 nn. 23 f.
    floral decoration, 5, 7
    Lechaion Cemetery, 139
    North Cemetery, 132, *138* f.
cross-squares, 25, 32
Cumae, 103 n. 13
cups, 28 and n. 16, 29 n. 6, 34, 36, 42, 45, 82, 84, 112 n. 4, 117 nn. 6 and 13, 128 n. 5, 135, 147, 151, 154 n. 1
cup-*skyphoi*, 150 n. 10
Cyprus, 122 n. 7

Danae, 47, 215
dead person, represented at tomb, 223
death in battle, 64, 221. *See also* war dead
decree-reliefs, 225
Deianeira, see *lekythoi*, shapes of
Delion, battle of, 132
Delos:
    Heraion, 132 and n. 9, 151 n. 11
    purification of, 132
    'Temple of the Athenians', 70 n. 7
Delphi:
    Knidian Lesche, Figure 3d
    Treasury of the Athenians, 20, 112 n. 4. Figure 3 a, b
Demir Kapija, 141 n. 13
depth, illusion of, 71
Dexileos, 64 n. 20
dexiosis, 225
dilute paint, washes of, 29
dinoi, 115
Diocharian Gate, *see* Athens
Dion, 93
Dionysos, 120 f. n. 11
Diphilos, 86. See also *kalos*
Dipylon, *see* Athens, Kerameikos
diskos at tomb, 207, 210, 220
DL, see *lekythoi*, shapes of
dog on tomb, 51 n. 5
dolls, 40 n. 19
domestic deposits, 131 f.
Doris, 84
dots:
    black on reserved shoulders, 51, 104, 107, 108
    grouped in field, 153 and n. 10, 203
    linked in pattern, 22, 102, 106, 121
    reserved on shoulder, 43, 47, 48
doubleens, *see* neck-amphorae of special type
dress patterns, 5, 6
drink, offerings of at tomb, 218. *See also* libation
drip-ring, 77, 144
ducks, 67

egg pattern:
    at join of neck to shoulder, on *lekythoi*, 20, 24, 26, 43, 56, 61, 62, 68, 125
    at join of shoulder to body, on *lekythoi*, 71, 106 n. 1, 124, 139 n. 3, 225
eidola, 28, 52, 71, 83 n. 4, 205, 214, 216, 219, 226
Ekklesiazusai, 73 f.
ekphora, 211
Elektra, 204, 223
Eleusis, 108 n. 9, 117 n. 6
Eleutherai, 86 n. 10
embattlement pattern, 117 f. n. 13, 127, 128 n. 2
emotion, rendering of, 55, 56, 215. *See also* gestures and mourning
Endoios, 105
epitaphios agon, *see* funeral games
Eretria, 53, 57, 59, 85 n. 3, 136, *137* f., 141 n. 2
Eridanos Cemetery, *see* Athens, Kerameikos

Eros, 21, 30 ff., 92, 102, 103, 107, 119 n. 7, 125 n. 5, 127 f.
Etruria, 116, 141
    bucchero, 12, 117 n. 5
    Corinthianizing vases, 116
    figured vases, 72
Euboea, 56, 136, 144. See also Eretria
Eupheros, grave-relief of, 221. Plate 46.3
Euripus, 137

face:
    profile view, 68, 222 ff., 71
    three-quarter view, 60, 222 ff.
false interior, 40, 41, 46, 55, 86 f., 133, 212
'family plots', 207
fawn hunt, 133
feather pattern, 70 and n. 11
feathery petals of palmettes, see palmettes
Ferrara, 146
fight at tomb, 222
Fikellura vases, 91
fillets, 36, 45, 50 f., 61 f., 67 n. 9, 86, 103, 203, passim
    rolled, 61 and n. 18, 203, 221
    tubular, 38, 39, 46, 49, 52, 212, passim
'flame palmettes', see palmettes
food, offerings of, at tomb, 218
François Vase, 7. Figure 1 d-f
funeral games, 65 and nn. 8 f., 219. See also tomb, fight at
funerary iconography, xix f., 20, 28, 34, 36, 40, 45, 46, 51, 53, 54, 57, 61, 64, 71, 82, 83 and n. 4, 85, 86, 97, 131, 133, 136, 137, 138, 139, 140 n. 4, 141, 142
funerary legislation, xix f., 74, 136, 205

Gela, 44, 59, 82, 125, 132 n. 10, 139 f., 207
Gelon, 140 n. 1
gem, 221. Plate 46.4
gestures, 52, 71, 203, 207, passim. See also mourning
Gigantomachy, 122 n. 2
Gorgos, 120 f. n. 11
grave-reliefs, 37 n. 2, 40 n. 19, 62 and n. 4, 70, 136
    represented on vases, 83 n. 4, 205
graves, excavation of, see cemeteries

Hades, 223
hair, 68, 71
    cut in grief, 209, 216
    styles, 62 and n. 7
    torn in grief, 83 n. 4, 209
half-palmettes, 109. See also Painter of the
halteres, at tomb, 207
hand-clasp, see dexiosis
handle of vase:
    clay attachments, 11, 12, 95
    floral decoration beneath, 34 f., 81, 91 f., 95 f., 126, 148 n. 14. Figures 25 to 27a
hands, representation of, 60
hare hunt, 17, 41 and n. 3, 121, 211, 219
hare surmounting tomb, 51 and n. 5, 216
hatching, see shading

head, elevation of, in prothesis, 209, 226
heads, see busts
head-vases, 25, 123, 127
hearts of palmettes, see palmettes
Helicon, 49
helmet, 109, 111 n. 2
    on tomb, 211
hemidrachms, 110 n. 1
hen, 123 ff.
Heraion, Delos, see Delos
Herakles, 96, 97, 98, 100, 105 n. 12, 122 n. 2
'Herculaneum Marble', 222
Hermes, xx, xxi, 28, 49, 50, 63, 83 n. 4, 215, 223
'hero' at tomb, 207
horsemen, 64, 65, 83, 85 f. n. 16, 221 f.
horse monument, 214
hunter, 101
hydriai, 10, 13, 20, 38 n. 4, 93, 94, 115, 124 n. 2, 144, 148 n. 12
    kalpis type, 15, 97, 109, 120, 124
    white neck or mouth, 94

Ialysos, 144
incision, 115 ff.
'interior' views of grave mounds, 83 n. 4
interment, 133
Ionia, 117 n. 6
'Ionian dress', 5
Iphigeneia, 140
Iris, 83 n. 4
Italy, 59. See also Etruria, South Italy
ivory, 5 n. 4, 83 n. 4
ivy, 17, 21, 117 f. n. 13
    dress pattern, 67
    leaves on shoulder of lekythoi, 121 and n. 3
    with berries, 21 and n. 5, 85, 152, 153, 154, 202

janiform vase, see head-vase
jewellery, 62

kalos inscriptions, 27, 40 n. 11, 43, 45, 46, 101, 123, 127, 140 n. 15
    Alkimachos, 46
    Axiopeithes, 46
    Diogenes, 25, and n. 6, 125 n. 1, 127 n. 12
    Diphilos, 44, 46
    Dorotheos, 93, 94
    Dromippos, 44, 46
    Epilykos, 123
    Euphiletos, 12 and n. 1
    Hygiainon, 46
    Karystios, 11 n. 14, 117 f. n. 13
    Kephisophon, 93
    Kleinias, 42 and n. 10, 43
    Leagros, 93
    Lichas, 42 and n. 11
    Megakles, 93
    Meletos, 42 and n. 12
    Memnon, 93
    Menon, 25

kalos inscriptions (*cont.*):
  Olympichos, 127
  Olympiodoros, 93
  Smikrion, 117 f. n. 13
  Zephyria (*kale*), 93
kantharos, 37 and n. 2, 100, 135, 203
Kerameikos, *see* Athens
Kerch style, 72 n. 5
key pattern, *see* meander
kneeling in grief, 55, 56, 57, 83 n. 4, 217 f.
Kolonos Hippios, 132
komast, 102, 103
korai, 30
  Acropolis 674, 25
  Antenor's, 6
  Euthydikos, 6
  Lyons, 5. Figure 1g
  Merenta, 5
  Peplos, 6
Korakou, 139
Koropi, 137
kouroi, 93
Küyünjik, ivory from, Figure 1b
kyathoi, 10 n. 5, 14, 15, 81
kylix, *see* cups
Kypselos, chest of, 211

LL (Little Lion), see *lekythoi*, shapes of
Lacedaimonians, grave of the, 132
lagobola, 121, 211
landscape, 63, 67, 68, 72.   *See also* rocky landscape
lattice pattern, 154
laurel pattern, 152
Lechaion Cemetery, *see* Corinth
lekanis, 69
lekythos, 73 and n. 10
  Type I, 116, 138
  Type II, 115, 116, 131 n. 1, 143
  Type III, 131 n. 1
  'standard', 8, 14
  'secondary', 8, 9
  shapes of: 77 ff.
      ATL, 9, 34, 79, *82* f., 122, 154 f. n. 17
        ('refined version'), 82, 140 f. n. 15, 204
      Athens 581, 21, 81, 146, 150, 151
      Beldam, 151 n. 11
      BEL, 9, 19, 79, 84 ff., 104, 111 f., 122, 152, 153, 154
      BL, 16, 23, 25, 43, 79, 84, 91, 98 n. 8, 100, 120, 122
      chimney, 22, *87*, 102, 109, *111* f., 150, 151, 152
      CL, 28, 79, *84*, 103, 108 n. 8, 122, 154
      'compromise', 13, 20, 21, 78, 92, 123 ff.
      Deianeira, 116, 138
      sub-Deianeira, 153 n. 6
      DL, 79, *80* f., 82, 98, 99, 100, 102, 119, 120, 149, 151, 152
      Haemonian, 151 n. 11
      LL, 80, 81, 93, 98 n. 3, 118, 120 and n. 4, 125, 146 n. 3, 150, 153 f. n. 10

Phanyllis, *118*, 119 n. 3, 146, 154
  PL, 34 f., 35 n. 1, 79, *81* f., 102 f., 150
foot, form of, 15, 23, 79 and n. 10, 80, 84, 112
mouth, form of, 66 f., 68, 69, 80, 81, 82, 84, 85, 87
  separate from body, 70
neck:
  decorated with patterns, 85 and n. 4, 154
  painted black, 15 f., 19, 20, 23, 79, 121, 123, 125
  painted white, 68, 69
shoulder:
  painted black with figures, 3, 16, 43, 49, 124 and
    n. 7, 126, 127
  reserved with florals, 15. *See also* palmettes
  with palmettes:
    classification of, 33 ff.
      IA, 35, 37, 40, 44, 46, 48 f., 125, 142
      IB, 43, 44
      IIA, 39, 40, 46, 48, 49, 50, 53, 54, 55, 56, 57, 61
      IIB, 40, 43, 44, 45, 46, 48, 51
      See also palmettes
  represented on vases, 65 f.
  large clay, 65 ff., 68 ff., 136, 224 f. *See also* Group of
    the Huge *Lekythoi*
  picture panel, 77 f., 78 n. 2, 80
  squat, 38, 54, 73, 77, 95 n. 11, 96, 103, 141 n. 14
  stone, 65, 67, 69 and n. 13, 70, 73 f., 136, 203, 204, 225
Lenormant Street, *see* Athens
libation, at grave, 57, 218, 219. *See also* drink offerings
lines painted at neck of *lekythoi*, 54, 57, 61
lion (lioness):
  on shoulder of *lekythoi*, 24, 27, 31, 120, 125
  surmounting tomb, 47, 214, 215
  on neck of *pelikai*, 115 f., n. 15
Locri, 141
'Locrian vases', 142
lotus buds, 4. Figures 1, 2
  on body of *lekythoi*, 21
  on shoulder of *lekythoi*, 13, 18, 77, 81, 99, 101, 102, 120, 147, 149, 150
  with added white, 8, 120, 144
loutrophoroi, xx, 14, 35, 38 n. 4, 49, *64* f., 66 n. 1, 72 n. 5, 85 f. n. 16, 86 n. 10, 103, 133, 204, 214, 220, 221
  stone, 64, 70, 136, 204
lozengy, 152, 154
Lupoli, 142
lyre, 108
  at tomb, 202, 205, 208, 210
'lyre palmettes', *see* palmettes

maenad, 80, 103, 119
'mantle figures', 213
Marathon:
  battle of, 131, 148
  tumulus, 147
Markopoulo, 137
matt paint, xx, 33 f., 37, 47, 49, 55, 56, 57, 59, 65
  red, on shoulder florals, 19, 28, 39, 85
    on body florals, 152, 154

meander, 47, 54, 57, 58, and n. 2, 61, 62, 66, 68, 106, 120 f. n. 11, 122, 152, 154. Figures 4, 5
   'crossing', 17 f., 32, 123 f.
   'false', 61
   'linked', 105, 106 ff.
   springing from vertical edge, 36 and n. 2, 120 f. n. 11
Medusa, 98
Megara Hyblaea, 141 n. 8
'Melian plaques', 204
'Melian vases', 7. Figure 1c
Melos, 57 and n. 6
Mesogaia, 137
metal vases, 11, 38, 70, 91, 117 n. 6
Metaponto, 141
minotaur, 119 n. 7, 124 n. 7
mint, reopening of, 110
'mistress and maid', 40, 45, 46, 49, 52, 208, 213
mock inscriptions, 17, 94, 102, 106, and n. 16, 107, 108, 122, 203
modelled clay handle attachments, 94, 119 n. 7, 123 n. 21
moon (crescent) added to coins, 110
mound, 29, 49, 50, 61, 83 n. 4, 106 n. 17, 204, passim
mourning, gestures of, xxi, 40, 49, 56
music at grave, 49. See also lyre
mythological scenes, xx, 50, 63 f.

Naucratis, 44
Near East, 143 n. 5
   florals, 5 ff.
neck-amphorae of special type:
   Andokidean, 10, 117
   doubleens, 14 and n. 1, 98, 118 n. 4, 124 n. 7, 126
   Nikosthenic, 12, 93, 117 f.
   Nolans, 14, 42, 44, 48, 49, 64 n. 11, 125, 213
neck-pelikai, 115 and n. 15
Negroes, 64 n. 14
Nekyia, 63 n. 1, 205, 215
net pattern, 15, 23, 24. See also dots, linked
Night, xxi, 211
Nike, 34 f. n. 16, 83 n. 4, 100, 103, 107 n. 11, 108, 128 n. 6
Nike Temple, Athens, 64 n. 19
Nolan amphora, see neck-amphorae
'North Cemetery', see Corinth

Oedipus and the Sphinx(?), 142, 143 n. 1
offerings at tomb, 36, 37 n. 1, 38
oil, xix, 73 f., 136
oinochoai, 11, 15, 21, 37, 38, 92, 93 ff., 104, 107 n. 7, 109, 115, 117 f. n. 13, 125, 126, 144, 148 and n. 14
Olbia, 35 n. 1, 102 n. 12
olive leaves on helmet, 110
olive sprig on vases, 84
olpai, 109
Olympia, 211
Onatas, 143
onos, 94, 119 n. 7, 123 n. 21
Orestes, 124 n. 2, 204, 223
'Oriental archer', 83 n. 4

'Orientalizing style', 116
'Orientals', see Persians
Oropos, 47, 49, 50, 137, 215
Orpheus, 102
Orphism, 62
ostraka, 131
owl lekythoi, 84, 108
owls, 104 and n. 9, 105, 108, 109 ff.
'owls' (coins), 110
owls on tomb, 202

PL, see lekythoi, shapes of
Paestum, 102, 141 n. 9
painting (panel and wall), xix. See also wall painting
palmettes, see also lekythos, shoulder
   Type alpha, 147
   Type beta, 147
   addorsed, 95
   Bowdoin black on reserved shoulder, 13, 27, 33 f., 35, 43, 45, 79 f., 82, 84, 85, 99, 101, 104, 120, 122, 132 n. 1, 148, 150, 154
   black ('elegant' Achillean), 35, 37, 43 f., 79, 132 n. 1
   enclosed by S spirals, 125 n. 5
   'feathery' petals, 147 and n. 22
   'flame', 71
   'hearts' of:
      red, 146, 149
      reserved, 94, 111 n. 6, 149, 151
      with dotted arc, 146, 151
   horizontal, 20 ff., 30, 80 n. 8, 94, 115 f. n. 15, 121, 140, 149, 151, 152
   on lekythos body, 18, 118 n. 4
   'Leagran', 13, 92, 121
   and lotus buds:
      on shoulder of lekythoi, 26 ff., 35 f., 45
      on body of lekythoi, 148
   'lyre' type, 96, 152, 153
      'sunken' 153, 154 f., n. 17
   on neck of pelikai, 115 f. n. 15, 118 n. 4, 126 n. 3, 146
   upright-on-Os, 115 f. n. 15, 117 n. 8, 118 and n. 6, 146, 147, 151, 153
   with white arc, 146
Panathenaic amphorae, xx, 12, 14, 42, 48
Parrhasios, 60, 71, 223
pattern lekythoi, 22, 54, 78 n. 2, 81, 86, 87, 122 and n. 7, 131 ff., 138, 139, 143 ff.
pattern squares, Figure 4
patternwork, execution of, 3
Pegasus, 99
pelikai, 36, 124 nn. 2 and 7
Peloponnesian War, 60, 138, 139
Perseus, 46, 98, 215
Persians (representations of), 41 and n. 6, 83 n. 4, 112
Persians (victory over), 110, 127, 132
perspective, 72, 226
Pheidias, 209, 210
phialai, 108, 116 nn. 8 and 13, 117 n. 6, 219
Pikrodaphne, 137
Pila, 141 n. 9

pitch, 74

plaques, 11, 133

'plastic attachments', *see* modelled attachments

plate, 42 and n. 17

plemochoai, 37 and n. 1, 52, 202

polos, 5, 25. Figure 1 a, g

polyandrion, 132 n. 1

polychromy, xx, 127, 128

Polyidos and Glaukos, 205

Polygnotos of Thasos, 50, 63 n. 1, 205, 215

Polykleitos, 210

Potnia Theron, 7, 77

predella friezes, 10, 95

preliminary sketch, *60*, 99 n. 1, 197

proskynesis, 210

prothesis, 36, 56, 66, 71, 72, 103, 135, 205, 224

proveniences of *lekythoi*, xx, 53, 131, *136* ff.

pyrrhicists, 15, 24 and n. 14, 84 n. 12

Pythagoreanism, 62

Pythis, 93

pyxides, 93 n. 16, 94

'rays', 4, 9, 15, 34, 70, 82, 84, 118 and n. 4, 147, 150. Figure 2 f–h

red-figure shoulders on white *lekythoi*, 25 ff., 46 f., 140 n. 13

red lines, 115 n. 9, 116 and n. 13, 118 and n. 9, 120 and n. 4

reeds, 62, 63 and n. 17, 64, 65, 205, *passim*

reservation, 115

Rheneia, 132 and n. 9

Rhitsona, 132, 146

Rhodes, 59, 116, 122 n. 7, 144

ribbing, 115

ribbons, *see* fillets

rocky landscape, 50, 83 n. 4, 211, 215, 218, 223

'rolled ribbon', *see* fillet

Sabucina, 100, 102 n. 10, 104 n. 8, 139 n. 18

'Sacred Way', *see* Athens, Kerameikos

Salamis, 59

saltire squares, 39, 66

sanctuary scene, 109

satyr, 84 n. 12, 119, 120 f. n. 11

scaraboid gem, *see* gem

sculpture, 70, 71, 74, 136. *See also* grave-reliefs

seated mourner, 223

second white, 28 f., *36*, *44* f., 49, 86, 140 n. 13, 142, 197, 203

Selinus, 29, 140 and n. 14

semi-outline, xx, 16, 19, 79, 80, 85, 91 n. 5, 98, 104, *105* ff., 119, 122, 202

shading, *60*, 68, *69*, 71, 72, 224

'shadow monuments', 61, 66, 67, 68, 224 f.

shield at tomb, 67, 224

shield blazon, 117 n. 2, 118

shoulder-figures, see *lekythos*

shoulder palmettes, *see* palmettes and *lekythos*

Sicilian expedition, 140

Sicily, 122 n. 7, 127, 132, *139* ff., 207

side-palmettes, 3, 77, 78 n. 2, 80, 81, 87, *91* ff., 96, 127 n. 14, 139, 149. Figures 27b to 34

silhouette, 16, 26, 29, 85 f. n. 16, 100 and n. 4, 105, 106 and n. 9, 107, 122, 154 n. 1

siren, 84 n. 12

Six's technique, 10, 12, 80 n. 15, 97, 98 n. 7, 101 n. 5, *116* ff., 120, 123

skenographia, *see* perspective

skiagraphia, *see* shading

skin tones, 72

skyphoi, 104 n. 9, 133

snakes on tomb, 221

south Italy, 141 f.

  vase-painting, 72

Spain, 143 n. 5

spandrel buds (tri-lobed), 31, 95, 125 n. 5

spears, 68

sphinx, 83 n. 4, *142* f.

Spina, 59, 72 n. 5, 141 n. 13

Spintharos, 93

Stadium Street, *see* Athens

stag hunt, 121

stamnoi, 92 n. 9, 115 n. 4, 120 n. 1

stamped decoration, 115

statue bases with relief decoration, 93

statues at tomb, 213 f.

stele, 40, 45, 52, 61, 83 n. 4, 202. *See also* tomb projecting into shoulder on *lekythoi*, 85 f. n. 16, *203*, 207

stool on tomb, 40, 47, 212

strigil, 102, 222 f.

Styx, 49. *See also* Acheron

sumptuary legislation, *see* funerary legislation

sword, 83 n. 4, 209, 224

Syntagma Square, *see* Athens

Syracuse, 140

'tablets', 62. *See also* fillets, rolled

Talos, 72 n. 5

Tanagra, 112

Taranto, 141

technique of white *lekythoi*, 197

Telamedes, 124 n. 7

textiles, 6 f.

Thanatos and Hypnos, xx, xxi, 63, 64, 66, 211, 215, 223

Themistoklean Wall, 93

Themistokles, grave of, 74 n. 1

Theseus, 119 n. 7, 122 n. 2, 124 n. 7

Thespiai, 132 n. 1

Thorikos, 143 n. 5

Thracian woman, 102

tomb, fight at, 64, 65 and n. 7

  visit to, 36, 61, 63, 64, 67, 70, 202

'Tomb of the Diver', 141 n. 9

tombs, representation of, 29, 44, 62, 83 n. 4, 85 f., 86, 142. *See also* acanthus, grave-reliefs, 'shadow monument', *stele*

tombstones with painted decoration, 38 n. 4, 50

tongue pattern, 23 and nn. 13 f., 24 and n. 4, 26, 79, 101 n. 5, 122 n. 6, 123

torch, 220
   race, 138 and n. 6, 220
Trachones, 137
tree, 221 f.
   reed-tree, 62, 63, 64, 65, 92, 96, 100, 104, 105, 107,
      108, 149
triglyphs, 67, 224
tripods, 117
Troad, 44
tymbos, see mound

unguentaria, 74
upright palmettes-on-Os, *see* palmettes

v's reserved on shoulder of *lekythos*, 43, 47, 48
valediction, 85 f. n. 26, 133, 203, 204
Valle Pega, 141 n. 13
vases:
   bought for funeral, 148
   displayed at tomb, 36 ff.
   overturned and broken, 38 n. 4, 86, 202, 209 f., 210,
      211
vent hole, *see false* interior
Villanovan, 117

volute-craters, 95 n. 5, 115 and n. 10, 117 and n. 8, 124 n. 2
Vouliagmeni, 139

wall painting, 44, *69*, 71, 72
Wappenmünzen, 110
war dead, 86 n. 10.
warriors, 65, 119, 122 n. 3, 209, 219. *See also* battle scenes
wells, 132, 146
'wet incised lines', 85, 151 n. 11
white pattern bands, 154 f. n. 17
white slip, xix, 9, 11, 14, 147 n. 16, 197
women seated at tomb, 39 and n. 5, 49, 56, 57, 61, 62 n.
   9, 83 n. 4, 204, *222* ff., *passim. See also* seated mourner
wooden grave markers, 86
wreaths, 38, 86, 202, *passim*

X-ray photography, 86

Yugoslavia, 141 n. 13

Zeus, 73
Zeuxis, 69, 71, 72
zig-zag pattern, 54

INDEX OF PAINTERS, POTTERS, AND WORKSHOPS

Acheloos Painter, *13*, 20, 78, 95

Achilles Painter, 15, 33 f., 35, 36, 38, 40, *41* ff., 49, 50 f., 52, 54, 58, 64, 79, 126, 132 n. 11, 137, 140 n. 9, 211 ff.

Achilles Painter's *Pelikai*, Class of the, 51 n. 8

Acropolis 606, Painter of, 7

Agora P 1256, Class of, 115 n. 9

Aischines Painter, 9, 82, 83 n. 4, 142 n. 1, 204

Ama Group, 11

Amasis Painter, 7, 11, 118, 144

Amasis Potter, 11

Andokides Painter, 10, 13

Andokides Potter, 10, 12, 117

Antimenes Painter, 9, 11 f., 13, 18, 92 n. 9, 94, 115 nn. 10 and 11, 117, 118 n. 4, 123

Athena Painter, *14* ff., 19, 23 f., 30, 31, 78, 79, 85, 98 n. 8, 101, 104 ff., 120, 121 f., 123 n. 6, 148 n. 8, 153

Athena-head *Pyxides*, Group of the, 110 n. 16

Athens 581, Class of, 18, 79, 81, 144 n. 8, 146 and n. 3, *147*, 150, 153

Athens 581, Workshop, 8, 9, 119

Athens 1810, Group of, 138 f.

Athens 1826, Painter of, *27* ff., 45, 51 n. 1, 85 f. n. 16, 140 n. 15, 141, 142 and n. 1, 203, 206 f., 216

Athens 1934, Painter of, *53*, 155, 217, 218

Athens 1943, Painter of, 51 and n. 8

Athens 2020, Painter of, 209

Athens 2025, Group of, 82 n. 14, 204

Beldam Painter, 9, 15, *18* ff., 22, 38 n. 4, 45, 79, 82, 84 ff., 87, 111 n. 6, 112, 133, 137, 138 n. 1, 148 n. 5, *153* ff., 202 f.

Beldam Workshop, 84 ff., 87, 96, 103, 150, 151 nn. 8 and 11, 152 n. 3, *153* ff.

Berlin 2464, Painter of, 62, 67

Berlin Painter, *14*, 15, 23 f., 25, 26, 31, 34, 36 n. 2, 42, 43, 48, 64 nn. 11 and 14, 80, 100, 115 f., n. 15, 120 f. n. 11, 123 n. 3, 124 and n. 7, 125, 126, 127, 128 n. 6, 140, 154 n. 9

Berlin Painter's Workshop, 47

Bird Group, 34 n. 2, *52* ff., 66

Bird Painter, *52* ff., 56, 58, 214, 216 ff.

Bosanquet Painter, 33, *37* f., 40, 51 n. 2, 57 nn. 8 and 14, 203, 208, 209 f., 213

Bowdoin Painter, 15, 23 f., 25, 30, 43, 79, 82, 83 n. 4, 84, 95, 100 and n. 4, 108, 109 ff., 122, 123 n. 3, 128, 140 n. 15, 142 n. 1

Bowdoin Workshop, 15, 41, 104 n. 5, 120, 121, 128, 132 n. 1, 141 n. 9

Brno Painter, 152 n. 3

Brygos Painter, 15, 26, 27, 30, 72, 102, 127, 140, 141 n. 9

Brygos Potter, 34

Cab. Méd. 218, Class of, 12 n. 15

Cactus Painter, 8, *21*, 91 n. 4, 96 f.

Cambridge 3.17, Painter of, 111 n. 6

Cambridge 28.2, Painter of, 34 n. 2, *54* f., 216 f.

Carlsberg Painter, *53*, 55 n. 10, 66 n. 8

Carlsruhe Painter, 19, 28, 58, 82, 83 n. 4, 84, 86, 103, 104, 111, 112, 154

Cartellino Painter, *25*, 84

Charinos Potter, *25* f., 107 n. 7

Chariot Painter, 85 n. 4, 118

Clio Painter, *51* and n. 8

Cock Group, *118* f., 121 n. 3, 123, 144, *146*, 147 n. 22

Copenhagen 3830, Painter of, 99 f., 102

Copenhagen 4986, Class of, 67, 224 f.

Corinth *Lekythos*, Painter of the, 139

Dessypri Painter, 15, 79

Diosphos Painter, 8, 12, 14, 17, 22, 79, 80, 81, 82, 94, 96 ff., 99, 101 f., 105, 112, 115 f. n. 15, 118, 119, 120, 123 n. 21, 126, *149* f., 152 n. 3

Diosphos Potter, *101* ff.

Diosphos Workshop, xx, 8, 17, 91 ff., 104, 121, *149* f.

Dolphin Group, 120, 137 n. 8, *114*, 146 and n. 3

Douris, *25* f., *29* ff., 78 n. 2, 125, 126, 127, 128, 132, 140, 148

Dresden Painter, 85 n. 4, 95, 96, 100 n. 4

Dubois Class, 144 n. 13

Dutuit Painter, 14, 24, 35 n. 1, 80, 95, 100 f., 102, 125, 126

Edinburgh Painter, *13* ff., 17 f., 78, 79, 98, 115 f. n. 15, 120 f., 123, 146 n. 5, *148* f.

Emporion Painter, *22*, 87, 109, 112, 139, 152

Epiktetos, 12

Epilykos Class, 123

Ethiop Painter, 28

Eucharides Painter, 27, 95, 123, 124, 126

Euphiletos Painter, 12

Eupolis Painter, *51* n. 8

Exekias, 10, 115 n. 11

Fat-runner Group, 121 n. 3, 144, 146

Floral Band-cups, *146* n. 10, 147

Floral Nolans, Group of the, 14, 24, 26, 27, 44, 47, 78 n. 2, 80 n. 8, 125, 126, 140 n. 9

Flying-Angel Painter, 82, 140 f. n. 15, 204

Gales Painter, 13, 78 n. 2, 79

Gela Painter, 10 n. 7, *17* f., *21*, 22, 26, 85 n. 4, 92, 97, 109, 118 n. 4, 121, 124, 140 n. 7, *148* f., 151

Golonos Group, 94, 123 n. 21

Goluchow Painter, 11 n. 5

Golvol Group, 115 n. 10
Group R, *58* ff., 73, 221 ff.

Hague Class, 21 n. 2
Haimon Painter, 9, 10 n. 7, *22*, 81, 82, 87, 102, 109, 112, 118 n. 4, 139, 146, 148, *150* ff.
Half-palmettes, Painter of the, 109, 152 n. 3
Harrow Painter, 123
Head-vases: Class B, 123
Hermonax, 42, 45, 48, 64, 126, 140 n. 9
Huge *Lekythoi*, Group of the, *68* ff., 73, 225 f.
Hypsis, 97 n. 15

Icarus Painter, 84, 102 n. 12, 103, 108 n. 8, 110, 142 n. 1, 152 n. 3, 154 f. and n. 17
Inscription Painter, *20*, 45, 82, 86, 153 f. n. 10, 202 ff.

Kephisophon Painter, 92 f., 94
Kleitias, 6, 7
Kleophon Painter, 43 n. 11, 64, 219 f.
Kleophrades Painter, 27, 80
Klügmann Painter, 15, 79

Leagros Group, 8, 9, *13* ff., 17, 18, 78, 92, 94, 95 n. 1, 97, 98, 115 nn. 10, 14
Lid Painter, 154 n. 1
Light-make Class, 144 n. 8
Little Lion, 80
London B 620, Class of, 12 n. 15, 93
London B 632, Class and Group of, 12 n. 15, 95 n. 8
London D 65, Group of, *19*, 85 n. 4, 86, 202, 203
London D 72, Painter of, *62*, 220
London E 342, Painter of, 28, *35* and n. 13, 63 n. 2
Louvre F 6, Painter of, 144
Louvre F 118, Painter of, 12 n. 15
Lupoli Painter, 142
Lydos, 133 n. 11, 144

Marathon Painter, 8, 18, 21, 22, 119, 147, 149
Marlay Painter, 154 n. 1
Meidias Painter, 60
Meletos Painter, *42*
Michigan Painter, 21 n. 2
Munich 2335, Painter of, 36 n. 2, 41, 52, 53, *55* ff., 57, 86, 207, 217, 218
Munich 2774, Painter of, 34 n. 11, 140 n. 15, 204
Mys, 85 n. 4

Negro *Alabastra*, Group of the, 127
New York 07, Painter of, 92
New York Hypnos, Painter of the, 57 n. 8
Nikosthenes Potter, 12, 115, n. 10, 117
Nikosthenic Workshop, 14, 95, 118

Oinophile Painter, 79, 81, 147
Oltos, 12
Onesimos, 147
Oxford 218b, Painter of, 115 f. n. 15
Oxford 1920, Group of, 95 n. 11
Oxford 1949, Painter of, 13

Paidikos *Alabastra*, Group of the, 94, 118
Palermo 4, Painter of, 34 n. 16, *35*
Pamphaios Potter, 12
Pan Painter, 27, 127, 128, 140
Panaitios Painter, 25, 81
Paris Gigantomachy, Painter of the, 126 n. 15
Paseas, 10, 11
Pasiades Painter, 94 n. 4, 101 n. 5, 149, 151
Pasiades Potter, 99, 101 n. 5, 118, 149
Penthesilea Painter, 45
Petit Palais 336, Painter of, 81, 103
Phanyllis Group, 118, 119, 121 n. 3, *144* f., 147
Phanyllis Painter, 81, 85 nn. 4 f., 109, 118, *144* ff., 147
Phiale Painter, 34 n. 2, 43, 47 n. 6, *48* f., 51, 53, 126, 137, 140 n. 9, 215
Philon Painter, 126 n. 3
Pholos Painter, 112, 152 n. 3, 153 f. n. 10
Pioneer Group, 13, 17, 124
Pioneers, 8
Pistoxenos Painter, 27, 45, 128
Pistoxenos Potter, 127
Praxias Group, 29 n. 1
Proto-Panaetian Group, 93
Providence Painter, 37 n. 8, 42, 43, 45, 48, 126, 140 n. 9, 206, 214 f.
Psiax, 9 ff., 11, 13, 14, 17, 20, 21, 94, 95 n. 2, 117 and n. 13

Quadrate Painter, 54, 57, 61, *63* and n. 17

Reed Group, *58* ff., 138, 220 ff.
Reed Painter, 58 ff., 71, 141 and n. 13, 220 ff.
Revelstoke Group, 58 n. 5, *66*, 67
Roundabout Painter, 13, 78 n. 2
Rycroft Painter, *21*

Sabouroff Painter, 33, *34* ff., 38, 40, 41, 51, 52, 53, 55, 56, 61 n. 18, 63, 64, 71, 78 n. 2, 81, 96, 141, 142, 208 f., 217
Sappho Painter, xx, 8, 12, 17, 79, 80, 81, 92, 93, 94, 97, 99, 101 n. 5, 118, 119, 120, 123 and n. 21, 133, 149 f.
Seireniske Painter, 142 n. 1
Skythes, 123
Sophilos, 6, 7
Sosimos Potter, 117 n. 6
Sotades Painter, 205
Syriskos Painter, 31, 125 n. 1, 126, *127* f.
Syriskos Potter, 127 f.

Talos Painter, 72 n. 5
Terpaulos Painter, 80, 95
Thanatos Painter, 36 n. 2, 37, *38* f., 51, 53, 54, 56, 57 n. 14, 61 n. 18, 69, 203, 209 ff., 213, 215, 217, 218
heseus Painter, xx, *14* f., 19, 79, 85, 98 n. 8, 104 n. 9, 106, 109 n. 12, 115 f. n. 15, 133, 153
Timokrates Painter, 27 ff., 45, 51 n. 1, 63 n. 2, 140 n. 15, 142 n. 1, 206
Torch Painter, *137* f., 220

Triglyph Painter, 63 and n. 8, *66* and n. 8, *67*, 68, 69, 71, 224, 225
Trophy Painter, 35 n. 6, *36* and n. 2, 39
Two-row Painter, 34, 39, 96, 152 n. 3, 154 f.
Tymbos Painter, 9, 34 n. 11, *82* f., 204 f.
Tymbos Workshop, 9, 41 n. 6, *82* f., 138, 141
Tyszkiewicz Painter, 123

Uprooter Class, 115 n. 14
Utrecht Painter, 86

Vatican G. 49, Painter of, *21*
Vatican G. 52, Group of, 144

Villa Giulia Painter, *28*, 51 n. 8
Vlasto Painter, 103
Vouni Painter, *27* ff., 45, 86, 142, 207

White Heron Group, 14
Woman Painter, 54 n. 13, 55, 56, *57*, 58, 62, 65, 66, 71 n. 8, 214, 218 f., 224
Wraith Painter, 92
Würzburg 517, Painter of, 99

Yale *Lekythos*, Painter of the, 34 f. n. 16, 37 n. 8, 100, 102, 139 n. 18

INDEX OF LITERARY REFERENCES

Aischylos
Choephoroi 9 — 85 f. n. 19, 209, 219
Niobe, fr. 78 — 223
Apollonios of Rhodes
Argonautika 4. 1638 ff. — 72 n. 5
Aristophanes
Ekklesiazusai
538 — 73 n. 9
744 — 73 n. 8
877 — 74 n. 2
904 — 74 n. 2
929 — 74 n. 2
996 — 73 n. 8
1032 — 73 n. 9
1072 — 74 n. 2
1101 — 73 n. 8
1111 — 73 n. 9
Demosthenes
60.13 — 219
Euripides
Alkestis
24 ff. — 64 n. 1
158 f. — 49 n. 12
161 — 219
261 — 64 n. 1
843 — 64 n. 1
Helen
1165 — 203, 212
Hesiod
Theogony
763 ff. — 211

Homer
Iliad
24.710–12 — 226
Lysias
2.80 — 219
Pausanias
1.26.4 — 105
1.29.6 — 64 n. 19
2.16.2 — 215
2.25.7 — 215
2.29.2 — 205
5.18.1 — 211
6.21.3 — 205
8.4.9 — 205
8.11.14 — 205
8.16.3 — 205
10.28.1 — 63, 205
Plato
Menexenus 249b — 219
Pliny
N.H. 35.60 — 60, 69, 71, 72, 223
35.67 — 60
Plutarch
De Glor. Athen. 346 — 72 n. 2
Sophokles
Elektra 1374 f. — 210
Thucydides
4.1–2 — 140 n. 1
6.1–5 — 139 n. 15
Vitruvius
7.2 — 72

3c

2. Athens, Agora Museum, P 5002. Psiax

3b

1. Paris, Musée du Louvre, F 71.
Amasis Painter

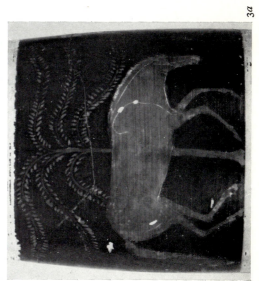

3a

3a-c. London, British Museum, 1900.6-11.1. Psiax

2

2. Hartford (Connecticut), Wadsworth Atheneum, 1961.8. Psiax

1. Minneapolis (Minnesota), Institute of Arts, 61.59. Antimenes Painter

2 *a*, *b*. Bochum, Ruhr University, Funcke Collection, S 496

LEAGROS GROUP

1. Vienna, Kunsthistorisches Museum, 75

4

4. Oxford, Ashmolean Museum, 512 (1895.75). Cactus Painter

3. Berlin (West), Staatliche Museum, 3261. Cactus Painter

2. Vienna, Kunsthistorisches Museum, 753. Rycroft Painter (near)

1. Athens, National Museum, 2246. Chariot Painter

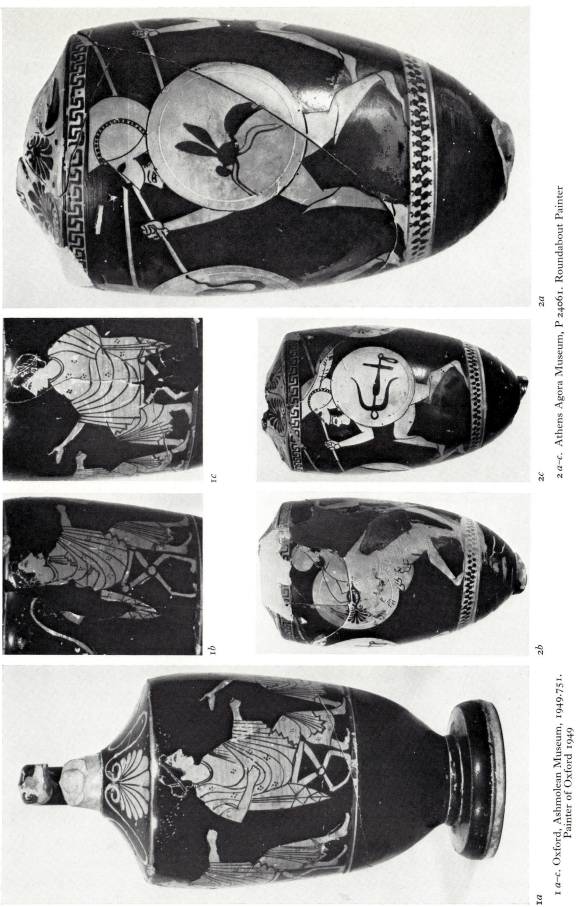

5

1 *a–c*. Oxford, Ashmolean Museum, 1949·751.
Painter of Oxford 1949

2 *a–c*. Athens Agora Museum, P 24061. Roundabout Painter

1*a*

1*b*

1*c*

2*a*

2*b*

2*c*

6

4. Columbia (Missouri), University Museum of Art and Archaeology, 58.12. Diosphos Painter

3. London, British Museum, 1922.10–18.1. Oinophile Painter

2. Agrigento, Museo Civico, 23. Terpaulos Painter

1. Boston, Museum of Fine Arts, 13.195. Gales Painter

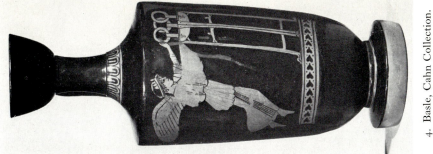

4. Basle, Cahn Collection.
Berlin Painter

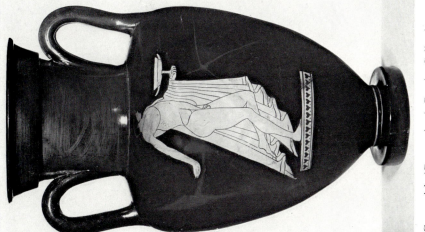

3. Greenwich (Connecticut), Bareiss Collection, 15.
Berlin Painter

2. Swiss Private Collection.
Edinburgh Painter

1. London, British Museum, B 188.
Edinburgh Painter

2 a, b. Bologna, Museo Civico Archeologico, PU 321. Douris

1 a, b. Berlin (East), Staatliche Museen, 2252.
Syriskos Painter

3a

3 *a, b*. Athens, National Museum, T.E.556

4. London, British Museum, E 768

3b

DOURIS

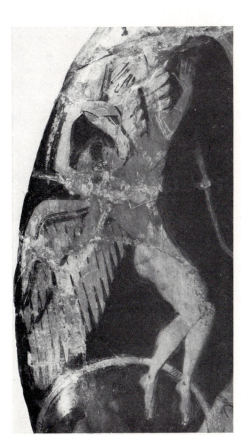

1. Berlin (East), Staaliche Museem, 3168

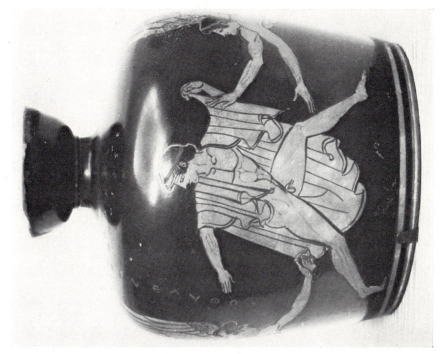

2. Athens, National Museum, 15375

1. Palermo, Museo Nazionale, N.I.1886 2. Cleveland, Museum of Art, 66.114

DOURIS

a   b

c

1 *a–c*. Cleveland, Museum of Art, 66.114

DOURIS

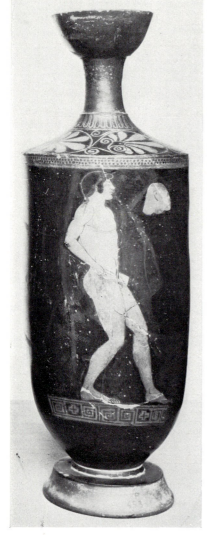

1. Boston, Museum of Fine Arts, 95.41
Douris

2. London, British Museum, E 573.
Bowdoin Workshop

3. Bochum, Ruhr University, Funcke
Collection, S 502. Bowdoin Workshop

4. London, British Museum, 63.7–28.45.1. Bowdoin Workshop

1. Paris, Peyrefitte Collection   2. Palermo, Museo Nazionale, 2792

BOWDOIN WORKSHOP

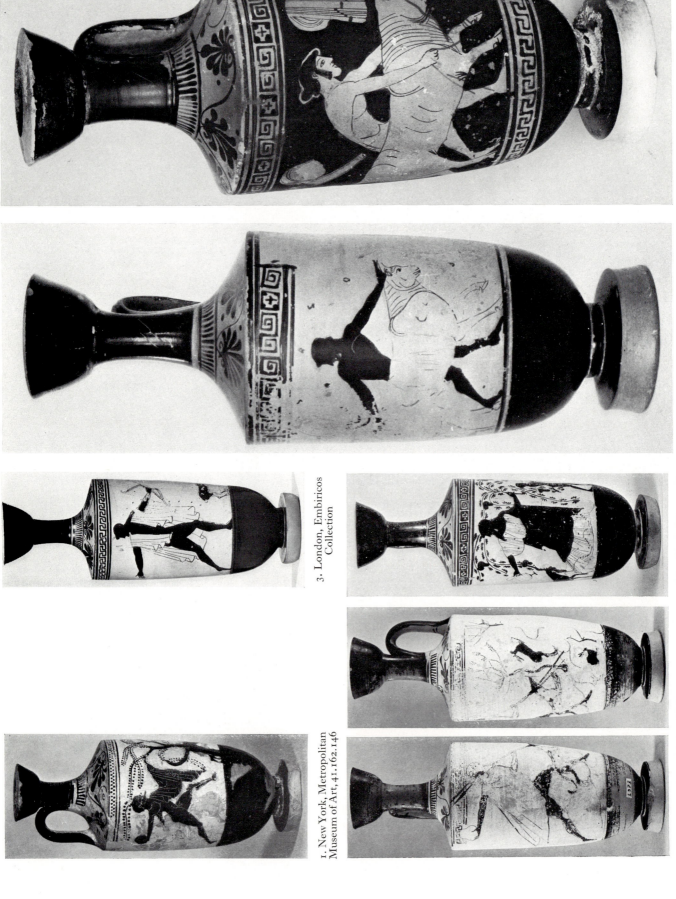

6. Lucerne Market (A.A.)

5. Bonn, Akademisches Kunstmuseum, 538

BOWDOIN WORKSHOP

3. London, Embiricos Collection

4. New York, Metropolitan Museum of Art, 08.258.28

1. New York, Metropolitan Museum of Art, 41.162.146

2 a, b. Athens, National Museum, 1973

1 *a, b.* Brussels, Musées Royaux d'Art et d'Histoire,
A.3131

2 *a, b.* Brussels, Musées Royaux d'Art et d'Histoire,
A.3132

BOWDOIN PAINTER

1 b

1 a

2 a

2 b

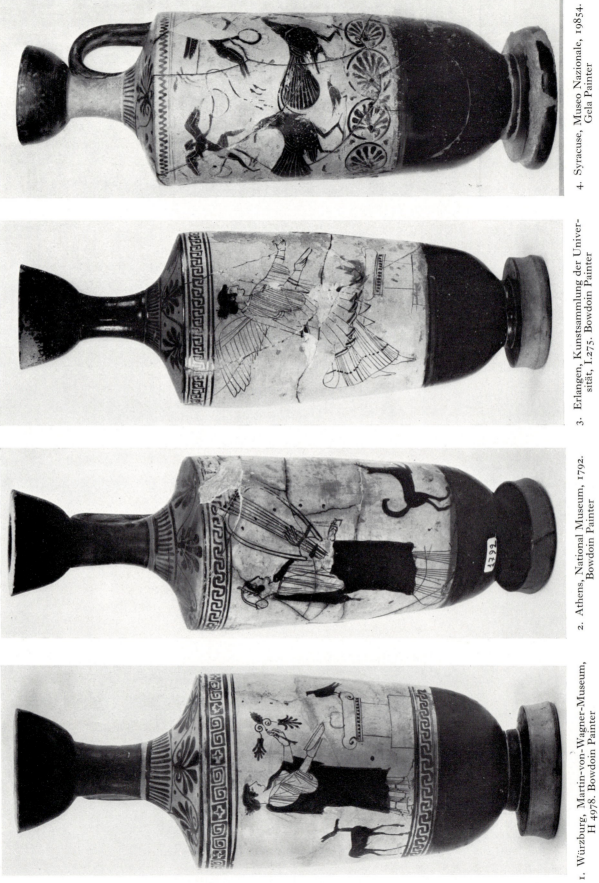

4. Syracuse, Museo Nazionale, 19854.
Gela Painter

3. Erlangen, Kunstsammlung der Universität, I.275. Bowdoin Painter

2. Athens, National Museum, 1792.
Bowdoin Painter

1. Würzburg, Martin-von-Wagner-Museum,
H 4978. Bowdoin Painter

1. Göttingen, Archäologisches Institut der Universität, ZV 1964/139. Gela Painter

2. Boston, Museum of Fine Arts, 99.526. Gela Painter

3. Vienna, Kunsthistorisches Museum, 84. Gela Painter

4. New York, Metropolitan Museum of Art, 41.162.13. Haimon Painter

18

3. London, British Museum, D 65. Group of
London D 65

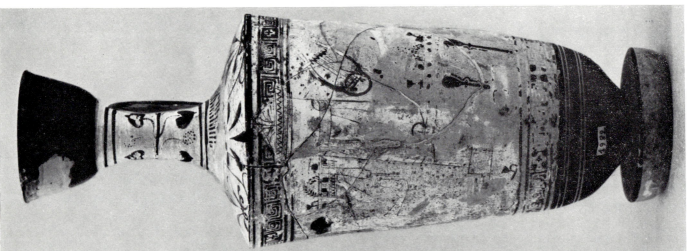

2. Athens, National Museum, 1982.
Beldam Painter

1. Athens, National Museum, 12801,
Beldam Painter

3. Athens, National Museum, 1958

2. Athens, National Museum 1790

Inscription Painter

1. Madrid, Museo Arqueológico Nacional,
19 497

20

1. Paris, Musée du Louvre, CA 1640

2. Boston, Museum of Fine Arts, 1970.428

3. Athens, National Museum, 1975

4. London, British Museum, D 33

1. London, British Museum, 1914.5–12.1.
Painter of Munich 2774

2. Basle Market (M.M.). Aischines Painter

3. Athens, National Museum, 2025.
Group of Athens 2025

4. Athens, National Museum, 1875.
Group of Athens 2025

2 *a, b*. Oxford, Ashmolean Museum, 1956.14

1. Paris, Musée du Louvre, MNB 3059

TYMBOS PAINTER

3. Paris, Musée du Louvre, CA 3758

2. Oxford, Ashmolean Museum, 547.
Tymbos Painter

1. London, British Museum, D 35.
Tymbos Painter

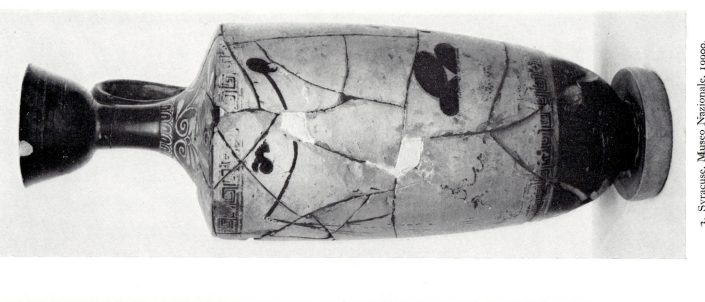

3. Syracuse, Museo Nazionale, 19900.
Pan Painter

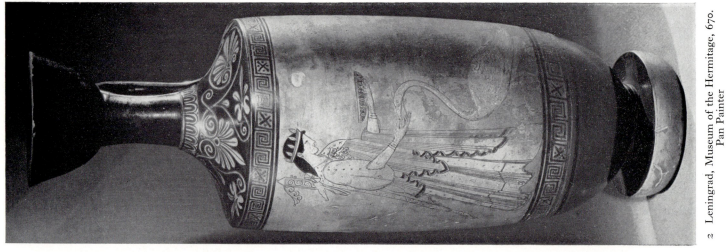

2. Leningrad, Museum of the Hermitage, 670.
Pan Painter

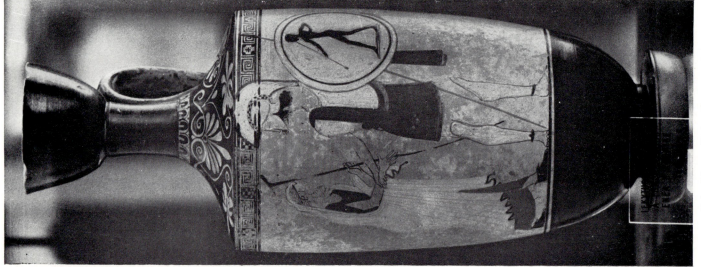

1. Gela, Museo Civico, Brygos Painter

3. Paris, Musée du Louvre, CA 3758

2. Oxford, Ashmolean Museum, 547.
Tymbos Painter

1. London, British Museum, D 35.
Tymbos Painter

24

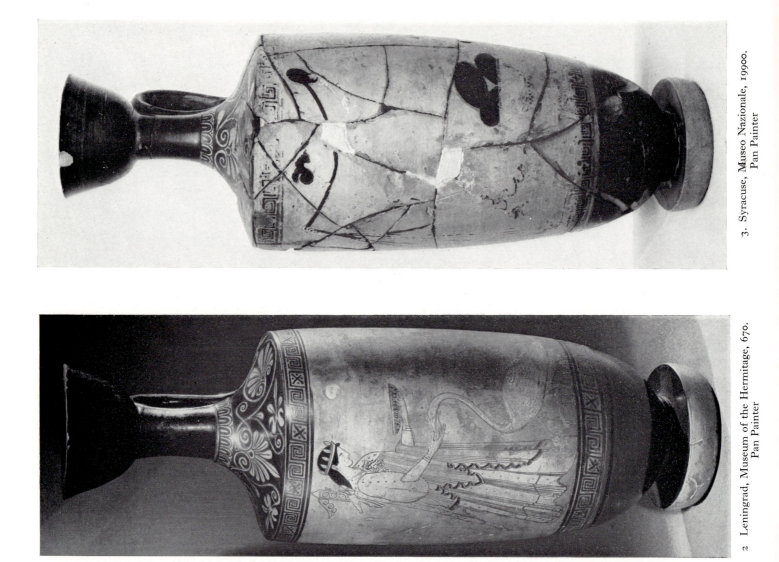

3. Syracuse, Museo Nazionale, 19900.
Pan Painter

2 Leningrad, Museum of the Hermitage, 670.
Pan Painter

1. Gela, Museo Civico, Brygos Painter

4. Athens, National Museum, 2032. Painter of Athens 1826 (near)

3. Madison (Wisconsin). Elvehjem Art Center, EAC 70.2. Timokrates Painter (near)

2. Athens, National Museum, 1929. Timokrates Painter

1. Paris, Musée du Louvre, CA 1142 (4175)

25

26

1. London, British Museum, 1928.2–13.1. Painter of Athens 1826

2. New York, Metropolitan Museum of Art, 35.11.5. Vouni Painter

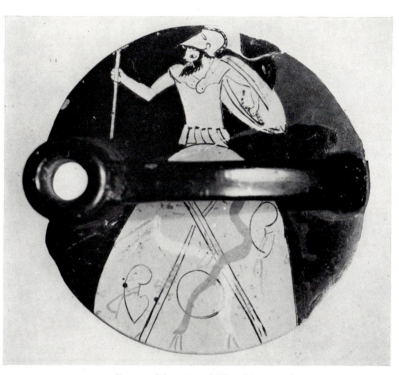

1. Boston, Museum of Fine Arts, 13.169

2. Oxford, Ashmolean Museum, 1966.854

3. London, British Museum, D 47

4. New York, Metropolitan
Museum of Art, 06.1021.134.
Villa Giulia Painter (near)

5. New York, Metropolitan Museum
of Art, 57.12.24

6. Zürich, Roš Collection.
Dresden Painter

3. Athens, National Museum, 164 22

2. Berlin (West), Staatliche Museen, inv. 3262. Sabouroff Painter

1 a, b. Honolulu, Academy of Arts, 2892. Sabouroff Painter

1. New York, Metropolitan Museum of
Art, 07.286.40. Sabouroff Painter

2. London, British Museum, D 62.
Sabouroff Painter

3. Athens, National Museum, 2021.
Painter of Athens 2020

4. Toronto, Royal Ontario Museum, 929.22.7.
Sabouroff Painter (manner)

BOSANQUET PAINTER

3. London, British Museum, 1907.7-10.10, fr.

2. New York, Metropolitan Museum of Art,
23.160.39

1. New York, Metropolitan Museum of Art,
23.160.38

2 a, b. New York, Metropolitan Museum of Art, 11.212.8

THANATOS PAINTER (near)

1 a, b. Boston, Museum of Fine Arts, 01.8080

THANATOS PAINTER

1. Boston, Museum of Fine Arts, 00.359

2. London, British Museum, D 67

3. London, British Museum, D 60

4. London, British Museum, D 58

33

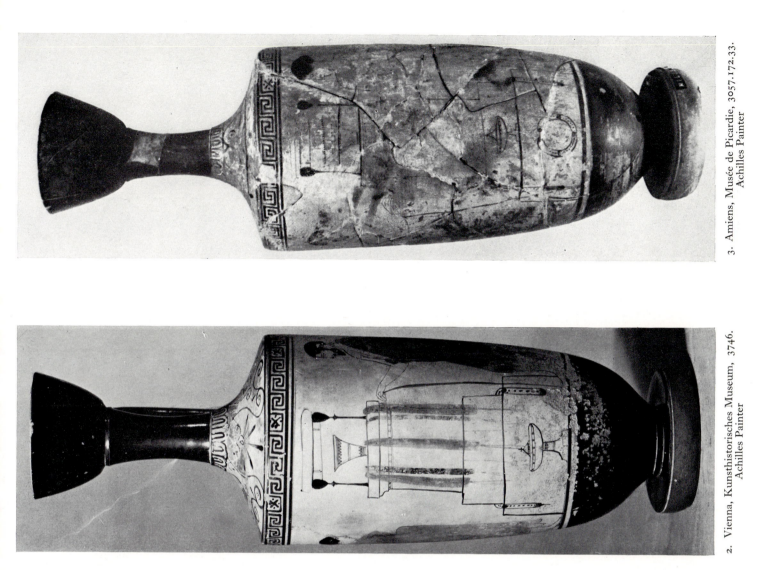

3. Amiens, Musée de Picardie, 3057.172.33.
Achilles Painter

2. Vienna, Kunsthistorisches Museum, 3746.
Achilles Painter

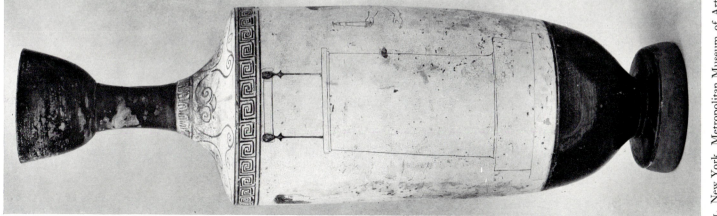

1. New York, Metropolitan Museum of Art,
12.229.10. Thanatos Painter

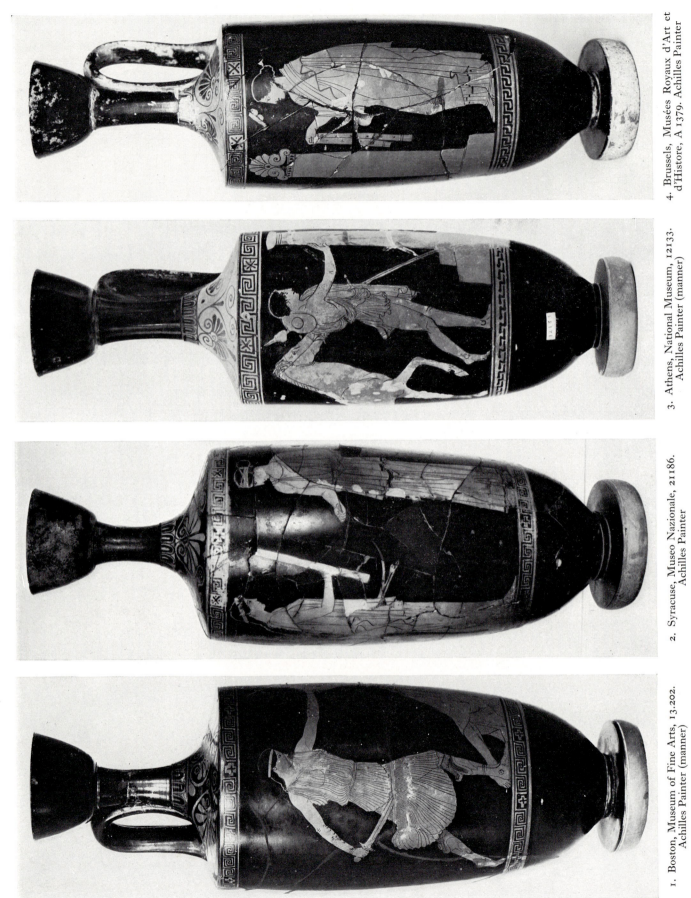

4. Brussels, Musées Royaux d'Art et d'Histore, A 1379. Achilles Painter

3. Athens, National Museum, 12133. Achilles Painter (manner)

2. Syracuse, Museo Nazionale, 21186. Achilles Painter

1. Boston, Museum of Fine Arts, 13.202. Achilles Painter (manner)

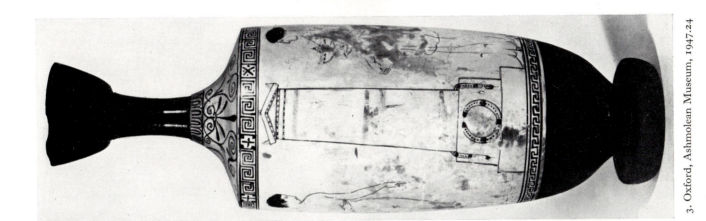

4. Brussels, Musées Royaux d'Art et d'Histoire, A 1379

3. Oxford, Ashmolean Museum, 1947.24

2. London, British Museum, D 48

1. Berlin (West), Staatliche Museen, 2443

1. London, British Museum, D 54.
Achilles Painter

2. Oxford, Ashmolean Museum, 545 (1896.41).
Achilles Painter

3. Athens, National Museum, 1938

1. Berne, Jucker Collection

2. Toledo (Ohio), Museum of Art, 69.369

4. Athens, National Museum, 1995

3. Athens, National Museum, 1943.
Painter of Athens 1943

2. Munich, Museum antiker Kleinkunst,
2798. Phiale Painter

1. Athens, National Museum, 1940.
Achilles Painter (manner)

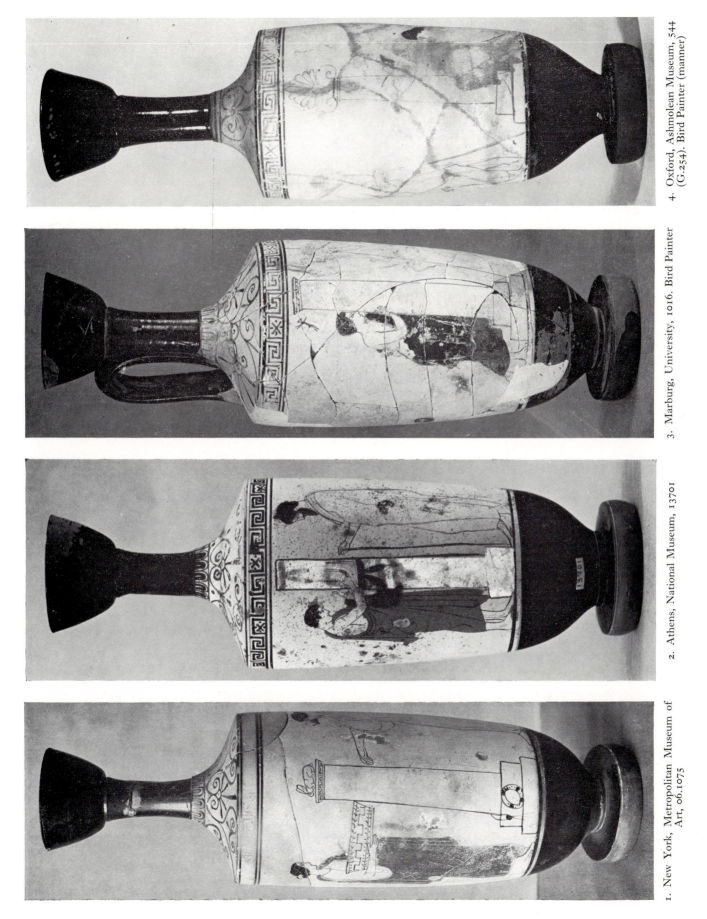

39

1. New York, Metropolitan Museum of Art, 06.1075

2. Athens, National Museum, 13701

3. Marburg, University, 1016. Bird Painter

4. Oxford, Ashmolean Museum, 544 (G.254). Bird Painter (manner)

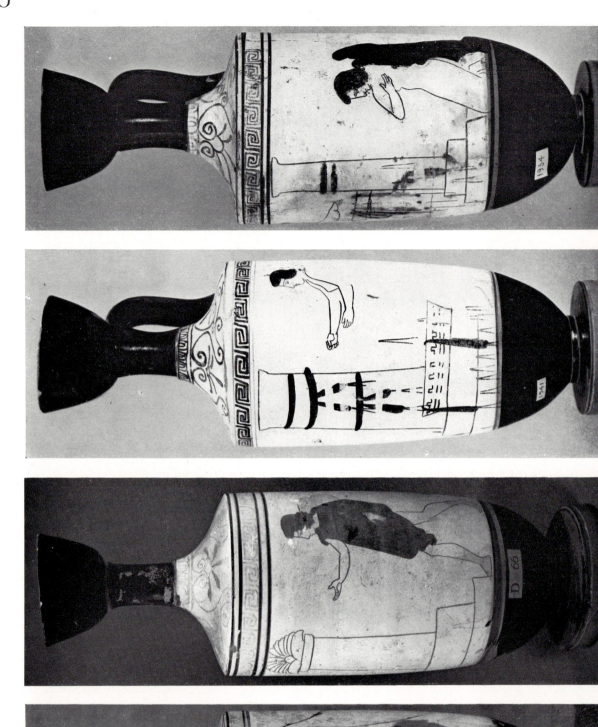

4. Athens, National Museum, 1934.
Painter of Athens 1934

3. Athens, National Museum, 1941

2. London, British Museum, D 66.
Bird Painter

1. Cambridge, Fitzwilliam Museum, GR
2.1928. Painter of Cambridge 28.2

41

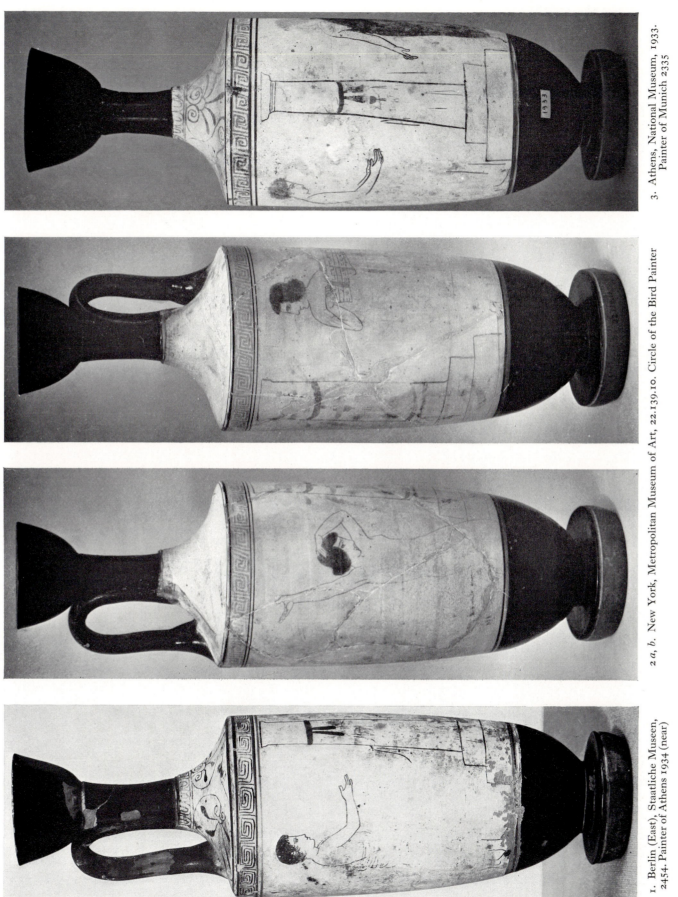

1. Berlin (East), Staatliche Museen, 2454. Painter of Athens 1934 (near)

2 a, b. New York, Metropolitan Museum of Art, 22.139.10. Circle of the Bird Painter

3. Athens, National Museum, 1933. Painter of Munich 2335

1. New York, Metropolitan Museum of Art, 09.221.44   2. New York, Metropolitan Museum of Art, 34.32.2

PAINTER OF MUNICH 2335

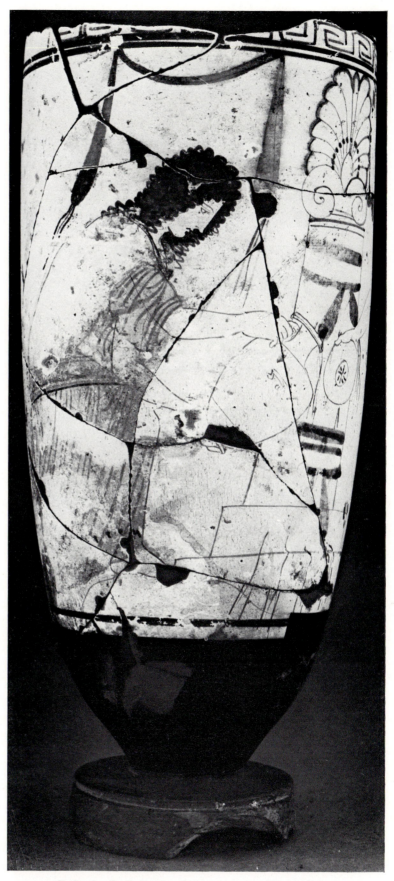

1. London, British Museum, 1928.2–13.2. Painter of
Munich 2335

2. Carlsruhe, Badisches Landesmuseum, 234. Woman Painter

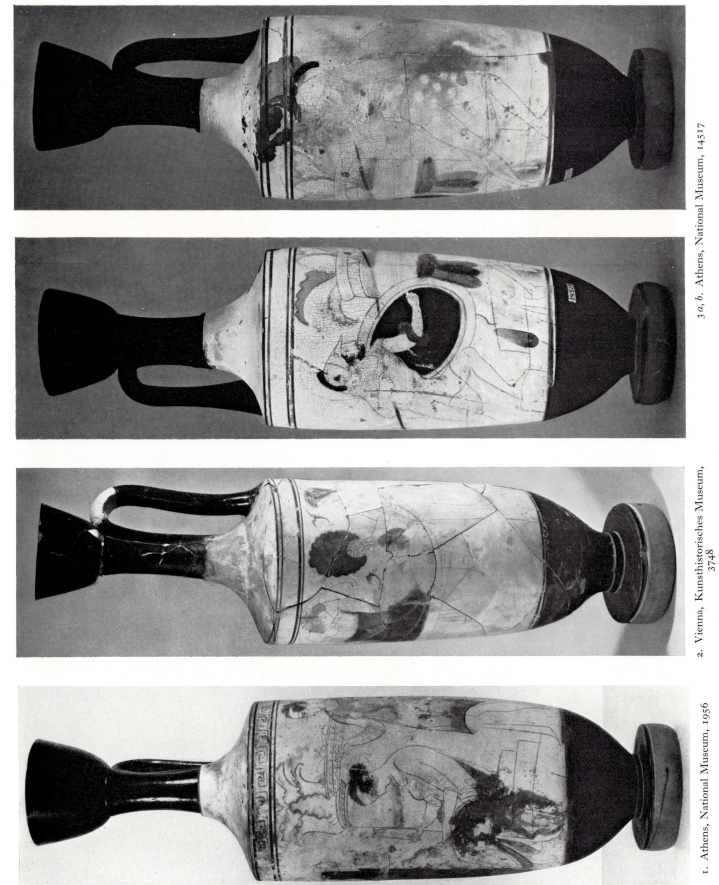

3 *a*, *b*. Athens, National Museum, 14517

2. Vienna, Kunsthistorisches Museum, 3748

1. Athens, National Museum, 1956

WOMAN PAINTER

4

3

2

2. Athens, National Museum, 1985.
   Torch Painter

3. Athens, National Museum, 1979.
   Torch Painter

4. Athens, National Museum, 1970.
   Torch Painter

1 *c*

1 *a*
1 *b*

1 *a–c*. Athens, National Museum, 1700. Kleophon Painter

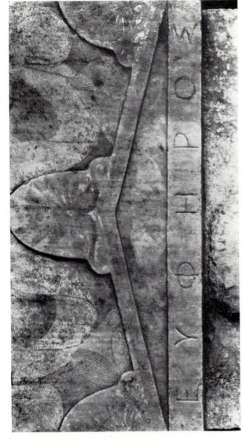

3. Athens, Kerameikos Museum, P1169, Grave-relief of Eupheros

4. Private Collection. Scaraboid gem (impression)

2. Paris, Musée du Louvre, MNB 616. Reed Painter

1. London, British Museum, D 72. Painter of London D 72

1. Hamburg, Museum für Kunst und
Gewerbe, 1917.817

2. Basle Market (M.M.)

3a, b. London, British Museum, D 61

3. New York, Metropolitan Museum of
Art, 41.162.12. Reed Workshop

2. New York, Metropolitan Museum of
Art, 41.162.11. Reed Workshop

1 a, b. Paris, Musée du Louvre, S 1161. Reed Painter

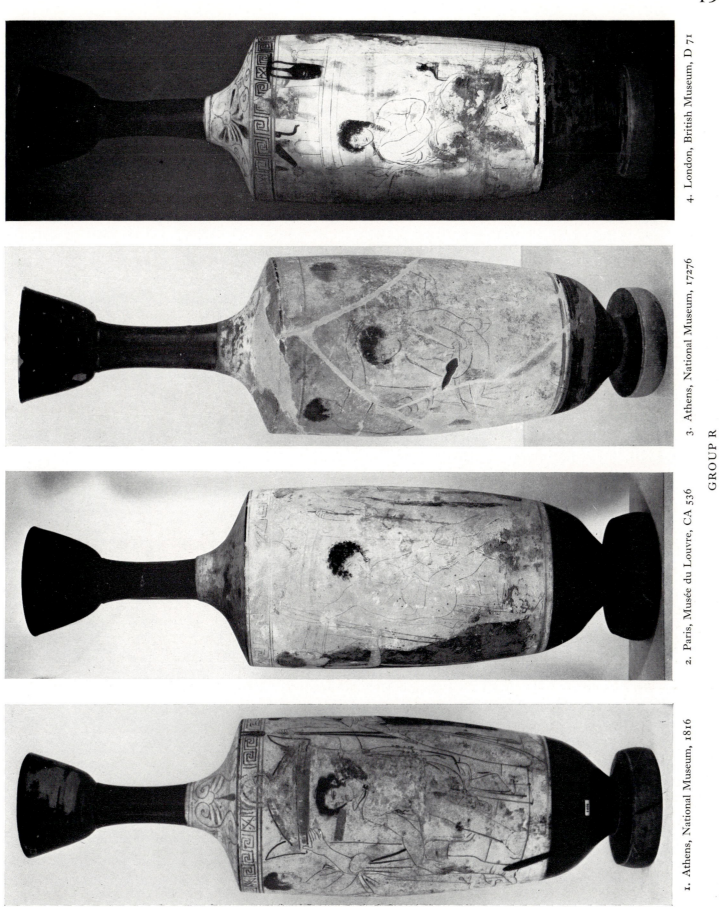

4. London, British Museum, D 71

3. Athens, National Museum, 17276

GROUP R

2. Paris, Musée du Louvre, CA 536

1. Athens, National Museum, 1816

3. Athens, National Museum, 19280, fr.

2. Paris, Musée du Louvre, CA 1264

GROUP R

1 a, b. Paris, Musée du Louvre, CA 537

51

4. Athens, National Museum, 1756.
Triglyph Painter

3. Zürich, University, 2518.
Triglyph Painter

2. Athens, Kerameikos Museum, 3146

Chicago, The Art Institute, 07.18.
Reed Painter

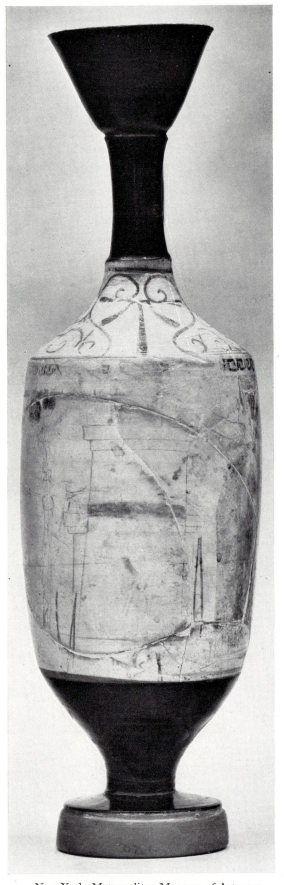

1. Copenhagen, National Museum, 4986   2. New York, Metropolitan Museum of Art, 07.1

CLASS OF COPENHAGEN 4986

4. Athens, National Museum, 1756.
Triglyph Painter

3. Zürich, University, 2518. Triglyph Painter

2. Athens, Kerameikos Museum, 3146

Chicago, The Art Institute, 07.18.
Reed Painter

1. Copenhagen, National Museum, 4986   2. New York, Metropolitan Museum of Art, 07.1

CLASS OF COPENHAGEN 4986

1. Ithaca (New York), Museum

2. Copenhagen, Ny Carlsberg Glyptotek, 221.
Stone Lekythos

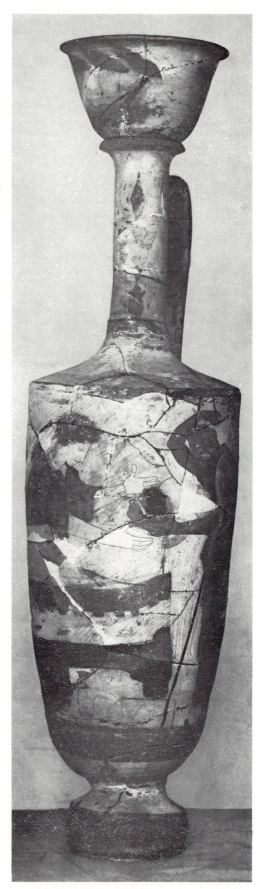

1. Madrid, Museo Arqueológico Nacional 11.194

2. Berlin (East), Staatliche Museen, 2684

GROUP OF THE HUGE LEKYTHOI

1. Carlsruhe, Badisches Landesmuseum, 167. Sappho Painter

2. Vienna, Kunsthistorisches Museum, 3607.
Diosphos Workshop

3. Paris, Musée du Louvre, G 203. Dutuit Painter

4. St. Louis (Missouri), Washington University, 3283.
Terpaulos Painter

56

3. Athens, National Museum, 2185, fr. Golonos Group (near)

4. Paris, Musée du Louvre, CA 4176

2. Once New York, Gallatin Collection.
Kephisophon Painter

1. Toronto, Royal Ontario Museum, 963.59.
Kephisophon Painter

3. Paris, Musée du Louvre, CA 4176

2a, b. London, British Museum, B 632. Class of London B 632

1. Munich, Museum antiker Kleinkunst, 2447. Class of London B 632 (related)

1 a–c. Paris, Musée du Louvre, MNC 650

2 a–c. Paris, Musée du Louvre, MNC 909

DIOSPHOS WORKSHOP

1. Boston, Museum of Fine Arts,
99.528

2. New York, Metropolitan
Museum of Art, 06.1070

3. New York, Metropolitan
Museum of Art. 51.163

4 *a–c.* Paris, Musée du Louvre, MNB 911

DIOSPHOS WORKSHOP

60

4. Athens, National Museum, 1827.
Bowdoin Painter

3. Richmond (Virginia), Museum of Fine
Arts, 56.27.4. Bowdoin Painter

2. Athens, National Museum, 1809.
Bowdoin Workshop

1. London, British Museum, 1920.3–15.1.
Athena Painter

4. Oxford, Ashmolean Museum, 1927. 4460

2. Copenhagen, National Museum, 3882. Two-row Painter (near)

3. Oxford, Ashmolean Museum, 1927.4467. Icarus Painter

1. Oxford, Ashmolean Museum, 1922.18. Vlasto Painter

62

3. Amsterdam, Allard Pierson Museum, 3754. Athena Painter

2. Athenian tetradrachm

1. London, British Museum, B 359. Painter of the Half-Palmettes

4. Bonn, Akademisches Kunstmuseum, 84.
Bowdoin Painter

3. Oxford, Ashmolean Museum,
1965.129. Bowdoin Painter

2. London, British Museum, D 22.
Bowdoin Painter

1. Marburg, University.
Bowdoin Workshop

64

1. Cambridge, Fitzwilliam Museum, GR 1.1895 (G.138). Carlsruhe Painter

2. Basle Market (M.M.)

3. Cambridge Fitzwilliam Museum, GR 3.1917 (3.17). Painter of Cambridge 3.17

4. Boston, Museum of Fine Arts, 99.928. Syriskos Painter

5. Paris, Musée du Louvre, CA 987, Epilykos Class

1a

 1 a, b. Oxford, Ashmolean Museum, 1932.733

2. Paris, Musée du Louvre, CA 987. Epilykos Class

 1b

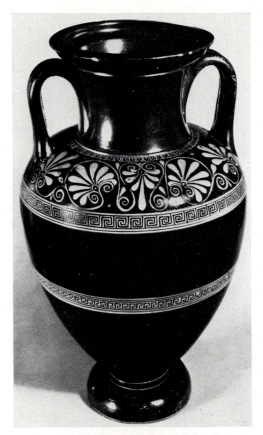

1. Birmingham, City Museum and Art Gallery, 1616.85

2. Brooklyn (New York), The Brooklyn Museum, 29.1

3. Copenhagen, Ny Carlsberg Glyptotek, V.26

4. Adolphseck, Landgraf Philip of Hesse, 50

FLORAL NOLAN GROUP

1. Oxford, Ashmolean Museum, 1936.113

2. Oxford, Ashmolean Museum, 1928.41

3. Oxford, Ashmolean Museum, 1935.2

4a

4a, b. Oxford, Ashmolean Museum, 1889.1013

4b

5. Oxford, Ashmolean Museum, 1938.732

6. Oxford, Ashmolean Museum, 1935.229

BLACK-BODIED LEKYTHOI

1. Athens, Agora Museum, P 24532

2. Oxford, Ashmolean Museum, 1872.1248A

3. Oxford, Ashmolean Museum, 1836.68

4. Oxford, Ashmolean Museum, 1938.736

5. Athens, National Museum, 12714

6. Oxford, Ashmolean Museum, 1934.329

7. Athens, Agora Museum, P 20750

8. Athens, Agora Museum, P 24546

PATTERN LEKYTHOI

1. Athens, National
Museum, 12271

2. Oxford, Ashmolean
Museum, 1927.4456

3. Eden Collection, Corsham
(Wiltshire)

4. Toronto, Royal Ontario Museum,
923.13.40 (335)

5. Oxford, Ashmolean
Museum, 1940.148

6. Oxford, Ashmolean
Museum, 1927.4458

PATTERN LEKYTHOI

1. London, British Museum, B 659

2. London, British Museum, 36 2–D 341

3. Basle Market (M.M.)

4. Oxford, Ashmolean Museum, 1927.4457

5. Athens, Kerameikos Museum

6. Oxford, Ashmolean Museum, 1940.149

7. Oxford, Ashmolean Museum, 1879.210

8. Corinth, Museum, T 566–118

PATTERN LEKYTHOI

1. Athens, Kerameikos Museum

2. Oxford, Ashmolean Museum,
1879.209

3. London, British Museum, 64.10–7.1722

4. Oxford, Ashmolean
Museum, 1930.617

PATTERN VASES

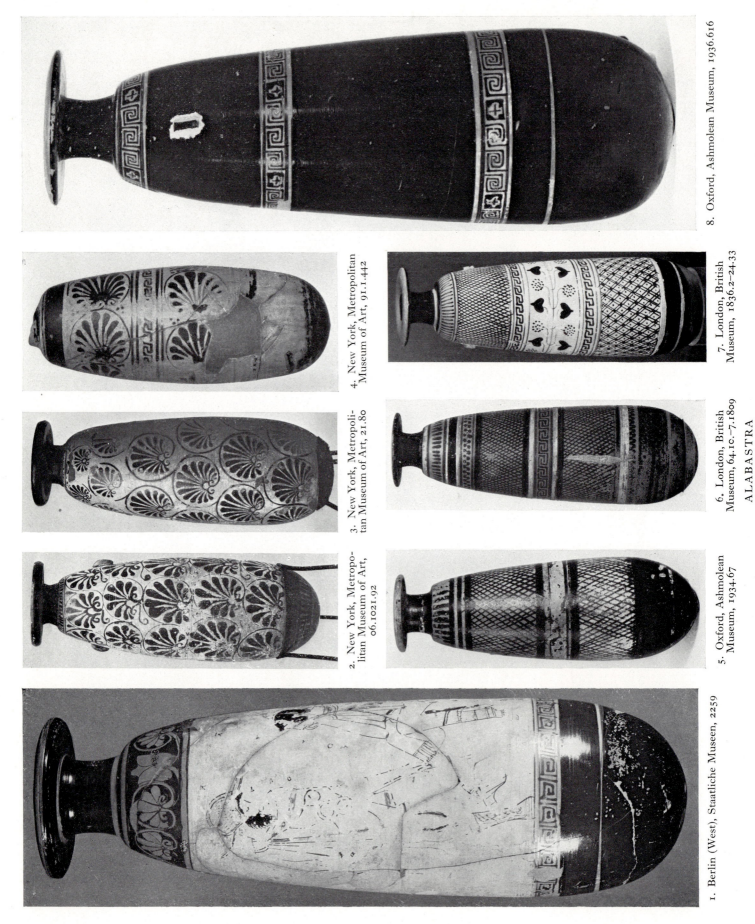

8. Oxford, Ashmolean Museum, 1936.616

4. New York, Metropolitan Museum of Art, 91.1.442

7. London, British Museum, 1836.2–24.33

3. New York, Metropolitan Museum of Art, 21.80

6. London, British Museum, 64.1c.–7.1809

ALABASTRA

2. New York, Metropolitan Museum of Art, 06.1021.92

5. Oxford, Ashmolean Museum, 1934.67

1. Berlin (West), Staatliche Museen, 2259